IS GOD REAL OR IS IT JUST ME?

THE ULTIMATE REALITY AS EXPRESSED IN "DIVINE AUTHORITARIANISM"

JOWELL L. PEDEN, JR.

TATE PUBLISHING, LLC

Published in the United States of America

By TATE PUBLISHING, LLC

All rights reserved.
Do not duplicate without permission.

Unless otherwise indicated, all scripture references are taken from the
Living Bible. Wheaton: Tyndale House, 1997, c1971 by Tyndale House
Pubishers,Inc. Used by permission. All rights reserved.

Book Design by TATE PUBLISHING, LLC.

Printed in the United States of America by

TATE PUBLISHING, LLC

127 East Trade Center Terrace

Mustang, OK 73064

(888) 361-9473

Publisher's Cataloging in Publication

Peden, Jowell

Is God Real Or Is It Just Me? / Jowell Peden

Originally published in Mustang,OK:TATE PUBLISHING:2004

1. Christianity   2. Science & Technology

ISBN 0-9759124-9-6 $19.95

First Printing: August 2004

DEDICATION

In memory of my mother and father: Emma Lee and Jowell Peden. My mother–a most loving and nurturing mother. My father–the universal man and great male role model. A man of men.

In honor of Dr. Lee Ball–perhaps the "smartest man I know." The professor who taught me to appreciate the abundance of life.

To my wife Debbie for her love and understanding even when I have demonstrated my shortcomings.

For the many family members, friends and teachers who have shared their lives in love and kindness.

Special thank you to The Word For Today, Chuck Smith and Mark Eastman, Ligonier Ministries and R. C. Sproul, Lifetime Guarantee and Bill Gillham for allowing my inclusion of their material.

CONTENTS

INTRODUCTION...7

SECTION ONE: THE ULTIMATE REALITY
Chapter 1 What Is The Ultimate Reality?.............................17
Chapter 2 Philosophy of Life - The Two Views 23

SECTION TWO: EVIDENCE OF GOD
Chapter 3 God Almighty 31
Chapter 4 Science: Closing In On God 59
Chapter 5 Evolution: A Big Horse With A Bunch of Guys Inside 71
Chapter 6 Science: The Biblical View 101
Chapter 7 Miracles: Something to Believe In 127

SECTION THREE: THE SOUL, THE PSYCHE
AND THE HUMAN INTELLECT
Chapter 8 For The Good Of Man, God Must Exist 161
Chapter 9 Philosophy: God's Will Be Done,
Despite Human Resistance 171
Chapter 10 Comparative Religion: What Do We Find? 189
Chapter 11 Theory #1: Noah Survived the Flood
With The True Revelations Of God..193
Chapter 12 The Human Intellectual Connection 217
Chapter 13 Theory #2: Every Human Being Intuitively Knows God .223
Chapter 14 Myths, Dreams, Symbols and Religion 237
Chapter 15 Myths and Christianity 259

SECTION FOUR: JESUS - WHO WAS HE?
Chapter 16 Jesus of Nazareth 277
Chapter 17 What Happened To The Body? 293
Chapter 18 Jesus, King of The Jews! 319
Chapter 19 Jesus' Message 339
Chapter 20 Jesus of Nazareth and the Honesty of the Gospels 347
Chapter 21 The Will of God Is Passionate! 353

SECTION FIVE: MODERN TIMES
Chapter 22 A Glance at The Revelation 365

EPILOGUE 407

ENDNOTES 409

INTRODUCTION

EXISTENCE

It truly is like we are on one long trip
and we are all on board - going.
But no one knows where we are going or why.
Yet, we are all going.
And we play cards along the way
because things get boring,
and there seems little else to do.
Why we are going and where we are going,
no one seems to care.
- the imagined determinism.

The writing you hold is not 'just' a book; it is a trip into deepest Reality. On this trip you will examine things taken for granted. You will question what really is and what is not. Please get ready; leave your preconceived and mind restricting baggage behind. It is time - the journey begins.

We hear of other realities or dimensions such as heaven and hell, but we do not genuinely recognize them as actual forms of reality. Nor do we recognize their validity outside the realm of religious expression. But, ignoring true boundaries of existence is unacceptable behavior for human beings. So, are there any apprehensible reasons to believe in such things? Moreover, we must question, is there a god or is there a God? And, if God does exist, who is he/she/it? These are not only mysteries for confessed agnostics, but are also puzzles for a significant number of people of various religions. A recent article by Netscape (internet) states: "Ten percent of Protestants, 21 percent of Roman Catholics, and 52 percent of Jews do NOT believe in God."[1] This book is the product of a common man's search for Truth. Because I was brought up in a Christian home, I have always believed in God and loved God. I have always expected God to be with me. I expected God to answer my prayers, lead me down the correct path and 'watch over me through the night.' Yet, through time, my relationship with God has changed.

While in high school, I thought God must be hard to reach. How could I explain my concerns in such a way that Almighty God might understand? I did not question God's concern for my expressions. Rather, my concern might better be expressed by the query: How does a mere human (a young human at that) relate to and communicate with the Great Being who runs this universe? Yet, through the counsel of Ken Hay (minister of my past), and personal study and prayer, I began to accept the premise that God has a personality and, therefore, God is relatively easy to communicate with. Through such logic and faith, I began to believe God knew my thoughts and my concerns before I could express them. Yet, because He encourages a loving relationship with mortals, He wanted to hear my concerns from me. Thus, I began to visit with 'my friend, God' or 'God, my Father,' instead of God, 'the Creator and Ruler of the universe.' These early prayers of mine were about others, my family, my friends, my country, etc. They only contained generalizations about me, i.e., 'Watch over me through the night.' I did not rely heavily upon God, because I had not yet experienced tragedy nor the feeling of personal helplessness.

I had heard that God controls the outcome of everything in the universe. Yet, I did not comprehend this authoritarian nature. Thus came another change in my relationship with God. While in college, I crossed a barrier in understanding God's role in world affairs. As a student, I worried that man might destroy God's creation by war, pollution and human greed. This worry, along with a fundamental understanding of conservation (which I learned as a Boy Scout) moved me to work through my school's Science Department to develop an environmental 'watch dog' group. I considered my environmental work to be in defiance of man and a strike for God. Yet, again through study and prayer, I found comfort in the realization that God already had a plan. I began to understand that man's selfishness is no match for God's unlimited authority and powers. God, the GREAT I AM, is omnipotent. The end of civilization would not be contrary to God's schedule; alas, the end will come, but it is part of the Divine Comprehensive Plan. God is in control. God has already determined when, where and how earth will be destroyed.

If I should mark a high point in my search, it came during a most disastrous period of my life. Through a sequence of events, I experienced great loss. I cannot express my emotions, the frustration, the helplessness and loneliness. Perhaps any rejection I felt was unjustified. Perhaps family and friends did not understand what I felt, nor would they have known how to help. Even the loving comfort of my wife could not fill my sadness. I then realized I did not have the valid perspective. Previous to this disaster I had relied too heavily on rationalizing my feelings, thoughts and attitudes. I had taken comfort in myself and had deduced I was too valiant for this world's troubles. I had concluded that 'self' was given to me by God to handle every problem I would meet. I would, some future day, return to God and hear 'well done, My child.' In those days my life was centered around my profession and private fun. I spent too much time at 'the office' and I put too much emphasis on sports, 'going to the lake' or other social events. After tragedy struck my life I decided to scrutinize reality and determine what was truly important. Then, I would make an effort to center my entire being around those values. I wanted to examine important things like God, family, friendship and country. I began to investigate the tough questions. It is not my intention to expound upon my journey, but to express its ongoing conclusions, for they verify the strength of our human foundations.

IS GOD REAL?

The problem most people seem to have believing in God and thus heaven, hell and the like, is two fold. *First,* they do not find any evidence for God. In fact, many believe that the entire scientific community has rejected God as some form of wishful thinking. Furthermore, the teachings in the Bible seem mythical while the teachings of evolution fully explain our existence without the interference of God. Thus, there is no need for God. *Second,* they have not experienced a relationship with God to the extent that it surpasses any personal doubts.

THIS WRITING

This book will address the first issue. I will give evidence that God not only exists, but controls the universe. All things function within the bounds of God's Will. I will also give evidence that miracles are both scientifically and logically probable. I will further postulate that all 'material' things on this planet are interrelated and yet subservient to man. Of course, this includes plants, animals, the soil and the air, but also such things as the particles of atoms, unseen bacteria, lasers and radio waves. We are indeed the caretakers of the world and are either sole caretakers or perhaps partner caretakers of the universe. Finally, I will investigate the question, "Was Jesus of Nazareth God?"

My original concept for this writing was to allow myself an opportunity to share some of my personal philosophical and theological beliefs with atheists and agnostics. Their search is not unique. I have asked their very questions. Many times we feel incapable of researching these intuitive puzzles for ourselves. Where does one look for a confirmation of God and the realities of a supernatural world? Quite frankly, there is an abundance of relevant information available. But, it is information which might elude the average person. Much of this knowledge is not expressed in the standard church sermon–nor is this material found in holy books, or sacred writings. Such wisdom is hidden from the average scholar, but is waiting for a scientist who understands the laws of the universe or an archaeologist who understands the significance of a Middle Eastern clay tablet.

A secondary part of this same resource dilemma involves the accessibility of material. One must search over a large number of books to get a reflective view of existence or, more correctly, human reality. Unfortunately, a psychologist does not have time to keep up with all of the studies going on in psychology, much less have a working knowledge of astronomy, biology and theology. To understand reality, however, one must do exactly that - have a wide view of all which is. I often wished for a book to be co-authored by some of my favorite writers in a variety of fields. The impracticality of such an undertaking and the variety of informational topics which play a role in an understanding of 'being' stymie such a venture. Yet, it is imperative, if I am fair with my own conscious, that I grasp a loose summary of what is 'real' as I understand 'reality.' This report you hold is the conclusion of such an examination.

Although, this material may bring insight to the nonbeliever, it is the believer who will really benefit from this book. It has been my personal experience that the atheist and the agnostic are not as open-minded to such evidence as is a theist. Jesus reportedly said, *"But Abraham said, if they won't listen to Moses and the prophets, they won't listen even though someone rises from the dead."*[2] He was alluding to a 'miracle' or action from outside our realm of comprehension. Yes, the atheist must accept God before he will accept the awesome activities and inspirations of God.

Though modern man rationalizes his own 'Truth' to account for his miscalculations, history of civilization confirms that the human being is drawn to God. Man is a most miserable and corrupt creature when he chooses to separate from the Creator of all that is. Judaism and Christianity, as well as a number of other religions, begin with this concept. The Holy Bible assumes that all humans have some knowledge of God. My writings will focus on this assumed knowledge.

Because churches are not equipped to research the psychological makeup of primitive man, etc., they leave such activity to the scholarship of universities. Yet, philosophically, our universities seem to be closed-minded about spiritual matters. For example, the above-mentioned miracle, (Jesus Christ rising from the dead), is both possible and logical if Jesus is God.[3] One most interesting possibility is 'extra dimensional structure' which, by the way, is consistent with our modern understanding of physics. We should at least suppose that, if we can describe the mechanics of a miraculous action through science, then an all-powerful being could perform that action. Nonetheless, many university professors would not even consider such an explanation, because they automatically rule out anything supernatural. They justify this unconditional disbelief by blindly advocating that 'miracles just do not happen.' In my opinion, these professors are limited thinkers dealing from a limited world view. They will go with the intellectual trend, the politically correct, before they will seriously consider other valid possibilities. However, such professors will never understand the true envelope of human potential until they accept God as the major force of all reality and recognize three philosophical points.

First, only God's presence gives purpose to the existence of a universe. God is the logic behind universal order, as well as the substance which developed order out of nothingness. A godless universe assumes that something spontaneously generated and developed through random chaos into a meticulous, integrated system of organized matter. Let us, for the moment, consider the implications of a godless reality. From this position, the earth, the universe and all that is, is one huge mistake. The immediate problem is that this ideology erases all meaning and value and worth. In essence, we do not exist, because in a godless universe, there is no meaning.

A *second* point is the existence of God adds value or credibility to 'personal purpose.' Only through God's being do we discern reason for each human and every living creature. Only through God do we have objective standards for behavior. Conversely, if we deny God, personal life also becomes meaningless. Personal actions are completely subjective. Philosophically, our personal existence is insignificant, because only with purpose do we find meaning.[4]

The *third* and final point: God loves each one of us and desires a love relationship in return. Amazingly, the real possibility of such a relationship may be the only reason for our existence.

In conclusion, the information I share will be very precious to those who are aware of a spiritual reality in life - those who either feel at peace in their relationship with God or are seeking to know the truth about these concepts.

I wish to emphasize that this work should be regarded as a *treaty* of philosophy more than a *comment* on theology. This work proposes that the *Divine Authoritarian Philosophy* is the true life philosophy; it takes the position that God is in control of everything known or unknown. It is important to me that I do not mislead anyone with my thoughts and conjectures. Theologically, I am a Christian in the traditional sense. Briefly, I believe Jesus Christ is the Son of God (and, thus, God on earth) and the Savior of mankind. He is the Way, the Truth and the Light. No man enters the Kingdom of God except through Him. My study, however, cannot be considered traditional. It is a contemplation of specific possibilities regarding an essence (God) of all force, and a related natural-supernatural structuring of all existence through Gods Will.

One of my personal objectives is to write a refined book which is easy to read and understand. This is particularly important considering the wide variety of disciplines to be discussed such as science, philosophy, logic, symbolism, theology, etc.

Because this book is based upon my perceptions, I will use certain sources as major references. These people listed below are not my only sources, but have had a great influence upon my thinking. In all cases, these individuals are easy for me to understand and seem to be very logical and philosophically sound:

I will use an astrophysicist, Dr. Hugh Ross, Ph.D. as my major source in science. Dr. Ross received his B.S. in physics from the University of British Columbia and his M.S. and Ph.D. in astronomy from the University of Toronto. Dr. Ross is a writer and lecturer. Ross also hosts a radio program and is the author of a number of popular books. Summing up his studies on the cover of his book, *The Fingerprint of God,* Dr. Ross claims "recent scientific discoveries reveal the unmistakable identity of the Creator."

Among the authorities on historical theological background I rely on popular Christian researcher, lecturer and author, Josh McDowell, noted Christian pastor and author Chuck Smith, William Bell Ph.D., Professor of Theology at Dallas Baptist University and author Paul Maier, a professor of ancient history at Western Michigan University. Also William Lane Craig, Professor of Philosophy at Talbot School of Theology.

My discussions on logic are highly influenced by Dr. R.C. Sproul, Ph.D., Chairman of Ligonier Ministries and professor of Systematic Theology at Reformed Theological Seminary and Dr. Thomas B. Warren, Ph.D., professor of Religion and Apologetics at Harding University.

I include the guidance of Dr. Bill Gillham, Ph.D., a psychologist, Christian counselor, my college professor and friend. His insight into the relationship of the Will of God to the purpose of man is particularly pertinent to a study on the Ultimate Reality.

I want to recognize a great number of ministers and teachers who have influenced my intellect and personal philosophy. Among these men and women are Dr. Lee Ball–a leader by example and the one who taught me to enjoy learning, Col. Ralph Smith–both a military and civilian chaplain and U. S. Army Ranger, Joe Ed Goolsby, George Strickland, Bob Price, Ken Hay, Larry Crocker, Steve Solomon, Robert Goodrich, W. A. Criswell and others.

I wish to thank my wife, Debbie, for her understanding in this endeavor. Without her love and encouragement, this book would have been much harder to write. I also thank both Debbie and my sister, Emily Momary, for proofreading my manuscript and giving me advice about many of my comments.

I also recognize those colleagues who provided encouragement and inspiration. Most notably, I include DareBorn McCullough, E. Pete Rose, David Harris, Archie Sims and Larry Dutton.

Finally, I thank one unnamed atheist (now agnostic). It was through our early discussions that I decided I needed to share this investigation with those holding similar questions.

This work is a probe into the spiritual significance of human life. Though the *Divine Authoritarian Philosophy* is not often expressed, I think most people would agree this view of life is possible and, perhaps likely. However, they have not found it apropos to their everyday life. My sincere hope is that other published studies will follow and investigations into human reality will expand into a more God centered experience.

SECTION ONE:

THE ULTIMATE
REALITY

CHAPTER 1

WHAT IS THE ULTIMATE REALITY?

"In the beginning God created the heaven and the earth."[1]

On July 11, 1978, a rock group recorded one of the greatest hits in the history of rock and roll. Though the group had people all over the world rocking to their music, it was their words that grabbed the minds of the masses. Even so, few listeners realized that the song held a deep hidden meaning. In fact, the message was so deep that the performing rock group probably did not even realize what they had done. What went unnoticed was that this hit tune unwittingly expressed the human search for meaning. A group known as The Who sang, "Who are you? I really want to know . . ." and, with this question about humanness, their recording framed the intellectual window for both philosophy and modern psychology. Thus, despite foul lyrics, the song could have been the apotheosis in self analysis. Of course, The Who wrote this song for reasons other than its distinct analytical insights. Yet, 'Who are you?' is a provocative question. Understanding ourselves is not easy. I freely admit - sometimes I think I know who I am and, at other times, I have to wonder. Sometimes I do things that are 'nice,' 'considerate' and 'good' and I can do them for no reason at all! Often, however, I do things that I wish I had never done. So, from time to time, I have to ask myself, "Who are you?" Interestingly, I am no different than the average person. Even Saint Paul wrote, "I don't understand myself at all, for I really want to do what is right, but can't." Paul continues to explain that the problem is not him, but sin within him.[2] People seem to be on a battlefront between good and evil. Psychologists, philosophers and theologians tell us this tug of war within our beings is normal. Yet, psychological disorders occur when a person cannot moderate this antithetical nature of the human soul.[3]

Such an inner search about ourselves sometimes leads to other provocative questions. There are existence questions even more elementary then "who are you?" Many people have wondered beyond spectrum of self, into the boundaries of deep reality, with questions like, "Does anything exist?" The senses can be unreliable, but reason proves our existence. Though we will later consider this query from the cosmological position, the more personal answer rests in the celebrated statement by Rene Descartes: "I think, therefore I am" (Cogito Ergo Sum). This deduction is considered by many to be the true beginning point of modern philosophy. Descartes' logic reminds me that if I can *think,* then I must *exist.*

IS THERE A GOD?

I would assume that most people consider the question, 'Is there a God?' the major incertitude of life. Naturally, it is a vital probe, because only from this foundation can all truth follow. On the personal level, the answer determines the factualness of who I am, and what is real and what is fiction. Yet, other awareness questions quickly follow because, 'Is there a God?' is only a problem for the agnostic. Most people have already asked the 'God' question and found some acceptable answer. They either accept the proposition that 'God exists' or they reject it. Biblical researcher, Grant Jeffrey, expresses the frustration enveloped in the 'Does God exist?' debate: "I will not debate you about whether or not God exists for the same reason that I would not debate someone about whether or not the world was round. I believe that those who claim 'There is no God,' in the face of overwhelming evidence of design found throughout nature, are either fools or liars. Any person who honestly believes that all of the marvelous complexity of this universe simply happened by chance is a fool. If he is not a fool, yet claims to believe that this incredibly complex universe is a result of random chance, then I must conclude that he is not being honest. In either case it is clearly a waste of time to argue the obvious."[4] Although, for the sake of philosophical understanding, I find it necessary in this book to investigate the reliability of God's existence, there is great merit in Grant's view.

Because of the above precursor, the big question for most of us should be the broader and more complicated question, "What is the Ultimate Reality?" Why is this the true litmus test for the philosophical self? The term 'Ultimate Reality,' calls forth a wide array of concepts. From Plato's idealism, to Dietrich Bonhoeffer's *Ethics,* to Mahatma Gandhi's belief in Truth, we find divergent perceptions of an Ultimate Reality. I personally find most definitions lacking. Instead of reviewing all of the classical ways humanity has distinguished the Ultimate Reality, let me simply state that the concept varies from philosopher to philosopher. Generally, the Ultimate Reality implies that which is most sacred, or of greatest value, or the foundation from which everything derives. From this understanding, Truth or absolute Truth would fit this category. However, Truth implies the knowledge of something and not the source of that knowledge. Absolute Truth would imply knowing what the Ultimate Reality is. I suggest the Ultimate Reality reaches further into the confines of realism, to the source of reality itself! The reality of which I speak

---

SO, IF GOD EXISTS, THEN THE UNIVERSE AND EVERYTHING IN THE UNIVERSE EXISTS BECAUSE GOD WILLS IT TO EXIST.

relates 'all that is,' with the source or essence of 'all that is.' It is the connection. Thus, this book proposes the Ultimate Reality is God plus God's Will (or, for the atheist the lack of God and the lack of God's Will). This distinction (the separation of God and God's Will) may seem subtle, but is actually very significant. Let us assume that God does exist and that God created the universe and everything in and outside of the universe. God did exist without a universe (this must be true if we assume that God created everything). Therefore, God's 'Will' was necessary for the existence of the universe. Furthermore, if this is true, then it probably is also true that nothing can exist in this universe without the approval or the Will of God. If God is powerful enough to *create,* God is probably also powerful enough to *destroy.* So, if God exists, then the universe and everything in the universe exists because God *wills* it to exist. Thus, we begin to describe what many theologians express as 'the personality of God.' Assuming God is the Creator of all that is, if there are any dimensions in or out of the universe, whether or not we are aware of them, if life exists in or out of the universe, if there are spiritual beings such as angels, ghosts and demons, it seems only natural that all of these things must be affected by the Will of God and live in a relation with God's natural and/or supernatural laws.

There are two other viable choices. One alternative is that the universe was created, but God either had no plan or the universe was 'by chance' formed by God. This option suggests that God has little or no intellect. But, this, like the atheistic view, goes against the evidence (discussed in latter chapters). The final alternative is that God created something too big to control. However, if we consider God to be great enough and intelligent enough to plan and create the universe, then we must also assume that God must be great enough and intelligent enough to control His creation. This does seem to be the most logical conclusion. We will investigate scientific evidence concerning this view. Thus, from this exercise in logic one could conclude that if God exists and God's Will exists and everything in the universe exists with the consent of God's Will, then God must have a reason for our existence and God would hope we would try to fulfill His Will in our lives.

Only from such a logical position can we start considering the perimeters of a willed relationship between God and man - the possibilities of a divine plan, the role of determinism and freedom of choice in our lives, and objective truth questions, i.e., what is life, is there a heaven, is there a hell, is there life after death, are there existing dimensions other than the four we recognize? To what extent does the actuality of all things affect self? Or more precisely, "Who are you?"

HOWEVER, IF WE CONSIDER GOD TO BE GREAT ENOUGH AND INTELLIGENT ENOUGH TO PLAN AND CREATE THE UNIVERSE, THEN WE MUST ALSO ASSUME THAT GOD MUST BE GREAT ENOUGH AND INTELLIGENT ENOUGH TO CONTROL HIS CREATION.

Scientists, such as Steven Hawking, have searched for a 'unified theory' to explain the interrelationship of all of the forces of the universe. In the book, *Steven Hawking: Quest For A Theory Of Everything,* Hawking gave an explanation: "If there is a Theory of Everything, we and everything in the universe must be obeying its principles, even while we try to discover what they are."[5] One might conclude such a theory would hold many governing rules. To the contrary, the rules of the universe may be few. Hawking stressed this view in the following comment: "The fact is that science is often less complicated than it first appears. The idea that all of it may come down to some thing remarkably simple isn't new or farfetched."[6] A number of scientists feel the String Theory explains how strong and weak nuclear forces, the electromagnetic force and gravity, could be joined into one united field. However, the theory does not explain what triggered the beginning event—the Big Bang. Taking Hawking's logic to its ultimate conclusion, one can easily understand how the nature of the universe may indeed center on a single creating force which would dictate everything known and unknown. Its essence would necessarily be the Ultimate Reality. Thus, a God force, in some way not understandable to mankind, spoke the universe into existence . . . "Let there be light!" It is theorized that shortly after the 'Big Bang,' gravity broke away from the other unified forces. Then, as the universe aged, expanded and cooled, the other unified forces separated.[7] Yet, we have no plausible understanding of how this force could be unleashed.

As mortal beings we can look from earth—our ground level reality, into the vastness of the night skies. Look beyond . . . beyond into a great sparkling sea called 'The Milky Way' . . . and beyond still! We cannot see much farther, so we must build a telescope to continue. Now look! We find seas and seas of 'Milky Ways!' Consider the ocean of galaxies spread toward what seems like infinity. Awesome is the drifting silence. Things that seemed important in our own world have faded away. Material values, self-centered desires and arrogant 'me'isms tend to seek their level of non-importance. So we contemplate! What really is important? What really does exist? As scientists probe the interrelated vastness of that which is, human relevance diminishes in a dramatic way. We become as noticeable as a bump on an electron. Our problems, from this view of reality, are not even mentionable. All human vestiges are virtually non-existent. In fact, all that now matters is GOD AND GOD'S WILL! Our honors, our awards are non-existent! "You are Man (or Woman) of The Year!" Such an honor has no meaning. "You are President of the United States!" MATTERS NOT! Remember, in reality, we are but a bump on an electron. Now we see more clearly our true existence.

Perhaps we can better understand, if we accept the factor of 'God,' that the only meaning to existence is GOD AND GOD'S WILL! In other words, through the Ultimate Reality we are allowed to focus on a bigger and truer picture of existence, one that holds the answers to all questions. Such a reality is not only God, but that which exists by the Will of God. And that, my friends, is the scope of this book.

If God does exist and God controls all of reality, then God and the Will of God should be more important to each of us than anything else in or out of the universe, including life itself.[8]

The following chapters give evidence to Divine Authoritarianism and the supposition that God does exist and has implemented a well-conceived plan for His creation. Thus, for everything there is a reason. Sometimes we are blinded to Truth by our self indulgences and prejudices and hatred; yet, it is we who are short-sighted and out of step. Reality does not change because of our misconceptions. Nothing is important but God and God's Will.

It is because of all this evil that you aren't finding God's blessings; that is why he doesn't punish those who injure you. No wonder you are in darkness when you expected light. No wonder you are walking in the gloom.[9]

If your eye is pure, there will be sunshine in your soul. But if your eye is clouded with evil thoughts and desires, you are in deep spiritual darkness. And oh, how deep that darkness can be![10]

CHAPTER 2

PHILOSOPHY OF LIFE: THE TWO VIEWS

Science is not the enemy of theism, for theism is compatible with science.
The enemy of theism is the intellect who does not comprehend true wisdom.

History has proven that many philosophical truths become antiquated relics of days gone by. With such change, human rationale seems to be only foolish naiveté. Though the big questions remain the same, our answers are based on what is right for the day. In an earlier time, man looked at the wonders of life and concluded God had ordained them–therefore, they existed. Whether it be the beauty of a jagged mountain range or the ravenous nature of a violent storm, God was the author and the enabler. Yet, through the guidance of our men of science, humanity began to realize that there were natural answers to all of life's mysteries. There were scientific reasons for mountain ranges and weather storms. Thus, many found no need for God. However, philosophical reflections which radically deviate from traditional human spirituality have generally proven to be only conjectural trash heaped upon a huge pile of hypothetical waste. We have seen materialistic theory after theory become passe, while a growing number of discoveries seem to point to intangible worlds beyond cause and effect logic. Once again man has begun to wonder if God ordains all that is. Nonetheless, our intellectual adeptness forbids a return to a spiritual based reality. The intellectual's politically correct philosophy has always been a political force. Make no mistake about this statement. The intellectual exerts a great political force which is particularly relevant to the field of science. Thus, we must recognize that science is a political tool before we can evaluate its real value to society.

Current academia proclaims God is not scientifically provable; therefore, God cannot be discussed in science. In earlier days, virtually everything was open to study. Science was then grounded in Greek Philosophy and functioned through rationalism (truth is knowable through reason). As one might expect, rationalism opened the doors to all questionable matters and, in particular, foundational questions. Yet, rationalism was often unverifiable or completely wrong. Major contributions during the sixteenth to eighteenth centuries began to change science methodology from rationalism to empiricism (truth is knowable through experience).[1] Empiricism became entrenched in intellectual circles through the philosophical works of Immanuel Kant and, later, through the philosophies of Hegel, Kierkegaard and others. As we will discover, Kierkegaard's concepts might well be considered most significant in the area of existential philosophy. However, Immanuel Kant has been the most influential modern philosopher in the field of science. Ironically, Kant was a theist and thought he was coming to the aid of 'theology' with his philosophical position, a combination of rationalism and empiricism. Simply put, Kant's concept of 'knowing' is similar to discovering truth through science. First, a concept is analyzed 'on paper' to the point where it becomes a theory. Then, experiments support or reject the theory. However, Kant stated that certain concepts could not be subjugated to cause and effect procedures. God is one such concept. (To Kant's credit, he also stated that the concept of 'God' could not be disproved). Thus, he theorized 'faith' is necessary to accept the concept of God. This philosophical stance seems reasonable enough, yet, 'faith' as Kant defined it, took God out of the scientific vocabulary and, thus, out of the realm of the absolute. Nonetheless, Kant's argument is antiquated, circular and based upon the assumption that God is unable to communicate with human beings. Scientist Dr. Hugh Ross questions Kant's logic.[2] Contrary to Kant's understanding, studies indicate that certain events occur which surpass statistical probability and common human experience. These events suggest there are mysterious forces at work which are often construed as conduits of divine intervention.[3]

Nevertheless, the contemporary intellectual perspective declares that God is not objectively discernible. In fact, any serious reference to God or anything supernatural automatically designates the discussion to be metaphysical and not scientific. Therefore, God's influence is negated. Moreover, with this 'scientific' point of view guiding our 'official' concept of reality, man has wrongly condemned himself to a life of hopeless despair.[4]

It is important to realize that Kant was viewing things from his perspective. Thus, Kant could not objectively 'know' God from a scientific point of view.[5] However, had he realized how much evidence related to God's existence would be disregarded by the intellectual community as a result of his position, Kant would have been quite hurt. Therefore, Kant's philosophical theory has become a paradoxical tragedy.

Actually, modern man has unmistakable scientific knowledge indicating God exists. Thus, a growing number of scientists are suggesting the existence of God is (to an extent) 'knowable.' Like humans have done with outmoded philosophies of the past, it is time for us to move to a new ration-

---

ACTUALLY, MODERN MAN HAS UNMISTAKABLE SCIENTIFIC
KNOWLEDGE INDICATING GOD EXISTS.

ale. As a matter of fact, I propose the evidence is so strongly weighted toward a theistic view that an atheistic view and virtually all other opposing views are implausible positions.

In this light, let us consider these two major camps (theistic and atheistic) and their philosophical influence on science through a discussion on the development of matter. They are as follows:

1. *The atheistic view:* There has always been matter or, for some unexplainable reason, matter developed from nothing and without cause. By chance and without reason, matter aligned to form the universe. By chance, non-organic changed to organic. This means rock like compounds became lifelike. Ameba-like creatures developed into millions of diverse life forms and/or species of life, including man. In a similar matter, there was a separation of sorts and, by chance, another event was happening in the plant world. Remember, when we say, 'millions of species,' we are not just talking about the millions of species of animals, but we are also referring to the many varieties of plants. We should also realize that animals cannot exist without plants and vice versa. Nonetheless, incredible balances and links of nature seem to align into an awesome structure of cosmic sophistication known as 'universe' and this conglomerate mix was synchronized by the 'dumbest of luck.'

Many atheists feel humans have evolved, or are evolving to such a state that we are now or eventually will be 'gods.' I find this concept particularly interesting because it reflects the human rationale expressed in certain Biblical stories, mainly the Genesis account of the fall of man, the Great Flood and the Tower of Babylon. As for the world religions, atheists feel God worship is deeply based in and, thus, part of mythology. The religious stories, rituals and other activities are man's attempts to explain natural occurrences by supernatural powers.

2. *The theistic or creationist view* - God created all matter and (through whatever process) developed all that is in the universe. Spiritually, everything in the universe is now, always has been, and always will be subservient to God.

PUSH–PULL

These two divergent views of reality (atheist and theistic) can be examined using a number of philosophical models. An example is the PUSH and PULL explanation:

A force pushes - The push concept describes the atheistic understanding of reality, a strict mechanism position. 'Push' is based on the ration-

---

NONETHELESS, INCREDIBLE BALANCES AND LINKS OF NATURE SEEM TO ALIGN INTO AN AWESOME STRUCTURE OF COSMIC SOPHISTICATION KNOWN AS 'UNIVERSE' AND THIS CONGLOMERATE MIX WAS SYNCHRONIZED BY THE 'DUMBEST OF LUCK.'

alism of French Philosopher, Henri Bergson. He proposed that an 'élan vital' life force pushes evolution 'ever upward' into more complex self-organization. The push originates as atoms bounce off each other and form molecules. The molecules blindly merge to form life. Thus, life is but a coincidence of nature. As a result of nature, man will continue to push upward. Eventually, humans will push themselves into another form of life superior to modern man.

A force pulls - The pull view is based upon Vitalism. Life is structured in terms of final causes. The creative force of life is grounded in a pre-established purpose. There is a timeless 'ghostly blueprint' in the future toward which life is being shaped and pulled. There is an 'Ultimate purpose for the universe.' Plato called it the 'form of the good.' Aristotle called it 'god.' As a seed becomes a tree and an egg becomes a chicken, we too were designed to 'become.' There is a reality of life that cannot be understood by simply analyzing its parts. An infinite, omnipotent Creator/God, through whatever means He has desired, has pulled life up to the present human plateau. Through God's Will, humans are unique. We are the only 'creatures' formed in His image.

THE LOGIC BEHIND PHILOSOPHICAL FAITH

Reconsider the *atheistic position:* There is no God. To take this stance, one must also state that he or she has access to all information and all information dictates there is no God. This atheistic statement does seem to fall into Kant's philosophical arena of 'faith,' for this position must be quite impossible to prove. There is a pencil and paper exercise in theological logic that I invite you to experience. Begin by drawing a circle on the paper. The circle will represent everything that can be known, the entire spectrum of knowledge. Now, within that circle, mark the area which represents your knowledge. Of course, this comparison is a perception changer. If your knowledge is like mine, such a dot would not even be noticeable. Therefore, let us assume that we cannot measure what little the individual knows. Now, consider the knowledge of the entire species. What we know as a species is like 'spit in a bucket!' (If there ever was an opportune time to use this Texas colloquialism, it is now.) It is foolish for anyone to embrace atheism. With such a big circle and such a little speck of a dot, one cannot possibly make a valid statement, "I know that there is no God." Writing about this concept, Kenneth Boa and Larry Moody concluded, "One would have to be God to know that God does not exist." Thus, one cannot confirm the atheistic view.[6]

Now, consider the *agnostic position.* This is a more reasonable and logical view than atheism. As a matter of fact, I don't think any reasonable

EVENTUALLY, HUMANS WILL PUSH THEMSELVES INTO ANOTHER FORM OF LIFE SUPERIOR TO MODERN MAN.

person alive today can be so factually sure of God that he or she does not have moments of question. Of course, this is where 'faith' indeed plays a role in our relationship with God. So, it might be said that from one time or another, all of us are at least on the edge of agnosticism. When I was growing up, one of the big events was the first man to walk on the moon. I remember to this day sitting in front of the television, excitedly, waiting for that first step. I'll bet most everyone alive who remembers this 'event' also remembers those famous first words on the moon: "One small step for man, one giant leap for mankind." However, I also remember the rumor that shortly followed. Someone accused NASA of faking the whole moon mission. As I recall, there was a book released and, later, a movie alleging that the moon walk took place on a movie set!

I personally believe that we went to the moon, but I have no real proof. I have seen spacecraft at museums and I have read scientific articles which indicate space adventure is not only possible, but factual. So, like the fine human being that I am, I have taken the best information and come up with a conclusion. As another example, I actually do not know that the world is round. I have not seen the round world. However, I've seen maps. I have seen pictures. I have heard the reasons for believing in a round world. I accept this information as true; for me, the world is round. Notice that both references to 'faith' are related to events considered factual by the science community; however, 'faith' is still involved. So now, with the understanding that faith is pertinent to virtually all things believed, including things provable by science, let us consider God. As for 'knowing God,' there is some good news and there is some bad news. The good news is that, from the information we now know, the atheist view seems impossible! This conclusion does not come from some exercise in logic, but from actual information gathered. Moreover, there is a flip side to strengthen this point: "The design in the universe demands a Creator" (a favorite saying of Hugh Ross). It is in this sense which we find unquestionable scientific evidence of God. And yes, Dr. Kant, I do imply empirical knowledge. The related evidence is not circumstantial or secondary, for scientists are staring face to face with a factual God. This will be examined in other chapters, but the implications have real philosophical value and, thus, eliminate the position of Kant. His presupposition is no longer valid. Now, how about the bad news? Well, the bad news is, from the best evidence we have, God is multi-dimensional and spiritual. (We also find scientific evidence of His multi-dimensional and spiritual existence). Unable to deny His existence any longer, some scientists have begun building a model of God in the same manner they would design a model of an atom. Many in this group,

---

AN INFINITE, OMNIPOTENT CREATOR/GOD, THROUGH WHATEVER MEANS HE HAS DESIRED, HAS PULLED LIFE UP TO THE PRESENT HUMAN PLATEAU.

uncomfortable with the spiritual realm, consider God to be a mechanical, benign non-involved god . . . a huge non-feeling force. The problem with this presupposition revolves around the predication that God is not a knowing, feeling intellectual being. A scientist who does not explore spirituality cannot know God. To know God on some personal basis takes a spiritual move on man's part. Looking for God is not like standing on a corner in a parade and seeing the Queen of England pass by in her carriage, or the Pope riding in his Popemobile. A spiritual process must take place. That is good, however, for man has a spiritual awareness or a spiritual value which can be honed and developed in the same manner as all human talents are honed and developed. Thus, if design is important, it seems we were designed to need a relationship with the Creative-force. By the way, Mister Scientist, the human need to communicate with God should be a huge hint that God is not only a Super-force, but also a multi-dimensional, intellectual Super-spirit. So, really, there is no bad news, only good and (the secret) good news. And, there is profound evidence (outside of holy books or holy writings) that, by GOD'S WILL, the individual human's spirit will survive mortal death and continue to exist.

Thus, I conclude this chapter with some of the basic philosophical problems that the atheistic position (man and all else that exists is the result of the dumbest of luck) must resolve. These questions were brilliantly posed in an oral debate at The University of North Texas, September 20–23, 1976, between Dr. Antony G. N. Flew, Professor of Philosophy at Reading University in England and Dr. Thomas B. Warren, Professor of Philosophy of Religion and Apologetics at Harding Graduate School of Religion in Memphis, Tennessee. Though this debate took place a number of years ago, Dr. Warren's points are fundamental and, thus, are just as relevant today as they were at the time of the debate.

Dr. Warren proposed that, before the atheist can know the proposition, "God does not exist" is true, he must first know:
1. Matter exists non-contingently.
2. Matter is the only thing that exists.
3. Matter is eternal.
4. No piece of matter has more value than any other piece of matter.

In addition, an atheist must know that by 'sheer chance':
1. Rocks and dirt turned into living matter.
2. Rocks and dirt developed a consciousness.
3. Rocks and dirt became human.

UNABLE TO DENY HIS EXISTENCE ANY LONGER, SOME SCIENTISTS HAVE BEGUN BUILDING A MODEL OF GOD IN THE SAME MANNER THEY WOULD DESIGN A MODEL OF AN ATOM.

4. Rocks and dirt developed in such a way that a woman was first on earth before any woman.

5. Rocks and dirt developed in such a way that a baby was first on earth before any woman.

6. Rocks and dirt developed the human female breast so that it could change blood to milk.

The atheist must also know that:

1. There is no law higher than civil law.

2. When a person passes away, his (or her) death is the absolute end of him (or her).

Finally, the atheist must know that by sheer chance, rocks and dirt developed:

1. A conscience (distinguishing right from wrong).

2. A spiritual capacity (relationship with God, hope of eternal life, etc.).

5. Intelligence.

6. A respiratory system.

7. A circulatory system.

8. A digestive system.

9. A reproductive system.

10. An endocrine gland system.[7]

Dr. Warren summarized his argument by declaring that, for the atheist to be correct, "the ultimate source" of every human being is rocks and dirt. If the atheist is correct we (humans) are nothing but organized matter. Warren continued, "Our alleged 'creator' has been rocks and dirt. If this is the case, then everything we are and do is the result of dead, non-intelligent, non-purposive matter. Given atheism, there is no real objective right or wrong." The atheist position contends that when we die our lives are over. It does not matter how we have lived. There is "no accounting or judgement or punishment." Hitler, Stalin, Mao Tse-tung, Ben Laden—whoever you consider to be evil is of no matter because death ends all debt. But, in fact the atheist cannot know any of these things, thus he or she is assuming much without justification.

However, Dr. Warren concluded, if God does exist there is "objective right and wrong," there is "objective moral good and evil." If the theistic view is accurate, we "have a real obligation to recognize the evidence for God and to obey God. And each and every one of us will live on as a unique cen-

AND, THERE IS PROFOUND EVIDENCE (OUTSIDE OF HOLY BOOKS OR HOLY WRITINGS) THAT, BY GOD'S WILL, THE INDIVIDUAL HUMAN'S SPIRIT WILL SURVIVE MORTAL DEATH AND CONTINUE TO EXIST.

ter of personality after this life on earth is over. And each one of us will give an account to God for how he or she has lived."[8]

So, again I ask, "Who are you?" What are we humans trying to prove? Are we trying to simply demand God doesn't exist? Are we trying to hide from reality? If we accept God and the Will of God as our guiding authority, why do we compromise His love by indulging filthy passions like lust and greed? Why do we crumble at the feet of hedonistic pleasure? Why is our pride satisfied through the humiliation of others? Where is our love for God? Finally, what is human love worth? Whatever that worth may be, love and hate and all of the feelings in between are the attributes which give human life its meaning and purpose.

SECTION TWO:

EVIDENCE OF GOD

CHAPTER 3

GOD THE ALMIGHTY

"That man is a fool who says to himself, 'there is no God!'"[1]

Evolution verifies God's existence. Admittedly, this is a different way to approach the old evolution vs. creation debate. It is not my intention to detract from conventional creation thinking and beliefs. My conspicuous omission of traditional creationism is for a purpose, as I maintain that any evolution theory is inapt without some form of a God force. Moreover, any evolutionary theory requiring God's participation is a creation theory unmasked. Thus, I propose, all plausible evolution theories are creation theories. Whether God only used seven days or took billions of years, all plausible theories require God's involvement. Furthermore, a planned universe is necessary if Divine Authoritarianism is truth and a planned universe is what we seem to observe.

Interestingly, science makes some important statements on behalf of God. As a matter of fact, much of our understanding and sureness of God's existence comes to us through scientific and intellectual revelations. As we discover scientific absolutes, we can develop a 'profile' of the characteristics of God, which, to a limited extent, describe God's character[2] Yet, when we discuss scientific realms which apply to our Creator, we find ourselves enveloped in the heart of the evolution vs. creation debate.

As stated in chapter 2, we seem to have only two legitimate choices pertaining to the existence of life. One choice is the atheistic view which proposes that all reality is material and evolved by chance, or, the more descriptive reference - by 'the dumbest of luck.' If this atheistic view is true, life has no meaning; the universe has no meaning. The second choice is the theological view which implies all reality has been planned and created. If this second theological premise is true then short-sighted speculations of contemptuous scientists limit our human understanding of existence and, thus, the meaning of reality.

Even though the latest published materials from scientists are crammed with information indicating both God's existence and that the universe is finely tuned, many scientists are reluctant to point to their professional

---

WHETHER GOD ONLY USED SEVEN DAYS OR TOOK BILLIONS OF YEARS, ALL PLAUSIBLE THEORIES REQUIRE GOD'S INVOLVEMENT.

works as affirmations of a 'Vast Intellect' or Supreme Being. This is particularly interesting when one considers the number of scientists who 'believe' in God. Scientist and author, Dr. Jim Brooks writes, "Many people believe that science and faith are incompatible, and are surprised to learn that scientists, especially those involved in studying the origin of life and the nature of the Universe, are also Christians. But the combination is a good deal more common than usually thought."[3]

Unfortunately, many scientists who would express the logical need for a creator God, no matter how convincing, might also find their professional works banned from our schools' bookshelves. We all know that slumping sales are not good for books nor for professional careers. As shameful as it is, a large percentage of our 'institutions of learning' are no longer interested in that which is real or true. Instead, they are preoccupied with that which is politically correct. "Separation of Church and State" has abandoned its intentioned protection of religious beliefs in favor of the criminalization of any discussion related to the relevance of God. Dr. Hugh Ross, concludes that there is only one religion "permitted to be discussed" in public schools. It is atheistic materialism.[4]

Institutional science took a great 'leap of faith' when it chose to accentuate the atheistic position. However, this leap included a 'belief' that future discoveries would provide substantial evidence to support a godless universe. That future has now come and much of it is gone. Instead of supporting atheistic rationalization, scientific discoveries are continuously shrinking any 'chance' of reality forming and developing through random accidents. Yet, some researchers enamored by the miracles of 'randomness,' seem to play the fool. Astrophysicist, George Greenstein wrote a book entitled, *The Symbiotic Universe*. In a summery note on his cover he states, " . . . our existence depends on a network of unlikely circumstances, a remarkable series of coincidences."[5] Greenstein discusses many random 'coincidences' which, to a logical minded person, might indicate that the universe was designed by an intelligence - a God. In fact, due to the strange and highly unlikely nature of said events, Greenstein believes randomness, in and of itself, cannot adequately account for reality as we know it. To better understand Greenstein's position (a seemingly popular position in intellectual circles); consider the foundation of the cosmos. In a universe that supports life, a synchronic pattern of 'miracles' must take place. For example, it is necessary that hydrogen and helium be the first atoms formed followed by beryllium and carbon. These atomic structures must be completed in a precise and time sensitive manner. Greenstein explains how the universe was uniquely shaped to accommodate

---

AS SHAMEFUL AS IT IS, A LARGE PERCENTAGE OF OUR 'INSTITUTIONS OF LEARNING' ARE NO LONGER INTERESTED IN THAT WHICH IS REAL OR TRUE.

this process and how smoothly these early atomic particles must have inter-acted with each other to make life possible. In the words of Greenstein, "It strikes me I'd like to know the explanation for that coincidence of resonances between helium, beryllium, and carbon. Is it an accident?"[6]

Greenstein then speculates, "The answer to that question depends on one's point of view. On the one hand, there is nothing supernatural going on. In this regard the analogy of the car, the bicycle, and the truck is a good one: We know how they're built. If by some chance these three vehicles were to vibrate in resonance with one another, engineers poring over the blueprints would be able to come up with an explanation. Similarly, the principles of nuclear physics are relatively well in hand. If we but knew the fine details, we would have been able to predict the resonances from a knowledge of the struc-ture of those nuclei."[7] Notice that Greenstein, like a number of other scien-tists, immediately rules out the ultimate concept, God designed the universe. This is a political statement and is not based on known facts. Moreover, if we recall the earlier circle and dot exercise regarding human knowledge, one must conclude an atheistic bias is anti-scientific. When and if we find answers to how atoms work in "resonance with one another," we will still be unable to explain why, and the why is needed to understand the reality supporting unique activity. As one might expect, Greenstein does propose a mechanical solution. Yet, he does not find a qualified mechanic. I truly believe he must realize this void. The car, the bicycle and the truck may vibrate in resonance, but their structures are not the result of accidents. Furthermore, they mechan-ically perform. Why? Because they were designed and created to do so by an intelligent being.

Greenstein later continues, "Suppose I were to shoot an arrow at a target by squeezing my eyes tightly shut, spinning about madly on one foot, and then loosing the bow completely at random only to find, upon opening my eyes for a look, the arrow lodged exactly in the bull's-eye. The fact is irrele-vant that in its flight it obeyed precisely the laws of ballistics, that even as I spun, the motion of my body followed known physical principles. The situa-tion would still be a matter for some surprise."[8] If laws of nature were the only forces which guided the arrow why would Greenstein be surprised? Greenstein does not have a problem accounting for the laws of nature; his problem is with the blatant 'dumb luck.' No matter the laws of nature, an acci-dental shot such as described would indeed be an eerie surprise. The 'dumb luck' factor is his obvious flaw. If you were to see Greenstein make the shot he described, would you really think it was a random shot? I would be very suspicious. Logic would lead an intelligent observer to conclude that there

NOTICE THAT GREENSTEIN, LIKE A NUMBER OF OTHER SCIENTISTS, IMMEDIATELY RULES OUT THE ULTIMATE CONCEPT, GOD DESIGNED THE UNIVERSE.

must be more involved than 'blind luck.' I would be inclined to suspect Greenstein was an expert archer. His 'luck' was not a fluke of his bow, but the product of his skill. Furthermore, I would be willing to bet he could repeat that shot any time he wished. His amazing 'luck' would be similar to that of a magician pulling a rabbit out of a hat. A rabbit does not accidentally appear. The magician plans to have a rabbit appear. It's a trick.

If conventional thinking is correct, once upon a time, such an arrow was propelled from a sea of nothingness. It was called the *Big Bang,* a term which describes the formation of the universe. From this arrow (Big Bang) came other consequences. Yes, laws guided the transaction, i.e., the flight of the arrow, but who dictated those laws and who set the circumstances? Who would command such skill to successfully negotiate such a feat? Who has that kind of authority? As in the case of Greenstein's shot, I do not think the beginning of the universe was a lucky accident. The material universe was no mistake.

So why do I claim that Greenstein realizes his obvious void? Because, time and time again, his text recognizes his shortsightedness. He looks at the facts and he asks "WHY?" Therefore, his book virtually makes my case. As further example, he writes, "Why should the rules of the game nurture life so carefully? Nothing in all of physics explains why its fundamental principles should conform themselves so precisely to life's requirements. The laws of nature could have been laid down only in the very instant of the creation of the universe, if not before, and this occurred long before the origin of life. In that instant, how could the universe have foreseen that billions of years later, on some tiny blue-white mote of dust, living creatures would have emerged - foreseen and adjusted itself accordingly?"[9] If a scientist is too political to publicly recognize that which is necessarily correct, if he is too closed-minded to presuppose the obvious, then I suggest he must intuitively know, 'dumb luck' does not rule the universe. Empirical science demands an Absolute Authority - a position reserved for God.

When the facts are presented in an unbiased manner, human intellect is left with but one valid choice; God rules. So convincing is the proof of God's authority that a growing number of scientists, who probably once would have scoffed at any possibility of a Supreme Being, are now faced with undeniable evidence. Granted these are only 'small steps for mankind.' It is understandable that the scientific community must be skeptically cautious. In fact, in their search for a credible alternative, many scientists try to limit God or put God into a box.

We discussed above George Greenstein's intrigue with a number of

> IF CONVENTIONAL THINKING IS CORRECT, ONCE UPON A TIME, SUCH AN ARROW WAS PROPELLED FROM A SEA OF NOTHINGNESS. IT WAS CALLED THE *BIG BANG,* A TERM WHICH DESCRIBES THE FORMATION OF THE UNIVERSE.

seemingly unexplainable 'coincidences' regarding the creation and evolution of the cosmos. His solution? He replaces the concept of God with the term 'cosmos.' According to Greenstein, the universe came into existence. It felt the need of a "conscious mind" to observe itself. This proposal conforms to the philosophical puzzle, if a tree falls in the woods and no one is there to hear it, did the tree really fall in the woods? If Greenstein's explanation seems novel it is not. It is a new twist on an old concept traceable to the Greek Sophists, particularly Protagoras who proposed 'man is the measure of all things.' For Protagoras nothing outside of man determines reality.

According to Greenstein, the Universe created life so the cosmos would factually exist. Cosmos + conscious mind(s) = 'Symbiotic Universe.' Thus, Greenstein uses Protagoras' theory removing the egocentric aspect and substituting the Universe as the determinate of human consciousness. However, Greenstein seems to dispute his own philosophical precept, 'There is nothing supernatural going on.' A cosmos of rocks, etc. that 'knows' about concepts like life, is certainly supernatural. Furthermore, like the traditional concept of God, Greenstein's cosmos of rocks is intellectually creative - thus, it must have an intellect. In like manner, Greenstein's metaphysical solution does not consider how the cosmos knew that no one existed to observe it or how the cosmos conceived of the concept of observing life forms previous to the factual existence of life. Nor does he discuss how a cosmos of rocks can be so philosophical. Thus, for Greenstein, the cosmos is actually a vast intellect. Make no mistake, to Greenstein, God does exist. The cosmos + conscious minds (life) is his god. Nonetheless, it is difficult for any scientist to observe the design in the universe and not feel the need for God.

A recent article in World Magazine by Nancy Pearcey held statements on this subject from Heinz Oberhummer, an astrophysicist at the University of Vienna, Austria. Oberhummer stated, "I am not a religious person, but I could say this universe is designed very well for the existence of life." And further into the article, Oberhummer said, "We have no idea why the strengths of the forces are fine-tuned" (to support life). Pearcey ended her article with the following conclusion, " . . . the simplest explanation is that it (the universe) was tailor-made."[10]

I once heard Carl Sagan, (the man known for the quotation,"billions and billions of stars") suggest he saw evidence of the god of Spinoza. (Spinoza's concept of god is, more or less, a force without a personality. Spinoza's god is everything, including the whole of the universe). This is a similar god concept to Greenstein's vision. I hesitate to categorize Sagan as Spinozian only because this confession seems unrealistic for a man whose

---

EMPIRICAL SCIENCE DEMANDS AN ABSOLUTE AUTHORITY - A POSITION RESERVED FOR GOD.

public projection was that of an atheist or, perhaps at best, agnostic. As small of a step from atheism as this might be, his disclosure is an attempt to give an explanation for the unmistakable empirical evidence for a Creator. Dr. Sagan recognized the 'God factor.' However, Sagan built his public reputation, in part, on his educational explanation of evolution - which made the whole evolutionary process seem quite by chance. Furthermore, throughout his life, he promoted the neo-Darwinian view of life. Thus, Sagan had to rationalize that God was impersonal and weak.

Other prominent scientists, realizing the enormity of these coincidences in the cosmos, the synchronized pattern of cosmic and microbiological events, and seeing an apparent master plan in nature, openly express their discontent with traditional evolution. In fact, many have 'dumped' neo-Darwinian evolution for other theories. For example, a very respected scientist, Dr. Fred Hoyle, proposes that life on earth is the result of intelligence in outer space. This particular scientist seems open to a pre-existing intellect/God being the prime cause. Dr. Francis Crick, co-winner of the Nobel prize for the discovery of DNA, concluded that DNA could not have evolved by chance and, therefore, was the seed of an advanced race of space aliens. In Click's hypothesis, space aliens replace God as the Creator. Frankly, with the growing number of seemingly impossible problems facing natural evolutionary thought, space alien 'explanations' are in vogue. To many, space aliens seem to be the best alternative to the supernatural Creator explanation. But God cannot be replaced that easily. If, by chance, our existence is explained by the seed of space aliens, how did an advanced civilization of aliens evolve without a plan maker or creator? Space aliens do not explain away the enormous number of 'natural' events which were determined at the moment of creation (or before) and made life possible in the universe. Furthermore, if space aliens are advanced enough to design DNA, which by Crick's belief (DNA) is too sophisticated to have evolved on earth, then how did their DNA (and/or other life form controls) evolve? How did an advanced intellect from another planet spontaneously 'become' when we (inferior earthlings) were too sophisticated to have a natural origin? Thus, neither life form (earthling or alien) seem to be the product of 'blind luck.' The vast odds 'demand' a Creator of all things including DNA and all space aliens. So, if you believe that aliens were the source for earth life, then my discussions of such things as the impossibilities of DNA evolution on earth also apply for the impossibilities of DNA evolving on planet 'Ultimatastic.' Additionally, an excuse that a different environment would change the 'blind luck' odds does not prove true. Assuming there is a positive environmental change found in another position in space

TO MANY, SPACE ALIENS SEEM TO BE THE BEST ALTERNATIVE TO THE SUPERNATURAL CREATOR EXPLANATION.

(which in itself is questionable), there is not enough matter in the universe for a 'by chance' assembly of DNA and proteins. Thus, it seems these 'natural' processes are impossible.[11]

The greatest changes in science in regard to theology may come from discoveries in physics. For an example, Dr. Frank J. Tipler is a professor of mathematical physics at Tulane University and specializes in global general relativity. According to Tipler, " . . . mathematical physicists (primarily Penrose and Hawking) have developed in the past thirty years the intellectual tools to analyze an actual infinity. Physics is no longer limited to the finite; technical advances inside physics itself have forced physicists to become concerned with the physics of the infinite."[12] Tipler proposes that physics can account for spiritual action. In Tipler's words, "Either theology is pure nonsense, a subject with no content, or else theology must ultimately become a branch of physics."[13] Tipler then made some interesting related remarks, including the following, " . . . physicists can infer by calculation the existence of God and the likelihood of the resurrection of the dead to eternal life in exactly the same way as physicists calculate the properties of the electron."[14] Tipler continues to explain why physics implicates the above 'theological,' i.e., Judeo-Christian-Islamic postulates: "The key concepts of the Judeo-Christian-Islamic tradition are now scientific concepts. From the physics point of view, theology is nothing but physical cosmology based on the assumption that life as a whole is immortal."[15] Whether or not Tipler has actually discovered 'God' might well be questioned. Tipler seems futuristic in the fashion of science-fiction and dimensionally limited in his thinking. After all, mathematics (Tipler's specialty) consists of cold, hard numbers. Thus, it can only deduce a model of reality. Furthermore, science cannot successfully examine the attributes of a supernatural being, because 'supernatural' is beyond the scope of scientific examination. Nor can science anticipate God's predetermined script. After all, mortal man cannot contemplate the mind of God. What physics has discovered and what Tipler and other physicists seem to be intellectually attempting to cope with is the growing number of physical universal constraints which eliminate a natural cause universe and infer that God does indeed exist and that God is a personal and loving Creator. Furthermore, if science were to accept a 'Supreme Being as a Creator' theory, the Biblical explanation of existence is remarkably reasonable. So, I suggest that scientists are trying to contend with the growing number of supernatural inferences arising in modern science.

THE HUMAN STUPIDITY FACTOR

The facade of a godless universe made by chance is but snake oil 'sold' to the public through a controlling media and a politically corrupt educational system. Rather then explaining the existence of life, neo-Darwinian evolution exemplifies a known sociological factor enveloped in human nature: If our society hears a falsehood often enough, it will accept it as fact. Thus, it is no wonder that the Bible analogizes God's people as sheep who need protection from the world's influences. Sheep are not considered to be very intelligent animals. They wander about in a herd for no logical reason. The greater the number of sheep in a herd, the 'dumber' the sheep seem to become. It is said that they will follow each other over the side of a cliff. Thus, another Texas colloquialism is humorously disparaging by suggesting a designated person is 'dumber than a hundred head of sheep.' We now live in a community which seems to be dumber than 250 million head of sheep. Our society functions in a 'virtual reality' world of fantasy. However, we pay a gigantic price. My atheistic friends often rationalize that society 'needs' to continue promoting the now traditional neo-Darwinian evolutionary fantasy. Of course, they hope someone will prove this fantasy is actually reality. Yet, their point is that theology should not be taught as science. I agree with them. I do not think the Biblical view of creation should be automatically adopted as fact in a science class. However, if science looks into the domain of theology, which would include the origin of life, then any scientific data suggesting God as a controlling force cannot be disregarded simply because it is also theological. You cannot see evidence of a "Vast Intellect" and proclaim that vast intellect to be cosmological dirt without even considering the more logical possibility, i.e., a Creator-being, yes a God, with an intellect! In other words, it is not scientific to deny the existence of a supernatural God if, in fact, evidence suggests a supernatural God does exist. Aforementioned lunacy, i.e., the misconstrued separation of Church and State, reminds me of Jefferson Airplane's greatest hit of the 60's which vehemently expressed youthful disgust for the blatant hypocrisy in society. Grace Slick blasted the establishment by singing:

> *When the truth is found to be lies*
> *when all the joy within you dies,*
> *Don't you want somebody to love . . .* [16]

We must consider the ramifications of our hypocrisy. If God does exist and God had a role to play in the evolutionary process, then everything our schools are teaching children about life is based upon lies. With such a perverted foundation, their world is about as relevant as a Saturday morning cartoon. No wonder so many of our children are violent and confused. No wonder our society seems to be crumbling before our very eyes. The USA no

---

THE FACADE OF A GODLESS UNIVERSE MADE BY CHANCE IS BUT SNAKE OIL 'SOLD' TO THE PUBLIC THROUGH A CONTROLLING MEDIA AND A POLITICALLY CORRUPT EDUCATIONAL SYSTEM.

longer accepts God's authority because our cultural infrastructure is now selling Nietzche's antiquated rumor: God is dead.

PROOF OF GOD: PRIME CAUSE

Most presuppositions about existence choose to ignore the 'first cause' of existence. This first cause was developed through Aristotle's position on motion. Aristotle was unhappy with Parmenides' (Aristotle's teacher) position on movement. His response came in his work, *Physics* (Book VIII, chapter 9), where he recognized that there has been motion from the beginning of time. Yet, there must be a first movement or "Prime Mover." This later became the essential position of St. Thomas Aquinas' *unmoved mover.* Now, the idea has become foundational to modern science because the 'cause and effect' thought process is the method by which scientists have developed material reality. Therefore, when students of logic read papers on evolution or hear debates about evolution vs. creation, they must realize that all such arguments are trivial antidotes to the prima or first cause factor. This 'prime' argument must be debated before any other point. All other concepts build on and are subjective to the first cause axiom. Naturally, the 'cause' of the universe must have had the capacity to form or 'create' the universe. Thus, the term 'sufficient cause' means a cause powerful enough to produce the resulting effect.

The application of a 'first cause' action today may seem contradictory to what you learned in philosophy class. Many people have the mistaken understanding that Emanuel Kant disproved the first cause issue with his book, *Critique on Reason.* However, what seemed true in Kant's day goes against recent scientific knowledge. Kant's view was based on the premise that the universe is eternal. Today, an infinite universe is no longer considered sound science. Thus, a first cause event is once again a logical expectation. At this point in time, logic presumes a first cause beginning.

The laws of logic are basics for all debates in science. One such law is known as the "law of noncontradiction." It states something cannot be A and non-A at the same time within the same relationship.[17] In regard to the prime cause question, the law of noncontradiction tells us that, if something exists today, then something always has existed. If anything exists, if I exist, if you exist, if this book exists, then 'something' is eternal. Because eternal existence is essential to all existence that which is eternal is described as a necessity.

To view this axiom from its opposite perspective we would state: "out of nothing, nothing comes."[18] The functional value of the concept, 'out of nothing comes nothing,' insists there is no such thing as spontaneous genera-

IF OUR SOCIETY HEARS A FALSEHOOD OFTEN ENOUGH,
IT WILL ACCEPT IT AS FACT.

tion. I use the term in a general manner to include any spontaneous formation over any period of time (long or short term). With our knowledge of science today, the debate over whether or not God is, can start and end with this simple law.

If you are a science student, there is a superb experiment related to this point. I suggest trying it before you completely accept what your public school or college is teaching on evolution. Take a test tube. Sterilize it thoroughly. Create a vacuum in it. Close it in such a way that it insures an interior sterile environment. Let it sit in an isolated place through class. Ask yourself what gas might evolve from the vacuum. In fact, ask what element, any kind of element, might spontaneously generate? After class, check the test tube. Under spontaneous generation, time is not necessarily a factor. Everything is 'spontaneous.' Therefore, your test tube may be full of life or rocks or something. However, assuming in your case you have nothing, leave the sealed tube out over night. Check it the next day. What has formed? If nothing is in the tube, leave it and check it in a week . . . a year . . . a decade . . . at the end of your life. Nothing will generate. Nothing can be made from waiting for nothing to become something. The mathematical equivalent is 0+0=0. We could watch for millions of years. Neither matter nor no form of matter would or could form. 0+0=0 also applies to chemistry, physics and every field of science and logic. (Quantum physics and related quantum systems are possible exceptions to this scientific foundation. Quantum theory makes certain contradictory phenomena theoretically possible for an instant, yet impossible from a practical understanding. Because these changes in subatomic structure seem to be miraculous, I will discuss this quantum activity in greater detail in later chapters). Actually, the above demonstration is a simplification of Louis Pasteur's experimentation which proved spontaneous generation to be false. Pasteur's work, however, certainly did not end the quest for self-creation concepts.

Science is once again beginning to reject spontaneous generation. Many scientists finally understand the absurdity behind 0+0=1.[19] If they are honest with themselves, scientists know the profound creation implications underlying this law of noncontradiction. Again we must consider the problems these new revelations hold for our schools. As we have previously mentioned, it is politically incorrect to teach creationism. Yet, the dynamic effect of the 0+0=0 rule is unmistakable. It destroys the primary concepts behind natural evolution. This absolute (0+0=0) value in the universe, of and by itself, subverts the neo-Darwinian evolutionary theory. Whether we accept evolution or not, if we live in a finite universe and 0+0=0, then natural evolution becomes

NOTHING CAN BE MADE FROM WAITING FOR NOTHING TO BECOME SOMETHING... WE COULD WATCH FOR MILLIONS OF YEARS.

only a dogmatic, but erroneous, theory intended to make man the center of his universe. Unfortunately, the choice for our schools is also clear. By both law and the pressures of intellectualism, they must teach the equivalent position to 0+0=1, and the truth becomes lies.

Nonetheless, no one can block the influence of universal truths on modern science. In fact, some of the categorical laws of science begin with the 'noncontradiction' logic and suggest the same theological conclusion. A great example is the "First Law of Thermodynamics." It too proclaims, "energy cannot be created (or destroyed) but simply converted from one form to another within certain limitations."[20] In reference to the First Law, research scientist Robert Gange comments, "A natural process cannot bring into existence something out of nothing."[21] According to Gange, "If the First Law is correct, which seems to be the case, and if the universe had a beginning, which seems to be scientifically accepted, then one conclusion is that something unnatural created the universe. If the world didn't result from a natural process, then it came from an unnatural process."[22]

As one might imagine, atheists try to avoid this causation problem by all possible means. Usually, when faced with such questions, they will conclude with a nonsensical 'faith' answer such as, "Evolution must have occurred without God." Of course, no one has a valid reason why such a conclusion 'must' be true. No one knows how such a universe (or anything else in the classical sense) could have happened without a cause. Yet, atheists unequivocally state, "There has to be a way." Can something the size and weight of the universe 'be' without a cause? Obviously, such atheistic rationalism ignores the foundations of science. Science does not blindly choose what its axioms will be. Consistency determines which theories become law. Unproven theories are but pragmatic ventures. However, in science, if a law is a law, there is no variance. If we have allowed a variance in our law, then science is a fable. If science is fable, than everything about science is nonsense and we live in a chaotic universe . . . or perhaps the universe is my own dream, though I really do not exist and you do not really exist and nothing is. Ah, the comfort of chaotic illusion.

Such inclusion as the statement just above opens all of the windows to the question: What is reality? Over the years, many philosophers have suggested that the 'Ultimate' human question is: "Is reality rational or irrational?"[23] Such a question might preclude a rather philosophical discourse on how logic should lead one to conclude what is real. Quite frankly, to suggest that reality is an illusion is illusionary in itself and therefore, nonsensical.[24] However, in regard to the origin of the universe, our philosophers have exam-

OVER THE YEARS, MANY PHILOSOPHERS HAVE SUGGESTED THAT THE 'ULTIMATE' HUMAN QUESTION IS: "IS REALITY RATIONAL OR IRRATIONAL?"[23]

ined the basic questions. Leibniz and Sartre brought such questions into focus with their query, "Why is there something rather than nothing?"[25]

As for the essence of existence, logic suggests that there are but four actual possibilities. They include:

1. The universe is an *illusion* and does not exist.
2. The universe is *self-existent* and eternal.
3. The universe is *self-created,* i.e., it emerged from nothing.
4. The universe is *created by something which is self-existent,* i.e., an eternal Being.

Other options seem to be variances of these four statements.

The first possibility that the universe is an illusion and does not exist relates to the above concept that nothing is real. Everything is part of a dream. If, in fact, the universe is an illusion, then we must still account for the illusion. This is the cosmological position referred to by Rene Descartes' logical explanation, "I think, therefore, I am." In the words of R. C. Sproul, "If it is a 'true' illusion, then something or someone must exist to have the illusion."[26] I might add, I find some hypothetical positions of clinical psychologists bordering on the illusionary. These statements mainly deal with the relationship between electrical impulses and brain functions. Electrons are carried on cords from the cortex to the rest of the brain. The electronic impulses are directly related to our perceptions. When we feel happy or sad, it is because of electronic impulses. From this clinical perspective, humanness becomes only a chemical reaction. This view totally erases the meaning behind all human emotion and a four dimensional reality. When a man and a woman meet and enjoy each other's company, are the love and romantic feelings they share only a reaction to electrons exciting brain stems? I say no. Feelings are real, sights are real, sounds are real and life is real. What happens is not totally related to electronic impressions. The brain does respond to internal commands. However, the brain functions similarly to a television in that electrons travel up the brain stem which acts as an antenna. From the brain stem, the electrons are moved up the correct wiring to provide a human being with an accurate understanding of 'physicalness' according to the four dimensions in which we were designed to function. What we experience and best understand are those things that fit within this four dimensional reality. We have a complex communication system which can be measured. Such a system does not mean our perceptions are only products of a mechanical and chemical system which borders on uncontrollable directives. More realistically, the electronic impulses project a reliable understanding of the world in which we live. This view is more in line with the latest neuro-scientific studies which indicate the human mind "generates a flow of imaginary visual scenes" which are inspired by "a variety of sources."[27] Moreover, the brain's reaction to these "imaginary visual scenes," is not what one might expect if this clinical perspective were true. One would assume that all brains function in the same manner. However, that is not what we find. Some brains are dominated by the right side while others are dominated by the left side. Moreover, some brains work best with visual stimuli, some with auditory impulses, some by tactile stimuli and some with kinesthetic contact. Furthermore, the human brain operates differently than other animals studied. According to Pasko Rakic of Yale University School of Medicine, "There must be small differences between brain development in humans and in other animals . . . these small differences can have a big functional impact on how the brain works."[28]

However, what if an *illusion is reality and nothing exists?* In the above case, what if the brain function only suggests earth and life on earth but, in reality, the electrons are part of the illusion? What if, somehow, the brain is also part of the illusion? What if there is no brain, no electrons and no life? If nothing exists, then there is no illusion and no questions to be answered because 'nothing exists.' [29] Therefore, because there is at least an illusion ("I think, therefore, I am"), 'something' does exist. The only rational conclusion about whatever is having an illusion can be expressed by the following: If something exists, it is either ultimately self-existent or created by something self-existent.[30] This logical conclusion points us back to our original concept regarding the necessity of an eternal being: If something exists today, then something has always existed. Additionally, because this something is necessarily eternal, it is self-existent. Would this mean that this same something is necessarily self-existent? Of course! If this something were not self-existent, it would not be eternal but would be created.

What about the second possibility? *Is the universe self-existent and eternal?* No! By our scientists' own admission, the universe is finite. It had a beginning and it will have an end. Could the initial driving force within the universe be both a creation of the universe and sufficient enough to form the universe? Such a force would include the Spinozian answer of a mechanical force of one kind or another. I question whether such a force could self-create. Does gravity exist without material bodies of various sizes moving and spinning at tremendous speeds? No! Matter and energy seem to be required for the mechanical model of the universe to hold any definable 'force.' Yet logic demands the existence of an eternal force of sufficient magnitude to cause or form the universe. Thus, if there was no universe, but there was an eternal force, would not that force be better explained by a transcendent God who needs no heavenly bodies, etc., rather than a gravitational force without material movement? Here is the dilemma science finds itself in. God is now needed in the equation. Sproul states the problem well; "If we argue that one part of

IF SOMETHING EXISTS TODAY, THEN SOMETHING HAS ALWAYS EXISTED.

the universe is self-existent and has the power of being within itself by which it can generate lesser levels of existent reality, then we have attributed to this mysterious being-within-the-universe the attributes of a transcendent God."[31] Thus, even if we accept the mechanical god concept we imply a transcendent omnipresent God similar to the Biblical understanding.

The third option is quite similar: *The universe is self-created.* This is the argument of the neo-Darwinian evolutionist. No doubt we live in a finite universe. As above, however, does the material universe create the force that drives the universe or does the force create the universe? We must assume that the material universe creates the known mechanical force. For example, you cannot have gravity without mass. Therefore, it is mass that 'creates' the force. This one fact destroys the mechanical or Spinozian view of cosmology. The mechanical argument assumes gravity, with the help of electromagnetic and weak and strong nuclear forces developed the mass when, in truth, all these forces derive substantial power from the existence of mass. Then, how could the universe self-create? How did mass self create? Can a universe self-create by chance? If we mean 'chance' to be the driving force, then the answer is NO! Chance has no power. Chance is no force. Chance has no 'being.' It cannot create anything in and of itself. Chance is only an expression for determining mathematical possibilities of a given situation.

What about random selection? Would random selection lower the odds for self-creation? If random selection does affect chance, which in itself is a highly debatable proposition, chance is still involved. Therefore, random selection is an "action-without-a-cause" and, by its very nature, is a nonsensical concept to scientific thought.[32] Furthermore, if the Big Bang came from a mass of infinite density as scientists suggest, there would be nothing to select from. Infinite density is one hundred percent broken down. Therefore, for all practicality, there is nothing. If one starts with nothing (but infinite density), any chance added to nothing still leaves nothing. The gamblers will confirm that you must have something to gamble (to win or lose) in order to 'take a chance.' Actually, this statement, 'The universe is self-created,' is both an illogical and a self-destructive statement. To self-create would again infer spontaneous generation and we have already seen the faultiness of that concept (I refer to the earlier discussed school experiment on spontaneous generation, as well as to the work of Louis Pasteur). I hope the degree of certainty in the rebuttal of this statement puts an end to spontaneous generation in your mind. I am sure Louis Pasteur thought he had crushed spontaneous generation years ago. Anyone who still believes this concept does not accept the uncompromising nature of the laws of science and logic today.

CHANCE HAS NO POWER. CHANCE IS NO FORCE. CHANCE HAS NO 'BEING.'
IT CANNOT CREATE ANYTHING IN AND OF ITSELF.

There is another Law of science which must be considered in a discussion on the origin of reality. The *New Generalized Second Law of Thermodynamics* places restrictions on the materials of the universe in a way that would make any 'chance' of self creation virtually nonexistent. Essentially, this Second Law explains that "things mix."[33] And when they mix and time passes, natural processes "destroy patterns."[34] In general, when things mix, patterns are destroyed. The converse situation then is, in order to create a pattern, "things will need to be separated."[35] Things by nature do not separate. They mix. The natural process demands the erosion of any given pattern. By natural processes, the universe should generally be losing information. What we observe is just the opposite. We find things have separated to create patterns, i.e., living plants, animals and people. Because natural law generally tells us things can only be separated if information is produced, we must conclude that the creation of a pattern infers an intellect.[36] Consider the relevance of this awesome concept. It speaks to the validity of everything that exists. An intelligence is essential to a creative activity.

You might be wondering what happened to the original Second Law of Thermodynamics? That was the 'old' law. Actually, there is nothing wrong with the old law. It still works today. However, it is limited in that it only describes physical things at rest. The 'new and improved' law replaced the 'old' law. The New Generalized Second Law of Thermodynamics, is an outgrowth of modern physics and is particularly compatible with quantum physics.[37] I have alluded to the fact that, in some ways, quantum physics has had an 'unstable' effect on science. The New Second Law, however, is an example of its positive effect. It was quantum theory influences on the Second Law of Thermodynamics which helped us to increase the accuracy of our conclusions. What has been the result? The New Second Law seems to be a comment about the importance of information in the universe and, as such, extends our view of reality beyond the material. Those who deal in quantum mechanics must leave classical reality and learn to think in terms of a quantum world run by another set of rules. In the words of Robert Grange, "Modern quantum laws do not describe independent physical things, but instead are statistical relations of our observations."[38] This ability allows us to "measure the information needed to describe an object's complexity."[39] Thus, we begin to think with a broader yet fuller concept of reality. The material or physical world is but an observation and, thus, is limited by human interpolation. What is real is the information that describes it. What allows us to change energy into matter is information. We have not understood this because of past limitations on observation. Through the New Second Law of Thermodynamics and the quantum world, we have greatly increased our ability to observe and measure existence, and information has become the consummate yard stick. With our expanded vision regarding information, we can cross the lines of perceptive reality. Perhaps information is even the great connector among all worlds and all dimensions, for mass and energy are secondary to and reliant upon information. Information then becomes a description of something greater than material things.

Yet, information is a tool reserved for an intellect. Through measurements, information researchers are finding empirical evidence of God's authority over nature. Some scientists now believe they are capable of deciphering information to the point that they can consistently detect and separate intelligent design from possible random generation. Intelligent design, one of the latest interests of science, has actually been debated for years. However, in 1996, the subject grew respectability with Biochemist Michael Behe's book, *Darwin's Black Box: The Biochemical Challenge to Evolution.* Behe's reference is to the complexities of the living cell. According to Behe, some biological systems could not have developed over time through 'blind luck' evolution. It is more likely that they were designed. In Behe's words, "No one has been able to explain the complex system in terms of Darwinian gradualism . . . There have been a number of objections to the arguments of the book (*Darwin's Black Box*), but I've looked into them. When you look at them closely, they don't hold up-both scientific objections and philosophical objections."[40] Perhaps the leading authority in the 'intelligent design' movement is William A. Dembski. According to Dembski, what makes said distinction is "the complexity of information." Information that is both complex and specified is called complex specified information (CSI). CSI is distinctively complex insuring that its distinctive number will not be "dialed randomly (at least not too often)." The specificity insures this outcome is unique.[41] Thus, it seems reasonable to assume that the Creator God is an intelligent being who is able to create 1) information, and 2) creatures who can examine that information.

An example of a popular concept which questions whether or not we observe a self-created universe (it is also open to the concept of a God created universe) is the previously mentioned grand unified theory. The idea behind such a theory is that all of the foundational concepts of science could be structured into one underlying equation. The unified theory was popularized through books by the celebrated theoretical physicist, Stephen Hawking. He assumes that our finite universe has no boundaries and is self contained. Would such a discovery verify that the universe self-created itself? Let me list a few problems which would preclude a unified theory from proving a self created universe.

First, we must be realistic. In 1970, Hawking and Roger Penrose

---

THROUGH MEASUREMENTS, INFORMATION RESEARCHERS ARE FINDING EMPIRICAL EVIDENCE OF GOD'S AUTHORITY OVER NATURE.

proved that the universe began with 'singularity.' Space, time, matter and energy had a common beginning at the moment of the Big Bang. Just because Hawking and others might be dissatisfied with the finality of this state does not change the profound implications of his work. The only 'self-created' rebuttal to singularity seems to be that quantum physics gives quanta certain attributes, such as size and wave length. When these attributes are factored into the Heisenberg Uncertainty Principle (HUP) the very concept of singularity becomes nonsensical. This is because no measurement can be made with 100% certainty. As an example, Hawking used HUP to break the hold of black holes. Perhaps, however, quantum measurements are 100% accurate in this instance. Black holes are tinker toys in comparison to singularity of the universe. With the dynamical power of the universe being the bond, would quantumness even exist? No, by definition, quanta would be crushed. Using HUP as an excuse to refute singularity is like a CPA looking at different accounting methods to explain away zero (0) dollars. Or, it is like the nonsensical parlor quizzes, "If God has infinite power, can He create a rock even too heavy for He to lift?" The most logical answer to quantumness is, if there was singularity (and Hawking and Penrose have proven there was), then there was no quantum cause previous to the existence of space, time, matter and energy. Quantum mechanics is dependent on these parameters. Therefore, quantum mechanics cannot function without them.

A second reason deals with the laws of thermodynamics. In his book, *A Brief History Of Time,* Hawking writes that there is a distinct thermodynamic direction for the universe which points from ordered to disordered. He illustrates this by referring to a thermodynamic directional arrow.[42] However, if one is to use quantum theory to refute singularity, than quantum mechanics destroys time. There cannot be different times for separations of particles. There can only be 'once-and-for-all probabilities' for each conceivable arrangement. Nonetheless, Hawking does not describe what many onlookers observe. Instead of a straight thermodynamic flow, we find a winding path moving from order to disorder. Occasionally a mysterious creative intelligence seems to separate 'things' causing order and thus information to appear. The best example of this creative force may be that life seems to be the highest form of order in the universe. Yet, as far as we can tell, life is a relatively recent event in the time line of the universe. Therefore, the arrow assumption is incorrect.

Hawking continues by commenting, "The no boundary proposal for the universe predicts the existence of a well-defined thermodynamic arrow of time because the universe must start off in a smooth and ordered state."[43] However, if the universe began in a no boundaries thermodynamic situation where time is infinite, one would expect a chaotic beginning. Mass would not explode (referring to the Big Bang) with excessive power, but finitely deteriorate. The pre-universe would only be a black hole and, according to black hole theory, "evaporate away and finally disappear."[44] In other words, nature left to itself would not create a Big Bang. It would only let an infinite density of matter decay. Yet, if matter was of infinite density how could it decay and 'finally disappear?'

Let us assume that a scientist somehow resolves the problems behind a grand unified theory, as some suggest has happened. Why would I propose the above theory does not prove self-creation nor does it diminish the cosmological need for a Creator God? Even if we were to assume that our finite universe has no boundaries and is self contained, something would still be missing. What would be missing is the intellect. The universe would still lack an introspective knowledge. Could space-time self-organize by the dumbest of luck? Could it then cultivate matter? Could it know which things should be done and then know how to do them? Some scientists try to cover this problem with a concept known as the "anthropic principle." The universe somehow knew life was needed to observe the universe's existence. Is this possible? Logic says no. The needed intellect is missing. The needed wisdom is missing. As was pointed out in the discussion about Dr. Greenstein's book (a number of others are just as fanciful), an infinite and intelligent Prime Mover seems essential. Patterns suggest an intellect; information infers an intellect. If we are as objective as possible and interpolate all of the information we have gathered to this point, then we must conclude there is an infinite something with an intellect.

The last possibility then is that the universe is created by something which is self-existent. This last choice, of course, is the category which encompasses an intelligent God as the casual force behind the universe. Furthermore, such a position seems to be the only valid choice because it does not break any laws of logic or science. As we take the beginning of the universe to whatever degree we wish, we still find reasons for a Creator.

Would any circumstances produce the Big Bang and not imply an intelligent Creator? Are there any alternatives? The earlier discussed quantum influence on singularity is erroneously considered a choice. Some scientists speculate that the Big Bang was one gigantic quantum jump. Other quantum possibilities are becoming just as popular. An example is Alexander Vilenkin's ideas about quantum creation. Vilenkin's theory makes some radical assumptions. For instance, he circumvents Big Bang singularity by presuming the fantastic. Vilenkin writes, "Rather than a virtual particle popping into existence, a whole universe, along with matter and energy and space and time and everything else, pops into existence from nothing."[45] There are several obvious problems with this kind of thinking. Most important, if quanta 'appear' to self-create it is only for an instant. They disappear as quickly as they appear. This is referred to as virtual probability of quanta. Dr. Gary McCartor, professor of physics at Southern Methodist University, describes virtual quanta's behavior as 'twinkling.' Anyone who has looked into the heavens understands this meaning. Virtual quanta do not suddenly appear and then stabilize for billions of years as the universe has done. They twinkle. A second problem area of Vilenkin's proposal is his related accompanying suggestion that universes "could be popping into existence all of the time."[46] Besides the impossibilities already expressed, the more practical answer is that we never observe universes appearing out of nothing. We do not observe Big Bangs or even mini-bangs. In fact, we have no reason to suspect anything permanent has ever popped into existence. Science writers, Robert R. Caldwell and Marc Kamionkowski, jointly wrote "You need not worry, though, about virtual apples or bananas popping out of empty space, because the formula applies only to elementary particles and not to complicated arrangements of atoms."[47] Why do we not read newspaper headlines like: MAN AND WOMAN KILLED BY QUANTUM INDUCED ROCK EXPLOSION! "They were just sitting there eating lunch when, all of the sudden, rocks exploded out of thin air!" We do not read such articles because that is not how quantum mechanics work. Quanta abide by a strict set of laws just as do all natural phenomena. I do not mean to make light of this premise, because the multi universe concept is becoming an alternative to a singular universe. In fact, some scientists suggest many Big Bangs occur in dimensions uncommon to our experiences. However, if Vilenkin's assumptions (or other similar multi universe assumptions) were, through some process, found to be accurate, it would not diminish the necessity for an infinite God with sufficient power to create all existence. Who or what tells nothing it is time to pop out a universe? Where did the laws that govern the popping out of a universe come from? How does nothing know how to form a universe with the right sequence of events and exact timing? Astrophysicist Paul Daves, once a major believer in the non guided quantum leap universe theory has recently claimed, "If new organizational levels just pop into existence for no reason, why do we see such an orderly progression in the universe from featureless origin to rich diversity?" Daves new conclusion is that " . . . there is 'something going on' behind it all."[48]

Obviously, there is a creative force which bears all of the signs of an intelligence. Factually, we could only say we think we know how singularity was circumvented. (Circumventing singularity will be a hard problem to solve even with a 'cooking' quantum field). Quantum physics does not negate the laws of classical logic and physics. It only broadens our understandings. Frankly, quantum reality is unsettling to both philosophers and scientists. Thus, they often resist its inclusion or perhaps blow it totally out of proportion. Here lies an enigma for the naturalists. Instead of adding some level of doubt to first cause logic, quantum mechanics destroys the materialistic view of our post-modernist society. Quantum reality is a foreign environment holding possibilities which seem to depend upon a perfect set of boundaries. Thus, we discover yet another complex level of organization in our universe, revealing even greater empirical evidence of a designed world and thus an intelligent Creator or God.

One of the most respected concepts of quantum theory has been the Copenhagen interpretation formulated by Neils Bohr. It consists of two basic premises. The first is that deep reality does not exist. In the words of Bohr, "There is no quantum world."[49] As an example, from a quantum practicality, electrons have no dynamic attributes, but only potential dynamic attributes. In related matter, the second part of the Copenhagen interpretation states that the observer creates reality.[50] This is a way of saying as the observer measures quanta, he/she updates the knowledge about that quanta. Thus, the probabilities of what a quanta will do are updated as the quanta is observed. Electrons only gain dynamic attributes when they are measured by an observer. Therefore, an observer is essential. For example, when quanta with the attributes of a wave are measured, they may change and show the characteristics of a particle. In this way, the nature, structure and attributes of quanta are affected by the observer. However, the observer does not know what will happen, only the probability of what could happen. Though, most scientists do not suggest anything radical or metaphysical about the importance of the observer, I suggest this understanding might change as we learn more about the quantum world. The outside or non-local observer may, in fact, affect the outcome.

My inference comes partly from the realization that there are even more provocative quantum concepts such as Bell's theorem. So significant is Bell's theorem that Kafatos and Kafatou feel it may be "the most profound discovery of science."[51] Bell's theorem simply states that quanta, are affected by non-local influences. If this is so, non-local influences are around us (human beings) and in us all of the time. Physicist, Nick Herbert has written that non-local influences "underlie all the events of everyday life. Non-local connections are ubiquitous because reality itself is non-local."[52] We somewhat understand the gravitational pull going on between the sun and the earth, but that is not what is meant by non-local influence. We are discussing something much more mysterious than gravity. A better understanding might come from some of the theorem's more interesting implications.

In his book, *Quantum Reality,* Herbert lists the characteristics of non-local influences as follows:

Non-local influences, if they existed, would not be mediated by fields or by anything else. When A connects to B non-locally, nothing crosses the intervening space, hence no amount of interposed matter can shield this interaction.

Non-local influences do not diminish with distance. They are as potent at a million miles as at a millimeter.

Non-local influences act instantaneously. The speed of their transmission is not limited by the velocity of light. (They travel faster than the speed of light).

A non-local interaction links up one location with another without crossing space, without decay, and without delay. A non-local interaction is, in short, unmediated, unmitigated, and immediate.[53]

This and the other quantum concepts are deep and far reaching. Not only do they present a surprising foundation foreign to all classical reality, but they might also provide a communication system for a non-local observer; i.e., a medium designed to apply God's Will. We are beginning to see this concept being discussed. As an example, Dr. Lee E. Warren insists that 'non-local' intimates the Spiritual world. He has further commented, "Bell's Theorem proves another realm exists that theology has talked about, but was unable to prove in a theoretical or empirical (experimental) sense."[54] If we accept the Copenhagen interpretation and assume the observer's conscious mind plays a role in measuring reality (as in a wave to a particle) and if Bell's theorem is correct and all quanta are influenced by non-local forces (which includes spiritual reality) then we may have found a system where the non-physical world influences the physical world. Furthermore, if a quantum jump somehow created the universe, then it is very logical to assume reality was created by the command of a non-local intelligence. Yet, regardless of the mechanics, when we consider the precision that was needed and unleashed in the Big Bang, we must conclude that a creative intelligence seems essential.

If we look further into the quantum implications of the beginning, we realize that we live in a universe which began by the cosmological force which utilized ten or more dimensions of space and time. Some theorists propose that we live in a multi-dimensional world, but we do not comprehend more than four dimensions. Others suggest there are two separate dimensional universes. As an example, the entirety of Kaku's book, *Hyperspace: A Scientific Odyssey Through Parallel Universes, Time Warps, And The 10th Dimension,* deals with a theory about the multi-dimensional universe.[55] Kaku alludes to a concept known as Vega's "string theory." This theory, like the grand unified theory, attempts to harmonize quantum mechanics and the theory of relativity into one theorem. Generally, string theories suggest that there exists ten or more dimensions. For example, one such theory suggests that, at the Big Bang, these multi dimensions split, forming two 'universes,' perhaps of six and four dimensions. However, strings do not adequately explain the universe we observe. Thus, we find string theories advancing to include membranes that are like 'bubbles.' These changes have given rise to the M-theory. In this theory p-dimensional objects, as if by magic, 'sweep out' into an added dimension. Therefore, an object with no dimensions gives "a one-dimensional trace" (or 'worldline').[56] Yet (as in the case of the grand unified theory), such theories do not well explain what existed before the Big Bang. Scientists do speculate with multi universe theories, etc., but most hypotheses need cause and cause suggests a first cause and Creator. Those theories, which suggest reoccurring universes are infinite, ignore the perfection and probable uniqueness of the only universe that we have observed. It is very hard for scientists to suggest this universe is only a mistake or a fluke of M-theory 'magic.'

Furthermore, the M-theory (or string theory) does not explain where or what the other dimensions are. Are they physical? Are some of these time dimensions as a number of scientists now think? I must reiterate that Hawking and Penrose proved time began with the Big Bang. General relativity suggests time and space are entangled in a conceptual union, as time began only when there became two or more objects. Of course, these mysterious extra-dimensions may, in some way, be spiritual. Furthermore, when we look closer at such proposals, we realize that a string or M-theory's dimensional splits describe a changing environment. Thus, there is a theoretical history of change. Such a historical record suggests all dimensions are finite and not eternal. Again we must think in terms of cause. What could 'cause' a dimensional split? What eternal force would be the logical first cause and sufficient cause of such a complicated theoretical universe as the one developed so perfectly through Vega's string theory? Bell's Theorem and the Copenhagen interpretation of Quantum reality indicate that the starting force might have been a non-local intellect or observer. Furthermore, the first cause would necessarily be infinite. Thus, an infinite, non-local, first cause (whatever it might be), must be defined as God. Most scientists would recognize this explanation as a legitimate conclusion, but might be afraid to infer (out loud) a God.

Interestingly, if we were to assume dimensions existed before the material universe, we should also ask how is this possible? The only meaning of a dimension is a measurement of space or time, and space and time did not exist. But, what if it did? Perhaps we have a solution to the grand unified theory. According to our assumption (dimensions existed before the Big Bang), there must be a more profound meaning to existence than material structure, simply because dimensions would have existed previously to material structure. This is particularly pertinent if we consider p-dimensional or 'magical' changes of something from a zero dimension to a material dimension. The alternative to the material existence is often described as the spiritual realm of reality. Obviously, a spiritual/nonphysical primal reality has even more profound implications as it easily allows for such abstracts as p-dimensions as well as the traditional concepts of heaven and hell. Yet, at present, multi-dimensional existence falls well beyond human understanding.

If such dimensional thinking opens the door to metaphysical alternatives, string theories and such lend well to early Jewish mysticism of Kabbalah. In fact, the Kabbalahian explanation of a multi-dimensional non-material procedure which might have produced a Big Bang explosion is a very good one. Daniel C. Matt, in his book *The Essential Kabbalah: the Heart of Jewish Mysticism,* summarized such a procedure. According to Matt's inter-petation of Kabbalah, there was the infinite known as Ein Sof. Before the Creation, Ein Sof withdrew its presence in every direction leaving a vacuum which was surrounded by the light of Ein Sof. The light spread outward from the vacuum and " . . . all the opacity and density of judgment within the light of Ein Sof–like a drop in the ocean–was extracted. Descending into the vacuum, it transformed into an amorphous mass, surrounded in every direction by the light of Ein Sof. Out of this mass emanated the four worlds: emanation, creation, formation, and actualization. For in its simple desire to realize its intention, the emanator relumined the mass with a ray of the light withdrawn at first–not all of the light, because if it had all returned, the original state would have been restored, which was not the intention."[57] If you assume the emanator is the breath of God at the time He commanded the universe to come into existence, this explanation could hold the secret to the alteration of singularity.

PHYSICALNESS VS. GOD

Spinozians and like thinkers revere one isolated product of God's Will and call it God. To them, god is the unified laws of the universe. These laws created everything–the universe itself. Furthermore, said axioms are the only things that are unmitigated; they are consistent throughout the universe. They are perfection in science.

However, such searchers are missing the spiritual and personal nature of God; both facets are experienced daily. Every time Dr. Kaku holds his son's hand or councils him about life, he experiences innate, yet common, forces of the personality as ordained by something greater than the individual psyche. Moreover, through such experiences, Kaku should better understand God's control of His creatures (determinism), yet the freedom He allows (free will). But, like common man, Kaku will repress these intuitions and allow them to become yet another file in the subconscious.

> WE ARE ONLY REAL TO THE DEGREE GOD DICTATES, AND WE ARE UNREAL, IF THAT BE GOD'S PLEASURE.

This should be the end of the story–God created the laws and God created the proper relationship between God and man, and man and man. However, science may be on the verge of uncovering something much more awesome. Something much more spectacular may be what is *real*.

Astrophysicists have detected evidence suggesting the alpha value is greater today than it was billions of years ago. If so, this could be revolutionary because alpha is a constant used to measure "the electromagnetic force that governs how electrically charged elementary particles interact."[58] If a constant in nature varies, then the foundations of science must be questioned. Thus, alpha should never change its value. According to Barry N. Taylor of the National Institute of Standards and Technology, "If alpha didn't have the value it has, Earth as we know it wouldn't exist."[59]

Perhaps the absolutes some scientists worship are not constant, but are changing. Perhaps, like time and space, everything is relative. Perhaps God and God's Will are the only things that are substantial. Everything else may be relative. (If we were another form and from other dimensions, such as angelic, perhaps we would not be able to interact in the universe without expanded perceptions. This premise would also justify the existence of human extrasensory perceptions). The John Templeton Foundation proposes that science has found evidence of a Creator "molding the universe over time."[60] In truth, however, the implication of alpha is much greater. We must be only a quark in the mind of God. Like a dream, we drift to whatever level of relevance our Creator desires. Physicalness has no meaning without a Creator's decree. We are only real to the degree God dictates, and we are unreal, if that be God's pleasure. Such a wide boundary might well explain our relativity, because One who controls time and dictates the perimeters of nature can easily prescribe existence.

THE FACTS

What we can be sure of is that there was a beginning. Furthermore, there was singularity (or God so structured creation to imitate singularity). No scientist or mathematician has ever found anything substantial to the contrary. The laws of physics claim such a beginning. Even the universe's extravagant loss of energy proves it's finality and a finality suggests a beginning. Moreover, the surety of a cosmological beginning increases with new information. The old Big Bang theory has been updated by the New Inflationary Theory of the Universe. Through this modernized version, we have increased the accuracy of our understanding of the beginning.

From time to time, scientists, such as Kaku and Hawking, will spec-

WHAT WE CAN BE SURE OF IS THAT THERE WAS A BEGINNING.

ulate on the pre-Big Bang possibilities. When this occurs, the pre-Bang topic can become very complicated, perhaps unexplainable and highly theoretical. For example, we discussed the highly speculative concept that our universe is one of many universes. Frankly, one of the major reasons this idea has been proposed is that our universe is too perfect to be the only universe. Thus, ours became the lucky universe. Yet, as we have discussed, there is no scientific evidence to support such a view. Moreover, even if we entertain the notion that 'the universe is only one of many universes to bubble forth,' such a concept suggests a line of history caused by a creative process with an initial universe. There still seems to be a need for a beginning. Additionally, logic insists–above all else–that there must be 'something' eternal and powerful; i.e., a sufficient cause in existence prior to those forces which account for the functions of the present universe. If a force existed before the universe, then it has to be independent of the universe. Yet, we must remember that our laws of science have well established that nothing we recognize as natural existed previously to the Big Bang, not even time. Furthermore, both quantum mechanics and the theory of relativity suggest an awesome, but simple, beginning - a created universe. In fact, if we eliminate the prejudices of the inquirer, then an all-powerful, eternal God becomes the essential factor. Thus, what we should hypothesize above all else is "In the beginning there was God." Of course, if we allow for a supernatural being, there is always a possibility that God created the universe in a shorter period of time than we can measure. In doing so, God would have given the universe certain characteristics which we mistakenly take to look as if it started with a bang. However, such a supernatural feat is totally foreign to our human abilities to measure and understand as reality. Either way, the universe must have had a beginning and, thus, a cause by an extremely powerful creative force.

      Though Kaku seems to be one of the scientists who believe that a mechanical force is god, many former agnostics are coming to grips with the scientific evidence of God, the All Powerful Creator. In his lectures, Hugh Ross occasionally will refer to articles from newspapers about the change in the scientific attitude. One such example, came from Frederic B. Burnham, "The community of scientists now considers the idea that God created the universe 'a more respectable hypothesis today than at any time in the last hundred years.'"[61]

      Reader's Digest is known for profound quotations. One such quotation came from a John Noble Wilford article originally printed in the New York Times. In the article, cosmologist Allan R. Sandage stated, "Science can-

---

FURTHERMORE, BOTH QUANTUM MECHANICS AND THE THEORY OF RELATIVITY
SUGGEST AN AWESOME, BUT SIMPLE, BEGINNING - A CREATED UNIVERSE...
THUS, WHAT WE SHOULD HYPOTHESIZE ABOVE ALL ELSE IS
"IN THE BEGINNING THERE WAS GOD."

not answer the deepest questions. As soon as you ask why there is something instead of nothing, you have gone beyond science. There has to be some organizing principle. God to me is the explanation for the miracle of existence - why there is something instead of nothing."[62]

Therefore, given the total knowledge of the day, can we, as rational humans, take science (or science theory) and conclude God is a fantasy constructed and explicated by human need or wish? No - such a presumption does not conform to the constraints of science. Rather, modern scientific theories seem incredulous without a Designer. In fact, our contemporary theories do adequately explain how a divine infinite Creator could 'speak' a force of energy from 'His mouth.' Moreover, the M-theory and quantum mechanics explain a way in which His words could become physical dimensions of time and space. We must assume that such an energy force was needed to cause a Big Bang explosion, as even the smallest particles hold nuclear energy unimaginable even to this day. We have no choice but to conclude that an infinite God is a very logical explanation for our finite universe. Yes, in the beginning there was God–one awesome GOD!

CHAPTER 4

SCIENCE: CLOSING IN ON GOD

"For some men, admiring the world itself rather than the Creator of the world, have represented it as existing without any maker, and eternal; and as impiously as falsely have represented God as existing in a state of complete inactivity, while it would have been right on the other hand to marvel at the might of God as the creator and father of all, and to admire the world in a degree not exceeding the bounds of moderation."[1]

I have a grievance with many of the 'science' articles found in major newspapers and magazines. Often, when they address issues like the theological implications of Science, their work is filled with unfounded conclusions. For instance, the article, "What Does Science Tell Us About God?" is in the December 28, 1992 issue of Time Magazine, and deals with the religious ramifications of science. However, the author ruined his article by including statements apparently designed to make the 'believer' of God look foolish. For example he wrote:

> . . . the current documentary *A Brief History of Time,* like the best-selling book of the same name, ends with physicist Steven Hawking's uplifting hope that someday humankind will 'truly know the mind of God.'
>
> Of course, when Hawking says God, he doesn't mean God. He isn't talking about a personal deity any more than Einstein was when he doubted that God would 'play dice' with the universe. Similarly, 'the God particle' doesn't exactly refer to a giant photon in a white beard and robe, beaming down benignly on all creation.[2]

First, the author, Robert Wright, uses a bad Einsteinian quote for his purpose, as it does not justify his point about Hawking. Einstein's problem with the personality of God was more philosophical than scientific. Einstein questioned why God allowed free will, as well as the accompanying pain and suffering, in His creation. He concluded that God did create the universe, but was not a personal God and, thus, did not get involved with people's lives.

When you look at the evidence for God working with man, such as the relationship of Abraham and God, one does not look to science. One looks at historical records, etc. However, what scientists have found are patterns (alluded to in the previous chapter) so exact or deliberate and so seemingly providential that God seems the best explanation. Such evidence is so over-whelming that humanity cannot ignore it or overlook it or even explain it away. There are those who do, but they are now out of step relics of days gone by.

Second, Mr. Wright's statement has little to do with the meaning of Hawking's comment. When I debate atheists who are knowledgeable in science, I often quote Hawking and point to him as an agnostic (with perhaps loose deistic leanings). When I do this, the opposition calls foul. Some atheists view Hawking as a flaming Christian. Why? Because the Hawking-Penrose proof of singularity is a landmark discovery, as it seems to prove God's existence. Though my opponents could be right about Hawking's beliefs, most 'believers' (in God) would argue that Dr. Hawking is, at best, an agnostic. My guess is Hawking leaves his religion at home; his comments are strictly related to the scientific evidence. Like most of us, Dr. Hawking may not fully understand the total implications of the term 'God.' Whether or not Hawking sees a need for a God with a personality is irrelevant from a scientific point of view. What is important is that, assuming a beginning, Hawking understands the scientific necessity for God, the 'Prime Force,' and he sees the Creator's handiwork. Dr. Hawking knows what he is saying and he means exactly what he says. If there was singularity, then there must be God. From a scientific position, at this point in time, 'God' is simply indescribable. Robert Wright of *Time,* you rascal! You are wrong!

With this understanding, the most offensive comment Mr. Wright made was not related to the meaning behind a statement of a scientist, but of the general perception of God Almighty. If he thinks of 'God' as a white bearded being in a robe, than he is certainly right about Hawking. Furthermore, he can add me to the list of nonbelievers. My God is not a cosmic bearded photon. My God is the most powerful force in (and out of) the universe. My God is an awesome being of boundless dimensions. He is not reconcilable to the limitations of human contemplation.

Finally, any scientist who would not describe God as Designer of all reality, Creator of all that is, nor anything other than compassionate or gracious in His creation, must have a skewed perception of value. For as previously hypothesized, assuming there is God, man does not exist without His decree.

To appraise the profound scientific evidence of a Creator/God, we will probe the beginning. . . ."In the beginning God created the heaven and the earth." My favorite scientist to discuss the 'evidence of God' is the previously mentioned astrophysicist, Dr. Hugh Ross. On the cover of Dr. Ross' book, *The Fingerprint of God,* Ross boldly proclaims, "RECENT SCIENTIFIC DIS-

COVERIES REVEAL THE UNMISTAKABLE IDENTITY OF THE CRE-ATOR." Ross believes the discovery of general relativity by Albert Einstein in 1917 began the accumulation of verifiable evidence which 'demands' a Creator. It is a matter of record that Einstein was an agnostic prior to his discoveries. Yet, afterwards, he reluctantly but firmly declared the obvious existence of a creator. Other scientists of the day were confronted by the same dilemma. The problem they faced was that general relativity proves the universe had a beginning and will most likely have an end. The important point is that if the universe had a beginning, then there had to be a beginner. This outcome is required by the principle of cause and effect. Cause and effect logic is the foundation of all science and philosophy[3] This is a very simplistic explanation of what general relativity is and does. Nonetheless, the discoveries which follow even to this day, only strengthen the evidence of the existence of God.

The following are comments from some of the more reluctant scientists. One of the most celebrated astronomers of our day is the previously mentioned Steven Hawking. Hawking has written:

> *The idea that space and time may form a closed surface without boundary also has profound implications for the role of God in the affairs of the universe. With the success of scientific theories in describing events, most people have come to believe that God allows the universe to evolve according to a set of laws and the laws do not tell us what the universe should have looked like when it started - it would still be up to God to wind up the clockwork and choose how to start it off. So long as the universe had a beginning, we could suppose it had a creator. But if the universe is really completely self-contained, having no boundary or edge, it would have neither beginning nor end: it would simply be. What place, then, for a creator?[4]*

What is really being discussed here is the viability of singularity in the Big Bang Theory vs. the Steady State, Oscillating universe theories, and 'popping out' quantum theories, etc., and the ramifications thereof. We have previously covered the problems with the 'popping out' theories. The Steady State model proclaims the universe is eternal. But this model is contrary to the evidence we have gathered from the heavens. Probably the most damaging observation is that all of the galaxies are middle aged. Their relative age indicates 'a moment of creation;' this and other points of evidence tend to confirm the Big Bang and disprove the Steady State theory. However, instead of accepting the Big Bang and its implications about our origins new presuppositions were introduced.[5] One of the most popular was a model that allowed the universe to expand from a beginning Big Bang and at a point in time col-

lapse back again. According to the theory this cycle repeats into 'indefinitely.'
[6] This model acknowledged an exploding universe which began only a few
billions of years ago. But, the science world asked, 'Why limit the universe to
one beginning? Perhaps the universe will produce an infinite number of Big
Bangs? If the universe has enough mass, gravity should halt expansion and the
universe will collapse upon it self. Then, for some unknown reason there
could be another Big Bang and the universe would begin to expand again.' [7]
Physicists inferred that an unknown bounce mechanism caused the whole system to "rebound" into an expansion, then collapse, then expand, collapse,
expand, collapse, "ad infinitum."[8] Our universe was on a lucky bounce causing atoms to self assemble into life. The theory was discussed in the 1920's by
Cal Tech physicist Richard Tolmand among others. Yet, Dr. Ross proposes,
that the true origin of the Oscillating Universe Theory is "Hindu and Buddhist
theology," because, these theologies have long claimed that everything rein-
carnates including the entire universe.[9] However, research in astrophysics
indicates that the universe is not efficient enough to support the Oscillating
Universe Theory. The universe wastes entirely too much energy to be involved
in any such process. So, no matter the religious (proof of God) connotations,
'Big Bang' theories now monopolize scientific thought.

One of the scientific experiments of the space shuttle made headlines
for its implications about the Big Bang theory. These findings were significant
enough to be mentioned in most major newspapers and magazines. The front
cover of the May 4, 1992 edition of Maclean's Magazine (a Canadian secular
news magazine similar to Time or Newsweek), read, "Looking at God:
Scientists Proclaim That Space Images Show The Origins Of The Universe."
The magazine briefly covered the history of our human search of the skies
before focusing on this purported major discovery. The article continued,
"Then, last week, American scientists announced the discovery of radiation
patterns in space that may mark the beginning of time itself. Said physicist
George Smoot, leader of the research team: "If you're religious, it's like looking at God. The order is so beautiful and the symmetry so beautiful that you
think there is some design behind it." Further in the article came quotes from
related scientists. "Nancy Boggess, a NASA scientist who was a member of
Smoot's 18-person team, compared it to archaeologists stumbling on a billion-
year-old fossil that confirms theories on the beginning of life. 'This is the oldest relic, the oldest fossil of the universe,' she said. 'It shows what the universe
must have been like after the Big Bang.'" Finally, Arnold Wolfemdale,
Britain's astronomer royal remarked, "I think one could argue that these
results firm up one's view of the presence of some deity whose purpose is

OUR UNIVERSE WAS ON A LUCKY BOUNCE CAUSING ATOMS
TO SELF ASSEMBLE INTO LIFE.

being worked out."[10] Of course, Wolfemdale's observation accurately describes the teleological position of Divine Authoritarianism. In our earlier discussion of the nature of the universe, Dr. Hawking said that if the universe had a beginning - NASA says that the Big Bang was the beginning, then a creator is quite the logical conclusion. We know from our study in logic (Chapter 3) that something has always existed (eternal) with the capacity to cause the Big Bang. However, what if we did not know of the Big Bang or the universe's boundaries? Hawking said that, if the universe has no boundaries, it could have no beginning or end. If there was no beginning there would be no related evidence of a creator. We logically know that, in such a case, the universe could then be self-existent. A self-existent universe, however, is not a valid approach. Hawking's own work proves there was singularity at the time of the Big Bang. In addition, the space shuttle and other recent discoveries have measured the universe and proclaimed there was a beginning.

I must emphasize one previous point. Because the scientific community feels they have uncovered real evidence of God through the Big Bang theory, one must not then conclude that they understand the awesomeness of God. Some scientists have looked into the cosmos and discovered an awesome all-powerful God, while others have seen a relatively weak and confined 'god.' Though few feel they can understand the universe without including a God (or creative) presence, many propose God is only what they (scientists) require God to be. Even Christians may think that, because they know certain things about the universe, they 'know' some limits to God. As an example, there are events once considered miracles but now hold scientific explanations. When they were considered miracles they were attributed to acts of God. Yet, now that science has found a natural solution to the mystery, the Divine nature has been neutralized. Thus, scientists and laymen alike should know it is a mistake to limit the boundaries of God by scientific discoveries or anything else. Dr. Jim Brooks remarks:

> *Such reasoning is incorrect and unnecessary and is often called the '-God-of-the-gaps' approach - where Christians or others claim room for God only in areas where human knowledge has not reached. This 'God of the gaps' is a wrong and pathetic substitute for the infinite, all-powerful God of the Bible, who is present within every part of His Universe and yet at the same time immeasurably transcends our every thought. To find God only where there are gaps in our scientific knowledge is unnecessary, misleading and indeed blasphemous. Since the gaps are rapidly decreasing, it suggests a shrinking God. But the*

THUS, SCIENTISTS AND LAYMEN ALIKE SHOULD KNOW IT IS A MISTAKE TO LIMIT THE BOUNDARIES OF GOD BY SCIENTIFIC DISCOVERIES OR ANYTHING ELSE.

*God of the Bible is not limited. Either He is there in the whole
Universe and in every part of it, or He is not there at all.[11]*

AN INTELLIGENT CREATOR

The second implication of this new scientific information is that the creator of the universe is vastly intelligent. Obviously, the natural realm holds a well defined and structured environment. In fact, the universe is so well designed, it seems to run itself. Isn't that what one would expect to find, if the universe was created by an all knowing God? Would God of the Bible create a universe and comment "it is good," if it were not sufficient to do its job? God's superior intelligence can be seen in all things. If one examines each scientific discipline independently and then considers all information in total, the resulting conclusion would probably be, "There must be an intelligent designer or 'God.'"

There is an allegory used to emphasize the importance of 'design' in the universe. Although it was probably first used by William Paley in reaction to David Hume's principle of uniformity, it has been used many times in many ways. So, for this writing, I will try to shorten it and personalize it. Let us say Albert Einstein was walking down the street. As he walked, he noticed a wrist watch lying beside the sidewalk. Now, in this story, Einstein had never seen a wrist watch before . . . nor had he ever heard of one. If Einstein were to pick up the watch and examine it, he would realize the watch had a designer. He would know the watch did not just happen by chance or by 'the dumbest of luck.' He would know the watch had a beginning and, I might add, a purpose for existing, a purpose for being created or put together. This is the scientific dilemma. The universe and everything in the universe seems to be designed or planned. Science, with its laws of nature and other rules and revolving theories, has not come up with a believable 'chance' explanation for this puzzle. Many scientists would like to find new information that might explain this designed appearance. But, the truth is, every new piece of scientific information seems to point to an intelligent Creator. Thus, in virtually every area of existence, there is empirical evidence of an intelligent God.

Richard N. Ostling, in a similar discussion, offered the following observation: "Yale physicist Henry Margenau, concludes that there is 'only one convincing answer' for the intricate laws that exist in nature: creation by an omnipotent, omniscient God." Ostling then considered the impact of such logic on the whole of science, "While many scientists are skeptics or are still seeking their own theologies, others are true believers - not just in some mysterious cosmic force, but in the God of the Bible or the Koran."[12]

Continuing with this topic regarding the religious beliefs of other scientists, Ostling wrote, "In his 1990 book *Genesis And The Big Bang,* Israeli nuclear physicist Gerald L. Schroeder argues in detail that there is no contradiction between the Bible's account of creation and current science. Schroeder also notes that the Ramban, the great medieval commentator of Scripture, had the remarkably modern insight that at the moment after creation, all the matter in the universe must have been concentrated in a tiny speck."[13]

Although the above descriptions paint a simplified picture, the evidence seems overwhelming. This possesses problems for both the believer and the nonbeliever. For the nonbeliever, this evidence is hard to swallow. If we consider the 'God force' of the universe to be only a unique, but natural, creative force in everything or a force similar to the god of Spinoza - if we believe only in an impersonal 'higher power,' then we have to heavily discount the logic of science. Physics suggests a beginning for all powers in the universe. However, something had to start the creation process. Furthermore, a beginning implies a reason for existence. A force does not just happen. It is produced. If there is a creative force sufficient in and of itself to form the universe, then the vast chain of 'coincidental' events which allowed life to form was not based on luck. Such luck, even assuming natural selection, is very improbable as it is incalculable beyond comprehension. Thus, a blind luck explanation is a foolish and absurd assumption. No longer can we imagine that such a mechanical force started the creation process. There must have been intelligence behind this force, and intelligence implies a personality. Furthermore, a command of this magnitude indicates the source is a vastly intelligent personal being and probably more exemplary of these traits than anything we can imagine. Quite logically, God would be much more intelligent and personal than a human being.

Yet, science is not ready to officially include God as a factor. We must now use 'code' words. We must not refer to God. We must only refer to an undistinguished 'intelligence.' I am reminded of a cartoon I once saw of a husband and wife arguing. The caption read, "Don't confuse me with facts, my mind is made up." However, for the believer, an ethical question of sorts has to be raised. I will sum up this situation using a statement from a philosopher friend of mine. I will call him 'Larry Plato.' He said something like this; "I do not want to hear of any more findings or theories or observations of science which have a factor of evidence about God. Science is to the point of proving God. What happens to faith? How can obedience through faith have meaning when God is a scientific fact? With such sureness one loses his freedom to act. Who will choose evil if God is fact? For God did not design man to be a robot, but to function as a free-willed being." Larry Plato made a very good point. In fact, Larry Plato might interpret Hebrews 11:3 as a verification of this view:

By faith, by believing God, we know that the world and the stars - in fact, all things - were made at God's command, and that they were all made from things that can't be seen.[14]

The prudent physicist would recognize that this Scripture brings even greater credence to the factualness of the Bible; not only does it state there was a beginning to creation (of which science now confirms), but it also seems to accurately reference subatomic particles - the building blocks of creation (also confirmed by science). In regard to Larry Plato's point, I do not think man will ever know God without first discovering the spiritual connection between God and His creation. As God waves His might in our face, we wonder in amazement, but we will never hear His loving words until we intellectually grasp the realization that His design is part of His spiritual expression. Scientists will never know God until they discover the spiritual world. Science is about natural experience. It can answer what is, but not why it is. Classical science cannot answer the philosophical question: Is there anything other than nature? Nonetheless, many intellectuals are allied to antiquated naturalistic concepts. They are not open to the newer and broader understanding of realism. However, because of the growing pressures, such thinkers are beginning to admit that there may be a 'god force' in the universe. Yet, scientists like Dr. Hugh Ross understand the 'spiritual nature of man' and the amazing depth of true reality. They are very special people. Only a few human beings have both the scientific and spiritual aptitude to stare through the cosmos into an awesome multi-dimensional organization of indescribable proportions, and grasp a look at a loving, but omnipotent Creator and God. A scientist at the now-scrapped super collider facility in Texas spoke of this same awesome ability. He said:

"I can look at one set of data and say it's miraculous. It shows the handiwork of God. I can look at the stars and say how wonderful. I can look at the whole evolution of the universe and so forth; from the Big Bang and say what a wonderful (pause - seemingly for a lack of words to accurately describe his feelings). The Psalmist would say the heavens proclaim the glory of God. I can see how much more they proclaim the glory of God. A nonbeliever can look at it and say isn't it marvelous, it is beautiful, but he doesn't see God there . . . It prepares the way, but if I am not ready to let God in, I'm not going to see it."15

Personally, I think the limited materialistic understanding of 'God' tells much about the atheist's mindset. As an example, Astronaut and Senator John Glenn, while preparing for his 'senior citizen' flight into outer space, recalled Soviet cosmonaut, Yuri A. Gagarin's (the first man in space) statement that, while in space, he did not see God. The implication being the atheist's view was the correct view. On the other hand, Glenn, at the time of his first flight, did not expect God to be so small that he would see him in such a limited manner. The implication being God was too magnificent to be confined by space.

This has been a very brief, historic glance at two of numerous scientific points which indicate an intelligent Creator. They are 1) Prima or First Cause and 2) design. These are two very significant points, but there is much more evidence. As we will continue to see, science indeed reveals much about God.

In closing this chapter on God Almighty, I wish to leave those who question God or His power with the Great I AM's own description of Himself. His words are directed to a believer who forgot God is in charge. God reveals the following to Job:

> *Why are you using your ignorance to deny my providence? Now get ready to fight, for I am going to demand some answers from you, and you must reply.*
>
> *Where were you when I laid the foundations of the earth? Tell me, if you know so much. Do you know how its dimensions were determined, and who did the surveying? What supports its foundations, and who laid its cornerstone, as the morning stars sang together and all the angels shouted for joy?*
>
> *Who decreed the boundaries of the seas when they gushed from the depths? Who clothed them with clouds and thick darkness, and barred them by limiting their shores, and said, "Thus far and no farther shall you come, and here shall your proud waves stop!"*
>
> *Have you ever once commanded the morning to appear, and caused the dawn to rise in the east? Have you ever told the daylight to spread to the ends of the earth, to end the night's wickedness? Have you ever robed the dawn in red, and disturbed the haunts of wicked men and stopped the arm raised to strike?*
>
> *Have you explored the springs from which the seas come, or walked in the sources of their depths? Has the location of the gates of Death been revealed to you? Do you realize the extent of the earth? Tell me about it if you know! Where does the light come from? Can you find its boundaries, or go to its source? But of course you know all this! For you were born before it was all created, and you are so very experienced!*
>
> *Have you visited the treasuries of the snow, or seen where hail is made and stored? For I have reserved it for the time when I will need it in*

war. Where is the path to the distribution point of light? Where is the home of the east wind?

Who dug the valleys for the torrents of rain? Who laid out the path for the lightning, causing the rain to fall upon the barren deserts, so that the parched and barren ground is satisfied with water, and tender grass springs up?

Has the rain a father? Where does dew come from? Who is the mother of the ice and frost? For the water changes and turns to ice, as hard as rock.

Can you hold back the stars? Can you restrain Orion or Pleiades? Can you ensure the proper sequence of the seasons, or guide the con-stellation of the Bear with her satellites across the heavens? Do you know the laws of the universe and how the heavens influence the earth? Can you shout to the clouds and make it rain? Can you make lightening appear and cause it to strike as you direct it?

Who gives intuition and instinct?

Who is wise enough to number all the clouds? Who can tilt the water jars of heaven, when everything is dust and clods?

Can you stalk prey like a lioness, to satisfy the young lions' appetites as they lie in their dens, or lie in wait in the jungle?

Who provides for the ravens when their young cry out to God as they try to struggle up from their nest in hunger?16

God revealed much more to Job about His power, but I wish to move to (God's) Biblical commentary on how *human* abilities compare to His. To accomplish this, God spoke to Job from a whirlwind:

Stand up like a man and brace yourself for battle. Let me ask you a question and give me the answer. Are you going to discredit my jus-tice and condemn me, so that you can say you are right? Are you as strong as God, and can you shout as loudly as he? All right then, put on your robes of state, your majesty and splendor. Give vent to your anger. Let it overflow against the proud. Humiliate the haughty with a glance; tread down the wicked where they stand. Knock them into the dust, stone-faced in death. If you can do that, then I'll agree with you that your own strength can save you.17

Before you take God lightly or discredit Him, please remember two points:

First, if these are indeed His Holy Words and you are not committed to His service, take a realistic view of your total waste of value, lack of purpose and eternal failure.

Second, if this is what He might say to a believer who took a moment to ponder, consider what His message is for the nonbeliever: perhaps, it is the promise of a coming death and destruction.

Anyone today who would argue that there is no God has a great mountain to climb, because the foundations of our cosmological understanding, along with many laws of both science and logic clearly state, "God exists." As in the case of Job, the power of God includes what the physical scientists see and understand. Thus, even the most reluctant atheistic scientist intuitively knows that science demands the presence of God.

CHAPTER 5

EVOLUTION: A BIG HORSE WITH A BUNCH OF GUYS INSIDE

"Why not consider the possibility that life is exactly what it seems to be, the product of a creative intelligence? . . . What scientists would lose from such conjecture is not an inspiring research program, but the illusion of human mastery of nature. They would have to face the possibility that beyond the natural world there is a further reality which transcends science."[1]

One lazy winter afternoon while driving down a Dallas freeway, I turned my car radio on and listened to the David Gold Talk Show. David's guest was an archaeologist who had been an evolutionist, but was now a creationist. During Gold's program, a skeptical caller ridiculed the guest by saying, "No archaeologist from a good school can believe in creation."[2]

I think this caller's opinion reflects the mindset of a majority of people in the USA. Yet, this common perception is not based upon the inferences of science. Instead, it has been ingrained into society through massive doses of Skinnerian brainwashing via the media and our public schools. As in the movie 'Matrix,' what seems to be real is a fashioned perception. The evolution paradigm covers our land like a blanket spreads over a bed; thus, it smothers alternative logic.

SKINNERIAN AMERICA

If you ask people why they accept traditional neo-Darwinian evolution, or any other hypothesis of evolution, most do not know. They might respond that a teacher said it is true or a chart on the wall showed exactly what had happened. However, if you question them further you will usually find they have naively accepted evolution; they assumed evolution must be fact because 'everybody' knows it to be fact. The teacher thinks it is fact. The Discovery Channel and PBS present it as fact. This, of course, is the postmodernist's rendition of the infamous 'leap of faith.' People have been 'programmed' to follow the crowd and accept whatever 1) television and, 2) the NEA proclaim. Both of these Skinnerian programmers are extremely political. However, both must also realize they are not teaching factual information. This is one reason David Gold asserts that only five percent of the public know how to think for themselves. In fact, most evolutionists do not seem to

be aware of the many fundamental evolutionary problems that have been discovered. In a debate featuring evolution versus creation, Dr. Philip E. Johnson
recalled a conversation he held with "a very famous molecular biologist" who
is also one of Johnson's colleagues at Berkeley. The biologist stated that he
accepts evolution from the cell on (presumably he meant from the cell through
the development of human beings). However, he "knew" evolution could not
explain the formation of the cell. Dr. Johnson pointed out to him that the cell
was "the only thing he knew about," meaning the only part of the evolutionary process in which he was involved.[3] This scientist is a perfect example of
a sheep following the herd. Many people simply do not question evolution.

One reason traditional evolution goes unchallenged is that virtually
every fact found over the last fifty or sixty years has either been shaped to fit
the evolutionary scheme, or dismissed and forgotten. Quite frankly, the public
has been 'misled' by our scientific community. Johnson proposes that science
tries to give an answer for every facet of reality. Thus, at times, it will "theorize extravagantly" from a selective portion of evidence and ignore the implications of any evidence not fitting the paradigm theory. Johnson calls such
scientists "culture-bound producers of texts."[4]

As an example, consider the supposed evolution of man. Most people accept ape-to-human evolution as fact. Yet, the evidence supporting this
'fact' is essentially a small number of skull and bone parts which might well
fit inside of a small box. Related research on these remains leads one to be
very skeptical. Donald Johnson made what has been considered by many to be
science's greatest anthropological find. He discovered a group of fragmented
bones known as 'Lucy.' Yet, in addition to a well-documented argument over
how many species are actually represented by Lucy's bones, the world renown
anthropologist, Richard Leaky (also an evolutionist), assured us, "on the basis
of molecular anthropology," that Lucy was an ape, not a human.[5]
Furthermore, I remind you of the *'Hesperopithecus haroldcookii'* or Nebraska
man. This 'first man' is known as the 'missing link' of the Scopes 'monkey
trial' (although not introduced as scientific evidence). Nonetheless, the entire
reconstruction of the Nebraska Man was based on the remains of a molar tooth
which turned out to belong to a peccary (an extinct pig).[6] (On a lighter side,
some women reading this book are equally convinced that man evolved from
the pig - not the ape). This 'pig's tooth' fooled a number of leading scientists.
In fact, Henry Osborn of the American Museum of Natural History claimed
that the Nebraska Man's tooth appeared to be "more human than ape."[7]

Another find, *'Eoanthropus dawsoni'* or Piltdown Man was
acclaimed as one of man's greatest archaeological discoveries. Instead, it

---

QUITE FRANKLY, THE PUBLIC HAS BEEN 'MISLED' BY
OUR SCIENTIFIC COMMUNITY.

proved to be one of man's greatest rues. Moreover, Piltdown was authenticated by some of Britain's most renown scientists. Unfortunately, it was a complete deception propagated for forty years by scientists who were either totally fooled or part of the 'cover up.' [8]

In the 60's, Neandertal (also known as Neanderthal) was considered to be yet another missing ape-to-human link. Scholars even assumed that this creature drug his hands on the ground in an ape like manner. However, we discovered that the evolutionists were wrong. Neandertal walked upright. More surprisingly, Neandertal had a larger brain capacity then modern man. Brain size has long been a measuring rod in the evolutionary processes. As the brain became larger, the hypothesis presumed, the creature evolved into a higher intelligence. Today, mainly because of Neandertal brain measurements, size is not as important as brain sophistication, i.e., how a brain is wired. We now think modern man is intellectually superior to all other creatures because of the evolution in brain wiring. Yet, we have no idea how the Neandertal brain was wired nor how he functioned. He might have been our intellectual superior, but perished in some natural disaster. Again our scientists had touted mistaken assumptions as fact.

Java man was portrayed to resemble modern man except for a noticeable difference in the shape of his forehead. However, now many scientists feel this difference occurred from an environmental disease such as 'rickets.' Perhaps we only have fossil remains of a diseased and disfigured race of human beings.

New technologies have caused other problems for presumptive evolutionists. Though there has been some disagreement about the interpretation of genetic data, DNA tests have confirmed that neither Neandertal nor Homo erectus of Africa are linked to the genealogy of modern man.[9] Thus, the 'experts' cannot explain how humans are related to monkeys. In fact, a number of scientists feel that DNA evidence is contrary to natural evolution. Furthermore, some of the existing fossil bones thought to validate evolution might only be the remains of ancient apes. Or, they might be the fossils of human races now extinct. As we find in all families of creatures, some races-/sub-species/species 'make it' and some are 'wiped out.'

Yet, the real intellectual 'sin'—what evolutionists sometimes 'forget,' or make misleading statements about, is the vast amount of information which is contrary to their neo-Darwinian picture of life. *The Blind Watchmaker* focuses on this point rather well. Writing about the scarcity of fossils conforming to the evolution theory Dawkins stated, "Nevertheless, however small the proportion fossilized, there are certain things about the fos-

PERHAPS WE ONLY HAVE FOSSIL REMAINS OF A DISEASED
AND DISFIGURED RACE OF HUMAN BEINGS.

sil record that any evolutionist should expect to be true. If a single, well-verified mammal skull were to turn up in 500 million year-old rocks, our whole modern theory of evolution would be utterly destroyed."[10]

ANOMALIES FOR DAWKINS

If such is the case, then consider the following abbreviated list of human like fossils which do not fit with natural evolution and by the intellectual's 'political' rules are either forced to fit or excluded from all evolutionary discussion.

For starters, anthropologists do not attempt to explain the "humanoid" footprints found by Dr. Wilbur Burroughs. Dr. Burroughs is head of the department of geology at Berea College in Kentucky, which should add to the creditability of his find. The footprints he found were measured by "authenticating tests" to be approximately 250 million years old.[11] Michael A. Cremo and Richard L. Thompson, co-authors of the provocative book, *Forbidden Archeology,* explain the importance of this find: "Scientists say the first appearance of apelike beings was not until around 37 million years ago, and it was not until around 4 million years ago that most scientists would expect to find footprints anything like those reported by Burroughs from the Carboniferous of Kentucky."[12] Burroughs seemed particularly interested with the physiological inferences of the print. Thus he stated, "The foot curves back like a human foot to a human appearing heel."[13] Cremo and Thompson also referred to the unique clarity of these prints: "These humanlike tracks are thus quite distinct, unlike the more famous but indistinct Paluxy 'man tracks' reported in Biblical creationist literature."[14]

Trilobites became extent 280 million years ago. Yet, in Antelope Spring, Utah there is a fossil of a "sandaled" human-shaped foot stepping on a trilobite. This print may be 300 to 600 million years old.[15] William Meister, discovered this ancient print and described it as follows: "The heel print was indented in the rock about an eighth of an inch more than the sole. The footprint was clearly that of the right foot because the sandal was well worn on the right side of the heel in characteristic fashion."[16] How does that compare with the skull parts called 'Lucy?' Because Lucy fits the contemporary paradigm, and the shoe print does not, Lucy has been studied and the shoe print seems to have been forgotten. How can this be?

There are many similar pivotal, but little known, archeological finds. A "perfect imprint of a human-shaped foot" was presented to the Ohio State Academy of Science. As amazing, the imprint was fourteen and a half inches long.[17] A broken rock in the Cumberland Mountains revealed both humanoid and animal tracks thought to be "300 million years old."[18] Is there a scientist who can explain the giant human-like print "16 inches long, 13 inches wide at the toes and 5 inches wide at the ball of the heel" found in the Tennessee River close to Braystown, North Carolina?[19] A human-shaped footprint found on the banks of the Mississippi River at St. Louis is considered to be 270 million years old.[20] We have found ancient footprints at White Sands, New Mexico.[21] There were giant footprints (18 to 22 inches long) of "a human wearing shoes" near Carson City, Nevada.[22] We have even found a fossil print of a "hand stitched" leather shoe, considered to be 180 to 225 million years old. This shoe print was found in Fisher Canyon, Nevada.[23] In 1973 two human-shaped skeletons were found embedded in rock near La Sal, Utah. The skeletons thought to be 100 million years old "had a relatively modern appearance"[24]

Yet, the most interesting find may be one reportedly unearthed from 1786 to 1788 in a limestone quarry near Aixen-Provence, France. A large amount of limestone was being removed to remodel a government building. After removing eleven (11) layers of rock and reaching a depth of approximately 50 feet, workers came upon a bed of sand, and made a shocking discovery. They had apparently happened upon the remains of an ancient civilization. Removing the sand, workers found "stumps of stone pillars and fragments of half-worked rock . . ." Later, they found coins and petrified wooden handles to hammers and other tools. The limestone they had cut through was an estimated 300 million years old.[25] This report can be found in the American Journal of Science of 1820 (v01.2, pp. 145–146). To this regard, Cremo and Thompson comment, "today, however, it is unlikely such a report would be found in the pages of a scientific journal. Scientists simply do not take such discoveries seriously."[26] The question then is who inhabited the civilization under the 300 million year old rock? And, if this is factual, could a civilization move under said rock? How can these things be?

Lucy, the lady considered by natural cause evolutionists to be Eve, is only about 3 to 4 million years old. So, how do we explain these anomalies? Are all of these fossils hoaxes? Perhaps the most publicized human-shaped tracks are found near Glen Rose, Texas—the previously mentioned 'Paluxy man tracks.' If these questioned tracks are indeed human, they indicate that dinosaurs and a human-like being roamed Texas together. The problem this creates is that dinosaurs are thought to have been extinct 60 million years before humans even existed.[27]

Dawkins has commented on these Texas tracks. He made a bold accusation when writing about the treacheries of people who believe in creation: "Ironically it is also the reason why creationists are so keen on the fake human footprints, which were carved during the depression to fool tourists, in the dinosaur beds of Texas."[28] I do not know where he got that information but, from what I have found, he is wrong.

First, we must realize Dawkins 'despises' creationists. Actually, Dawkins claims all natural evolutionists (both puncuationists and gradualists) "despise so-called scientific creationists equally."[29] Unfortunately, his comments, as well as those of others, give creditability to the accusations of those 'despised' creationists who report threats by evolutionists, etc. For example, the Institute for Creation Research sponsors a radio program called *Science, Scripture and Salvation.* One episode featured an orthodontist (perhaps the first researcher "to take orthodontic x-rays of Neandertal fossils") who claims to have found obvious differences in growth patterns of the Neandertal creatures which are contrary to those accepted by evolutionary science. He stated, "Many men have staked their entire lives and their entire reputations on the faith of macro evolution . . . And much evidence has been altered in order to prove (evolution). I have only seen the tip of the iceberg."[30] This orthodontist further noted that he had been denied access to study Neandertal bones in a museum in Nairobi Kenya which is headed by Richard Leakey.

He also has claimed to have been followed, threatened, chased, and had his car window shot out by a bullet. Do we believe him? Such accusations are not uncommon among those 'despised' researchers. How can we not find some credence in his claims when creationists are so openly hated? And how can we not believe in cover-ups when we know of such cover-ups (as the above Nebraska Man)?

Second, I am not aware of any valid studies which found these humanoid footprints from "the dinosaur beds of Texas" to be anything other than authentic. I called the Dinosaur State Park of Texas which is named for the dinosaur prints in question. They would not comment on the humanoid prints. The Chamber of Commerce of Glen Rose, Texas felt the prints were authentic and the Science Department of nearby Howard Payne University could only suggest contacting Dawkins about his comments. Other people, from the area, who are well-informed about the credibility of these unique fossils seemed to be confused by Dawkins' claims and assured me of their authenticity. I have personally viewed the footprints in question and they look authentic. I do not understand how someone could 'fake' such prints in rock and have them look as authentic as these. The neighboring Creation Evidence Museum not only claims they are authentic but has other objects of interest, such as a fossilized human finger preserved in rock.

Perhaps Charles Dawkins understands these footprints to be 'enemies' of natural evolution. Using these prints as proof, some 'creationists' claim man lived with the dinosaur. I think it is important to mention there is other evidence that humans witnessed dinosaurs. As a matter of fact, there are two descriptions of animals in God's discussion with Job which must be one of the following 1) fictional animals or 2) extinct animals which would include very accurate descriptions of two known categories of dinosaurs. The first description is in Job 40:15–24. God is speaking to Job:

Take a look at the behemoth! (Modern theologians suggest this is an extinct hippopotamus). I made him, too, just as I made you! He eats grass like an ox. See his powerful loins and the muscles of his belly. His tail is as straight as a cedar. The sinews of his thighs are tightly knit together. His vertebrae lie straight as a tub of brass. His ribs are like iron bars. How ferocious he is among all of God's creation, so let whoever hopes to master him bring a sharp sword! The mountains offer their best food to him - the other wild animals on which he preys. He lies down under the lotus plants, hidden by the reeds, covered by their shade among the willows there beside the stream. He is not disturbed by raging rivers, not even when the swelling Jordan rushes down upon him. No one can catch him off guard or put a ring in his nose and lead him away.[31]

Some creationists think this might be a description of an Apatosaurus style or sauropod (lizard hipped) dinosaur. It certainly sounds more like a dinosaur than a hippopotamus. The other mysterious description follows the above and is found in Job 41:1–33. Again, God is speaking to Job. This time the topic is an animal called a leviathan which is often considered to be an extent crocodile. Some believe it better fits the characterization of a Tyrannosaurus style or theropod dinosaur.

According to traditional thought, dinosaurs were unknown in Biblical times. In fact, dinosaurs were 'discovered' only about 150 years ago. Of course, the above Biblical descriptions are thousands of years old. In addition to these mysterious depictions, there are hundreds of stories regarding the dragon's spiritual position of power by ancient tribes around the world - even in the most isolated places. The inference here is dragons are mythical relics of actual creatures, i.e., dinosaurs. For an example, a myth from Sumer, which dates back thousands of years, refers to Gilgamesh slaying a huge dragon. Humans have also recorded eyewitness accounts. Greek historian, Herodotus wrote of reptiles which flew over Egypt. Primitive humans left cliff drawings shaped like dinosaurs. It was a common rite of respect for early man to reproduce forms of powerful animals on walls of caves and cliffs. It would not be out of character for humans to have hunted and killed such creatures for meat, for ritual or just because they were a nuisance.[32] One such 'dinosaur' drawing has been found in the Grand Canyon. Others are scattered over North America.

As to the human type prints found in Texas and around the world, they do not necessarily prove Dawkins wrong. Perhaps some are hoaxes. However, one cannot suggest all of these prints are both genuine, but non human, because some of them are of shoe prints. There are scientists who suggest these prints are not as old as they seem (which, by the way, includes Dr.

Burroughs of Bera College). They are forced to conclude that the rock forma-
tions happened in stages and the various stages are, for some reason, indistinguishable. Of course, such a presupposition overlooks the fact that when
creationists suggest modern methods of measuring the age of artifacts is incorrect, they are ridiculed for their ignorance. Moreover, it is irrelevant, in this
case, that such an explanation does not sound reasonable, because this explanation cannot solve the mystery anyway. Reader's Digest considered this evolutionary dilemma:

> *There are two problems with this explanation. First, anomalous fos-
> sils (abnormal in that they do not fit the evolutionary picture) are
> found not only at the junction of sedimentary layers but deep within
> rocks that show no sign at all of discontinuous formation. Second,
> out-of-place fossils (footprints, etc.) are often inconsistent not only
> with the ages of associated fossils but also with the rock strata and the
> age conventionally ascribed to them.[33]*

Such anomalies can only be shrugged off by natural evolutionists.
Even Robert Shapiro, who is a skeptic of both natural cause evolution and
causal creation, complains, "Creationists collect anomalous results, and criticize faulty procedures and logic used by scientists."[34] Obviously Shapiro is
trying to excuse evolutionists' disregard of anomalies. Yet, his comments only
go from bad to worse as he continues by stating, "Anomalies and artifacts
exist in every scientific field."[35] Does Shapiro realize what he is admitting?
His comments suggest that these and other 'anomalies' represent a weighty
percentage of the evolutionary record. Plainly, Shapiro has executed a 'faux
pas' by stating that which he knows to be truth. Please recall that Dawkins
claimed one well-verifiable anomaly destroys the theory of evolution. Yet,
Shapiro states that a wide variety of anomalies do exist. The apparent (yet
unstated) conclusion is, we base 'science' on only a part of the discovered artifacts and throw out all evidence that does not fit our predetermined conclusions. Thus, one must ask, what is the condition of evolution science?

Ironically, one of the problems skeptics have in accepting evolutionary speciation is the lack of confirmation in the fossil record. Thus, not only
do we throw out non-supportive factual evidence, but we do not find the fossils we would expect to find - those which prove neo-Darwinian evolution.
There are only bones of the Stegosaurus. There are no bones for a Stego-
apatosaurus. There are only bones of alligators. There are no bones for
alligata-snakes. There are only bones for bears. There are no bones for bear-
lions. If anomalies indeed exist as extreme as the footprints listed above (and
in every evolutionary field), yet fossil finds are dissatisfactory - not what one
would predict of an evolutionary model, then the evolutionary model must be

wrong. Think about what 'science' asks us to do. It wants us to pretend certain existing fossils do not exist and pretend that many non-existent (but extremely significant) fossils do exist. Any reputable scientist must realize that evolution as we know it is only a myth. Even if it holds some truth, a workable model is but a mirage in the desert of cogitative mystification.

We have previously discussed the scarcity of the fossil record as it applies to the development of humanness. Frankly, there are many more 'forgotten' or 'not important' (or whatever term 'scientists' wish to use), but embarrassing fossils which do not fit our preconceived ape-to-human evolution in natural history.

However, the real problem Dawkins and other like minded evolutionists have with the above anomalous fossils is that, if the Glen Rose prints are valid, then 'Lucy' becomes an ordinary find. Are 'creationists' simply misinterpreting quirks of nature? Come to Glen Rose, Texas and see this mystery for yourself.

For further information, I include the address and telephone number for the Creation Evidence Museum. (I would gladly list others, but they seem to be the only organization willing to forgo political pressures and discuss this subject in depth) P.O. Box 309, Glen Rose Texas, 76043; Telephone number (817) 897–3200.

THE EFFECT OF ANOMALIES

Unlike Dr. Robert Shapiro, I cannot discredit all anomalies without reason. Furthermore, I cannot disregard the comments of the Creation Evidence Museum just because its anomalies seem to defy conventional evolutionary assumptions. As for Charles Dawkins' logic, I do not think "our whole modern theory of evolution would be utterly destroyed"[36] by one or more anomalous human fossils. Obviously, one can find such anomalies. The problem lies in the numbers of anomalies which, as Shapiro put it, "exist in every scientific field."[37] Such a large number and variety of anomalies does concern me and should be of concern to everyone searching for Truth.

So, what do we do with such deviations? How can we and/or the scientists explain them? Do we continue to sweep them under a pragmatic rug and pretend they do not exist? Do we make derogatory and unsubstantiated accusations about them and anyone who dares to refer to them? My question is mainly directed to natural cause evolutionists, because creationists have answers. Short term creationists claim contemporary methods of time dating are wrong. Long term creationists are not bothered by time dating, because they are not constrained by time in the way that natural cause evolutionists

ANY REPUTABLE SCIENTIST MUST REALIZE THAT EVOLUTION
AS WE KNOW IT IS ONLY A MYTH.

are. We must exclude punctuation evolutionists from this evolutionary dilemma as their time factor is structured similarly to long term creationists. In fact, the economy of time is the most appealing factor of the punctuation theories. Like the long term creationists, most punctuationists postulate that positive change could be extremely rapid and cyclical. Therefore, almost any evolutionary activity would fit in both the punctuation and the creation timelines.

Additionally, when we contemplate the beginnings of humanness, even the definition of humanness must be questioned. Many creationists do not accept the secular criteria. For example, secular anthropologists sometimes base humanness on such activities as the burying of dead or using tools, etc. Yet, varying degrees of such behavior can be observed in other mammals, birds and insects.

Judaic/Christian theology clearly states that human beings were designed to communicate with and worship God. Interestingly, many philosophers have attempted to define humanism in relation to a desire. To Plato, humanness exhibited spiritedness (thymos). Machiavelli thought humanness entailed a desire for glory. To Hegel, this special attribute was the desire for recognition. Even Nietzsche described it as "the beast with red cheeks."[38] Yet, if the philosopher is correct, this human 'spiritedness,' which is easy to discern but hard to describe, also seems to be related to the mechanism which allows man to communicate with and worship God. Therefore, one might suggest there is some degree of agreement between the philosopher and the Judaic/Christian theologian.

A CLOSER LOOK AT EVOLUTION

For the sake of argument, I will be a gracious creationist and I assume (for the moment) that all of these unsettling anomalous finds are invalid. All of the above 'anomalies' and the thousands more awaiting an intelligent explanation are meaningless puzzles. Let us assume there is some reason to excuse every piece of evidence that does not fit the evolutionary timetable. Perhaps the examiners used faulty dating procedures, or all are indeed hoaxes, or we have not found all of the answers, but when the answers are found, they will prove evolution. Again, for the sake of argument, let us assume everything found in science suggests life came from rocks or cousins of rocks. Life progressed from rocks to slime to alligators to monkeys to humans. (I know I missed many species, but that is the general direction of the evolutionary ladder).

Instead of continuing with the multitude of unsolved mysteries, let us

JUDAIC/CHRISTIAN THEOLOGY CLEARLY STATES THAT HUMAN BEINGS WERE
DESIGNED TO COMMUNICATE WITH AND WORSHIP GOD.

discuss some of the problems related to the foundational suppositions of the natural evolutionary position.

ORIGIN OF LIFE

Perhaps the best place to begin is the origin of life. To accept natural evolution, it seems one must accept the premise that 'some form of spontaneous generation initiated life's beginning.' Yet, it should be clear by now that, for all practical purposes, spontaneous generation is not a natural process. It seems to either be a supernatural process, perhaps directed by God, or a fallacious hypothesis. Spontaneous dissolution is the only proven natural spontaneous process; thus, the scientific community hangs its hat on a fantasy.

Interestingly, in 1953, a process thought to link non-life material to the generation of life (a connection in the spontaneous generation process), was allegedly formed by student, Stanley Miller, in professor Harold Urey's research laboratory. Although, in this famous experiential exercise, Dr. Miller did not actually prove spontaneous generation, he was thought to have discovered the primal process which evolved after the needed molecules were available in the earth's atmosphere. Thus, he proved life evolved out of non life. That, at least, was what the American public was led to believe through educational television and the atheistic position of the NEA.

When I think of the Miller-Urey experiments, I recall watching Dr. Carl Sagan, on his NOVA Cosmos series, as he explained the importance of these experiments. According to Sagan, all of the needed elements were available in abundance. I assume these included water, ammonia, hydrogen, carbon dioxide, etc. The mixed condition of these ingredients formed a pre-biological 'soup.' Add a little lightning to energize the soup and you have life. Today, this sounds like Miller watched Frankenstein too many times. Yet, Carl Sagan assured us life was easily created. His summarization of Miller's conclusions looked and sounded very positive and accurate. He left no question as to the actual outcome; the first amino acids formed quite abundantly. The answer to life was right there. Life did spontaneously arise!

However, in the 70's and 80's, we began to hear of 'problems in the soup.' The structure of Miller's discovery weakened and crashed. At the present time, virtually all in the scientific community have rejected the validity of the Miller-Urey experiments as a connector to the original formation of life.

THE MIXED CONDITION OF THESE INGREDIENTS FORMED A PRE-BIOLOGICAL 'SOUP.' ADD A LITTLE LIGHTNING TO ENERGIZE THE SOUP AND YOU HAVE LIFE.

TIME PROBLEMS

Time dating procedures indicate the origin of life (i.e., the evolution of rocks or cousins of rocks into living organisms) must have been a rather simple procedure. The earth is thought to be approximately 4.5 billion years old. However, it would need to cool. Therefore, the starting date for any evolutionary process would have been more like 4.2 billion years ago. Additionally, it is generally thought that life could not have existed on earth four billion years ago, due to comet activity. Huge comets were striking the earth on a regular basis. One obvious reason for the comets was the absence of atmosphere.

However, using the accepted evolutionary timetable, rather complicated organisms were formed on this planet at least 3.5 to 3.8 billion years in the past. This early life, of and by itself, creates problems for the gradual evolutionist. Evolutionist Gordon Rattray Taylor writes, "The earth was formed some 4.5 billion years ago. It did not cool to reasonable temperatures until perhaps 4.2 billion years ago. Yet life manifested after only 15 percent of its entire existence, when conditions were, one would have imagined, highly unfavorable. This does not give long enough for the series of happy chances which seem to have been needed."[39]

Andrew Knoll, a paleontologist at Harvard University, points out, "By the time we really have our first good window to look at the record, there is already evidence that (photosynthesizing microbes) were in place."[40] We have found this evidence in a number of places to include well publicized fossils in Greenland. As referenced above, the general scientific community speculates that there must have been a 300 to 400 million year old window for life to have originated and become functional. Three to four hundred million years is a very short period of time for evolution to change non living rocks or cousins of rocks into living photosynthesizing organisms. Consider the sophistication. Anyone who has taken a biology class should know photosynthesis is a very complicated process. Today, this process is still not totally understood. Thus, photosynthesis poses a real evolutionary problem and the neo-Darwinian evolutionists have no answers. As an example, after explaining that gradual evolution can bring about dramatic change, Dr. Taylor comments, "Even so, it is very hard to swallow the idea that chance - or rather a long series of chances - built up such an extremely elaborate mechanism as photosynthesis, a mechanism which depends on substances far more complex than the raw materials which it transforms. Unless there was some inner necessity, some built-in, primordial disposition to consolidate into such a pattern, it is past belief that anything so intricate and idiosyncratic should

ADDITIONALLY, IT IS GENERALLY THOUGHT THAT LIFE COULD NOT HAVE EXISTED ON EARTH FOUR BILLION YEARS AGO, DUE TO COMET ACTIVITY.

appear."[41] Again, the real difference between natural evolutionists and long term creationists on this point is not the age of life, but how life formed. Was life created by a creative force, or was it a chance accident? Was there a "built-in primordial disposition" that somehow knew to formulate a photosynthetic reaction? If so, what could have implanted that disposition?

Creationists and evolutionists alike realize that the odds for inadvertent life forming and existing on earth or anywhere in the universe are incredibly bad. Yet, whatever we designate to be the odds for a string of accidents causing life, those 'bad' odds are dramatically better than the actual possibilities - further complicated by the known behavior of matter. That is, we must figure into the equation the behavior of the raw material. I refer to the effects of The New Generalized Second Law of Thermodynamics, introduced in chapter 3. As a reminder, this Second Law explains that "things mix."[42] When they mix and time passes, natural processes "destroy patterns."[43] In general, when things mix, patterns are destroyed. The converse situation then is, in order to create a pattern, "things will need to be separated."[44] Things by nature do not separate. They mix. The natural process demands the erosion of any given pattern. Thus, the natural spontaneous activity (that which would be expected) is dissolution. (We will discuss dynamical systems, commonly called the Theory of Chaos or Complexity, later in this chapter. Under certain conditions patterns will form in nature but only for temporary periods of time. Then the patterns mix. At this writing, there does not seem to be any reason to suspect Chaos could create the series of patterns required to create life. In fact, what is generally observed as natural behavior is the above conclusion that "things mix.")

What if the material earth were to somehow defy natural processes by creating patterns and generating organisms? The obvious question would be: How did this 'magical' (or unexplainable) activity occur? If there were some 'magical' way to defy natural law or if there were some unknown method to compromise the laws of science, what would be needed to insure life as we know it? It is at this point of conjecture that one might figure the odds for the origin of life. Of course, most scientists (even most natural evolutionists) recognize the miraculous connotations imbedded in these odds and declare life on earth to be a statistical improbability. "The point is that not just any pattern will do, but only the one that is desired."[45] There are millions of evolutionary possibilities, but only one specific chain of events could have developed life as we find it today. Thus, by our own existence, we can surmise that there is a creative force with a selective design. The New Generalized Second Law of Thermodynamics both confirms the existence of this ultimate

---

CREATIONISTS AND EVOLUTIONISTS ALIKE REALIZE THAT THE ODDS FOR INADVERTENT LIFE FORMING AND EXISTING ON EARTH OR ANYWHERE IN THE UNIVERSE ARE INCREDIBLY BAD.

creative force, and infers the force has an intellect. (Whether or not this 'Creator' is an intellectual being, whatever its essence - whether it is mechanical or a personality, this force must be considered to be God or, more appropriately, the Will of God in action. Why? Because it is the source of creation for everything in the universe and the essence of all information.) Why does 'information' require an intellect? Simply put, our experience with "information-intensive systems" has taught us that an intelligent agent is required to create information. Stephen Meyer put it well, " . . . what philosophers call 'agent causation' now stands as the only cause known to be capable of creating an information-rich system, including the coding regions of DNA, functional proteins, and the cell as a whole."[46] (As Meyer's statement suggests, not only is this inference of information important at the beginning of life, it continues to have its effects throughout the animal kingdom.)

For evolutionary theory to be correct, life must have formed extremely quickly after the asteroid activity subsided. Remember, according to the accepted evolutionary theory, the organisms of 3.5 to 3.8 billion years ago would have been photosynthesizing. In this timeline come paradoxes. To whatever extent organisms were photosynthesizing, the process must have been functionally simple. Yet, from a chemical standpoint, it must have been an extremely sophisticated procedure, especially for rocks or cousins of rocks. Nonetheless, the time line suggests that the origination of life may well have existed at the earliest possible moment. The obvious question looms: Was this process a coincidence or the result of a preconceived cosmic plan?

A COSMIC SUPER-INTELLECT?

There are several points to make here in regard to an intelligence behind the universe. First, it is very provocative that everything in the universe is intrinsically functional and works so precisely. Everything seems in sync. There does not seem to be any 'down time' or wasted opportunities. Moreover, all 'natural' occurrences seem to add relevance to existence, not only to life but to all that is. Life begins at the earliest possible moment. Even the natural evolutionists suggest that all of the diverse activities needed for the formation of life happened in a precise (synchronized) movement. For example, ultraviolet light was the most abundant energy source on the early earth. Certain ultraviolet waves are not considered to be a good energy source for the formation of some intermediates to amino acids.[47] However, the energy from the shock waves of meteorites and thunder would be a very amenable energy source for a "synthesis of amino acids" from simple gasses.[48] If evolutionists are right and life did evolve from rocks or cousins of rocks, isn't it interesting

---

EVERYTHING SEEMS IN SYNC.

that asteroids and meteorites bombarded earth just at the right time . . . and then, for some unknown reason, the asteroids and meteorites were greatly decreased so life could survive and flourish. But look at the dilemma. One would think that the asteroid bombardment could only cease with the buildup of the atmosphere through photosynthesis. But, photosynthesis would be difficult in ultraviolet light because ultraviolet light waves would have stymied the formation of the building blocks of life. Dr. Michael Denton explains, "Nucleic acid molecules, which form the genetic material of all modern organism, happen to be strong absorbers of ultraviolet light and are consequently particularly sensitive to ultraviolet-induced radiation damage and mutation."[49] Furthermore, without amino acids, the atmosphere could not develop and the asteroid bombardment could not be stopped. Actually this is the simplified version of the early atmospheric conditions of earth as the dilemma is much more involved. One major problem pertains to the formation of oxygen. When the delicate atmosphere began to form, any oxygen found in that atmosphere would be very destructive to organic compounds. Yet, the oxygen was needed. According to Dr. Denton, oxygen is required to develop "an ozone layer in the upper atmosphere." And, the ozone was needed to shield the planet's surface from excessive exposure to ultraviolet radiation. In an oxygen-free scenario, "the ultraviolet flux reaching the Earth's surface might be more than sufficient to break down organic compounds as quickly as they were produced."[50] Denton calls this a Catch 22 situation, explaining, "If we have oxygen we have no organic compounds, but if we don't have oxygen we have none either."[51]

New studies make the new earth theory even more perplexing. Virtually the entire science community has assumed the young earth was warm. Warmth is what one would expect from a volcanic and asteroid active earth. So, it seemed obvious, that the earth was warm. However, the most recent studies indicate that just the opposite would need to be true if life were to form. The bonds of the nucleotide bases are heat sensitive. According to these studies, the genes in life's ancestral cell could not have withstood temperatures of about 70 degrees centigrade.[52] This is just one small detail of a much greater temperature problem. In fact, a variety of the RNA and DNA molecules, necessary for life, require extraordinary temperature variations. Of the four required elements, cytosine and uracil require "near boiling water temperatures." Yet, adenine and quanine require "freezing water temperatures." Thus, it seems rather impossible that these four elements would gather together "under natural conditions" and "in adequate concentration" at any time as needed to structure life.[53] But, they did assemble . . . in the right place, the right time and the right amounts, just like one would expect if life was prearranged.

No matter what happened, it must have been perfect timing because the evidence suggests that life came into existence rather quickly. In fact, the word 'miraculous' seems appropriate here. This was one of the multimillion (or perhaps multi-trillion) evolutionary activities which suggest that an ultra-powerful intellect or 'consciousness' formed the universe and developed an organism known as the human being.

Despite the fact that our scientists are unsure of the chemical makeup in virtually all phases of early earth, most seem to agree, there would need to be a perfect situation to create life. This by no means takes away from the overwhelming belief that there was a period of trial and error before the environment 'found' just the right conditions; young earth experienced variant temperatures and volcanic activity, earthly actions and reactions. However, with the proper mixes of atmospheric chemicals, the asteroid bombardment and related circumstances, all the pieces came in line to form life. Assuming the above mingling explains the origin of life, it is apparent that when a perfect mix did happen, life came quick.

At life's inception, the environment must have changed again in a way that not only encouraged but incubated life. If any aspect of the multifarious early earth environment had been altered, virtually all evolutionists suggest life would not have formed nor survived. Secondly, even though educational television and our schools tell us that the formation of life is as simple as Sagan had once suggested, most of our scientists confess it is an extremely difficult puzzle. If life's origin was so easy, why do we not see rocks or cousins of rocks becoming life today? Whether through chance or through a mechanical force (perhaps a Spinozian type of god which would have started the universe quite accidentally, and yet could do nothing else) why was it so easy for life to start in an unprotected atmosphere yet, such simple origins do not spontaneously generate in today's protected atmosphere? Thirdly, our scientists do not yet have the solution to the origination of life. Quite frankly, science has not even produced much valid data about life's origin. Matt Crenson, a science reporter for the Dallas Morning News, confirmed this statement: "Research during the last three decades has cast doubt on old ideas about how life began, but it hasn't affected anything that's much more convincing."[54] Dr. Jeffery Bada, a chemist at the Scripps Institution of Oceanography has commented, "The origins of life remain one of the major unsolved problems of this century." He further remarked, "There's no evidence for anything so it's a wide open field."[55]

Many scientists involved in this mystery are feeling the hopelessness of the origin puzzle. This explains the above comment of the "very famous

---

IF LIFE'S ORIGIN WAS SO EASY, WHY DO WE NOT SEE ROCKS
OR COUSINS OF ROCKS BECOMING LIFE TODAY?

molecular biologist" who said he accepted Darwinian evolution from the cell on, but "knew" evolution could not explain the formation of the cell.[56]

We have not even touched on perhaps the hardest problem for evolution scientists to solve: the probabilities of random selection. What are the 'chances' of life being randomly formed by natural cause? First, I must remind the reader that chance has no power, is not a force, but a statement of mathematical possibilities. Chance in and of itself did not create anything. (This is the focus of Sproul's previously mentioned book, Not A Chance.) The highly acclaimed British astrophysicist, Sir Fred Hoyle, in his picturesque way, explained the extreme odds against the natural origin of life when he compared "the probability of life appearing spontaneously on Earth" with the success of a blind person solving the 'Rubik Cube.' If a blindfolded person made a random move every second, it would take on the average "three hundred times the age of the Earth, 1,350 billion years, to solve the cube." He further stated, "The chance against each move producing perfect colour matching for all the cube's faces is about 50,000,000,000,000,000,000 to 1."[57]

Hoyle next mentioned the fact that there are 200,000 different types of protein in the human cell. If the odds are the same for all 200,000 protein types, then these odds are "almost unimaginably vast."[58] How vast is "almost unimaginably vast?" It is like filling up 40 sheets of paper with zeros if contrasted to the number 1. These odds approximate using a normal pair of dice and throwing double six's 50,000 times in a row![59] If dice were ever rolled like this in Las Vegas, I can assure you, it would not be by chance.

Although some natural evolutionists argue that random selection substantially lessens the odds for the 'by chance' development of the other 200,000 protein types, this point is almost mute. Whether or not their argument is true is not relevant. Random selection could not improve the odds of the original protein. Until simple life became acquainted with a process to reproduce itself, the initial 'chance' did not change. Therefore, if we assume the only factor involved in creating life is placing molecules in a proper sequence, the odds would remain in the area of 50,000,000,000,000,000,000 to 1. Additional known factors can increase the odds much further.

Hoyle's most noted illustration dubbed 'junkyard mentality' was used to point out the impossibility of the earlier discussed prebiotic soup originating life. Probably, this comparison is not as mathematically measurable as his 'Rubik Cube' explanation but, from a practical bearing, it must be just as accurate. Hoyle wrote, "A junkyard contains all the bits and pieces of a Boeing 747, dismembered and in disarray. A whirlwind happens to blow through the yard. What is the chance that after its passage a fully assembled 747, ready to

CHANCE IN AND OF ITSELF DID NOT CREATE ANYTHING.

fly, will be found standing there? So small as to be negligible, even if a tornado were to blow through enough junkyards to fill the whole Universe."[60]

Charles Dawkins wrongly accuses Hoyle of forgetting the effects of random selection. Evidently Dawkins misread Hoyle's book. As I have previously pointed out, random selection can have no great effect on the correct development of biological processes until a life form can reproduce. Until such a time, every combination of the soup would be like a separate chance for a whirlwind to assemble a 747.

But, what if the cell was simplified? What if the life cell was of the simplest single cell animal? Would cell sophistication play a roll? Not according to Dr. Denton. All cells are fundamentally the same. No matter if they are cells from simple bacteria or from the most sophisticated mammals, in essence, they are the same. In each, the roles of DNA and mRNA and proteins are virtually "identical." The instruction abilities of the genetic codes are compatible. And, states Denton, "The size, structure and component design of the protein synthetic machinery is practically the same in all cells." As for the "basic biochemical design" of a cell, Denton maintains that "no living system" seems to be "primitive or ancestral" as related to "any other system." In fact, there does not seem to be "the slightest empirical hint of an evolutionary sequence among all the incredibly diverse cells on earth."[61] Dan McShea of the Santa Fe Institute has done extensive research comparing single cell organisms with multi-cell organisms. His surprising conclusions are even more disheartening to evolutionists. McShea has found that single cell life has greater internal complexity than cells of animals higher on the ladder of life. "People are sophisticated," states McShea, "but compared to paramecium, their cells are simple."[62]

It now becomes clear that if we accept the prebiological soup premise that is so popular in most evolutionary circles, we must also hypothecate well beyond that which science allows. Thus, according to Michael Denton, "The complexity of the simplest known type of cell is so great that it is impossible to accept that such an object could have been thrown together suddenly by some kind of freakish, vastly improbable, event. Such an occurrence would be indistinguishable from a miracle."[63]

The absurdity behind life originating through natural evolution is also expressed by nuclear scientist Robert W. Faid, who, by the way, is an ex-evolutionist now professing to be a creationist. Faid states:

If life was spontaneously generated out of non-living matter, without the benefit of intelligent planning, then it is this single cell life form (amoeba or something similar) which must have been first. But can anyone actually believe that this accident of creation was accompanied by the detailed instructions of the process of mitosis?

Can anyone really believe that this first amoeba-like creature had built-in instinct to seek and recognize food, to project a pseudopod for propulsion toward the food, then another to help the first pseudopod capture it, ingest the food through the membrane, excrete the waste products, and to initiate the proper procedure and in the proper order and timing for the chromosomes and centrosomes to divide, move toward one another along with half of the protoplasm, unite, and finally split in two with each of the daughter cells repeating the entire procedure, ad infinitum?64

Faid was alluding to the notion that, if we stripped life's structure to its simplest form, it would necessarily do certain things to sustain itself and multiply. It must be able to capture and ingest food. It must be able to excrete waste. It must be able to reproduce, etc. Considering these activities, the information needed to sustain life makes even the most fundamental forms seem extremely complex. This cell sophistication suggests, in yet a different way, that natural evolution is a mathematical impossibility. Each decision a life form would need to make is described as a "bit of information."[65] These "bits" are figured logarithmically and should not be confused with "computer bits."[66]

Mathematician John Von Neumann approached life as an organic machine. In so doing he wondered what would be the minimum information requirement of a machine capable of reproducing itself. Neumann discovered such a machine had to make approximately "fifteen hundred correct decisions, one after another without error," to successfully self-replicate.[67] We have since learned through the electron microscope that approximately fifteen hundred (1,500) bits of information also describe the needs of a "larger protein molecule."[68]

Because this seems to be a comfortable number for describing the complexity of the simplest form of life, it is more or less understood as a valid delineation. The protein may be the simplest form of indisputable 'life.' However, this is where the numbers cause major problems for natural evolution. To really understand the significance of the fifteen hundred bits of information required for the simplest form of life, we should look at some comparisons. According to Robert Gange, all of the information in "the world's largest library" is less than fifty (50) bits. All human knowledge accounts for only sixty (60) bits. The "information content" of the entire physical universe is about two hundred thirty-five (235) bits,[69] with the maximum estimate being two hundred ninety-three (293) bits.[70] Where does a 'fifteen hundred bit' protein molecule get so much information? I suppose a form of life might 'accidentally' stumble into reproduction, bypassing some of the need for so much information. But, what are the odds that organic materials would accidentally form a mixed 'soup' and then bypass enough dead end options to create the needed information to form life? Even though we know the New Second Law greatly limits matter and energy, is there even a chance that a natural 'soup' could defy natural law and create enough information to make life work? Could it randomly form fifteen hundred bits of such information?

It is these kinds of figures that lead a growing number of scientists to conclude that 'natural' evolution is a mathematical impossibility. In fact, this conclusion became the claim of a group of mathematicians in the 1960's. The improvement of computers and electron microscopes have only increased the confidence of these mathematicians that life occurring by accident is indeed an impossibility. Those who ignore such conclusions should remember that mathematics is 'the purest science.' 'Natural' evolution not only goes against the laws of nature, it is a mathematical impossibility.

We have only scratched the surface of such problems. Robert Faid believes there is at least one mystery in the creation of life which is unexplainable. It is well known that "every living organism," from the simplest to the most complex, require amino acids to produce the protein needed to form living cells–which, in turn, make up the living organisms. Though an organism may use many amino acids, only twenty are "absolutely essential" for life's structure. If life was "spontaneously generated," then the twenty amino acids would also have to be spontaneously formed from chemicals such as methane, carbon dioxide, water vapor and ammonia. These are the elements thought to have existed in the "primordial atmosphere" of early earth. There would have needed to be "random chemical reactions" creating chemical mixtures of carbon, hydrogen, nitrogen, oxygen and sulfur.

Nineteen of these twenty amino acids (the exception being glycine) are "optically active." This is an interesting characteristic. If "polarized light" were to pass through a solution of these amino acids, the light beam would shift either to the right or the left. Faid explains:

Any chemist will tell you that, in random reactions, statistically 50% of molecules formed would be right handed and 50% would be left handed.

But all of the optically active essential amino acids are left handed. This means that they were not randomly formed: they were created by God at the moment He created the first organism which needed them for life.[71]

ONLY AN INTELLIGENCE FAR BEYOND THE HUMAN INTELLECT
COULD HAVE CONCEIVED OF SUCH GENIUS.

Faid is exactly right, random chance is not a viable answer. Only an intelligence far beyond the human intellect could have conceived of such genius.

As a matter of fact, profound statements like the above lead one to believe that the only way evolution could have any validity would be as an expression of the greatest artistic 'naturalist' of all time, the Creator of all that exists, the Lord of Hosts - God Almighty. For traditional evolution to have been actualized, it seems one must rely on an extreme (to the extent that it seems unnatural) form of spontaneous generation. We have earlier discussed the absurdity of spontaneous generation. Yet, spontaneous generation seems vital to evolution. I suggest that only through a miracle of God could we hope to rely on any form of spontaneous generation. Nothing is impossible with God in command, even something as absurd as spontaneous generation. Through the authority of God, chance becomes a pawn of divine providence.

Amazing as the above argument seems to be, we are finding evidence that random chance may not even exist. If our universe was predetermined, then random selection may only be an illusion. How can this be? After all, the deterministic character of the universe does not seem to fit well with a world of quantum possibilities where anything is possible. However, if one controls the quantum world, then one could have predetermined the universe. If what we seem to be discovering is accurate, if the universe was predetermined and designed, then the quantum world is surely controlled and the universe exists as described in the Bible. So, was the universe predetermined and designed as Divine Authoritarianism would demand?

Such deep questions surface in the study of Dynamical Systems, commonly known as 'Chaos' or Complexity Theory. This relatively new field of study has developed through the growing capabilities of computer science. The trend in science has been to break matter down to its lowest denominator. Thus, we have quantum mechanics. However, Chaos is more of a managerial approach to problems. It considers systems as a whole and searches for patterns of order which are undetectable to a mainstream particle physicist. Research into dynamic systems indicates that order is not random. Patterns of order even exist in stable chaos. In discussing science and probability, mathematician John Hubbard remarked, "There is no randomness in anything I do. Neither do I think that the possibility of randomness has any direct relevance to biology. In biology randomness is death. Chaos is death. Everything is highly structured."[72] The team of scientists, Heinz-Otto Peitgen and Peter H. Richter (a mathematician and a physicist), in expressing the absurdity that 'randomness' could form patterns in the universe, sarcastically wrote, "Perhaps we should believe in magic."[73]

Thus, the agnostic scientist who claims the universe is 'deterministic' and yet finds no need for God, does not understand the implications of Chaos (nor the Heisenberg's Uncertainty Principle). The theory of Chaos suggests, 'everything is highly structured' with patterns. This view of extensive structure makes a controller (God) an attractive foundation.

Of course, there have always been scientists who understood the design and structure of the universe is empirical evidence of a designer and thus God. But, the study of Chaos gives even stronger evidence for this position. Recall for a moment my previous discussion on the involved and costly separating procedures required in the formation of information. Ian Stewart, in his book, *Does God Play Dice?: The Mathematics Of Chaos,* addresses this colossal question: How can patterns form in chaos? In Stewart's statement affirming he does not know he concedes, "I also won't ask what manner of brain Vast Intellect (God) would require to store, let alone think about, Its Master Equation for life, the Universe, and Everything. A brain bigger than the universe, clearly implying that Vast Intellect must stand outside the universe and peer in. Not a bad idea, on the grounds similar to Heisenberg's Uncertainty Principle - if Vast Intellect were part of the Universe, then every time It pondered the value of dx7345232115'dt It would change the very thing It was pondering."[74] Thus, it seems, if information is the ruler used to measure the universe and God has an intellect, then God is not just a beginning force within the universe, but a super being separate from the universe.

It would be unfair not to mention that there are some scientists who, disturbed by all of the new but very real scientific implications of God, find this order in Chaos reassuring for their point of view. I am sure they address all new areas of science in an atheistic manner, yet they can only draw for straws. Their assumption is that perhaps 'Chaos' holds a force of nature (without God) which created the universe. Yet, there is a real conflict here. Does 'Chaos' interact with the New Second Law of Thermodynamics? This question is paramount. Norman Packard, a researcher in the field of Chaos states, "At the pinnacle of complicated dynamics are processes of biological evolution, or thought processes. Intuitively there seems a clear sense in which these ultimately complicated systems are generating information. Billions of years ago there were just blobs of protoplasm; now billions of years later here we are. So information has been created and stored in our structure. In the development of one person's mind from childhood, information is clearly not just accumulated but also generated - created from connections that were not there before."[75]

However, there are some real problems with the structure of his proposal. First, humans and other living creatures are 'designed' to gather information. Additionally, they 'generate information.' When they do so, it comes 1) with a cost of energy and 2) through a needed intellect. The proof of this statement is plain if one considers that the more sophisticated a creature is, the higher level of information it can gather and generate. Therefore, there is no disagreement between creatures acquiring knowledge and the natural laws of thermodynamics. Secondly, in the beginning there were no 'blobs' which instantly became life. Logic demands that there must have been more to the formation of life. As we have discussed in this chapter, spontaneous generation of a blob or any life form is fantasy.

What the Dynamical Systems or Chaos has revealed is unique patterns that appear in a nonlinear application for a time in reaction to stimuli. A good example is boiling water. As heat is added to water new patterns do form. As boiling water gets hotter the patterns seem to break into smaller ones and become more chaotic. Unquestionably, under these circumstance new patterns are produced. And, Chaos or Complexity theory suggests that if a mutation were to have an influence on a species perhaps it would be at 'the edge of chaos' (when change is most likely to occur). However, it would be a stretch to suggest Chaos is the answer to evolution. If it were, we would see new species popping up about as fast as we find species becoming extinct. Long term, The New Second Law of Thermodynamics has proven to be accurate and reliable. Yet, atheists must suggest that Chaos is the superior force. Otherwise, the science of Chaos indicates that God must exist. (God may exist if Chaos is indeed superior. A number of scientists profess that said position would also validate a belief in God. But, Chaos controlled by or in harmony with the New Second Law seems devastating to the atheistic view.) Somehow, some way, the atheist must find thermodynamics subjective to undiscovered laws of Chaos–laws unknown to humanity. By such absurdity, we can again open all of the windows to reality and invite a new 'Dark Age' to take over our world. If we make thermodynamics subjective to Chaos, then we are in effect saying 'things' are not finite. Things only become better organized. Therefore, such theories as the ancient oscillating universe theory, which defies known laws of science, are back in business because the universe will never end. The universe will only better organize itself. Of course, science will not accept this concept without a great deal of supporting evidence–which has not been discovered. Thermodynamics is law and Chaos is an interpretation of a phenomenal system not yet totally understood. However, if forced to make a judgement, it seems reasonable to conclude that Chaos agrees with the rest of an organized universe and, thus, indicates a defining intelligence. Moreover, thermodynamics must be the superior (over dynamical systems), if laws are fact and things are finite. We have no reason to believe Chaos creates anything as substantial as life, nor will it keep the universe from decaying. It certainly holds no validation for spontaneous generation (spontaneous generation is contrary to the determinism of dynamic systems). I refer to the earlier suggested experiment regarding spontaneous generation by tracking a void in a test tube throughout one's life. At this point, the study of Dynamical Systems (Chaos) is but a managerial tool which allows us to look at structures from an overview instead of the traditional dissector view. It is a tool used daily in varying degrees in every field, i.e., science, business, sports, etc.

Let me attempt to simplify the theory's procedures. When I play golf and I want to sink a twenty foot putt, I find it valuable to walk away from the putt and look at my shot from a wider view. I hope to see all of the conditions involved. Is the ball going to go straight? Will it fade to the right or the left? Often, several movements are required. The ball might need to travel straight for ten or so yards and then roll slightly to the right and into the hole! Of course, my putts do not always go the way I plan. However, misses are usually the fault of the man physically making the shot (me) and not the logic behind the plan. Yet, this wider vision of a golf putt demonstrates why the total view of a problem is advantageous. If I were to add variables such as wind currents, the exact velocity of the ball, etc., with enough time and patience and a computer to see how varied conditions could affect the shot, I might develop a true dynamical expression. And, we could calculate how all balls from that spot might travel. Of course, a golf putt is not difficult enough to need a complex analysis. A more complicated problem, such as the effects of stress in a business office, would be more appropriate. As the variables increase, the behavioral activity would become divergent, never repeated, yet predictable. What is being discovered through the science of Chaos is not an exact answer, but tendencies or patterns. As in quantum mechanics, the behavior of the individual is not important. Granted, people do make choices. Some people handle stress better than others. Therefore, individuals will behave differently. However, it is the total behavior which is measured and it is in the total behavior that patterns emerge. As in so many areas of study, we once again discover patterns of design.

Finally, one other area of science must be considered when discussing the shortcomings of evolution. The previously mentioned mathematical inferences of complex specified information (CSI) seem to have its greatest impact on biological research. The physical sciences, such as physics, chemistry and astronomy are exact sciences for the most part because of their mathematical implications. Biology, on the other hand, is often subject to human conjecture. A scientist can look at an old bone and come up with a new presupposition on evolution's tree of life. What CSI tends to do more than anything else is make biology fit under the umbrella of exactness. This closes the windows in which the scholar might play. Biologists and related scientists do not like mathematics interfering with their freedom of conjecture. Nonetheless, not only does CSI point to intelligent design, but it also disputes the current paradigm of science and restricts the alternatives.

Looking to this realm of biology, William Dembski uses the bacterial flagellum as an example of intelligent design rather than chance. The flagellum is like a miniature boat. It is described as having a "whiplike rotary motor" complete with an "acid-powered rotary engine, a stator, O-rings, bushings and a drive shaft" which enables it to "navigate through its environment."[76] Dembski points out that this sophistication "requires approximately fifty proteins. Yet the absence of any one of these proteins results in the complete loss of motor function."[77] The flagellum's irreducible complexity seems to refute "Darwinian mechanism." Moreover, the information needed by it's structure fits CSI's requirements of complexity and specificity and, thus, bacterial flagellum implies that it is a product of intelligent design.[78]

SCIENTISTS LOOK FOR ANSWERS

There have been many inventive theories about the origins of life. Some theorists suggest that life conceptual molecules formed below the surface waters of a frozen earth. Another group of scientists propose that the first life formed in layers of clay. Yet another group prefers that life sprung forth within the protection of bubbles. There are even a number of very credible theorists who believe life-supporting materials of various kinds came from outer space. The scenarios seem endless. However, the most important query might be, what part of the cell developed first? What part of the cell is the most fundamental and what functions of the cell can be accomplished by environmental factors, etc. Can any of the cell activity be accomplished by outside forces? Tom Siegfried, science editor of the Dallas Morning News, has made some interesting comments related to this issue:

"So a central issue in life's origin has been which came first: proteins or nucleic acids - the construction workers or the blueprints? The problem with all the standard views of the origin of life is that all the reactions in biochemistry today require enzymes,' says biophysicist Harold Morowitz of George Mason University. 'So if you assume you require enzymes to do all this chemistry, then you say you need enzymes to make the molecules that make enzymes. It's the classic chicken and egg argument.'"[79]

Though some very knowledgeable people believe we will never understand how life originated, others think the answer is just around the corner. Virtually every neo-Darwinian evolutionist's book or paper written on this subject over the last thirty years seem to promise a 'soon coming' solution. I cite Laurie R. Godfrey's book, *Scientists Confront Creationism* as an example. It includes a chapter by Russell F. Doolittle who ends his chapter by stating, "Given the rapid rate of progress in our understanding of molecular biology, I have no doubt that satisfactory explanations of the problems posed here soon will be forthcoming."[80] I must point out that Godfrey's book was published in 1983 and because of the time factor involved in writing, the concepts expressed in his chapter were formulated twenty years or more before my thoughts (I write this in 2004 and I assume most of his ideas were formed years before he wrote his chapter). Yet, instead of satisfactory explanations, we seem to have found even more serious problems than were known in 1983. Therefore, I would think Doolittle has been proven wrong. The explanation was not 'soon forthcoming.' Of course, such misplaced optimism goes all of the way back before the previously noted Miller experiments. Many scientists around the world have spent their entire careers trying to create life with no success. They are the modern alchemists. I think we are now beginning to read and hear a strong opposing sentiment. As in the earlier mentioned words of Dr. Jeffery Bada, "The origins of life remain one of the major unsolved problems of this century . . . There's no evidence for anything so it's a wide open field."[81] Many of those scientists closest to the problem candidly state that we will never create life. Obviously, there is more to it then just putting together the proper sequence of molecules. Therefore, we can clone it and manipulate it, but I would not expect to see humans replicate life 'from scratch' in our life-time. However, I do not presume that we will never replicate life, for 'never' is an infinite term. I personally believe that if life can be created through experimental means, human beings can discover how to do it. After all, the resources are there. There are thousands of extremely intelligent and well edu-cated people working daily with very delicate equipment, plus some of the most sophisticated computers in the world, trying to solve the related problems.

So, for the sake of this discussion, let us simply forget the absolute impossibility of spontaneous generation and assume that one day we will find a way to artificially create life. So, I ask, if Stanley Miller were to recreate life today, what would it prove? Would this prove life originated and developed through a natural accident? No! It would only prove that human beings, with the help of incredibly intricate tools, have an ability to create. Humans found a way to make life. As mankind conquered the Rubic's cube by watching, experimenting and reasoning, so might they find a creation process. Thus, a creative force with an intellect (such as human beings) might discover a method to copy the original, i.e., a previous life form thought by many to be a creation of the ultimate creative being - God.

Certainly the vast majority of scientists would comment that this replication will be a complicated process. Yet, complexity holds another resounding problem. Though Sagan's enthusiasm for Stanley Miller's experi-ments mislead the public, his faith was not unfounded. Why? Because the paleolithic record suggests that the formation of life was a simple process. Thus, Miller's success should have lead to a quick solution. Of course, that human achievement has yet to come. So, when do we say, "The solution to this problem is too sophisticated to have evolved through natural causes?" When do we admit natural selection could not have performed this process in the given time frame? I suggest we have probably already passed that point of sophistication. Even though we have not replicated the process, anything we might discover today, through the wonders of the computer, etc., should be too sophisticated for a historically limited natural process. I think the watershed on replication came in the late 1960's to early 1970's. This was before the computers became prodigiously sophisticated and before we had sufficient insight into genetics, etc., because these overcompensate for the limits of time. However, even early computers were capable of bypassing the millions of unneeded trial and error steps required by genetics to replicate a living cell.

So, we might ask, what if this needed high level of cell sophistication can only be replicated through a sophisticated form of intelligence? What if there is more involved in life's origins than putting molecules in a given sequence? Such a discovery would emphatically destroy any assumption of random selection. Thus, science returns us to the previous metaphysical questions.

Microspectively, we might find that life is guided by an intelligence born within each molecule. An inherent intellect in all living things is yet another concept which attempts to justify random selection and is being proposed by some scientists today. Intelligence may, in fact, be the key to life. Yet, if life is born with intelligence, then it may well be guided by the Creator of all universal intelligence. So, comes the related questions: What is the origin of all intelligence? Is there a guiding force controlling the evolution of all things? As eluded to earlier, such a controlling intellectual force would necessarily be God.

Finally, if we do indeed find an answer to the origin of life, we will not know whether we have the correct answer. We will necessarily have to ask: Did life originate in the manner demonstrated in the laboratory? Life may have developed in an entirely foreign manner. For example, what if God made life with 10 molecules and we learn to do it with 250? How would we know, through whatever formula we derived, that we had indeed found the original formula? All we would be sure of is that life can be reproduced by an intelligent cause copying the previously engineered form of an unknown cause. In such a case, the origins of life would still suggest (through cause and effect logic) an intelligent cause. Yet, at this point in time, any discussion about replication is virtually meaningless. Regardless of our personal predictions, to assume human beings will ever recreate natural life is a dramatic fantasy which belongs only in science fiction novels, not science textbooks.

One last situation often comes up in such philosophical conversations. It seems that a number of very intelligent people have been frustrated by the seemingly impossibilities of a natural origin to life and do not want to consider the creationist view of a beginning, so they theorize that we are the result of outer-space organic materials or even space aliens.

What would be the implications if we find and verify organic materials or beings in outer space? Would that prove neo-Darwinian evolution?

No. First, we should find some organic debris on Mars.[82] However, these traces would come from earth. We lose organic particles to space which should be measurable at such short distances. But, to make the discussion more interesting, let us presume we do find something much more surprising. What would be the inferences if we found alien beings in outer space? Contrary to the belief of some people, aliens would not disprove creation by God. If God created the universe God created everything in the universe. If beings or organic compounds, etc. do exist and did not originate on earth, we would not have proof of an accidental form of evolution. There would still be a need for a first cause. However, such a discovery would present a more profound philosophical question—the same query asked above. That question is: Why do we find organic material 'naturally' forming in the universe when we cannot replicate that material with our sophisticated computers and related equipment? Modern computers can perform molecular calculations well beyond the inferences of nature. Philosophically speaking, what is in the universe is not as interesting as how it got there.

GOD IS THE REASONABLE ANSWER

In this chapter I have covered some of the major problems related to discovering a natural solution to the origins of life. I have further pointed to recent discoveries which totally change the understanding of such evolutionary terms as 'randomness' and 'spontaneous generation.' Perhaps the only truly empirical information science has given us is that everything has design and, thus, the sum of all things strongly favors a designer. Whether we are considering microbiology, astronomy or physics, everything seems designed and we can observe said design in a number of ways. If we take all of the studies on structured chaos, and complex specified information (CSI), regardless of the field, we systematically find order and patterns of information much to complicated then a 'by chance' explanation. All things great and small seem to exist by design. That is the awesome reality of matter and time.

Furthermore, today's educational systems are left believing in a theory which claims the human ancestor was a rock. Yet, they do not have a scientifically sound explanation as to how such changes could have happened. However, if there are good reasons, if Carl Sagan and friends were right about spontaneous generation, God would still seem to be the most reasonable answer to the universe's creation process. If God designed the 'natural' universe including earth and all life on earth, it seems reasonable that He would also design a 'natural' way for life to form. Whether God created our environment by a traditional creation method or through an 'evolutionary' creation method, it seems logical that God would have included life in the creation equation from the time of His original conception. It should be understood that the God who designed and created the universe is indeed ALL POWERFUL!

A final reason to believe in a planned universe (thus a super intelligent God) is that the engineering in our existence is observable. We live in a synchronized world. Scientists assume everything in the universe was set for life to form on earth. In the book, *Microcosmos, Four Billion Years of Microbial Evolution,* evolutionists Margulis and Sagan discuss the ease with which life formed on earth as in the following: "The presence of organic compounds in meteorites only seems to confirm that a hydrogen-rich environment exposed to energy in the presence of carbon - conditions that certainly existed throughout our solar system, if not the universe—will, by the rules of chemistry, produce the building blocks of life."[83] To whatever extent this is true, such favorable conditions (for life) suggest a planned structure. Margulis and Sagan continue, "It is the many other unique qualities of the earth, including its wetness, balmy temperatures, and gravitational properties, that made it a better environment for these molecules than other planets. The earth's conditions favored certain chemical combinations more than others, and over time a direction was set."[84] Margulis and Sagan name only a few of an astounding number of 'lucky' events which allowed life. Some others have been previously mentioned in this writing. To assume the universe is the result of an enormous string of haphazard incidents, that we are the benefactors of such incredible 'luck,' seems foolishly naive. Obviously, there is much more to the origin of life than incalculable odds of having all of the needed elements form and all of the required conditions congenitally blend. Remember, our most sophisticated technology can mimic all of the favorable conditions, but it cannot duplicate the simple chemical expression of changing non-life into life. Yet, at the exact moment required, the needed synchronization was there and the process was quick. Whenever and however life came, earth was a marvelous incubator. The process seems to have been perfect in every way. This fact is recognized by all. Therefore, the odds vehemently favor 'life' being an intelligent plan.

By the way, in reference to the beginning bias (scientists from good schools do not believe in creation), the Intelligent Design and Evolution Awareness (IDEA) Club of University of California at San Diego (a student organization) has as a web site disputing this thought. Included is a section entitled: "Scientists and other Intellectuals that Doubt Darwinism and other Naturalistic Theories of Origins." Contained within is a very long list of names including many mentioned in this book. These are some of the top scientists in the country with Ph.D.s from the "best universities."[85] (Web address is listed in footnote.) Thus, contrary to public opinion, it is no longer justifiable for a scientist to blindly accept traditional evolutionary theory. Moreover,

> TO ASSUME THE UNIVERSE IS THE RESULT OF AN ENORMOUS STRING OF HAPHAZARD INCIDENTS, THAT WE ARE THE BENEFACTORS OF SUCH INCREDIBLE 'LUCK,' SEEMS FOOLISHLY NAIVE.

the wise person should be introspective enough to recognize God's signature on his or her life. Assuming God is able to create a universe, balance its forces, command its dimensions as well as design and create many living species, all for the fulfillment of His Will, then He might well be powerful enough to 'know' your inner being. If He commands the dimension of time, He might have known before there was a dimension of time what problems each of us would face at any given point in our lives. He then could have spun 'timed' solutions to whatever problems He wished to solve, even at the initial action of universal conception. He could have known everything about each and every one of us - who would try to live good lives, who would love Him, who would pray to Him and for what reasons. Philosophically and theologically, I accept such a powerful God. I certainly do not believe God ALMIGHTY is an old man with a gray beard and spends His time going around putting out political fires. Nor does He follow behind His children changing His plans per their foolish requests. Rather, it is we who should follow and accommodate our awesome infinite Creator. God and the Will of God are all that matters in time and space. Most certainly, this is the Ultimate Reality.

GOD AND THE WILL OF GOD ARE ALL THAT MATTERS IN TIME AND SPACE. MOST CERTAINLY, THIS IS THE ULTIMATE REALITY.

CHAPTER 6

SCIENCE: THE BIBLICAL VIEW

" . . . but, test everything that is said to be sure that it is true, and if it is, then accept it."[1]

Some readers may feel this philosophical journey has been quite overwhelming. We have covered numerous reasons why God must exist. Yet, there are many others as science continues to gather information indicating God created and controls our universe. Yes even evolution seems impossible without God. To the dismay of the neo-Darwinian advocates, a world affected by the slightest force, such as the flapping of butterfly wings (exaggerated cause), screams of a planned, well balanced environment crafted by a great First Cause, the absolute God.

Yet, the political rules imposed on science greatly limit discussions about such things as the Ultimate Reality. For example, science does not address 'why something is.' It only seeks to know whether or not 'something is.' Yet, in our discussion about existence, "why" has major implications regarding the intendment of life. Frankly, in the shadow of these "why" questions, science is but an eccentric toy.

If you will recall, the most logical conclusion about the source of existence is that if something is, then something with sufficient cause is eternal. Let us further remember the sum total of our human knowledge is only like 'spit in a bucket.' There is much about our existence we do not understand - including matters of God. In fact, the very concept of God stretches human consciousness. Though we know many things about our physical universe, we know virtually nothing about the bounds of reality. If we were to assume gradual evolution is the answer to human existence, then what would said conclusion suggest about our spiritual existence? What would be learned about the spiritual planes of reality? Nothing! Gradual evolution would not disprove God nor heaven nor hell. Furthermore, any scientist who suggests evolution is possible without God is moving into subjectivism and not the boundaries of valid scientific deduction. Both atheists and theists who believe evolution diminishes the likelihood of a Holy God ruling over existence are badly mistaken. I refuse to allow any concept of science to be more than an explanation of the material world. Obviously, something exists outside of the material realm. Research in a number of areas validate a metaphysical world. Our origins clearly come from beyond a Big Bang. Our essence defies scientific law.

Most assuredly, pure logic and true science are not the enemies of God. I am a Creationist. However, the only objections I have to evolution are based on scientific evidence. I have no 'theological' reason to disagree with anything science has discovered about the beginning of the universe or evolution or human origins. I resolved the evolution issue back in the 60's when I was in college. At that point in time, from my perspective, the limited evidence for evolution seemed overwhelming! I took some science books and compared them with a Bible. In doing so, I affirmed that the Bible does not hold an in depth explanation about how God created the universe. The Bible is not, nor was it intended to be, a science book, as it holds much more depth and Truth than a discussion on science. The Bible answers the cosmological questions of ancient middle eastern shepherds. Yet, it also fits extremely well with the projections of modern science such as the formation of space, earth's atmosphere, the earth's crust, and the development of life. In fact, Biblical descriptions imply many of the newer concepts of science, including multi-dimensionalism, relativity, quantum mechanics and the science of Dynamical Systems (Chaos).

There seems to be two creation stories in Genesis. The first narration is a chronological accounting of creation. A second record may to be a summation of how creation appeared on earth with the changing density of earth's atmosphere. Furthermore, this latter discussion seems more philosophical and, perhaps, symbolic through its emphasis on relationships. Nonetheless, I am confident there is important information, in both of these creation explanations, which has yet to be grasped by the human mind.

It is significant that the order in the first Genesis account generally follows the 'scientific' explanation of evolution. I think many Judaic/Christian Americans who grew up in the 60's saw this agreement as a verification of the validity for both the Biblical and evolutionary explanations. Both described the same events. I find the Biblical wording, "Let the earth bring forth every kind of animal . . ."[2] an interesting choice of words. To this day, I do not understand what that means, and I cannot emphatically state it does not imply evolution. In college I thought, "Evolution? Why not? He is God. Let Him do as He pleases." Thus, I became a 'theistic evolutionist' or, more specifically, an 'evolutionary creationist.' I accepted the Darwinian concept of evolution as factual. I thought ancestors of rocks slowly changed into human form. The only difference between what Carl Sagan was preaching and what I accepted was I concluded that God's involvement was necessary and long lasting. I felt God conceived of, designed and commanded the process of evolution. Evolution was His providential tool. We humans were here because God used evolution to put us here. From this position, evolution makes the Bible very special. Considering all of the myths and all of the explanations of ancient creation, there is only one which expresses a world created in a chronological way generally compatible with instructional evolution. That expression comes from the Bible. The vast majority of atheists suggest the Biblical creation account was stolen from other Mesopotamian creation myths. Yet, the other ancient writings cannot meet this test. Thus, the Bible seems to have been written centuries before its sophistication. It is the earliest theological expression to introduce the generally accepted progression of life forms - from the most simple to the most sophisticated - as well as the first writing to declare God is eternal.[3] This 'eternalness' of God is a very critical point because physical evidence tells us something with proper authority must be eternal. Where does the Bible get its 'scientific' implications? How does the Bible hold such absolutes? How can the Biblical narration be the only ancient creation account to anticipate the concepts of relativity, quantum mechanics and modern ideas of logic? Such Biblical accuracy does not necessarily rule out the possibility that all creation myths carry a grain or two of truth. However, for me, science eliminates any notion that the Genesis account was founded and developed strictly from Sumerian, Babylonian, Egyptian or other previous writings. To continue believing this postmodernist fantasy seems foolish indeed. Many related questions have solidified my position. For example, how did Moses know about the order in the development of the animal kingdom? How did he know wild animals of one species do not breed with wild animals of another species? How did he know human beings developed later than the other general categories? The many points of similarity between the Biblical and traditional evolutionary theory go on and on.

I still find this collaboration of Biblical writings and scientific theory to be evidence of both an omnipotent God and Biblical truth. Even the crumbling neo-Darwinian view of evolution brings validity to the Biblical account. Similarly, the Biblical narration gives a level of credit to an evolutionary process. If, for example, the commonly held evolution theory involved a raven bringing mankind out of a hole in the ground, it would not fit any interpretation of the Genesis chapter one account. However, it would fit early Native American theology. Thus, evolution would give ancient Native American culture a level of credibility. Finally, evolution is totally different from any Native American traditional view and thus detracts from the validity of such American myths.

On the other hand, the Biblical creation explanation is much older than all modern evolutionary theories. If Biblical creation is correct, then one would expect the evolution hypothesis versions to correlate with the progression of creation because the Biblical pattern would be accurate. After all, evo-

---

EVEN THE CRUMBLING NEO-DARWINIAN VIEW OF EVOLUTION BRINGS VALIDITY
TO THE BIBLICAL ACCOUNT.

lution would be the imitator, for it would be based on the human experience—one part of the creation discovering other parts.

JUST THE FACTS

What do we know from science about evolution? What can we accept with a high level of certainty? We are somewhat certain through DNA sampling that subspecies evolve from a general species. For example, all breeds of dogs probably came from one dog species. All of the human race probably came from an archetype human being. Cosmologically, we infer the universe had a beginning. The earth and stars had a beginning. We also deduce that time and the three dimensions of space probably had a beginning. Though I am writing in generalities, the above assertions are virtually all we can reliably conclude about evolution. Interestingly, all of these beginnings are also Biblical. Yet, these Biblically correct statements are all we can demonstrate or even project about evolution without breaking laws of science or making revolutionary yet unverifiable assumptions. I state this to make two points. First, certain critical assumptions in the evolutionary theory seem unworkable without a source of superior intelligence and power. Natural evolution of and by itself seems unworkable, because it defies laws of science, i.e. the law of thermodynamics, and the doctrine of uniformity. Furthermore, most classical assumptions in evolution propose incalculably bad odds and then assume these bad odds were naturally fulfilled. Such assumptions should be unacceptable to any reasonable theorist. But, accepting the fantastic is necessary if one rules out the more reasonable supernatural possibilities. Finally, because of these obvious inadequacies, if a classical form of evolution was proven true today, it would still require a Creator and, thus, the resulting adjusted version of evolution would satisfy both my philosophical and theological positions. So whether through evolutionary creationism or traditional creationism, the Biblical accuracy is obvious and vastly superior to all creation myths.

TIME AND GOD

I would prefer believing that God created everything we know as 'reality' in humanly accurate seven day creation periods. This would make our human understanding of science and theology much simpler. I would like science to prove that everything we know as reality came into existence in six twenty-four hour days. Actually, I believe the Biblical God, had He so chosen, could have created the universe in a fraction of a second. Therefore, the term 'day' does not express a limitation on God's work, but is an expression of periods in God's creation activity. If God is All Powerful then whether these 'days' are 24 hours or not is insignificant. Furthermore, the Biblical use of 'day' may have a symbolic spiritual relevance yet to be discovered. Nonetheless, the more we study 'time,' the more we understand that 'time is relative.' And, the meaning of time depends upon how time is measured. A

Biblical 'day' is not necessarily an absolute statement of time. The correct interpretation of the Biblical 'day' is not a scientific mandate for substantiating the Biblical God. I cannot limit God by stating my interpretation of a 'day' is the one Moses intended. There are many variations in the Biblical usage. In most instances, a Biblical 'day' was from sun up to sun down or about a half of a twenty-four hour day. Apparently, this half day concept is not the 'day' in Genesis, chapter one. In this instance, the Bible seems to be using the creative 'day' in a more flexible manner. One commonly used interpretation comes from a Biblical verse of Scripture: "A thousand years are but as yesterday to you! They are like a single hour!"[4] Thus, many creationists suggest the world was created in six thousand years. Others suggest the Bible is speaking in even more relative terms. A day indicates an unspecified period of time. Therefore, 'day' was used to denote a separation of events. In the same manner, the Bible prophesies about a day of Judgement when God will destroy a world of sin. The time of this day is unknown to humans - one of God's surprises. We find a similar variance of time in modern speech. For example, the statement, 'this day is Wednesday,' contrasts with 'the day of the dinosaur.' The first statement is relatively definite; the second is relatively indefinite.

Over the years, a number of creationists have argued against taking a narrow view of time. This point was well made by Don England in 1972. This chemist and professor at Harding University wrote, "One is not obligated by Scripture to adopt a young earth view and we must avoid at all cost taking general impressions which we get from Scripture and crystallizing them into literal absolute truths."[5]

Demanding that time limitations in Genesis meet our expectations may be similar to a scientist accepting Spinoza's limitations on God. These limitations are unfortunate for the exact meaning of time is not critical to Biblical Truth. The message is that God created the universe. If we are indeed discussing a supernatural being, we cannot limit that being without reason. However, here lies part of our conflict and perhaps part of our solution. Time is extremely relevant to human science. It is the human standard normally used in measuring the rate of change. Yet, from our human perspective, time is becoming a friend to all who favor the creation theory and an insurmountable mechanical problem for natural evolutionists. Thus, time has become somewhat of a scientific enigma.

This position was well taken by Philip E. Johnson in a debate over creation vs. evolution. Dr. Johnson was asked if he was a thirteen thousand-year creationist. He responded:

I do not speak to such issues. I do not bring Biblical issues into the discussion at all and do not have any particular personal position about the age questions. In my work, I assume the official age that is

given, but I have not made an effort to make a personal study of radio-
metric dating for example, or whatever. So, I just leave that all alone.
Whatever age you want is fine with me. Take as much time as you
want, the mutation selection process did not produce and could not
have produced all of these complex structures.6

Dr. Johnson's statement captures my personal view. I am not concerned with time factors. From the macro-evolutionary perspective, time is
indeed relative and, perhaps, insignificant. Thus, if we allocate all the time in
the universe, there simply has not been enough time for the 'mutation selection process' of and by itself to produce life in its many forms.

OTHER PROBLEMS

Generally speaking, scientists feel that supernatural theories are not
verifiable and, therefore, must be treated as myths. This is where scientists
begin to reveal the political prejudices in science, because if the above is an
accurate statement, scientists should have a similar problem legitimizing any
natural evolutionary hypotheses. None can be tested by the 'scientific
method.' If, for example, we replicate life in the laboratory, we do not know
if we did so in the same manner and under the same conditions of the original
life - the initial life on earth. Therefore, all evolution theory, like creation theory, is based upon speculation. So, how can so many in the scientific community adamantly expect society to accept evolution as factual? I conclude that
natural evolutionary scientists have neglected their science. Dr. James Bales
has written:

Having ruled out the possibility of divine creation he (neo-Darwinist
evolutionist) is automatically committed to the position that matter
created life and its manifold forms. This is why he continues to cling
to faith in evolution regardless of its inability to pass the tests which
the scientists require before they accept many other positions as sci-
entifically established. They make an exception of the hypotheses of
evolution, because if nature is unable to account for life in all its
forms; their naturalistic world-view has been shattered. In such a
case, their determination to find a scientific - in other words, a natu-
ral - explanation for reality has proved to be fruitless. Rather than to
give up the quest for natural explanations of all reality, they are will-
ing to accept miracles, they are willing to believe that nature - con-
trary to the doctrine of uniformity - did in the past what she cannot
and is not doing today; but they are not willing to accept any miracle
worker except nature.7

This is indeed harsh criticism of the logic of evolutionists.

Philosopher Thomas Kuhn made other interesting observations related to the behavior of scientists. Most notably, he concluded that facts are not regarded as neutral. Observations are "paradigm-dependent."[8] Let us apply Kuhn's conclusion to evolution: Darwin, through virtually no experimentation, came up with the evolution hypothesis. Other scientists made Darwin's theory a paradigm of thought. Once accepted as fact, scientists did not and do not question paradigm thought. This would have labeled them as non-intellectual. They assumed future evidence would validate the evolutionary position. However, the accumulating evidence does not fit the evolution paradigm. Therefore, all conflicting data has either been forced to fit the paradigm or totally rejected.

FOSSILS

Fossils have been our most objective historical record of the plant and animal kingdoms. If an animal shows up in the fossil record, it did exist. Virtually everything else, from environmental changes to factors related to design, are matters of interpretation. Though fossils may also be explained in various ways, a fossil is a historical fact. Interestingly, the fossil record is not what one would expect to find if traditional evolution was accurate. Neo-Darwinian evolution proposes that life evolved slowly. Each new generation was slightly more advanced than the past. But, to the evolutionists' dismay, the fossil record indicates all life forms appeared suddenly.

This abruptness in the fossil trail and the stability and distinctiveness of the fossilized classes are major reasons for my philosophical shift from evolutionary creationism to what scientists would identify as a fundamental creationist position. Before I considered dumping the gradual change position necessary to evolutionary creationism, I needed to contemplate one politically controlled issue. If the above is true, if there is not a conforming fossil record, then how can professing evolutionists (who are also scientists) speak with such resolution on this matter? The answer is simple. The only real alternative to natural evolution is creationism.

If you read virtually any book about evolution, it will acknowledge shortcomings of the fossil record. However, it probably will claim the record is consistent with the theory of evolution. Many books might even state that the 'missing links' in the record are small and insignificant. Because authors seem to either ignore missing links or make misleading statements (as above) about them altogether, the late Stephen Jay Gould of Harvard has called the lacking fossil record 'the trade secret of paleontology.' Referring to Gould's term, Francis Hitching writes, "Reading popular or even textbook introductions to evolution, one sees what he (Gould) means: you hardly guess that they (gaps) exist, so glibly and confidently do most authors slide through them."[9] An example of these misleading statements can be found in Kenneth Jon

Rose's *Classification of The Animal Kingdom: An Introduction To Evolution.* Here he writes, "Even if there is a 'gap' between one genus and another, the gap is often so small that it is almost unnoticeable to the untrained eye."[10] Such books might show charts which place groups of animals in different branches of an evolutionary tree; the suggestion being that the record does support branches of animals originating from other branches. Then, the overview of the fossil record is dropped and a discussion normally begins about these natural forces which might have caused evolutionary change. If the evolution theory is again compared to the actual record, the book will make comments only on those adaptations found within a particular species. Of course, everyone understands these inner-species changes to be fact. Even well entrenched creationists accept such change.

Though there might be some variance over what constitutes a species, the most common biological description pronounces a species will breed freely within it's own species, but cannot successively breed outside of its species. Most people realize it is possible to breed dogs in a manner conducive to growing long or short ears. Furthermore, a subspecies of dogs can and will breed with another subspecies of dogs. Variations in an animal's habitat might also cause change. If a subspecies of birds cannot find enough worms, the sub-species may change its feeding habits and become marvelous insect hunters. Of course, environmental influences such as eating habits are 'learned' changes. Nonetheless, change can and does take place. Such non-contested points which are often used to explain evolution are frivolous. These types of changes have been labeled 'micro-evolution.' The real issues are the 'macro-evolutionary' questions. Such contested questions might include: How can a dog in a natural environment bring forth an entirely new kind of animal? Though that sounds like a valid question, it is the very sort of inquiry that creationists are ridiculed for asking.

The best response for traditional evolutionists has been that micro-evolutionary changes lead to gradual macro-evolutionary change. However, the fossil record does not support this supposition because there are no solid transitional links. Neither did it support such change in Darwin's day. Thus, Darwin wrote, "So that the number of intermediate and transitional links, between all living and extinct species, must have been inconceivably great. But assuredly, if this theory be true, such have lived upon the earth."[11] Darwin and his colleagues obviously thought we would find many of these missing transitional links. Over the last century we have found a vast variety of fossils from previously unknown life forms, yet there is virtually no evidence of the many transitional forms Darwin thought would be needed to validate his theory. In fact, quite the opposite is true. The record speaks of an abruptness in change. A number of scientists have found this very puzzling, because Darwin's logic on this point seems right. A gradual change from one species to the next should leave a continuous series of fossils beginning with the most simple life form and ending with modern man. Interestingly, this one problem has caused the evolutionist and the creationist to switch sides with Darwin. It is the evolutionists who must rationalize away problems with the fossil record. Creationists simply state the record is clear, traditional evolution did not happen.

Even in the sixties, creationists understood the magnitude of the fossil void. They concluded the lacking fossil record was an inexplicable impediment to the neo-Darwinian position. As an example, Dr. Robert T. Clark and Dr. James D. Bales, wrote a book, *Why Scientists Accept Evolution,* which was published in 1966. In their book, Clark and Bales proclaimed, "Evolution, if it actually took place, would now be a matter of history . . ."[12]

Because of these high stakes, scientists have promoted forgery fossils produced to mislead the scientific community about the existence of transitional specimens. The latest fraudulent attempt not only hurt the reputation of science in general but, most specifically, The National Geographic Society, as they promoted the faked bird-dinosaur Archaeoraptor liaoningensis. Now, other scientists have confirmed that bones from "up to five different animals" were used to create this fictional species. Paleontologist Timothy Rowe, of the University of Texas in Austin, stated, "Sadly, parts of at least two significant new specimens were combined in favour of the higher commercial value of the forgery, and both were nearly lost to science."[13]

Of the valid contemporary fossil finds, perhaps the one most often referred to as a transitional form is the fossilized remains of a bird known as Archaeopteryx. The Archaeopteryx is often hailed to be the first bird and a link between reptiles and birds. Because of the remains of this one animal, many scientists seem to have adopted the position that birds are the direct descendant of theropod dinosaurs. This concept was first proposed by biologist Thomas Henry Huxley, and more recently adopted by Yale paleontologist John H. Ostrom. Now, this transformation has become a litmus test for evolution. Unquestionably, the Archaeopteryx had some unique features such as a mouth full of teeth and a long bony tail covered by feathers. Yet, under further scrutiny the animal seems only to be a meat eating bird. Larry D. Martin, paleontologist at the University of Kansas, and a number of other scientists have concluded the feathers only prove the animals are birds and not dinosaurs.[14]

One must not lose sight of the fact that many of today's birds are meat eaters and many birds have unique features. Thus, the Archaeopteryx, instead of being an example of change, might be analogical of its modern cousins. As for the evolutionary implications of a bird with teeth, the Confuciusornis sanctus, from the Jurassic period of China, seems to predate the Archaeopteryx and is a primitive beaked bird without teeth. In fact, the Confuciusornis sanctus is thought to have had features more similar to modern birds.[15] If logic be our guide, the sharpest teeth with the deepest roots should belong to the oldest most primitive bird - the one closest in line to its dinosaurian heritage. However, Caudipteryx zoui had sharper teeth and deeper roots than Archaeopteryx and probably lived fifteen to thirty million years later.[16] Also, the Archaeopteryx's odd tail is similar to the tail features of the modern swan. Additionally, a number of experts suggest that the ostrich has "more supposed reptilian features than the Archaeopteryx."[17]

Some scientists suggest that, prior to the Archaeopteryx, the bird family had tree split into several branches. One became the ancestry of the modern bird and another branch became the "opposite birds" represented by Archaeopteryx.[18] According to the evolutionary logic of survival of the fittest, it seems likely that the older, toothless Confuciusornis sanctus adapted and propagated and the branch including the Archaeopteryx became extinct. Thus, the adaptation of teeth in birds did not take hold - perhaps too clumsy for its purposes.

If, however, the ostrich seems more reptilian than the Archaeopteryx, why do we not hear scientists raving about 'the ostrich, our dinosaur-bird?' The ostrich is a much later addition to the bird family and, therefore, no one would claim that it exhibits a reptilian-bird linkage. What it does exhibit is the flexibility of a species or the variety of features within each species. Similarly, experts do not feel that penguins link birds to the fish. Yet, we must wonder, if penguins were but ancient fossils, would we now theorize that birds evolved directly from fish? Over the years, penguin wings could have evolved from the fin. They are the perfect example of the amphibian learning to walk upright. What a find! However, the penguin is too late an addition to create such a question and a bird-fish link does not fit the paradigm.

What we have covered so far has been based upon speculation. What one scientist sees as a dinosaur-bird another scientist sees as an extinct bird. Yet, the collapse of the bird-reptilian discussion may have come very recently, via a one two punch, in the research laboratory. The first set of problems relate to homology and involves the development of the digits in the theropod hand or forelimb. Both the theropod and the avian hand develop from five digits. Because the theropod hand develops digits I-II-III, it was assumed birds develop the same digits. However, recent embryonic studies prove the avain hand develops digits II-III-IV. Some scientists may assume the avian hand originally developed from digits I-II-III and later evolved into II-III-IV, but there is no evidence of such a progression. Thus, such speculation is without merit. The digits in a bird's wings most probably could not have and did not evolve from the theropod's forelimbs. It can be assumed that the similarities between theropod and bird are synapmorphic and not homoplasic.[19] Moreover, the theropod's forelimb is much to small in relation to its body size to be compared to the Archaeopteryx. Finally, the theropod's wrist has a number of features which are not homoplasic with the Archaeopteryx.[20]

The second problem area involves the respiratory systems of theropods. John Ruben, a zoologist at Oregon State University, was interested in studying the Synosauropteryx (so called) 'feathered' dinosaur fossil finds in China. First, after examining the Sinosauropteryx fossil, he presumed that the assumed feathers were collagen fibers. This presumption is now shared by a number of scientists.[21] However, his research brought an unexpected surprise. Ruben found the first soft evidence that theropods had the same interior 'compartmentalization' of lungs, liver and intestines as do crocodiles - not birds. Ruben concluded form his studies that dinosaurs were incapable of "high rates of gas exchange." This means they were cold blooded and not the warm blooded animals that modern theory presumes. Naturally, it would be much more difficult for a cold blooded theropod to evolve into a warm bodied bird. That change alone would most likely fail any chance of theropod-bird linage. Thus, Ruben determined that the 'feathered' dinosaur's "bellowslike" lungs could not have evolved into the modern bird lungs.

Like so many times before, neo-Darwinian evolutionists did not wait for these new bird fossils to be evaluated conclusively. Instead, they forced the early interpretations to fit their foregone conclusions. Then they took their ill-formed findings to the public and sold them as fact. This recurring 'grasp for validity' by evolutionists makes it difficult for a skeptic to accept any of their conclusions. Alan Feduccia, an ornithologist at University of North Carolina, stated the probable consequences of the forged bird fossils: "In my opinion, the theropod origin of birds will be the greatest embarrassment of paleontology in the 20th century."[22]

Finally, if the 'feathered' dinosaur is the best fossil representative of evolution linkage, then there is virtually no evidence of transitional forms and no case for gradual change. This emerging pattern of non-existent links is consistent throughout the fossil story. The gaps are indeed real with no valid transitional forms. Francis Hitching adds, "But the curious thing is that there is a consistency about the fossil gaps: the fossils go missing in all the important places."[23]

Even writers sympathetic to evolution have felt obligated to address this gap problem. Gordon Rattray Taylor wrote, "But perhaps the most serious weakness of Darwinism is the failure of paleontologists to find convincing phylogenies or sequences of organisms demonstrating major evolutionary change." Of course, evolutionists have excuses for the deficient fossil record. But Taylor questioned the validity of their standard excuses: "Naturally many will have escaped fossilization or have been subsequently destroyed, but surely one or two should survive?"[24]

More perplexing is the fact that the earliest fossil specimens of each class seem to be distinctive and well defined. These animals do not appear as evolving creatures. They seem fully developed and distinctive members of a class in the 'Tree of Life.' According to Michael Denton, "It is still, as it was in Darwin's day, overwhelmingly true that the first representatives of all the major classes of organisms known to biology are already highly characteristic of their class when they make their initial appearance in the fossil record."[25]

Paleontologists work directly with fossil bones. Naturally, they are more knowledgeable about animal history than the other branches of science. Paleontologist G. G. Simpson was one of the first scientists to speak out regarding the abruptness of change and the gaps in the fossil record. On an occasion, Simpson commented that "most species appear without known immediate ancestors." He continued by noting "really long, perfectly complete sequences of numerous species are exceedingly rare." Thus, he concluded, "Gaps among known species are sporadic and often small. Gaps among known orders, classes and phyla are systematic and almost always large."[26] Simpson explained that such records should be expected for a variety of "biases" mainly centered on the small number of specimens recoverable.[27] Yet, why are all of the known specimens fully developed and not transitional? What Simpson describes does not fit the gradual model, but is applicable to what one would expect to find if the changes were more radical. Species (by the common biological definition) are necessarily closer in order than are classes and phyla. Yet, the pattern of gaps is not confined to one class, but is universal throughout the plant and animal kingdom.

THE GAPS

Let us consider this fossil record as it applies to the major periods of change. I begin my comments by referring to the earlier discussion on the origins of life. In chapter 5, I discussed how amazing it seems that life even generated on earth. Though the fossil record suggests that life arose with ease, it avoids being replicated in the science lab. In fact, humans may never replicate (initial) life. This paradox is frustrating to scientists. However, there are other paradoxes. If we compare the ease in which life first formed on earth (approximately one half billion years) to the development of the first complex life, we are again surprised.

According to conventional science, eukaryotes (nucleated cells) appeared approximately one billion years ago (and perhaps only 725 million years ago). Taylor comments, " . . . it took three billion years to get from prokaryotes (blue-green algae with no well-defined nucleus) to eukaryotes (nucleated cells), as against less than half a billion to form life itself. That doesn't make sense."[28] The fossil record implies life was relatively easily formed and the following complexities were extremely difficult. Yet, we know from experience the spontaneous generation of life was improbable at best and, based upon laws of science, more appropriately described as an absurdity. The mysteries surrounding formation and evolution of the unicellular animal are perhaps the most puzzling in the evolutionary process. We have no logical answer for these paradoxical impossibilities. Even though we are without a realistic solution, we must take a look at the next major step in the evolutionary ladder: the multicellular organism.

One of the most baffling changes occurred in the pre-Cambrian era when one cell life became multicellular. Granted, this period is also difficult to document, but the only historical evidence suggests an abrupt appearance of a multicellular metazoa. Interestingly, the structure of the first metazoans is very consistent with the multicellular organisms of today. Taylor explained the ramifications of this dilemma: "Because of the absence of fossils we do not know what the earliest metazoans looked like, or into what class they fell; nor do we know from what groups they evolved, though many guesses have been made. In these conditions it is possible to mount long controversies of the kind in which some scientists delight. Since they can never be resolved they can agreeably fill out a lifetime."[29] Taylor finished his statement with the following quotation: "Or, as Professor Bonner (J. T. Bonner of Harvard University) says in a classic understatement: 'There is some dispute among biologists as to the origin of the metazoa.'"[30]

After multicellular life formed an event took place often described as the Cambrian explosion. This term 'explosion' symbolizes a great change in the sophistication of life. However, it also is a period of great mystery. Here, the evolutionist faces some tough questions. How can evolution explain the vast changes that occurred in a comparatively short period of time? Why and how did life abruptly stop its transformation? Denton assures us that from the earliest view of the seas in paleozoic times "invertebrate life was already divided into practically all the major groups with which we are familiar today."[31]

Each abrupt new life form is uniquely designed. And, the same evolutionary problems hold true for plants. According to Denton, plants are also "highly specialized" when each "major group" shows up in the fossil record.[32] Thus, the record indicates that all new life forms are unique and not like any previous species. This fossil impression is quite clear when reading the works of other great paleontologists. Niles Eldredge (Curator at the American Museum of Natural History), intrigued by this Cambrian period, wrote: "With no obvious disturbance in sedimentation, there is no reason to assume that there is a gap in the time preserved in the rocks. And it is reasonable to conclude that the event - disappearance (of life) and replacement - was very quick indeed. If it was not literally overnight, then at least the turnover was so rapid as to appear instantaneous: a few hundred or even a few thousand years can look instantaneous in the Paleozoic rock record."[33] Devout neo-

Darwinian evolutionist, Charles Dawkins is another hostile witness for creationism. He further confirmed these statements about even the earliest fossils in his writings regarding the Cambrian gaps. He commented, " . . . the Cambrian strata of rocks, vintage about 600 million years, are the oldest ones in which we find most of the major invertebrate groups. And we find many of them already in an advanced state of evolution, the very first time they appear. It is as though they were just planted there, without any evolutionary history."[34]

Fish are very important to the evolutionary ladder, because all land animals are assumed to have evolved from the fish. However, we have no record of one fish group slowly distinguishing itself from its ancient ancestor. To the contrary, all fish groups appear in a time frame of less than "fifty million years." The time factor in and of itself seems to be an impossibility. There does not seem to be enough time for the gradual change of invertebrates to fish. Francis Hitching wrote the following about the fish gaps: " . . . one would expect the fossils to blend so gently into one another that it would be difficult to tell where the invertebrates ended and vertebrates began. But this isn't the case. Instead, groups of well-defined, easily classifiable fish jump into the fossil record seemingly from nowhere: mysteriously, suddenly, full formed, and in a most un-Darwinian way. And before them are maddening, illogical gaps where their ancestors should be."[35]

Thus, science finds that the earliest "representatives" of each group were "highly differentiated and isolated" when they were first discovered. Thus, no known species could be "in the remotest sense" considered intermediate. In fact, states Denton, "No fish group known to vertebrate paleontology can be classed as an ancestor of another; all are related as sister groups, never as ancestors and descendants."[36] It is quite obvious fish do not fit the evolutionary paradigm and constitute yet another devastating contradiction to traditional evolutionary theory.

Following the fish in the evolutionary ladder is the amphibia. Again, however, the fossil record shows no evidence of an evolutionary amphibian line of descent. As in every other case, the evolutionists assume there are fossils. We just have not found them. Granted, there is a very weak record of ancient amphibia. Evolutionists do speculate that, because fossils of fish and amphibians have a relatively comparable bone structure, sea animals gave way to land animals at this point. Yet, the fact remains that we have no hard evidence of the transformation of animal life from the oceans to land. As Gordon Rattray Taylor commented, "Though we have this clue of bone structure of the crossopterygian fin there are no intermediate forms between finned and limbed creatures in the fossil collections of the world. Once again the critical evidence for gradual evolution is missing."[37] Furthermore, there does not seem to be an amphibian line of descent after animals make contact with land.

According to Michael Denton, we find our first fossils of amphibia beginning about three hundred and fifty million years ago. At that time a number of "archaic and now extinct groups" of the amphibia family appear in the fossil record. Yet, once again, "each group is distinct and isolated at its first appearance and no group can be construed as being the ancestor of any other amphibian group."[38]

I think at some point in this discussion we must conclude that form (which permeates through repetition) defines personal biases by similarities. In other words, Frank Lloyd Wright's buildings have commonalities in expression. The alternative is equally convincing as Pablo Picasso's creative style differs from Sandro Botticelli's artistic expression. In keeping with identification through artistic pattern, God's creativity would, probably, reveal some degree of commonality. Most land creatures should have common features as most cars have wheels. Designs that work well should reappear.

Another major problem in the concept of evolution lies in the area of adaptations. Passing and improving upon special adaptations is considered to be necessary to the specialization found in all species of life. However, the fossil record gives no reason to speculate that structural adaptations are refined and passed down from one ancestor to another. As an example, we do not observe a fossil line where a species without eyes went through a long chain of evolutionary forms leading to the evolution of eyes. As Denton stated, "The absence of transitional forms from the fossil record is dramatically obvious (even to a non-specialist without any knowledge of comparative morphology) where a group possesses some significant skeletal specialization or adaptation which is absent in its presumed ancestral type."[39]

Why is the actual fossil record so different from what we would suppose? One reason is that random selection, which is the foundation for all natural evolutionary thought, does not explain what is observed. Random selection suggests animals are always randomly selecting and always gradually changing. Uniformitarian evolutionists try to rationalize their position by making exceptions, etc., inserting random selection as a 'catch all' excuse. However, besides the earlier discussed problems the newer sciences have with the concept, random selection is not compatible with the fossil record. What we do see and what fits with the cases discussed above is, once a species becomes established, it may exist for thousands of generations with virtually no known change. Then it often becomes extinct.[40] Furthermore, if random selection was relevant, one would expect to find even greater diversity in the tree of life. Ancient species would have gradually evolved into many new phyla. However, such changes are just the opposite of what is observed. There are no new phyla. Whatever evolution is, it seems to follow the Second New Law of Thermodynamics in that there seems to be a "decelerating process."[41] Today's phyla has existed for at least 500 million years. All phyla were established in the Cambrian age. No additional phyla have evolved since then. Today's classes were established in the lower Paleozoic era at least 400 million years ago. All of our orders were established by the Mesozoic era or about 60 million years in the past. Next came all of the families and then the genera, and last all of the species. Thus, since the beginning of life on earth, evolution has been working in smaller and smaller fields. This may be one reason we do not observe change in today's world. As the universe becomes more chaotic, we, human beings, only observe extinction. In the future, evolution may play itself out. Thus, change may be a thing of the past.[42] Therefore, random selection is not a valid answer and should be considered passe.

EVOLUTION'S COLLISION COURSE WITH CREATIONISM

In the 1960's, a number of scientists, particularly paleontologists, were growing dissatisfied with gradual evolution. The anemic condition of the paradigm (evolution) became obvious when young theorists began to bring forth radical new concepts. Of the new theories, punctuated equilibria seemed to be the most attractive. This theory was co-originated by two previously mentioned scientists, Stephen Jay Gould, was Harvard's most noted paleontologist, and Niles Eldredge of the American Museum of Natural History. Their theory suggests the transformation of a group of descendants from one species into a new species does not occur through gradual evolution. It occurs through more radical genetic change. According to the theory, generic mutations develop during periods of crises when the numbers of animals in a species are small. This might occur when a herd is isolated from other members of its own species, such as by a mountain range. Furthermore, a genetic mutation might randomly appear in any one animal of the segregated herd. After this change has been absorbed and spread, the segregated herd would be superior to other herds of this species. Now better adjusted to their environment, the stronger animals go through a long period with no change. At such times, these animals are said to be in a period of equilibrium. Because of the relatively small populations involved and the increase in the rate of change, there would be few if any transitional fossils to be found. Thus, the punctuated equilibria hypothesis reflects the gaps in the fossil record. Interestingly, Gould and Eldredge were not the first scientists to suggest transitional organisms come from small populations. However, their hypothesis seemed to be the best expression of the fossil record.

Yet, Gould, Eldredge and colleagues found their own dilemma. In several areas, punctuated equilibria falls short of being the consummate solution. One reason is that the punctuated equilibria model does not correspond

---

THEREFORE, RANDOM SELECTION IS NOT A VALID ANSWER
AND SHOULD BE CONSIDERED PASSE.

with real life observations. What we observe is that larger numbers of muta-tions will occur as a species' population increases. The more animals there are in a species, the greater the possibility of mutation. Conversely, when the numbers of a species are low, we find extension of the species, not drastic change! Because of the certainty of said conclusions, the ecologists most familiar with the environment and sociology of herds (which generally implies the African and European scientists) believe that punctuated equilib-rium is only explainable through creational cause. Thus, even though Gould was an avowed evolutionist, African and European scientists labeled him a creationist.[43]

Interestingly, studies in genetics (MHC polymorphism) confirm that larger populations are needed to pass change. Referring to the findings of one such study, *The Scientific American* states, "These estimates contradict the popular notion that species arise from small founding populations in which random fluctuations in gene frequencies provide conditions for greater effects of natural selection."[44]

One of the better publicized studies in Dynamical Systems seems to also agree with this contradiction. Sir Robert May demonstrated that herds have a point of 'boom' or 'bust.' A small and/or declining herd population leads to extension. However, with the rise in a population, comes a period of equilibrium. A continued rise would then produce a stable chaos. It is in this period of chaos that unexpected patterns arise.[45] Because of May's study, there is reason to believe that chaotic activities in a herd are predictably struc-tured. As discussed earlier, it seems reasonable to expect this chaotic period to produce the greatest climate for change. It seems most likely that a positive mutation might emerge within this period of chaos. However, if change takes place in a large herd atmosphere, then the number of transitional forms should be logarithmically magnified. This, of course, would suggest that there are many transitional fossils. Thus, such changes occurring in a large population would further intensify the problem of the lacking transitional fossils. Large herds would show more anomalies than small herds. I suspect this is the rea-son we have not heard much about May's study. It is devastating to evolution. Sir Robert May is now the Chief Scientific Advisor for the United Kingdom and Head of the United Kingdom Office of Science and Technology. I con-tacted Dr. May about this point and even he wished not to discuss it. He indi-cated his concept was very complicated. To the contrary, it seems very predictable. I suggest 'boom-and-bustiness' as it relates to punctuationism is too political for the head of a government's office of science; that is why he wishes not to discuss it.

As for the Gould and Eldredge hypothesis, in many ways punctuated equilibria seems more aligned to the historical account of the long day cre-ationists. The fossil evidence suggests punctuationism, but punctuationism seems to be as miraculous as creationism. J.P. Moreland once wrote, "But punctuated equilibrium appears to be empirically equivalent to creationism as far as the fossil record goes. Both seem to imply the same data, and it can be argued that punctuated equilibrium is either an ad hoc addition to save macro-evolution or a replacement of evolutionary theory preceding it and not a refinement of evolutionary theory."[46] Quite frankly, Gould and Niles inadvertently proclaimed that, as far as the fossil record is concerned (the best historical evidence), creationism has always been more accurate than the paradigm (gradual evolution). Though the 'punctuational model' was designed to account for the absence of transitional life forms, Denton states," . . . it's (punctuational concepts) major effect seems to have been to draw widespread attention to the gaps in the fossil record."[47]

Many traditional evolutionists such as Charles Dawkins, try to minimize the differences between traditional evolution and the punctuated concept. Even Eldredge and Gould seemed defensive about their controversial views. However, the evolutionary difficulties punctuated equilibrium was designed to resolve are real and substantial. Thus, the solidarity in the evolutionary empire is crumbling. Punctuated equilibrium exposes a great weakness in traditional evolution. Finally, the ecological interpretation of punctuated equilibria brings a new validity to theistic evolution. Rapid genetic change seems more compatible with divine intervention than with natural selection. The greater a positive one-step change in a species, the less likely that change occurred by natural selection.

Saltation is a punctuational theory similar to, but much more radical than, Eldredge and Gould's punctuated equilibria. Saltation proposes that major mutations could result in one step macro-evolution, thus creating a gap in the fossil record in just one generation. Such mutations would probably happen in the embryo stage of development. In so doing, one species might derive from another species through one mutational change. Saltation was first introduced in the 1930s when O. H. Schindewolf proposed that a reptile laid an egg which, when hatched, produced a full-fledged bird. This one action explained the 'reptile-to-bird' gap. Later, Richard Goldschmidt refine the theory. He suggested major progressive evolution could occur only through large mutations or macromutants.[48]

However, saltation is so extreme that it is considered by virtually all scientists to be a creation theory. Richard Dawkins makes this point rather well. Referring to Fred Hoyles' 747 illustration described earlier, Dawkins rightfully concludes: "747 saltationism is, indeed, just a watered-down form of creationism. Putting it the other way around, divine creation is the ultimate

RAPID GENETIC CHANGE SEEMS MORE COMPATIBLE WITH DIVINE INTERVENTION THAN WITH NATURAL SELECTION.

in saltation. It is the ultimate leap from inanimate clay to fully formed man."[49]

Most neo-Darwinianists argue that a saltation form of macro-evolution would produce a wide variety of 'monsters.' The great Harvard University biologist, Ernst Mayr has written:

If one had to rely on mutation pressure as the only evolutionary factor, one would need such a high rate of mutation that it would result in an enormous production of 'hopeful monsters.' All available evidence is opposed to such an assumption. Indeed, most mutations appear to have only a slight, if not an invisible, effect on the phenotype. More penetrant mutations are usually disruptive and produce disharmonious phenotypes, as correctly implied by Darwin, and will therefore be selected against.[50]

To Dr. Mayr I respond that even most creationists accept traditional evolution within structured limitations. For example, all dog breeds evolved from one initial breed, but all within the same species. Yet, saltation seems to be the most likely way to breach species delineation. Indeed, following Mayr's logic suggests, if saltation has taken place, then there has been some guidance or structural wisdom built into the sequence of mutations. Thus, it would seem, there is a 'Master' plan and a Creator. This is one reason scientists consider saltation to be a creationist theory. Though saltation is generally rejected, the overwhelming odds against a 'by chance' evolutionary theory has not bothered neo-Darwinianists regarding the origin of life. Nor do the other inconsistencies bring pause to their capricious logic. So, I accept Mayr's challenge. I will make a case for saltations. Not only will I give evidence that the related genetic mechanisms are indeed workable, I will give Mayr an example of how a distant influence can affect mutations.

There is another obvious saltation problem: How would a new species breed? Dawkins writes, " . . . if a new species really did arise in a single mutational step, members of the new species might have a hard time finding mates."[51] This brings up a good point. Continuation of a new species formed through saltation would probably require two muted embryos. However, what is true of saltation is also true to a lessor extent, yet with just as devastating an outcome, to punctuated equilibria. In both cases, there would necessarily be a first member of a species. Furthermore, the size of the population has a dramatic influence on the existence of the species. This point should be quite obvious if we consider why our society puts animals on an endangered species list. Such care is a necessity for saving a species when the animals' numbers fall below the numerical figure thought to be safe for its continued existence. Therefore, it seems likely divine intervention would be a necessity for either of these punctuated theories (saltation or punctuated equilibria) to be functional in both the production of a new species and for the development of a population large enough to survive. Nonetheless, comparing the problems of saltation with punctuated equilibria does not adequately address the above concerns. It only implies that both theories have similar problems.

Hopefully, the solution may come to us through the rapidly advancing study of genetics. One very promising saltation supposition involves a process identified as systematic differentiation. Though we do not totally understand the structure of DNA, some scientists think part of the DNA chain is not involved with the actual building of an organism. This unused portion has been called superfluous DNA. Of course, the superfluous DNA must also have a set of jobs. One is to improve the genetic blueprint. Part (or parts) of this superfluous DNA is considered a 'regulatory gene.' Its job might include implementing genetic change. Furthermore, because this portion of DNA is not expressed in the development process, it should be 'immune' to natural selection.[52] Therefore, the randomness, so important to traditional evolutionary concepts, may have been eliminated from the systematic differentiation process.

Part of the superfluous DNA might work internally and undetected, like a virus, slowly altering the DNA code until a 'predetermined' genetic restructuring was complete. Then, like flipping on a light switch, the regulatory gene could activate major genetic change. By behaving in this manner, the regulatory gene could simultaneously produce a number of individuals in a new species. Obviously, this procedure would solve the previously mentioned saltation mating problems. Furthermore, the parent species would continue to exist. Of course, coexistence of like species is what the fossil record suggests. Just as important, the regulatory gene would eliminate random selection from the evolutionary process. This is because the concept of gradual random change is replaced by macro-change and is totally controlled by the regulatory gene.

A related facility of DNA allows the genetic material to respond through directed mutations to those environmental problems which might otherwise be considered a threat to the organism. Transposors might be 'jumping genes' which have been observed in experiments.

Further research designed to focus on directed mutations bring credence to the above suppositions. Experiments by John Cairns of Harvard University indicated that the " . . . forces of selection seemed to be not merely weeding out unfit organisms but actively steering the mutations in a beneficial direction."[53] Another study by Barry G. Hall of the University of Rochester focused on the above-mentioned problems as caused by environmental change. In his experiments, "hungry bacteria needed two separate mutations -

neither of which seemed to confer any benefit alone - to use a new food source." Hall's calculations indicated that, " . . . the odds of both mutations occurring without encouragement were astronomically poor . . ." Amazingly, he found that a "surprising number" did select the two needed mutations.[54]

No form of an evolving specialization has been observed in nature. Yet, at least in artificial breeding, the mutational process does work. As Gregor Mendel discovered in his early experiments with pea plants, we can and do artificially crossbreed flowers or grasses, etc. We call the results a 'hybrid' species. However, it is important to note that we have not been able to successfully duplicate this artificial specialization in the animal world. With few possible exceptions, our experiences with artificial mutations in animals have led to genetic 'monsters' with deformed limbs and organs, etc. In nature, we generally observe macro-changes stemming from disasters, such as nuclear explosions. These lead only to negative changes similar to the above deformities and sicknesses. Yet, in the evolutionary process, saltation jumps seem to explain both the historical fossil gaps and the related problem of the infusion of new design. One such example is the evolution of wings. Genetic biologist, Dr. Jack Wood Sears, reflecting upon the disadvantages of a budding wing wrote, "It is not conceivable to me that an organism with developing wings, yet unable to fly, and without the help of the front legs, since they are now useless as they are being 'turned into wings,' could successfully compete with its more normal neighbors."[55] It seems that the only way evolving birds could survive is if wings could appear in one macro-change. Feathers are similarly puzzling. Growing feathers would be a disadvantage to an animal until they were developed enough to be used for gliding through the air. Yet, their design is delicately precise and sophisticated.

Because of the recent discoveries in genetics, I predict evolutionists must reverse their tough stance against rapid change evolution and embrace saltation as the obvious 'natural' evolutionary process. I do not think they have a choice. Similar to Darwin's belief that the fossil record would substantiate evolution, modern evolutionists suggest genetics will give conclusive evidence that life evolved as is hypothesized. Yet, continued findings have been very discouraging. As addressed in Chapter 5, genetics indicate human beings are not related to Neanderthals or Homo erectus.[56] Other recent genetic studies indicate little or no evolution has occurred in the homo sapiens species. Molecular geneticist Rebecca L. Cann, has addressed the issue in reference to studies of mitochondrial DNA.[57] According to Cann, human females have experienced relatively little or no evolutionary change since their inception (affectionately yet perhaps misleadingly, dubbed 'Eve'). Furthermore, "women can trace their lineage only a couple hundred thousand years at the most to a common ancestor."[58] This date moves human origins ever closer to the normally accepted Biblical range.[59] Furthermore, this shortened time period for human existence makes our early intellectual development even more amazing. Prior to these discoveries, the origins of our human intellect were the focus of much speculation. There did not seem to be a good answer. Thus, anthropologists and science fiction writers alike set forth wild hypotheses. This shortened time period will most assuredly add to the speculation.

A similar study on the male Y chromosome was conducted by Robert Dorit of Yale, Hiroshi Akashi of the University of Chicago and Walter Gilbert of Harvard University. To the apparent surprise of the experimenting scientists no genetic variation was found in men. A variety of races and ethnic backgrounds were purposefully involved, but such factors did not change the results. As to the male study, Dr. Ross stated, "This non-variation suggests no evolution has occurred in male ancestry."[60] Later studies continue to validate the above conclusions. There is little or no measurable diversity in the genetic background of human beings - male or female. One correlated study infers that there is little or no genetic variation within a species, but there is greater genetic variation comparing one species to another species. "When the Y chromosome of modern humans is compared with that of modern chimpanzees, gorillas, and orangutans, another great challenge arises. Large species-to-species genetic variations occur, but within each species very little, if any, variation is found."[61] Thus, through studies in genetics, homo sapiens (as well as all species of life) become a species with a mysterious, even questionable, line of descent. Perhaps there is no line of descent.

If this be true, how can scientists envision human prototypes negotiating the required nature changing jump from apes to man? Scientists are beginning to whisper synonyms to saltation. (Please keep this secret. Scientists do not want to be known for relying on the supernatural. It is not socially accepted in intellectual circles). Occasionally, terms like evolutionary tweaking are being used to describe a process which bypasses a number of genetic steps causing rapid change. Though no neo-Darwinian evolutionists would admit it, such cliche words like 'tweaking' are expressions of saltation.

MACRO MUTATIONS AND REGULATORY GENES

If macro mutations do occur and are governed by the actions of regulatory genes, then there are major philosophical questions that need to be answered. What tells the gene to flip on or off the switch? It cannot be a random process because, as stated above, the gene is 'immune' to random expression. Some biologists suggest change occurs because of environmental stress on the gene. Other scientists reject the 'directed mutation' hypothesis and look

---

"THIS NON-VARIATION SUGGESTS NO EVOLUTION HAS OCCURRED
IN MALE ANCESTRY."[60]

for other explanations. Richard Lenski of Michigan State University concludes, " . . . there does seem to be a physiological dependence to certain mutation rates."[62] A physiological dependence infers there is some fashion of an intellect within the gene. A natural mechanism which protects predetermined genetic change from outside influence or, as the situation arises, attempts to allow only a positive change, suggests a deterministic intelligence. Just as profound is a gene that must in some way be programed to flip the correct switch at the appropriate time. Philosopher, Robert Augros, Ph.D. and physicist, George Stanciu, Ph.D. rightfully argue that matter cannot predetermine this action: "It cannot be matter because of itself matter has no inclination to these forms, any more than it has to the form Poseidon or to the form of a microchip or any other artifact."[63]

If you will recall, one of the differences between nonliving matter and living things is 'information.' The massive information needed to establish life is so provocative that the most logical conclusion seems to be that there is a source of information or a programmer. The same is true of a regulatory gene. It would take a vast amount of information to develop a gene with the 'job' of switching on an incubated macro mutation. Augros and Stanciu addressed these phenomena: "Is there anything in our experience like this? Yes, there is: our own minds. The statue's form originates in the mind of the artist, who then subsequently shapes matter, in the appropriate way. The artist's mind is the ultimate cause of that form existing in matter, even if he or she invents a machine to manufacture the statues. For the same reasons there must be a mind that directs and shapes matter into organic forms. Even if it does so by creating chemical mechanisms to carry out the task with autonomy, this artist will be the ultimate cause of those forms existing in matter."[64] In conclusion, Augros and Stanciu state, "The artist is God, and nature is God's handiwork. Divine are - that is, nature - is more profound and more powerful than any human art because it constitutes the very essence of things."[65] Again, we find a great mass of evidence pointing to a Creator/God. Like so many others connected to the field of science, Augros and Stanciu are faced with overwhelming evidence that a Creator seems essential. Yet, few other scientists have been so bold as to discuss this enigma.

Scientists such as Gould, Eldredge, Dawkins and Sagan who arrogantly state that "God does not exist" or "God is mechanical and not an intelligent personality" are, in effect, claiming they know all of the information in the circle. They know everything there is to know. They have all of the knowledge needed to make this paramount decision and God does not exist. To the contrary, there is not a good scientist in the world that knows anything emphatically. In spite of all of the empirical evidence claiming God does indeed exist, including that evidence discussed in this book (which is only a small sampling of the total evidence), these men have the audacity to lead others into the dark hole of defiant humanism. "God does not exist because I declare this to be true," they cry. The shame of it is that each of these men (Gould, Eldredge, Dawkins and Sagan) are/were gifted scientists. They have been blessed with great talent. Yet, despite their talent, the Bible would refer to them as fools. For they seem to have ruled out the most probable cause for all that is . . . an intelligent God.

MAY I POINT OUT, GOD IS NOT DEAD; NIETZSCHE IS

I will argue with anyone that the Will of God is much more probable than the 'chance' of a whirlwind correctly putting together all of the parts of a 747 jet airliner. Furthermore, I suggest that a being's 'will' is needed to produce a 747. Aircraft are creations of an intellect. The chances of a tree becoming a rocking chair are virtually nonexistent without the factor of some being's will. Wooden rocking chairs are the direct result of a human being conceptualizing, designing and building a rocking chair from that which was once a tree. Only by the will or desire to produce an object conceived in a human mind does a rocking chair become an actuality. The laws of logic and classical (macro-world) science are based upon one premise: every cause has an effect and every effect has a cause. Everything that has happened had a cause. As we have previously discussed, one might argue that new discoveries in physics and quantum structure suggest some variance from cause and effect thinking. However, what new physics may actually acknowledge is that the observer affects the outcome of quantum action.[66]

CONCLUSION ON EVOLUTION AND GOD

One of the problems with classical evolution is it begins with a subatomic action and no observer. (As you might recall, an outside influence of a supernatural nature might be possible through the inferences of the Bell theorem of quantum mechanics. It states that quanta are affected by non-local influences.) The concept behind evolution is that somehow life began. Later, after a long series of cause and effect or causal events, mankind emerged from the ape family. All of these events were natural and resulted in logical conclusions. Even though neo-Darwinists conclude life began through the activities of subatomic particles with no input from an observer, they arbitrarily conclude that to allow for supernatural events would introduce 'discontinuity' to biology. Sullivan made this point rather well: "It (a supernatural event) introduces an unaccountable break in the chain of causation, and therefore cannot be admitted as part of science unless it is quite impossible to reject it."[67] However, have we not crossed that line when our brightest scientists begin introducing obvious creation theories, but call them natural evolution? Have we not crossed the line when we excuse unsolvable problems with unproved inferences, yet we ignore the logic of a first cause? I suggest the best explanation for the origin and evolution of life is a creation theory, ANY creation theory!

There are many variations of creationism. How did God form "a man's body from the dust of the ground" and breathe "into it the breath of life?"[68] We are not told and, I confess, I do not know. Furthermore, I do not think it wrong to speculate as long as we do not compromise God's spiritual truth. The creationist might seriously consider the 'punctuated' theories of Eldredge, Gould and others or the saltation implications discussed above. Furthermore, when neo-Darwinists ponder the path of evolution and the origin of life, they might also contemplate on the supernatural inferences of their only foundation - spontaneous generation. From my perspective, if causation is the answer to what is considered natural phenomena (the 'real world' is based on this axiom), then creation is the only logical answer to existence. A Prime Mover of Vast Intelligence, most certainly, commands the development of our causal world. Of course, this brings us back to our beginning concepts. If our general understanding about the universe is correct, if our general laws of logic and science are true, if we know anything to be true, then we know: in the beginning **there was God.**

CHAPTER 7

MIRACLES: SOMETHING TO BELIEVE IN

"The cosmic religious experience is the strongest and noblest main-spring of scientific research."[1]

In the early morning hours of February 25, 1998 Art Bell interviewed physicist Dr. Michio Kaku on Bell's radio program. They were discussing such things as space travel and the speed of light when Bell began to consider the spiritual side of life. Bell quizzed Kaku about his personal thoughts concerning God and Dr. Kaku stated, "Most scientists believe in the god of harmony. That is, there was a cosmic order to the origin of the universe. The universe could not have been strictly an accident of sorts. Polls taken of scientists say that most scientists have some kind of semi religious feeling, not necessarily organized religion, but they do believe that the harmony and the beauty of the universe is too gorgeous to be an accident." Art Bell then asked Kaku if he believed in the God of the Bible. Dr. Kaku responded, "I would say that the miracles that we see in the Bible are probably not possible." Kaku continued, "My son had an appeasing where he read a science book for the first time and he realized that miracles of the Talmud and the miracles of the Bible simply violated what he knew about science."

Yet, as the interview progressed, Dr. Kaku seemed to contradict himself regarding these impossibilities (of miracles). Once he said, "I think that scientists historically have laughed at spirituality. And I think their beginning to revise a lot of their early laughter, because they're beginning to realize that certain phenomena that are measurable in the laboratory are quite astounding. For example, Yogis that perform these marvelous feats have been tested in the laboratories and in controlled conditions and we now know they have spiritual power over their body that is physically impossible, but there it is in the laboratory. For example, they can lower their metabolic rate below the fatal level. They can be buried alive and have prayer beads sticking out of the dirt while they are buried alive underground . . ."[2]

Here is one of the leading scientists of our day (his understanding of universal creation discussed earlier) wanting to scoff at miracles of the past. Yet, he recognizes that science's view on the subject has been flawed, and he realizes that there are many unexplained 'miracles' happening every day all over our planet. Most of these contemporary miracles are manifested through the spiritual make up of man. However, most of the significant miracles in the Bible are authorized directly form God. So, Dr. Kaku, if the "harmony and the beauty of the universe is too gorgeous to be an accident" and modern man is the conduit for contemporary miracles, then what great works could the Creator of the universe call forth? What great force could 'speak' an explosion that spun the universe into existence? Perhaps, if God played a little trick with the world's nuclear structure, He would impress the doubters–if any survived the nuclear trick. However, God does not seem to 'do miracles' to impress us. History seems to indicate miracles are used for a nobler purpose.

Certainly many people, like Dr. Kaku and his son, look upon this subject with some degree of skepticism. However, many scientists are vehement defenders of the God of the Talmud or the Bible and believe in Biblical miracles. As for me, I too accept the premise that God can and has preformed miracles. When someone asks me if I believe in miracles, I always answer "yes." Yet, considering the Einsteinian quote found at the beginning of this chapter, my best response might be, "Yes, I believe in miracles, and I also believe in quantum mechanics!" My God can do as He pleases within or outside of His natural laws. The scientist who does not recognize the miraculous implications of our existence is quite foolish.

When we consider 'miracles' we are probing phenomena well beyond the range of science. The very word 'miracle' indicates that we do not understand something observed. Though scientists may have possible answers to some 'metaphysical' events, many such puzzles defy human understanding. But, living in 'secular relativism' has allowed us to distort truth. Thus, we cling to a premeditated ignorance and hide in the shadows of darkness–not knowing what is real, yet denying there is more. Yet, in darkness we shall wilt and die.

'Hiding in the shadows' well describes what is often seen in debates between learned Christians and learned atheists. The atheistic strategy is often one of ridiculing, name calling and stereotyping the opponents. But, as man has continued to grow in knowledge, Truth, it seems, has become an enemy of atheism. In such debates, evolution is a common topic. Yet, in regard to what we have previously covered, evolution theory has changed to fit the creationist models - not the other way around. Punctuated equilibria fits the early creationism motif better than it does Darwin's concept of gradualism evolution. No doubt this has been noted by numerous scholars, because many evolutionists believe that punctuated equilibria crosses the bounds of natural law. To this regard, the broader understanding of evolution seems impossible without a number of miracles to overpower a variety of insurmountable obstacles.

THE ATHEISTIC STRATEGY IS OFTEN ONE OF RIDICULING, NAME CALLING AND STEREOTYPING THE OPPONENTS.

Though evolution rejects the word 'miracle,' substitute words have been given analogous extraordinary powers. So, neo-Darwinian evolution rejects logic and hides in the darkness of a godless universe. In so doing, it claims the universe is controlled by Lady Luck, the goddess of hopeless despair. Her moral platitude being 'Eat, drink and be merry, for tomorrow we die.'

WHAT IS A MIRACLE?

What are the parameters of 'miracles?' The word *miracle* can mean various things to various people. Some people think of a narrow scope of phenomena such as healing miracles. Some consider all seemingly incredible events to be miraculous, whether it is the 'miracle of life' or the statistical oddity of picking winning numbers in a lottery.

From this writer's understanding, miracles are *acausal phenomena,* meaning with no apparent natural cause. In contrast, atheistic materialism is a pseudo-logic based on cause and effect determinism, but which ignores the miraculous implications even of the imperative first cause. An example of the materialistic determinism is that every human action is totally based upon the past and present (natural) environments. Therefore, human beings do not have a choice in their actions. From this standpoint, a child does not choose to be in a gang. He or she is destined to be in a gang. Thus, there are no miracles nor any other variation from cause and effect including freedom of choice.

In contrast, acausal phenomena (which would contain miracles) might include such phenomena as extrasensory perception (ESP) and other forms of telepathy, meaningful coincidence, as well as those more profound incidences proclaimed to be acts of Divine Providence. If something is unexplainable by the materialistic understanding of nature, then it could fit into the realm of acausal phenomena.

THE GOD FACTOR

If we assume God exists, then any *natural* explanation we may have for miracles are speculative at best. Despite the feelings of Dr. Michio Kaku, when we introduce God into a discussion, we are introducing virtually the entire realm of supernatural possibilities. As Kaku so amply testifies, this abstraction (intercession by God) is unfathomable to many logical minds. However, if we speculate about the meaning of the clues we humans have gathered about God, we must recognize the distinct possibility that God's logos brought nature into existence. Both logic and the Bible propose God is an infinite being, the prime cause and sufficient cause for existence. This implies God has unimaginable powers. We must also add, a God of creation would probably need to be a Vast Intellect. Therefore, God would not have to

---

...WHEN WE INTRODUCE GOD INTO A DISCUSSION, WE ARE INTRODUCING VIRTUALLY THE ENTIRE REALM OF SUPERNATURAL POSSIBILITIES.

play in recognizable boundaries. An infinitely powerful God can create miracles in many ways illogical to our limited understanding of divine power. I apologize for my clinical manner of describing God. However, we should realize the actual implications of the term 'God' and we should not take God's abilities lightly. Thus, with some understanding of our inferior position, let us continue our discussion.

SCIENCE AND MIRACLES

Over time, as science (a study of natural events) has grown in influence, *intellectual* thinkers became less enamored by supernatural events. They have continued to be curious. Yet, they have thought some *scientific* explanation awaits every discovery, an explanation that will bring the mystery out of the mysterious and give a questioned event a logical and natural explanation. This sounds reasonable and, of course, as science has acquired knowledge, it indeed has solved many such mysteries. On the other hand, science seems to have add varying degrees of validity to a number of supernatural events. To better understand the true substance of science, let me digress for a moment.

Do you remember when you were in high school? Remember how much emphasis was placed on 'who was dating who' and what car one drove? Do you remember how important it was to play football or basketball or be in the drill team and such? Your whole world revolved around students and activities at high school.

Today, things that seemed important in high school seem childish, perhaps silly. It is hard to believe that we focused our personal world on such foolishness. Nonetheless, if we compare our lives today with those 'wonder years' then we do find similarities. However, our major influences have shifted to a different society. For instance, if your neighbor is picked up in an ambulance and rushed to the hospital, you would normally be very curious and worried about his or her condition. Yet, probably, someone living fifty miles away would have no regard (except superficial) as to the related injury or sickness. From a cosmological reference, we have no contact with the events on Saturn; therefore, we know less about Saturn than we do about our favorite football team or movie. Yet, I would assume, Saturn's environment is more important to our universe than a form of entertainment.

From the above examples, one understands that our personal world is built around our contacts. Thus, it seems logical that a major reason many do not accept miracles is that they either do not come in contact with them, or they do not recognize them as miracles.

Three philosophers seem to have held the most influence in discrediting miracles. They were Voltaire, Spinoza and Hume. Based upon Newton's mechanical universe, the general argument became the following: If God designed this great and beautiful machine (universe), why would God interfere with its grand nature? Thus, a miracle became a "violation" of God's "immutable" Natural laws.[3] It seemed that God was in some way defiling Himself by causing a miracle. It is important to understand that most scientists, philosophers and other intellectuals who are closed minded to miracles are grounded in this philosophical position.

The *antagonist position* (pro-miracles) is: What we perceive as Nature is nothing more than God's Will in motion, "producing certain effects in a continual and uniform manner." Therefore, "a miracle is not against the course of nature," but is *part* of the course of nature, in that it is an *unusual event* executed by God.[4] Thus, known natural laws may be only partial measurements of reality which are mistaken for the whole of reality. If God's Will creates all reality, and each of us are limited by time and space, then we only experience a small part of that reality. Yet, the historical record proclaims reality is of the grander nature (with the inclusion of miracles) then the majority of us have experienced. Skeptics base reality only on their personal experiences and are not willing to accept super-natural experiences reported by others.

Have you ever wondered what an ant knows? Does an ant accept reality beyond its short experiences? If it has any conscious, it knows *ground stuff* and reacts to stimuli. It hasn't a clue about a more comprehensive reality. It may not even realize that water kills ants because it has not experienced water. As ants do not understand life beyond their experience, perhaps there is more to reality than our brief existence allows.

In a documented discussion, William Lane Craig supported Gottfried Less' position from *Wahrheit der christlichen Religion* with the following:

1) Nature is the order of God's Will; thus, "a miracle is just as possible as any event. Therefore, it is just as believable as any event."

2) One cannot refute testimony to an event simply based upon "experiences and observations." If we dismissed all other input, "nothing new would ever be discovered."

3) "There is no contradiction between experience and Christian miracles. Miracles are different events (contraria) from experience in general, but not contradictory events (contradictoria) to experience in general."[5] Thus, to assume we know everything about the way things work when we admittedly do not is quite foolish and illogical. As J. Vernet concluded, God's Will created Natural law and, therefore, Natural law is "subject to change." Natural law does not "flow from the being of God with inexorable necessity," but results from His choice. Therefore, "he does not violate his own nature . . ."[6] What Vernet is implying is, if God chooses what is reality, than anything that happens cannot be considered a violation of Nature, because everything is a projection of God's Will. Thus, everything is real by the 'grace of God' and nothing else exists. There are no violations by God's Will for God's Will is all

there is. This, of course, is the foundation of the Philosophy of Divine Authoritarianism.

EVIDENCE OF A GRANDER REALITY

We have logical and mathematical evidence of the existence of ten (10) or more parameters of time and space. Though human beings do not understand 'being' in more than four dimensions, nor do they perceive the forces enveloped in extra dimensions, these additional parameters were functional necessities in the formation of our universe.[7] However, it is not uncommon to find a physical scientist who can think in multi-dimensional terms. In his lecture *Fifth Dimension and Beyond,* Dr. Ross has described a conversation with other physicists about the miraculous appearance of Jesus after His crucifixion. His disciples were gathered behind locked doors and were afraid for their lives. But, they became even more "disturbed" by the way Jesus entered their hiding place. Though Jesus was a physical person of "flesh and bone," He entered through a wall and the wall was left intact.[8] Of course, observing Jesus' sudden appearance would have had a profound effect on one's perception of reality. This miraculous act has caused both the philosopher and the theologian conceptual problems. In fact, it has been excused as delusory behavior on the part of the disciples. Many have wondered why such an unbelievable report was ever recorded? Some have thought that it was invented so that the disciples could further argue their claim that Jesus had risen. Others have suggested Jesus did not appear in the physical sense, but instead was an apparition. Another theory suggests that the disciples were drunk and/or on drugs. It seems that any liberal excuse to desensitize this event's miraculous factor has been or will be used. However, the above mentioned physicists came to a different conclusion. They deducted that "Jesus must be five dimensional." These physicists intellectually understood the proposition that the Creator who designed the universe can control all dimensions of space and time. According to Dr. Ross, if one controls four spacial dimensions, i.e., length, width and height and another dimension just as real but unknown to humanness, one could eat the fruit of an orange without peeling the orange's skin. Even more amazing, with the addition of a fifth spacial dimension, one could move the orange through a table "without disturbing the orange or the table." Thus, concludes Ross, the Bible gives us proof that Jesus Christ held command of extra dimensions.[9] I further suggest to you, if there are extra dimensions of time and space and, if Jesus is God manifested on earth, then He should be able to appear in rooms. The question then is no longer do we believe in miracles? The question has become, do we believe in science? If we assume Jesus is God, as the Bible so states, and we still question this *miracle* then we must question the validity of science. Realistically, we would expect God to use all dimensions of time and space, to be able to appear in rooms, walk through doors and perform any miracle He wished. Conversely, it would be illogical to think He could not 'suddenly appear in a room.' He, the Creator, must have control of His universe. Therefore, if you cannot accept Jesus' miracles, it is not miracles you do not believe in; you either do not believe in extra dimensions or you do not accept the proposition that Jesus is the Son of God.

Actually, extra dimensions conform to Einstein's theory of relativity. Einstein discovered that space and time are relative. This *relativity* confirms God's existence. Ross and others have committed on the prodigious implications of the theory. Not only atheism but most of the world philosophical positions are based on the premise of an infinite universe. However, the Judo/Christian tradition is an exception. This credence states there was a beginning and a Beginner. Dr. Ross feels that the validity of singularity brings mankind "face to face" with that Beginner, the "cause-or-causer" of everything in the universe - from rocks and dirt to all life forms - in accordance with the cosmological argument for God.[10]

Our configuration in dimensional time and space might be compared to hues in the color chart. Colors come to our eyes in light waves. Both red and blue are concepts or understandings of constrained color. They are not true definitions of *color,* but they are as close as we seem to be able to distinguish. However, if red was the only color we ever perceived, then red would be our understanding of color. As a matter of fact, we would not understand the color 'blue.'

Science tells us there are colors we do not see. These colors definitely do exist, but we are not able to receive their message. Pit vipers find their prey by seeing body heat. Although we humans can feel heat waves with our hands, etc. we do not have the equipment to *see* heat like a snake. In fact, we cannot understand *seeing* heat, as a snake sees heat. We also know sounds exist that we cannot hear. It is common knowledge that dogs hear high-pitched sounds inaudible to us.

With this same certainty, we know that dimensions exist other than the human understandings of length, width, height and time. More important, with the same certainty, we can factually conclude that if Jesus Christ was indeed the Son of God, and had He used the laws of physics, He could have performed *miracles*. He would be the Lord of all dimensions of time and space. Miracles would be 'a piece of cake.' Previous to His appearance to the disciples behind the locked door, He fulfilled the atonement for man's sin - through His death and resurrection. As the Messiah, He was the long awaited

---

...IF JESUS CHRIST WAS INDEED THE SON OF GOD, AND HAD HE USED THE LAWS OF PHYSICS, HE COULD HAVE PERFORMED *MIRACLES*. HE WOULD BE THE LORD OF ALL DIMENSIONS OF TIME AND SPACE. MIRACLES WOULD BE 'A PIECE OF CAKE.'

Hero prophesied by both man and nature, and the fulfillment not only of Jewish prophecy, but of a world of prophecies, dreams, symbols and myths. After His resurrection, He was completely unencumbered. He was the proven Savior. Therefore, He moved as any astute scientist would expect a five (or more) dimensional Creator/God to move. Jesus needed to be in a locked room full of doubting disciples who were afraid for their lives. How did He handle it? The logical way; He appeared.

If Jesus is the Son of God, then this Biblical description is not so fantastic. In fact, it seems a logical Son of God response. Thus, these multidimensional revelations of science only accentuate and substantiate the claim that Jesus was and is the Promised One, the anointed Son of God.

This Biblical narrative should hold even greater meaning for the non Christian. Science gives us new evidence that Jesus was not two parts human (Mary and Joseph), but a unique being. In fact, He acted in a manner that modern science suggests would be compatible with a multidimensional God–not a mythological god. Obviously, Jesus was in control of invisible planes unknown when the Bible words were written. He was more than a *great prophet*. Jesus' actions indicate His Lordship over nature and law. One might even conclude that within Jesus' miracles lies a hidden Biblical message waiting our modern men of science. God may again be saying "man's wisdom is only foolishness to The Almighty God." God might also be saying (in yet another way), "This is my Son with whom I am well pleased and, P.S., He is in control of True Reality - the whole of Reality!"

There are other miracles for which we have no plausible answers and no technical understanding. One such event is the 'Immaculate Conception.' Was there an actual *miracle,* as man would define it, at the conception of Jesus' earthly life? If this event was, in fact, pre-planned by God, Jesus' miraculous conception is not as fanciful as a dimensionally limited human might first assume. God, the Creator of life, must know all there is to know about life and is quite capable of creating any type of life He desires. However, acceptance from an authoritarian source, i.e., the Bible is again, not sufficient for many people. Man has tried to rationalize away such miracles. In doing so, he has also explained away the profound meaning involved in this miraculous proposition.

When the story of Jesus' virgin birth is discussed, the usual response from non-believers often includes the following thoughts: "Jesus could not have been the only one to circumvent the natural procedure of conception. It takes two human beings to conceive of human life, not one person and a spiritual deity."

BUT I ARGUE THAT A VIRGIN BIRTH IS NOT ONLY POSSIBLE, IT IS LOGICAL.

But I argue that a virgin birth is not only possible, it is logical. The reaction to this Immaculate Conception proposition must also center around one's position about God., i.e., whether there is a God, how potent is God and what was the relationship between God and Jesus. Certainly, if God is more than a super force at work in the universe, or the sum of the forces in the universe, and, if God is coherent and an All-Knowing and All-Powerful Being, then He is capable of many things human science has yet to explain. I contend that God gave this 'miracle' as the sign of the Messiah. I suggest God told man at the earliest appropriate moment that humanity would need a Savior and God would send one. As an unmistakable sign, The Son of God would be born of a virgin. Certainly, no man could misconstrue the meaning of such a sign. It would be a feat only God could perform.

I further suggest that, if God implemented just five spacial dimensions of space, He would have greatly simplified the process of impregnating a virgin. Today, scientists, who are incapable of supernatural activities and ignorant of any processes which might manipulate extra dimensions, can artificially accomplish human reproduction. We seem to have mastered processes like artificial insemination and in vitro fertilization. Furthermore, we are successfully experimenting with cloning and gene analysis. It is apparent future experiments in genealogy will bring even more amazing knowledge about fertilization and mutation to include the removal of deformities and/or other characteristics. In fact, new findings suggest new moral questions. Realizing these advancements have come at our infancy in this field, we must assume there are many things about genetics we just do not understand. Therefore, any judgements we might make to date would be prejudicial. In regards to this point, we do not yet understand any processes of positive mutation, processes which logic would dictate are controlled by God, and which would have to exist for any from of progressive evolution and/or creation to be reality. Nonetheless, we must assume that either evolution or creation (or both) are realities. Similar positive mutation processes might have induced a virgin birth. Certainly they should not be automatically ruled out. We can be very certain on one point: manipulating genes can cause major changes. Because of our growing genetic knowledge - because we can do things today that seemed impossible only a few years ago - we should be more understanding and more accepting of the genetic capabilities of God. We must concede there may have been a point in time marked by a miraculous birth of the Son of God. This miracle would have happened if an All Knowing and All Powerful God made just one genetic change within one female egg.

Future experiments might very well give us a number of new ways

---

THIS MIRACLE WOULD HAVE HAPPENED IF AN ALL KNOWING AND ALL POWERFUL GOD MADE JUST ONE GENETIC CHANGE WITHIN ONE FEMALE EGG.

God may have superseded nature to proclaim the deity of His Son. However, we must not forget one very valid possibility. The easiest way for God to have generated a virgin birth would have been to command life to form in Mary's womb, and asking His Son to reside in it. I rather believe that this was the way God brought forth the Christ Child's special life. God set Jesus Christ aside from every other human being and gave Him the birth sign of the expected Savior.

I believe in the Immaculate Conception. You do not have to. But your non belief is not based on logical evaluation. Your non belief is based on your personal philosophy. Either you reject Jesus Christ as the Holy Son of God, or you reject the proposition that there is a God with an intellect that controls all of the dimensions in the universe. If Jesus Christ is the Son of God and God controls all forces and dimensions of the universe, then the Immaculate Conception is both very possible and logical.

The Immaculate Conception is not so amazing if it is compared to the foundations of evolution theory. If Louis Pasteur, or any reputable scientist after Pasteur, could be totally honest in assessing the possibilities of the Immaculate Conception versus those of spontaneous generation (the material-ist's rationalization for the initiation of life), he or she would probably state that the most likely miracle is the virgin birth. Even though spontaneous gen-eration (long or short form) is a necessity to all natural evolutionary concepts, any honest scientist must conclude that, from what we know at this point in time, both spontaneous generation and a virgin birth are unnatural phenom-ena. Both should be classified as miracles. Furthermore, both are quite simi-lar concepts. Like the miracle of life itself, no one knows how anything could be spontaneously generated from nothing. And nothing is the known begin-ning. Because of the ambiguity involved in the process, one might even spec-ulate that spontaneous generation (or a more palatable quantum generation guided by a distant influence) along with cell mutation are perhaps today's two best scientific explanations for God's involvement in the Immaculate Conception. Thus, if you believe in spontaneous generation, you should be equally accepting of Jesus' virgin birth.

To the neo-Darwinist, 'natural evolution' and 'spontaneous genera-tion' must be associated with each other. Nonetheless, they present one giant oxymoron. Because of its dependency on spontaneous generation, evolution is a miracle and could not have occurred without the divine guidance of God's Will. The vast majority of empirical information demonstrates the necessity of an infinite God. The humanist accepts evolution but finds his belief to be a contradiction. One simply cannot *believe* in evolution and reject concepts like God and miracles.

In the 1950's and 1960's, we did not have such strong proof of extra-dimensional worlds.[11] However, Carl Gustave Jung began to conceptualize the same extra-dimensional relationships. In fact, he believed that all acausal phenomena were the result of the consciousness' mastery of time and space.

In his book *Synchronicity,* Jung states, "For the unconscious psyche space and time seem to be relative; that is to say, knowledge finds itself in a space-time continuum in which space is no longer space, nor time time."[12]

Unfortunately, Jung chose experiments in astrology to examine his hypothesis on synchronicity. These experiments offered mixed returns with which he did not seem entirely pleased. In fact, he made suggestions regarding the way he could have improved his study. Yet, his experiments did indicate that life and the actuality of things intersecting with life have more meaning than blind chance. Jung accepted the proposition that there are phenomenal events which consistently defy statistical norms. In fact, these interactions are statically impossible.

In a relative way, the Big Bang and those activities which immediately followed, stand out as the greatest all time examples of 'meaningful coincidence.' If synchronistic activities are manifestations of an intelligence, then it seems an All Powerful intelligence would be necessary to cause an event of such magnitude. God seems a necessity of the Big Bang. The only apparent argument against the Big Bang is divine intervention or God creating the universe in such a way that it seems like there was a 'big bang.' Thus, if we accept the position that singularity was extinguished by a bang, then we must accept the real possibility of miracles. Furthermore, there was a trail of meaningful coincidences which followed the initial bang. Each coincidence had to occur with perfect timing and intensity or nothing would have formed in the universe. Other synchronistic events would follow on earth. Two good examples are the perfect timing of meteors previous to any life form and the timing related to the development of photosynthesis. Thus, evolution, as science perceives it, requires meaningful coincidences.

Many free thinkers such as Jung, Kant and Plato developed great philosophies which assumed multi-dimensional factors. Each perceived of Einsteinian relativity combining time and space. Each understood and endeavored to explain this much broader concept of reality. However, providence is not confined to philosophy and science. Many synchronistic points in time have occurred during the monumental events in human history. Therefore, we should ask, is there a force which guides certain moments of human existence? Is our history (or parts of our history) predestined by our Creator?

Some of the expressed miraculous events of the Bible do seem more akin to an act of synchronicity or providence than to a traditional miracle. An excellent example is the star in the heavens that lead the Magi to Bethlehem and the baby Yeshua (Jesus). Bethlehem was prophesied centuries before to be the birth place of the Jewish Messiah. Though the Magi were pagans (perhaps Zoroastrian priests from Persia), they were 'wise men' or scholars of the day.

It is generally thought that these men were students of *mystical* activities and, certainly, Biblical prophecies fit within their sphere of interests. Secondly, in the Babylonian tradition, they were astronomers and astrologers. The science paradigm of the day was that 'men of science' studied the heavens for cosmic signs because personal behavior was controlled by heavenly bodies. 'Wise men' would have expected signs in the night sky to announce something as important as the birth of a great ruler or Messiah. Interestingly, our modern astronomers have traced the movement of the stars and planets back to ancient days. In so doing, they found a conspicuously significant number of profound signs in the heavens just prior to Jesus' birth. For ten months during the year, 7 BC, Jupiter, Saturn and Mars traveled the heavens encased in the zodiac sign of Pisces. (For unrelated reasons, the fish would later be used as a sign of kinship by early Christians.) Three times in 7 BC, Jupiter and Saturn visually became one. This created one very large and bright star in the night sky. A number of modern astronomers have accepted this astrological movement as a logical explanation for the 'Christmas Star.' The Magi understandably found great significance in this combination. The giant planet Jupiter was the star representing the highest god. Albeit, Jupiter bears the name of the head god of the Roman civilization, this same planet represented Zeus, highest god of the Greeks, and Marduk of the Babylonians. There was likewise a very strong Palestinian connection. Saturn was the astrological "defender of Palestine." This suggested a coming event connecting the head god and Palestine. The celestial body 'Pisces' also represented the Palestine area, but was further associated with "epochal events and crises."[13]

Perhaps even more meaningful was Comet No. 52 (on the Williams list) which soon followed this initial grouping of heavenly bodies. Comets were considered a sign of a change as would include the birth of a new king. This comet was seen for some seventy days in 5 B.C.[14] Therefore, it may have been the actual Christmas star. The Biblical account states, "At about that time some astrologers (wise men) from the eastern lands arrived in Jerusalem asking, 'Where is the newborn King of the Jews?'"[15] Comet No. 52 traveled westward and would have led easterners toward Jerusalem. Perhaps it even seemed to point its sweeping tail to Bethlehem.

These are not the only star theories. There are other possibilitie; such as the Christmas star was a nova (Comet No. 53 on the Williams chart) seen in 4 B.C.[16] The most dramatic possibility, however, is that it could have been something totally supernatural and uncharted by human science. Even so, enough unusual heavenly activity did occur to alert any 'wise men' that something very profound was happening in Palestine. Historians have long con-

THREE TIMES IN 7 BC, JUPITER AND SATURN VISUALLY BECAME ONE. THIS CREATED ONE VERY LARGE AND BRIGHT STAR IN THE NIGHT SKY.

cluded that this period was the approximate time of the birth of Jesus of Nazareth. Surely the Magi did react. Reading mysterious signs in the heavens and knowing the Jewish prophecies, it would have seemed illogical for the Magi not to have traveled to Palestine to investigate. Furthermore, they must have expected Jesus to be royalty, or greater, because the report states that they came and worshipped Him. Some Church leaders have been embarrassed because God used pagan beliefs (astrology was forbidden in the Jewish faith) to announce the birth of His Son to the world. Others understood that God had a purpose for this startling announcement.[17] The most obvious reason might be to invite the pagan world to embrace His Son, because unlike other traditions, the Christ was sent into the world to save all mankind.

Despite the evidence, liberal historians and theologians discount Biblical providential accounts through seemingly flawed rationalizations. However, more recent historical records provide another set of miracles; many of which cannot easily be dismissed. Even so, while scholars must accept the authenticity of said documents, they can at least censor them. Thus, numerous corroborated events which had a profound influence in casting and shaping the American heritage are now deemed too provocative for public school textbooks and, thus, unfit for young minds. Why? Because of the providential and, thus, theological implications.

Many of our founding fathers believed in Divine Providence. Often, these men referred to such divine guidance in their writings. One such incident involved George Washington during the French and Indian war. The details surrounding this event seem so fantastic that we must remind ourselves that its accuracy goes unquestioned by many serious historians. Washington was a young officer commanding British ground forces. While on a mission, Washington and other officers were on horseback leading foot soldiers. As they crossed dangerous terrain, native Americans siding with the French began to fire. Washington was among those who moved forward of the main body to counter the attack. The engagement was heavy and the combined British and American colony forces took heavy casualties. The vast majority of the British troops turned and ran, leaving Washington and other officers totally exposed. The officers were swinging their swords and shouting for the troops to halt and return fire. Of course, the Indians placed a higher priority on killing officers than the shooting of enlisted soldiers. This is a common strategy in battle. So, sixty-three of the eighty officers were casualties. Naturally, George Washington on horseback in front of cowering troops was an obvious and very vulnerable target. To understand Washington's vulnerability, I quote historian, James Thomas Flexner:

MANY OF OUR FOUNDING FATHERS BELIEVED IN DIVINE PROVIDENCE.

During the same few moments, the sound of firing came running down both flanks, it seemed as if by magic, since the Indians moved so skillfully from behind one tree to behind the next that no enemy was visible. Bullets filled the air, striking particularly the officers who towered, conspicuous on horseback, as they rode in circles, hitting the men with the flats of their swords. Washington's horse sank under him. He leaped clear, his illness forgotten, As a riderless horse reared by, he caught it and sprang up.[18]

For the greatest part of the battle, Washington was an over exposed primary target yet, miraculously, he survived. After this battle, Washington wrote to his brother stating, "But, by the All-powerful Dispensations of Providence, I have been protected beyond all human probability or expectations; for I had four Bullets through my Coat and two Horses shot under me. Yet, escaped unhurt although Death was leveling my Companions on every side of me!"[19]

Fifteen years later, George Washington met the Indian chief who, during that battle, fought against him. The chief reportedly told Washington,

I called my young men and said, mark yon tall and daring warrior. Himself alone is exposed. Quick, let your aim be certain and he dies. Our rifles were leveled, rifles which but for you knew not how to miss. Was all in vain. A power mightier far than we shielded you. Seeing you were under the special guardianship of the Great Spirit, we immediately ceased fire at you. I come to pay homage to the man who is the particular favorite of heaven and who can never die in battle.20

Even if we dismiss this opponent's statement, Washington was a glaring target and, by all rights, should have been killed. Washington's apparent protection in battle was reported by a number of the witnesses to this conflict. Furthermore, this Providence is referred to in a number of unrelated papers. Colonel John Winslow wrote of the time: "And the conflict gave a young soldier named George Washington several opportunities to distinguish himself, creating a reputation that led directly to his selection as Commander in Chief of the revolutionary army."[21]

If we refuse to believe these witnesses, do we also refuse to believe the similar reports of Winston Churchill's many acts of bravery and his coincidental luck during the Boer Wars? These were intense moments of fighting and Churchill recalled the "'soft kisses' of the bullets as they 'sucked in the air' around him."[22] Of his vulnerability in one particular battle, he wrote that he was, " . . . continually under shell & rifle fire and once the feather in my hat was cut through by a bullet. But - in the end I came serenely through."[23] And on another occasion he wrote, "I was very nearly killed two hours ago by a shrapnel . . ."[24] Churchill stared death in the face many times. Yet, he lived to become one of the greatest world leaders in history and the correct person to lead Britain during World War II.

Today we have many leaders who, without God's providential intervention, would not be alive to lead. Bob Dole, wounded in World War II, was not expected to live, yet he did. Is his life not a miracle? He had a great effect upon the American political system and government. Is that meaningful? If we excuse these reports, how do we explain the documented miracles of the Vietnam conflict. The extraordinary story of Dave Roever is such an example. Gravely wounded on the battlefield, all medical facts indicate that he should have died. Yet, he did not. As a Christian evangelist, he uses his miraculous life as a tool to reach others. In the case of Dave Roever, do we ignore eye-witnesses and medical reports? Can we look at Roever's reconstructed face and not realize his life is a miracle? There are miracles around us every day too numerous to count. Many may never be known to the public, because they are not as fantastic or newsworthy as Dave Roever or Bob Dole.

There is one more person we must discuss. General George Patton's entire life seemed to be a demonstration of Divine Providence. He was a significant warrior for human freedom at a most desperate time. Even his death seemed synchronistic (in the psychological understanding) and peculiar, as if it were a sign from God. General Patton held a profound trust in God. Although he held some non-traditional Judaic/Christian beliefs, such as reincarnation, he held a passionate belief in Divine Providence. Early in his career, he let it be known that God's Will destined him to accomplish greatness on the battlefield. Of course, that is exactly what he did. With God as his inspiration, he drove the Third Army across Europe, and thus played a major role in defeating the German Nazi war machine. Perhaps Patton's finest moment in time came in World War II during the Battle of the Bulge. American troops were pinned down and surrounded at Bastogne. Patton, determined to rescue them, accomplished the impossible. His troops traveled for approximately 48 hours over harsh winter conditions and, though exhausted, fought and won a battle liberating Bastogne and crushing the German offensive.[25]

To save time, General Patton had moved with only three divisions. Patton explained, "General Eisenhower stated that I should wait until I got at least six divisions. I told him that, in my opinion, a prompt attack with three was better than waiting for six - particularly when I did not know where I could get the other three."[26] Yet, one of the major factors of the movement was contending with the horrid winter weather. Reflecting on this event, Brig. General Brenton G. Wallace wrote, "Our units traveled from 50 to 150 miles in the most impossible winter conditions. It was, without doubt, the fastest and greatest mass movement of an army in history."[27]

Unfortunately, it seemed evident that weather would also hamper the impending battle. Most noteworthy, it would eliminate the air support deemed essential for an offensive of only three divisions. The situation was even more tenuous because Eisenhower had imposed a 48 hour news blackout on Europe which eliminated all weather reports. However, Patton ordered a chaplain to write a prayer for good weather and then distributed it among his troops. Pattons' prayer was as follows:

> *Almighty and most merciful Father, we humbly beseech Thee, of Thy great goodness, to restrain these immoderate rains with which we have had to contend. Grant us fair weather for Battle. Graciously hearken to us as we may advance from victory to victory, and crush the oppression and wickedness of our enemies, and establish Thy justice among men and nations. Amen.* [28]

An immediate change in the atmospheric conditions brought a string of good weather days allowing for air support and a Third Army victory. General Wallace remembered the effect of this seemingly miraculous change in weather:

> *Then our planes came, and that made the day perfect. Hundreds and hundreds, they laced the skies until the vapor trails formed a white mist almost as thick as the ground mist that had been keeping them earthbound for so long. It was beyond words; the most marvelous thing that could have happened.*

> *At the Christmas day briefing, the Air Officer, Colonel Murray, announced: 'It is prophesied by our weather men that the present clear weather will continue for at least another seven days.'*

> *That brought a general laugh from the staff, because there hadn't been that many clear days all winter and it just seemed impossible that such a miracle could continue. But the officer went on to explain that 'through a freak of nature, two high-pressure areas from opposite directions had come together directly over us, that they were approximately of equal force, and that the clear weather would continue until one or the other weakened and gave way.'*

> *And that is what happened. Call it luck, a freak of nature, Providence, what you will, it was a thing that might not happen again at such a psychological moment for a hundred years. For seven days our air force blasted the Germans from the air, while our ground forces battered them on the ground.* [29]

As a secondary observation about the synchronicity in this battle, 'seven' is considered a numerological sign of completeness from God.

It is possible that Patton had, in fact, received a current weather report. A man in his position, with so many lives at stake, would do whatever it took to obtain the weather conditions for the coming fight. Yet, it is apparent that Patton had faith in God. Whether or not Patton did receive a weather report is secondary. The historical significance abides in the fact that the weather cleared at just the right time. There would not and could not be a delay for the right weather. Patton would have moved anyway. And, as important, the weather stayed clear seven days, long enough to assure a victory. If God has the abilities that Judaic/Christian theologians assume, then He would know Patton's prayer long before it was put on paper.

Thus, we are left with a question related to the supernatural. Did God answer General Patton's prayer? In fact, we might broaden that question and ask, does prayer *work?* Accumulating scientific evidence indicates it does and, in fact, it supports the traditional religious understanding of prayer. There are hundreds of studies which give evidence prayers are effective.[30]

Solemn prayer seems to hold true metaphysical gifts often taking human beings beyond their humanness. Renowned Harvard professor and philosopher William James had an interesting thought on the intimate power of prayer. He committed:

Religion is nothing if it be not the vital act by which the entire mind seeks to save itself by clinging to the principle from which it draws its life. This act is prayer, by which term I understand no vain exercise of words, no mere repetition of certain sacred formulae, but the very movement itself of the soul, putting itself in a personal relation of contact with the mysterious power of which it feels the presence, - it may be even before it has a name by which to call it. Whenever this interior prayer is lacking, there is no religion; wherever, on the other hand, this prayer rises and stirs the soul, even in the absence of forms or of doctrines, we have living religion.[31]

Of course, all prayers do not seem to be answered in a manner we might hope. If they were, no one would ever die and everyone would be rich! Furthermore, theologians warn we should be sincere about our prayers. For example, if we pray for patience we might encounter unexpected experiences where our patience is tested and stretched. If you will recall, Patton was frustrated because God did not move as fast as Patton would have liked. He was left in England when the Allied invasion started. When Patton got his assignment, however, it was one which seemed cut out for his abilities and manner. And, Patton was spectacular.

Larry Dossey, M.D., summarized the scientific experiments related to the healing effects of prayer as follows:

Remarkably the effects of prayer did not depend on whether the pray-

---

OF COURSE, ALL PRAYERS DO NOT SEEM TO BE ANSWERED IN A MANNER WE MIGHT HOPE. IF THEY WERE, NO ONE WOULD EVER DIE AND EVERYONE WOULD BE RICH!

ing person was in the presence of the organism being prayed for, or whether he or she was far away; healing could take place either on site or at a distance. Nothing seemed capable of stopping or blocking prayer. Even when an 'object' was placed in a lead-lined room or in a cage that shielded it from all known forms of electromagnetic energy, the effect still got through.[32]

Other studies imply the effects of prayer are actual and not psychological, i.e., not a result of 'the power of suggestion' or of a placebo effect. Prayer has proven to be effective even if the recipients are not aware of the prayers being offered on their behalf. In fact, studies have been conducted on a large number of non-human lives which held no *concept of prayer.* Despite the life form, *prayed for* groups showed statically significant improvement over *non prayed for* groups. Thus, prayer must reach beyond humanness into unknown dimensions of life and/or spirit.

Today the scientific studies continue. One patient, healed after nine months of a prayer study, is reported to have stated, "There's something weird going on here, and I love it."[33] Of course, physicians are equally impressed by such results. A 1996 survey from the American Academy of Family Physicians suggested that ninety-nine percent of physicians believe a patients "religious beliefs can heal."[34] Dr. Dossey has predicted how prayer will affect our future. Among his prognostications are the two following thoughts:

1. In a future day, it will be considered "medical malpractice" for a physician not "recommend" prayer as an "integral part" of the medical strategy.

2. We will acknowledge "some aspect of the human psyche" as "genuinely nonlocal." This observation will change our understanding of humanness, because "this nonlocal aspect of ourselves cannot die." If this 'human aspect' is nonlocal, "it is infinite in space and time, and thus omnipresent and immortal by implication."[35]

These are amazing predictions for a man who once rejected religious beliefs. Dossey appears to be amazed and perhaps perplexed with the *supernatural* corporeality of prayer. Though Dossey seems somewhat rebellious of traditional religious inferences, he recognizes a higher reality appearing to humanity through spiritualism. Yet, he was not the first person to examine the powers of prayer. His investigative report was basically an updated re-run of earlier studies consisting of various degrees of scientific and historical reliability. For example, Will Oursler investigated a number of themes related to prayer, including the reported healings at Lourdes and St. Anne Beaupre, faith healers and the effect of spiritual healing on specific diseases, such as cancer. Oursler's conclusion was similar to Dossey's, i.e., there are miraculous healings. Oursler made twenty-three points in his summary. Among them are:

1. Healings of a paranormal character occur cannot be questioned.

2. These healings are accomplished through "a variety of religious and spiritual techniques, beliefs
and rituals."
3. "These techniques, rituals and beliefs have at least one element in common: prayer to God."[36]

Yet, it did not take studies to influence many thinkers about the wonders of prayer. Its effects seem to have been an observable spiritual reality even previous to known scientific studies. At the turn of the century, William James wrote, "As regards to prayers for the sick, if any medical fact can be considered to stand firm, it is that in certain environments prayer may contribute to recovery, and should be encouraged as a therapeutic measure."[37] James continued his discussion on prayer with the following, "But petitional prayer is only one department of prayer; and if we take the word in the wider sense as meaning every kind of inward communion or conversation with the power recognized as divine, we can easily see that scientific criticism leaves it untouched."[38]

Prayer and love seem, in some way, to open human senses to parameters beyond that which we know and understand. Thus, humans are introduced to other paranormal experiences such as 'healing by laying of hands' and ESP (extrasensory perception), areas foreign to our laws of science and material existence. Often, these paranormal avenues seem connected to human spiritual insights. Yet, to some degree, each has proven to be actual and legitimate. So, we might ask, what connecting processes are utilized by prayer, spiritual healing, ESP and the like. How can messages get from God to man or man to God? If the messages do come from God or the divine, how do we receive them? Of the many theories, I think the most likely is that the quantum world provides the mechanical communication system. The quantum world may offer access to a reality quite foreign to the human concept of 'natural.'

QUANTUM PHYSICS

Quantum mechanics, a realm of reality which can be connected to Jungian logic, is devastating to materialistic philosophies. Of course, this relatively new field of physics centers around the appearances of the subatomic world. Though no one really knows all that lurks in the passages of quantum reality, there have been some bizarre, yet generally accepted, ideas. One comparative concept is sometimes referred to as the *Cinderella effect.* We, human beings, live in a predictable world. From our view everything seems to be

PRAYER AND LOVE SEEM, IN SOME WAY, TO OPEN HUMAN SENSES TO PARAMETERS BEYOND THAT WHICH WE KNOW AND UNDERSTAND.

based upon cause and effect activities. This 'cause and effect' realm of being is the basis behind deterministic thinking. Evidently, the quantum world - that world on which ours is built - has no cause and effect rules. So, we live in a Cinderella world. However, Alice In Wonderland is a better parody, for personal authenticity springs from a quantum foundation which has no actual reality, but must be viewed as a world of potential. This concept is so disruptive to our classical understanding that some physicists and philosophers have suggested we do not yet have a valid understanding of quantum behavior. One such person was Max Plank. Though he proposed the foundations of quanta, this non-classical feature kept him from accepting his own interpretation. Albert Einstein, a neo-realist, insisted the quantum theory was incomplete, and when the facts were known the quantum world would be actual and not based upon potential. He thought that when all of the facts were known 'quantumness,' would also be based upon cause and effect reality. Einstein wrote, "I still believe in the possibility of a model of reality - that is, of a theory which represents things themselves and not merely the probability of their occurrence."[39]

Though quantum reality does not seem to add any real meaning to our classical world, it holds gigantic inferences for the fields of science and philosophy. I have previously suggested that if information is the ruler used to measure the universe and God has an intellect, then God is not just a beginning force, but the designer of the universe and a personality separate and apart from the universe. Tied to this supposition is the Copenhagen interpretation of quantum theory and the possibility that the observer may well influence quanta through measurement. If we add the Bell theorem's profound implications regarding non-local influences and the Anthropic principle which suggests that, if there were no observer, information would be meaningless, then we find bold new reality and, perhaps, the connector between the natural and the supernatural.

Nick Herbert stated, "The greatest unsolved problem in quantum theory is: What is a measurement? What is there about an 'observation' that enables it to turn a wavelike possibility into a particle like actuality? After more than a half a century of speculation we simply do not have a good answer to this fundamental question."[40] Again, we find a new turn in Protagoras' philosophy accrediting man as the measure of all things. Now, we witness nature itself as the collaborator. This time, nature takes its satiric inferences a step further. Did the observer dictate the outcome? Did the observer cause the tree to fall? In other words, do subatomic particles perform for intelligent observers? This question has appeared in some well known metaphysical fiction writings. For example, James Redfield's *The Celestine Prophecy* asks "To what extent does the physical universe as a whole - since it is made up of the same basic energy - respond to our expectations?"[41] The viable answer is - none. However, perhaps we do not understand the influences of quanta because we have yet to discover the code. Thus, without the code there is no viable formula.

If there is a causal connection between quantum particles and material truth, it seems logical that a Vast Intelligence guides material reality. Yet, because of the Cinderella effect, scientists might not understand an implied role of a non-local, but guiding intellect. If we assume God does exist, quantum mechanics could lead to any miracle, any reality, any truth God wished to allow. The Many-Worlds or Many-Universes interpretation of quantum theory states, "Reality consists of a steadily increasing number of parallel universes."[42] For every possible quantum outcome, a new universe instantaneously forms. These universes have been referred to as static, frozen and unchanging. Of course, this concept seems preposterous to human reason. Yet, it is easier to accept the 'Many-Universes' quantum concept if we assume these to be potential universes (in harmony with the Copenhagen Interpretation). Certainly the potential exists for virtually any outcome. Therefore, miracles are easy if one controls quantum physics and, thus, every conceivable outcome.

However, what if these many universes are actual? Such speculation brings a number of concepts to mind. One of the most interesting is that these many universes are energy states and part of our everyday lives. M. R. Franks suggests that each of us move freely through a latticework of these multiple universes daily–the true universal traveler. Though the individual, or more accurately the perceiver is unaware of his or her abilities, nonetheless one moves through many such energy states. According to Franks:

> There is no one dynamic, changing universe; rather, each conscious being has his own personal dynamic universe. Time is the illusion experienced by sequentially visiting contiguous energy states. At each quantum event the universe does not split into parallel universes. (Strictly speaking, 'contiguous' universes would be perpendicular to three-dimensional space as we know it. 'Parallel universes' is a misnomer.) Rather, consciousness merely enters one of numerous contiguous static universes.[43]

By this understanding, Franks can, more clearly, explain miraculous events such as synchronicity. Franks states,

> A mind with the ability to move laterally, or sideways, through the lattice would perceive itself as having an ability to work miracles. 'Sideways' here means in the direction of parallel states differing from the present state only by the desired characteristic, and neither distinctly 'future' nor past' to the present state.[44]

As we gather more and more information we realize our understanding of quantum reality becomes increasingly foreign to that which we would assume 'quantumness' should be. So, what does this bizarre world, a world beyond our world, confirm about other realities? It proves that another world with another set of rules exists. Therefore, quantum physics proves the existence of supernatural reality. The quantum world is a supernatural world because it operates outside of the boundaries that we perceive as natural. Most scientists seem to minimize this fact. However, the problem Einstein had with quantum reality was that he realized its supernatural inferences. Einstein's 'missing link' in quantum mechanics could be further explained if we are to conclude that the quantum world is so infinitesimal that it combines spiritual dimensions with material dimensions. As ingredients for a holiday dish are combined in a mixing bowl, so might the quantum world conjoin spiritual and physical realities. When we refer to the human understanding of existence as a Cinderella world, we are really suggesting that we live in a limited world. Like the domain of the Mad Hatter of Alice In Wonderland, there is yet another world on another level of reality that is as strange as any fantasy. All of true reality must be unlimited (supernatural) except for our relatively small and limited place in existence.

The scientist who will not accept such a mystical explanation should remember that the total amount of information that we hold regarding our existence is 'like spit in a bucket.' Here is an example of our ignorance on this subject: We assume that the Higgs boson (hypothesised quantum building block used to describe the origin of masses through the Higg's field) is perhaps a particle or grouping of particles. Factually, we do not really know what it is nor do we comprehend much about anything regarding the quantum world. Moreover, we know less than five percent about our total environment, because data suggests that ninety-five percent of the universe is made with dark matter. We further assume there is dark energy, but we know little about it. In fact, dark energy has us still guessing about the true nature of gravity. Thus, we do not understand much about the classical world in which we live.

What proof do we have of the spiritual influence? If we now assume God does not exist, then we must also conclude that, at the conception of the material universe, there was no intelligence and, thus, no logical reason for the beginning of intelligence. There is no logical explanation for the Big Bang breaking singularity or for our Cinderella existence or any existence. Yet, we are miraculously here, and we are miraculously intelligent beings. Therefore, with or without God, miracles are a necessity. And, if there are miracles, God is the implied source of all miracles. So, Dr. Kaku, you might wish to re-think

IF WE NOW ASSUME GOD DOES NOT EXIST, THEN WE MUST ALSO CONCLUDE THAT, AT THE CONCEPTION OF THE MATERIAL UNIVERSE, THERE WAS NO INTELLIGENCE AND, THUS, NO LOGICAL REASON FOR THE BEGINNING OF INTELLIGENCE.

your 'off the cuff' remarks regarding God and miracles. Chances are, it is a miracle that you exist.

SELF

Related to the miracle of 'being' is the age old philosophical question, 'What is the relationship between mind and body?' This personal introspection (related to Rene Descartes proposition "I think therefore I am") often occurs when one discovers there is something internal (within us) which is profoundly different than anything else in the material world - the discovery of 'self.' As a matter of fact, the dominating miracle experienced in every person's life may be the sudden appearance of 'self.' What is self? I do not mean the dictionary term. I prefer a deeper and more practical understanding of self. One of my great memories as a youth is looking out of the four windows at the top of the Washington Monument. These windows are at 90 degree angles and thus each window brings a different view of Washington D.C.'s beauty. From one window you can see the Jefferson Memorial, from another the Lincoln Memorial, from a third the White House and, from the last window, the Capitol of the United States. Looking in these four directions from ground level is impressive, but looking from the top of the Washington Monument is awesome! Everything is so peaceful and serene. Yet, one feels the power of the United States government. At such a time, many feelings enter my consciousness including the pride I have for the United States, reflections of our heritage, the wisdom of our forefathers, my respect for George Washington, Abraham Lincoln and other leaders. However, there is a more personal feeling. Whether or not this personal feeling is related to my internal patriotic emotions, I do not know. For some reason, in the room at the top of the monument - looking out over Washington, D.C., I feel a dichotomy of 'self.' I feel as though my body is but a building, much like the physicalness of the Washington Monument, and I am peering out of my body while I experience looking out of a window. At that moment, I know my body is but a vehicle to be used by self. Self lives in my body, but self is also separate from my physical being. It is self which is called by God to bring good and greatness to that which lies before me. Anytime I wish to think about my being, I can experience this dichotomy. My body is the slave to self. The body does what self instructs. If self wants the right arm to rise and the body part is working properly, the right arm rises. In like manner, the self is called to be obedient to God. The difference is, self can think. The self has the choice. Self can determine whether to be godly and submit to God, or whether to live for self, in pride and selfishness. Many psychologists and psychiatrists understand there is

---

IT IS SELF WHICH IS CALLED BY GOD TO BRING GOOD AND GREATNESS TO THAT WHICH LIES BEFORE ME.

more to self than an animalistic behavior. Science does not understand why humans take pride in concepts like freedom and dignity and love and caring, nor why humans appreciate great works of art and the beauty of music. Science does not understand why humans around the world, no matter what their country or culture or race, desire to worship God. The most obvious example in modern history may be the spiritual revolution that occurred in Russia after the fall of the Soviet Union. We saw a spiritually oppressed society become free to express innate spiritual behavior. To the secularist, the Russians must seem depraved in their frantic obsession for spiritual Truth. However, for those who understand the innate needs of self, their actions are very understandable, perhaps necessary for a well rounded psyche. In fact, about one-third of adults have more dramatic spiritual experiences such as "a moment of sudden religious awakening or felt close to a powerful, spiritual force that seemed to lift them out of themselves."[45] Why do human beings react the way they do? Could it be that innately we understand God is important to our being? Could Biblical revelations be instructions from our Creator?

It is interesting to note that more and more areas of the Bible which were legitimate leaps of faith, are being validated by science, archaeology and alike. Thus, we discover yet another reason to believe that the commonly held materialistic view of man is not the realistic view. We are inclined to flatter ourselves. Humanism is romantic, shallow and, more than likely, completely fallacious. Conversely, theists seem more and more to be the realists.

CONSIDER THE EVIDENCE

We have looked at miracles from a theological standpoint, from a philosophical standpoint and from a scientific standpoint. Now let us consider miracles from the weight of the evidence.

What can be said about the credibility of those people who made the Biblical reports? Atheists believe that the Biblical reports came from men with vivid imaginations who felt the need to add miracles to important events. Thus, the Bible is composed of myths. However, when one looks deeper into the affairs of the Biblical manuscripts, one finds a unique account. I quote from the comments of R. C. Sproul, "One of the interesting elements of Biblical miracles involves the sobriety of their accounts. Compare, for example, miracle narratives of the New Testament with those found in the Gnostic literature of the second century. The Gnostic 'miracles' display a flavor and atmosphere of the bizarre and frivolous."[46] This is even more apparent in other literature of antiquity. We can reflect on the writings of the Greeks and the Romans and their mythological gods and goddesses. We can compare the Bible to writings of any ancient society's writings. Reported miracles of other gods and goddesses have the flare of a dream. Furthermore, they do not match up with the historical view of life. However, the writings about Jesus Christ are different. One might ask why? The disciples did not know to compare writings. Saint Peter and company did not have the benefit of the analytical studies of Freud, Jung and Campbell. They did not know what the history of mythology would hold. They did not even think there would be a history. They did not know other works written around 50 A.D., would be linked with dreams. Sproul, recognizing this uniqueness, wrote, "New Testament miracles take place in a context of a sober view of history and redemption."[47] The disciples knew the Truth. There was no room for faith in the context of what they observed. Faith was only a matter of accepting the promises that accompanied Truth. They witnessed or confirmed everything which was reported.

I invite you to question the integrity of the people reporting the miracles of Jesus. I again turn to R. C. Sproul's comments, "Those who claim them (miracles) are men of obvious profound ethical integrity and men who are willing to die for their veracity."[48] Saint Luke is considered to this day to be one of the greatest historians to have lived. Modern archaeology has proven the value of his veracity. According to Sproul, "The word of Ramsey tracing the journeys of Paul as recorded by Luke has so vindicated Luke's accuracy as a historian, that modern secular historians have called him the finest historian of antiquity. The Biblical historians have fared considerably better under close scrutiny and critique than have other ancient historians such as Josephus and Herodotus."[49] Therefore, we do not need to rely entirely on the works of Carl Jung to reveal to us differences between myths and the reported miracles of Jesus. We can let the disciples themselves answer this point in question. The following is a direct quotation from Saint Peter related to this exact matter. "We do not declare unto you cleverly devised myths or fables but rather what we have seen with our eyes and heard with our ears."[50] I encourage agnostics to question the sincerity of Saint Luke and others. If you want to know the truth about Jesus, then investigate both the theological and secular historical writings of the early days in Christianity and the earnest nature of their authors.

Yet, to the agnostic or atheist, the acceptance of any supernatural phenomena must seem illogical and nonsensical. Such a person is not swayed by reading someone's testimony about a miraculous event, but, like Thomas of the New Testament, he or she demands to examine the event. Nonetheless, if a authentic miracle is found, one must then accept the philosophical (and scientific) position that one indisputable miracle demolishes materialism. Some unmistakable samples may have transpired in our Cinderella existence.

LOOKING FOR LITERARY MIRACLES

There are some controversial studies in letter patterns and numerology in relation to the Bible. Some researchers claim to have discovered meaningful codes which have remained undetected until recent times. The supporters claim patterns as pronounced as those in question seem missing in other literature, even other holy literature. Their conclusion is such miracles further prove the Bible is the inspired Word of God. Other investigations suggest they are not special but found in many other books. Because there may be a degree of meaning in some or all of these studies I feel they should be mentioned.

These investigations interrelate the Arabic numbering system with the ancient Hebrew and Greek alphabets. The Hebrew and Greek languages were cryptically structured so that each letter has both a numerical and alphabetical value. It is common knowledge that the numerical symbols of the Bible have literary value beyond the clear symbolic structure. A great example is the number 666 (the number of the Beast). Numerologists have searched this number for a personal name or literal warning. Kabbalah, a form of Jewish mysticism, suggests that God exists beyond the universe. God created the universe using a beam of light (the Divine Will) which flowed into thirty-two secret paths or penetrations. Ten are emanations called 'sephirot' or numbers and can also be described as the attributes, faces or hands of God. The remaining twenty-two positions are essentially the letters in the Hebrew alphabet. (Interestingly, this explanation of creation sounds very similar to an advanced 'string theory.') Therefore, both the universal understanding of numbers (or the value represented by numbers) and the Hebrew alphabet are said to have a divine origin.

Amazingly, we can again go to Carl Jung for independent support. Jung writes:

It is generally believed that numbers were invented or thought out by man, and are therefore nothing but concepts of quantities, containing nothing that was not previously put into them by the human intellect. But it is equally possible that numbers were found or discovered. In any case they are not only concepts but something more-autonomous entities which somehow contain more than just quantities. Unlike concepts, they are based not on any psychic conditions but on the quality of being themselves, on a 'so-ness' that cannot be expressed by an intellectual concept. Under these conditions they might easily be endowed with qualities that have still to be discovered.[51]

The thought that numbers do not derive from a human origin is not a contemporary concept. Pythagoras, an early Greek philosopher and mathematician, preached that numbers contained an "intrinsic and living virtue" of God. Clearly, Pythagoras had a great respect for numbers. As an example, he is credited with discovering that the diatonic scale in music could be explained in terms of mathematics. Furthermore, because of his more mystical theories regarding mathematics, he is called the Father of Numerology.[52]

So, we realize that both numbers and the Hebrew alphabet have long been mythically connected with divine processes. However, unlike the religious rituals and philosophical theorems described above, the following Biblical codes are quite tangible.

In the fourteenth-century, Rabbi Rabbeynu Bachayah wrote about the coded messages he had happened upon in the Torah. In explaining his process, he defined odd patterns that comprised the codes as "equidistant letter sequences." In his research, Bachayah would start with a designated letter. He would then take, as example, every twenty second letter that followed in a Biblical chapter. This is a significant number if for no other reason than the fact that there is 22 letters in the Hebrew alphabet. As in the above Kabbalah explanation, the Hebrew alphabet is sacredly connected with God. Occasionally, Bachayah's process would produce a symbolic word or message. In the above example where he used the 22nd letter, he uncovered the word 'Torah.' However, Bachayah's work was, for the most part, ignored.[53]

In 1977 Jerry Lucas and Dan Washburn co-authored a book called *Theomatics*. Theomatics is a mathematical procedure which uncovered dramatic numerological Biblical messages in both the Hebrew and Greek languages. Though their formula did not include equidistant letter sequences, their results seemed even more impressive. Their theory recognized that various numerological values are divinely mathematical, or more precisely, theomatically associated with God, Jesus, Satan, etc. For example, the Greek word for God has a mathematical value of 484 or twenty-two squared. (Notice that again we find the numerical significance of 22). By figuring the numerical value of each Hebrew or Greek letter of a verse, and finding the summed total of that verse, one could find a mathematical relationship within each Biblical verse. Verses which are directly related to God will have summed values that can be factored by twenty-two squared. Thus, these summed values further demonstrate the divine nature of the writing. The interrelated concept of a mathematical signature of God to authenticate His message is not so fantastic. I am reminded of the mathematical messages we propelled into the outer limits of our solar system by way of a Voyager space probe. Furthermore, artists usually leave an authenticating mark on their paintings and authors usually have their names printed in the front cover of their books. Similarly, Theomatics proposed that: a) God was the designer and originator of both the Hebrew and Greek languages and b) God uses numerology to signal His approval of the Bible. Other 'holy books' cannot make such claims because they do not bear these unmistakable numerological patterns. No other religious work envelops these 'theomatic' patterns. In a discussion about the above discoveries, nuclear scientist, Robert W. Faid, stated:

Mathematicians have examined this theomatic design and have stated that even with the assistance of the most modern computers, they could not formulate even one language in which such a theomatic design would make any sense.

Even non-Christian mathematicians have agreed that they cannot explain the theomatic pattern of even one feature in terms of chance. The design had to have been placed there by intelligence, and this intelligence cannot be matched by the most sophisticated computers.[54]

Yet, there was a major hurdle facing Theomatics. Though it has a mathematical basis and therefore a 'scientific' medium, Theomatics was a mathematical mystery. Many Americans find mathematics boring or too complicated. Because of the sophistication involved in theomatic patterns, some people did not understand the message. Unfortunately, Theomatics has erroneously been compared with Numerology and Pythagorean occultism. For these reasons, Theomatics seem to have been somewhat ignored.

However, other mathematical relationships continued to be investigated. Rabbi Michael Dov Weissmandl of Czechoslovakia continued to examine the simpler 'equidistant letter sequences' discovered by Rabbi Bachayah. Though Weissmandl, like Bachayah, confined the bulk of his research to the Torah, he continued to uncover coded messages. Nonetheless, these discoveries were so amazing that even Weissmandl questioned whether they were significant finds or merely coincidental anomalies. Fortunately, with the advent of the computer the verses could be examined more thoroughly. The task has been adopted by a number of scholars. An in-depth study was performed at Hebrew University and the Jerusalem College of Technology. Their conclusions were published in the Bible Review, October, 1995. These incredible findings give further credit to the divine nature of the Scriptures. Grant Jeffery summed up the meaning of such studies:

This scientific discovery is earth-shaking in its consequences because it reveals a staggering level of mathematical design and intelligence which could only have been produced by a supernatural mind, providing unshakable mathematical proof that the Bible was truly inspired by God. The incredible data demolishes forever the false claim by liberal scholars and skeptics that the Bible was written and edited by uninspired men and that it is full of errors and contradictions. Despite the fact that numerous scholars and scientists have attempted to challenge the validity of this Torah research, the evidence has not been refuted.[55]

One researcher, Dr. Harold Gans, was a skeptic who developed his own related computer program. To his astonishment, Gan's program confirmed the validity of these mysterious codes. As a result, Dr. Gans began teaching classes on the divine implications of these coded messages.[56]

The clear alternative to the 'divinity of the Bible' explanation is that these coded messages have amassed by chance. To investigate 'chance,' the other choice, alternative literary works have been translated into Hebrew. Proponents argue they hold few, if any, cryptic messages. Therefore, it is illogical to presume that the Biblical codes can be explained by 'random chance.' If the messages are distinctively Biblical then we cannot assume they are delusions nor are they accidental quirks.

Up to now I have only discussed Jewish investigations. A natural question in western civilization might be, "Is the word 'Jesus' similarly coded?" Interestingly, 'Yeshua' (Jesus) is equidistantly coded and found in various passages pertaining to messianic prophecies. One such code actually reads, "Yeshua is My Name."[57] A Jewish student named Yacov Rambsel discovered Yeshua's name is revealed in some controversial verses. An example is Daniel 9:25–27, which is considered to be a messianic prophecy by Christians, but denied by modern rabbinical scholars. Daniel 9:25–27 reads:

(9:25) Now Listen! It will be forty-nine years plus 434 years from the time the command is given to rebuild Jerusalem, until the Anointed One comes! Jerusalem's streets and walls will be rebuilt despite the perilous times.

(9:26) After this period of 434 years, the Anointed One will be killed, his kingdom still unrealized . . . and a king will arise whose armies will destroy the city and the Temple. They will be overwhelmed as with a flood, and war and its miseries are decreed from that time to the very end. (9:27) This king will make a seven-year treaty with the people, but after half that time, he will break his pledge and stop the Jews from all their sacrifices and their offerings; then, as a climax to all his terrible deeds, the Enemy shall utterly defile the sanctuary of God. But in God's time and plan, his judgment will be poured out upon this Evil One.[58]

Rambsel discovered that the name 'Yeshua' is coded in Daniel 9:26. This verse holds the direct point of controversy by referring to "the Anointed One" who will be "killed" or, as most often interpreted, the one 'cut off.' Starting with the Hebrew letter for Y (yod) in the wording "the city" and counting to the right every 26th letter is found the word 'Yeshua.' Anyone with a Hebrew text (which can be purchased through any book store) can find this coded name. As unlikely as it is that, by chance, 'Yeshua' is coded in this strategic and controversial verse, consider the likelihood of finding this particular code in the exact messianic verse by the exact numerological count, i.e., found in the 26th verse by counting every 26th letter.

The inferences of the above coded messages are quite simple. Either these codes exist or they do not. Yet even if, through future study, we find further codes and messages, many will question and doubt. Are these real messages from God? Quite frankly, I do not know. I would heartily recommend reading *Theometrics, The Signature Of God,* and *Yeshua - The Hebrew Factor.*

PSYCHIC PHENOMENA

On the evening of August 8, 1994, I was watching an *Unsolved Mysteries* television show. This particular episode featured a story about 'psychic dreams.' The show discussed three different cases where people had dreams which revealed information the dreamer could not have known through conventional processes. In two of the stories, dreams prophesied to people about future accidents. The dreams were so precise that they envisioned detailed information, i.e., an exact bend in a road, etc. Things happened exactly as the dreams had prognosticated. The show also pointed to the fact that sometimes more than one person may have the same psychic dream. A mother and her daughter had the exact dream about a future accident which did indeed occur to their respective husband and father. The third and last segment was about a woman who had several dreams about hospital activities. Then she had a last dream in which she was visited by a man she had known in the past. He took her to a church and showed her himself in his casket. He told her how much he had loved her and kissed her goodbye. She stated this dream seemed more 'real' than her usual dreams. She regarded it as more of a vision than a dream. She later learned her 'old friend' had been sick and passed away at approximately the same time she had experienced her visionary dream. Of course, these particular dreams may have been fictional or made up. Yet, such visions are common. There are many stories about dreams which foretell futuristic events. As was suggested by *Unsolved Mysteries,* we may never be able to explain such events.

To live as rational beings, we must honestly consider reality from this larger, yet truer understanding of being. According to Dr. Charles T. Tart, *five phenomena* associated with parapsychology have been proven valid beyond any reasonable doubt. They are *telepathy, clairvoyance, precognition* (prediction of the future), *psychokinesis* (PK) and *healing.* There seems to have been enough study on these subjects to support paranormal conclusions. In fact, in an interview, Tart made the following statement, "And I am saying anyone who disagrees with me (on the above five phenomena) is being unreasonable."[59] Such human capabilities more properly fit within human spiritualism than they do the classical understanding of humanness. Perhaps that is only because we do not yet grasp the nature of humanness. Perhaps man is both a physical and spiritual being. Where in a materialistic reality do we categorize the indefinable? How can we validate such mystical events? Even more amazing these 'mystical' perceptions often seem to intensify in people at the time of death.

Jay Kesler tells a story about one of his good friends named Jim Smith. Jim was a clinical psychologist whom Jay describes by saying, "He is among the greatest 'no bunk' Christians I've ever known in my life . . . He loathed religion, but loved Jesus Christ." Unfortunately, Jim had lymphatic pancreatic cancer. Because he was in the last stages, Jim was taken to Baylor Hospital in Dallas. At this point, his sickness had progressed to the stage of termination. Jim would soon die. Jay and Paul Robins, of *Christianity Today,* also one of Jim's friends, traveled to Dallas. When they got to the Dallas airport, they were advised that Jim was in a coma and, thus, it would be too late for their visit. The travelers continued on to the hospital. When Dr. Kesler and Paul Robins arrived at Baylor Hospital, Jim was still in the coma and had not talked to anyone for several hours. However, as soon as Jay and Paul walked into Jim's hospital room, Jim came out of the coma. He immediately sat up in his hospital bed and informed the two visitors, "I've been waiting for you." Jim was functioning as if he had just experienced a total medical recovery. Jay recalls, "He was himself totally." In their discussion, Jim was quite frank. He knew his friends were concerned, because he was close to death and would soon die. When Jim stated, "This is near the end," Jay and Paul started crying. Jim responded to their tears with, "No don't cry. It's ok. It's really ok." Jim asked, "Jay, could you sing for me without a hymnbook the five verses of 'A Mighty Fortress Is Our God?'" Jay answered, "Jim, I can do a verse or two, but I cannot do five." Jim stated, "I can't either, but I woke up at three o'clock this morning and the angels sang to me five verses of 'A Mighty Fortress Is Our God,' and I wrote them down." Then Jim turned to Paul and he asked, "Paul can you quote 2nd Corinthians, Chapter 5?" Paul recalled a portion of it, but couldn't recite the whole chapter. Jim said, "I can't either, but I woke up after hearing the angels sing and I quoted the entire chapter . . . Guy's, I'm telling you this thing is real! It's bigger than our heads. It's bigger than our knowledge. It's even bigger than our faith. Relax guys. It's OK. We'd better pray." Of course, Jay and Paul are still in tears over their friend's situation. Jim was "dry eyed" while he prayed, "Lord, these guys are having a hard time. I'm going to see you soon, but they're going to be along quicker than they think. But Lord thank you for being so real to me, and the fact that I can tell them the truth; everything is OK." Jay concludes by relating, "So Jim laid down . . . and in a few hours he went to heaven."[60]

This is just one of many eye witness accounts I could have relayed to you on supernatural sensory encounters. It is interesting to find accounts where an observer brings back information such as five verses of a song about God, or recalls entire chapters from the Bible. Of course, this particular event could be explained away if one concludes that Jim has, in the past, heard both the song and the Biblical chapter. Jim's subconscious fed him the information in the midst of a drug-induced vision which was related to his traumatic state at the time.

Such an explanation might be possible in this particular case, but as we have pointed out, one cannot explain many other seemingly acausal phenomena. What I have been discussing goes far beyond the possibilities of miracles. It reaches right to the heart of the Ultimate Reality. Some people think we are "not equipped to understand" all that which we see. However, what we humans do perceive is a very creative supportive environment, or clinically speaking, a very efficiently ordered environment. This environment seems designed and equipped to insure the fulfillment of providential activity. I do not mean to imply that there are no other ways for God's Will to be known or fulfilled. We have discussed, in part, some of the machinery in place which satisfies the Will of God - the transcendental Will, the 'prima causa' as some scientist might describe it. Because of our lack of understanding, the transcendent holiness of God is a mystical concept to man. Moreover, there are many 'mystical experiences' in Christianity. For example, the cleansing power of the Holy Ghost is a mystical experience. There is a great difference, however, in the mysticism of Christianity and that of eastern religions. Christian mysticism is based on the transcendental love of God—God making a way for man—God stooping to help man. Forgiveness of sin, Jesus' healing of the sick, and salvation of a human's spirit are all acts of God's love. However, when we consider the eastern religions, these religions seem to be mechanically mystical. A general view of eastern thought suggests that man, through his own actions, must enter a mystical world and rise to the top. He, man, must do this for himself.[61] A clear example of eastern mystical thought comes from a quotation of S. N. Dasgupta, "Self will shine forth in its own light and he himself will be absolutely free in boundless, companionless loneliness of self-illumination."[62]

So, we find that one of the major struggles in religious philosophy is how to treat these types of mystical or miraculous events. Are they supernatural events—perhaps indications of a God who cares for life and controls reality? No matter how you perceive them, miracles happen every day!

SECTION THREE:

THE SOUL,
THE PSYCHE,
AND THE HUMAN
INTELLECT

CHAPTER 8

FOR THE GOOD OF MAN, GOD MUST EXIST

" 'God is, or he is not.' But to which side shall we include? Reason can decide nothing here. There is an infinite chaos which separated us."[1]

In earlier chapters, I presented sound logical evidence that God exists. I wish to continue by introducing a pragmatic view which makes a belief in an authoritative God valid, reasonable and desirable. This philosophical position is best known from 'Pascal's Wager' which advocates that whether or not there is a God, one is foolish not to believe God exists.

In an attempt to be fair, I will assume that the atheists are right. Presume for a moment that there is no God, no heaven, or hell. There is nothing spiritual anywhere throughout all that is. In fact, nothing exists. There is no matter. There is no time. There is no energy. There is no spiritual force. In the historical past, dating back prior to the pre-universe state, we find a period of nothingness. At a point in time, and through a single quirk of pure chance, energies of unknown origin came into existence. Perhaps positive and negative charges formed out of nothing. This in itself would have defied the laws of science because there was nothing to form into charges. Moreover, even if charges could form, opposite charges attract, which would logically neutralize a charge induced force at its inception. Yet, through some unknown quirk of fate, energy became matter - or something unplanned and (probably to us) incomprehensible. But, at an exact moment in time, matter came into being. This happening broke even more natural laws. However, for one instant in the history of the universe, energy and matter just happened– 'by the dumbest of luck.' It seems, within such a scenario, energy begot matter (both positive and negative matter). However, this energy was not available, but just happened, or maybe energy was present (though that is impossible because of singularity), and somehow changed by chance and without reason. There was no beginning force. There was no intellectual catalyst, no creation, no design; it just happened by 'the dumbest of luck.' To accomplish this formation, pre-matter and pre-energy aligned itself to explode into space. Pre-energy and/or pre-matter would necessarily perform the impossible and break singularity, but the impossible seems to be a necessity for a godless universe. So enormous was the explosion that it hurled gigantic galaxies of matter at great speeds through the unknown and incomprehensible reaches of that which is to be. Of course, everything we have assumed in this atheistic drama is nonsense. As 'smart' as we humans are, we do not have the vaguest idea of anything natural that could cause the needed mega-force. Like those actions above, such a phenomenon would break many of our scientific laws. The galaxies of gas, or whatever new form matter took, would become galaxies of stars. A really bizarre 'happening' in the recesses of chaos formed a delicately structured and extremely sophisticated cosmos—by 'the dumbest of luck.' This event happened so spontaneously that it could not be measured because it threw all mathematical projections off. Therefore, today's mathematical search into this area of history yields incalculable gibberish. All projections are invalidated. Time, in fact, is not even a concern. The further we inquire, the more we find even a greater sequence of extraordinary events and incredible events. Then came man. Though conceived by a continued improvement of dirt and rocks, he began to contemplate life. He formed all of these false perceptions; "If there was no God there could be no universe." Thus, say the atheist, man believes in a god that does not exist.

I suggest to you this atheistic position is not only fallacious, but dangerous to the structural foundation of civilization. It is dangerous because if there is no God, then everything—money, spouses, friendships, toys, sports, etc., is nonsensical. Nothing matters. Form the agnostic position, human perception is nebulous. Without a God, however, life and all that is—is only waste. Thoughts are waste. Ideas are waste. Even so, whether we like it or not, pragmatist William James changed this dictum. According to James' philosophy, if there absolutely was no God before man, there absolutely is a God now. In a like manner, there absolutely is a spiritual part of man. There is a common spiritual morality; there is a devil, there is a hell and so on. For if man believes in God (and any of the other above concepts) and this belief affects his actions, his life, his 'self,' then in human reality (which would be the only kind of relevant reality), there is a God. If man believes he is a spiritual being and spirit affects the way he lives, then he does in fact have a spiritual life. The effects of the concept 'spirit' are a testimony as to the validity of a 'spirit.'

If I want to love my neighbor (or the world of people) more completely, and I pray to God to help me become more loving and compassionate toward others or, if I want to be more understanding, patient, truthful or anything else and I pray to God for help and get the desired results, then, indeed, God does exist. If praying to God has helped me to improve myself or the situation of someone else then, in effect, there is a God and I am a spiritual being. Furthermore, to whatever extent I have learned to love, care, and tell

---

I SUGGEST TO YOU THIS ATHEISTIC POSITION IS NOT ONLY FALLACIOUS, BUT DANGEROUS TO THE STRUCTURAL FOUNDATION OF CIVILIZATION.

the truth, etc. with the perceived help of God, society as a whole has benefited. Most important to me, I will prosper, too. Our medical doctors and psychologists are learning, that the man who does not hate, but loves, generally lives a longer, happier and less stressful life. "Do unto others as you would have them do unto you" and "love your neighbor as yourself" now take on a real medical significance. I Kings 3:14 reads, "And I will give you a long life if you follow me and obey my laws as your father David did." It is ironic that ancient sheep herders, who were descendants of slaves, knew this medical truth thousands of years before our men of science.

Does all of this tie in with modern civilization? Let us reflect upon those symbols which relate to the power of sociological ascension. Consider Sir Thomas Moore's, *Utopia*. Utopia was a fictional society in which humanity had solved all of the problems of socialization. Today, Utopia is the 'word symbol' of the dream society. Human beings can make scientific advances, economic advances, etc. but, until we live with one another in harmony, we will not realize life's actual value. This is the goal of sociology - to form a society engineered by man so precisely and so perfectly that it will be void of all social problems. Forget God and all of His Laws. Man can build the perfect society. Whether it is Moore's *Utopia* or Plato's *Republic,* Lenin's Soviet Union or the futuristic concept of today's university professor, visionary societies seem to work on paper, because on paper they are but idealistic dreams. Such humanistic societies are envisioned to be one big happy family. The benevolent government is exceptionally fair and cares for each of its citizens. In like manner, each citizen seems to be the perfect neighbor—kind, trusting, courteous, well adjusted and happy; each is always ready to share everything with anyone who comes his or her way. However, utopian societies seem incapable of factoring in the true nature of man, a nature which is just the opposite of that expressed by Sir Thomas Moore.

Human nature seems more in line with the Machiavellian view; 'man is a liar, a thief, a cheat and a coward' (a favorite illustrative adage of Dr. Lee Ball regarding the Machiavellian philosophy). This leads to one extremely important function of God. God provides the world with objectivity. Humans need objective laws to exist. Furthermore, human beings need to assimilate— to live by God's specific precepts. Society will never approach utopian idealism until it embraces the natural laws of sociology set forth by God. "You must not murder. You must not commit adultery. You must not steal. You must not lie," etc. I submit these values represent more than yet another proof of God. I suggest they also describe God's Will for man's behavior and its (God's Will) relevance to a healthy society. An understanding of the role these

---

HUMAN BEINGS CAN MAKE SCIENTIFIC ADVANCES, ECONOMIC ADVANCES, ETC. BUT, UNTIL WE LIVE WITH ONE ANOTHER IN HARMONY, WE WILL NOT REALIZE LIFE'S ACTUAL VALUE.

absolute values play in the function of civilization give honor to their Author. The entire western civilization owes its development and thus all that it has produced to the laws put forth in the Bible. This brings us to a very crucial point about the relevance of God's Will and, thus, His Laws that moderate our lives. As human beings, we feel more comfortable contemplating our own will then we do our role in the Providence of God (our function in the 'Big Picture').

      There is a theological battle going on in each body. It is over ownership. It is similar to our daily battle with cancer cells. The medical field claims this cancer war goes on inside of everyone. Healthy cells fight off cancer cells. Sometimes our bodies grow weak and cancer takes hold. We all know the result of losing the war to cancer. Most of us have seen a loved one lose such a war. In the same manner, good and evil battle daily in our thoughts and actions. This is not just a theological description of human behavior. This battle is truly a natural human event. For some reason, the Creator/God/Force allowed us to exist in a world with real choices of opposites. We choose to do things that are considered good or we can choose to do things that are considered bad or evil. We may question what are the correct rules, which religion, which interpretation of the rules, etc. We may even question what is good and what is evil. We may find situations that do not have hard or fast rules, but we battle daily over choices. Just as white cells battle infection, our continuous battle of goodness versus sinfulness is a natural event and obviously part of God's Master Plan. It seems logical to me that the battle extends to all spiritual matter. As an example, if we accept the explanation for evil in the Bible, we know Lucifer (the devil) has already lost his war, and he will lead legions of spiritual matter down the path of sin. Whether we accept Lucifer as a real entity or simply a 'symbol' for sinful behavior, there is reality in the results of our actions. When we looked at the universe, and felt like a bump on an electron, we had a look at the 'Big Picture.' The sortation of good from evil must be an important part in the fulfillment of God's Master Plan. All humans have a conscience and this conscience may be a built-in control of God's Will over personal free will. This separation of good and evil is happening as naturally as the process of DNA. There is a process controlled by natural/supernatural laws. God the Creator had this process planned and structured from the beginning of time.

      Yet, even if we die of cancerous sin, what if our major test was learning to submit to God and we did not stress this submission in our lives? Perhaps, by our actions and/or words, we have encouraged others to 'do their own thing' instead of obeying Gods commands. We can discuss virtually any

THE ENTIRE WESTERN CIVILIZATION OWES ITS DEVELOPMENT AND THUS ALL THAT IT HAS PRODUCED TO THE LAWS PUT FORTH IN THE BIBLE.

morally affected sociological/psychological situation. Be it abortion, sexual promiscuity, lying, extreme desire for money or fame etc., all could fit under the same conscious choice. Do we think, "Spouse abuse is wrong for me, but I have no voice in what others do." Or, do we think, "Abuse goes against the Will of God. Perhaps I can be a positive influence in this person's life."

Thus far, our discussion has been a very simplified understanding of human rationale, but today human rationale seems to reject God's Will. Over a relatively short period of time we have witnessed a great deterioration of sociological ethics. We are experiencing a major change in the way our society views moral issues. We are attempting to discern correct behavior by invoking human relativism misconstrued as moral values. This human trend is what Friedrich Nietzsche expressed with the famous words of a madman, "God is dead." Though Nietzsche was an atheist, his point was not the atheist's position. His point, instead, was man no longer looks to God for answers. To do so (as with all old ways) would be to embrace a 'slave mentality.' But to do away with past conformity and look to himself for answers, man evolves toward 'overman' (growth into superhuman being). Interestingly, the term 'superman' became connected with Nietzsche. However, this is a mistranslation of overman.

To illustrate the problem, consider the following situations. We have been conditioned to rationalize why a man might abuse a child. By traditional thinking the solution to this problem is to condemn the abuser. But, we know a high percentage of child abusers were abused when they were young. Thus, the abuser's actions are not his fault but the fault of his parents. Perhaps he was not properly trained to communicate with children. So his abuse is society's fault. He was born an abuser. It is part of his psyche. Therefore, we might respond, it is natural he is an abuser. This excuse, perhaps the most heretical and dangerous position, is becoming a popular rationalization. Let us consider why a man would beat up his wife? Maybe he had a stressful day at the office and could not handle his obligations at home. Thus, his abusive manner was his bosses' fault. It is presumed that men rape women because they need to feel power over another person and civilization does not always supply them with that opportunity. Once again it is society's fault. We cannot hold individuals accountable for society's cruelties. Yet, with the loss of absolute values, violent actions have not only become common, but expected.

If you wonder how far our morals have fallen, ride with any policeman on any Friday night. A segment of United States children rationalize that killing others is commendable behavior. As a matter of fact, acts of violence, such as the killing innocent people, have become a right of passage or initia-

OVER A RELATIVELY SHORT PERIOD OF TIME WE HAVE WITNESSED A GREAT DETERIORATION OF SOCIOLOGICAL ETHICS.

tion into a number of street gangs. As we follow Nietzschian philosophy violence becomes the correct way to live. Here lies our dilemma; if there is no God then what is wrong with this violent premise? What is wrong with murder or rape or any violent act? There is obviously a pleasure in sadistic violence. Psychologists recognize such perverse pleasures as natural behavior. Freud recognized a human passion for destructiveness. He called it the "death instinct."[2] Freud further explained the human pleasure of sadism as a "blending of Eros (sexuality) and the death instinct, directed outside oneself."[3] Freud's explanation leads one to think in terms of sexual activity. True, sadism can be involved in sexual expression. The Marquis de Sade's writings and experimentation on sadism expresses these 'joys' as a human sexual desire.[4] However, whether exhibited in sexual relations or not, the sadistic thrill comes from having control over another being. Some children enjoy trapping insects and burning them to death with a magnifying glass. Some hunters kill game and do not eat it, but leave it to rot in the sun. In the early days of the United States, buffalo sportsmen were notorious for leaving dead buffalo behind. They killed for the enjoyment of killing, i.e., it was the pleasure of holding life and death powers over the creature. They were decadent men 'playing god.'

Some Satanists claim there is a pleasure in sacrificing life to Satan. In a filmed interview, a young woman spoke of such powers. She said, "Something about sacrifice, if you do it once - you want to do it all of the time. Once you have actually passed the barrier of sacrificing an animal you get this sort of blood lust, where you really want to do it. And I really wanted to do it." Following her confession a man described why Satanists desire to have their sacrifice suffer a slow painful death.[5] Human sacrifices to Satan have become the most sensational Satanic rituals. Women virgins are reported as targets, children and babies are considered targets too. Even Christians have been called targets. The innocence of the victim is rather important. At one time, such reports seemed to preposterous to be true, but today in these violent times, such reports seem quite plausible. A government official from Britain responded to a woman's confession that she had sacrificed her own baby by stating, "She said it herself, she said it in public. What does one make of it other than a heart breaking confession of something that has been a guilty secret for a long time?"[6]

The Columbine High School massacre is a different and more recent example of youth having a fascination with killing innocent people. According to the Jefferson County Colorado Sheriff report, Dylan Klebold wrote about killing (perhaps a daydream of things to come) in a notebook, " . . . killing enemies, blowing up stuff, *killing cops!!*" And, his last entry expressed his expectations at Columbine High School, "Park cars, set car bombs for 11:18 get out, go to outside hill, wait. When first bombs go off attack. *have fun!*" Eric Harris showed a similar fascination. His journal held these notes: "I will sooner die than betray my own thoughts, but before I leave this worthless place, I will kill whoever I deem unfit . . .," "I'm full of hate and I love it . . . You know what I hate? . . . MANKIND!!!! . . . Kill everything . . . Kill everything. . . ." He also wrote, "Its my fault! Not my parents, not my brothers, not my friends, not my favorite bands, not computer games, not the media, its mine." This comment leads one to wonder if some or all of these influences were negative factors. Plainly he thought investigators might question the effects of these areas of his life. At least one school board member, Patti Johnson, thought the school curricula might also be a factor. Johnson reportedly said in a speech that too many teachers in Colorado schools encourage students to question values taught at home and encourage them to talk about death. Of course the school system disagreed with Johnson's assessment.[7]

There is a pleasure in sin. A pleasure is realized through participating in premarital sex, being 'unfaithful' to your spouse, engaging in homosexual activities, beating someone over the head with a baseball bat, or holding a gun to a pleading man's head and pulling the trigger. All of these pleasures happen daily in every city in the United States. However, all of these and many other human failings are absolutely wrong and contentious to the Will of God and His Laws according to Judeo/Christian absolutes. I suggest everyone intuitively knows which activities are wrong. But, anyone can intellectually (through misconstrued 'rationalism') accept them as natural. Intellectually, we try to convince ourselves that our behavior is justified. We rationalize that we were born with sexual needs and therefore, it is natural to cheat on our spouses. In fact, an affair may be 'good' for the marriage.

As a cell fights to survive cancer, we fight for the survival of our spirits. Spiritually we grow stronger or we grow weaker. Without the guidance of God, we most surely lose. We can verify this from our human internal defense system. When we take advantage of others, make fun of others, rob, cheat or kill others, our conscience weakens. Almost anyone in law enforcement will confirm the presumable truth: repeat criminals will 'lose' or, more accurately, reduce the potency of their conscience. However, as we turn to God, and worship God, as we learn to give our love to other human beings, to help those who need our help, and to forgive those who cause us pain, we grow spiritually in 'harmony' with the Creator's Will for our lives. In accordance, our conscience grows and retains more authority or control over our decisions.

This simplified discussion of good and evil lays the ground work for some of the major questions concerning God. In the New York Public Library Desk Reference (a reference I frequently use for general knowledge) under "Philosophy" are three statements related to good and evil which seem to summarize man's greatest questions about the 'being' of God. They are as follows:

If God can prevent evil, but doesn't, then He isn't all-loving.

If God intends to prevent evil, but cannot, then He isn't omnipotent.

If God both intends to prevent evil and is capable of doing so, then how can evil exist?

In response, let us first recall the Biblical answer. Adam and Eve, through human free will, chose knowledge (which must have included both good and evil knowledge) instead of "the possibility of free and perfect enjoyment of life."[8] Of course, this choice was a sin because it went against the Will of God. Humans chose to know evil. Thus, the human encounter with evil is the product of humanism. Interestingly, this whole area of discussion is the bases of the ancient argument regarding free will vs. predestination. Does man choose evil or is he destined to be evil?

However, despite Adam and Eve, evil was not necessarily created by human choice. The Bible also depicts Satan's rebellion and a battle which will continue until a 'Day of Judgment.' Another Jewish writing, the Zohar of the Kabbalah, implies that evil had a 'mysterious' beginning and may have actually been a part of creation.[9] Such an addendum implies what many have felt; the Biblical account of Adam and Eve has much deeper meanings than it superficiality states. The text certainly is not about eating apples (apples are not even mentioned). Moreover, evil may be an unwilling tool of God. Though evil's purpose may defile God's Law, it vehemently demands a sincere appreciation for God's sovereignty and Holiness. To put it another way, our ancestor's (Adam and Eve) bad, yet free choice did not interfere with God's Will. Instead, it encumbered mankind. Our freedoms emphasize our frailties.

However, to better understand the value of evil let us move away from theology and consider the above three questions from philosophical position. My friend Larry Plato says; "How can you understand good if you have no evil?" From another perspective our question would go like this; "There is no good if there is no evil." Consider the following statements: If you are not aware of hell, how do you know of heaven? Without the possibility of hell, heaven loses meaning. In like manner, if no one dies, what is death? How could we even imagine death if we do not know what it is? Evil gives humanity reason to appreciate good. A child will learn through experience that 'mommy' will protect him or her. Likewise, we must suffer evil if we want to experience good. Our first postulate states; "If God can prevent evil, but doesn't then He isn't all-loving." God may, after all, be all loving and allow evil. From an omnipotent view, "evil" may actually be "good," if evil instructs our

OUR METAL IS FORGED THROUGH OUR EXPERIENCES WITH EVIL.

spirit to want for good. Therefore, postulate one may be invalid. If postulate one is invalid, than two and three have no basis. Thus, for our present world, evil with pain and suffering, has a purpose. Our metal is forged through our experiences with evil.

In a like manner we must ask the question Einstein could not answer, "Why does God allow suffering?" As with the above exercise of good and evil, suffering is necessary for one to appreciate pleasure. Again my friend Larry Plato made a very important point, "If you could own everything you wanted, there would be no pleasure to life." This is quite similar to a law of economics which predicts that a person with one pair of shoes gets more utility out of his one pair than someone might who had one hundred pairs. Any one pair of shoes has little value to the man who has an exhaustive supply. Similarly, pain and suffering allow us to appreciate the joys of our good fortunes. Larry Plato continued; "If we had no pain and no suffering, if there were no needs, then we indeed would be like gods." If everyone had a fifty million-dollar house (free and clear), a 57 Chevy convertible in mint condition and two separate electrical carving knife sets - one for Christmas and another for Easter, how could that person appreciate the real values of life? Perhaps the *more* you have, the *less* you appreciate life, and conversely, the more you suffer, the more you appreciate the value of life. From personal observation, I find it generally true that the more money one has, the less value one finds in the fraternal order of human kind. Owning 'Things' and placing excessive value on the importance of 'Things' alters the human bond. I further contend that extravagant behavior is a destructive behavior. The greatest example of this is the self abuse going on in Hollywood—specifically, the reported divorces and bed swapping, high use of drugs or alcohol, etc. Theirs is the searching for joy through a self imposed non-rational 'final experience.'

So, let us think of the perfect world. What if there were no death, and no pain? What if everyone had everything they could possibly want? Suppose everyone could eat all of the ice cream they might possibly want and not get fat or die? What if you could win at solitaire (card game) every time and without cheating? What if you could have everything you ever dreamed of? What value would be in life?

CHAPTER 9

PHILOSOPHY: GOD'S WILL BE DONE, DESPITE HUMAN RESISTANCE

"You're lost little girl . . . tell me who are you!"[1]

When I hear "You're Lost," by the Doors, (song above) I often think about the confused psyches of many of today's youth. This Doors' song is probably about a girl 'strung out' on drugs. However, the song does not focus on a bad habit. Instead, "You're Lost" speaks to one's inner self. Sometimes we go through a routine introspection of one's being, including personal experiences, conflicts, triumphs, search for love, affection, acceptance, etc. These intuitive analyses help us to develop patterns of both thought and action. However, unlike the edicts of the en vogue pseudo-rationalism philosophies which permeate within our hedonistic society, there is absolute Truth, there is but one objective Reality. Until we discover this Reality, then we are indeed lost.

In one of his intriguing sermons, Dr. James Boice gave a good example of how relativism (a rationalism philosophy) affects modern thought. While on an airplane flight Dr. Boice sat next to a lady who was an obvious relativist. During the flight their conversation got around to religion. When Dr. Boice made a comment from the Christian perspective, she would respond, "Well, that is your opinion." Dr. Boice would reply by saying something like, "You are right, that is my opinion, but that is not the issue. The question is, is it true?" Then Dr. Boice would continue with another Christian point and the lady would repeat her first statement, "That is your opinion." At which point Dr. Boice would again say, "Yes, that is my opinion, but that is not the issue. The issue is, is it true?" Evidently this conversation went on for some time and the responses continued in the above pattern.[2] This exchange must have become quite amusing for Dr. Boice. However, I am sure by the end of the flight, the lady had learned firsthand the philosophical differences between her 'relative' world view and the Christian authoritative philosophy or divine authoritarianism (God is absolute and in control of all that is). Relativism allows one to make moral choices based upon personal preferences. Likewise, relativism negates absolutes because one rationalizes his or her choices are as good as or better than those of most people. However, making opinionated choices can contribute nothing toward one's understanding of absolute Truth, because Truth, like all things, can be rationalized away. Truth can be twisted by the mind to the extent that it no longer seems true. At such times, what is reality to the self deceived is but a fantasy, and what is actual Truth and actual reality becomes a personal falsehood. Yet, logic dictates that absolute Truth must still exist. There must be an absolute Truth. There must be a common good. And, there must be an Ultimate Reality. It is extremely important for each of us to realize this fact and be honest and accurate in our search for Truth. Truth is like solving problems in math class. To a given problem, there is only one correct answer and a disciplined manner (formula) to get the correct answer. If you do not have the right answer, you are wrong. Moreover, if you think you have the right answer but do not know how to use the correct formula then you are lost. As an example, let us consider a fairly simple math problem: $2 \times 2 = 4$. If a person says the answer is "four" (4), but is only guessing, then he does not know 'why.' Therefore, he will miss when he guesses at the answer of $4 \times 2 = ?$. The meaning to the answer is missing. He simply does not comprehend $2 \times 2 = 4$. Thus, if he works on these types of math problems, his guesses will most often be wrong—he is lost! I believe the same thing is true with life. Even if you see the right path but do not recognize it, then you are not only wrong, you are lost.

When we explore those philosophical and historical submissions associated with the riddles of existence, we find God is a necessity. The pieces of life's puzzle fit best when God is the ultimate source. God is the initiator and in complete control of, the total sum of all reality. I am not only stating God is in control of one's life, (i.e., your life or my life), but God is the Supreme Ruler over the entirety of all that is—all life and all matter and all things. Only by His wisdom, only through His decision to allow sin to unveil its evil filth, do we exist in this present state. Through our freedom to choose between the fruit of good and evil, we allow either 1) God's love or 2) sin to rule our lives. This line of thinking is not only a theological position, but a philosophical position. The God/man relationship seems a central driving force of the human intellect. The major dilemma in every person's life is "What value will be given to God?" However, for the 'believer,' that dilemma expands to the earlier posed question, "What is God's Will for my life?" How one handles these queries determines one's perception of reality. Thus, subjective solutions in the above discussion become the foundation to one's personal philosophy.

GOD IS THE INITIATOR AND IN COMPLETE CONTROL OF,
THE TOTAL SUM OF ALL REALITY.

THE RULES OF LIFE

Some philosophers suggest that all human beings intuitively know God. Others propose that humans hold other divine information such as God's rules for human behavior. In this regard, all major civilizations (to one extent or another) have embraced authoritarianism. One interesting factor in civilization has been the relationship of a society and its values. Every society seems to intuitively understand the value of certain rules. Whether or not they accept the same God, they accept common authoritarian laws.

As one would expect, all God centered philosophies could be referred to under the umbrella of 'authoritarianism philosophy.' In fact, such a God centered philosophy was the foundation of the United States of America, as well as the entire Western Civilization. From the earliest of times, we find human society based upon objective laws (God's laws) of right and wrong. These laws may have varied somewhat from one culture to another, but all major societies over the history of the world have held similar laws.

Naturally, the Judaic Ten Commandments come to mind. Of course the Jews had other laws, but the *Ten Commandments* are usually considered to be the foundation of their culture. In abbreviated form, they are:

1. You may worship no other god than me.
2. You must not make yourselves any idols (or any graven image).
3. You shall not use the name of Jehovah your God irreverently, (or, use the name of the Lord your God to swear falsely).
4. Observe the Sabbath as a holy day.
5. Honor your father and mother.
6. You must not murder.
7. You must not commit adultery.
8. You must not steal.
9. You must not lie. (Or, you must not give false testimony in court).
10. You must not be envious of your neighbor's house, or want to sleep with his wife, etc. (be covetous of others).[3]

Christians have a different directive than other theologies, but suffice it to say the Christian doctrine is in agreement with the above Ten Commandments.

As one might assume from the authoritative religions, i.e., Judaism, Christianity and Islam, that the Muslims would hold similar beliefs. Mohammed taught there are five simple rules to live by. The *Five Important Rules* are:

1. Believe in Allah, and Mohammed, His Prophet.

FROM THE EARLIEST OF TIMES, WE FIND HUMAN SOCIETY BASED UPON OBJECTIVE LAWS (GOD'S LAWS) OF RIGHT AND WRONG.

2. Pray five times each day.
3. Be kind to the poor and give alms.
4. Keep the Fasts during the Month of Fasts.
5. Make the yearly pilgrimage to Mecca, the Holy City.[4]

All but one of these laws might be thought of as amendments to rule number one of the Ten Commandments. However, these rules can be considered over and above the Ten Commandments, as Mohammed understood their importance. As a matter of fact, Moses (the recipient of the Ten Commandments) is considered a prophet in the Jewish, Christian and Islamic beliefs. Actually the main differences in the various understandings of God through these three authoritative religions rests in the personalities of God. The *Islamic* understanding is of a strong autocratic Allah or God. The *Jewish* YHWH is a vengeful and jealous, but forgiving God. The Christian God is more sophisticated, represented in three distinct forms. But, the *Christian* God seems also to be more loving, accented by the concept that He is our Father in heaven.

Moral rules and a deep reverence for God would most certainly be expected in these authoritative religions. However, there are other popular religions which are not considered authoritarian. This grouping would include the *Eastern* religions. So, we might ask, do the Eastern religions follow this same authoritative pattern? Compare the Ten Commandments to the following *Buddha's Five Commands* of *Uprightness* (abbreviated):

1. Do not kill.
2. Do not steal.
3. Do not lie.
4. Do not commit adultery.
5. Do not become intoxicated at any time.[5]

Consider *Jainism's Five Commandments of the Soul* (abbreviated):

1. Do not kill any living thing, or hurt any living thing by word, thought, or deed.
2. Do not steal.
3. Do not lie.
4. Do not live an unchaste life and never become intoxicated.
5. Do not covet or desire anything.[6]

Because both the Buddhist and the Jainist are to some degree agnostic, they do not have specific rules related to a god. However, they are reverent to all beliefs in God. Furthermore, the rules they live by do express principles of life found in the authoritative religions.

As for the Hindu religion, it is hard to set *Hindu* beliefs to one group of rules because there are so many sects. However, in general, Hindu sects have a devout reverence for (their understanding of) truth. They have a belief in the sacredness of life and an opposition to murder. This reverence toward life applies even to the animal world. For comparison, the Taittiriya Upanishad teaches Hindus to "speak the truth, practice virtue (dharma), and treat mother and father, teacher and guest, as gods."[7] Furthermore, the Hindus have a high regard for the "heroic and chaste life."[8] Hindu beliefs are therefore loosely based upon these same objective rules.

If we consider those religions of the past which are rarely practiced today we tend to find many of these same patterns. As examples, The Egyptian Book of the Dead and the Babylonian Code of Hammurabi hold similar spiritual laws.[9]

C. S. Lewis alluded to this truth (all mankind intuitively knows God's laws) with a statement in his book *Mere Christianity:*

I know that some people say the idea of a Law of Nature or decent behavior known to all men is unsound, because different civilizations and different ages have had quite different moralities.

But, this is not true. There have been differences between their moralities, but these have never amounted to anything like a total difference. If anyone will take the trouble to compare the moral teaching of, say, the ancient Egyptians, Babylonians, Hindus, Chinese, Greeks and Romans, what will really strike him will be how very like they are to each other and to our own.[10]

Virtually all societies were based on these absolute rules. Without exception, all great societies abided by that which C. S. Lewis and others have referred to as the 'Law of Nature.' Humans recognized moral absolutes. However, absolutes presuppose an antithesis, (right infers there is a wrong). Therefore, humans thought in terms of right and wrong. All human activity was either right or wrong. Furthermore, Lewis made divisions in the virtues of man. Cardinal virtues are those held by all civilized peoples. These virtues are prudence, temperance, justice, and fortitude.[11] We will continue to examine this human intuitive knowledge in other chapters, especially in references to the studies of Carl G. Jung and Joseph Campbell. (I refer to my chapter on Myths, Dreams, Symbols and Religion.) The communality of these social relationships (i.e. rights and wrongs) suggest a common and supernatural source for general human law, a source which communicates with the human soul.

Around the turn of the century, philosophical man began to ignore his obvious common knowledge, including the intuitive rule book, his 'conscience,' given to him by some a priori source. (A priori refers to knowledge supplied through the mind independent of experience). There was a self induced 'evolution' of human thought. We find a massive shift from moral order or 'Natural Law' mentality to the destructive pseudo-rationalism of today. We gave up absolute right and wrong and replaced it with human 'choice.' This one gigantic change in human thought must be considered a bench mark in human existence. Science recognizes human cognizance, the process humans use in deliberation, as one measurable distinction between human beings and all other life forms. The implication being: How man asserts his cognizance, determines the type of creature he is. There is a great difference between the cogitative skills of the monkey and the human. However, by the adoption of relativism, the scales of human reason have shifted and we witness the destruction of all human values. The modern application of rationalism proclaims there is individual Truth. Each individual can obtain Truth through human discernment. This corruption of human rational erases absolute Truth (objective right and wrong) in favor of selective Truth (subjective right and wrong, i.e. personal choice). Through this pseudo-rationalism definition of 'Truth' all objectivity has ceased. From a theological basis, rationalism destroyed the concept of sin, for what is sin if there is no absolute Truth? Thus, modern rationalism created a dilemma for philosophical man.

The destructive aspect of modern rationalism was perhaps best described through Frances Schaeffer's "line of despair." Schaffer explained his line of despair by the following, "Notice that I call the line, the line of despair. Above this line we find men living with their romantic notions of absolutes (though with no sufficient logical basis). This side of the line (below the line) all is changed. Man thinks differently concerning truth, and so now for us, more than ever before, a presuppositional apologetic is imperative."[12]

KANT

Though the beginnings of rationalism have been around at least from the 1600's, Schaeffer suggested that the line of despair came to Europe about 1890 and to the U.S. around 1935. Early rationalistic philosophies such as Kant's were placed above the line of despair for they still recognized absolutes. Only after rationalism had matured do we find philosophical man falling below the line. In other words, the line of despair represents the previ-

FURTHERMORE, DIVINE AUTHORITARIANISM IS THE MOST ACCURATE INTERPRETATION OF THE TOTAL OF ALL ANALYTICAL KNOWLEDGE.

ously mentioned change in human thinking. Above the line, human beings thought in terms of right and wrong. In the early 1900's intellectual rationale crossed below this line. Thus, today, society no longer affords absolutes.

Do not confuse the modern understanding of rationalism with rational thinking. Schaeffer warned against such confusion. Rational thought means thinking logical, i.e., within reason. Divine authoritarianism philosophy (God is in charge) embraces rational thought. Furthermore, divine authoritarianism is the most accurate interpretation of the total of all analytical knowledge. According to Schaeffer's proposition, "The line of despair indicates a titanic shift at this present time within the unity of rationalism. Above the line (pre-despair side) men were rationalistic optimists. They believed they could begin with themselves and draw a circle which would encompass all thoughts of life, and life itself, without having to depart from the logic of antithesis. They thought that on their own rationalistically, finite men could find a unity in the total diversity. This is where philosophy stood, prior to our own day. The only real argument between these rationalistic optimists was over the circle that should be drawn, (Kant, Hegel, etc.). One man would draw a circle and say, 'You can live within this circle.' The next man would cross it out and would draw a different circle. The next man would come along and, crossing out the previous circle, draw his own—ad infinitum.[13] Schaeffer concluded, "But at a certain point this attempt to spin out a unified optimistic humanism ceased."[14] It is interesting that Schaeffer found humanism and philosophical rationalism inner changeable because rationalism is the backbone of the humanist movement. Humanism stems from the atheistic compromise; simply stated, God is humanity. Humanity alone can create a human utopia. Therefore, as we evolve and progress we will become 'god.' Though the individual may die humanity lives on. Therefore, "Our worship must be dedicated to humanity. Our hymns must be sung to the highest object of devotion, to a humanity which is a composite of all noble souls from every age."[15] I must reiterate, what value does one give to God?

Schaeffer continued by stating:

In the end (with no absolutes) the philosophers came to the realization that they could not find this unified rationalistic circle (they had no agreement as to what determined truth) and so, departing from the classical methodology of antithesis (good and evil, etc.), they shifted the concept of truth, and modern man was born.

In this way modern man moved under the line of despair. He was

---

HUMANISM STEMS FROM THE ATHEISTIC COMPROMISE; SIMPLY STATED, GOD IS HUMANITY. HUMANITY ALONE CAN CREATE A HUMAN UTOPIA. THEREFORE, AS WE EVOLVE AND PROGRESS WE WILL BECOME 'GOD.'

driven to it against his desire. He remained a rationalist, but he had changed.[16]

Many theological and secular thinkers seem to believe the change in human value was initiated by Darwin's Theory of Evolution. There is no question but what the evolution theory gave great impetus to this erosion of values. However, evolution was not the initial corrosive. Dr. Hugh Ross states the change came with the theories of Immanuel Kant.[17] Kant suggested that a separation existed between knowledge and faith. This separation assumed knowledge was "limited to the phenomenal world."[18] One then would conclude the apparent alternative—the supernatural world could not be understood outside of faith. However, Warren Young reminds us, "Faith is recognized to be the basic assumption to knowing of any kind."[19] Though Kant's theories did bring change, he was a theist addressing this very problem (whether or not there are objective values) in its infancy. Perhaps Voltaire (Francois Marie Arouet, 1694–1778) should be considered as the one who began the move to liberate man from God's Laws, for he was an advocate both of the freedoms of the individual and the ineptness of God. However, previous to him came such rationalists as Benedict Spinoza. Both his concept of God (non-personal) and his belief that evil does not exist, must be considered factors in the change in human perception. The point is, there were many philosophers who brought forth an array of God destructive concepts prior to Darwin's theory. Therefore, a changing of the guard was well in process before Darwin was born.

Despite whom was responsible, there has been a descent of human values. Schaeffer claims it was Hegel who actually was "the door" to this line of despair. Before Hegel's philosophy, man had begun to question objective value. However, humanity still held to conceptual (objective) knowledge in relation to cause and effect. Yet, Hegel proposed human thought developed through a "synthesis." It was this sophistication of the thought process which began to move man away from a belief in simple right and wrong.

Though Hegel may have been the door, it was Soren Kierkegaard who actually crossed "the line of despair" and began the walk downward with his "existentialism" philosophy. A major change in human thought sprang forth through Kierkegaard's search for Truth. Though the despair of his philosophy came from his acceptance of the Hegelian idea of synthesis, it was his search for Truth which set his works apart from those of Hegel and Kant. Kierkegaard's "despair" came from two philosophical positions. The first came in Keirkegaards' concepts of objective and subjective reasoning. Both Kant and Hegel suggest Truth can be obtained through a "balanced blend of direct experience (subjective) and abstract, conceptional (objective) knowledge."[20] Kant and Hegel stated, that both 'subjectivity' and 'objectivity' were valid tools to use in our human search for Truth. Keirkegaard absolutely and totally denied this concept. The path to Truth is not found in objective absolutes, which would include absolute right and wrong, but from an individual sorting through a situation and determining what seems right to him. Kierkegaard's second disastrous step was a logical extension of his first concept. This extension is what became known as a "leap of faith." He concluded Truth is subjective. Therefore, "faith" is the essence of religion. It is important to note, Kierkegaard did not argue against the existence of objective Truth, only that man is unable to understand objective evidence because man is partial. Thus, Truth is subjective to human reason. I cannot emphasize the impact of his position too strongly! It is a misconception which spells disaster! Keirkegaard flatly denied any suggestion that objectivity could play a roll in the discovery of Truth. The most amazing thing is Keirkegaard was a devout Christian man. I think he was misguided, but he evidently had a burning passion for God. His whole philosophy seems to be built around his attitude toward the human to God (man looking to God) relationship. Moreover, his "leap of faith" concept may have been based upon his reverence for the human decision to accept Jesus as Lord and God. If this was the reasoning behind his famous "leap of faith" doctrine, then Keirkegaard was a bit of a romantic and certainly out of touch with the human situation. Christianity is not an irrational or illogical choice. I would suggest to you that Keirkegaard was a Christian because he was brought up a Christian. Had he been brought up as an Inca Indian, he might have taken that same "leap of faith" in proclaiming humanity lives on the back of a giant tortoise. I do not mean to suggest (as do some) that Kierkegaard was not a faithful dedicated Christian man with the high ideals and values which go along with Christianity. Kierkegaard had dedicated his life to being the servant of his Lord Jesus Christ. Walter Kaufmann hails Kierkegaard as "a Protestant's Protestant."[21] However, the falsity in his philosophical line of thinking is obvious. Objectivity should play a roll in the human search for Truth. The risk in trusting human perception is documented by a historical record of false impressions and human disasters. Our understanding of the nature of man confirms that virtually every human mental concept exists in a state of constant change. The history of philosophy is a great example of our human frailties and misconceptions. We have alluded to these frailties with Schaeffer's illustration of philosophers crossing out each other's circles and drawing new ones. Only when we accept objective Truth do we find any historical consistency or stability in philosophical inquiries. It is our subjectivity which leads humanness down a path of ruin and decay. One of my concerns about Christians such as Kierkegaard is how they seem to build their

---

KIERKEGAARD'S SECOND DISASTROUS STEP WAS A LOGICAL EXTENSION
OF HIS FIRST CONCEPT. THIS EXTENSION IS WHAT BECAME KNOWN
AS A "LEAP OF FAITH."

whole theological center on intuitive awareness and personal interpretation of spiritual matters. By doing so they are not as prepared and, thus, not as strong in their theology as are Christians who search for validity in all things including the objectiveness of the laws of science, the facts of history, etc. I suggest the Biblical model of knowledge supports knowing God through both subjective and objective input. As a matter of fact, Christians are directed by their God to seek and worship the entirety of God (Father, Son and Holy Spirit) with hearts, souls and minds. In truth, Christians are to worship God with the entirety of their being. The human body is God's temple.

One problem that today's Christian movement holds for a casual observer is that Christianity seems to be based upon emotions and not realism. Emotional worship of God is very important. However, many worshipers are filled with emotional feelings, yet seem to have no understanding of the factualness of the Christian message. It is plain to many observers that worshipers can be manipulated into believing and acting as the 'teacher' wills. Scriptures can be twisted and reinterpreted to mean whatever the 'church' leadership wishes. This is a real ecumenical problem. For an example, I know people who have left the Christian Church because a minister repeatedly preached that if one 'believes' enough, and gives enough money, he or she will become rich. To the contrary, monetary wealth is not a high priority in Christendom and such deceit is devastating to the Christian movement. Yet, when humans begin to intellectually understand the awesomeness of God and the factualness of God and His Will, then a reverence for God must follow. Worshipful emotions become much richer and more valid. Such knowledge allows us to better understand the authoritative nature of God's Will and the value it holds for our lives. However, it is this very experience which Kierkegaard's theories poisoned for much of modern society.

Unfortunately, Kierkegaard's existentialism did not just live and die on the desks of the intellectuals. Once it had been examined, accepted and expounded upon, existentialism became a great force. When a stone plunges into a lake there are ripples that rush out from the point of impact and flow through the waters. So was the effect of existentialism. Once accepted, it created ripples which were to be felt throughout society; first in philosophy, then in art, next came music, then general culture and finally theology. The existential line of despair made its way throughout all American life.

ONE OF MY CONCERNS ABOUT CHRISTIANS SUCH AS KIERKEGAARD IS HOW THEY SEEM TO BUILD THEIR WHOLE THEOLOGICAL CENTER ON INTUITIVE AWARENESS AND PERSONAL INTERPRETATION OF SPIRITUAL MATTERS

(KANT)

PHILOSOPHY > ART > MUSIC > CULTURE > THEOLOGY

←————————————————————————————————→

(KIERKEGAARD)

↕

EXISTENTIALISM

A good description of the religious accommodation of Kierkegaard's view is found in *Philosophy Of Religion Contemporary Perspectives*. It states:

> *Truth for existentialism consists in knowing it to be true in one's existence. We do not know truth by speculating, reflecting, thinking; we become the truth. This is not to deny that there is objective truth. Many times we must choose and take a risk. Kierkegaard has made this point famous by his description of the 'leap of faith.' Thought only gives us possibilities. As long as we think about someone, something, or some action, we remain in the realm of possibility. 'Truth as subjectivity' is choosing one possibility and making it actual in our existence. So while the possibility may be objectively uncertain, subjectively one is in the truth. Atheism or theism is just such an objective uncertainty. To choose either to be true is a leap of faith in which one becomes the truth of that choice. But there is always the doubt that one may be objectively wrong. But choose we must! For not to choose is itself a choice!*[22]

Sounds sincere enough, or perhaps innocent enough, but very misleading. A "leap of faith" in the understanding of Kierkegaard's philosophy might better be described as a lack of faith or a search for faith. There are many solid reasons for believing in God from both empirical and a priori standpoints and in Christ from both historical and empirical standpoints. This book just scratches the surface. Every flower is adorned in a glorious coat of beauty. This is a natural event happening millions of times on the same mountain side. The wild flowers teach us about our Creator. Yet, we do not take time to appreciate their beauty nor contemplate their splendor. Man should recognize such natural wonders as human blessings—love letters from God to mankind, because only human minds seem to realize the world's natural beauty. This is objective Truth in empirical knowledge. Natural beauty is only for God's stewards to see and ponder. Yes, man alone sees and understands such wonders. It is through these blessings that we realize even the flowers of the field praise Abba God and confirm His love for the world, but most assuredly, for all mankind. Humanity does not take giant leaps of faith into some dark abyss of nothingness. We do not hope on chance. The sound position on Truth would seem to be more in line with Christian realism which proposes that reality is both natural and supernatural. Furthermore, there is a "revealed knowledge as well as a natural knowledge."[23] C. S. Lewis agreed with this statement in his general discussion of Christian faith. He stated, "I am not asking anyone to accept Christianity if his best reasoning tells him that the weight of the evidence is against it. That is not the point at which Faith comes in."[24] However, it is by faith which we accept and react to facts. One of Lewis' illustrations is of a boy learning to swim. This made a special impression on me because I have been a swimming instructor. Therefore, I feel compelled to make some additions to Lewis' comments. He begins, "...take a boy learning to swim. His reason knows perfectly well that an unsupported human body will not necessarily sink in water: He has seen dozens of people float and swim. But the whole question is whether he will be able to go on believing this when the instructor takes away his hand and leaves him unsupported in the water . . ." I find this comment on faith even more relevant to adult students. Adults are much more logical students. They are more aware of the facts. Physiologically they are swimmers. Adults know all they have to do is follow instructions and they will swim. Yet, adults are much harder to teach because, despite the facts, they have a greater fear of water. Unless they have had a serious problem (like nearly drowning), then this reaction is an illogical fear. Ask any YMCA or Red Cross swimming instructor, adult 'non-swimmers' generally have an unrealistic fear of water. As a point of interest, I learned a great way to teach adults to swim. The secret is to rid them of their fear; then swimming does become a natural activity. The first thing I always do with an adult is put a towel on the bottom of the shallow end of the swimming pool. Then, I have the adult stand over the towel, reach down, put their head in the water, open their eyes and pick up the towel. Sometimes it is quite entertaining to watch the extent students will go to pick up the towel without getting their heads wet. However, they must reach for it over and over until they can reach down, put their head in the water, look at the towel and pick it up. I will not let them do anything else until they can pick up the towel. After they can do this without visible stress, they are very easy to teach. You might ask, why am I so dogmatic about this procedure? I found it fruitless to have adults try any other exercises (even blowing bubbles) until they have bridged their unfounded fear with a "faith" in their ability to conquer water. All they

---

HUMANITY DOES NOT TAKE GIANT LEAPS OF FAITH
INTO SOME DARK ABYSS OF NOTHINGNESS.

need is faith to do what they know their bodies are factually able to do. I can continue to list example after example of situations where we know the facts, but need faith to act on the facts. Such is our faith in God. Faith in God is not the "leap of faith" Kierkegaard theorized. Faith in God is that understanding which allows us to obey God. Faith is what allows humans to 'live a godly life,' to trust God and take those steps in life God would have us take. Faith is following His example. Faith is picking oneself up after failing and believing God will be there for us even if no one else is.

Perhaps we should understand Kierkegaard's personality and some of the situations in his life which might have affected his thinking. There were several events which are said to have had a profound effect on Kierkegaard. The first formed through his relationship with his father. Kierkegaard came from a deeply religious Christian home. He developed a strong love and respect for both his God and his father. However, he became somewhat disillusioned when he learned that his father had not and did not lead a perfect life. His father was a 'sinner,' as are all human beings (with the exception of Jesus Christ). Though Kierkegaard continued to walk in the light of God, his disillusionment with his father continued to haunt him throughout his life.

A second event hurt him deeply. He fell in love with a young woman named Regine Olsen. Kierkegaard was a man of honor and principle. However, he was not a virgin and was too ashamed to tell his bride to be. Yet he was too honorable a man to marry Ms. Olsen without telling her of his own sin (some might disagree whether or not such a position was one of honor or cowardliness or self flagellation). However, his solution was painful. He simply gave up the woman he loved. Reportedly he carried a broken heart throughout his life. His disappointment in these events seems to be reflected in his philosophy, for Kierkegaard appears to be a man searching for perfect love. This sentiment is obvious in his following writing:

> *What I really lack is to be clear in my mind what I am to do, not what I am to know, except in so far as a certain understanding must precede every action. The thing is to understand myself, to see what God really wishes me to do; the thing is to find a truth which is true for me, to find the idea for which I can live and die. What would be the use of discovering so-called objective truth, of working through all the systems of philosophy and of being able if required, to review them all and show up the inconsistencies within each system; - what good would it do me to be able to develop a theory of the state and combine all the details into a single whole, and so construct a world in which I did not live, but only held up to the view of others; - what good would it do me to be able to explain the meaning of Christianity if it had no deeper significance for me and for my life; - what good would*

it do me if truth stood before me, cold and naked, not caring whether I recognized her or not, and producing in me a shudder of fear rather than a trusting devotion? I certainly do not deny that I still recognize an imperative of understanding and that through it one can work upon men, but it must be taken up into my life, and that is what I now recognize as the most important thing. That is what my soul longs after, as the African desert thirsts for water. That is what I lack, and that is why I am left standing like a man who has rented a house and gathered all the furniture and household things together, but has not yet found the beloved with whom to share the joys and sorrows of his life.[25]

Such a passionate man was Kierkegaard. However, a problem looms. Though he was a man of great passion and a man of romantic fervor, he was a man of weak fabric. He was easily hurt and he found it difficult to bounce back. Thus, the backbone of his philosophy was 'man exists.' Nothing else is certain. We do not know if God exists or if life is meaningful or if man has purpose. Left to itself, this one declaration is a despairingly bleak foundation. 'Man exists' raises fears and questions and insecurities.[26] However, 'man exists' is the backbone of our philosophy today. Kierkegaard, a man of weakness, set the foundation for intellectual thought in the modern world! Kierkegaard, who could not deal with the fact that his father was human and therefore subject to human indiscretions—Kierkegaard, who could not bring himself to discuss his own past indiscretions with the woman he loved and thus chose to solve his dilemma by giving up the love of his life, was the founder of existentialism. (This does not mean Kierkaggard appeared weak to his colleagues, however, he obviously did not handle life's challenges in a healthy manner). This weak man's solution to life became the philosophy of intellectuals and instructors in universities and schools of learning.

Existentialism became the foundational concept of other philosophers like Heidegger and Nietzsche. Many viewed man as nonsensical, having no reason to live except to die. Thus, the existential philosophy became the basis for Humanism—the philosophy of atheism and the foundation for Utopian concepts such as Nazism (Hitler was an ardent fan of Nietzsche) and Communism (Marx was perhaps the epitome apostle for Humanism). Through the "transcendence" of man (Heidegger's concept conveying man's continuance to rise and to become) we will evolve. From the hopelessness of this existentialism came the philosophical basis of modern thought. Kierkaggard's solution to life became the philosophy by which school children in the United

...WE THE PEOPLE OF THE UNITED STATES PLUMMETED BELOW THE LINE OF DESPAIR AND WE ENTERED INTO A WORLD OF DEGENERATING MORALS.

States would learn to look at life and deal with problems. Yet, when his philosophy became the model philosophy for our modern society, we the people of the United States plummeted below the line of despair and we entered into a world of degenerating morals.

Today we live in a society gripped with existential confusion. We need a circle drawer, one who knows what behavior is best for humanity. But, who is wise enough to be the circle drawer? Who even knows how to define the terms needed to have a circle? Take the meaning of 'ethic.' Ethics are defined in various ways. As a matter of fact, the discussion of 'what determines ethics' goes back to Greek philosophies and to the most ancient theologies. Many major philosophers have worked on this definition problem and have found it very perplexing and even elusive. As an example, Immanuel Kant after writing, *Groundwork Of The Metaphysic Of Morals,* discovered weaknesses in his theories and thus revised his concepts in his work, *Religion Within The Limits Of Reason Alone.*[27]

If we could solve this circle drawer problem, then perhaps we could determine an objective law. However, determining an objective law is only a beginning. To illustrate, let us assume the existence of God's Law. Other questions naturally follow. Such questions might be: If man has an intuitive understanding of objective law then how is that law transcendent? What is the extent of human comprehension? To what degree can humans interpret their intuitive understanding? What is the relationship between personal freedom and the human obligation to abide by objective law? These problems cannot even be addressed by existentialism and therefore they create havoc within existential morality. Yet, such difficulties are totally eliminated by authoritarianism.

The major problem of existentialism for our modern society is not which philosopher will draw the circle, but the value of the rules. If we define ethics as standards—a universal and systematic set of rules understood by all (whether God sent or not), then we now live in a valueless society. This modern ethical void is quite obvious and problematic. To illustrate, let us consider the United States of America's current sexual ethics . . . there seems to be no rules for sexual conduct. Even child pornography is becoming acceptable. As a matter of fact, the U.S. government has often sponsored what (I suspect) the majority of its citizens would consider 'child porn' through the National Endowment of the Arts. The value of 'ill-tasteful' art has become a continuous battle for the National Endowment of the Arts. Modernists often rationalize away valued absolutes by a number of expressions we have all heard. Examples might be, "Times have changed. We cannot expect people to live by old standards, for we live in a modern world." But, is time really a factor in determining a moral standard? Moreover, ethics have been vulgarized by complicating ideas such as 'situation ethics.' Thus, ethical descriptions like 'value' and 'valueless' have lost their definitive nature and seem to flow into one vast stream of uncertainty. Some of today's most relevant statements concerning morals and values are, "You decide what is right for you; each to his own; different strokes for different folks." Actually, such a rationalistic view of morality is based in spiritual Paganism and has been expressed quite well by both the Greek and Roman mythological gods and goddesses. This direction of moral expression, if carried to its logical conclusion, bares the fundamental values of Satanism. To contrast the two lines of thought, the authoritative religions such as Judaism, Christianity and Islam are based upon the *authority of God's law or natural law.* In contrast, Satanism could be described as a *defilement of natural law.* Whether we accept Satan as actual or not, for all practical purposes Satan does exist. Satanism, a cousin of Wicka, advocates the antithesis to the traditional concept of absolute values. Thus, what is good is evil and what is evil is good. Instead of the Christian concept; 'love one another,' the Satanist advocates, 'there are no limits to using another for self gratification.' Furthermore, if the existentialist is right and there are no absolute values then there are absolutely no limits on behavior.

Because of this growing anti-ethical behavior (no limits on behavior) in modern society and the related destruction it brings, even many atheistic existentialists understand the need for absolutes. However, they have procrastinated on this problem by integrating their only standard—evolution. In essence, man is in a state of evolution which will culminate in a (before mentioned) utopia. Guided and acceptable human behavior will also evolve. Therefore, behaviorists will form absolutes (in the traditions of B.F. Skinner) and thus define human happiness. Yet, through all of this, we still do not know which behaviorist will draw the circle. We do not know who will decide what is 'correct' behavior. We have seen these behavioral pressures through political correctness. It is fashionable and thus acceptable to have extramarital affairs, but it is vulgar to wear furs, smoke or collect guns. But, to what extent? How far do we go with extramarital affairs and if we cannot wear furs can we eat meat? The answer to these questions vary depending on the circle drawer you ask. A 'Hollywood Starlet' and renown singer is an environmental advocate, but flies around the country and world in her private jet. (Private jets are big polluters compared to commercial travel). Obviously, she does not feel obligated to the environmental standards she places on everyone else. So, do we live by her political correct words and not consider her lifestyle? Who then do we follow?

It is this revolutionary factor (the question, Is there limits?) which destroys the existential thought process. It is a factor which pushes man below

---

SOME OF TODAY'S MOST RELEVANT STATEMENTS CONCERNING MORALS AND VALUES ARE, "YOU DECIDE WHAT IS RIGHT FOR YOU; EACH TO HIS OWN; DIFFERENT STROKES FOR DIFFERENT FOLKS."

the line of despair. The negativity is not in question, for its negativism is well understood even by the friends of existentialism. Jean Wahl's book, *A Short History Of Existentialism,* points to the ravage of existential thinking. In the following quote, Wahl begins by announcing the existential rejection of God and the chaos resulting from this rejection. In fact, notice Wahl's final point, a conformation that man only lives to die.

> *Obviously, we have abandoned any classical scheme, any hierarchy of realities at the top of which is God, the most perfect Being. Now we see only existents, flung for no reason upon the earth, and essences are merely constructions from existences. No doubt one may seek out essences of material things and implements, but there can be no essence of an existent individual, of man. Here we see most clearly the essence - if we may so speak! - of the philosophy of existence, as contrasted to nearly all classical philosophy, from Plato to Hegel, in which existence always derives from essence.*
>
> *The existence of man, this being, flung into the world, is essentially finite. Limited by death, his existence is a 'being for death'. . .* [28]

Assuming there is no God, then the existential view of life is correct. If there is no God, there is no grand plan. There is only a cosmic metamorphosis of no meaning, except to the selfish self. Therefore, Hitler was right (and so was Nietzsche). Take all that you can get and eliminate anyone who gets in the way. Take the football jacket the boy is wearing and shoot him if he protests too much. Do the wildest sexual acts with whomever you please—for love and marriage have no meaning, nor is there any merit in values. No meaning exists except self gratification and that too will pass.

However, assuming there is God, then everything exists for God. God and God's Will are the only truly important concepts in (or out of) the universe, because without them (God and God's Will) life has no meaning.

I suggest our society (the United States Of America and the freedom for which it stands) is on the decline because society has rejected God, God's Laws and thus, God's Will. And, this is not a trend limited to the United States. Peter Brierley, a church attendance specialist, has predicted "the Christian church in Britain will be dead and buried within 40 years time."[29]

Yet, we can expect to find a much greater emphasis on the eastern religions in our society, for they are existential in nature. They allow man to live by his own rationalizations and ignore the Will of the Creator. However, we are also witnessing extremists, of the authoritative religion of Islam, con-

I SUGGEST OUR SOCIETY (THE UNITED STATES OF AMERICA AND THE FREEDOM FOR WHICH IT STANDS) IS ON THE DECLINE BECAUSE SOCIETY HAS REJECTED GOD, GOD'S LAWS AND THUS, GOD'S WILL.

trol an alarming segment of the Islamic culture. These radical Muslims seem to have lost the objective nature of "thou shall not murder" and are intent on wiping out alternative beliefs through terrorism and mass murder. The extremists have been successful in exterminating most of the Christians and Jews in several middle eastern countries. Now, they seem to be attacking Americans on American soil. Again, the question is, who draws the circle?

CHAPTER 10

COMPARATIVE RELIGION

Everyone knows GOD.

I have presented empirical evidence which supports the proposition that God created the universe, and everything in the universe. I find it extremely provocative that a growing number of distinguished physical scientists admit the laws of physics and other avenues of science imply God's existence. Yet, many scientists question who God is. Some do not see any physical reasons to believe in a personal God, so they follow Einstein's alternative by suggesting God may be a dynamic super-force. They cannot deny the logical need for something grand, such as a mega-force or mega-factor or mega-thing which, up to now, has been unexplainable by modern science. Virtually all see the need for God, whether or not they want to admit God's existence. The problem is that, in the USA, God is not 'politically correct.' The United States Supreme Court has determined that God's existence is not scientific. Yet, if God is real, as the natural evidence seems to indicate, then God's existence is indeed 'scientific.' If this is the case, then the courts are wrong and our entire society is warped.

It is also interesting to find a number of psychologists who do see evidence of a 'personal God,' but do not find a need for a cosmic God. Many consider God to be a symbolic 'supreme archetype' (mental representation). Both the physical mega-force and psychic archetype are considered scientific in nature and acceptable conclusions in their perspective disciplines. Yet, many theorists deny the obvious: combine the findings of both fields and there is profound evidence for the God of the Bible. It seems reasonable to think that combining these conclusions would give a more definitive understanding of God—a more complete image. Generally, scientists are centered in their own field of study and do not realize the significance of the 'big picture.' Others in the scholastic world are totally lost. They appear to be the political puppets of 'intellectualism.' This is an arrogant, self destructive, egocentric position. I submit to you my premise on this point: considering the whole of all evidence: all physical and psychological input indicates God 'the Creator' is both real

---

THE PROBLEM IS THAT, IN THE USA, GOD IS NOT 'POLITICALLY CORRECT.'

and personal in nature. Therefore, He is intellectual and has a Will for our lives which effects the intuitive nature of man.

If God is a personal being, and God does have a Will, then is there a path to His presence? Can we form a relationship with the Creator? Do all religions lead to the same end or is there a 'True' religion and how do we recognize or distinguish it from all of the others?

Like most people who seek to know God, I have held common theological views about the different world religions: Religion A was devised to rip people off; Religion B is sincere in man, but was devised by Satan; Religion C is not really a religion, but a philosophy, etc. I must again state my personal belief: The man, Jesus of Nazareth, was and is both God and the Savior of mankind. One day, all of humanity will humbly bow and every tongue will confess Jesus Christ is Lord over all which has been or will be.

Yet, if I consider religion either from an all inclusive whole, or from the 'one on one' comparative religion mode, I seem to focus on a number of interesting universal understandings. In fact, some of these similarities are quite prominent. Let us step away from our personal theologies for a moment and take a philosophical look at religion.

Let us begin with a closer look at my premise: *all physical and psychological/sociological evidence indicate God 'the Creator' is both real and personal in nature.* We looked at much of the physical evidence in section 1. Now let us consider the psychological/social evidence. In accordance with said premise, I have certain presuppositions. I suggest most of what we 'understand' in academia related to early history is predicated by presumptive scholars who mold facts to fit their understanding of past existence. Therefore, much truth about ancient religions has been lost. Because of this presumptive view of history, we may have a false understanding about human spiritual development.

As you can see, my writing will be somewhat controversial. Had I wished to be safe, I would have limited my discussion to the 'here and now' and I would not have irritated academia. I would have stated how each of the modern world religions differ from one another and how all of them are similar. Fortunately, there are many books which do just that. Therefore, my intention is to be a little more probing and profound than just a regurgitation of material which is already easily obtainable. I am sure there is more to the relevance to the total of all world religions than the academic sentiment, i.e., a bunch of folksy myths passed down from generation to generation. I intend to express several possibilities.

Finally, I hope to point to some of the fallacies in modern man's common perceptions. These are perceptions which seem to have been purposely shaped by the arrogance of our deviated intellectualism. The most notable misconception is 'all religions lead to the same end.' Let me quickly point out some of the fallacies of this line of thinking with the logic of R. C. Sproul. He inquires:

> *How can Buddhism be true when it denies the existence of a personal God and at the same time Christianity be true when it affirms the existence of a personal God? Can there be a personal God and not be a personal God at the same time and in the same relationship? Can Orthodox Judaism be right when it denies life after death and Christianity be equally right when it affirms life after death? Can classical Islam have a valid ethic that endorses the killing of infidels while at the same time the Christian ethic of loving your enemies be equally valid?[1]*

Immediately Sproul has destroyed the New Age concept that all religions are equally valid. We know there are many similarities in the world's religions, yet there are also some real inconsistencies and differences. So, what is valid and where did all of these religions come from?

In pursuit of my stated premise that all physical and psychological evidence indicate God the Creator is both real and personal in nature, I present to you *two intriguing theories* or, perhaps more accurately, speculations about the origins of these religions.

THEORY #1

Noah did survive 'The Great Flood.' He stepped out of the Ark with the true revelations of God, perhaps to include writings or hieroglyphics from the first men (Adam or his kin). As 'true religion' was spread, different aspects would lose meaning in one area of the world, while other aspects would gain strength or even find new meanings.

Let me stress that the true importance of the Great Flood story is the message of the text. This is a profound narrative with deep significance to the human soul or psyche. In fact, this is perhaps the classic morality story. It is not so important that we find the skeleton of an ancient artifact. To find the physical remains of the Ark, yet miss the wisdom within the related Tanakh (Old Testament) narrative, would be a tragic disparity. It is the 'meaning' that validates the concept, not the remains of an artifact. To illustrate the importance of 'meaning' in historical fact, consider an unrelated event. We know that Jerusalem was destroyed by Roman troops in 70 AD. However, despite this solid fact, those who do not accept Jesus Christ's divinity find it most difficult to accept Jesus' prophetic warning. Thirty plus years earlier, Jesus prophesied that Jerusalem would be destroyed. In like manner, if we found an 'Ark,' could we not say the 'Great Flood Story' was only a primitive man's explanation for a natural disaster?

If, instead, we consider the ancient symbolic inferences, and depth of spirituality intertwined within this narrative, we will discover a magnificent work of art. The psychodynamics of the Noah account hold deep psychological and spiritual revelations wrapped in paradoxical undertones. Of course, the predominate message is one of Divine Authoritarianism, i.e., that God is in total control of His creation. He can conceive and destroy as He pleases. Nonetheless, the great conflict revolves around a continuing battle between good and evil. Not only do we find evil personified in man before the flood, but we also find humans returning to evil after the flood. In fact, in the end times, humans will have chosen evil, over good, even to the extent of those immoral days which necessitated 'the Great Flood' (God's physical expression of His repugnance for evil). Implied within are the awesome powers encompassed within God's creation and the human vulnerability to these powers. Other symbolic themes include the natural relationship between God and man or, more specifically, the loving communion between God and man. Also expressed is a somewhat similar though lessor relationship between human beings and animals. Furthermore, we become aware that all humans belong to one human family with a common ancestor. There is a wholeness of life, an inclusion of all things from the great to the small. Enveloped are environmental, physical and spiritual connections we have yet to fully understand. Finally, there is a righteousness in the creation which seems to justify our journey in time. All existence has great purpose and we humans must continue to accomplish our part of that purpose for the fulfillment of creation. Whether or not we find an Ark, this story is significant to the human quest for meaning.

The second theory has actually been introduced through the last chapter. However, I will go into much greater depth.

THEORY #2

The major world religions were products of a universal doctrine and 'natural law' which has been stated in a variety of ways. That law essentially declares, *'mankind innately knows God.'* This innate understanding would include the knowledge humans acquire in dreams and relay to others through myths.

I realize the controversial nature of these two speculations. However, I think human knowledge blatantly points toward both a world wide flood and a God-centered collective unconscious or awareness. Therefore, I feel the above two theories better explain the historical puzzle than do our ever changing and illogical institutionalized concepts. With this brief explanation I begin my theories.

CHAPTER 11

THEORY 1
NOAH SURVIVED THE FLOOD
WITH TRUE REVELATIONS
OF GOD

(Writing about the Jewish historical position) " . . . not only is Noah the first real man in Jewish history: his story foreshadows important elements in Jewish religion."[1]

A rocklike formation in the shape of a huge ship rests on the side of Mount Mahser Dagi (the Doomsday Mountain) of the Ararat range. Some theorist suggest this object was buried by mud for thousands of years. Amazingly, this object rose from its burial—a symbolic resurrection. It seems as if the 'ship' waited until a special time to be discovered and that time is now. A number of explorers have proposed that this may be 'Noah's Ark.' If this is the legendary 'Ark,' it does not have the rectangular 'box' shape characterized on television programs. Instead, it is shaped like an ancient Egyptian watercraft similar to the one used by Elizabeth Taylor in the movie "Cleopatra," only much larger! Quite possibly, the 'Ark' had anchor and drogue stones similar to the ancient Egyptian vessels. (Drogue stones were large rocks with a carved hole near the top to run rope through. Drogue stones were used to steady a ship.) This 'ark' find is not a 'hearsay' or an allusive sighting as the more popular television version seems to be. Amazing pictures of this 'Ark,' anchor and drogue stones can be seen in several books; among them are Charles Berlitz's work, *The Lost Ship of Noah: In Search of The Ark at Ararat,* David Fasold's *The Ark of Noah,* as well as a summarized version by Ron Wyatt, *Discovered: Noah's Ark.*

So positive is the belief in the existence of the Ark that a Turkish National Park has been dedicated to the vessel. This, too, is very impressive since the Muslim faith (the major religion of the Turkish people), claims the Ark did not come to rest in Turkey or Iraq, but Arabia.

When discussing the Ark, I am almost always amused and amazed by one perpetual question: "How would they know the boat found on Mount Ararat was Noah's?" Why does this question amaze me? It comes from the question's emphasis, because whether or not it is Noah's Ark does not matter. If, indeed, this is a boat it could be Bob's boat, but *someone's* ancient craft may have sailed to a high surface of the mountain range mentioned by the Bible as the 'Ark's' resting place. And, such evidence would substantiate the myth—a flood of Biblical proportions did occur around the Ararat range. Albeit, there are a number of potential sites which satisfy the Biblical criteria and, thus, should be discussed. However, for brevity, I will concentrate on the Magser Dagi find.

If, and/or when there is verification of such an Ark, many feel the remains would have a dramatic influence on humanity. Dr. John Morris of the Institute for Creation Research states, "The significance of finding the Ark would extend into the personal lives of each one of us, for we would be reminded of God's past method of purging the world of sinful people, and our attention would be focused on God's promise of another judgment in the very near future."[2]

THE PROBLEM

Many scholars and theologians alike question the authenticity of this Mahser Dagi find. I must add, they have good reasons for their caution. The experts honestly do not know what this boat-like object is, or how it got on the Ararat mountain range, or how it got its' Biblical proportions, or how it became shaped like an ancient ship.

Yet, the shape is indeed startling. It is interesting to note the late explorer David Fasold was a 'marine salvage expert.' Yet, after visiting this object he declared, "Anyone who can't recognize this as a shipwreck either wouldn't know Noah's Ark if he was standing on it, or should have his 'theological cataracts' removed!."[3] This conspicuous resolution resonates in the statement of a Muslim witness named Resit who, in viewing the site at an earlier time, is reported to have commented, "I can recognize a ship when I see one."[4] I must note, Fasold later had reservations about this artifact, not because of the shape, but because of the quality of finds at other 'Ark' sites and perhaps as a result of growing personal problems between Fasold and Ron Wyatt. Mahser Dagi is considered Wyatt's site.

Perhaps even more relevant to the obscurity of this boat-shaped object is that it is politically incorrect. It is not the kind of Ark the experts would have hoped to find. Any archaeologist who proclaimed this object the 'Ark of Noah' would sustain political fallout from both atheists and most of the religious community. Perhaps this likelihood alone explains why the find is not often discussed on television. In the first place, an atheist would deny any Ark exists, because an ancient ark does not fit well with the humanist

IF, AND/OR WHEN THERE IS VERIFICATION OF SUCH AN ARK, MANY FEEL THE REMAINS WOULD HAVE A DRAMATIC INFLUENCE ON HUMANITY.

understanding of history. The Noahian Flood is especially damaging to all popular evolutionary models.

Secondly, the Biblical statement of the Ark's amazing size is hard for a skeptic to believe. Consider the Biblical proportions, "Make it 450 feet long, 75 feet wide, and 45 feet high."[5] Frankly, an ancient boat of such size would suggest a divine architect. The Ark may well have been the largest wooden ship ever built. Modern man holds no concept of the magnitude of such a feat. We must remember Noah had no computers to check the buoyancy of his design. He had no knowledge of what the most advantageous length, weight and height ratios of a ship might be. Furthermore, he did not have the sophisticated ship building tools we use today. He was a primitive man living in a primitive age. Frederick A. Filby explained what was involved:

> *Noah's Ark was the largest sea-going vessel ever built, until the late nineteenth century when giant metal ships were first constructed. The Ark was approximately 450 feet by seventy-five feet; but as late as 1858 'the largest vessel of her type in the world was the P&O liner Himalaya, 240 feet by thirty-five feet . . . ' In that year, Isambard K. Brunel produced 'the Great Eastern, 692 feet by 83 feet by 30 feet of approximately 19,000 tons . . . five times the tonnage of any ship then afloat. So vast was Brunel's leap that even forty years later in an age of fierce competition the largest liners being built were still smaller than the Great Eastern . . . [6]*

Remember, Noah's Ark would have measured quite a bit higher than even Brunel's ship, The Great Eastern. An atheist simply could not contend with such a find.

Conversely, many theologians do not think this particular Egyptian styled ark meets Biblical standards. There seems to be two general theological problems with this find; both are related to Biblical interpretation. The *first* problem is, *the ark was found on a side mountain* of the Ararat range and not near the peak of the tallest Ararat mountain where everyone expected to find it. However, the Bible does not define exactly where on the Ararat range the Ark came to rest. The passage reads, "So the flood gradually receded until, 150 days after it began, the boat came to rest upon the mountains of Ararat."[7]

The *second* problem is *the shape of the Ark.* This Egyptian styled ship was not rectangular as the Bible seems to indicate, but has the shape of a more streamlined boat. Let us have a closer look at the Biblical description; "Make it 450 feet long, 75 feet wide, and 45 feet high."[8] Suffice it to say this modern translation is not totally accurate. The meaning would change simply in the translation from Hebrew to English. Moreover, there would be problems understanding the exact dimensions from any translation. We can only have an approximate idea of the size, because the original script described the Ark's dimensions using a cubit. But which cubit? What was the length? There is an Egyptian cubit and other cubits. Yet, what if these Biblical dimensions do not describe a rectangular ship, but reference volume? What if we are perceiving a physical shape and the Bible is describing a voluminous proportion? Some scholars think the cubit used to build both Solomon's Temple and the Pharaoh Khufu's Great Pyramid, was 20.6 inches. If 20.6 inches was the length of Noah's cubit, then the voluminous dimensions of the above Ark shaped object are extremely accurate with regard to the Scriptures, i.e., the exact length, width and height given in the Bible. Thus, this Egyptian boat-shaped 'rock formation' could very well be the genuine Noah's Ark. Such an Ark would have been a massive ship. John Whitcomb writes of a mental exercise to understand the volume in which we speak: "For the sake of realism, imagine waiting at a railroad crossing while ten freight trains, each pulling fifty-two boxcars, move slowly by, one after another. That is how much space was available in the Ark, for its capacity was equivalent to 520 modern railroad stock cars."[9] Whitcomb's exercise is based on the modern translation. If a larger cubit was used, the number of these box cars would increase proportionately.

Just as interesting is the profound state of the actual—that which has been discovered. Think of the symbolism of a rock shaped exactly like a ship with the same dimensions of the Biblical Ark found on the side of mountain designated in the Bible as the Ark's resting place.

NOAH: A JEWISH MYTH?

For those of you who consider the story of Noah's Ark a Hebrew fantasy, the Bible is not the only document that discusses the flood. There is a diversity of flood stories from virtually all ancient civilizations. Some scholars suggest the Jewish version was borrowed from earlier Mesopotamian stories. However, whether or not the Jewish version is 'borrowed,' a common flood story is what one would expect to find if the Noahian flood was an actual disaster. Perhaps broader than the Biblical story (yet not as accurate) is an account generally known as the Epic of Gilgamesh. There are several Sumerian, Babylonian and Assyrian versions of the Gilgamesh Epic. The Sumerian account is the oldest version. The 'Noah' or hero of this Sumerian story was called Ziusudra. The Babylonian hero was named Utnapishtim. Assyria named their hero Xisuthros, Sisuthros, Sisithros or Seisithros.[10] Simply put, each of these versions, to one degree or another, affirm the

> THERE IS A DIVERSITY OF FLOOD STORIES FROM VIRTUALLY
> ALL ANCIENT CIVILIZATIONS.

Genesis record. This in itself suggests a dissemination of Noah's knowledge. Quite likely, there have been even older Mesopotamian accounts. These Middle Eastern stories are but the beginning of a long trail of flood stories. Some Indian and early Aryan/Indus/Hindu records could also be narratives of the flood. For example, the Vedas have references which may have originated from the flood. One is a hymn to Indra - the god of the thunderstorm. Initially, Indra was the supreme god of Aryan shepherds who dominated Indian culture and who, along with native Indus, forged the Hindu religion. The Aryans were nomadic people—actually travelers from Europe, or natives from Iran. In our search for a great flood, let us consider the beginning passages of a hymn to Indra:

1. I will extol the most heroic Indra who with his might forced earth and sky asunder;

Who hath filled all with width as man's upholder, surpassing floods and rivers in his greatness.

2. Surya is he: throughout the wide expanses shall Indra turn him, swift as car-wheels, hither,

Like a stream resting not but ever active: he hath destroyed, with light, the black-hued darkness.11

One can easily imagine Noah composing something similar to his God after he survived the 'Great Flood.' Therefore, I suggest, the dominant Hindu god may have originated from the God of Noah.

There are also several references to the prehistoric Indian Puranas and Mahabharata. More important may be a reference to "Manu and seven survivors" landing on a mountain in India. Of course, the number of survivors (eight) is consistent with the Biblical account.[12] Manu, the Sanskrit name for Noah, may have evolved from 'Proto-Indian-European' roots. An ancient meaning of 'Ma' was 'water' (as in maritime). 'Manu' became the word for 'man.' One easily draws a connection between these Sanskritian roots and Noah, because Manu (or Noah) was the father to 'post-flood' mankind.[13]

Some Egyptian rituals and stories may have originated from the Noahian flood. Even more remarkable, societies separated from the rest of the world have flood myths quite similar in many respects to the Biblical and Gilgamesh versions. A great example is the flood legend of the Samo-Kubo tribesman of New Guinea. For continuity's sake, I will greatly simplify the Samo-Kubo version. The Samo-Kubo story (as in the *Epic of Gilgamesh*) explains that people were making noise (misbehaving). This made the lizards mad (gods in *Gilgamesh*). The Lizard Man made it rain for days. People began to climb the mountain peaks, but to no avail. Water rose and finally covered the mountains. Only two brothers built a raft and survived. Morris focused on the importance of this myth:

The significant thing, however, is that a hitherto unknown tribe, deep in an almost impenetrable jungle with almost no contact with the outside world, has in its traditions a story remarkably similar in many ways to the story of Noah's Flood that we find in the Bible. True, many local embellishments have been added, as would be expected, but the essence of the story remains.[14]

Morris lists more than two hundred distinct ethnic versions of the flood story from all over the world including jungle wilds and other isolated places. I share with you the uniqueness of this diversion by the following sampling of his list: Babylon, Egypt (Pharaoic and Priestly), Bapedi Tribe (South Africa), Masai Tribe, Persia (Ahriman, Bundehesch, Testrya, Yima and Zala-Cupha), Hawaii (Mauna-Ka Tribesmen and Nu-U), Samoa, Tahiti, China (Fo-hi, Joa and Toa-tse), India (Rama), Celts, Druids, Lithuania Rumania, Russia, Athenian, Arctic Eskimos, Cherokees, Arapahos, Aztecs, Mayan, Cuban, Peruvian, Rio de Janeiro, Incas and Brazilian Mountain peoples to name a few.[15] According to Berlitz, who is a linguistic expert, this number can be broken down even further as he distinguishes "over 600 variations" of the Noahian story.[16] Certainly, the universal nature of this disaster message must indicate something significant about its credibility.

In addition to this 'Myth' proof, there is also a great deal of geological, archaeological, and historical information to support evidence of a great flood.

GEOLOGICAL DATA

Uniformitarianism proposes that evolutionary change occurs at a consistent but gradual rate over a period of time. It is quite apparent that a Noahian scale flood would move geology far away from this traditional evolutionary model. Geological rejection of a world flood is related to a categorical rejection of all detracting explanations of the fossil record. I must stress that a large number of today's 'in crowd' educators must not only reject the flood, but all creation models and all 'fast' evolution models including punctuationism. However, there are scientists who claim *the existing fossil record is better explained by a great flood* (or a number of great floods) than by the 'long day' evolutionary models. Yet, evolutionary geologists argue against basing any theories on existing fossil records because many fossils have deteriorated and thus vanished from the record. For some reason, only homogeneous ones have survived. We have perhaps thousands of fossils of one specific specie, of ancient animal, but no confirmed link. How unlucky can we get? Early evolutionists, including Darwin, thought the fossil record would prove their theory was correct. To their discredit, the fossil record has become perhaps evolutions greatest problem (that is excluding the impossibilities imposed on the theory by the physical sciences). It is important to understand the political nature of the 'flood' position and the havoc it creates for the 'programmed' educator. It is also important to understand what the fossil record may actually be telling us. It may be a snapshot of a fateful day in time.

Furthermore, the objective nature of the fossil record is a two edged sword. The problem for evolutionists is not only what the record does not show, but what it reveals. During the brief age of man, the earth's environment has experienced some major changes. Previous to the Noanian age much of the earth was covered in tropical vegetation and rain forests. This understanding is consistent with the pre-flood Biblical model, for a thick, protective, vaporous atmosphere might well produce a homogeneous warm tropical climate. This tropical world must have existed when the earliest human explorers measured and mapped our earth's surface. There is amazing evidence suggesting this conclusion. As an example, an existing ancient map unveiled Antarctica without ice and divided into distinct land masses. This land division was not rediscovered until 1958. In fact, most maps today show the ice mass and not the actual land. Few in our modern culture even realize this dichotomy. More impressive is the detail of the ancient map which included topographical information yet to be re-measured. Included were locations of rivers and valleys, etc. Interestingly, this early geographical sophistication does not end with Antarctica. Other ancient maps show a land bridge between Siberia and Alaska suggesting a great change in either land mass or water level. Another map designates the Sahara forest before it became a desert. Only recently has modern man recognized this change in the Sahara region.[17]

We find evidence of a *massive flood in all parts of the world,* from South America to Russia. Mammoths and other animals were frozen in the arctic ice. Some of these animals were extremely well preserved, even with undigested vegetation in their bellies. Some were standing, some kneeling. One mammoth, studied by the Leningrad Museum, had buttercups on its tongue. One suggested solution to this ecological puzzle is that the animals froze in an erupted vaporous atmosphere caused by an enormous flood.[18] But why would millions of animals be eating vegetation in the arctic? The only possible answer is that the arctic region was tropical.

Additionally, we know ocean floors move. Continents 'drift' away from one another. Scientists tell us the *continental shelves and plates have made major shifts.* Moreover, there are tremendous underground water reserves. Perhaps, after a massive disaster which reshaped the earth's surface, water masses were poured from one massive holding area to another. This is the same kind of fluid shift one might expect to see if water broke through a dam, only on a much greater scale.

Finally, despite the protests of evolutionary geologists, I must mention *fossils and seashells* of ocean life have also been found high on mountains around the world. Besides the obvious question of how the bones of a whale wash up the slopes of the Himalanian mountains, there is another interesting puzzle for the evolutionist. We find no evidence of "large-scale fossilization" occurring in today's world. Whitcomb states the problem well, "When fishes die in the oceans they do not sink to the bottom and become fossils. Instead, they either decompose or are picked to pieces by scavengers."[19] Of course, Whitcomb took the geologists excuse for evolution and gave it as proof of a worldwide flood. A flood could quickly cover plants and animals with a protective covering of mud and sludge. Thus, geological world data might confirm the Biblical view that a flood covered "all the high mountains under the whole heaven,"[20] However, these are only a few of many pieces of evidence which relate to both the pre-Noahian and Noahian days.

Even though we have geological evidence to support the Biblical account, many geologists claim a flood of such magnitude is impossible. John Whitcomb writes, "Geologists are certainly correct when they insist that a world wide, mountain-covering flood could not occur today on the basis of observable geologic processes, and the present balance of sub-oceanic and continental masses. There is no known force or combination of forces in the crust of the earth sufficiently powerful to elevate all the ocean floors and to submerge all the continents and then reverse the process within one year."[21] However, there are extraordinary things which might well have caused such devastation. A particularly large asteroid striking the earth at precisely the right angle could bring about immediate and major changes in the earth's environment and topography. In fact, this is exactly what many Noahian theorists suspect happened. The evidence of 'heavenly bodies' striking the earth has been found around the world. (Some paleontologies now suggest this very thing may have killed the dinosaurs). Such a collision might even knock the earth off of its axis. Circumstantial evidence suggest this was the case. I would list in this category the massive transformation of earth calendars from 360 day years to 365 day years. We should remember, ancient humans were very good at measuring seasons. I find it hard to believe they would disregard five days. Yet, a number of ancient calendars consisted of 360 days.

Furthermore, such a disaster would cause *massive volcanic activity.* Eruptions could increase the height and dimensions of land masses and drastically reshape the contours of the earth's surface. Interestingly, there is a geological theory that the earth has expanded or 'grown' in size. According to this theory, all of the land mass was, at one time, connected. As the earth's core expanded, the continents began to shift and move away from one another. Of course, a major eruption in the earth's surface could also erupt the great underground springs and water systems referred to above (similar to massive underground systems known today). The release of such underground resources could, by itself, cause massive flooding. If we consider a gigantic catastrophe of this nature perhaps involving a magnetic loop collapse or a reversal of magnetic forces, and the moving land masses exposing immeasurable forces, the possibilities of a massive flood greatly increase.

ARCHAEOLOGICAL DATA

Further evidence of a massive universal flood is found in archaeological data. Underwater explorers find columns of ancient buildings, stone walls and ancient roads laying on shelves strewn across ocean floors. Such evidence of a past global disaster is often tied to other great myths. The most famous is the Story of Atlantis. It has often been suggested that the destruction of Atlantis was related to the Great Flood. Interestingly, both stories were common to the Greeks. An example in ancient literature comes from the Babylonian flood account of Berossus, the Babylonian priest/historian. He stated that a god named Chronos directed his 'Noah' (Xisuthrus) to collect and bury many records prior to the flood. Perhaps not so coincidentally, Chronos (Cronos or Cronus) is both the name of the Greek god and the "legendary name of the last king of Atlantis."[22]

Another interesting point is found in the wording of Sumerian texts. The Sumerian society probably would have been either contemporary with or the closest known society to the Noahian era. Related to this connection is a list of ancient Sumerian kings which enumerates kings before and after 'the Flood.' According to archaeologist Seton Lloyd, "Great floods were a commonplace of Mesopotamian history until quite recent times . . ."[23] If that is true, why would one 'Great Flood' be singled out in an ancient list of kings? Was it because one flood was much worse than all others? Was it so devastating that it ended the reign of kings? At a later date, did a new reign of kings began? Perhaps the less severe floods which followed were similar to an earthquake's aftershocks. Perhaps great changes in the ecological strata precluded these later and lessor floods. Thus, lessor floods continued for many years until the earth's atmosphere became stable.

In the Mesopotamian region, ancient cities were built on top of the ruins of even older cities. Some researchers believe they have dug down through a number of levels of a city and into flood devastated ruins. Perhaps the most dramatic example was found by E. Mackay on the site of ancient Kish. Kish undoubtedly was one of the oldest cities ever built on planet earth. According to Mackay's field notebook, the remains of a "ziggurat terrace was founded directly upon an easily recognizable 'flood stratum' which covered the whole site."[24] Cities built on flood cites may be the case of Middle

Eastern cities, as well as the Egyptian delta area. Because of the general location of the entire Biblical account of early man, i.e., the accepted location of the Garden of Eden, the location of Noah's Ark, the city of Babylon, etc., I suggest yet another option to our perception of early man.

CAVE MAN

Like so many others, I wonder about the hominid beings (like Neandertal). Gene analysis indicates humans are not related to these primitive 'ape man' creatures. Therefore, at this date in time, I conclude hominids were large apes. However, if we use our imagination and disregard gene analysis, as neo-Darwinian evolutionists must, then one can make a case that Neandertal or Cro-Magnon or their descendants were the mysterious Biblical giants created by sexual relations between human women and spiritual beings. The Biblical story goes as follows:

In those days, and even afterwards, when evil beings from the spirit world were sexually involved with human women, their children became giants. When the Lord God saw the extent of human wickedness, and that the trend and direction of men's lives was only toward evil, he was sorry he had made them. It broke his heart.[25]

Though the Neandertals were not tall, they were apparently very strong. If brain size is related to intelligence, Neandertal may have seemed to be an intellectual 'giant.' In fact, fossil remains have led some anthropologists to speculate limited inbreeding between humans and Neanderthal did occur.[26] Yet, perhaps the Biblical giants were not Neandertal, but the taller Cro-Magnon creature. 'Cro-Magnon man' may have had similar features to the modern human—described as "big boned, powerful and tall." Some may have grown to be "six feet four inches in height" or taller.[27]

Then, perhaps, either Neandertal or his rival Cro-Magnon were, on some level, related to the mixed breed beings which became extinct through the great flood. At first this suggestion seems ludicrous. But a closer look might change that view. As earlier discussed, the Neandertal had a larger brain cavity than modern man and thus a larger brain. Using the "mean" as our figures, modern man's brain capacity is 1,350 cc. From our limited sample, Cro-Magnon's capacity was extremely close to that figure. However Neandertal's capacity was 1600 cc.[28] Thus, Neandertal's brain was of greater size then our own and, therefore, had greater intellectual (and, perhaps, spiritual) potential. The discovery of this larger brain capacity sent scientists scurrying for an explanation. They concluded that the size of the brain is not as important as its sophistication, i.e., how the brain is wired. The Neandertal brain is not thought to have been wired as intricately as modern man's brain. Though their conclusion makes sense, it is based purely on speculation. No one actually knows the intelligence level of the Neandertal. In fact, if we speculate on brain wiring we might also consider the possibility that Neandertal had superior wiring. Neandertal may have been more intelligent than modern man. Furthermore, we know Neandertal lived in the Biblical centered Eden/Ararat/Babylon area. Actually this particular Neandertal community extended across Iran, Iraq and up into Turkey. Archaeological reports state that some skeleton finds in said area were "unmistakably exhibiting the characteristics of Neandertal man."[29] Neandertal seems to have held an orientation for blood sacrifices, and, in fact, adopted an occultic prototype rationale. The Neandertal fervor for debauchery and brutality remind us of rituals of later 'evil' human societies. According to E. O. James, what appears to have occurred in various separate excavations would include ritual sacrifice and cannibalism. A dead and perhaps sacrificed Neandertal would be decapitated, his or her brain extracted and eaten as a "soul substance or trophy."[30] The skulls could then be made into "drinking cups."[31] These decapitated skulls were placed very precisely indicating a Satanic expression. One site included twenty-six severed skulls which were marked by red ochre (paint) and facing west in ceremonial fashion. Close by were another group of six such skulls.[32] As referenced by James, archaeologists speculate that the Neandertal ate a victim's brain to gain the dead person's spiritual or intellectual knowledge. If this is the case, one must wonder, how did they know the brain stored knowledge? These less then human creatures determined the brain, not the liver nor the heart, stored knowledge. Ask yourself a question: if you had no information about the inner workings of the body, if you were one of the first people to have lived, would you know where human intellect is stored? Would you have realized the brain held knowledge? Would you determine the brain had any function at all?

If James is correct, Neandertal may have also held some concepts related to mathematics. Perhaps one of the first mathematical instruments ever conceived and produced by an earthly creature was found in the Lake Edwards area in Africa. We have named this people as 'Ishango.' Ishango is described as Neandertaloid in that he was related to and perhaps a descendant of the Neandertal. The mathematical instrument was a bone deliberately marked in a manner suggestive of a measuring device. It is thought the Ishango's deliberate lines were grouped in such a way as to anticipate the moon's cycles.[33] If so, it was a simple but ingenious tool. The kinds of activities we have discussed lead us to believe that the Neandertal was not some kind of 'idiot' animal with an inferior brain, but a calculating being. Secondly, we must ask ourselves, if this tool is contemporary to Neandertal thought, how many of their tools have disintegrated over thousands of weathering years? The anthropologist would state, "If one assumes that there was a great flood, Neandertal died out prior to the time prescribed to Noah." However, by their own admission, they do not have enough fossil records to substantiate their beliefs. They factually do not know when Neandertal died out. From any scientific point of view, the actual Neandertal time schedule is only a guess. However, as we consider flood evidence from other parts of the world, we might remember Neandertaloid.

Egypt also holds physical evidence of a Noahian class flood. For example, The Queen's Chamber in the Great Pyramid seems to have a salt line.[34] Even if there had been a heavy rain which caused the kind of flood we might expect from a 'normal' disaster, how would a salt line form in the Queen's chamber? Furthermore, I would expect the flood water to be much higher outside the pyramid then inside simply because of interior air pockets. It would certainly take an amazing flood to make such a mark.

The flood evidence around the Great Sphinx is even more intriguing. There is a revolutionary theory concerning the weathering of the Great Sphinx at Giza. John Anthony West has proposed that the erosion of the Sphinx was caused by water rather then wind or sand. The normal erosion of Egyptian monuments produce a 'layered look.' The softer stones erode much faster than the harder stones, leaving a series of rough hard layers with the eroded soft stones in between. However, the Sphinx seems to have a rounder and smoother surface. There is also some crevice erosion, like the erosion one might find on a mound of dirt after heavy rains.[35] If West's theory is correct, it changes the current beliefs of both the age and development of human civilization. It puts a civilization in Egypt perhaps thousands of years before our current thinking allows. These radical effects have made West's theory interesting enough to be produced for a television program and later released to the public in video form entitled "The Mystery Of The Sphinx." This video uses a computer to illustrate how such a flood would have affected this structure.[36]

There is another Egyptian controversy involving the Sphinx. Whose face is on the Sphinx? Many researchers have suggested that it is of the Pharaoh Chephren. However, in a study regarding this question, an expert took facial measurements of both the statue of the Sphinx and that of Chephren. I must stress that the ancient Egyptians were extremely fine craftsmen. It is obvious they were meticulous in their work. The shapes of the statues were probably very accurate. The referred to inspection determined that the frontal slope (the angle formed by the position of the outer eye and a vertical running just in front of the chin) of Chephren's head was 14 degrees while the same slope on the Sphinx was 32 degrees. This Sphinx face has a dramatic slope. If these statues are at all representative, the Sphinx is not the face of Chephren.[37] I suggest this radical facial measurement may not be of an Egyptian. I am reminded of the Mayan practice of re-shaping the slope of the forehead of their noble class. They were the intellectuals. Evidently, they would place weights or other devices in strategic areas of the head to change the slope of the front of the face. Both the Sphinx and the Mayan noble class had heads that more closely resembled a Neandertaloid being. These are but a few creations of ancient human beings which could be reflections of a Neandertaloid legacy. Perhaps Neandertal descendants were a great people and the builders of a pre-flood civilization that was the greatest of its day. Perhaps the Mayan and other primitive peoples ritualized the memory of a giant Neandertaloid. I must add that I am personally skeptical of such a Neandertal influence. However, historical questions (such as who was Neandertal) go unanswered.

WORLD LAND MASSES SUGGEST A GREAT FLOOD

There is even more evidence of a Great Flood. Ocean fossils have been discovered on virtually every land mass around the world. Furthermore, great lakes covered some of earth's major land masses. For example, current thinking dictates a large part of Africa (particularly the desert area) was once covered with lakes.[38] These lakes may have been the remains of flood pools which, over time, dried up leaving a water basin with no foliage which resulted in The Sahara Desert.

Other ancient civilizations show signs of a Great Flood. Tiahuanaco, Bolivia is an often cited example. Tiahuanaco sits about two miles high on mountains in South America. Amazingly a "salt line" around surrounding mountains indicates this ancient village was once an ocean port.[39] Tiahuanaco has other evidence of a great flood including the ancient ruins discovered beneath Lake Titicaca.

HISTORICAL REPORTS

If there was a flood, there is always the possibility of finding survivors in other parts of the world. When the Spaniards explored the Canary Islands they found tall, light skinned inhabitants. Some were even blonde haired, blue eyed. These natives were amazed to learn that the Spaniards or any other people existed in the world. Their ancestors had survived a great flood so tragic that they assumed that they were the only inhabitants of the world. This seems perfectly logical because the Noahian flood would probably have occurred 3,500 years (or more) before the Spaniards landed. These people indicated that their ancestors managed to survive by evacuating to mountain tops which became the Canary Islands. Unfortunately the intruding Spanish soldiers killed the remaining members of this lost family.

Interestingly, there are reports of shipwrecks on other mountains around the world. Some of these ships hold markings unfamiliar to our understanding. Such a ship was found in the mountains close to Naples. Another large ship was discovered by miners in Switzerland. This particular ship bore human skulls presumably of its crew. Another ancient ship was found in Peru by Spaniards and yet another in Alaska during the gold rush. This Alaskan ship was reportedly 300 feet long.[40]

If these crafts are genuine ancient ships and not hoaxes, they do not necessarily suggest other flood survivors. This wreckage may have happened before, during or after the Great Flood. However, such artifacts do reveal at least two things. First, any historical find is a *message* from the earth to human intellect. And the message of a ship on a mountain emphatically states, "This area of the world has experienced major changes and man has witnessed those changes." Second, primitive man may have been far more *advanced* then we realize. I do not think building a ship for sailing would have been as difficult as the construction of the towering structures found virtually all over the world. For example, how did the Egyptians built the pyramids?

RELIGIOUS TRADITIONS

Of the secondary topics related to the "Great Flood Theory," perhaps the most interesting is connected with Easter. Conservative Christianity holds a degree of contempt for the Catholic Church's timing of the Easter celebration. Most likely, the Easter date came from a compromise with Roman Empire pagans. In like manner, the Easter egg and the Easter bunny have nothing to do with the resurrection of Jesus Christ, but were associated with fertility rites which accompanied pagan festivals of Aster. Such festivals denoted a change of winter to spring, and were related to harvests, having babies, the coming of good weather and so forth. To the Roman Catholic Church, tying Jesus' resurrection to an existing springtime festival seemed like a good idea at the time. It brought converts to Christianity. However, the Aster festivals may have originated from deeper meaning and an earlier beginning than a pagan spring festival. Perhaps this festival began with the landing of Noah's Ark. Fasold suggested that the opening of the Ark was a symbolic cracking of the egg shell.[41] Freedom from the confines of the Ark signified a new birth and new life. Perhaps it was celebrated with the first Easter egg. Decorating an egg for pagan festivals was not just a Babylonian tradition. It seems to have been a unified custom which spread throughout the world. The Hindus in distant China and Japan used painted eggs in sacred festivals. Athenians used eggs in their celebrations to Dionysia or Bacchus (the Greek and Roman god of wine). It is interesting to note that much of the Bacchus myth includes things related to the story of Noah. The most obvious of these is the invention of wine and the activity of sailing.

The dispersion of mankind after the flood can be tied to the human need for water and the tendency of life to follow the water beds and rivers. John Morris writes:

> *Another interesting feature of Mt. Ararat is that the snow on its peak melts and runs down into a system of shallow rivers and underground streams which eventually form the headwaters of the Euphrates River. This geographical characteristic might explain the early population*

migrations of the Mesopotamian region. Such migrations generally follow the paths of water. Thus, one would expect a number of Noah's descendants to migrate down the banks of the Euphrates River. Interestingly, approximately seven hundred miles south of Ararat, in the Tigris-Euphrates Valley (the Fertile Crescent), lie the remains of the ancient city of Babel.[42]

If we remember this archaeological migration principle when we read Fasold's explanations, then we find a most intriguing statement which may tie all of ancient middle eastern and eastern civilizations directly to the Ark. He writes, "The custom of the sacred eggs hung in the temples of Egypt can be traced back through the classical poets and the mysteries of Babylon, for it begins on the banks of the Euphrates, or the river FIRAT in Turkey, near the Ark."[43] Fasold is pointing to much more than the very beginnings of the Easter egg. He is allowing us to experience the rehabilitation of earth. Fasold backs his observation with the following documentation: "Hyginus the Egyptian, keeper of the Palatine library in the time of Augustus, reports, 'An egg of wondrous size is said to have fallen from heaven into the river Euphrates. The fishes rolled it to the bank where, the doves having settled upon it, hatched it and out came Venus, who afterwards was called the Syrian goddess Astarte.'" [44] Reading this passage closely, we find many similarities with the Biblical story of Noah. For example, the dove lands and the Ark is opened. Assuming this connection to be accurate, perhaps the pagans built their Aster celebrations around an already existing Noahian celebration. Perhaps 'goddess Astarte' was Mrs. Noah, the matriarch of human life in post flood age. The Noahian celebration naturally would have begun as a thanks-giving to God for His salvation. Might it have evolved to include a sacred "mothers' day" to bring blessings on Mrs. Noah's ability to nurture children? Factually, she was the most important survivor. Human survival revolved around her reproductive abilities. Such speculation may not sit well with some theologians. However, if one considers the traditions which have risen through Christian celebrations, such as the Christmas tree and the Easter egg, then per-haps we can better understand how historic events become paganized.

There are a number of other appropriate speculations relative to the 'Great Flood' which could change our understanding of historical procession of human thought. A study in ancient creation myths provides a variety of sto-ries around the world suggesting the universe formed from a water beginning. The 'Great Flood' may have been the historic impetus of these stories. Early in the Egyptian creation story, Tem lays an egg into a universe of "watery waste." From this egg is hatched Ra, the Egyptian sun god. From Ra descend the other Egyptian "gods and goddesses."[45] Considering the previous discus-sion regarding Aster, and realizing eggs which hung in the Egyptian temples may have originated with the Noahian myth, it seems plausible that this creation myth might also be based upon a flood. The Hindus likewise believe "the Self-Existent" made the waters and placed a golden egg (made from His seed) in the waters. The golden egg bore Brahman—"the World Parent."[46]

An additional Noahian tie to the Egyptian culture comes from the Great Pyramid of Egypt. Contrary to Berlitz's suggestion of a pre-flood great pyramid, Fasold suggests a Noahian influence in its construction. Whether this structure was built before or after the flood, the builder/contractor may well have used the very same measuring rod designated by God for the construction of Noah's Ark. There are some other intriguing mysteries related to the construction of the Great Pyramid. An ancient record of Herodotus claims its construction to have been supervised by "strangers to Egypt."[47] One must ask, why would the great civilization allow "strangers to Egypt" to begin such a massive undertaking? If Herodotus is accurate, there must be more to this story than what Herodotus has relayed. Furthermore, many pyramidologists and theologians, suggest that the Great Pyramid was built primarily as a receptacle of prophecy. In arguing this position, many point to a passage in the Bible which states:

In that day shall there be an altar to the Lord in the midst of the land of Egypt, and a pillar (Hebrew "Matstsebah" correctly translated means monument) at the border thereof to the Lord of Hosts in the land of Egypt.[48]

Some researchers suggest the location of the pyramid has special meaning. E. Raymond Capt has written, "The Great Pyramid was placed in the exact center of all the land area of the world. Lines drawn through the north-south and east-west axis of the Pyramid divide equally the earth's terrain. The north-south axis (31~ 9' meridian east of Greenwich) is the longest land meridian, and the east-west axis (29~ 58' 51' north), the longest land parallel."[49]

Several questions immediately come to mind. Was primitive man able to measure exactly the widest and longest axis on the face of the earth, or was this a 'spiritual' decision connecting man with the Supreme God? Was this location predetermined by fate or providence? Was freedom of choice, at least in this case, an illusion?

In ancient times, if the center of the earth were to be determined, it would not be decided by measurements, but dictated by the dominant country of the day. How else would one choose? Mankind did not even know the earth was round. So, again I ask, how did the human race arrange to put that most spectacular monument in such a meaningful location?

Capt continues, "Since the full official name of the pyramid, the

Great Pyramid of Giza, means, in English, the Great Pyramid of the Border, the answer to the apparently contradictory definition of Isaiah is found in the Great Pyramid. The only spot on the face of the earth that completely answers this description, both geometrically and geographically, is the precise place where the Great Pyramid actually stands."[50]

Capt's facts may be questionable to some, but nevertheless, he uses this beginning to unveil a fantastic theory about the prophecy of the Great Pyramid. In his theory, he proclaims that this pyramid prophetically pinpoints the exact date for specific events such as the Passover of the Jews in Egypt and the Crucifixion of Jesus of Nazareth in Jerusalem.[51]

I have been very skeptical about prophecy theories related to Egyptian structures including the Great Pyramid. However, I do believe there was a Noah who was a very spiritual man. God confided to him many secrets of life. One of those secrets was that His promise to Adam (recorded in Genesis 3:15) would come true. A Messiah would come and physically suffer from man's transgressions. However, by His suffering He would defeat sin. God continued to explain other events. The world would eventually regress to an evil age similar to those days immediately prior to the flood. Finally, humanity will try God's patience for the last time. The world will be destroyed, not by a flood, but by a final Great War. God will allow man to venture so far away and to become so debased that man would destroy himself by his own hands. The final event is the Battle of Armageddon. With humanity ready to destroy itself, God will step in and end the world as we know it. As we shut God off from our schools, our sporting events, our work places and our lives, we are proving that God is the glue that makes us successful, because without God we are only evil dust floating through space. There is no reason for our existence and we will not survive. (I refer to the loving God who commands humans to love one another. I do not believe God condones murder nor do I find it logical that God would want radicals to kill innocent people in His name. Such murders may be a direct cause of the great abomination—the coming buildup to and battle of Armageddon—and must face God and account for their transgressions).

Noah was the bearer of Truth. Assuming Noah knew God, obeyed God and worshipped God as God wished, then what happened to humanity and why do we drift away from God? If Noah and his family were indeed the only human beings left on earth, what happened to God's divine wisdom? According to the Bible, after Noah died, humans once again began an intellectual slide away from Truth. From a secular historical view, we really have

AS WE SHUT GOD OFF FROM OUR SCHOOLS, OUR SPORTING EVENTS, OUR WORK PLACES AND OUR LIVES, WE ARE PROVING THAT GOD IS THE GLUE THAT MAKES US SUCCESSFUL, BECAUSE WITHOUT GOD WE ARE ONLY EVIL DUST FLOATING THROUGH SPACE.

no reason to doubt this explanation. Changes in theological concepts have been a common phenomenon in the human community. As earlier noted, we have seen the same human process affect Christianity in the United States of America. In fact, some of our traditional Christian churches have discarded Christian theology in favor of ancient pagan and secularist answers to 'modern' problems. Likewise, Noah's spiritual Truth did not remain pure. The Bible tells us a humanist movement festered until its culmination in Babylon. From the little that we know about early Mesopotamian theology, we might piece together what could be considered the degeneration discussed in Genesis. Archaeologists suggest the community of Eridu was one of the first Mesopotamian cities to erect a distinguishable shrine to a god. It was a simple building to their patron god. Yet, it was one shrine to one god. This endeavor suggests, at this stage of development, Eridu and perhaps the rest of Mesopotamia believed one god dominated their lives. Later, in the kingdom of Sumer, we find evidence of polytheistic practices. Particularly apparent are the polytheistic practices of Uruk. We also find polytheistic practices in Ur, Lagash and Nippur. By the time Babylon came into prominence, man may well have lost all spiritual Truth and begun to indulge in a plethora of magical and occultic concepts. There seems to be a disregard for Noahian principles. Nimrod or Namra-uddu, an ancestor of Ham and the son of Babylon's founding father, was deified and associated with Babylon's chief god 'Marduk.' [52] It seems that human spirituality moved to a radical experimental position. Humans believed they could control the earth's magic. Humans had become so self-centered, pompous and were determined to meet God on His own ground. They endeavored to build a "tower" which would reach to heaven. We have found secular records of such Babylonian spiritual towers called ziggurats. The Biblical story of Babel building a tower (ziggurat) to the heavens is often hard for the reader to understand. The Bible gives few details. However, the sin of man was not building a ziggurat, but *why* it was built. The tower was not to be built for the glory of God, but as a demonstration of the greatness and glory of humanness. The tower was symbolic of the arrogant pride of man.[53] Man would endeavor to determine on what grounds he would encounter God. Man would determine his own destiny. Yes, man was determined to intrude on God's turf. However, YHWH (a sacred Jewish name for God closest translation is 'Lord') has a plan and a history that man must fulfill. Yes, history is preordained. God's Will cannot be denied. YHWH had to slow down the process of history. Human civilization was moving at a fast pace toward an ultimate destruction and Day of Judgment. Evidently, God was not ready to initiate the day of destruction. In order to save His creation, God would command great forces against man. Unquestionably, the universe would revolve around the Will of God, not the will of man.

When considering Babylon's common spiritual worship, it is important to note, Babylonian society was practicing astrology and other occultic activities, perhaps even witchcraft. These 'crafts' involve supernatural forces outside of God's approval. That was partaking of forbidden fruit (like Adam and Eve). Scripture further suggests their magical practices were communicated through a dominate language. From Babylon, God confused humans by giving them many languages and scattered them throughout the world.[54] Interestingly, genetic comparisons of some primitive African tribes indicate there may have been an early common language that included sharp clicking sounds.[55] It is also now accepted that Mesopotamia had an early common language. If true, man could have easily carried with him a common but false theology. This may, in part, explain the similarities in ancient worship or the primary level of human religions. Such a religion would have included the animism practices including deification of animals. Obviously, Babylon participated in such practices, because deified animals decorated Babylon's famous gate of Ishtar.

Most of civilization's ancient religions recognized the concept of "animism," or a natural world that is controlled by spirits. These spirits might effect every aspect of life. A culture might have a god of the forests, a god of the wind or the god of water. When there was a devastating storm, it could be rationalized as an act of the gods; the gods were mad, etc. There were also gods who regulated the powers of man, most notably human *sexual* powers. Usually a desire for sexual powers was expressed through a horned or erect male god, or fertile, erotic female goddess. The goddess Venus is perhaps the most recognized of these ancient sexual deities. Likewise, spirits were considered the cause of illnesses, etc. This remains a belief of some of the primitive populations of today. Tribal medicine men or shamans were spiritual leaders as well as the earliest doctors. Thus, the rituals which went along with curing illnesses were often intended to effect spirits.

Another religious expression fundamental to animism is the deification of animals such as the eagle, raven or buffalo. This deification was the result of yet another human intuitive understanding - the recognition of the 'soul.' Today, most cultures would agree, not only does man have a soul, but so do many living creatures. Yet, animism (or deification) concepts are unquestionably polytheistic.

The earliest and most primitive of peoples may have practiced animism. In fact, animism may have been the human Self's first step in self rationalization of an internal tugging of spiritualness. Polytheistic animism was not an isolated concept. It did not just fester in a Middle Eastern culture. Among those thought to be primitive animism practitioners were the followers of the Shinto religion, some of the Indus peoples (pre-Hindu India), the ancient Druids, the Egyptians, virtually all African religions and tribes of both the North and South American natives. Of course, the occult and witchcraft activities, fundamental to some of the early distinguishable religions, included animism concepts. Thus, man's discovery of the soul was not a hidden accident, but an examination and understanding of one's personal 'Self' and the projection of the same or similar life experience in other human and animal lives. In actuality, it was an awakening of Self. It was one of the first answers to the question, "Who am I?"

Some post-modernists have tried to explain away the human spiritual significance of early religious activities. Perhaps the most sensational attempts suggest many spiritual writings are related to visitors from outer space. Erich Von Daniken wrote several popular books on this subject in the 1970's. It seems as though Von Daniken thought every spiritual act and all human myths were expressions related to space invaders. Many of his arguments were nonsensical. One of the most dramatic of these offerings came from his book, *Chariots of the Gods*. He explained drawings of countercrossed straight lines and "enormous" symbolic figures on and around the plains of Nazca in Peru as landing fields for space ships. Von Daniken seemed to believe no human could have drawn such straight lines without the aid of space vehicles. Aliens must have hovered over the earth and gave humans instructions on how to draw straight lines.[56] The factual matter seems quite different than Von Daniken's suggestion. Those lines considered to be landing fields were more likely to have been measuring rods used to sight the movement of the heavenly bodies and were used to determine when to plant crops, etc. Such creations were used by many 'primitive' peoples. For instance, there is the more sophisticated, but less tedious 'Sun Dagger' (calendar) of Chaco Canyon in Arizona. This calendar was designed and constructed by the most primitive of peoples. These ingenious tools do prove that the ancient human had vast knowledge in the science of astronomy. I would also like to note that the straight-lined paths from the wilderness to the sacred village in Chaco Canyon in the southwestern United States are more amazing to me than the lines of Nazca. However, there is still the great Nazca question: How did primitive people draw those amazing straight lines? There are a number of related theories but, to date, no one knows for sure. One of the more interesting theories is a 'pre-Inca' tribe actually made hot air balloons. A man would go up in a balloon and direct the development of the designs.[57]

What Von Daniken has expressed as "enormous drawings" (presumably to signal space travelers) actually were figures of a spiritual nature—like zodiac signs. One often portrayed drawing is a prehistoric Indian deity referred to as the 'Blue Hummingbird.' Interestingly, this god would be worshipped and passed on through a number of early Indian civilizations finding its zenith during the Mayan culture.

Though they were probably not landing fields for alien space ships, the Nazca drawings are important marks in human ingenuity. They display a sophistication in the ancient humans' observance of the cosmos and a well defined spiritual awareness. There are many things about ancient man we cannot explain, but I think the human spiritual drive and researching mind, as well as geographical changes, are better explanations for most of these secrets then the visitation of aliens. Yet, even Alienists understand there is deep meaning in humanity's common ideas of myths and religions. They further understand secular explanations involving such phenomena are, at best, ignorant attempts to explain things which are bigger than man, things humans cannot materialize and make their own. I certainly agree with Von Daniken when he stated,

I think the psycho-analysts should curb the adepts of their science if they themselves want to remain credible. Our research into myths and legends and the interpretations of archaeology are - as far as they concern prehistory - tied up in a straitjacket of preconceived views. Eyes have grown blind, ideas become dead. Science says that it cannot accept imaginative solutions because they have no empirical or demonstrable foundation. But now serious conclusions become more and more fantastic every day, while at the same time the disparaged fantasies acquire a firmer background.[58]

Many writers like Von Daniken believe aliens brought to man his expressions of wonder. I, however, believe most of these common expressions are evidence of God's power within the human experience. Nonetheless, the Von Daniken theories give arguments which strengthen both the 'Noahian' (Theory #1) and 'Communality' (Theory #2) concepts.

In addition to Alienists and other sensationalists, many anthropologists and historians have tried to explain away the spiritual feelings of man through the human motives of fear or superstition. Sigmund Freud popularized this concept. Such explanations may well have merit. However, as in the case of spectacular alien alternatives, these secular speculations fall short of a complete understanding. From a wider and more careful examination, such motives as fear and superstition do not explain the total of the parts; the larger pattern of intuitive expression of man. There is one fact about the intuitiveness of human beings no scientist can refute. Simply put, humans must worship. We might not worship God. We might express our worship to musicians, actors, athletes, beautiful women, gorgeous men, inspiring paintings, creative works of architecture, the slick lines of a car or any one of a number of things. Yet, an inescapable fact of life is, humans must worship! Humans are built either by chance or by design to worship something.

Through these feelings of worship man became aware of the human soul—a part of humanness which may live after physical death. This soul became the backbone to the human association with God and understanding

SIMPLY PUT, HUMANS MUST WORSHIP.

God and His Will. From the earliest detectable days, humans have exhibited a sense of the eternal destiny awaiting the human soul.

Though the evidence indicates earlier suppositions, the Sumerians are generally given credit for the initial understanding of a post human existence in an underworld. The Sumerian underworld was known as the 'House of the Dead,' and the Sumerians buried possessions with their dead. It is assumed this was done so the dead could use these earthly things in the world to come. Some of the ancient cultures understood human behavior might have an effect on life after death. According to the Egyptian Book of the Dead and other sources of hieroglyphics, there was a "cult of Osiris" composed of priests and pharaohs. This cult would re-enact the experience of Osiris, their first 'god-king.' Osiris was to have been resurrected from the dead. The cult members would volunteer to experience what we post-modernists call "near death experiences." They would lie in a casket and allow fellow members to seal the coffin. One of the witnessing members would carefully count off approximately eight minutes before the casket could be reopened. Their texts indicate these near death experiences are similar to our own. Melvin Morse and Paul Perry described the Egyptian reasoning: "Each new king was supposed to be a direct reincarnation of Osiris. An important part of the ceremony was to re-enact his entombment. These rituals took place in the depths of the Great Pyramid and were a prerequisite for becoming a god-king."[59] Many slaves must have died in experiments designed to determine how long the casket should be sealed. Yet, the sophistication of the Egyptian religions and the major steps Egyptians made toward understanding life, death, God, good, evil give evidence of wisdom acquired through near death experiences. "An NDE (near death experience) gave Egyptian rulers a sense of all-knowing. Before they were sealed into the casket, they only acted like kings. Afterward, they felt as if they had deeper knowledge of the world around them."[60]

Morse and Perry conclude: "I also believe that an NDE as part of a king's prerequisite may account for the unusual peace and prosperity that Egypt enjoyed for the nearly two thousand years that the pharaohs reigned. As happens with those who experience NDEs today, these kings were transformed by the humbling and exalting experience of near death. They developed a reverence for the love that people share with one another. They became kind and caring and interested in the universe and the world around them."[61]

Other societies may have also used near death experiences to shape their belief systems. The Tibetan Book of the Dead and the Aztec Song of the Dead are two records which have wording which suggest such experimentation. Of particular interest to my writing is an Aztec reference to a twisting transformation of the first king, Quetzalcoatl, into a "a body of light" - the Morning Star.[62] This description suggests the Aztecs may have known about and perhaps used NDE.

Finally, ancient tablets have been found which not only verify Babylonian pagan religious practices, but indicate common spiritual relationships between ancient civilizations. One example is the Ebla Tablets, approximately 17,000 tablets recovered from a middle-eastern city. The tablets may date back as far as 2,300 to 2,400 B.C. Though these tablets have not been fully translated, they do seem to verify the saga behind the Babylonian theology. Dr. Clifford Wilson wrote:

There are literary texts with mythological backgrounds, incantations, collections of proverbs, and hymns to various deities. Rituals associated with the gods are mentioned, many of these gods being known in Babylonian literature of a later period. These include Enki, Enlil, Utu, Inana, Tiamut, Marduk, and Madu. The god of the city of Kish is also mentioned.[63]

Ebla was on a trade route between the Mediterranean Sea and the Euphrates River. It was located southwest of Mount Ararat (Noah's mountain) in the general vicinity of Ur. Referring to literature discovered prior to the actual recovery of Ebla, Dr. Wilson states, "The kingdom of Ebla had previously been known in Sumerian, Akkadian, and Egyptian texts . . ."[64] Thus, intellectual and spiritual concepts may have been widely expressed and exchanged throughout the known world.

CHAPTER 12

THEORY 1 (CONTINUED)
THE HUMAN INTELLECTUAL
CONNECTION

*(Speaking on divergent religious philosophies) - "It is in answering
these questions that the various theologies perform their theoretic
work, and that their divergencies most come to light. They all agree
that the 'more' really exists; though some of them hold it to exist in
the shape of a personal god or gods, while others are satisfied to
conceive it as a stream of ideal tendency embedded in the eternal
structure of the world. They all agree, moreover, that it acts as well
as exists, and that something really is effected for the better when
you throw your life into its hands. It is when they treat of the experience of 'union' with it that their speculative differences appear most
clearly. Over this point pantheism and theism, nature and second
birth, works and grace and karma, immortality and reincarnation,
rationalism and mysticism, carry on inveterate disputes."[1]*

As we continue to probe the religions of the world, we find some
interesting perplexities. Certainly, there are the numerous, uncompromising
differences which have caused conflicts throughout the ages. Just as obvious,
however, are the similarities and universal truths found throughout a multitude
of divergent ancient texts and scrolls. This conundrum may lead to a number
of interesting questions, including the following: Is there an eastern tie to the
religious heritage from Noah's ark? Is it possible that eastern thought had
access to fundamental Hebrew teachings?

Before we delve into the related historical background, I feel it necessary to make a few observations about eastern religions. Eastern religious
thought can generally be defined as existential. Confucianism may be the most
existential, for it is based on the agnostic teachings from one man's questions
about life. Of the common eastern disciplines, Hinduism, Shinto and Taoism
are perhaps the most theistic in their views. These 'most theistic' are also the
oldest of the eastern religions. If one understands human thought and is aware
of the philosophical changes which have taken place in the modern west, it is
easy to assume the early eastern intuitive understandings of God gave way to
the more modern human-centered or existential positions. There is no surprise

in the fact that a supreme God theology has evolved into a human-centered position because, to some extent, we find this same evolution occurring in the United States of America today. Eastern thought now declares that the human being has total power over his or her life and can even determine the path to heaven (or Nirvana or Nothingness, etc.).

In our consideration of world religions, let us look at an age outline of the major world religions. Using the New York Public Library Desk Book as a reference, the abbreviated time line for the founding of these religions is as follows:

2000 B.C. Judaism, founded by Abraham.

1500 B.C. Hinduism, developed from various Indian regions and imported Aryan religions.

604 B.C. Taoism, founder Lao-tzu is reported to have been born on this date in China.

588 B.C. Zoroaster, traditional date of revelation to Zoroaster.

563–483 B.C. Buddhism, founded by Siddhartha Gautama.

551–479 B.C. Confucianism, founded by Confucius.

4–6 A.D. Christianity, Jesus of Nazareth is born.

500 A.D.   Shinto, introduced in writing. (Actual founding date may be prehistoric).

570–632 A.D. Islam, founded on the writings of Muhammad, the prophet.

There is some question as to the age of Shinto. However, if we assume that it is perhaps a contemporary to Taoism, we will probably have a fairly accurate picture of the known foundations of the major world religions. When considering the above timeline, one might question if there is a guiding connection involved with these religions.

Let us presume that for some time after the days of Noah, the world worshipped one God. They worshipped the God of Noah, the God who proved His power by commanding the Great Flood. However, this original Noahian relationship with the supreme power was diluted over time by human super-stitions and intellectualism. Earlier, we discussed a scenario based on Mrs. Noah's reproductive responsibility. According to the scenario, she was the major child bearer survivor; thus, she became revered. In time, this ancient lady may have been worshipped through ceremonies and festivals originally begun to celebrate her success in bearing children. Mrs. Noah's fate would stimulate human questions. Two pagan concepts may have easily evolved. First: It is the woman that bears life and not the man. Thus, the one who 'cre-ated' (confused with begot) human beings was a female. Therefore, God must be female. Second: God (a male) cannot bear fruit. Thus, there must also be a female goddess who is the bearer of life. Therefore, God was mated to and created through a goddess. This divine marriage concept has been justified throughout history. Mythological 'god' hierarchies seem to be built on soap opera mentalities where gods mate with goddesses and bear other gods and goddesses. They feud, fight, make up, etc. It is not hard to imagine humans trying to analyze God in their minds as they wonder how God makes things happen. Through human reasoning, the entire world slipped out of touch with divine truth and into a pagan world culminating with the Babylon 'tower' incident. But, then, God again introduced Truth to humanity through Abraham. It was pure Truth not diluted by rationalism.

At least five hundred years before a sophisticated eastern religion existed, Abraham brought the Jewish (and Muslim and Christian) monotheistic God out of this age of "animisms." Previous to Abraham, the entire world may have practiced the superstitious spiritual activities which spread throughout the world from Babylon. (Egypt may have been a brief exception. It is widely accepted that Akhnaten, the Egyptian Pharaoh believed in a monotheistic god—Ra, the sun god). In this dilution, the Jews may have lost sight of Noah's impression of one universal God and, in fact, worshipped many gods, including a god associated with the characteristics of the wind. Some scholars have proposed that YHWH was originally thought of as a wind and weather 'god.' It may have been through this wind or weather deity that YHWH—the God of Noah revealed Himself to Abraham. Whether or not this was the case is secondary. What is important is that Abraham did meet the God of Noah, the great I AM, an All Powerful God whose name is too sacred to be spoken. YHWH, the wondrous and awesome, who is, was and will be the one God and only God of the universe. Through this awesome divine revelation, Abraham may have been the founding father of modern religious thought. If the Bible is correct, Abraham became the servant of the God of Truth and the true Word of God was once again to become part of human understanding. This revival predated all modern eastern and western religions. If this event was factual, then one might conclude the short Biblical account of Abraham's lessor known sons, the sons of his servants etc., may have been the source of sophistication in eastern religious thought. The Bible states, "Abraham deeded everything he owned to Isaac; however, he gave gifts to the sons of his concubines and sent them off into the east, away from Isaac."[2]

These eastern lands are considered to have included parts of Iraq, Iran, perhaps Pakistan and Afghanistan. In like manner, historical records reveal Aryan shepherds pushed into eastern soil. It is thought they also pushed through the very lands Abraham's other sons (by his servants) had settled. As suggested, Abraham began Judaism around 2000 B.C. At approximately that time, the Middle East experienced the re-emergence of monotheism—the

WHAT IS IMPORTANT IS THAT ABRAHAM DID MEET THE GOD OF NOAH,
THE GREAT I AM, AN ALL POWERFUL GOD WHOSE NAME IS
TOO SACRED TO BE SPOKEN.

belief in one universal 'God.' It is also thought that around 2000 B.C., the Persians (Iranians) were developing sophisticated Hinduistic and Taoistic concepts. This includes concepts regarding the inner actions of good and evil forces.[3] From these same concepts, Persian Zorasterianism would develop. Perhaps Persian beliefs formed from a mixture of Abrahamian and early Sumerian theology, along with invading foreign influences. Included in these foreign influences would be migrant Aryan tribes.

Sumerian ancestors may have wandered into the Mesopotamian region from the northeast. We know very little about these people. Perhaps they maintained some semblance of Noahian thought, because their god dwelled on the top of Mount Sumeru. Earlier, Noah worshipped God on Mount Ararat. Some scholars feel the Sumerian influence carried religious traditions to various ancient civilizations including Babylon, Egypt, India and China.[4]

Additionally, the Persian theological mixture may have played a major role in the development of the Greek and Roman god hierarchy. Both the Greek god, Zeus and the Roman god, Jupiter are thought to have evolved from the European sky and weather god, Dyaus Pitar.[5]

No one is certain what exactly happened in India. Certainly, the nomadic Aryans carried their new, sophisticated spiritual concepts to India which helped shape modern eastern philosophy and religion. It is assumed a number of Aryan tribes brought with them a variety of foreign beliefs, experiences and customs. For example, the Aryans may have introduced a supreme god called 'Indra' with a host of lessor gods which were associated with nature. Previous to this influx of Aryan culture, the Indus must have developed a polytheistic theology. These native Indus are believed to be the outstanding influence in the early Rg (Rig) Vedas. Thus, these early Rg Vedas offer the best examples of the Indus polytheistic beliefs.

In modern Hinduism we find an unmistakable layering of ancient deities influencing a variety of other gods. During the late Paleolithic and Neolithic areas, goddess worship in one form or another swept through Europe, Siberia, down through Mesopotamia and continuing into the far east. Just previous to the Aryan invasion, goddess worship seems to have been an influence in the Indus religion. This period of influence is referred to as the 'Harappa culture.' The modern Hindu mother goddess who is 'guardian' of the home as well as the village was an outgrowth of the Harappa culture.[6] Also from this (Harappa) era is found a prototype of the male god Shiva with three faces, one frontal and two profiles. Additionally, this god sits in a 'Yoga posture.' Shiva as Pawupati is "Lord of the Beasts and Prince of Yoga."[7]

It is thought that the later Rg Vedas and the Upanishads were greatly influenced by the Aryans. Thus, these later Rg Vedas and Upanishads unmistakably embrace monotheistic thought. These Aryans were the dominate force after their invasion and they had developed a supreme god deity previous to their arrival in India.[8] Not only did the Aryans hold a primitive but evolving monotheistic understanding of Brahman as an "all-pervading power," but also, to one extent or another, an understanding of a god personality because "it (Brahman) knew itself."[9] We can further imagine that, over time, the subordinate Indus added their own influences. Here lies much of the confusion. With so many sources of theology being introduced in India, determining the source of each idea is perplexing. For example, the belief in the transmigration of the soul, generally known as reincarnation, is assumed to be an ancient (pre-Aryan) tradition. Furthermore, transmigration of the soul of humans into animals is considered to be a rather common expression of the ancient polytheistic 'animism' theologies. After the Aryans conquered the Indus, this transmigration theology was apparently repressed. However, over a period of time the concept was enveloped into the Hindu beliefs.[10]

Nonetheless, the Aryans may well have understood reincarnation, for this was also a Persian concept. The Persian influence in reincarnation seems to have become an influence throughout Mesopotamia to include some of the celebrated Greek philosophers, as well as area religions including the Jewish Kabbalists and Gnostics.

So, where is the Abrahamian influence on Hinduism? When we segregate those concepts thought to have originated with the pre-Iranian Aryan invaders, and extract concepts which would seem to have originated from or favor a polytheistic theology (influence of the Indus), we discover a Middle Eastern 'type' of religion. We find a religion with primitive monotheistic tendencies, or at least a belief in a supreme ruler, good and evil forces struggling with one another, and a spiritualness of life perhaps to include a human soul. Where did these sophisticated religious concepts come from if not from an Abraham influence? Why not deduce they came from the oldest possible source? One might very well suppose Abraham's belief was dogmatic. Therefore, one would have expected to find monotheism passed down and around. If my conjecture is correct, then Hinduism was both a melting pot of theological thought and an eroded version of Abraham's teachings. The next question seems quite logical. Modern Hindus do not believe in a God like YHWH. If the Aryans brought monotheism to India, what happened to their infusion of monotheism? The answer is quite simple; however, it is also profoundly important to the understanding of human logic in relation to spiritual concepts. Much of the Aryan sophistication was rejected by the rationalism of Vedic thinkers. Their efforts to establish a harmony or their own one (little) world religion eventually led to monism.

Because this is so important to the historical differences between Hinduism and middle eastern theology, I am compelled to post a quote by

Gregg M. Sinclair on this theistic evolution and the reasoning behind such change:

> *Even the single great Being of the monotheistic period did not escape criticism. The mind of man is not satisfied with an anthropomorphic deity. The seeking mind did not so much care for personal comfort and happiness as for absolute truth. Whatever the emotional value of a personal God may be, the truth sets up a different standard and requires a different object of worship. Monotheism failed to satisfy the later Vedic thinkers. And thus monotheism eventually gave way to philosophical monism, the doctrine of the impersonal, unknowable One.*[11]

Thus, the Hindu religion was shaped to meet the Indian 'thinkers' existential understanding. Hinduism was not focused on intuitive understandings. Instead, it focused on human reason and philosophical synthesis. This seems quite logical for we are witnesses to Christianity being exposed to the existential view. Given enough time, these existentialism could produce radical changes in fundamental Hebrew/Christian doctrine. In fact, Calvin's great contribution to Christianity was his re-emphasis of the fundamental Truth in Scriptures. Calvin's logic removed much of the human philosophy which had infiltrated Christianity. Thus, an existential position mixed with an eroding objective Truth very adequately explains such changes to the Aryan religious concepts.

As we continue with this evolution of thought, we find even clearer examples of existential influence on eastern religion. Hinduism was the 'mother' of modern eastern religion. But, from the human position, Hinduism did not adequately explain certain human theological conflicts. The obvious example is Buddhism. It originated primarily because Hinduism did not adequately explain the divine reason for human pain and suffering. This, of course, is a major problem in all religious thought. If you will recall, accepting the theological view of pain and suffering kept Einstein separated from traditional religion.

The Noahian influence may partially explain the growth of religious practices, but it does not address the common acceptance of certain traditions and concepts. My second theory may come closer to addressing these issues.

CHAPTER 13

THEORY 2
EVERY HUMAN BEING
INTUITIVELY KNOWS GOD

*"The further limits of our being plunge, it seems to me, into an alto-
gether other dimension of existence from the sensible and merely
'understandable' world. Name it the mystical region, or the supernatural region, whichever you choose. So far as our ideal impulses
originate in this region (and most of them do originate in it, for we
find them possessing us in a way for which we cannot articulately
account), we belong to it in a more intimate sense than that in which
we belong to the visible world, for we belong in the most intimate
sense wherever our ideals belong. Yet the unseen region in question
is not merely ideal, for it produces effects in this world. When we
commune with it, work is actually done upon our finite personality,
for we are turned into new men, and consequences in the way of
conduct follow in the natural world upon our regenerative
change."[1]*

As discussed earlier, we humans have a common mindset regarding
many soulful matters. My interest in these common grounds began while taking a Greek Philosophy course at SMU. A number of Greek philosophers,
including Plato and Aristotle, perceived basic moral and spiritual concepts.
Some of these perceptions are akin to that of the Hebrew values. Perhaps these
great thinkers were also able to find a spiritual contact with the Creator God
Almighty, or perhaps God's concepts are so logical and real that even 'pagan'
man could find them reasonable. What Plato and Aristotle did was discard the
mythological gods. Then, through the instruments of science and reason, each
designed philosophical models of life which, in many ways, complimented
Hebrew principles. With these revolutionary ideals the Greeks began a logical
examination and deduction of human and natural values. It was this examination which led to many of their celebrated philosophical truths. With the
Hebrew religious/Greek philosophical similarities being so obvious, and the
Hebrew/Greek regions geographically aligned, I held the same mental quiz
many historians must have pondered. I thought it quite logical that the Greeks
'borrowed' ideas from the ancient Hebrew (or vice versa) in a crossover of

values and thought. Though this crossover would initially seem logical, there are obviously major fundamental differences. The Greeks looked at their religion in a totally different manner than the Jews. Greek culture did not accept the mythological affairs of the 'gods' as actual events but were more in the form of explanations for otherwise unexplainable natural occurrences. This mythological, theological approach was necessary because the Greeks had 'out-grown' the spiritual wisdom of their day. Therefore, both Greek theology and other intellectual ideologies needed a way to grow. Their concepts were first crude, but evolved into a sophisticated, yet always changing understanding. The Jews, on the other hand, had an entirely different attitude. From the earliest of records, the Hebrew theological principles were much more advanced, stable and absolute than that of Greek pantheism. Any serious student must realize that the Jews would not have changed their basic theology in the slightest way for any Greek myth or philosophy. Obviously, much of what the Greeks had discovered about the human soul by logic, the Jews had received from YHWH in a purer and more meaningful form. Simply put, while the Greeks were advancing in logos, the basic Hebrew spiritual concepts were ancient, showed little change and were sophisticated well beyond their time. Furthermore, it seems reasonable that a crossover of concepts from Hebrew to Greek would also have a noticeable influence in the mythological beliefs of the common Greek. Yet, Hebrew thought was not embraced by the Greek populace. So, what caused the difference between the spiritual intuitiveness of the Greek philosopher and the Greek populace? Why did the philosopher understand the human soul more than the Greek priest? It was the philosopher's use of human intellect. Though it would be hard to find evidence of the Greeks 'borrowing' moral or spiritual concepts from the Hebrews, it is quite obvious that man 'knows' certain laws intuitively.

The similarities between religions are amazing. Instead of looking at religion in the usual way, let us compare the earliest religions from an essence perspective. What is it that early religions say about themselves? To begin, let us expound upon the previously mentioned anthropoogical view: Religious expression evolved from primitive ceremonies which are believed to be centered around survival. They include rituals to bring good fortunes in hunting, weather, crops, etc. Besides being "animisms," the "gods" were tribal gods as described above. There was a god of the wind, a god of the sun, a god of the hunt, a god of fertility, a god of love, a god for war, etc. These gods began to grow up and become more and more sophisticated. Men began to claim that their god/gods were communicating with them, i.e., leading them, giving them signs, etc.

ON BEING HUMAN

I assume the psyche and the soul have separate functions in the human makeup, but both play important roles in the human condition. However, post-modernists have focused on the psyche and neglected the soul. They have treated the ancient man's spiritual behavior as only an activity of human superstition and non essential to our human makeup. Carl Jung, the great psychoanalyst, developed a theoretical description of the mechanics involved in this psyche/soul relationship and exposed the disheartening results of our modern neglect. The concepts in both theories (Noahian and intuitive man) overlap, for each probes the function of our human soul and the birth of theology.

SPIRIT AS ARCHETYPE

Anthropologists generally state that the above-mentioned animisms developed from crude superstitions. What if the anthropologists are only partially right? Perhaps, animisms are more 'psychically' involved in humanness. Perhaps, they are primary expressions of the spiritual nature of man in his environment. Perhaps, if we post-modernists were more in tune with the plumbing of our psyche or 'self' and its connection to the human soul and/or spirit, we would have a greater reverence for these primitive intuitive expressions and realize that they declare hidden truths. We are becoming more and more aware that things outside of our physical condition affect our health. A positive attitude and personal happiness support good health. Hate and other evil thoughts might negatively affect our health. However, our 'modern' world does not allow the individual any freedom for self understanding. Our society dictates psychic 'relativism.' Yet, the psychic experience is only valid relative to the understanding of psychology - an inexact science; thus, intuitive spiritual feelings are considered naive superstitions.

Freud in his book, *Totem and Taboo,* used his popularized psychoanalytical approach to explain intuitive religion. In his creative logic, he wildly speculated about the foundations of primitive human lifestyles. Freud suggests primitive man headed a kind of human herd mainly composed of females and offspring. The man was the protector and head of the unit. However, on an occasion, a young male youth had a sexual desire for his mother, so he killed his father and ate his dead parent in a 'ritual' fashion. Guilt set in and the young male perhaps removed himself from the group and remembered this violent act through animal sacrifice.[2]

Though Freud's concept was interesting, it was mainly an attempt to allow a godless evolution to explain existence. Thus, it was lacking in depth. Doesn't it make more sense to propose the earliest man understood the force of God in his universe? Even if we give Freud the benefit of the doubt and

WE ARE BECOMING MORE AND MORE AWARE THAT THINGS OUTSIDE OF OUR PHYSICAL CONDITION AFFECT OUR HEALTH.

accept his theory as fact, it still does not get to the bottom of human religion. One must continue to ask, "Why does the Freudian man have a discerning conscience and yet the dog, the cat, the monkey, the elephant seem to lack such an intellect." Animals do not reason right from wrong on a moral basis. As man became more in touch with God, the earliest of the world's religions matured and grew in sophistication.

Interestingly, some researchers may have located a 'God Nodule' in the forehead of the human brain. If this is true the nodule may be related to the human need to search for God. Yes, humans may be 'wired' to worship God.[3] Nonetheless, it is obvious that the entire human race has an intuitive need to connect with God. Mohandas K. Gandhi is an excellent example of a human searching for God. Gandhi rejected the traditional Hindu understanding of God, because he did not think God was polytheistic. To him God could be expressed as Satya or Truth. Of course Truth exists everywhere, thus Gandhi spent his life searching for Truth. In this quest Gandhi became familiar with western religion. However, he rejected Jesus as the Son of God because he did not believe only one man could be the Son of God. Some interesting comparisons can be drawn between Gandhi's position on Truth and the Jewish reverence for God's Law. Gandhi claimed, "Ahimsa (nonviolence) is my God, and Truth is my God. When I look for Ahimsa, Truth says, 'Find it through me.' When I look for Truth, Ahimsa says 'Find it through me.'" On another occasion Gandhi explained how one can know Truth. He proposed Truth was, "what the voice within tells you."[4]

A great portion of the world's spiritual beliefs are based on the voice within, i.e., man's intuitions of God. Perhaps these intuitions consist of that part of God which God wishes to reveal to a particular people at a particular place and time. Perhaps that is done through some biological connector such as a 'God Nodule.' In my opinion, Gandhi's weakness was he did not understand his inner voice; he relied almost completely on philosophical religion and human logic to interpret 'Truth.' Problems arise when existential man tries to use intellect to define God, that is, when humans put God into a man-made philosophical box enforced by human pride. This becomes even clearer in the Spinozian 'archetype' of god. The Spinozian god theory is based totally on personal philosophy. This human creation of a god model is encouraged by Keirkagaard's existential thought, for God becomes relative to the subjectivity of man. Spinoza's god would allow the human to evolve into the intellectual giant of the universe. However, in many of the monotheistic religions, God has revealed Himself to be not only 'Almighty,' but multi-faceted. This aspect of God's personality is quite obvious in the Christian tradition of the

---

NONETHELESS, IT IS OBVIOUS THAT THE ENTIRE HUMAN RACE HAS
AN INTUITIVE NEED TO CONNECT WITH GOD.

'Holy Trinity.' However, it is also apparent in the Hebrew religion. For example, in Genesis we read that God's Spirit hovered over the waters. These concepts differ from the eastern pantheistic religions. Generally stated, Hinduism promotes the belief that everything is God. Yet the Buddhist does not have any concept of God, as God is beyond description.

There is a better way to compare eastern and western religions. It is important to consider a religion from its philosophical position. I think the above example of the Spinozian god model says much about Spinoza's outlook on God, i.e., his position in his search for Truth. Even by generalizing religious philosophies we find some interesting analogies. Similar to the Spinozian model, the eastern religions are fundamentally existential. In this tradition, man reaches for God, not knowing God through divine revelation, but subjectively through the examination of nature and self. Thus, he does not have an authority 'God.' The eastern understanding is based on the existence of man in relation to whatever he communicates with, i.e., whatever he touches, whatever he feels, whatever he senses, whatever he knows, etc. The dilemma then is: When man seeks God through 'self,' there is no one to point the way. This, as we will soon see, has been and is a major problem for mankind.

The western and/or middle-eastern religions bridge this dilemma through what they understand to be objective revelations. These 'revelations are proclaimed to be directives from God. Christianity, Judaism and Islam, the major examples of these religions, are authoritarian in nature and demand the personal worship of one God. In Judaism and Christianity, we find a God to man objective relationship—God reaching to man and allowing man to accept or reject His authority. In the Islamic belief, it is man who reaches to God or Allah. However, the Koran (the Islamic Holy book) is believed to be God's objective revelation through His prophet Mohammed. In all three cases, Christian, Jewish and Islam, worshipers seek God's authority in their personal lives.

THE SYMBOLIC CONNECTION IN RELIGION

As stated in the introduction, *all humanity intuitively knows God.* Enveloped in this intuitive spiritual nature lies a reverence for certain ritual symbolism. These symbols are often regarded as religious archetypes (mental representations). Likewise, the vehicle of communication for these "religious archetypes" is the dream state. It would be well to note that most religions claim their spirituality came to humanity through dreams and/or visions.

When we consider this 'religious' connection of a collective uncon-

---

IN JUDAISM AND CHRISTIANITY, WE FIND A GOD TO MAN OBJECTIVE
RELATIONSHIP—GOD REACHING TO MAN AND ALLOWING MAN
TO ACCEPT OR REJECT HIS AUTHORITY.

scious, the significance lies in the distinct similarities of ritual symbolism shared by the various world religions. I am referring to physical religious rituals which are actual reflections of needs of the subconscious. Although not normally introduced as Jungian analysis, 'symbolic ritualization' is a common area of study in Comparative Religion classes. Yet, from this perspective we encounter real identifiable evidence of a deep profound intuitive acknowledgment of God. Perhaps this intuitiveness could even be described as a spiritual calling for the subjugation of 'self' to God. There are many such examples. However, it is perhaps more important, to recognize the common connection or intuitive 'collective unconscious' of these religious activities.

THE SACRIFICE AS AN ARCHETYPE

A common ritual widespread in ancient god worship was the offering of sacrifices. In fact, sacrificial rituals are one of mankind's oldest common spiritual expressions. Man universally feels unworthy to approach the deity. He feels a theological need to appease and please the gods. In ancient rituals, there were two distinct types of sacrifice. 1) the *sacrifice of produced crops.* 2) *blood sacrifice,* both animal and human. We have a description of both types of sacrifice in the Biblical story of Cain and Abel—children of the first human family on earth.

Abel became a shepherd, while Cain was a farmer. At harvest time, Cain brought the Lord a gift consisting of his farm products, i.e., grains, etc. Abel brought the fatty cuts of meat from his best lambs. The Lord accepted Abel's offering, but not Cain's. This made Cain feel rejected and angry. His face grew dark with fury.[5] The divine choice of animal sacrifice set the precedent for the Hebrew tradition.

Yet, other religions did practice the ritual sacrifice of crops. The Anasazi (ancient American native) offered grain to the Sun god. The Anasazi native would hold grain out to the sun and let it blow away in the wind. Halfway around the world ancient pagans across the European continent also sacrificed some of their harvest to the gods and goddesses. This too, is evidence of a common understanding of sacred symbols.

However, blood sacrifices are certainly the more dramatic. Blood rituals were part of the human religious experience even back to the most ancient times, a fact which gives credence to the Biblical account of Cain and Abel. God addressed Cain after he had slain his brother. In His remarks to Cain, God declares His abhorrence for the shedding of innocent human blood: "Your brother's blood calls to me from the ground. What have you done? You are hereby banished from this ground which you have defiled with your brother's blood."[6] Likewise, God later states, "And murder is forbidden. Man-killing animals must die, and any man who murders shall be killed; for to kill a man is to kill one made like God."[7]

To understand the true ancient Hebrew meaning of these Biblical statements, let us look at Philo who lived from about 20 B.C. to about 50 A.D. and wrote extensively about Jewish religious matters. Philo commented on the importance of blood in regard to God's directions to Noah (thus man) given in Genesis 9:4: "But never eat animals unless their life-blood has been drained off." Philo also stated:

> *God appears by this command to indicate that the blood is the sub-stance of the soul; I mean of that soul which exists by the external senses and by vitality, not of that which is spoken of with a certain especial preeminence, being the rational and intellectual soul; for there are three parts of the human soul; one the nutritive part, another that which is connected with the external senses, and the third that which exists in reason. Therefore the rational part is the substance of the divine spirit according to the sacred writer Moses: for in his account of the creation of the world, he says, 'God breathed into his face the breath of life,' as being what was to constitute his life. But of that part of the soul which is connected with the external senses and with vitality, blood is the substance; for he says in another place, 'The blood exists in every breath of flesh.'*

> *It is with great propriety in fact that he has called the blood the breath of all flesh, because*

> *there are in the flesh senses and passions, but not intellect not thoughts. But again by the expression 'the spirit of blood,' he inti-mates that the spirit is one thing and the blood another; so that the essence of the soul is truly and beyond all possible question spirit. But that spirit has a place not by itself separately, apart from the blood in the body; but it is interwoven and mingled with the blood.[8]*

As previously mentioned, Noah made blood sacrifices. His first act on Mount Ararat, after releasing the animals, was to make a blood sacrifice unto God. Noah built an altar and sacrificed those animals God had designated for ritual sacrifice.[9]

One might also recall the directions God gave Moses about the Passover:

> *From now on, this month will be the first and most important month of the Jewish calendar. Annually, on the tenth day of this month (announce this to all the people of Israel) each family shall get a lamb (or, if a family is small, let it share the lamb with another small fam-ily in the neighborhood; whether to share in this way depends on the*

size of the families). This animal shall be a year-old male, either a sheep or a goat, without any defects.

On the evening of the fourteenth day of this month, all these lambs shall be killed, and their blood shall be placed on the two side-frames of the door of every home and on the panel above the door. Use the blood of the lamb eaten in that home. Everyone shall eat roast lamb that night, with unleavened bread and bitter herbs. The meat must not be eaten raw or boiled, but roasted, including the head, legs, heart, and liver. Don't eat any of it the next day; if all is not eaten that night, burn what is left.

Eat it with your traveling clothes on, prepared for a long journey, wearing your walking shoes and carrying your walking sticks in your hands; eat it hurriedly. This observance shall be called the Lord's Passover. For I will pass through the land of Egypt tonight and kill all the oldest sons and firstborn male animals in all the land of Egypt, and execute judgment upon all the gods of Egypt - for I am Jehovah. The blood you have placed on the doorposts will be proof that you obey me, and when I see the blood I will pass over you and I will not destroy your firstborn children when I smite the land of Egypt.[10]

The Jewish tradition of sacrificing sheep also became one of the most important symbols in Christianity. Most Christians believe the Jewish blood sacrifices were symbolic expressions of God pointing to the divine significance of the coming suffering Savior - Jesus Christ. This is the same Suffering Savior referred to in Psalms. Because of Jesus' crucifixion for the sins of humanity, Jesus is often lovingly referred to as the "Lamb of God." Thus, the salvation of the Passover blood is symbolic of the blood of Jesus. The roasted meat is symbolic of the flesh of Jesus. Even the unleavened bread bears the prophetic marks of the crucifixion. Unleavened bread has small holes laced throughout which are symbolic pierce marks from the nails in Jesus' limbs. Lines across the bread are representative of the lash marks on Jesus' body. God's insistence of wearing traveling clothes while eating the lamb is symbolic of a Christian's need to be ready to travel with Jesus through the sorrows and triumphs of life.

In addition to these historical Hebrew/Christian sacred rituals, there are many primitive myths, stories and legends of a religious nature which bear similarities to the death and/or resurrection of Jesus. We find one such example in the Philippine Islands where legend held that humans annually sacri-

MOST CHRISTIANS BELIEVE THE JEWISH BLOOD SACRIFICES WERE SYMBOLIC EXPRESSIONS OF GOD POINTING TO THE DIVINE SIGNIFICANCE OF THE COMING SUFFERING SAVIOR - JESUS CHRIST.

ficed other humans for "good fortunes" during their seasonal harvest. Here is a description of the proceedings:

> *Early December, when the constellation Orion appeared at seven (God's universal number) o'clock in the evening, the people knew that the time had come to clear their fields for sowing and to sacrifice a slave. The sacrifice was presented to certain powerful spirits as payment for the good year which the people had enjoyed, and to ensure the favor of the spirits for the coming season. The victim was led to a great tree in the forest; there he was tied with his back to the tree and his arms stretched high above his head, in the attitude in which ancient artist portrayed Marsyas hanging on the fatal tree. While he thus hung by the arms, he was slain by a spear thrust through his body at the level of the armpits. Afterwards the body was cut clean through the middle at the waist, and the upper part was apparently allowed to dangle from the tree, while the under part wallowed in a pool of blood on the ground. The two portions were finally cast into a shallow trench beside the tree. Before this was done, anybody who wished might cut off a piece of flesh or a lock of hair from the corpse and carry it to the grave of some relation whose body was being consumed by a ghoul. Attracted by the fresh corpse, the ghoul would leave the mouldering old body in peace.*[11]

Many analogies between this variety of ritual and the death of Jesus can be drawn. The most important might be the sacrifice of the servant's life and the shedding of the servant's blood for the well being of others. Human sacrifices have been ritualized around the world, from the Maya Indians of Central/South America to African tribes in the deepest world jungles.[12]

On the other hand, we find an antithesis or perhaps evil power symbolized through blood in human sacrifice and terror in the name of Satan. Periodically, a police officer or FBI agent, etc. will be interviewed on T.V. and indicate that the rumors of Satanic terror and human sacrifices are unfounded. To those of you who might question the validity of Satanic activity, let me remind you that Richard Ramirez, "the Night Stalker," was a "disciple of the Devil."[13] The satanic Matamoros gang led by Adolfo de Jesus Constanzo and Sara Maria Aldrete murdered Mark Kilroy, a student at the University of Texas. Their human sacrifices were to appease Satan.[14]

Serial killer, Jeffrey Dahmer is of particular interest to me because of his ritualistic behavior. However, others have, to one extent or another, practiced these same rituals. Yet, Dahmer was sensationalized to an extent that his behavior became clear to the public. He decapitated victims, painted their heads and kept these heads and other body parts in a refrigerator. If you were to substitute the refrigerator for other manners of saving heads and bones, etc. Dahmer's actions mimic any one of a number of ancient societies. Furthermore, he experimented with brain surgery attempting to make his victim a 'zombie.' He also practiced cannibalism. It is interesting to note, Dahmer explained his cannibalism as an attempt to ingest the essence of his victim, to have the victim closer to him, perhaps to 'become one' with the victim. Subconsciously he was imitating ancient 'rites' generally tied to Pagan or Satanic rituals but also related, in a perverted way, to the Christian practice of communion. In pre-Christianized Rome, Christians were sometimes connected with the practice of cannibalism because the Romans did not understand such Christian behavior as the ritual of communion.[15] In the Jewish tradition, when two people ate a meal together they symbolically became 'one.' In similar fashion, when a Christian practices the ritual of communion, he or she becomes one with the body of Christ.

In a related comparison, if we weigh the importance of God and Satan, it is not as important for a person to recognize the actual existence of Satan as it is to have a relationship with God. Yet, truth should dictate a human search for sources of good and evil. Enveloped in our intuitive knowledge is a recognition of right and wrong. Such dichotomy leaves room for both a good and an evil spirit or force. Within the theme of comparative religions, the existence of an evil force has long been recognized by virtually all world religions.

GOOD AND EVIL

However, the extent of our common religious expression extends well beyond our ritualization of symbols. A significant communality which groups a great number of ancient religions was their distinction between good and evil. A knowledge of good and evil may date back to the beginnings of human life. We are certain there was a clear understanding in the Egyptian, Sumerian and Babylonian cultures for each had both good and evil gods. Furthermore, the Egyptians may have been the first known culture to state that at death, good people were rewarded and the evil punished. I suspect this sophistication may have resulted from their previously described experiments in 'Life after Life' experiences.

Zoroaster was one of the first sophisticated religions which was based on the concept of good and evil. In many ways, Zoroaster is similar to Judaism. Zoroaster even declares 'righteous' people will pass on to paradise, while the 'wicked' will be 'purified' in hell. Yet, Zoroasterism embraces two supreme gods. One god is good and one god is evil. These two gods constantly battle.

Eastern thought, to a lessor degree, wrestled with good and evil. The yin and yang forces of the Chinese Tao are sometimes misconstrued as representations of good and evil. Actually, they are opposite forces. Yang is the positive force. Yin is the negative force. All things in the universe contain both yin and yang. From this point, the credibility of yin and yang greatly diminishes. Though many psychologists, etc. still refer to yin and yang, their practicality can be likened to that of the physical theories of an ancient Greek philosopher, Anaximander. He concluded that the world is the product of dueling qualities of nature; such as hot and cold, wet and dry. However, his concepts of science were so limited that he could not have mentally grasped the concept of the elements which are fundamental to modern science. Like Anaximander, the ancient Chinese philosophers and priests intuitively understood the presence of design and structure in the universe and expressed it through yin and yang, concepts comparable to, but less sophisticated than, Western spiritualism. It is often suggested that man 'collectively' knows it is 'morally' wrong to kill another human. Humanists argue that this ethic stems from an instinctive self preservation of man. Thus, it would seem, our instincts lead us to a common religious doctrine: Thou shalt not murder or harm another human being. Yet, humanity has been based on and owes its survival to an understanding of good and evil.

THE CONCEPT OF ONE GOD AND JUDAISM

Because a majority of people in the United States base their personal beliefs on the Hebrew and Christian theological teachings, it is interesting to note that numerous scholars believe the Jewish faith was greatly influenced by beliefs of other cultures. To whatever extent that may be true, perhaps the greatest outside influence on the Jewish religion were the Persians. These were the same Iranian people whose teachings brought the Aryan influence to India and, thus, developed Hinduism. The Babylonians enslaved the Jews. The Persians conquered the Babylonians. Thus, the Jews became property of the Persians.

Yet, by that time, the Persians' belief system had evolved into the Zoroastrian religion with both a good god and an evil god. It is extremely important to note, the Jews did not 'buy' the duel god concept. They had bonded with YHWH and YHWH was Ruler over all. In which directions the Jewish people moved, in whatever way Jewish thought changed, they never lost this one great and unique concept. YHWH was their one and only God. The fact that no other ancient people bonded to the belief of one God, Supreme Ruler, Creator and Almighty separates them from all other peoples. The Egyptians had the monotheistic concept but discarded it and returned to polytheism. The Aryan/Indus somehow found the monotheistic concept and then lost it to monism. Other civilizations may have understood and embraced

---

IN WHICH DIRECTIONS THE JEWISH PEOPLE MOVED, IN WHATEVER WAY JEWISH THOUGHT CHANGED, THEY NEVER LOST THIS ONE GREAT AND UNIQUE CONCEPT. YHWH WAS THEIR ONE AND ONLY GOD.

this concept for a brief while, but Judaism applied the bond. They made the concept of one All Mighty God the backbone of their existence.

SIMILARITIES BETWEEN EASTERN AND WESTERN RELIGION

Often popular writers in the west bring forth eastern philosophical ideas. This seems to be particularly true of the "self help" books. For example, in his writings, Dr. Wayne Dyer integrates some concepts from both eastern and western religions. Such books should be digested like any other philosophy book. I would hope one might gain insight about the sacred innuendoes of life. The obvious point of his book, *Real Magic,* is that Dr. Dyer recognizes the magic in human life. He recognizes a spark pointing to God. He recognizes the evidence of God's presence. And, though we might express these intuitive rules differently, all men have access to them. They are recognized around the world and in virtually every culture. If humanity continues to drift away from this understanding, it will fall even further from God. When we try to explain away the significance of both the worldwide evidence of God and His glory, we not only deny ourselves the true facts of life and the magic in life, but we are out of God's grace and out of His touch. In reality, He does not force us to accept His authority. Rather, He will allow us to live our lives in defiance. In this case, *Real Magic* is a statement on some of the same intuitive understandings expressed in C. S. Lewis' writings, but from a strictly existential perspective. Naturally, a diversity of observers expressing the 'magical' effects of spiritual activity builds an intellectual case for a God presence who is communicating with and working within humanity (activities which many secular psychologists would like to deny).

DIFFERENCES BETWEEN EASTERN AND WESTERN RELIGION

This 'magic' seems to play a major role in all inquisitorial religions (humans seeking Truth as in the Eastern tradition). They examine the magic and the synchronicity and the miracles of everyday life. But here is where the east and the west part. The east is preoccupied with the message. We must realize the signs of 'magic' are elements of creation or perhaps the by-products of creation. They themselves are not 'God' nor are they some pantheistic revelation of the way to a god state for humans. The magic is but part of creation. Our ability to witness life beyond the physical materialism is one of the joys of being stewards to the creation. We are able to experience and express ourselves through these miracles, magic and synchronicities. God, through His creation, allows us to understand the wonders of His power and His Glory. (The God of the Bible warns us about worshiping nature and its magic or even becoming reliant upon it).

A UNIVERSAL SAVIOR

Everything so far in this chapter has been related to my theories about a special relationship between world events and beliefs. However, there is another unifying factor which speaks to one of the two major functions of all world religions. Since the earliest days of human existence, man has been looking for a Savior. Most people do not realize the universal reality of this human search. Virtually all world religions have prepared the way for a 'Savior' in one form or another. Most people probably realize the Jewish faith awaits a Messiah. Judaism expects their Messiah to step forward at any time. Furthermore, different individuals have been suggested as possible candidates for that position. As far as I am aware, no 'modern' Jew has publicly proclaimed the mission and accepted the Messiahship. Jews feel this Savior will make Israel the center of the earth. However, Muslims also await a Savior who will unite the Muslim believers and make them the conquerors of the world.

The eastern religions are somewhat different from most other religions. As I have previously discussed, they are philosophically existential. Therefore, it is harder to focus on broad statements. Yet, generally stated, they too await a Savior. As eastern holy men share wisdom, their following grows as they are revered and even deified. I am reminded of the 1960's when eastern holy men became celebrities in the American culture. People would travel to India and other eastern lands to serve a Maharaja. The famous 'Beatles' rock band seemed to change their entire life and music styles after making such a trip. However, the Maharaja cannot be the one who will save man for, when holy men die, they do not rise from the grave, but only turn to dust. The Buddha's life story is remarkably similar to Jesus' life. Furthermore, some of Buddha's teachings have been compared to Jesus' teachings. However, The Buddha did not rise from the dead and he did not forgive sin. Krista, considered mystical, also holds some of the spiritual uniqueness of Jesus. It is interesting to note the similarity in the Hindu deity's name 'Krista' and Jesus' title, the 'Christ.' I have philosophically wondered if the writings about Buddha and Krista and others were not, in some way, prophetic messages to the eastern man about a historic Son of God who did come to give the entire world instruction on how to love one another and exist in harmony.

When we look at a comparison of Persian theology to Judaism, one fact becomes very relevant to this discussion. That fact is that the Zoraster believers had a concept of a Messiah. Those early Jews, enslaved by Persia, must have found this Zorasterian similarity quite interesting. In fact, many scholars believe the Zorasterian messianic concept may have influenced the Jewish understanding. The Persians awaited 'the Redeemer,' who was more than a national figure. Joseph Gaer wrote, "From the Persians the Jews learned that they, too, awaited a Sayoshant, a Redeemer. But the Redeemer of the

---

HOWEVER, THE MAHARAJA CANNOT BE THE ONE WHO WILL SAVE MAN FOR, WHEN HOLY MEN DIE, THEY DO NOT RISE FROM THE GRAVE, BUT ONLY TURN TO DUST.

Zoroastrians was not to be just a national hero who would bring glory and power to the Persians. Their Sayoshant would redeem all of mankind from the powers of the Evil Spirit."[16] Perhaps, from this enslavement, the Jews began to realize that the coming of their Messiah would not only be the greatest physical-historical event in Jewish history, but would be a great event for everyone in the entire world. The Messiah would bring peace to all mankind as well as the entire animal kingdom. This experience, i.e., the understanding that others would be positively affected by the coming of the Messiah, must have had both positive and negative effects on the Jewish conscious. On the one hand, it would be good to bring peace to the world. On the other hand, the Jews were a segregated people by choice. And why not? They had been enslaved by their neighbors. Could they give up their nationalistic political view? How much true joy did they find in this expanded understanding of the Redeemer. Did the rest of the world deserve a Redeemer? I wonder if the Jewish leadership was not shaping their unique theological Truth to meet a political design.

As we probe this intuitive nature of man, we continue to find evidence of an intuitive human understanding of God's merciful salvation. Some exciting, but unexpected and, perhaps, ignored findings come from some of our most prestigious scholars. These dramatic findings have simply been shoved under the carpet by both the scholar and the theist. The scholar must be embarrassed to even suggest this most logical conclusion of these studies. To do so would be to admit that there is a universal and personal God who loves human beings. The findings to which I refer are that many of humanity's primitive myths and rituals may be common reflections of this human desire for God's promise to Adam of a coming Messiah.

CHAPTER 14

MYTHS, DREAMS, SYMBOLS AND RELIGION

Atheists believe life is a product of chance. In accordance, they must also assume all religions are factious myths, perpetuated by wishful thinkers. Their perception ignorantly embraces the works of some major modern philosophers including Carl Jung and Mythology researchers such as Joseph Campbell. To the contrary, these men collectively brought exciting discoveries related to the spiritual nature of man and the verification of an intelligence beyond our understanding!

Carl Gustav Jung is an enigma, a wild card, a black hole in the expanding purview of human logic. As we humans progress in understanding our own existence we are amazed at the complexity of even the simplest things. Jung's findings accentuate this axiom; his theories are so profound that we still do not fully appreciate their meanings. Scholars and laymen alike read into his thoughts things which are not there, and limit his works to measured conclusions without venturing into new frontiers, those areas of humanness most exciting to Carl Jung. Though a panorama of the human soul lies dormant at our feet, torn and mangled, we know little of its nature. All the while, Jung's roadmap to soulful expression seems abandoned for political delusion.

In an article entitled "Spiritual Questioning," the author suggests some people worship a human communication system developed and popularized by Jung. The point of the commentary was that such people do not understand that which they worship. The article began: "Embarked On A Search For Meaning—More And More Americans Are Turning to The Mythic Psychology Of The Late Carl Jung." The article then compared the atheistic approach to life as expressed by many psychotherapists to the traditional avenues of religion. Afterwards, the article addressed the reasoning for becoming some sort of Jungian mystic.[1]

Conservative critics rightly conclude Jung's psychoanalysis has no room to ask what is right and wrong, no basis for moral judgement. Thus, to Jung, emotions are the yardstick to understanding self. But, Jung was not dealing with right and wrong issues, only with human processing avenues. Most certainly there is a difference between right and wrong. Yet, this being true, a blatant question looms, i.e., why do people make bad or wrong choices? Why would anyone even consider making wrong or bad or evil choices if they can make good choices? Why is evil so exciting when, intellectually, we would rather do good? To whatever extent Jung's thinking brought about value clarification issues, one must realize the field of psychology must address these human behavior problems. Obviously, each human being holds different values which have been shaped from birth forward. That is what psychologists like Jung must deal with. Moreover, we have previously discussed the philosophical reasoning behind the switch from the human concern for right and wrong to the relative philosophies. It was the philosophers who introduced relativism to the fields of science.

This chapter is not a deliberation of the values nor the evils of psychology. Frankly, those spiritually oriented people who oppose secular psychology would be much more accepting if it validated objective values. However, because I intend to use Jung and other philosophers and psychologists in this chapter, I feel compelled to begin with a closer look at some of Jung's theories. Jung was not a theologian nor did he claim to be. Those who 'worship' anything related to the psychoanalytic process misunderstand Jung, but this misunderstanding is a problem for anyone who makes any part of creation their god. Finally, Jung has been misrepresented by the media and secular psychology picturing him as a fanatical atheist. I find it ironic that anyone acquainted with his works would call Jung an atheist.

However, for the sake of argument, let us consider a more pragmatic view of Jung. Assume for a moment that Jung *was* an atheist. Let us discount Jung's personal writings and assume (as Schaeffer assumed) Jung believed God is but the "supreme archetype (a symbol) arising out of the evolution of the race."[2] Jung's personal theological inclination is only 'incidental' to his theories. It is his findings which interest us. As a scientist, Jung found an observable spiritual world. This world is hidden from the modern materialistic man. Yet, it verifies what theists proclaim, i.e., there is a spiritual existence in the human journey and, therefore, the work of Jung should give humans yet another reason to believe in a personal God.

Those who question his motives or personal beliefs should read Jung's book, *Answer To Job*. This was a controversial book for both the secularist and the Christian. Jung may or may not have embraced Christianity in the traditional sense. Apparently, Jung's understanding of the spiritual world accumulated through a number of sources. Jung's family background included a grandfather who was a Christian minister and a mother who was a mystic. Moreover, Jung had personally experienced the paranormal, including a near-death experience after a heart attack in 1944.

Jung's expressions suggest that he had a knowledge of and a respect for the secrets of Kabbalah, a mystical branch of Judaism which may reach back to the days of Abraham. Ancient Kabbalahism could explain why some of Jung's concepts seem occultic in nature. Yet, his professional expressions might have simply been based on his experience with symbolism in dream states rather than from his personal theology. Nonetheless, he was no atheist. Jung deeply believed in God. Once asked about his belief in the existence of God, he retorted, "I don't believe. I know!" This declaration was not a Keirkegaardian "leap of faith." This was a scientist looking at the evidence and coming up with an unmistakable conclusion. Thus, the topic for this chapter could have been, "What Did Jung Know?" Psychiatrist James A. Hall, professor at Southwestern Medical School and consultant at Southern Methodist University, concludes Jung came to believe the dream state 'Self' was somehow an association to God. That is to say, God, the being in heaven, the Almighty One, Ruler of the Universe is somehow manifested into our dream state through that phenomenon labeled the archetype 'Self.' Simply put, the archetype Self is the awareness of higher values in a dream, as opposed to the self awareness or personal self of a dream. These higher values are sometimes brought into dreams by a God image, such as Jesus Christ or the Buddha.[3] I suggest Jung discovered a God to man connection which is much grandeur then an atheist can understand. From my perspective, God sometimes expresses His Will to us through our dreams. Additionally, I suggest Jung 'knew' God as 'personal' in the Christian sense. In fact, he understood God as personal in ways most Christians have yet to discover.

In an editorial note, Gerhard Adler recalled a message Jung had sent to a friend. Jung wrote, "I had to wrench myself free of God, so to speak, in order to find that unity in myself which God seeks through man. It is rather like that vision of Symeon the Theologian, who sought God in vain everywhere in the world until God rose like a little sun in his own heart."[4] Jung saw a sacredness in the world, a sacredness of Creation and a sacredness of mankind. That is the totality of his claim. If Jung's personal theological views were not traditional, so much the better, for his research into the human psyche, found to favor traditional theology, can not be judged as prejudicial. Thus, Jung's studies not only confirm the influence of God, but also the real human need for a human relationship with God the Savior (Jesus Christ).

Though Jung revealed his reverence for God, he only expressed himself as a scientist. He did not intend to be the founder of a new religion. He was not a theologian, and he did not publicly advocate any religion. In the introduction to *Answer to Job* Jung exposes his feelings on this very position:

> *In what follows I shall attempt just such a discussion, such a 'coming to terms' with certain religious traditions and ideas. Since I shall be dealing with numinous factors, my feeling is challenged quite as much as my intellect. I cannot, therefore, write in a coolly objective manner, but must allow my emotional subjectivity to speak if I want to describe what I feel when I read certain books of the Bible, or when I remember the impressions I have received from the doctrines of our faith. I*

do not write as a Biblical scholar (which I am not), but as a layman and physician who has been privileged to see deeply into the psychic life of many people. What I am expressing is first of all my own personal view, but I know that I also speak in the name of many who have had similar experiences.[5]

There were only a few exceptions to Jung's clinical demeanor as a scientist. As a matter of fact, his biggest theological problem seems to have been the same problem many of us experience in our own professions of life. He did not know when to take himself out of the psychology department and become a child of the Almighty. The fault in Jung's theological views became most apparent in *Answer To Job;* one cannot psychoanalyze God, and Jung tried. From my point of view, Jung had about as much success in this endeavor as my dog might have analyzing me. A dog cannot possibly understand human perception. Looking from a humanly logical position, a human cannot possibly understand the personal depth nor the multi-dimensional focus of God. Jung's discovery of the uncharted spiritual plains of reality should have led him to realize he is inadequate to perceive the awesome being of God. This brings us back to the same human frailty we have earlier discussed. Jung's analysis of God would naturally be from an existential position. His logic made 'mere man' the judge of God's actions and thus Jung's human understanding took authority over God. Though he realized his point of weakness and so stated his deficiency (in the above paragraph), he could not help giving his professional opinion about God. He saw God through psychoanalytic eyes. Quite naturally, this is a great example of an occupational hazard of the psychoanalysis. We are cautioned that "God never treats man as a thing, an it, and if man treats God in this way it is a grave abuse of fellowship."[6]

A second problem Jung seemed to have was also based on his professional existential view. Jung saw and understood the a priori meanings of symbols and myths. He experienced a spiritual osmosis of concepts from a world beyond the human. Obviously, this was extremely exciting to him. The mysteries of the unconscious and the related wonders of symbolism became the focus of his life. In addition, his conclusions hold spiritual value. However, the questions necessarily become: "What value do we use?" "How much merit do we put in ancient myths?" Modern religions suggest good and evil constantly wrestle within every individual's mind. As a scientist Jung saw this same struggle between these two great forces. It was the mythical hero's duty to slay the dragon; this expressed our inner struggle. Jung was convinced everyone had a sophisticated shadow side that had to be confronted and controlled. Yet, like most psychologist and psychiatrist, Jung saw evil in human life at a much greater frequency than the general populace might. Furthermore, as a professional, he witnessed the awesome destructive power of evil and the effect it had on both our subconscious and conscious states. He saw evil do psychological battle with good and often win. He saw evil appear in human dreams. He saw evil consume human reason. He saw evil take over peoples lives. Therefore, as a psychoanalyst, he had a much greater respect for the power of evil than you or I might have. Nonetheless, I suggest that Jung mixed the foundations of ancient myth and Christian dogma too thoroughly. It is understandable that he would involve the wisdom of symbols and myths in his understanding of Truth, i.e., his personal belief system. From this psycho-analytical view, 'evil' must seem much more evenly matched with 'good' than most people might imagine. Therefore, he obviously acquired both a great dis-dain and an enormous respect for 'evil.'

Jung's writings often seem 'deep' or overly complicated, his logic brilliant and provocative. Yet, his perceptions are beautifully simple. Jung's studies only uncover some curiosities regarding the human experience and draw logical conclusions about human mental processes. His system does not explain away God. He is not suggesting humanism. To the contrary, he was acquainted with a world beyond the material. Jung recognized the extreme structured form at the core of the human personality. He found an amazing infrastructure of ideas, thoughts and values which often surfaced in human dreams and myths. He designated this phenomena as the 'collective uncon-scious.' In addition, he broadened the human understanding of reality with his writings on issues like 'synchronicity.' Synchronicity is Jung's term indicating "meaningful coincidences."[7] Synchronistic events indicate that life is more than a 'crap shoot.' There are events taking place in our lives which defy any laws of chance or probability. There are relationships which seem to be pre-arranged by a mysterious source. Jung's conclusions certainly give validity to the term 'Divine Providence.'

I find it interesting and relevant that Jung was inspired by Einstein's early studies in relativity (of time and space) when Jung developed his con-cepts of the relativity of time in 'psychic' activity.[8] Thus, there is a connec-tion between relativity of time and space and Jungian synchronicity. Because of this synchronistic and relativity connection, one easily draws assumptions involving an outside influence or divine determinism.

It is important to note that the entirety of this chapter's discussion will be focused on the scientific (psychological and social) evidence of a human spirit and the existence of God. I write of a universal language which seems to be on a higher plain and more sophisticated than any spoken tongue. Jung has not been alone in conceptualizing such events. Suggestions of syn-chronistic relationships come from a variety of scientists and philosophers such as Gottfried Leibniz and his 'law of preestablished harmony.' [9] Additionally, common words like "serendipity" and "déjà vu" confirm that humans have a history of 'meaningful coincidences' and these seemingly meaningful events have been noted in previous times. Finally, this language is not confined to Christianity or Judaism or Islamic traditions or any other religious 'isms' but an intuitive function of the human being—a communication system which appears to connect the human spirit to human self. I am reminded of Lawrence Ferlinghetti's poem, *As in a play by Jean-Paul Sartre:*

> *And the dice*
> >*have already*
> >>*been thrown*
> *The hero swims in circles*
> >*returning & returning*
> *And arrives at the same*
> >>*whirlpools*
> >*and the same conclusions*
> *by different paths each time*
> *Arrives at the same final choices*
> >*by totally different arguments*
> >>*but always dictated by the same still voice*
> >>>*within himself*
> *(the road not taken always the same)*[10]

SYMBOLISM

According to Carl Gustav Jung, "What we call a symbol is a term, a name, or even a picture that may be familiar in daily life, yet one which possesses specific connotations in addition to its conventional and obvious meaning. It implies something vague, unknown, or hidden from us."[11] Of course, the linguist would contend all words are symbols. However, symbolism as related to this discussion implies an elevated meaning of an object which gives it an expanded and greater value than its true functional or material worth.

MYTH

The term 'myth' may be a bit misleading. When this term is used, most people probably think of a fairy tale, etc. But to the mythologist, it simply means story. The term does not necessarily judge the validity of the story. It does not mean true or false. It simply states 'story.' Considering the 'myth' in this fashion, one might say there are two popular myths about the John F. Kennedy assassination. One 'myth' being that a single gunman killed J.F.K. and the other 'myth' being a group of people killed J.F.K. Obviously, one myth is factual and one is not.

DREAMS

Dreams are the products of a complex internal communication system of inner self-expression. Through dreams, a person integrates information between the unconscious and conscious, giving insight to his or her behavior. According to Joseph Campbell: "Dream is the personalized myth, myth the depersonalized dream; both myth and dream are symbolic in the same general way of the dynamics of the psyche. But in the dream the forms are quirked by the peculiar troubles of the dreamer, whereas in myth the problems and solutions shown are directly valid for all mankind."[12]

Dr. John Freeman suggests, "The dreamer's individual unconscious is communicating with the dreamer alone and is selecting symbols for its purpose that have meaning to the dreamer and to nobody else . . . the communication of the unconscious are of the highest importance to the dreamer - naturally so, since the unconscious is at least half of his total being - and frequently offer him advice or guidance that could be obtained from no other source."[13]

I must stress the fact that John Freeman recognizes an 'advice or guidance' which comes from within self. This insight must be considered very significant to human spirituality. Furthermore, Freedman's recognition of "the ability to establish communication with the unconscious is part of the whole man" is equally important. This recognition correlates well with the understanding that man is more than a simple animal. He receives and evaluates information from expressions within. All of this leads to a profound point made by Dr. Freeman. "Those who have limited themselves to living entirely in the world of the conscious and who reject communication with the unconscious bind themselves by the laws of conscious, formal life. With the infallible (but often meaningless) logic of the algebraic equation, they argue from assumed premises to incontestably deducted conclusions."[14] Statements such as this cannot be easily dismissed. Human beings have intuitive resources which seem to reach beyond the boundaries of human reason. Yet, a meaningful discussion of dreams and dream analysis must involve the study of symbolism. It can be argued that there is a communality within the symbolism of dreams. Though each person's dreams are individualized and unique, certain symbols (often called achetypes) tend to stand for the same or a similar idea regardless of the dreamer.

Another psychological trait of man—the perceiving spiritual being, is the connection of these symbols to both dreams and myths. The Campbell/Jung influences lead one to believe most myths may have come from dreams. How else would one expect to find such a communality of symbols?

THE WISDOM OF MYTH

In like matter, researchers have found similarities in culturally isolated myths. Moreover, there seems to be common links between mythical concepts and religious ideals. Because of this communality of value, some scholars assume that both myths and religions are of a humanly conceived origin. An example of the similarities of values comes by way of the Roman myth of Cupid and Psyche. Psyche was a beautiful woman and Cupid was the son of Venus. Because Venus resented Psyche's beauty, she directed Cupid to shoot Psyche with one of his famous darts causing this attractive creature to fall in love with some unworthy suitor. However, Cupid fell in love with Psyche and talked Venus into accepting Psyche. This, of course, made Psyche immortal and Cupid very happy. The mythological conclusion is that "you can not separate Psyche (soul) from Cupid (love)." Or "the soul and love must be connected." This is just one of many myths that seem to seek and define intuitive values.[15]

THE VALUE OF SYMBOLS

No matter how this communality occurs, there is reason to expect some form of collaboration between dreams and myths. Many researchers suggest there exists certain trigger concepts or, more simply, symbols. For example, in a collection of myths and dreams, the figure of a bull stands for power while the figure of a peacock (and the many eyes of the peacock) stands for immortality. These same mythical concepts are not only found in literature but, also, in many forms of art. The fascinating thing about this 'dreams to myth collaboration' is these symbols were found in many separate areas of the world and used by many primitive and isolated peoples. In addition, modern people utilize the same symbolism in their dreams and fantasies.

Furthermore, there is a mysterious communality through a number of religious symbols in a variety of religions regardless of historical time and culture. One assumes these symbols came to prophets or 'holy men' in dream or altered states. Again, these phenomena of common dreams, common symbols, common myths and, thus, common values, etc. were philosophically branded by Jung as "collective unconscious." With these findings, the 'politically correct' intellectuals jumped for joy and pronounced, "God is definitely dead this time." Science had found a common imagination. Through this imagination, God came into existence. Every one collectively wanted God to exist. Every one wanted something greater than human beings to exist, for such a presence would explain weird things that happen around people, and to people.

I think this God-myth theory does make for an interesting discussion. However, the problem is, this theory is illogical. Think for a moment. What do we factually know about intuitive man? We know there is a unification of

WITH THESE FINDINGS, THE 'POLITICALLY CORRECT' INTELLECTUALS JUMPED FOR JOY AND PRONOUNCED, "GOD IS DEFINITELY DEAD THIS TIME."

sacred symbols, a consciousness that tries and convicts man's soul, a universal awareness of specific rights and wrongs and a common understanding of specific values - all this regardless of geographic location, cultural segregation, religious background, position in life, sociological factors, and the like. Does it make any real sense for a primitive tribesman in the wilds of Borneo to have the same spiritual dream symbols as a business man in New York City who's concept of "roughing it" is a golf game without a cell phone? Even though similar symbols sometimes have different meanings in different cultures, doesn't it seem odd that one finds the 'cross' as a religious symbol both in the Catholic churches of Rome and the ancient Inca ruins of south America? Even if we assume the meanings of these two crosses are somewhat different, could they be sacred symbols meant to trigger deified projections?

Actually, If we investigate the symbolism of the pre-Christian cross, we find it generally held concepts similar to those secondary meanings of the Christian symbol. Of the pre-Christian crosses, the Ankh or 'Egyptian' Cross is perhaps the most popular. As a matter of fact, it is easily purchased in the jewelry section of many well known department stores. It is also used in other forms as stylish decoration. On a recent trip to Las Vegas, I visited the Luxor Hotel. The hotel building is a magnificent structure decorated in an Egyptian theme. Many Egyptian symbols were built in and around the hotel grounds. As one might imagine, the Luxor designers seem to have used the most common Egyptian symbols and these Egyptian crosses are easily found. The Ankh is similar to the Christian Cross except for an expansion at the top. This expansion becomes an imperfect circle and represents the zodiac. The entirety of this Egyptian cross symbolizes the path of the soul as it travels the heavens and ascends downward to humanness. G. A. Gaskell writes, "When the soul enters upon the limitations of the cycle of life (Zodiac) it is no longer wholly divine, but its lower part gravitates towards desire and sensation. The 'Galaxy' is a symbol of the celestial regions (atmabuddhi) from which the soul has come. The world-soul descends to be involved in the matter of the lower planes, that it may rise again in the myriad souls of humanity."[16] From the standpoint of the human soul, this Egyptian meaning sympathizes with the meaning of the Christian cross. I do not suggest the Ankh should, in any way, be connected to Christian doctrine or included in the Christian mindset. I think such inclusiveness is clearly rejected in Biblical references. In fact, the inclusion of symbols from other gods is considered idolatry.[17] Therefore, we realize these two crosses (Christian and Egyptian) are not theologically compatible. Furthermore, we must also realize the major differences in their underlying mystical concepts. However, if we examine the symbols strictly as a detective might, we must conclude there is an implied common understanding. Of course, when we think of the Christian cross, we probably reflect on the sacred meaning of the crucifixion of Jesus, which in itself was the fulfillment of the divine sign of the Messiah spoken of from the very beginning of human life. The Christian belief declares that only through the death and resurrection of Jesus is it possible for human souls to leave this world and travel into a peaceful spiritual dimension, i.e., life in heaven. From the Christian view, Jesus is certainly the key to the meaning behind the cross symbol. If I took the Ankh and put a crown of thorns at the place where the soul comes and leaves humanness, I would feel much more comfortable about its symbolism. Even though Jesus came after the Ankh was conceptualized, both crosses state the ultimate human hope. It is the symbolism of both crosses which takes human beings out of this life to a better afterlife.

Perhaps the earliest uniform crosses were actually figurines of a Neolithic 'goddess' with her hands stretched out as if to give comfort. We also find crosses being used as letter symbols in the earliest written alphabets. Many times designs on pottery included crosses. These early representations were often tied to divinity and/or the passage into eternal life.

In Mesopotamia, the earliest crosses were generally Maltese like shapes known as *'cross formee.'* This symbol lasts through the Sumerian age. In the Babylonian Kassite Period a cross was found that suggests the sun deity.[18] Utu was this sun god who characterizes "the brilliant light of the sun."[19] On his daily journeys across the heavens, Utu would set the horizons to bring warmth. He also represents "truth, justice and right."[20] Utu had a cult following that seems to go back to "the earliest times."[21] It is interesting to note one early Uruk king on the celebrated Sumerian King List was considered a son of Utu.[22]

The Aztec god Yacatecuhtli, patron god of the merchants, carries a cross on his back. His cross symbolizes the crossroads merchants must travel. This sounds far from any Christian meaning, but a better understanding of the Aztec concept brings yet another similarity. The prehistoric *Central American cross* symbol stood for the world.[23] One unusual point to note, however, is the positioning of this cross on Yacatecuhtli's back. It is obviously a heavy burden to bear and very suggestive of the factual cross Jesus had to carry.[24] As *Yacatecuhtli's cross* symbolizes the burden of the crossroads in the world, even so does the cross of Jesus Christ.

Similar to the crossroads of the *Mayan cross,* many Africans used the cross to symbolize the intersections between the "path of the living and the dead."[25] This message is even more suggestive of the cross of Jesus. As discussed above, it is through the crucifixion and resurrection of Jesus that the Christian finds forgiveness of sin and the gift of eternal life. A final comment on the 'crossroads' symbolism; the 'crossroads' deity is found in many cultures. Often, he is the messenger or communicator for the other deities, in some ways similar to Jesus' position as the Christian's intercessor between God and man.

Some prehistoric crosses are mysteries. In South America, a window in the shape of a small cross stands over a doorway to a Yarra building (pre-Inca tribe). Scholars have assumed the shape was made for war. The cross would allow archers from inside to aim with little risk. However, if this cross-shaped window was made to protect warriors, why not make only a slit or a small circle? Furthermore, the Inca, who controlled the Yarra, also had a cross which they kept in a "sacred place." They "revered" this cross for reasons unknown.[26] Perhaps, then, we have yet to discover the full meanings of all South American pre-Conquistador crosses. However, it seems clear that they had more meaning then simple design or protection from an invasion.

As we study antiquity through modern technology, we may find other mysterious cross discoveries. *In Search Of* was a television series filmed in the 1970's and 80's. In a show on the possibilities of alien earth visitors, *In Search Of* pointed out something very unusual. Through modern photography and graphics, we have discovered that twelve great Grecian temples, separated over an entire civilization, are aligned in the shape of a perfect *Maltese cross*. The Maltese cross is one of the most ancient middle-eastern cross figures discovered. The program suggested this feat did not happen by chance. For this alignment of temples to have occurred by chance would have been a mathematical long shot. Therefore, the program concluded, the alignment must have been done by aliens. On the other hand, I think there is a better explanation. If this symbolic cross is more than temples being placed at random, if there is any intelligence behind this 'cross' phenomenon, then humans unconsciously formed the cross and were guided by a force through the collective unconscious. The resulting topographical symbol was not for the contemplation of ancient Greeks, but for a future generation who would have the technology to discover the mystery.

Throughout the world, we find symbols of edified crosses, perhaps designed to be identifiable with a specific tribe or community. Among these adaptations, we find crosses with tails (much like the cursive letter 't'), forms of Greek-style cross (the arms of the cross are the same length*), St. Andrew's crosses* (the cross is not vertical, but tilted as in the letter 'x' which denotes how St. Andrews was crucified) and the most notorious adapted cross, the ancient *swastika*.

Although the swastika is found in various forms around the world including Europe, the Far East and Native American tribes, it gained its greatest notoriety when the German Nazis embraced it as their dominant symbol. This must have been embarrassing to the United States Army who had chosen the swastika as a troop patch in honor of Native Americans. The German symbol, borrowed from the Druids, was worn as a charm by many German solders during World War I. It was adopted as the official symbol of the Nazis party on May 20, 1920. Originally, the swastika, held a majestic meaning. In addition to being the Nordic symbol for the sun, it also signified the act of creation. Unfortunately, the swastika further symbolized the "mystical destiny of Aryan man." Because of this Aryan symbolism, the Nazis expected the swastika to replace the Christian cross.[27] The occultic Druids, builders of Stonehenge, thought they would form a superior race. One might argue that such a concept is a perversion of the Biblical principle of salvation. As the cross was bent, so was the unconscious understanding of salvation. Adopting this ancient belief and encouraged by Darwinian evolution and Nietzsche's concept of 'over-man,' Hitler's Nazis proclaimed that the Aryan race was the superior race.[28] Doctors began to examine children for Aryan qualities. Favorable (Aryan) traits were noted and developed. Had the Nazis succeeded, there would be no racial unrest, for only one race would officially exist; the 'super' race. Everyone who was not Aryan would be enslaved or eliminated. Over time, Aryans would evolve into gods. That, of course, was salvation to the Nazis. All of their perverse activity was the direct result of the human act of ration-alization. Hitler's Nazism was based on the perversion that man can solve all of his problems through science and intellectualism. Human beings rational-ized away laws that the Almighty God gave society. Included are laws like, 'love your neighbor' and 'do not murder.' In this particular instance, the per-version of the cross could be expressed as a parallel to the perversion of the intuitive Word of God. The Nazis abomination occurred after the days of Jesus of Nazareth, but the rationale goes back previous to the Druids, even back to the beginning of confrontations between God and man in the Garden of Eden. There seems to be a common tie that extends far beyond any conceivable human logic and which culminates at a cross through the crucifixion of the Messiah.

The universal nature of religious symbolism has been observed by other parties unrelated to the theological and the psychological Jungian argu-ments of communality. It is interesting to note that people who believe in aliens from outer space also see the universal nature of symbolism. They base much of their beliefs on the same collective unconscious experiences as dis-cussed above. However, alienists are unsympathetic witnesses to this phenom-enon. Therefore, they have yet another perspective. Von Daniken, for example, made comments about the global discoveries of "circles, wheels (with spokes), the sun, concentric circles, squares inside circles and variations on crosses and stars. Just as if all prehistoric artists, even those in the most remote parts, had visited the same art school!"[30]

According to Von Daniken, most researchers are amazed by this uni-formed structure. Von Daniken had been aware of the discoveries of various

BECAUSE OF THIS ARYAN SYMBOLISM, THE NAZIS EXPECTED THE SWASTIKA TO REPLACE THE CHRISTIAN CROSS.[27]

researchers in this field. In fact, he made a very interesting comment about one such expert: " . . . Oswald O. Tobisch has shown in tabulated form that rock drawings in Africa Europe, Asia and America are related to each other." At the end of his comparative studies Tobisch asks in amazement: "Is it possible that once there was a unified concept of God on an international scale simply inconceivable to our present way of thinking and that mankind in those days was still in the 'field of force' of the 'primordial revelation' of the one and almighty creator, to whom mind and matter, the whole universe with the heavenly bodies and living creatures, were and are subordinate?"[31]

I cannot stress enough the relevance of this point. The humanist position on all matters of the universe, including human life, is based on one proposition: everything is by chance. The humanist believes that despite Jung's findings, despite Campbell's findings, despite Tobisch's findings, despite all of the other scientists and discoverers who have intimated anything other than chance has caused everything—all of them are wrong. Despite scientists who conclude that some activities defy the laws of probability and do so on a recurring pace, or draw similar conclusions from activities such as ESP, out of body experiences, paranormal synchronicity or anything unusual, the atheist must protest. There can be no exception. Everything is by chance!

Again we find that all theists (all believers of God, regardless of denomination or religion) are in the more objective position to judge both scientific and historical facts, because any evidence of a paranormal or supernatural event can be evaluated by the evidence of an event instead of an immediate rejection of the facts of the event on ideological or philosophical grounds. A Christian who evaluates the possibilities of ESP may accept or reject such phenomena on the merits of ESP events. If ESP should fall into the category of possible or probable, the decision can be based purely on the merits of the facts. Personal judgment as to whether ESP is good or evil i.e., a work of God or a work of Satan, can be deferred as I am suggesting Jung deferred theological judgement. However, the event itself can be judged on its merits. If a humanist should argue ESP is possible because ESP is a result of human evolution - the natural development of an evolving brain, one could counter that many paranormal events, synchronistic events in particular, cannot be relegated to human or animal evolution.

From my perspective, to suggest that "common" manifestations of unconscious symbolism, found within every human being, regardless of culture, regardless of race, regardless of sex, regardless of religious affiliation, etc., give proof that man's religious consciousness is some sort of 'common human wish' is a major stretch of the imagination. To the contrary, the collective unconscious is more likely to be a psychological probe into the human self. It suggests the human spirit has a divine spiritual influence. In other words, humanity has a 'collective' spiritual awareness because every human being has a spirit. As a matter of fact, it seemed obvious that Joseph Campbell accepted many human myths as encounters with the 'many faces of God' (used by Campbell as a book title). A popular book entitled *The Power of Myth* is the result of a Bill Moyers interview with Joseph Campbell. In the introduction, Bill Moyers explained the reason behind Campbell's earliest interest in study of mythology. Moyer wrote:

> *He (Campbell) wanted to know what it means that God assumes such different masks in different cultures, yet how it is that comparable stories can be found in these divergent traditions - stories of creation, second comings, and judgment days. He liked the insight of Hindu scripture: 'Truth is one: the sages call it by many names.' All our names and images for God are masks, he said, signifying the ultimate reality that by definition transcends language and art. A myth is a mask of God, too-a metaphor for what lies behind the visible world. However, the mystic traditions differ, he said, they are in accord in calling us to a deeper awareness of the very act of living itself.[32]*

The collective unconscious seems to hold a connection between physical man and spiritual man. It is important for us to realize that the spiritual area of human uniqueness is recognized by all investigators, both secular and theological. Many Christian writers have found similar answers as Jung. The difference being, Christian writers are interested in the spirit over the psyche, where secular sources, such as Jung, tend to focus on the psyche. An example of a Christian work which deals with this subject is C. S. Lewis' masterpiece, *Mere Christianity.* In his first chapter, Lewis discussed what he called the Law of Human Nature. He began his book with some observations including the following:

> *'Give me a bit of your orange, I gave you a bit of mine' - 'Come on, you promised.' People say things like that every day, educated people as well as uneducated. and children as well as grown-ups.*

> *Now what interests me about all these remarks is that the man who makes them is not merely saying that the other man's behaviour does not happen to please him. He is appealing to some kind of standard of behaviour which he expects the other man to know about.[33]*

Though I hesitate to probe too deeply into a psyche and/or soul understanding and dissemination of higher values, I feel compelled to touch on a related point made by Schaeffer. Certain words have always held meaning to man beyond the dictionary definition. These are words such as love, morals and purpose. Schaeffer wrote, "The use of such words trigger responses to a greater degree in line with what the specific race has thought they mean and how it has acted on their meaning, and to a lesser degree in line with what really is and what man is."[34]

The Jewish followers of Jesus realized that all humanity receives messages form God. In the Biblical New Testament, we find Romans 1:18–19: "But God shows his anger from heaven against all sinful, evil men who push away the truth from them. For the truth about God is known to them instinctively (literally 'is manifest in them'), God has put this knowledge in their hearts."[35] Furthermore, the Bible states, "He will punish sin wherever it is found. He will punish the heathen when they sin, even though they never had God's written laws, for down in their hearts they know right from wrong. God's laws are written within them; their own conscience accuses them, or sometimes excuses them."[36] C. S. Lewis alluded to the collective unconscious with his previously mentioned statement, "If anyone will take the trouble to compare the moral teaching of, say, the ancient Egyptians, Babylonians, Hindus, Chinese, Greeks and Romans, what will really strike him will be how very like they are to each other and to our own."[37]

SPIRITUAL WAR AND MYTHS

History records some extremely interesting events which validate a foundational Biblical perception. Human beings are participants in an invisible spiritual war. Therefore, conspicuous evil natures often emerge. Unlike positive spiritual influences, history also records evil spiritual powers which have influenced cultures and societies. Sometimes, the cultures 'bought' these evils without outwardly acknowledging their decision. They rationalized away their path of evil. The previously discussed German Nazis immediately come to mind. They based their 'super race' concepts on the religious mythology of the Druid culture. Extrapolating from the findings of Jung and others, I suggest that the German people intuitively knew attacking their neighbors was wrong. Furthermore, Hitler's henchmen knew the extermination of other races was evil. Interestingly, Hitler became the human answer to the long awaited Antichrist. Yet, many of the German people rationalized that Hitler was their savior. He had been sent by divine providence and his mission was to set the foundation for the 'Aryan millennium.' [38] In like manner another evil man would be conceptualized as the savior of the Russian people. Like Hitler, he would rely on science and human intelligence to lead the masses into a new era. His name was Joseph Stalin.

Today, we see another phase in this war of the evil empires. The Al-Qaeda (Islamic terrorist organization) have declared war on the Western

---

HUMAN BEINGS ARE PARTICIPANTS IN AN INVISIBLE SPIRITUAL WAR.

world. To them, all people who are not Muslim are evil. Thus, their goal in life is to exterminate all Christians, Jews, Hindus, Buddhists, as well as atheists and occultists—everyone who is not Muslim. Yet, to American logic *they* are the evil ones. They are breaking universal laws of God by killing innocent people and spreading terror throughout the entire civilized world. This struggle goes to the earliest days of sin and is a very interesting struggle from the good vs. evil conflict perspective. Yet, as the above examples were not the first evil cultures, neither will they be the last.

Throughout history, some cultures have chosen to pursue evil. Perhaps the most perverse of the major cultures was the Aztec civilization of ancient Mexico. The Aztecs had many gods, but their two major deities were Quetzalcoatl and Tezcatlipoca. These two gods may have been borrowed from an ancient Teotihuacan society and were passed through the Toltecs. The Toltec culture was the last great society in the Mesoamerican region (ancient Mexico) before the Aztecs (also known as the Mexicas). Quetzalcoatl was considered the protective strength of the Toltec peoples and Tezcatlipoca was the god who caused their downfall. After the demise of the Toltecs, these two gods were adopted into the Aztec world. The two deities could take different forms. Quetzalcoatl was revered as a feathered serpent (perhaps indicating both his eternal existence and his ability to fly). He was also represented in the morning star (his heavenly nature) and the wind god (signifying his awesome omnipresent power).

Tezcatlipoca often took the form of the Blue Hummingbird (Huitzilopochtli) which is so clearly depicted on the famous plains of Nazca. The Blue Hummingbird (Huitzilopochtli) was recognized by the Aztec culture as the god who gave them magical powers and visions. Throughout the course of the Aztec culture, there would always be a spiritual war between these two deities. To our way of thinking, Quetzalcoatl might be considered the good power and Tezcatlipoca the evil power. However, the Aztecs had evolved away from the terms of good and evil. To them, this spiritual dichotomy would have been better expressed by the concept of "yin and yang." This is a good example of how Eastern and Judio/Christian philosophy have similarities but are also profoundly different. This rationalization diminishes the powers of consciousness and replaces the concepts of good and evil. The two gods were opposites. Religious myths explained how Quetzalcoatl had been tricked by sorcery. Therefore, he was forced to leave the Aztec people. Essentially, the Aztecs had been left in the hands of Tezcatlipoca. Now they chose to ingratiate themselves in Tezcatlipoca's favor. Tenochititlan was Tezcatlipoca's form on earth. Tenochititlan "ruled over all . . . He was Tezcatlipoca's surrogate on earth, his voice, his action: 'he speaks within you, he makes you his lips, his jaws, his ears . . . He also makes you his fangs, his claws, for you are his wild beast, you are his eater-of-people, you are his judge.'" [39]

Though they knew Tezcatlipoca reflected the 'shadow' or dark side of human nature, he brought them great power and wealth. He promised to make them "lords and kings of all that is in the world."[40] It is important to note that the Aztecs expected Quetzalcoatl to return on the day celebrated as the birth date of the first priest-king, Chiconaui Ehecatl (the priest-king was distinguished with the title of Quetzalcoatl) and in the year called "Ce Acatl." Ce Acatl was the Aztec designation for Quetzalcoatl's appearance as the Morning Star. This symbolic combination transpired every fifty-two years. It occured only once in the lifetime of Montezuma. That day was in the spring of 1519.[41] Amazingly, this one day would seem to be providential. Perhaps, it also brought a spiritual message to the world.

Certainly, the most hideous examples of Aztecan perversion came in their practices of human sacrifice. They practiced human sacrifice often and, sometimes, in large numbers. Perhaps the largest number to be sacrificed at one time came on a day in 1487 when there were a reported 80,400 human sacrifices. The National Geographic described this as "the greatest orgy of human sacrifice in the history of the Aztec Empire."[42] The Aztec methods of sacrifice can only be described as extreme. I wish to relate to you, as tastefully yet as accurately as I can, one of the most atrocious of their sacrificial rites. This particular type of sacrifice must have taken place on various ceremonial days. However, it is most often associated with an agricultural festival designated to appease the god Tlacaxipeualiztli. In this instance, the sacrificial victim was usually a captured warrior. The prisoner's humiliation began as he was led by his captor through Aztecan streets. He was then imprisoned to await the hour of his gruesome death. On a day in March he was drugged to one degree or another, laid prone on an alter and skinned alive. Cuts were made around his legs, arms, neck, etc. Next, his skin was skillfully ripped from his carcass. The victim's heart, still beating, was torn out of his chest (probably torn out in a similar method as portrayed in the Indiana Jones movie - *Temple of Doom*). The sacrificial heart was offered to the gods and the bloody carcass disposed of. The privileged warrior who had captured this warrior/sacrifice would wear the dead man's skin to even included covering his face with the dead facial skin. In this hideous dead man's skin, the Aztec warrior would dance for Tlacaxipeualiztli. After this celebration the Aztec warrior would continue to wear the rotting skin. In a number of days the skin began to crack and break open. The warrior's shedding of this dead human skin was symbolic of the "bursting of the skin of the maize seed."[43] Interestingly, this Aztec ceremonial practice of wearing a human sacrifice's skin can be traced back to the pre-national days when the Aztecs were little more than a wandering tribe. At this particular point in time, the early Aztecs were starving. After begging the Culhuacan people for and receiving mercy, they asked a "Culhuacan Lord" to allow his daughter "to become a goddess and wife" of the Aztec god. I am sure the Culhuacan thought his daughter would be honored by becoming the queen of the tribe. To the contrary, the daughter was ceremoniously sacrificed. Even more perverse was that which followed. One of the Aztec priest wore the daughter's skin in the presence of her visiting father. This 'honor' was a shocking and disgusting act of violence to the girl's father. Needless to say, the father called for war against the Aztec people.[44]

SYMBOLIC MEANING

This human play of sacrificial death was really an attempt for Aztecan salvation. In their rituals, we find a perverted mixture of symbolic incarnation and reincarnation. The blood that was spilt was food of the gods. Yet, by their sacrificial deaths, victims became incarnations of gods. On the other hand, through eating of sacrificial human skin, the Aztec people "were performing a kind of communion with the divinity . . . they believed that their bodies would be mingled with that of the divine host and that they would miraculously receive the benefits of the communion."[45]

This explanation only strengthens my earlier statements regarding a structured and collective unconscious as it is related to spiritual activity. Evil has often been connected to the symbols of good. Furthermore, this common structure suggests there is a personality or intelligence guiding evil. For those of us who believe in a literal Satan, I do not doubt Satan's participation, but how did he do it? Is there some inexplicable innate understanding of a human need? This evil representation is confusing to psychologists and theologians alike. For example, the psychoanalytic expressions Jung used in his references to the relationship between God, Jesus and Satan was a major problem between him and conventional Christianity. What many failed to realize is that Jung's explanations were not about theological relationships, but psychological representations in this most important and timeless battle of good vs. evil.

Many questions about human consciousness arise from the lives of the Aztecs. What was the innate 'self' expressing in these people? What about the communion of flesh and the spilling of blood for the sake of others? The Aztec people connected a perversion of life and death, of human sacrifice and the communion of sacrificial flesh and, thus, the blood sacrifice with their search for validation. Obviously, this was a desecration of a sacred symbol—blood.

The same question might be asked in regard to the symbolism of the serpent. The Aztec symbolic reenactment of the 'bursting of the skin of the maize seed' - the wearing of the sacrifice's skin until it dries and cracks open is also similar to a serpent shedding its dead skin. "The fact that snakes periodically wriggle out of their old skins and seem to go on as a new 'edition' may have helped to perpetuate these ideas about the immortality of snakes."[46] The doctors of ancient Greece used the symbol of the caduceus—

"a staff entwined by two snakes" to represent the "life giving powers" of their medical profession. We use this symbol in our medical field today.[47]

The Aztec society reached its ebb point during the period of the Great Speaker (priest-king) Montezuma. Though Montezuma was born on the sacred day of Morning Star, he felt his loyalties bound to the Blue Hummingbird. Yet, he must have realized the divine signs which pointed to the end for his society. Throughout his reign, Montezuma saw discouraging signs in the heavens.[48] The Aztecs also began to suffer from increasing natural disasters. For example, sixteen thousand Aztec warriors were decimated on a mountain side by heavy winds and rain.[49] In other instances, temples dedicated to Huitzilopochtli were destroyed; one through fire and one by lightning.[50] Montezuma's aunt had a terrible fall and went into a coma. Perhaps, she even had an afterlife experience. When she awoke, she spoke of visions of white-faced men dressed in black stone. They rode "hornless deer." The Aztec people and cities were to be destroyed.[51] Montezuma believed the vision was from Quetzalcoatl warning of the terrible things to come. Other signs and visions of destruction were reported. Interestingly, the Spaniards did land on the exact day predicted as the day of Quetzalcoatl's return - the year of Morning Star (Quetzalcoatl) and the day of the first Quetzalcoatl. Because it was Good Friday and the Spaniards were Catholic, they were dressed in black. Hernando Cortes and the Spaniards were thought to be sent by Quetzalcoatl and, in fact, they did overthrow the Aztecs.

Did the Aztecs indeed receive divine messages of their impending destruction and were those messages from an unknown God, the God of all that is good—YHWH? Was YHWH revealed to some of the Aztec Leaders? One Aztec (Texcoco) king named Nezahualcoyotl did not approve of the gruesome human sacrifices and turned to "The Lord of Everywhere." No images could represent this god. One of Nezahualcoyotl's prayers began, "God, our Lord, is invoked everywhere. Everywhere is He venerated. It is He who creates things. He creates himself: God."[52] Nezahualcoyotl's understanding of god, although not yet monotheistic, and certainly not of the Almighty and eternal God YHWH, was a giant step away from a polytheistic balance of deities. Perhaps, YHWH did reveal Himself to Nezahualcoyotl as He did with Abraham. Obviously, Nezahualcoyotl was honestly and earnestly seeking a relationship with the one real God. As a result, Nezahualcoyotl's theological premise introduced the important concept of single cause to the Aztec world.[53] This understanding about God should be considered much to sophisticated for Aztec culture. Yet, we find the same revolutionary belief that developed in Mesopotamia being conceived in primitive Mexico. However, the big difference between the Middle East and Mexico is that the Aztecs felt bound to the darkness of Tezcatlipoca/Huitzilopochtli. They did not pursue the path of the one Almighty God as did the Jews of Mesopotamia. It is evident that, no matter what the degree of theological sophistication, no nation which has turned from God's prescribed laws for society has survived. The divine providence of the Aztec people was laid out before them. They knowingly chose the dark way. Ironically, their prophecies foretold of the destruction to come from their path into darkness and it was their prophecies which were fulfilled and in a most ironic way.

Do not misunderstand the importance of myths, religious or otherwise. They do mean something. They go beyond man the machine. They go beyond electric impulses in the brain. They express parameters inexpressible by mathematics. They express intuitive visions of universal knowledge. They express things which the human intellect can only question. Yet, this logos lies within each of us. Perhaps our historical basis does not have the dimensions of unencumbered reality, or perhaps our human basis is encumbered by the limitations of time and space and human understanding. Perhaps, all intuitive truth is greater than historical reality and in that way redefines Plato's concept - the mortal is but a shadow of the divine. Perhaps, we are indeed imprisoned by our flesh and shackled from true understanding.

If we accept the proposition that some input of a divine nature is delivered to man by way of a complex self-communication system, that sometimes God communicates and advises through our dreams, or that we sort through God's input both in our conscious and unconscious state, then Biblical Scripture takes on new scientific significance. "If you want favor with both God and man, and a reputation for good judgment and common sense, then trust the Lord completely; don't ever trust yourself."[54]

I suggest to you that it is by this exclusive human connection to God's logos that we are allowed spiritual communication. When humans pray for guidance, it is through the intuitive Self that God advises us of His Will. Yet, we humans know we cannot live up to the legal requirements of God. We are not capable of living within spiritual perfection. Thus, we intuitively know of many transgressions through what we call our conscience. When we try to live 'godly lives' we convict ourselves of our own evil. There lies our curse, and there lies the human separation from God, who is our creator and the origin of our intuitive laws. God is perfect and good. Man, is flawed and evil. Yet, intuitively, flawed man longs for a relationship with this perfect God.

GOD IS PERFECT AND GOOD. MAN, IS FLAWED AND EVIL. YET, INTUITIVELY,
FLAWED MAN LONGS FOR A RELATIONSHIP WITH THIS PERFECT GOD.

THE TOWER

There is a tower on a mound
standing majestically.
Its power and presence
abidingly sure
this palace of mystery.

It is pleasing to gaze over the grounds
which clothe the tower's land
and ponder it's soothing
serenity,
and beauty oh so grand.

The ladies and gents of fine repute
wonder - "What finery must abide?"
What gold and silver trims
and frames
the lavish ambiences inside.

Yet, on it's gate
a sign clearly states
a message for all to read.
"Life is sacred and YOU have sinned
NO TRESPASSING!
by the KING!"

CHAPTER 15

MYTHS AND CHRISTIANITY

"Is it possible that there are no coincidences?"[1]

One major question people ask regarding Christianity is, "Could the 'Jesus story' be a fabricated tale, a form of mythic folklore?" Actually, when one compares ancient works, numerous parallel concepts are found in both Christian mysticism and mythological expression. Antagonists assume these analogous characteristics somehow lower the 'expectation bar' of religion making it less credible than it might otherwise be. However, the major factor of such issues must always be 'what is real and what is fiction.' In this regard, most historians believe Jesus of Nazareth was a real person, and He was probably crucified on a cross. Moreover, these scholars would be just as accepting of Jesus' resurrection if it were not for its miraculous implications. There is more than enough evidence to authenticate His resurrection under normal circumstances. For example, it is clear that those who were in contact with Jesus after the crucifixion believed He had resurrected from the dead. Thus, it is hoped this writing will delineate the differences between the life of Jesus of Nazareth and mythic folklore. We will closely examine this issue for obvious reasons.

Regrettably, the abstruseness in the above relationship exposes a postmodernist ignorance toward the human self. Most great, soulful concepts have come to humanity from a higher conscious state, such as a dream state. So, one could logically theorize that there is a divine to human 'osmotic' like process which conveys information including the prophesies found in Daniel and The Revelation. Though there are major differences between religion and mythology, one would also expect to find similarities. Obviously, both avenues provide rare looks into the human soul. Both grasp human innate understandings as well as allow for explanations of things which happen in life beyond our comprehension. Nonetheless, the scientist would necessarily ask, why have virtually all humans, from postmodern to the most ancient, held similar reoccurring intuitive expressions? More specifically, why would humanity have a continuous inspiration of a god-king, born of a virgin, who dies and resurrects from the dead? One presupposition is that we have been programmed by our Creator to watch for certain important events in human history. Such prophecy does not seem out of place if the Creator is a loving God. In fact, one might expect a benevolent God to continuously remind us that He has a master plan and, despite our preference for independence, our well-being is incased in His plan. Thus, it should be no surprise that the collective human psyche, on every meaningful occasion, relays to us significant information about life.

THE PROBLEM

We humans cannot live up to those standards we intuitively feel required to meet. We feel inadequate. As we grow older, we watch our loves and dreams decay and crumble. So much of our lives are wasted on distractions and perversions of various kinds; thus, we fall short. We cannot, by ourselves, fulfill our aspirations. As an illustration, most of us learned at a young age the differences between right and wrong. Generally, we vow to do 'good' throughout life. Yet, in our decadent world, bad or evil activities are often acquainted with the lifestyle society refers to as the 'good life.' In fact, history affirms that our cultural celebrities are generally great examples of human degeneration. Thus, our moral commitment is often softened; our preferences become skewed; good intentions are postponed or forgotten. Time and time again we ignore the good we wished to do and live for the moment. Sooner or later, our lives will end and our good intentions will become meaningless. In essence, they never existed.

It should be no surprise that mythology affirms this reality. Humans have 'collectively' become aware of specific signs apropos to the 'Hero' or expected savior, the universal Messiah. Thus, our collective mindset has assimilated the divine story and produced numerous examples of virgin births, tests of character, deaths and resurrections - all related to the coming Hero. Because these are mythical symbols, they reappear cyclically in conjunction with the seasonal growth of crops. Moreover, through repetitious patterns, these myths continue to remind mankind of human shortcomings. Yet, surreptitious activities which operate from the depths of the human psyche, when exposed to historical wisdom, appear to identify Jesus of Nazareth as the one authentic person who satisfies this Savior archetype. I do not suggest the life of Jesus of the New Testament was based on repetitious mythical stories. There are obvious differences between the dream-like discussions of ancient gods and the narratives about Jesus. Historical facts indicate Jesus was both a real being and a prophetically 'marked' Savior. These and other distinctions separate Jesus from the dream like mythology of ancient civilizations. Yet, ancient mythological pronouncements suggest Jesus, who fulfills the 'Hero' formula, was more than the Jewish Messiah. He seems also to have satisfied the messianic inferences in the stories of Egypt, of Sumer and Babylon, the Celts, Greeks, the Africas, the Americas and the entire historical world.

When we consider the various ways Jesus brings symmetry to psychodynamic patterns, particularly those related to spiritual matters, we find something truly amazing. Jesus seems to be a focal point for the human consciousness. Though it would be a mistake to build one's Christian faith on psychodynamic patterns, it would also be wrong to ignore Jesus' powers over the human condition. We do not understand reality if we do not understand the preeminence of Jesus in Self. Thus, I will begin this subject matter by listing a few of these unique factors.

SYMBOLS AFFIRM JESUS

I have previously discussed some of the symbolism related to Jesus' life. Particularly significant is the relevance of blood sacrifices and the metaphorical expressions of the cross. These two symbols bind together intuitive rituals and knowledge which reach back to the most ancient of times. Jesus' actualization through crucifixion of mythic structure and the resulting unification of the two sacred symbols into one superior symbol should, of and by itself, hold great spiritual relevance for all mankind.

Yet, the historical implications are even more profound. Besides his historic being, Jesus was a bystander, not the instigator, of His inherent destiny. Jesus did not, in any human way, control many of the events which led to His Messianic fulfillment. It was through a humanly contrived act of torture and the gross mutilation of a prisoner that many of the Messianic symbols mysteriously converged on Jesus' shoulders. Moreover, the known facts are so bizarre that Jesus' death appears to have been preordained. The Pharisees (the Jewish Priesthood) seem to have been the predominant group who found it necessary to eliminate Jesus. Yet, it appears they broke both Jewish custom and law by putting Jesus to death. The fact that Jesus was crucified instead of stoned to death in and of itself makes the Jesus story provocative. According to the New Testament, they made several attempts on Jesus' life prior to His crucifixion. Had they been successful, they would have stoned Him instead of crucified Him, leaving part of the messianic prophecies unfulfilled. Stoning was the death sentence of Jewish tradition and their attempts were to no avail. The time was not right; thus, Jesus always escaped. However, the Pharisees were successful in capturing Him just prior to the Jewish Feast of the Passover.

Passover was the sacred remembrance of the day when God sent death to all Egyptian first born males - both humans and animals. However, Jewish families were forewarned to do certain symbolic acts in order to have their first born males spared. Among these acts was a stipulation that every family must pick a male lamb "without any defects,"[2] kill the lamb and spread it's blood on the family's door frame. In fact, the explicit instructions were, " . . . take a cluster of hyssop branches and dip them into the lamb's blood and strike the hyssop against the lintel above the door and against the two side panels, so that there will be blood upon them . . ."[3] Recall that Jesus has been considered the Lamb of God. The blood at the top and sides of these doors seem symbolic of the span of the future cross stained with Jesus' blood and the striking of the hyssop is symbolic of the stripes from the whips bursting Jesus' flesh.

In conclusion, a death angel is said to have passed over the Jewish homes leaving them safe because of the lamb's blood. As for those dwellings with no lamb's blood, the angel killed each of the first born males.[4] Was the Passover God's representation of the coming Savior? Jesus is described as God's Son who died for the sins of the world. As the blood of the lamb spared the lives of the chosen (Jewish) people, so it is Jesus' blood that saves the chosen who are followers of Jesus.

According to Jewish law, Jesus could not be executed on the Passover. Therefore, He would need to be put to death prior to that date. As suggested above, the Pharisees did everything in their power to kill Jesus well before the Passover. However, providence would bring a number of problems which postponed His demise. The Jewish leadership's 'chance' to capture and execute Jesus finally came the morning before the first day of the Passover celebration. (There is some argument as to whether or not the Passover had already begun). If this report is true, and there seems to be little or no reason to doubt it, the Jewish spiritual leaders had lost control of the timetable. Pilate, the Roman Proctor, was so frustrated by the pressures of these rushed proceedings that he actuated a symbolic gesture by washing his hands of the affair. Neither the Jewish leadership nor the Roman ruler wanted Jesus crucified on the Passover. So, Jesus was 'destined' to be crucified the day before the Passover. Yet, after Jesus' tortured body was hung, another important event would follow. "The Jewish leaders didn't want the victims hanging there the next day, which was the Sabbath (and a very special Sabbath at that, for it was in the Passover), so they asked Pilate to order the legs of the men broken to hasten death; then their bodies could be taken down. So the soldiers came and broke the legs of the two men crucified with Jesus; but when they came to him, they saw that he was dead already, so they didn't break his."[5] Jesus' unbroken bones are thought to be a fulfillment of prophecy. "He keepeth all his bones: not one of them is broken."[6] Interestingly, the lambs used in the actual Passover event were to be without defects.[7] Of course, that would exclude animals with any broken bones. Assuming both the original Passover day and the Crucifixion of Jesus were historical events, the Passover ordeal seems to leave a metaphoric sign on the man called Jesus.

There are a number of other symbols which are also fulfilled in dramatic ways through the Christian legacy. Included would be Pisces (the fish), the circle, the sheep, the lamb, the lion, light, fire, and many others. When I was a child, I found it confusing that Jesus was intertwined in so many symbols. For example, I wondered, "Was Jesus the Lamb or a Shepherd?" I would later learn, metaphorically, Jesus was both.

A second point is that Jesus' traits seem to satiate an innate spiritual longing within the human collective unconscious. Jesus, in and of Himself, seems to be the archetype for spiritual leaders. In one way or another, Jesus has been fused into the doctrine of Muslims, various Hindu sects, the Christian faith, as well as many of the religions which have grown from these major branches, i.e., Jehovah's Witnesses, the Mormons, and a number of mystery and New Age religions. Others, such as the Branch Davidians and the Black Muslims suggest that their leaders, in some way, fulfill Jesus. According to this grouping of religions, either Jesus died before He fulfilled His work and the present church leader is fulfilling the rest of the work or Jesus was a prototype of a leader or leaders to come. The inference is that a divine leader now on earth is the Messiah.

The Jewish faith gives honor to Jesus in a very different way. Even though Jesus of Nazareth was Jewish, and Christianity was initially a form of Judaism (some people argue it continues to be), the nation of Israel seems to be concerned over Jewish conversions to Christianity. This reverse position is yet another form of respect in that it acknowledges the power of Jesus' message. No other person has achieved such respect from virtually all major world religions and cults at any one time on planet earth. This alone speaks highly of His message and purpose.

Additionally, throughout the ages, there have been personalities that reportedly held some of the same attributes or life dramas as Jesus. Included would be the previously mentioned Krishna (Hindu) and the Buddha. These similarities are so great that some suggest early Christians came to the far east telling of the life of Jesus. Many of His attributes were adopted by the prevailing major religious deities. Others suggest these similarities were captured in ancient myth to mirror the 'Anointed One.' However, for whatever reason, we do find familiar divine traits in each example. Assuming there is more to these eastern figures then legend or fable, then these men must have also been very special people. Certainly, each had an earnest desire to walk in Truth. However, they did not die on a cross and rise from the grave. Neither did Mohammed, nor did Ghandi, nor did Julius Caesar. They did not fulfill the collective understanding of the coming Savior. Only Jesus of Nazareth can stake that claim.

THE MANY SYMBOLIC HERO MYTHS AND JESUS

There have been many myths which paralleled the life of Jesus Christ. I have previously referred to the Aztec mythical god, Quetzalcoatl. Many Mormons (and others) assume Jesus visited the Americas as Quetzalcoatl. Part of the confusion may result from the belief that, over a

number of years, the Quetzalcoatl god-king myth grew from an actual historical person named Ce Acatl Topitzin. After demonstrating his spiritual knowledge, Topitzin was awarded the title of Quetzalcoatl (meaning the feathered or
plumed serpent). Later he became leader of the Toltecs. But, as his reputation
for goodness grew, he became a liability to the Priests. It is assumed they plot-
ted his murder. From this point on, the historical Quetzalcoatl becomes a
mythical being and his legend follows the classical mythical form of many
ancient gods and goddesses found around the world. Unlike the perfection
personified by Jesus and YHWH, Quetzalcatl held weaknesses similar to
humans. As in many hero myths, Quetzalcoatl was fooled into a compromis-
ing situation. Of course, Jesus was tempted by Satan, but did not fall for
Satan's tricks. Had He done so, there would have been no resurrection,
because He would have forfeited His Messiah status. Thus, Jesus' infallibility
disassociates Him from the symbolic mythical format; a standard trait of the
mythic gods is their fallibility.

Deeper analysis would connect Quetzalcatl to other intuitive issues.
However, the great paradox was related to the arrival of the Spaniards which
ended the Quetzalcatl mythical cycle. In a strange way, these honored quests
brought a 'day of judgement' to the natives of Central America. Thus, the
recycling god-king myths may be better represented by Osiris, Tammuz,
Orpheus and Balder. At least, these myths seem to be the one's most often
referred to by researchers.

As noted above, there are major differences between mythical heroes
and Jesus of Nazareth. One substantial difference is that myths revolve around
a cyclical or reoccurring story line. In Jung's words, "It is the finality of the
Christian concept of the resurrection (the Christian idea of the Last Judgment
has a similar 'closed' theme) that distinguishes Christianity from other god-
king myths. It happened once, and the ritual merely commemorates it."[8] What
Jung refers to is that the god-king myths revolve around a death and resurrection cycle which reoccurs year after year. It seems death and resurrection were
always in some way tied to the fertility celebrations and agriculture.
Quetzalcoatl, Osiris, Tammuz, Orpheus and Balder kept reappearing as did
other mythical characters. As it turns out, Jesus' finality, a single historic
event, distinguishes Him from the world of reoccurring Hero myths. To put
this another way, the celebration of Easter is not commemorating a new resurrection but a recognition of a past but single historic event.

The myth of Osiris holds at least two important points which might
subconsciously refer to a coming man called Jesus. The first point is, Osiris is
considered to be "the first mortal to have risen from death."[9] It was thought,
at least in part, that through rituals (associated with the Cult of Osiris) Osiris
would annually resurrect from the dead causing a renewal of earth's vegetation.[10] Of course, reproduction was also connected to this renewal of life, i.e.,

fertility. Secondly, the myth of Osiris explained the reasoning behind Egyptian mummification. Because of Osiris' fortunes, the Egyptians mummified and prepared their deceased for a life after death. Similarily, Christians proclaim that only through Jesus can a person find life after death.

The myth of Orpheus has often been considered to be the most similar to Jesus. Yet, according to Jung, there are major differences between Orpheus and Jesus. Like Osiris, Orpheus had his own mystery cult. Orpheus was a great minstrel and, with his music, he could control the certainties of nature. Like earlier examples, the Orphic mysteries were rooted in a sexual and seasonal agricultural god which echoed the sacredness of fertility rites. As Jung remarked, "Christianity, on the other hand, dispelled the mysteries. Christ was the product and reformer of a patriarchal, nomadic, pastoral religion, whose prophets represented their Messiah as a being of absolutely divine origin."[11]

I personally think the Babylonian god, Tammuz or (his more ancient Sumerian name) Dumzi is the mythical god most similar to Jesus. Tammuz fell into this same divine death and rebirth pattern to celebrate the harvest of crops. Tammuz was sometimes ritualized by a form of the cross; this too, in part, symbolized the life cycles of the harvest. However, Tammuz's cross (like the cross of Osiris and the cross of Horus and perhaps many other known and unknown crosses) was a psychodynamic projection and Jesus' cross was factual. Crucifixion was conceived of well after the origin of Tammuz, but was thrust upon this self proclaimed Messiah by those trying to discredit Him. (Jesus proclaimed His Messiahship at the beginning of His ministry).[12]

I do not question whether or not there is a pattern of myths typifying Jesus' life, particularly in regards to a birth, death and rebirth cycle. I only question the meaning of these myths. Likewise, Jung suggested there are other ideas with similar correlations. For example, the Christian concept of the Last Judgement holds "a 'closed' theme" while the mythical equivalent holds an 'open' or recycled understandings.[13] Thus, the Hero myths seem to be more of a continual rationalization of the possibilities of eternal life than a discussion of historical events. One can point to the myth's familiar cycles as well as the related predictability of story progression. However, just the opposite appears to be true of the New Testament documents. The finality of these Biblical events are certainly a surprise to all involved except for Jesus of Nazareth.

Therefore, a very intriguing question comes to mind. Could the cross of Jesus and, thus, the historical act of crucifixion be universally marked as a sacred moment in time? Could the collective unconscious of man have been waiting for this fulfillment of the sacred symbol? Whether one accepts the resurrection of Jesus as fact, certainly the crucifixion stands on its historical merits and, as such, was also the most dramatic manifestation of symbolism in recorded history. However, I think it was more than a historical event. I am suggesting something bigger, grandeur and more meaningful than 'literal.' I am suggesting something more real than 'factual.' This one historical death and related resurrection event crossed all human spiritual, intellectual and physical barriers. It became the pinnacle phenomenon of every dimension and every parameter of reality–the most prodigious mark in that which is existence. Jesus' sacrificial act and the resulting resurrection was the culmination of all spiritualism in one super synchronistic event. From the human perspective, it was the fulfillment of the reoccurring myth that soothed humanity's spiritual dreams, hopes and fears, yet this time it was an actuality. Thus, the combined crucifixion and resurrection of Jesus was the superior act of psychodynamic fulfillment.

Even from a scientific standpoint, this event seems to be an apex in time and space. I am referring to the distinctions that would necessarily need to be made regarding complexity-specification. According to William Dembski, there is a major distinction between a miracle and a sign. Even though a miracle is an unexplainable event and has a unique attraction, it is the sign that is that is important to the scientist. The sign is a "mark" and "derives from the Latin verb signare."[14] Thus, scientists look for 'signs' in their investigations. Dembski further explains, "Ideally, a sign should be uniquely specific to the sign giver, just as a fingerprint is uniquely specific to the human being."[15] In this way, Dembski feels the resurrection is of interest to complexity-specification analytic scientist: "Jesus bodily resurrection signifies mastery over death, because Jesus himself connects the two (death and resurrection) . . . Yes, the resurrection is a miracle. But more importantly it is a sign that confirms both Jesus' and our own mastery over death."[16] Dembski is inferring that God's signature is found on Jesus' resurrection, the single event that demonstrated death is mastered. Life exists after death.

However, neither the psychodynamics nor the complexity-specification of this death and resurrection phenomenon negate the theological implications. I firmly believe those who ask Jesus to be Lord of their lives do in fact receive a pardon for their human crimes against the divine nature of God. Of course, this salvation is the supreme message of the cross. Assuming this to be 'Truth' (in the context of Ghandi and other holy men who search), could the communality of symbolism also suggest a common spiritual influence? (This seems to be more in line with the findings of Jung/Campbell then the layman's understanding of myths and symbolism). Moreover, wouldn't such symbolism be the suggestion of an outside force? Could some things or one thing be relaying a similar message to a variety of people? Mankind is

COULD THE CROSS OF JESUS AND, THUS, THE HISTORICAL ACT OF CRUCIFIXION
BE UNIVERSALLY MARKED AS A SACRED MOMENT IN TIME?

drawn to the cross and a number of other spiritual intuitions because of their divine origin. The human 'Self' is unconsciously decoding the Will of God through religious symbolism.

As for those Christians who associate the above as occultic, if YHWH used astrological 'signs' to send pagan scholars to the Messiah's birth, then we should not be surprised to learn He pointed to the salvation of His creation in even more extraordinary and unmistakable ways. Even today, the universal nature of Jesus' being suggests all mankind intuitively knows Jesus Christ is salvation.

I think Jung would agree with the above position because he wrote:

For the believing Christian, Christ is everything, but certainly not a symbol, which is an expression for something unknown or not yet knowable. And yet he is a symbol by his very nature. Christ would never have made the impression he did on his followers if he had not expressed something that was alive and at work in their unconscious. Christianity itself would never have spread through the pagan world with such astonishing rapidity had its ideas not found an analogous psychic readiness to receive them. It is this fact which also makes it possible to say that whoever believes in Christ is not only contained in him, but that Christ then dwells in the believer as the perfect man formed in the image of God, and second Adam.[17]

This mystical face of Christianity is not sacrilege to traditional Church thinking but embedded in its very foundation. The earliest Christian leaders claimed the entire 'Old Testament' is one big prophecy of the future coming of Jesus Christ, the Holy One. Thus, as one might expect, there is a great outpouring of symbolism. Each word produced a progression of symbols and prophecies, describing the coming Savor of man. In contrast, the 'New Testament' discussion of the life of Jesus is based upon witnessed reports. Thus, with the exception of The Revelation, new symbolism is relatively sparse; predominately the 'Old Testament' holds the primitive symbols and dreams - not only those of the Jews, but, as discussed above, of the entire ancient world.

Furthermore, the 'Old Testament' includes perhaps the oldest Hero story. The Book of Genesis account of Adam and Eve may come from some of man's earliest records. Moses is considered to be the author of Genesis. With his position, he must have had access to the ancient writings of the Jewish tradition, those of the great nation of Egypt as well as most of those in the Mesopotamian region. Such documents were lost to man ages ago. When God visited with Adam and Eve and the serpent, whether it was through thoughts, dreams or through some actual form of verbal discourse, God referred to the coming Savior. Speaking to the serpent, God said: "And I will put enmity between thee and the woman, and between thy seed and her seed; it shall bruise thy head, and thou shalt bruise his heel."[18]

Referring to this verse, Henrietta C. Mears comments: "In mercy God promised One who would redeem men from sin (Genesis 3:15). The seed of the woman (the virgin-born Jesus) would come to destroy the works of the devil (1 John 3:8)."[19] Mears point is obvious, but just as clear is that this coming 'Hero' would, in some way, be seriously wounded by Satan. Straight out of the Old Testament, many years before Jesus of Nazareth is born, comes the foundation to these very ancient god-king myths discussed above. Thus, all mankind has looked for the Promised One of the woman's seed. Assuming this was to be a divine gift to all humanity from a loving Creator and God, doesn't it seem logical to find a path of dreams coming to all mankind in the form of myths to reinforce this divine promise? Perhaps these myths were raised through the power of suggestion, for those relevant symbols (such as the cross) had already been established.

Though the premise fits without the efforts of 'Satan,' the unified Christian response to the mythological rendition of a miraculous birth, death and rebirth cycle is that such manifestations are ploys of Satan. Most assuredly, Satan could find great benefit in using this (God's) prophecy for his brand of disguising and twisting truth. However, the Biblical Satan does not seem to fabricate as much as he distorts and rationalizes (for the sake of man). Logically, he would take an anxious man with subconscious information about a coming Savior and infuse human pride. Would not the 'savior' then be coming only to make one human division great (that of the Jews, or the Egyptians, or the Muslims, etc.) instead of redeeming all people who accept His lordship? I suggest such an equation would indeed offer both myths and human claims of grandeur. Yes, human psychological and racial priorities might well influence a culture's understanding about the coming Messiah.

However, such an explanation may not be complete. We might also find culture plays a role in the myths surrounding the Messiah through the nature of communication. Studies in dream analysis suggest dreams have personal meaning. Therefore, Osiris, Tammuz, Orpheus and Balder may be a personalized interpretation of the same spiritual message, i.e., "The Messiah will be marked at birth. During His life He will die, resurrect and save those who are His followers." The ambiguous and unreliable nature of pagan prognostications seem to be as much the fault of the interpreter of God's message as with the message itself. A great Biblical example is found in Daniel 2 when the then Babylonian King Nebuchadnezzar needed Daniel to interpret his nightmare. However, Christians declare the same allegations about the Jews. Christians claim the Jews did not correctly interpret their Scripture when they refused to accept Jesus as the Messiah. As in the above explanation, the pride of the Jewish leadership (the Pharisees in particular) played a major role.

It is important to remember the difference between myths and Jesus of Nazareth. We have a historically documented case that Mary was impregnated before marriage. We can be fairly certain, Jesus was either a bastard child or He was God on Earth. If Jesus was but a bastard child, his rise from this stench to a leader among men - more precisely Holy Leader, is in itself extremely amazing. Such a defilement would have been reason enough for Mary's death and an unshakable mark against the child. In the case of Jesus, the sign of His virgin birth was obvious. There is no middle ground on this point. Some scholars try to explain away the virgin birth. They substitute middle ground excuses, such as Mary was in a school for Hebrew women and was 'sort of married.' Such arguments are not relevant. The historical record is clear. There are a number of historical references from ancient documents which seem to point to Jesus' unique conception and birth. Most of these references are from hostile witnesses and are expressions like "the bastard of a wedded wife."[20] Evidently, St. Matthew, and, thus, other early Christian authors, were aware of these personal attacks. Therefore, Matthew stresses that Joseph received an unmistakable message from God emphasizing Jesus was His divine Son and would "fulfill God's message through the prophets."[21]

THE MOVIES

May I suggest that you rent the movie, *Who Killed Roger Rabbit?* In my opinion, this movie was an artistic bonanza! Roger Rabbit was a "toon" (a cartoon character) and he was being helped by a real human being. The movie incorporated cartoons and real actors on the screen at the same time. Thus, the two worlds came together on the 'golden screen.' The totality of the worlds were separated, but each world would fade in and out while the characters of each world mingle together. Perhaps Roger Rabbit was a blind paradox of truth. Consider the following scenario: The world we live in is like the "toons" and a more sophisticated world exists independently of our world. From a scientific view, this scenario is more than just a creation of science-fiction. As discussed earlier, there are calculated realities of other dimensions of space and time. There are quantum worlds of probability we cannot understand. Yet, multi-world thought dates back to Plato and before. What if the three dimensions of space and one dimension of time which we consider 'reality' actually limit our utility. What if humanness is like "Toonville" and we are the "toons?" We do cross over once in a while and get a somewhat limited view.

> WE CAN BE FAIRLY CERTAIN, JESUS WAS EITHER A BASTARD CHILD OR HE WAS GOD ON EARTH...THERE IS NO MIDDLE GROUND ON THIS POINT.

We call this, "life after life" or "out of body" experiences, etc. These are generally experiences where people die and are resuscitated or brought back to life. When that happens, those dead who come back to life often tell stories of a waiting beautiful world filled with love and joy. What if that world is reality and this world is "toons"? This is not so preposterous. Quantum physicists refer to our world as a 'Cinderella' world because our reality is both unique and relative.[22]

Consider further how ignorant we must seem to an unlimited and perfect world. From such a vantage point, even our most intelligent beings must always seem to be doing foolish things. What if our Creator, the cartoon artist, left word that one day a human man would come to help us? What if Jesus was who He said He was. What if He was a superhuman being inclusive of both God and man and He was here visiting? According to the Bible, He had all of the answers. What if the Bible is true? What if He had all of the answers from the real world, but we were so insensible that we wanted to get rid of Him and we did? As silly as it sounds, that might be exactly what happened and the myths and dreams we express may actually be probes into the Truth of Reality.

In fact, that is what these psychodynamic patterns proclaim. The entire human race 'instinctively' watched for the Savior. The Anasazi (ancient Native Americans) knew of His coming. The ancient Chinese and the Celtic tribes were looking for the Savior. Early man may have passed the expectation by mouth. God told Adam and Adam told Cain and Abel and so on and so on. But all human beings may also have 'instinctively' received the message. That is what the Savior's dream/symbol/myth experience is saying to the human collective unconscious. You see, Carl Gustave Jung was right! Joseph Campbell was right! They just did not extend their conclusions far enough. Jesus Christ was the long awaited 'Hero.' Jesus Christ was indeed 'the Promised One' of God.

When atheists proclaim all human religions are myths, they are actually partially right, but not in the sense they imply. Of course, human religions and myths are connected because both are products of our human search. Carl Jung felt 'Self' was the human's unconscious connection with God. A closer walk with God is what all humans seek. Why then are there so many religions? Because mankind seeks God through limitations, and thus the flesh binds the spirit. If we unfettered our inner knowledge we would valorously seek ultimate truth and denounce filth and we would know the Ultimate Reality as it relates to our personal lives.

Perhaps this distinction in individual being, this realm of perception without the limitations of a spatial existence, is still a major human problem.

WHAT IF JESUS WAS WHO HE SAID HE WAS.

Perhaps our humanness has bound us. Perhaps we are encumbered by our 'fleshiness' perceptions. Perhaps Gentiles (non Jewish) are so acclimated to the fables of flesh that spiritual Truth is hard to recognize. Perhaps, to post-modernists, the symbols are of greater Truth than the reality for which they stand. In the chapter on miracles, we are reminded of new scientific concepts which might give us mortals some insight regarding the playing field of total being, i.e., mind, body and spirit. Moreover, such discoveries give us tangible knowledge unavailable to Saints Matthew, Mark, Luke and John. Yet, we hold unwarranted resistance to the authority of the Ultimate Reality.

Though I certainly do not suggest psychoanalysis is the root to solving all human problems, I do think a fundamental tool used in understanding self is the common language of the unconscious. Any open-minded psychologist, whether secular or theological, who understands this language must recognize that the deepest most fundamental need of humanness is communion with God. Tied to this ultimate need is the realization that we are unworthy of Holiness. We are, by nature, attracted to evil.

THE CHRISTIAN AND MYTHS

For the Christian, the study of intuitive nature of man, should be only academic. Myths, along with other intuitive understandings, are primarily directed to pagan man and not to the dedicated God fearing Christian. The intuitive voice of myths speaks to man for a different reason than does the spiritual message of YHWH, Jesus Christ or the Holy Spirit. This does become quite interesting because the Christian and the Jew are warned time and time again by YHWH not to become involved in pagan theistic practices. In fact, a most interesting warning comes to Christianity through 1 Timothy. Paul explains to Timothy the reason for myths and religions and laws for human beings. His explanation will be quite surprising to most readers:

> *As I said when I left for Macedonia, please stay there in Ephesus and try to stop the men who are teaching such wrong doctrine. Put an end to their myths and fables, and their idea of being saved by finding favor with an endless chain of angels leading up to God - wild ideas that stir up questions and arguments instead of helping people accept God's plan of faith. (This sentence in the King James states, Neither give heed to fables and endless genealogies, which minister questions, rather than godly edifying which is in faith: so do.) What I am eager for is that all the Christians there will be filled with love that comes from pure hearts, and that their minds will be clean and their faith strong.*[23]

WE ARE, BY NATURE, ATTRACTED TO EVIL.

The city of Ephesus embraced many of the 'mystery' religions. It is not clear exactly to which myths and genealogies Paul is referring. It seems someone like an early Gnostic or Marcion is taking myth and adding it to Jesus' message of Christian love—a doctrine we are about to probe. However, this quotation gives us further reason to believe the accounts about Jesus' life, i.e., His miracles, birth, crucifixion and resurrection, were witnessed affairs and considered to be literal events and not myths.

Next comes a message for theologians.

But these teachers have missed this whole idea and spend their time arguing and talking foolishness. They want to become famous as teachers of the laws of Moses when they haven't the slightest idea what those laws really show us.[24]

It is "FOOLISHNESS." Perhaps in reality our arguments about science and evolution and what did or did not happen in ancient days is only trivial. Perhaps the heart of man should be our true concern. Thus, only the information in the following chapters is of true importance. This expresses what God's intuitive message to humanity seems to articulate.

Those laws (the laws of Moses) are good when used as God intended. But they were not made for us, whom God has saved; they are for sinners who hate God, have rebellious hearts, curse and swear, attack their fathers and mothers, and murder. Yes, these laws are made to identify as sinners all who are immoral and impure: homosexuals, kidnapers, liars, and all others who do things that contradict the glorious Good News of our blessed God, whose messenger I am.[25]

One very interesting point about 1 Timothy is that Paul indirectly tied 'The Law' of Moses to myths. As we have discussed, both the law and repetitive myths are intuitive to all humanity. Paul did not have the knowledge of Carl Jung. He did not understand the human collective unconscious. Though he was well schooled and widely traveled, he probably had general knowledge about the many pagan religions of his day. Though Paul probably did not understand the universal nature of mythical symbolism, he certainly did understand the communal human cry for a Savior. Paul knew God's voice which is innate and speaks to all who will listen. And he knew why God speaks.

More importantly, we must realize that Paul separated the mythological from the real. Certainly, he knew of the mythological gods of both Greece and Rome. He must have also heard of ancient virgin birth stories including a few of those listed above. These were already established legends. He knew about some of the fabled gods and/or super human beings arising from the dead. Yet, he professed Jesus was actual and not mythological. It was Paul's choice, and others likened to Paul who accepted Jesus as actual. This legitimized Jesus and separated Him from the numerous myths. Most assuredly, Paul fell in love with Jesus, because Jesus is the Messiah.

Sitting silent wearing Sunday best,
The sermon echos through the walls.
A great salvation calls to the people
who stare, into nowhere
and can't feel the chains
on their souls.
He's more than the laughter
or the stars in the heaven.
As close as a heartbeat
or a song on our lips.
Someday we'll trust Him
and learn how to see Him.
Someday He'll call us
and we will come running
and fall in His arms and the tears
will fall down and we'll pray,
I want to fall in love with You.[26]

SECTION FOUR:

JESUS—
WHO WAS HE?

CHAPTER 16

JESUS OF NAZARETH

"Who do you say that I am?" The entire world of religion seems to revolve around this one question of Jesus. Yet, there seems to be only one good answer. He was God visiting earth. He came in the material flesh so we could recognize Him . . . but, we didn't . . . and He knew that we wouldn't . . . yet, He came anyway . . . because He loves us.

I hope everyone who picks up this book has some Biblical knowledge about the life of Jesus of Nazareth. It is not the intention of this writing to "tell the story of Jesus." Rather, it is my pleasure to validate His historical being, His life's purpose and the fulfillment of His purpose. In so doing, I will involve only moments in His life.

For me, the amazing thing about Jesus is not who He claimed to be, or the life He lived, or anything related to His ministry; it is the great theoretical assumptions people make in order to cast shadows on His creditability. Many atheists seem to deny Jesus of Nazareth even existed. I have listened to debates where atheists argued Jesus was not a historical person. Such arguments do harm to the atheistic cause because His human existence is considered factual by virtually every credible historian. Furthermore, we can be just as sure that Jesus was an extraordinary person.

COURSES

If you take a course in college pertaining to the life of Jesus Christ, your professor will most likely try to be accommodating to all sides of the 'Jesus story.' This is both understandable and probably commendable. I do recognize the professor's situation. He or she must extend the normal civilities to all students. Such niceties would include not offending other religious doctrines, i.e., the Jews, Muslims, agnostics, atheists, etc. Therefore, any lecture would give the associated Hebrew leaders, Sanhedrin council, and Jewish people the benefit of whatever doubt may exist. Yet, often these common courtesies go too far and the profound nature of Jesus is lost to hospitalities. Such a classroom oration will often include 'politically correct' perspectives such as, "Jesus had only a small following. Most Jews had no feeling, pro or con, toward Jesus." Many times the professor will soften the perception of Jesus' wisdom with comments like, "Matthew, Mark, Luke and John only relayed 'the good stuff' about Jesus. Naturally, these men only wrote about the great things Jesus said. They did not relay the 'dumb' or 'nasty' comments He may have made. Why would they report these things if Jesus was their friend?

As for the virgin birth, resurrection and all of those miracles reported to have been performed by Jesus, the disciples were writing and speaking in a form of double speak. These things had great symbolic meaning. Thus," the professor will conclude, "the miraculous events may not have been factual. Furthermore, the Sanhedrin did not look at Jesus as a man of miracles, but as a man of magic. However, whether or not Jesus was the awaited Messiah, He was a good man who had a great influence on the entire western civilization."

Such a statement would lead one to believe Jesus could have been divine, perhaps the Son of God as the Christians believe, or perhaps a prophet such as the Muslims and other traditions suggest. Yet, maybe He was just a nice guy that a few people grew to love. However, such a commentary is extremely misleading, for it is widely speculative and intentionally devoid of some rather amazing historical realities. Finally, these 'watered down' courses fail to address what is perhaps the greatest issue in the history of human civilization and certainly the major reason to take a course on the History of Christianity. Jesus asked: "Who do you say that I am?" That is the real question—the question waiting an answer by every human throughout the ages. Who was Jesus of Nazareth?

In this and following chapters, I intend to provide the reader with substantial historical evidence indicating Jesus was both the long awaited Messiah of the Jews, and for all mankind, as well as the Son of God (God on earth).

JESUS AND MIRACLES

We have previously discussed reasons to believe in miracles. Through these discussions, we exposed a major doctrine of the divine authoritarian philosophy, i.e., both natural and supernatural events are alike for God. Samuel Clarke presupposed that the only true course of nature resides in God's Will for producing predestined events in a "continual and uniform manner."[1] Miracles reflect the interposition of God in the normality of affairs. Therefore, miracles are not genuinely foreign to the course of nature.[2] Historian Paul Maier, commenting on David Hume's supposition that natural law cannot be violated, wrote, "Hume's position may not be entirely valid even in terms of the natural sciences, and it overlooks the quintessential issue, namely: the only way that the super-natural dimension could ever demonstrate itself in the natural realm would be, in fact, by intrusion into natural law."[3]

Yet, some people just do not accept supernatural events as reality. In fact, a number of people accept Jesus' existence as a historical fact and perhaps acknowledge Him to be the true Son of God, yet, they assume the mira-

THAT IS THE REAL QUESTION—THE QUESTION WAITING AN ANSWER BY EVERY HUMAN THROUGHOUT THE AGES. WHO WAS JESUS OF NAZARETH?

cles of Jesus were fictional tales. The problem with such thinking is that Jesus' miracles set Him apart from the common man. Jesus' ability to command the elements and reach beyond nature attest to His super-nature. Moreover, if Jesus could not interpose His Will with natural law, why would anyone accept such a natural man as God? Most assuredly, I cannot command the elements, I cannot call on the extra-dimensions of the universe nor expect miracles to be performed at my will. Then again, I do not claim to be God. Nonetheless, if I were God, I would expect to be able to command the universe. I would expect all dimensions, all the elements, all laws of physics or quantum physics and all of everything that exists to bend to my whim. If we are intellectually honest, such powers are not unfitting or amazing for an all powerful God.

So, if Jesus is God, why would He not make use of miracles? It does not take a great 'leap of faith' to believe that He performed such feats. It only takes the acceptance of a solid and uniform historical record. In a variety of documents of antiquity, Jesus' miracles are brazenly conspicuous. In fact, His most common characteristic seems to be that He was a great man of miracles. It is quite clear to many modern historians that Jesus was both respected and feared by all, most certainly by His enemies, because of His perceived miraculous capabilities. Make no mistake, Jesus performed mighty deeds which seemed distinctly supernatural.

HISTORICAL EVIDENCE OF JESUS' MIRACLES

Many people have read the New Testament references defending Jesus Christ. However, most are unaware that the Bible is substantiated by numerous historical documents. Included are such sources as the Jewish Talmud. As one might imagine, official Jewish records are antagonistic towards Jesus. However, said documents make it obvious that the Jewish establishment perceived Him as a very dangerous man. We find approximately twenty references to Jesus in the unexpurgated Talmud records. Fredric Farrar's book, *The Life of Christ,* holds an interesting discussion about some of these references. To better understand the Jewish fear of Jesus, Farrar refers to a Talmud record which states, "That man, He whom we may not name, the Nazarene and the fool." Also found is a coded grouping of letters which imply the following, "May his memory be destroyed and his name be blotted out."[4] The practicalities of such statements are likewise convincing, as the historical Jewish struggle with Jesus is obvious; His challenging nature is clear and His influence conspicuous. Thus, it seems, the method the Jewish establishment used to clear their collective conscience was removal of all related records. Yet, as one might expect in the case of such an important historic figure, the fingerprints were there. The cover-up has been discovered and documents were found.

For a historian, negative comments like those above carry great weight. Hostile records are written to hurt someone's credibility (in this case Jesus Christ). Yet, the hostile documents verify Jesus' existence and His reputation. Ask any attorney about the strength of a hostile witness' testimony which, in fact, verifies their client's position.

Other official documents scorned Jesus for using magic and breaking laws. As an example, there is a reference in the Talmud to Jesus' crucifixion. In this comment, Jesus is referred to as "a sorcerer and a law breaker."[5] Historian Paul Maier is attuned to the inferences of words in ancient texts. Maier writes, "By definition, sorcery is something extraordinary or supernatural accomplished with help from below."[6] Thus, the demonic association could include awesome displays of power. Maier contrasts miracles with sorcery by the following, "A miracle is the same (as sorcery), though achieved with help 'from above.' In any case, the supernatural is conceded."[7] The point is that both sorcery and miracles were considered supernatural feats and not human manipulations. Between 95 and 110 A.D. Rabbi Eliezer ben Hycanus of Lydda made another reference to Jesus' magic arts. A common reference indicates that, "Jesus practiced magic and led Israel astray."[8] We must remember that, in the days of Jesus, magic did not refer to entertaining parlor tricks but, like sorcery, was another reference to supernatural abilities. With that in mind, what do you suppose was Jesus' magic and why was He a law breaker? Do you think He healed the sick on the Sabbath Day as the Bible indicates? (Healing on the Sabbath, aside from being miraculous, would be against the Jewish law as it was wrong to do any work including miracles.) Or, do you think Jesus was pulling rabbits out of hats and spitting on sidewalks? No, the official reaction to Jesus brings exegetical credibility to the Biblical account.

Referring back to the period around 95–110 A.D., we find a "controversy" in Palestine related to whether or not it is "permissible to be healed in the name of Jesus."[9] This statement suggests that Jesus Himself healed. Evidently, the tradition of Jesus Christ, the man of miracles, spread throughout the ancient world. Even the Roman Empire took notice. This is extraordinary, as there were a number of possible messiahs living in Judea at the time. Generally speaking, Jewish messiahs were considered unimportant and ignored by the Roman Empire. For the Empire to break their 'messiah custom' and deal with the 'Jesus problem' speaks to the power of the early Jesus movement. According to Marvin Hunt: "To the pagan Greek and Roman writers, Jesus was just an insignificant flicker in the history of a nation and people they despised. They considered him as just one of many so-called messiahs who had come to lead the Jewish people to liberation."[10]

Yet, in a relatively short time, Jesus' influence became a notable factor outside the Jewish state. The Roman Emperor, Julian the Apostate, (361–363 A.D.) has been labeled as "one of the most gifted of the ancient adversaries to Christianity." Plainly, he was a hostile witness and, thus, a more valid witness for the defenders of Christianity. Julian the Apostate wrote, "Jesus . . . has now been celebrated about three hundred years; having done nothing in his lifetime worthy of fame, unless anyone thinks it a very great work to heal lame and blind people and exorcise demoniacs in the villages of Bethsaida and Bethany."[11] The fact that these are the words of a Roman Emperor emphasize the magnitude and sincerity of the Christian movement. The dedication of the average Christian must have been considered a serious threat to be recognized by at least two emperors, Julian the Apostate and Nero.

I further wish to emphasize that these references are excerpts from historical documents other than the Bible. They were not written about a mythical hero, a statue, or a relic, but about a real human being who was feared because of His miraculous powers. If you question the historicity of Jesus or the secular documents dealing with His deity, then I suggest reading Josh McDowell's books, *Evidence That Demands A Verdict, Vol. I and II.* McDowell's books have everything from quotations of leading archaeologists referring to the physical foundations of the Bible, to many references about Jesus made by ancient 'hostile' historians such as Cornelius Tacitus (born 52–54 A.D.) who wrote the following:

But not all the relief that could come from man, not all the bounties that the prince could bestow, nor all the atonements which could be presented to the gods, availed to relieve Nero from the infamy of being believed to have ordered the conflagration, the fire in Rome. Hence to suppress the rumor, he falsely charged with the guilt, and punish with the most exquisite tortures, the persons commonly called Christians, who were hated for their enormities. Christus, the founder of the name, was put to death as a criminal by Pontius Pilate, procurator of Judah in the reign of Tiberius: but the pernicious superstition, repressed for a time broke out again, not only through Judah, where the mischief originated, but through the city of Rome also.[12]

Tacitus next confirmed that the early Christians did indeed suffer horrible deaths for their faith in Jesus. He wrote, "They (the Christians) were covered with wild beasts' skins and torn to death by dogs; or they were fastened on crosses, and, when daylight failed were burned to serve as lamps by night."[13]

As far as I am aware, there are no records which state that only three people believed Jesus' claims, or only fifteen people came to Jesus for healing. Though the Talmud Sanhedrin 43a states, "Our Rabbis taught that Yeshu had five disciples: Matti, Necki, Netsur, Burni, and Toda,"[14] the overwhelming written evidence is that Jesus had some followers in various areas of Judah. Of course, the best records are the books of the Bible which state Jesus did not want large followings, but found great acceptance as He performed wondrous miracles.

As His reputation grew, the crowds grew. When He was finally publicly acknowledged as the Messiah, He became very popular. This Biblical narration of events seems quite logical. If I am a Jew walking down First Street and my friend, Joseph, comes up and tells me, "There is a guy over on Third Street who may be the Messiah and He is performing some really neat miracles," I think I would head over to Third Street. If Jesus was indeed the miracle man history dictates, then He would have found quite a following regardless of His intentions or whether or not He sought fame.

Indications are that Jesus did acquire a strong following which seemed to peak on or around Palm Sunday as Jesus triumphantly entered Jerusalem on a young donkey. This entry was thought to have been earlier prophesied: "Rejoice greatly, O my people! Shout with joy! For look - your King is coming! His is the Righteous One, the Victor! Yet, he is lowly, riding on a donkey's colt!"[15] To further identify Jesus as the Messiah, the following verse seems to have prophesied about Jesus' coming crucifixion: "I have delivered you from death in a waterless pit because of the covenant I made with you, sealed with blood."[16]

Some historians explain that these Palm Sunday crowds were only the normal Passover travelers and not assembled to praise Jesus on His entrance into Jerusalem. However, if His reputation for miracles preceded Him, the natural response of these crowds, no matter why they were on the road to Jerusalem, would have been to gather around this man—the one some openly called the Messiah.

This is exactly what the Bible indicates. In fact, Jesus' popularity resulting from miracles became the political reason for His Crucifixion.[17] A Jewish council convened to discuss Jesus of Nazareth . . ."What are we going to do?" they asked each other. "For this man certainly does miracles. If we let Him alone the whole nation will follow Him - and then the Roman army will come and kill us and take over the Jewish government."[18] From the historical perspective, this narration agrees with the earlier secular and Jewish references to Jesus' "magical" abilities. If His popularity were the only problem, then they could cope with Him. There have been many popular political prisoners. However, Jesus' popularity was only the symptom. The miracles were obviously the cause of the Jewish council's query. He seemed to be supernatural. Some, or all of the council, probably wondered if Jesus was not the Messiah. Yet, they may have rationalized, "He cannot be the Messiah, because when it comes to confronting the Roman conquerors, He is a pacifist." They certainly did not perceive Him as the Jewish Savior when they considered Jesus' view of peace toward the Roman legions. They assumed that the Jewish Messiah would be more like King David. He would lead them in battle and

Judah would become a great nation. If there were to be any future political relationship, Rome would be Judah's servant.

The Biblical record explains what the Pharisees and Sadducees decided to do with Him. We do not know how many were ready to quiet Jesus 'permanently.' Perhaps only a few. However, we do know that those in this group were powerful and prevailed. "And one of them, Caiaphas, who was High Priest that year said, 'You stupid idiots - let this one man die for the people - why should the whole nation perish?'"[19] Caiaphas' statement seems brutally honest and logical. Yet, history tells us these religious leaders had interests other than the Jewish state. Caiaphas had succeeded his father-in-law Annas as High Priest. Thus, he was in control of the sacrifices offered to God. Peter Marshall referred to these other 'interests' with the following:

> *Annas and Caiaphas controlled the market in the temple porch, where sacrifices were sold to pilgrim worshipers and Roman money was exchanged for the statutory half-shekel required as a temple offering. The priests determined the rate of exchange and made money shamelessly. Moreover, they drew rent from the ground on which the sellers of animals for sacrifice put up their stalls and stacked their dove cages. The People knew this and resented it, but what could they do? . . . An income equivalent to about a million and a half dollars a year was flowing into the temple treasuries. Jesus knew all this; it was common knowledge . . . The most scathing words ever reported to have come from Jesus' mouth were spoken against the men who perpetrated this wholesale theft.[20]*

It is important to point out that the American dollar has inflated considerably since Marshall's commentary. These leaders must have worried about their well-being. They, above everyone else, had so much to lose, as they had reached a high status of wealth, power and fame under the status quo. It would have been idiotic by worldly standards for those Jewish leaders to have given up their massive fortunes and power for what they rationalized to be the ideas of a vagabond sorcerer.

The Jewish priests began to look for a political solution to their conflict with Jesus. By invoking authoritative pressures, they involved the Sanhedrin, the governing body of the Jews. Thus, Jesus became a political criminal. Naturally, Jesus' followers became afraid. Each individual must have examined the strength of their faith in Jesus. Each was growing increasingly aware of the probable repercussions stemming from an affiliation with this "Nazarene." Furthermore, records indicate other men of the day proclaimed themselves to be messiahs. Probably most were ready to lead Judah into battle. The conditions were certainly right for a messiah. Many Jews must have been confused. Some began to believe that the Jewish Scriptures were wrong or God had failed them, because the prophetic time for the Messiah's appearance had already past.

Naturally, when Jesus failed to rise up against the Romans some of the once amenable Jews began to discount Jesus' Messianic claims. This rationalization process would seem to be the politically correct procedure. After all, a group of the Jewish leadership now openly rejected Jesus. They often declared Him possessed by a demon![21] The common people must have wondered, "Is this the way the Jewish Messiah will be treated by our priests?" Because of these added political pressures, the relevant question was no longer, could Jesus be the Messiah, but should one take an active position supporting Jesus as the Messiah?

What if Jesus hadn't come when He did, but appeared today in Cleveland. What if, while He was marching toward Washington, D.C., Oral Roberts, Jessie Jackson, Pope Paul II and Dan Rather all went on Night Line and claimed, "Jesus was not the Messiah as the people of Cleveland had reported, but instead was a very clever and well-disguised Charles Manson. In fact, He is going to get many people killed - so, stay away from Him!" How many of us would say, "I'm going to go join Jesus on His march on Washington?" Moreover, if Jesus arrived in Washington and was grabbed by the F.B.I., how many of us would rush to His defense? Most of us would probably say, "We don't need another dangerous radical running around causing political problems. Let us get on with the business of life and wait for another and better messiah." This allegory may seem a little far fetched. However, it is probably a more realistic comparison than most of us might want to believe.

Thus, human nature seems to agree with the Biblical account. Here lies our dilemma. While acknowledging that there are good reasons for our conditioned minds to question miraculous events, both the historical record and human nature confirms the events in Jesus' life. Therefore, Jesus' miracles may not be the cause of our disbelief. The deity of Jesus Christ is the true problem. His deity must either be accepted or rejected. The question has always been, Who was Jesus of Nazareth? In his book, *Theology In Reconstruction,* T. F. Torrance discusses the importance of Jesus' question, "Who do you say I am?" Torrance wrote:

> *It was the interplay of question and counter-question that lay behind the Cross. Indeed it was precisely the interaction between the questioner and the questioned in which the Truth of God in Jesus penetrated more and more deeply into the inner secrets of men that led directly to the crucifixion; for by the life he lived in their midst Jesus questioned his contemporaries down to the roots of their being, and forced them to the boundaries of their existence where they had either*

to take refuge in their own preconceptions and crucify him in self-protection, or give themselves up wholly to the scrutiny of God that both slays and makes alive.[22]

THE CRUCIFIXION

How do we know within reason, that Jesus was crucified? Besides the Biblical accounts, we have a number of other historical confirmations in Jewish literature. One such record comes from the Babylonian Talmud in Sanhedrin 43a:

It has been taught: On the Eve of the Passover, they hanged Yeshu. And an announcer went out in front of him, for forty days saying: "he is going to be stoned because he practiced sorcery and enticed and led Israel astray. Anyone who knows anything in his favor, let him come and plead in his behalf." But, not having found anything in his favor, they hanged him on the Eve of the Passover.[23]

Fredric W. Farrar is emphatic that this Talmud reference to "The Hung" is about Jesus of Nazareth. In fact, he refers to other writings which designate Christians to be "worshipers of the Hung."[24] Thus, this rabbinical source is yet another voice confirming Jesus as a sorcerer or man of miracles. Moreover, it is most interesting that a rabbi confirms the New Testament's statement about the illegal timing of the crucifixion. Eastman and Smith explain:

According to Jewish law it is illegal to perform capital punishment on the eve of the Passover. However, this record verifies something that we wouldn't expect to find in a rabbinical source, the fact that the Sanhedrin acted illegally in condemning and crucifying Jesus on Passover.[25]

One final point needs to be made about this statement. It further confirms that the disciples, at the time of the crucifixion, went into hiding, because they would not speak in His favor. Of course, one would naturally doubt that the Pharisees controlled Jesus for forty days and then rushed to crucify Him on the Eve of the Passover. More realistically, the Bible refers to earlier Pharisees attempts on Jesus life. Nonetheless, both the Jewish and Christian sources confirm that Jesus' disciples were afraid. Moreover, the crucifixion does not deify Jesus; nor does it necessarily make Him the Messiah. It would take the resurrection to historically separate Jesus from the rest of humanity.

THE RESURRECTION

Of the supernatural events, the resurrection of Jesus is the most miraculous. From a personal view, it is not important whether Jesus healed one leper or a thousand lepers. It is, however, important whether or not He raised Himself from the dead. The entire relevance of Jesus Christ rests on this point. In Matthew 12:38–42 Jesus Himself made this very pronouncement. The resurrection of this 'Holy One' was predicted by the Jewish leader David in Psalms 16:8–11. Peter explained the meaning of Psalms 16:8–11, as did Luke by his recording of Peter's words in Acts 2:24–35. Both declared Jesus to be the Messiah by His fulfillment of this Jewish Scripture. The resurrection is the sign of His authority and of His might. In fact, it can be claimed that the resurrection was the sign spoken of by dreamers, prophets, myths, prognosticators and soothsayers in virtually every part of the world since the beginning of religious man. It is the awaited sign of authenticity, because mere man cannot resurrect himself from the dead. Dead men turn to dust. Chuck Smith has stated:

> *That one man out of all of them rose from the dead unto eternal life does seem rather incredible because it (resurrection) is so unique. Many people have been resuscitated, brought back to life, but that was only to die at a later date.*[26]

Yet, the witnesses' statements indicate that there was no later death for Jesus, but an ascension into heaven.[27] Biblical scholar James Orr felt the incredible resolution of the early martyrs demonstrated that, " . . . the Resurrection of Jesus Christ came to be regarded as a solid and unquestioned fact."[28]

Orr once made this insightful comment regarding the resurrection of Jesus:

> *Here then, is a conceded point - the belief of the Apostolic Church in the Resurrection of the Lord. It is well to begin with this point, and to inquire what the nature of the belief of the earliest Church was. Was it belief in visionary or spiritualistic appearances? Belief in the survival of the soul of Jesus? Belief that somehow or somewhere Jesus lived with God, while His body saw corruption in the tomb? Or was it belief that Jesus had actually risen in the body from the grave? That He had been truly dead and was as truly alive again?*

> *If the latter was the case, then beyond all question the belief in the Resurrection of Jesus was belief in a true miracle, and there is no getting away from the alternative with which this account of the origin of Christianity confronts us.*[29]

The early record is quite certain about the physical status of the resurrected Christ:

> *During the forty days after His crucifixion He appeared to the apostles from time to time, actually alive, and proved to them in many ways that it was really He Himself they were seeing. And on these occasions He talked to them about the Kingdom of God.*[30]

As we have previously discussed, the resurrection was the ancient sign of a coming human deity and messianic Savior. What dignifies the resurrection of Jesus Christ? What takes the story of Jesus from the realm of myth and places it in the realm of reality? Why believe Jesus of Nazareth over all of the mythically resurrected?

Acknowledged resurrection myths seem to be ingratiating concoctions of the imagination. Yet, the narratives about Jesus of Nazareth seem void of such markings. The New Testament narratives are direct and matter-of-fact. But, the differences are much greater than apparent style or contents. *First, there is a problem with access.* There does not appear to have been any cults spreading resurrection fables around ancient Palestine.

Second, the resurrection of an individual was foreign to Jewish logic or understanding. Many Jews believed in a resurrection of all humanity at the end of the world. This abrupt deviation from a fundamental Judaic belief by Jesus' followers is quite remarkable in its own right. There seems to be no reason for this revolutionary change other than a profound event leading to radical change. Had they not been challenged in such a manner, William Lane Craig suggests, the followers would have reacted in a very different way: "The disciples, therefore, confronted with Jesus' crucifixion and death would only have looked forward to the resurrection at the final day and would probably have carefully kept their master's tomb as a shrine, where his bones could reside until the resurrection. They would not have come up with the idea that he was already raised."[31] Of course, Craig is assuming the disciples would have accepted Jesus as their leader after death. As later discussed, that premise alone is unthinkable.

Third, essentially all historians now believe the New Testament writings were completed and circulated during the "lifetime of the eyewitnesses."[32] Thus, most scholars realize there was not enough time to develop a mythical story of this magnitude, so radically aberrant to the Jewish culture and traditions.

Fourth, there is no historical reason to believe resurrection stories about any other man. Moreover, as the Messiah relates to Jung's theories, all of the resurrection myths might be symbolic representations of the collective unconscious, i.e., intuitive knowledge of an awaited Savior. Finally, as historian Paul Maier relates, "Mythical personalities are not involved in authentic episodes from the past. Nor do they leave hard evidence behind. In the life and ministry of Jesus of Nazareth, however, there are many points of contact between His record in the Gospels and the surrounding history of His times."[33] Thus, great evidence supports the historical resurrection of Jesus.

Aside from the absurdity of the mythology angle, other radical departures from Judaic tradition are witness to the honesty of the resurrection movement. The fact that women found the empty tomb is a great testimony to the factuality of the Biblical account. Women were not considered reliable witnesses at this time and place in history.[34] We have some idea of the status of women of the ancient middle eastern world by recognizing the fundamental Muslim observance of the traditional role of women. Without question, if these resurrection reports were fictional, the writers would have held that men found the open tomb. Though there are some discrepancies between the witnesses of this event, this single disclosure goes along way toward validating the honesty of these accounts.

One Biblical/historical event essentially gives credence to every statement the Bible makes about the life of Jesus of Nazareth and emphatically proclaims His resurrection. That great event transpired on the first Pentecostal festival following the crucifixion of Jesus Christ. Those Pentecost activities were to culminate a chain of many miraculous events. Only days after Jesus is reported to have ascended into heaven, the disciples took to the streets preaching about His resurrection and telling of the miracles, the wonders and the Old Testament prophecies fulfilled through His life. The disciples were preaching the Gospel to everyone in Jerusalem and most likely within feet of the empty grave, the empty tomb of Jesus Christ. Had their message been made of lies, they would have been laughed out of town! Remember, the same people hearing this Christian message were also eye witnesses to many of the things spoken of by the disciples. They had witnessed the miracles. They had seen the crucifixion. They saw a mutilated Jesus die a horrible death. Yet, they intently listened, and many of them dedicated their lives to the man crucified on a tree. They became 'worshipers of the Hung.' Concurring with this conclusion, Dr. Orr wrote, "There is not a hint anywhere that the fact of the empty tomb was ever questioned by either friend or foe. It would have been easy to question or disprove it when the Apostles were boldly proclaiming the Resurrection in Jerusalem a few weeks later. But no one appears to have done so."[35]

I must emphasize the importance of this particular moment in the history of man. Indeed, the reaction of the Jewish people to the empty tomb was

THUS, GREAT EVIDENCE SUPPORTS THE HISTORICAL RESURRECTION OF JESUS.

the beginning of the Christian religion. Yet, it was more. Despite any discourse about the validity of Jesus' claims of being the Son of God and the Messiah, this phenomenon would permeate virtually all theological concepts. This same historical disposition would have an astounding effect on most major philosophies and thought processes coming to the human race. Finally, the political reaches of this spirit would be most particularly demonstrated by the great democratic movement in western civilization. Thus, one might assume, this is the Age of the Gentile spoken of in the Bible.

Logic calls out! It breaks through our selfish humanness and our preconceived notions of godness or godlessness. Logic insists that the Resurrection message was perceived as true from its very beginning. Had Jesus' body been laying entombed during the Pentecost, then the people would not have listened and Christianity would never have begun. Yet, a large number (about 3,000) of one audience in Jerusalem were baptized after St. Peter's 'Pentecost' sermon.[36] Peter exclaimed:

O men of Israel, listen! God publicly endorsed Jesus of Nazareth by doing tremendous miracles through him, as you well know. But God, following his prearranged plan, let you use the Roman government to nail him to the cross and murder him.[37]

In Peter's statement, we again see reference to Jesus' miracles, those activities which Jewish documents designated as "magic" and "sorcery." Peter's proclamation that Jesus' miracles confirmed God's endorsement suggests a "magic" no one else could do, or had ever done.

As to the sincerity of those involved, it does not seem logical to question the knowledge of the growing numbers of Jewish followers. Would the people of Jerusalem have converted to Christianity to worship a dead 'coward.' However, we know massive crowds did convert! Moreover, history dictates that the followers of Christ existed under extreme persecution. All Jewish converts must have been willing to die for Jesus - their Messiah. Therefore, these conversions must be regarded both as further evidence of the factual nature of the resurrection and an exposing of Jewish discontent with their government's explanation. The converts reveal the people of Jerusalem had problems accepting the official explanation that "Jesus' body was stolen." I strongly believe most Jews knew Jesus was "The Promised One." However, it was a message for the bold. The conventional Jewish citizen would be unwilling to circumvent the Pharisees authority. Traditionally, the Jewish people followed the dictates of the religious establishment, and their authority extended

---

HAD JESUS' BODY BEEN LAYING ENTOMBED DURING THE PENTECOST, THEN THE PEOPLE WOULD NOT HAVE LISTENED AND CHRISTIANITY WOULD NEVER HAVE BEGUN.

beyond theological boundaries. The people may have discussed the wisdom of their leaders, but the Jewish leadership held the authority. Despite the reality of the day, despite what they knew to be Truth, many of the Jewish country-men may have rationalized, "Perhaps things are not as they seem. Perhaps the Rabbis and their friends were right; they do have a direct line of communication with God. They are the righteous. Surely they would not mislead us. Furthermore, Peter may not know all of the facts. Peter cannot protect our future. There must be some other explanation." Add to this chaotic dilemma the known fact that Jesus had been executed. The people may have further rationalized, "It was too late to do anything for Jesus because He died. Despite the fact that His followers jubilantly cried, 'He has Risen' - despite the obvious empty tomb - regardless if Jesus had risen from the grave, He is now gone. Therefore, He will not be there to save us." This was especially relevant since the Jewish people had allowed His death! Why would He now help them? They would have to find another way to freedom besides Jesus of Nazareth. Reluctantly, the people would yield to the traditional Jewish cultural and political pressures.

Historic records indicate that from the resurrection of Jesus until the destruction of Judah, a period of about 38 years, the Jewish people were traumatized. Followers of Christ have generally held this reality as an outcome of a Jewish mob's self-condemnation. Pilate gave the assembled Judaic crowd an opportunity to let Jesus live. However, they demanded His crucifixion. It is often assumed that the crowd did not hold the common Jewish perception of Jesus, but was in some way hand picked by Caiaphas or his loyalists. Nonetheless, part of their cry was, "His blood be on us and our children."[38]

The Jewish population was very uneasy. I assume it was much like Czechoslovakia during the 1950's or the 'Eastern Bloc' nations in the 1980's just before the fall of Communism. Many wanted change, but only a few were brave enough to take a leadership position in a movement for change. The reality of accepting Jesus Christ as the Son of God was a great risk. This reality brought confusion and anxiety. "We killed the Messiah" rang throughout Israel, if not by the gossips at least by Peter, James, John, and the other early Christians. The accuracy of this statement is as unquestionable as is the existence of Christianity itself.

In spite of the constriction of the negative factors, Christianity exploded throughout Judah and all of the known world. This early growth proves beyond a shadow of a doubt that the message was convincing. In fact, numerous proclaimed messianic leaders died trying to lead the Jewish people against the Roman Empire. However, all were forgotten after death. Only one called for love even for one's enemy. Large numbers of people accepted Jesus as the Lord of their life, people who were willing to die grotesque and painful deaths just for the honor of worshipping a man they had seen crucified and buried . . . a man named Jesus of Nazareth.

CHAPTER 17

WHAT HAPPENED TO THE BODY?

"He didn't die for nothing.
This is the one thing,
The one thing that
I know."[1]

      That Jesus was crucified and buried does seem true. We can be reasonably certain about the historical legitimacy of Jesus' death. However, a following corollary is hard for many people to accept. This succeeding event was a miraculous resurrection. Accordingly, Paul Maier clarified the historian's problem with Jesus' Resurrection:

> . . . two or three sources in agreement generally render the fact unimpeachable. In the case of the first Easter, there are at least seven ancient sources - the four Gospels, Acts, and the letters of Paul and Peter - but this has not led to universal acceptance of the resurrection as a datum of history. Why not? Because the more unlikely the episode, the stronger the evidence demanded for it . . . Nevertheless, important historical evidence - quite apart from the Gospels - can be assembled to show that the tomb, at any rate, was empty on Easter morning.[2]

      Therefore, the obvious next step is to ask: What happened to Jesus' body? If this is where history leads us, it is no great surprise to find the above question addressed many times by many authors and scholars. The correct answer is of great relevance to the Christian faith, because to consider the options from a logical view unveils the mystery which surrounds the faith. Therefore, let us contemplate the above question: What happened to Jesus' body?

THE JEWISH LEADERSHIP
      The Jewish leadership would be the obvious group wanting to discredit Jesus of Nazareth. After all, they are the ones who demanded His execution. Therefore, we ask: Did the Jewish leaders take Jesus' body? The answer is an emphatic, NO! If they had, they would have produced the body when the disciples began to preach about the resurrection. Furthermore, the evidence shows these Jewish leaders were quite confident that either Jesus'

body was stolen by the disciples, or He was indeed whom He claimed to be—the Messiah and the Son of God. As we will see in a later chapter, this latter option may have weighed quite heavily on their consciences. But, the deed had been done. They, with the help of the Roman conquerors, had put Jesus to death. Caught off guard by the opened tomb, their quick-witted declaration was, "The disciples stole the body." From the Pharisees' position, which denied Jesus' deity, the disciples were the logical scoundrels. Moreover, historical documents verify the authenticity of this Biblical explanation. Records clearly show this hastily concocted explanation was still the official position in the days of Justin the Martyr.[3] Plainly their response was a very logical immediate reply. In fact, in a very short time, their logical response became a bad answer. On this point Maier has remarked:

> *But, it is the reaction of the priestly authorities that, even for the neutral historian, must constitute evidence for an empty tomb. The Temple establishment did not do the obvious to counter the apostles' preaching: they did not lead an official procession out to Joseph's tomb, where, for all to see, they could have given the death blow to the dramatically growing kernel of Christianity by opening Joseph's sepulcher and revealing the moldering body of Jesus of Nazareth. They did not do so because they knew the tomb was empty, even if they had an official explanation for this: the disciples had stolen the body.[4]*

Thus, we must conclude that at least the Jewish leadership, and perhaps everyone in Jerusalem, realized that the tomb was empty and the authorities were not responsible for the missing body.

Had the Jewish leaders taken more time to consider the facts, they would have found a better explanation. Considering the zeal of the disciples, the Jewish leaders' best retort may have been something like this: "We took the body and destroyed it. We wanted to further humiliate the followers of this dangerous man. Let our actions be a warning to all of you!" Such a lie would have ended much of the speculation about Jesus being the Messiah. However, this deception would have created other credibility problems in the future. They would have to explain away numerous post-resurrection appearances of Jesus witnessed by great numbers of Jewish citizens. Yet, because they did not have all of the facts and likely assumed the disciples had taken the corpse, they instead gave an honest answer. The historical record confirms that the Jewish leadership were concerned about this very possibility. Therefore, Jesus' internment was well guarded by soldiers, perhaps by an entire squad of

---

...AFTER THE REPORT OF JESUS' MISSING BODY, THE JEWISH LEADERSHIP
TOLD THE GUARDS TO LIE, TO CLAIM THAT THEY FELL ASLEEP
AND THE BODY WAS STOLEN.

Roman soldiers. These soldiers were some of the best trained fighting men in the history of the world. They were fierce and dedicated soldiers sworn by their lives to serve the Roman Empire. There would be no such theft; that was certain.

THE ROMAN GUARD

Could the soldiers have removed the body? This is a totally absurd question, but one that must be asked because it is a major stumbling block to all conspiracy theories. The Roman soldiers would never take it upon themselves to remove the body of Jesus, because they would die if His body was missing. It is inconceivable that so many soldiers would surrender their lives for an illogical prank designed in a way that would discredit the Roman state and cheapen the value of the Roman legion. Neither would they fall asleep on the job as was reported in the official Judaic response. The Biblical explanation seems very reasonable; i.e., after the report of Jesus' missing body, the Jewish leadership told the guards to lie, to claim that they fell asleep and the body was stolen. In return, their lives would be spared. However, because the Roman guard had such a stellar reputation, I question if this official response was convincing to the people of Judah. The conquered people were well aware of the ruthless traditions of the Roman legion. Again we see the weaknesses of a hastily composed response. As we continue with the possibilities, we begin to see severe holes in this official explanation.

SWOON THEORY

The swoon theory (associated with fainting before death), also known as the "scheme theory," involves a faked death scenario where a group of Jesus' followers successfully planned and carried out the greatest ruse of all time. Most resurrection skeptics seem to favor a swoon option. However, most historians discount any such possibility. (David Friedrich Strauss is attributed with discrediting this theory in 1835 with his famous book *The Life of Jesus*).

If the New Testament description of events is factual, the removal of Jesus' body by anyone would involve a major conspiracy including some bizarre and unbelievable partners. When one considers the depth of problems in a swoon theory, the complexity of this mission becomes very apparent. What would one have to do to pull off the swoon theory?

Let us assume Jesus ingested some herb, drug, or poison to render Himself unconscious during the crucifixion. As we have already discussed, the Roman legion was perhaps the best trained fighting machine ever assembled. In their customary fashion, the Roman soldiers carried out the execution of Jesus of Nazareth. Such Roman units included an executioner. Like the other soldiers, these executioners were superbly trained in their work. These men were very precise and even artistic at inflicting torture. They were able to keep a man on the edge of death for days, just for the profound impact these atrocities would have upon onlookers. The Roman executioners knew when a man was dead or alive. Had there been any question, the executioner would have broken Jesus' legs, thus keeping Jesus from forcing His body up in the proper position to receive air. Therefore, Jesus would have suffocated.

Mark Eastman, M.D. is acquainted with the dangers of damage to the human body. Considering the 'Swoon Theory,' Eastman wrote, "From a medical, as well as a logical point of view, this is the least rational (theory) of all. This theory virtually ignores the character of the wounds that a crucifixion victim received."[5] Eastman continued to describe, from his medical position, the ramifications of hanging on a cross for six or more hours. Of course, there would be massive blood loss and dehydration. Eastman further explained what all doctors know: even a sword wound in the side would bring "brain death" within a matter of minutes.[6]

Yet, let us assume for some unknown reason, Jesus was not dead when placed into the tomb. Of course, He would have been in critical condition. Thus, it definitely would have been a miracle if He had lived another three days. Yet, to make the swoon option work, Jesus must have experienced a drastic recovery. In three days, He would have recovered from being nailed to the cross and close to death, to the point where He could roll away a huge, heavy stone. His next major obstacle would have been to sneak past that squad of highly trained Roman guards. Most likely, less obvious problems would have also surfaced. Yet, let us assume that He negotiated all obstacles necessary to reach the security of His disciples. His toughest challenge was still to come. He would have to convince His followers that He was resurrected. He would have to gain much of His strength and hide His great pain.

James Orr pointed out another aspect which should be addressed. That is the honesty factor. Orr wrote:

The hypothesis (Swoon), in fact, cannot help passing over into one of fraud, for, while proclaiming Jesus as the Risen Lord, who had ascended to heavenly glory, the Apostles must have known the real state of the case, and have closely kept the secret that their Master was in concealment or had died.[7]

Yet, why would the disciples carry a farce to such extremes? The real problem with the swoon theory or any other idea which might involve the disciples is that they were very badly hurt by Jesus. They had placed their trust in Jesus—a man destined to be the Messiah of the Jews! "Then Peter began to mention all that he and the other disciples had left behind. 'We've given up everything to follow you.'"[8] The disciples had put everything at risk for Jesus. It seemed as though Jesus had betrayed and deceived them! I am not aware of any historically validated piece of evidence that contradicts the disciples' fear nor the Biblical report of their abandonment of Jesus. There is no historical or logical reason to doubt this point. Even most Swoon theorists acknowledge the frightening position of Jesus' followers. They, not unlike the Jewish leadership, had been aggravated by Jesus' passivity toward the Roman oppressors and must have wondered if Jesus was not testing their loyalty! Jesus must have understood their anxieties, for He told them many times in many ways, "My time has not come." In John 7:6 Jesus makes this point unmistakably clear and Saint John emphasizes Jesus' position in John 7:30. Obviously, His followers must have believed that, Jesus was the Messiah! He was fulfilling all of the prophecies about the Messiah! As a result of the miracles He performed, many people were convinced He was indeed the Messiah. However, Jesus didn't trust them, for He knew mankind to the core. No one needed to tell Him how changeable human nature is.[9] Similar to the early expectations of some Pharisees, the disciples must have reminded each other: "Any day now Jesus will claim the entire world for the Jews. Yes, He will take up His sword and ride toward Rome. Judah (Israel) will rule the world!" Recall with me the conversation about who was going to sit at Jesus' right hand? The disciples expected Jesus the Messiah to set up His kingdom within days! They were expecting Him to fulfill the prophecies of Isaiah 60, 61 and 62. They thought He was the Messiah and would ride to Rome capturing and killing all rebellious Gentiles. The dreams and fantasies of many Jewish loyalists must have centered around this man of miracles. You can almost picture Simon the Zealot riding off into the sunset, yelling, "Praise to thee Jesus of Nazareth, King of Kings and Lord of Lords. Let us kill all except the baptized Jews! And may Judah be the Capitol of the world for ever! Oh hail to thee Messiah Jesus! You are our leader and our Savior!" What applied to the Pharisees and the masses also applied to the disciples . . ."they were not truly acclaiming Him as king of heaven but an earthly king - their earthly king - is implied by their swift falling away . . ."[10]

Unfortunately, Jesus was arrested and tried for very serious crimes against the Empire of Rome. This action was facilitated by the deeds of one of His disciples, Judas Iscariot. It is thought by many that Judas was trying to force Jesus into proving He was the Messiah. Judas must have been aware of the frustration of his people, and Jesus would soon lose their favor. Certainly Jesus needed to act now! Although Jewish Scripture said otherwise, many may have thought that the Jewish Messiah would not die. Judas may have been one of these people. Therefore, Judas would force the invincible Jesus to begin His aggression toward Rome. The Bible indicates that, in his cleverness, Judas unknowingly acted as Satan's agent. He would not allow Jesus' Will to control destiny. Unfortunately for the disciples, Jesus did not call for an uprising! He just stood there. He stood before His accusers and calmly accepted the verdict of death by crucifixion.

The best documented reaction of all the disciples was Simon Peter. I think there is a reason for this. Peter seems to be the bravest of the apostles. He was definitely one of the spokesmen. From his description, I expect he was one of the most dedicated of the pre-crucifixion followers. Yet, Peter showed his true loyalties before Jesus' trial had even begun.

Peter had been very bold during the time Jesus was performing miracles. Reread the Biblical accounts of Peter's flamboyant style of bravery while Jesus was ministering to the needs of others. However, when Peter realized that Jesus was not going to fight, he became fearful. This was apparent when he denied Jesus three times within hours after Jesus was arrested. He may have even cursed Jesus. "He began to curse and swear. 'I don't even know this fellow you are talking about,' he said."[11]

In one of his great sermons, Peter Marshall made this point quite clearly:

"He (Peter) used language he had not used for years.

It was vile . . . even the soldiers were shocked.

They all looked at him in amazement."[12]

John Shelby Spong summed up the honesty of this Biblical account by stating: "That was Peter before the Easter Moment. I see no reason to doubt the accuracy of the main lines of this biblical portrait . . . there is no motive I can imagine in the early Christian writers that would cause them to create this devastating portrait of one whom they regarded as a hero. If the record were going to be doctored, it would seem far more likely for it to be doctored in a favorable manner."[13] This is a very important point, for we know Peter to be the early 'great giant' of the Christian movement and the patron saint of the Roman Catholic Church.

If this is an accurate account of the 'brave apostle' called Peter, if this was indeed his reaction to the capture and arrest of Jesus, then the other apostles were probably more frightened than he. To risk their lives in some crazy swoon theory would have been totally out of the question. If the unknown conversations of the other followers could have been recorded, I am sure their responses would have seemed just as confused, cowardly and devastated as that of Peter's. Certainly they would not have seen any reason to try to save Jesus' life. Instead, I think they were more than willing to let Jesus die. I imagine they would have spoken to one another more in the terms of the following: "What a COWARD! What an embarrassment to Peter and Thomas and to all of those zealots hiding out in the mountains! Should we save Jesus from death? I don't think so. In the first place, I am afraid to show my face in public. If the Roman soldiers find out that we are Nazarenes (Christians), we will

OUT OF ALL OF JESUS' FOLLOWERS, I BELIEVE JOHN CAME
CLOSEST TO UNDERSTANDING HIS MESSAGE.

surely die. So what would be the point of risking our necks to keep Jesus alive? Had He chosen to be the (earthly) King of Judah, He would have been given His glory. He would not have to die. So, why didn't He at least try? He had a great following. Many people believed in Him. He could have at least optioned to attack Rome. The entire Jewish population would have followed. This man could have been the promised king of Judah. All He had to do is say, 'I am the promised one! I am He for whom you await. Let's go kill Romans!' He could have been known as 'the guy who will lead the country into its age of beauty and greatness.' Why did I follow Him? I am such a fool! I have ruined my life and my family's life . . . for what reason should I continue to stick my neck out for this man who hurt me so deeply? And why should I try to save Him? What would be the point? He cannot be our Savior. He will not fight. All He does is embrace our (Jewish) enemies . . . However, there is Barabbas, the reactionary. At least he will fight Rome!"

As hard as it is for us to understand, the man whom many of us deeply love was considered a loser, a deceiver and a very dangerous man. He was totally rejected and abandoned.

When He hung on the cross, His mother (Mary) stood at His feet. A mother's love for her child is like no other love. Yet, like the other onlookers, Mary could not have understood what she witnessed. I must assume she was in a hysterical state of emotional shock. If she was visited by an angel before conception, as the Bible states, she would have to be a very confused woman. As she viewed her son's horribly painful death, she must have wondered what had happened? Within her cries for her suffering son, Mary must have questioned God: "My God, my Father, what went wrong? Please have mercy on my son! Please don't let Him suffer! I love Him God. I just don't understand what went wrong!"

John was the only disciple mentioned in the New Testament bold enough to be with Jesus at His death. John seems to have been a very compassionate and spiritual person. Out of all of Jesus' followers, I believe John came closest to understanding His message. I do not think John expected Jesus to rise from the dead, but perhaps he understood some of the beauty in "love one another." John was there because of his heart. He was there to say goodbye to his dear friend. He was there to console a heartbroken Mary. Some women stood close by. Some other followers stood in the distance, but all were crushed. Other than these few onlookers, Jesus was abandoned. This Roman crucifixion had done its job. Everyone understood the reality of the situation. The Jesus movement was dead before Jesus was dead. Jesus was not the leader the disciples thought Him to be. In a very dramatic way He had shown His

WHY WOULD ANY JEW OR ANYONE ELSE (EXCEPT PERHAPS HIS MOTHER), AT THAT POINT IN HISTORY, WANT ANYTHING TO DO WITH JESUS OF NAZARETH?

intentions to the entire Jewish population. Even if He was saved from death, there was never any reason to believe that He would ever take up the sword and proclaim the kingdom. Clearly that is what the 'Jewish Messiah' was suppose to do. This is why, despite any earlier popularity created by His miracles, Jesus was not to be accepted by the Jewish people as the Messiah and why it would be useless for anyone to pull off a scheme to make Jesus into the 'traditional' Jewish Messiah. He had failed the 'true' test. None in Judah, including the disciples, thought Jesus had the perceived messianic will, and no 'scheme' would cause Jesus to fight Rome.

The historicity and logic which certify this to be the Jewish perception at Jesus' death prove its truth. This is the major reason any and all swoon theories are preposterous. Forget the danger of such a crazy venture, the messianic view of the Jewish culture would logically subtract Jesus from their list of possible messiahs and make any human attempt to confirm His claims completely futile. Ask yourself this one important question: what mortal Jew would have wanted Jesus as a messiah? Ask yourself what ex-disciple, now hiding from the authorities, wanted Jesus to be the Messiah? Why would any Jew or anyone else (except perhaps His mother), at that point in history, want ANYTHING to do with Jesus of Nazareth?

If there had been any explanation, even a hint of a swoon hoax in the minds of those closest to the situation, there would not have been a Christian movement, for the movement started with a dramatic change in the heart of Jesus' followers. The discerning question regarding Christianity has always been, why the great change? If Jesus was not going to bring independence and riches to Judah, why was there such a momentous change in the hearts of Jewish men and women? The resurrected Jesus Christ of the New Testament came not only to save Judah, but to save the entire world! This global messianic concept was much more provocative than the simplistic Jewish version. Thus, it was heresy to the traditional thinking Judaic leaders. Yet, it was willfully overlooked. What could have been so fantastic about this Messianic Jesus for any Jew? Why would so many Jews instantly change their total perspective about the mission of the Messiah, i.e. what the Messiah was going to do? These followers must have known they would be killed over the 'new Messiah' concept and they must have realized Judah would remain a ward of the Roman Empire. Why would they save Jesus and continue to protect Him if He was going to have them die for Him? Why would they throw away all that was important to Judaism, disclaim their Jewish traditions, accept Gentiles as spiritual brothers (an extremely distasteful concept to religious Jews), lose their children, spouses and loved ones to the sword, taste death many times and suffer many other heartbreaks to proclaim Jesus to be Immanuel - "God with us."

If Jesus was not God on earth and, by some strange reason, all of the

Roman guards were suicidal and Peter was really from another planet in the form of a superman or whatever it would take to pull off a conspiracy, then, whomever were the conspirators, all were terrible people. Yet, logic dictates that these outrageous requirements are far more preposterous than Jesus' deity. Perhaps even more convincing is the philosophy of Jesus. Such a deceitful scheme does not sound like the plan of a man who stressed "love your neighbor as yourself." In fact, this is direct evidence that any religion which suggests Jesus Christ was anything less than the eternal God on earth is wrong! Jesus was not just a prophet. He was not an angel or messenger. He was not just a good man. He was either that which He signified He was—the one eternal God, or He was the worst of men. If Jesus was a fake, whether dead or alive, those who conspired with Him while their friends and loved ones suffered unnecessary pain were indeed horrible and demented people.

LESS POPULAR THEORIES

Did any of the minor 'characters' take Jesus' body? This group would include Joseph of Aramatheia and/or other silent followers. It seems even more ridiculous to think that Joseph of Aramatheia, or any other Jewish leader, or any man or woman of wealth and power would have done anything as perverse as to steal Jesus' body. Of everyone involved, the leadership had the most to lose. For the above reasoning, to give up so much for an illusionary dead man makes no sense. There was nothing to gain and much to lose. Moreover, had anyone stolen the body, he/she/they, most likely, would have told Jesus' friends and disciples what had happened. I cannot imagine anyone who was not a great friend of Jesus taking His body and risking certain death. Yet, if such were the case, the natural thing to do would be to go to Jesus' other friends and brag, "Look what I have done." Yet, let us assume the body snatcher(s) did not tell anyone. These subversives would still face many of the same problems covered in the swoon theory. For example, they still had to get beyond a squad of conscientious Roman soldiers. Realize the implications unfolding here! The Jewish leaders had taken great precautions to insure the fate of Jesus. Theirs was a well-devised plan which would have foiled the attempts of any mortal man. By all that seems 'scientifically' or 'historically' viable, their precautions should have silenced all nonsense about Jesus being the King of the Jews. Yet, to their surprise, these precautions had certified Jesus' immortality and their fate as curators of the most scandalous of botched 'official stories' in the history of the world. Yes, their well-planned security insured Jesus' validity! As earlier pointed out, the ensuing official response was probably the worst conceived cover-up ever known. They had set out to silence a troublemaker. Instead, they unwittingly devised an environment that would substantiate His claims—Jesus, the Messiah, the Savior of all mankind!

Many skeptics have speculated about Jesus' crucifixion and resurrection. They focused on everything from the prophets' writings to philosophical suppositions. However, all of these theories seem to go against the reality of the facts. Nonetheless, skeptics will continue to speculate because, without such speculation, Jesus must be God. Therefore, it would not surprise me to find controversial papers suggesting Jesus was friends with Pilate and thus spared from death. In fact, I would expect to find people trying to profit from such an amazing suggestion. Someone might proclaim, "Jesus had children and I am His descendant . . . He spent the summer of 72 A.D. right here in this very village." Keep in mind such alternatives cannot and will not be collaborated. For example, there is a rumor suggesting Jesus left Judah before the Crucifixion. Jesus went to France to live out His life. Someone *else* was crucified in His place.

The most popular crucifixion substitute has been *Judas*. Sects of the Muslim religion seem to be the major proponents of this concept. Because the variations of this substitute concept have been so persuasive, we should look at this particular theory further. Let me state from the outset, I find this substitute theory much harder to believe then many other alternatives. In my opinion, there are two major problems with the logic of this view, and these problems make a substitution theory extremely hard to accept.

First, if we suggest that Jesus' followers knew that someone such as Judas died on the cross, then we run into the same problems we found in the swoon theory. How do you explain the extraordinary change in the disciples? Why would they lay down their life for a man that was a fake? Why would they radically change their theological view about the Messiah? Why would they suddenly change their Judaic view about Gentiles? Why a change in their nature regarding the Roman Empire and the world? These changes are well documented and not a matter for speculation. In fact, they are the foundations of the Christian movement and are contained in the earliest writings of the New Testament.

Second, if there was a divine substitution, the substitution was undetectable to onlookers such as Saint John or Mary, the mother of Jesus. An undetectable switch suggests a supernatural Jesus, not a mere prophet. Thus, this supernatural act would have to be considered a sign from above and reinforce all of Jesus' claims of deity. The only thing it would not do is provide humanity with a Savior. (The Messiah must die. Innately, all humans know this to be truth—so states Biblical Scripture as does the before discussed 'Hero' mythology). Thus, if we assume Jesus was not the Son of God but involved in a switch, the switch would have been known at the crucifixion.

A substitution was not the testimony of St. John and the other witnesses to the crucifixion. Remember, there were people who knew Jesus like a brother or a son. To discount any of the claims of Jesus, one must call His early Jewish believers liars. One must say the witnesses were lying when they said He reminded them that in three days He would rise from the grave. The writers Matthew, Mark, Luke and John, as well as Peter, Paul and many of the other writers and witnesses who may have had a hand in producing the New Testament books were quite adamant about their witness.

Yet, other smaller but messy problems would also exist. For example, wouldn't such a switch need to be planned with the aid of Herod, Pontius Pilate, the Sanhedrin and the Pharisees?

Let us also remember the New Testament did represent all sides fairly. The opposing positions were treated accurately and are verifiable through other historical sources. Thus, there has been no serious argument about the postures of the various parties involved. In fact, the majority of the disputes over the truthfulness or honesty of the record came years after the deaths of the involved eye witnesses. For a man in another land and in another time to state that he knows the eye witnesses were lying, or knows the facts are wrong, or knows the true status of Jesus, seems pretentiously arrogant. Furthermore, such a position ignores the factual sacrifices of the believing Christian martyrs.

Additionally, there have been levitation theories suggesting Jesus did not die on the cross, but used a 'New Age' *mediation force* to survive the crucifixion and resurrection, etc. All of these theories seem to be perpetuated by philosophers or prophets living in a far off land or sitting on a mountain top contemplating the way things should be. Let us pass up the more bizarre explanations, such as those which suggest that Jesus wasn't really a person, but a *ghost* or spirit. Equally bizarre is the theory of mistaken identities in which the gardener at the tomb may have looked like Jesus and, thus, was *mistaken* for Jesus. Let us skip the radically off the wall leaps into fantasy and consider one last reasonable speculation. This is the most obvious choice, but the acknowledged least likely answer to the puzzle.

DID THE DISCIPLES STEAL THE BODY?

Even the most skeptical of historians tend to dismiss this choice. The resulting dedication and determination of Jesus' disciples declare the sincerity of their belief. Chuck Smith makes several pertinent points about this topic. Therefore, my comments will combine reflections from his sermons, *The Credibility of the Resurrection* and *Resurrection*.[14] Smith said:

You may think it an incredible thing that God should raise the dead. However, you have to deny a rather powerful witness. The Church has been witnessing for nineteen centuries that God raised Jesus from the dead. But those first witnesses, they're the tough ones. For you see, if you assume that God did not raise Him from the dead, if this be your assumption, then some how you've got to explain what happened. You are stuck with this - either God raised Him from the dead or these guys got together and cocked up a wild story among themselves. "We will go out and tell everybody that He rose, that we saw Him. Now, you two guys say that you saw Him when you were on the road to Amayus. Make up a story about walking along and how He appeared with you and talked to you . . . you finally recognized Him and He disappeared. Then we will all say that we were in a room together and suddenly He appeared. We will say that we were up fishing at the Galilee and He was standing on the shore. He had some coal and some fish and He invited us to eat. We'll make up these stories that we saw Him in these different places and then we'll go out and tell everybody. Otherwise, we'll have to go back to fishing for good and we don't want to do that. So lets get this story going and maybe we can live off it for a while." However, in time, each one of these men, who told the story of the Resurrection, were put to death by violent means.

Because James said, "Yes, I saw Jesus; He is risen!" The sword severed his head from his body. He could have saved himself. He could have said Caesar is Lord, but he said Jesus is Lord. Thus, James was killed. Peter was crucified up side down. He was originally sentenced to death by crucifixion, but he requested to be crucified up side down because he didn't feel worthy to die in the same way as Jesus Christ. Others were beaten to death; others were stretched to death on the racks, others were burned at the stake. The other James . . . his feet were tied with a rope and a donkey was harnessed and they pulled him until his brains were bashed out on the pavement. Anywhere along the line he could have cried out "Stop! It's a hoax; it's not true." But, every one of these disciples held fast to the story, "Yes, Jesus is risen." Now, wouldn't you think that among that many, one of them would have cracked under the pressure. When Stephen was there and the stones were pelting him, don't you think that he would say, "hey fellows, all right quit throwing the rocks. I'll tell you the truth. It's all a big hoax. We made it up." But, he doesn't. Instead he looks up toward heaven and says, "Ah, I see the heavens open and I see the Son of Man standing at the right hand of the Father on high. Oh Lord, don't charge them with this sin. Into your hands I commit my spirit." And another stone crashed into his skull and he was gone. Come on Stephen, give us a chance to not believe. Break down . . . but he doesn't. Each one of them goes to a violent death with the story of the Resurrection being affirmed from his lips rejoicing in the risen Christ, singing praises to his Lord! That makes the story very credible indeed.[15]

Actually, Chuck Smith only discussed the 'tip of the iceberg' in regard to the validity of the early Messianic Jews. Robert W. Faid gave a brief run down of the martyrdom of some of the other known followers of Jesus. Here is the remainder of his list:

> *Andrew, Peter's brother, preached in Scythia, Greece, Asia Minor, southern Russia, and was finally crucified at Patros on a cross which would ever after be known as 'St. Andrew's Cross.'*

> *Phillip, missionary to Phrygia, possibly visited Gaul (France), was stoned and crucified at Hierapolis.*

> *Bartholomew, missionary to Armenia, was flayed (skinned) alive.*

> *Thomas preached in Parthia, Persia, and India. He was killed with a spear near Madras, India.*

> *Matthew preached in Ethiopia and Persia. He was killed on a missionary journey to Egypt.*

> *James, the Younger, preached in Palestine and Egypt. He was crucified in Egypt.*

> *Jude preached in Assyria and Persia. He was killed in Persia.*

> *Simon, the Canaanite, was a missionary to Egypt, Africa, and was crucified in Britain.*

> *Matthias preached and was martyred in Ethiopia.*

> *John, the beloved disciple, preached in Asia Minor, was imprisoned on the Isle of Patmos; then he was freed, and he died a natural death at an old age at Ephesus.*[16]

These are many of the known (by name) early martyrs. Of course, there were many more. Though this list includes the traditional group of men, historians might question some of these methods of death. Perhaps they might even question the identity of some of the disciples. Yet, none can question the actuality of the atrocities that awaited any and all professing Christians. From that standpoint, this summary is very inadequate. For many willingly lost their lives to gruesome torturous deaths.

For example, a common historical reference of Christian martyrdom comes to us from Flavius Josephus in *Antiquities of the Jews*. Josephus relates the ordering of the stoning death of Jesus' brother, James, and unspecified companions. James was head of the Church, which leads one to conclude that his companions were Christian brothers and/or sisters, " . . . so he (Ananus) assembled the Sanhedrin of the judges, and brought before them the brother of Jesus, who was called the Christ, whose name was James, and some others, [or some of his companions;] and when he had formed an accusation against them as breakers of the law, he delivered them to be stoned."[17]

Chuck Smith reminds us, "Satan once, in talking to God and evaluating man, said: 'Skin for skin, all (that) man has, will he give for his life.' Satan was saying: As far as man is concerned, the most precious thing he has is his life and he will give anything to save his life."[18]

Philosopher, Georg Wilhelm Friedrich Hegel, might argue that man's capacity to sacrifice his life is what makes him human. Yet, Hegel would also contend life is precious. There would need to be a cause worth the risk. Though each human must ask himself or herself, "What price for life?" Jesus' resurrection was not 'over valued' by just one distorted individual or a few radicals. There were thousands of men and women who experienced agonizing deaths because they proclaimed Jesus was risen and, thus, was Lord of their lives. Additionally, if the resurrection was a hoax, as so many people became involved, most likely one would have gotten the details different from what was agreed between them. When their lives were on the line, one of them, in weakness, would have recanted his or her belief. We have only to look at any other life-risking conflict to find human beings who have became cowards and did whatever was needed to save their lives. The deserters and cowards in war are the most obvious illustrations. As an example, in World War II, there were Jews who, in fear for their lives, abated the Nazi cause. Yet, there are many other World War II illustrations. Recall the incident when Patton slapped a 'coward' soldier for bringing disgrace to a place where brave and wounded men served with honor. Psychologists contend fear is caused by the instinct of self-preservation and is a natural phenomenon shared by all human beings. However, Christians so defied 'human nature' - none of the earliest would cower. Thus, certain words became associated with them. Smith relates, "The word *witness* is the word 'martus' (in Greek) from which we get our word martyr, and is why the word martyr came to mean witness: because all of these men died for what they witnessed (in Jesus Christ)."[19]

Certainly, these earliest Christians 'knew' Jesus was God. I use this term in the unconditional sense. To 'know' is an important philosophical concept in modern thought. There is a difference in 'knowing' and 'being certain.' To 'know,' as I am using the term, means there can be no mistake. There can be no illusion. To 'know' expresses a relation between the observer and a fact. However, 'being certain,' or 'being sure,' etc. is a state of mind. Such terms express a relation between a person and a proposition. There may be a particular circumstance where one might be 'certain' and be wrong. Human logic cannot produce the certainty of 'knowing.' Human belief cannot give us the certainty of 'knowing.' *Knowing* lies beyond any capability of being wrong.[20]

I have an atheist friend I will call 'Thales,' who once said to me, "There is no difference between the Branch Davidians believing David Koresh was the long-awaited Christ and Jesus' disciples believing Jesus was the long-awaited Christ." My answer to him was, "If David Koresh rises from the dead, then I will consider your comparison." Basically, 'Thales' could have made his correlation between Jesus and any cult leader. However, his point should be examined. What is the difference between Jesus of Nazareth and David Koresh or Jim Jones or anyone else claiming to be the Messiah? Evidently, David Koresh made statements that would lead one to believe he considered himself to be the Christ. He made some generalities that were taken to mean that he was a form of the Messiah. Moreover, he did some of the things the Messiah would have been expected to do. He obviously prophesied. He held authority over his church. Koresh's followers had great faith in his spiritual guidance. In fact, they seemed 'certain' that Koresh was the Messiah. Nonetheless, any belief in Koresh's Messiahship was based on 'blind' faith. From the reports of the few Koresh devotees that did survive the 'Waco fire,' as well as from the evidence collected after the fire, we find similarities in the reactions of devotees. Jesus' disciples abandoned Him when He was captured. They feared for their lives. In like manner, many Davidians cherished their lives more than their mission. In fact, many tried to escape the flames. Up to the moment of each leader's demise, there were only debatable differences in the loyalties of their respective followers. However, Mr. Koresh did not come back to life after his death. Jesus did. That is the difference. Koresh was only man. Jesus was boundlessly more. Additionally, if a group of Koresh's followers were to claim he did resurrect from the dead, then the real question would be how many would be so sure of Koresh's resurrection that they would willingly undergo gruesome tortures and death? Would they stand by their beliefs while they were being flayed (skinned) alive or crucified? Such conduct constitutes extraordinary behavior. People hide from extreme torture. Yet, history is quite insistent that many of Jesus' disciples boldly defied the threat of such persecution. Though many may have traveled away from Jerusalem to escape the Phariseen scorn, it should also be pointed out that to take the Christian message to all parts of the world was, and still is, the Christian directive. Furthermore, death awaited Christians around the world. Though it is evident that a small number of later followers succumbed to fatal pressures, there are no records of these earliest Christians retracting their claims.

Everything we know about Jesus of Nazareth indicates He was special. Unlike other so called Messiahs, Jesus' claims are based on historical fact, the human observation of a historical crucifixion, the observation of a resurrected Messiah and the fulfillment of the awaited signs. From all credible historical information known, we can be sure that Jesus was not the kind of Messiah the disciples expected and Jesus most certainly died on the cross. Furthermore, His crucifixion did not transpire or conclude the way anybody, friend or foe, expected. However, those who closely observed, 'knew' the truth. Thus, it is the lives of thousands of early Christians that validate Jesus' resurrection and divinity.

Without the personal experience of observing this historical event, we cannot 'know.' We can believe, we can be sure, we have a variety of good reasons to believe, the propensity of information may lead the prudent person to conclude, etc. However, unless we were in a room and observed a physical Jesus, whom we had seen die on a cross, walk through a door and say, "Put your hands on my spike wounds so you will have no doubt," only then do we 'know' Jesus is God. That is why Jesus said, "You believe because you have seen me. But blessed are those who haven't seen me and believe anyway."[21]

However, make no mistake, the disciples 'knew.' They were not playing games. They were not living a lie. Jesus Christ had proven Himself to be both the Messiah and the Son of God. He had, in fact, risen from the dead, and they had seen Him alive after death. They were even encouraged by Jesus to examine His scarred and tortured flesh.

I hope you understand the significance of this exercise in logic. The amazing behavior of Jesus' closest companions has been reexamined and scrutinized beyond that of most other historical beings. Of course, there were other amazing historical facts about those earliest days of Christianity, but the dedication and sacrifice of Jesus' companions seems too incredible for mortal man. In an earlier chapter, I quoted one of my philosophy friends. Larry Plato made a very profound statement which I leave to its own merit because Larry is factually right! I believe his statement is the only thing that would logically explain the behavior of Jesus' early followers. The philosopher said, "I do not want to hear of any more findings or theories or observations of science which have a factor of evidence about God. Science is to the point of proving God. What happens to faith? How can obedience through faith have any meaning when God is a scientific fact? With such sureness one loses his freedom to act. Who will choose evil if God is fact? For God did not design man to be a robot, but to function as a free willed being."

In the case of Jesus and His disciples and followers, Larry Plato is right! His reasoning answers the mystery! If you give proper consideration to the lives of many martyred men and women, many being witnesses to the resurrected Jesus, there can only be one honest conclusion. They knew the Truth. Their faith in Jesus' holiness was no longer a matter of 'believing,' but a matter of 'knowing.' Their whole perspective on life changed. They had stepped

REPORTS INDICATE THAT NOT ONE OF THE EARLIEST CHRISTIANS (THOSE WHO KNEW JESUS) DENIED JESUS TO SAVE HIS OR HER LIFE.

away from their traditional values and concepts. Now they grasped a whole new understanding of reality. They KNEW Jesus Christ is the Holy Son of God! If we accept the theological implications related to the Son of God as fact, then this particular Christ experience transcended the normal boundaries of human perception and most assuredly carried human beings into areas beyond that of all other human knowledge and joy. Certainly, if indeed this be true, it was the most thrilling event in the collective human experience. It must have cut through the fabric of human reality, giving humanity an understanding of the Ultimate Reality. Obviously, we cannot conceptualize the feelings of those chosen to witness for all mankind.

HISTORICAL PROOF

Jesus' Resurrection is also apparent from *secular historical sources.* First, there is no other known reason for the *explosive growth of the early Christian Church*—even in Jerusalem among the witnesses to the crucifixion. Second, shortly after the crucifixion, the Jewish *followers of Jesus radically changed life long religious and racial traditions* even to include the most difficult task of accepting people of all races and nationalities as spiritual brothers and sisters. This is perhaps the only time in the history of the world that virtually all ethnicities were sincerely loved and accepted by a cross section of a discriminating race. Third, Jesus' *followers were determined to travel the world to proclaim Jesus' message* unto all mankind. Archaeological discoveries bring a growing collection of evidence of their global successes. Again, we find perhaps the only such episode in the history of the world. This zealous undertaking seems impossible even today with our modern modes of travel. However, these early Christians used antiquated forms of travel and went to unknown lands and dangers. Fourth, there is *no other explanation for the unique demonstration of martyrdom of Jesus' saints.* As grotesque as the tortures were, these martyrs joyfully went to their deaths, singing and praising Jesus' name. They were anxious to once again be with their Lord and Savior. Reports indicate that not one of the earliest Christians (those who knew Jesus) denied Jesus to save his or her life. Fifth, there is *no other logical explanation for the Roman Empire's historical position nor for the traditional Jewish position that the body was stolen.* Both Roman and Jewish leaders were caught by complete surprise. Therefore, as hostile witnesses, they proclaim Jesus' Resurrection. Because of the turmoil and unrest in the land, it is apparent that the loss of Jesus' body was more than just a mild concern for the leaders. They must have worried about possible uprisings against both powers in Judah. There was nothing to gain and many problems to come. Even if one does not accept the Messiahship of Jesus, the treatment He received, as described in the New Testament, would indicate grave concern on the part of the authorities.

One more historical document seems particularly relevant to this discussion. A Roman historian made an interesting reference to Jesus in his writings. Furthermore, he was a contemporary of the younger eyewitnesses to Jesus' life. Flavius Josephus was born A.D. 37 of Jewish heritage. He lived an adventurous and honorable life before becoming one of the most noted historians of the Roman Empire. In reference to Jesus Christ, Josephus wrote:

> *Now there was about this time Jesus, a wise man, if it be lawful to call him a man, for he was a doer of wonderful works, a teacher of such men as receive the truth with pleasure. He drew over to him both many of the Jews, and many of the Gentiles. He was the Christ, and when Pilate, at the suggestion of the principal men among us, had condemned him to the cross, those that loved him at the first did not forsake him for he appeared to them alive again the third day; as the divine prophets had foretold these and ten thousand other wonderful things concerning him. And the tribe of Christians so named from him are not extent at this day.*[22]

What makes his historical account so amazing are two facts. *The first is that Josephus was a Jew in the traditional sense.* He would not have held the position he did if he had been a 'Christian' Jew. Thus, it is difficult to imagine Josephus giving such a flattering description of a man considered by the authorities to be a sorcerer and lawbreaker. *Secondly, Josephus was employed to record history for the Roman Empire.* It is generally thought the Roman Empire saw Christianity as a threat to the worship of the Empire. So, the critics felt Josephus' statement 'too fantastic' to be authentic. Someone must have tampered with the text. However, generally when such tampering occurs, other non-tainted copies are found, proving once and for all that the counterfeit text was not authentic. In the case of Josephus' statement, there has been only one deviation found. Dr. Maier suggests that a document uncovered by Professor Schlomo Pines of Hebrew University presents "a differing and probably original version of this passage." The variance states:

> *At this time there was a wise man called Jesus, and his conduct was good, and he was known to be virtuous. Many people among the Jews and the other nations became his disciples. Pilate condemned him to be crucified and to die. But those who had become his disciples did not abandon his discipleship. They reported that he had appeared to them three days after his crucifixion and that he was alive. Accordingly, he was perhaps the Messiah, concerning whom the prophets have reported wonders.*[23]

Allowing for interpretation inflections, these two statements are very similar. Because the first version is more laudatory of the Christians, one might assume this second document is essentially an original version.

Doubters may wonder if some scholar changed Josephus' writing to sound only partially friendly toward Christians. To the contrary, the document seems to convey the sincere observations of a historian. Dr. Maier had some interesting thoughts from a historian's understanding: " . . . Josephus does not seek to scotch the resurrection claim by any information at his disposal that Jesus' body still lay in its grave. Certainly this is an argument from silence, but the silence is especially eloquent in view of Josephus' known habit of roasting false Messiahs elsewhere in his histories, in contrast to the near-favorable reference here."[24] In fact, this says much more than even Dr. Maier is willing to concede. Josephus, a man in good graces with the Pharisees, a man in good standing with the Romans, seems to have wondered about the true nature of Jesus as he writes "Accordingly, he was perhaps the Messiah . . ." Again the question comes to mind, how many Jews believed Jesus was the Messiah, but were too pragmatic to defy the Jewish leadership? As for Josephus' work, the Christians of the day were not in a position to make such changes. Therefore, there probably will not be any finds that conflict to any great extent from the above documents.

When one looks closely at this period, taking its writings at face value, a strong case can be made for a strained Jewish population. There had been a united front in the Jewish hatred for Roman (Gentile) rule. Now, the Pharisees, with the approval of the Roman garrison, were requisitioning the slaughter of known 'Christian' Jews. The rest of the population was theologically and politically restrained and confused. Through defiant sympathizers, a frustrated society expressed its resentment. Part of that frustration may have been a reaction to the official response to Jesus. Too many Jews were defiantly dying for Jesus. To many 'saints' were throwing cautions to the wind and openly 'witnessing' - even in Jerusalem! Many Jews must have been caught in this serious challenge. Individually, they would have to ask, "Do I risk my life and follow Jesus?" Politically, it was not a good time in Jerusalem. The entire population lived in turmoil. Other writings suggest this turmoil lasted until the fall of Jerusalem in 70 A.D. One has to recall the words of Jesus just prior to His crucifixion. A pro-Phariseeian crowd had previously cried out their choice to crucify Jesus and had acknowledged that Jesus' blood was on their hands. As Jesus carried His cross to the spot of execution, a number of "grief-stricken women" followed along behind. Jesus may have turned around to acknowledge them as He said, "Daughters of Jerusalem, don't weep for me, but for yourselves and for your children. For the days are coming when the women who have no children will be counted fortunate indeed. Mankind will beg the mountains to fall on them and crush them, and the hills to bury them. For if such things as this are done to me, the Living Tree, what will they do to you?"[25] It is plain that Jesus was speaking prophetically of a coming disaster for Jerusalem at the hands of the Romans. The coming destruction in 70 AD was horrendous by all accounts. Even the Temple was destroyed and never rebuilt.

THE IMPACT OF RESULTING DOCUMENTS

Jesus has had a profound effect on many researchers who have examined the historical facts surrounding His crucifixion and resurrection. I think of Frank Morison, author of the popular book, *Who Moved The Stone?* Frank began the book with the intention of ridiculing the belief in a risen Christ, but ended his research as a firm believer in the resurrection. Mark Eastman, M. D., coauthor of *The Search for Messiah,* a book used as a source in this writing, had a similar life experience. He was a skeptic until he studied the actual historical record. Then he became a believer.

Perhaps the most prestigious legal scholar in modern history was Simon Greenleaf. Dr. Greenleaf (1783–1853) became a Royal Professor of Law at Harvard University, and later was awarded the position of the Dane Professor of Law of Harvard. In reference to his tenure, H.W.H. Knott has stated that the direction of Dane Professors of Law Story and Greenleaf lifted "the Harvard Law School to its eminent position among the legal schools of the United States." As to his reasoning, Greenleaf produced *A Treatise on the Law of Evidence,* which is acclaimed as "the greatest single authority on evidence in the entire literature of legal procedure."[26] Being an inquisitive man, Greenleaf obviously looked long at the above question. His resulting work was *An Examination of The Testimony of the Four Evangelists by the Rules of Evidence Administered in the Courts of Justice.* In this inquiry, Greenleaf "examines the value of the testimony of the apostles to the resurrection of Christ."[27] Here is his summary statement:

> *The great truths which the apostles declared, were, that Christ had risen from the dead, and that only through repentance from sin, and faith in Him, could men hope for salvation. This doctrine they asserted with one voice, everywhere, not only under the greatest discouragements, but in the face of the most appalling errors that can be presented to the mind of man. Their master had recently perished as a malefactor, by the sentence of a public tribunal. His religion sought to overthrow the religions of the whole world. The laws of every country were against the teachings of His disciples. The interests and passions of all the rulers and great men in the world were against them. The fashion of the world was against them. Propagating this new faith, even in the most inoffensive and peaceful manner, they could expect nothing but contempt, opposition, reviling, bitter persecutions, stripes, imprisonments, torments, and cruel deaths. Yet this faith they zealously did propagate; and all these miseries they endured undismayed, nay, rejoicing. As one after another was put to a miserable*

death, the survivors only prosecuted their work with increased vigor and resolution. The annals of military warfare afford scarcely an example of the like heroic constancy, patience, and unblenching courage. They had every possible motive to review carefully the grounds of their faith, and the evidence of the great facts and truths which they asserted; and these motives were pressed upon their attention with the melancholy and terrific frequency. It was therefore impossible that they could have persisted in affirming the truths they have narrated, had not Jesus actually risen from the dead, and had they not known the fact as certainly as they knew any other fact. If it were morally possible for them to have been deceived in this matter, every human motive operated to lead them to discover and avow their error. To have persisted in so gross a falsehood, after it was known to them, was not only to encounter, for life, all evils which man could inflict, from without, but to endure also the pangs of inward and conscious guilt; with no hope of future peace, no testimony of a good conscience, no expectation of honor or esteem among men, no hope of happiness in this life, or in the world to come.

Such conduct in the apostles would moreover have been utterly irreconcilable with the fact that they possessed the ordinary constitution of our common nature. Yet their lives do show them to have been men like all others of our race; swayed by the same motives, animated by the same hopes, affected by the same joys, subdued by the same sorrows, agitated by the same fears, and subject to the same passions, temptations, and infirmities, as ourselves. And their writings show them to have been men of vigorous understandings. If then their testimony was not true, there was no possible motive for its fabrication.[28]

LOGIC AND JESUS

Obviously, the interpretation of the historical record has been the focus of my work. Virtually all of my conjecture has come from historical documents. However, for the time being, let us intellectually dissociate Jesus from the human experience of history. As a matter of fact, let us discount all limited personal experiences such as a human spiritually or emotionally felt relationship. Let us consider Jesus purely from the divine logic behind God. If there is a God, and if He is all powerful, then He can do whatever He wants to do. A divine Messiah/Savior/Son of God would have to be set aside from all other human beings. From the beginning of time, God had alerted humanity through prophecies, dreams, myths, etc. as to what the signs would be. The

GOD'S REASON FOR CREATING US AND ALLOWING US TO EXIST IS THAT HE WAS LONELY AND WANTED OUR COMPANY.

major sign would be the resurrection. "Does it seem incredible to you that God can bring men back to life again?"[29]

If the Will of God allowed the laws of nature to become functional, then the Will of God could, in all probability, alter said laws. Chuck Smith has said:

> ... if you have more or less created your own God in your own image and you have this anthropomorphic concept of God, 'if I were God, this is what I would be, this is what I would do, this is how I would respond and react,' and if you have been guilty of creating your own god like yourself, then your god is definitely limited and has great problems and it would be a very incredible thing for him to raise the dead. But, if you have accepted God's revelation of Himself in the Bible, then, that God who is revealed in the Bible talks about the res-urrection of the dead - you have no problem at all.[30]

Whether you are an atheist or a theist consider for a moment the truth within this statement of Dr. James Orr: "If Christ was what His Church has hitherto believed Him to be - the divine Son and Savior of the world - there is no antecedent presumption against His Resurrection; rather it is incredible that He should have remained prey to death."[31]

Dr. Orr's quotation is profoundly perceptive. Consider his point for a moment. Forget the world around you and the laws therein. Forget reality from the human ability standpoint, for we are now contemplating the super-natural. We can confidently state, if God does exist, there is something greater than the laws of the universe. For the sake of argument, let us restrict God. Let us say God believes in the Spinozian 'hands off' policy. However, for one inspirational moment in time He put Himself in an 'earth suit' of flesh, and walked around visiting people. He wouldn't need an occasion, but, for our understanding, let us say He wanted the experience of being human. What would happen, if for some spiritual reason, He allowed us to kill Him? Would He stay dead? Would He continue to live? The Bible claims death cannot hold the Father's Son. "Then God released him from the horrors of death and brought him back to life again, for death could not keep this man within its grip."[32] If He lives, would He not let those who loved Him know that He was not dead, but alive? Would He not at least let those who contemplated His divinity know He was still alive and in control?

Assume with me the Biblical perspective. God's reason for creating us and allowing us to exist is that He was lonely and wanted our company.

WHY HE WOULD WANT TO SAVE ANY OF US IS THE BIG MYSTERY TO ME.

God has 'Willed' a spiritual link with us and, therefore, He factually is our 'Spiritual Father.' If He considers us His 'spiritual children' or, if there is another similar kind of spiritual relationship that would manifest itself through a loving God, why would He not try to show us that He is real? What if He did some amazing supernatural acts for us, such as creating a beautiful world in which to live? What if He created a world so perfect and so grand it took billions of stars and a special set of natural laws to make human life work? What if things on earth got really crazy and people lost the joy of life and, therefore, they would not treat each other with the intended kindness and respect, but instead would take advantage of one another and abuse one another and even murder now and then? What if God knew that people needed a special sign from Him? What would be the best way for Him to let people know He was real? What if He knew that people remembered Him as a vengeful God and He wanted people to know Him as a loving God? What if He loved people so much that He was willing to make a major sacrifice for the human race? Is that not the kind of God you would like to have? Well, it seems He did that. He put on an 'earth suit' and came down to see us. He gave us a chance to know Him better. He showed His great love for each and every one of us. He stressed love. The jest of His message, "Love your God with all of your heart, with all of your soul and with all of your might and love your neighbor as yourself." His message is beautiful in its lucidity. He did not give us a conglomerate of rules. Instead, He edified and simplified the Ten Commandments. Thus, everyone could understand and live by a compassionate 'Law' - not a restraining Law. He said love! God still has to judge (someone has to hold the universe together), but we are to love. Is that not a wonderful message? Would that not make a perfect world? Think about a world of love. Women could walk down streets late at night without fear of being raped or murdered. Men could help people stranded on the side of the road without fear of being robbed for their kindness. People without food would have food. People without shelter would have shelter.

But, we didn't like His message, so we decided to torture Him to death. We chose one of the most prolonged and painful forms of execution ever devised by man; a most bizarre death for a man of love. I know this is a much simplified summation of events. There is much more involved here, such as, "the salvation of mankind." However, these are the basics of what happened. Why He would want to save any of us is the big mystery to me. People are moral weaklings. Men and women are so evil compared to the pure Holiness of God Almighty. God said:

No one is good - no one in all the world is innocent.
No one has ever really followed God's paths, or even truly wanted to.
Every one has turned away; all have gone wrong.

No one anywhere has kept on doing what is right; not one.[33]

I hear people say, "If there is a heaven, I deserve to go there as much as anybody." Well, understand this, if heaven is a Holy place, then no human being deserves to go to heaven. Forget doing more good then evil, for in a truly 'Holy' heaven, good would be the expected conduct all of the time and 'good' would not be a distinguishable factor. However, we humans are filthy in sin and are unclean in our thoughts. In the divine system of 'good' as the Ultimate Reality would seem to be, all consciousness abides by the spiritual good expressing God's Will. If 'the wages of sin is spiritual death,' this spiritual law would be as relevant to spiritual man as the Law of General Relativity is to our physical universe. If this is so, then the human being who does five thousand good deeds and only one sin is condemned. The five thousand good deeds are expected. However, the one sin would be an act of rebellion against God's holiness. Thus, even though we try to offset our sins with good deeds, we are not fit to live in heaven. We are not qualified to walk among angels. We deserve to die with our sin. In the history of the world, man has proven to be a disgrace to all that is Holy. The angels, and the sleeping ones (those who have gone before us) must weep for our transgressions. It seems logical that, if anyone is allowed to live with the Holy One, the choice would be God's. It would be God's rules, and He would want only those spirits/souls who recognize His authority. I am convinced God's grace is the only way to heaven. So, Jesus' love for His Father and love for humans and the world at large was so great that He willingly stepped down from His position united in the Father and accepted a subservient role. He became our defender and spokesman. He became subservient to the Father, gave away His multidimensional existence and took on flesh. Why? To forge a kinship between Abba God and humanity.

I have heard a story, from a number of ministers, which makes my point rather well. My version is paraphrased from Chuck Smith's sermon, *Call His Name Jesus*. It is about a man who only went to church once a year. He always went to church on Christmas eve for the Christmas program. His children were usually involved in the program and it was such a festive and family-centered time of the year that he would do the 'church thing' for his family. One year he decided that this was hypocritical. He said, "I do not believe in the incarnation of Jesus. That is actually what is being celebrated at Christmas. It is hypocrisy for me to go to church on Christmas. I do not see why God would have to become man. I do not understand it. I don't see the need for it." Thus, he announced to his family his resolve not to go to church that Christmas. The children kept begging and imploring, but he stood his ground. When Christmas Eve came, though the weather was bad and there was a blizzard outside, he waved goodbye to his family as they left for the Christmas Eve service. He went back into the house and sat before his fire, got out a book and settled in for the evening. Suddenly, he was disturbed by a strange noise and he looked up and saw a little bird trying to fly through the window into the room where he was drawn by the warmth and the light of the fire. Because it was cold and trying to find shelter, the little bird kept flying up against the window beating against it. He ignored it at first hoping it would go away, but, as it continued in its efforts, he began to see the blood stains on the window from the bird. He decided to help the bird, so he put on his overcoat and went to the barn and opened the barn doors. He put a light on hoping to attract the little bird to the barn so it could be sheltered. He waited for a while but the little bird did not come to the barn. He went back to the house and found the bird still flying against the window. He began to swing at the bird to get it to go toward the barn. As he began to swing at it, the little bird started to panic and tried all the more desperately to fly through the window. The man said, "Little bird, you don't understand me. I'm not trying to hurt you. I'm trying to help you. I've opened the barn for you. There is a place of shelter for you. I'm not trying to destroy you. You don't understand me little bird." He kept trying to shoo the little bird and it became more and more panicked until finally he said, "Oh I wish I could communicate with that little bird the fact that I don't want to hurt it. I only want to help it. If I could only become a bird for a moment, I could communicate." Then all of a sudden it hit him. Why the incarnation? Because men had such wrong ideas about God. They thought God was angry. They thought God wanted to harm them. They thought God wanted to judge them. In reality, God had provided a place of shelter and God was only trying to turn them to Himself so they might discover His love and the shelter He had provided. Now the man understood. His perspective changed. He got into the other car and went to the Christmas program. God had revealed to him the reason for the incarnation. God was seeking to identify with man for man had lost his identity. So Jesus became what we are so that He might make us what He is. God willed Him to suffer for our sins and, though He was rich, for our sake He became poor that through His poverty we might know the riches of God.

So what about Jesus, the one called The Savior? What proof is there that He was the special one, the one all mankind has been waiting for since the beginning of spiritual man? Was He the one from the ancient writings that God proclaimed to Satan in Genesis 3:15? "And I will put enmity between thee and the woman, and between thy seed and her seed; it shall bruise thy head, and thou shalt bruise his heel." Here lies the importance of the grave. The test of the truth of Jesus Christ is the credibility of His death and resurrection. I am thrilled to confirm to you the overwhelming evidence provides no other realistic conclusion. The resurrection of Jesus Christ cannot be discounted logically, historically or any way except philosophically - and only philosophically if, in your own mind, you put limits on God.[34]

THE GREAT QUESTION

You are now privileged to make your own choice. Was Jesus Christ The Son of God, the Messiah, the Promised One? Or, was He the greatest liar of all time? If Jesus Christ was indeed our Creator, our God and our only hope, then He is a most extraordinary Sacrifice—from a real and loving God, the One who loves us infinitely more than we deserve.

CHAPTER 18

JESUS, KING OF THE JEWS (AND EVERYONE ELSE)

"The Jewish leaders surrounded him and asked, 'How long are you going to keep us in suspense? If you are the Messiah, tell us plainly.'"[1]

Before Jesus was arrested, the Jewish leadership seemed particularly perplexed by His miraculous powers. A very interesting question might now be considered. How did Jesus' resurrection affect the Jewish leadership? Of all the people on earth, the Pharisees - the Jewish priests, were the obvious authorities on the Tanakh or 'Old Testament.' They knew the signs of the Messiah. They also knew the Scriptures which referred to the Jewish nation. It is important to note that by the time of Jesus' birth, all of the Old Testament prophetic Scriptures had been accumulated and those fulfilled had proven to be extremely accurate. Yet, before Jesus became a known personality, the Pharisees had rationalized their way around such Scriptures as Zechariah 11:15–17.

Then the Lord told me to go again and get a job as a shepherd; this time I was to act the part of a worthless, wicked shepherd.

And he said to me, "This illustrates how I will give this nation a shepherd who will not care for the dying ones, nor look after the young, nor heal the broken bones, nor feed the healthy ones, nor carry the lame that cannot walk; instead, he will eat the fat ones, even tearing off their feet. Woe to this worthless shepherd who doesn't care for the flock. God's sword will cut his arm and pierce through his right eye; his arm will become useless and his right eye blinded."[2]

Yet, a problem was developing. Jesus was making accusations that seemed to equate these Pharisees with the wicked shepherd. Therefore, it had become increasingly difficult for them to be open minded about Jesus' words and deeds. This is illustrated in John 9:39–41:

Then Jesus told him, "I have come into the world to give sight to those who are spiritually blind and to show those who think they see that they are blind."

The Pharisees who were standing there asked, "Are you saying we are blind?"

"If you were blind, you wouldn't be guilty," Jesus replied. "But your guilt remains because you claim to know what you are doing."[3]

Thus, while addressing the Pharisees, Jesus seemed to be referring to the blindness in the wicked shepherd's right eye. (The right side is symbolic for spiritual righteousness and honor.) The inference in Zechariah 11:15–17 as with John 9:39–41, is the wicked shepherd is only partly or prejudicially blind. He cannot comprehend the spiritual Truth, but can see facts (perhaps symbolic of the left eye).

Though the Pharisees did know the prophetic pattern of the Messianic Scriptures, and had rationalized about their meanings, they were frustrated and perplexed by Jesus of Nazareth. This is quite obvious in the New Testament when we consider such writings as John 7:25–27 and John 7:46–52.

In John 7:25–27, some of the 'common' people of Jerusalem were speaking about Jesus: " . . . Isn't this the man they are trying to kill? But here he is preaching in public, and they say nothing to him. Can it be that our leaders have learned, after all, that he really is the Messiah? But how could he be? For we know where this man was born; when Christ comes, he will just appear and no one will know where he comes from."[4]

Plainly these people were watching the behavior of the Pharisees regarding Jesus. They wondered if Jesus was the Messiah. Yet, they clearly expected the Messiah to mysteriously appear. They assumed the Messiah's background would be unknown; apparently Jesus' past was common knowledge. Of course, The Revelation indicates a 'second coming' (of Jesus) where Jesus the Messiah will 'just appear.' Perhaps the most familiar of these Scriptures would be Jesus' message to John pertaining to how Jesus' followers should live in His absence: "Go back to what you heard and believed at first; hold to it firmly and turn to me again. Unless you do, I will come suddenly upon you, unexpected as a thief, and punish you."[5] Similar references can be found in The Revelation 16:15, 1 Thessalonians 5:2 and 2 Peter 3:10.

Now consider John 7:46–52 which reflects on the thoughts of the Temple police during a Phariseeian meeting:

"He says such wonderful things!" they mumbled. "We've never heard anything like it."

"So you also have been led astray?" the Pharisees mocked. "Is there a single one of us Jewish rulers or Pharisees who believes he is the

Messiah? These stupid crowds do, yes; but what do they know about it? A curse upon them anyway!"

Then Nicodemus spoke up. "Is it legal to convict a man before he is even tried?" he asked.

They replied, "Are you a wretched Galilean too? Search the Scriptures and see for yourself - no prophets will come from Galilee!"[6]

It seems the Pharisees were correct about this. There were no prophets mentioned from Galilee, nor does there seem to be any prophecies about the Messiah coming from Galilee. But, it is just as obvious that they are overlooking the profound nature of Jesus and the many prophecies He had fulfilled. Furthermore, a few (at least two) of these leaders were sympathetic towards Jesus. Obviously, their admiration was from a distance. Nonetheless, these men, and perhaps all of the leaders, must have known Jesus' birth place (the city of King David) and its prophetic importance. Yes, Bethlehem was quite significant. Moreover, Jesus' miraculous birth may have been commonly known. Some early historical documents mentioning Jesus make inference to His virgin birth. One would think if there were conversations about His birth, His place of birth would be part of that discussion. Perhaps the Pharisees consciously ignored the birth issue. Nonetheless, the Scripture makes it clear this 'verbal jousting' was the dominant Phariseeian strategy to repudiate Jesus' authority.[7]

Yet, if it was common knowledge that Jesus was born in Bethlehem, as logic would suggest, then had the common citizens known the Scriptures they would have recalled Micah 5:2 which plainly states the Messiah will be born in Bethlehem:

O Bethlehem Ephrathah (this ancient name of Bethlehem-Judah is an extremely significant Jewish location, reference Gen. 35:16 - 19 and 1 Sam. 16: 1–13), you are but a small Judean village, yet you will be the birthplace of my King who is alive from everlasting ages past.[8]

One should also notice Micah 5:2 makes reference to the infinite nature of the coming Messiah. He is "alive from everlasting ages past." Could the ancient Jewish scholars have missed the eternal nature of the Messiah? But the Pharisees, for whatever reason, did overlook these prophetic indicators. To compensate for situations in Jesus' life which seemed to fulfill messianic prophecies, these leaders tried to change the course of Jesus' destiny. However, the records of the witnesses state that their efforts were to no avail.

For example, we are told in John 8: 59 and again in John 10: 31–39 that Jesus called on His miraculous powers to escape from being stoned.

Then Jesus told them this: "If I am merely boasting about myself, it doesn't count. But it is my Father - and you claim him as your God - who is saying these glorious things about me. But you do not even know him. I do. If I said otherwise, I would be as great a liar as you! But it is true - I know him and fully obey him. Your father Abraham rejoiced to see my day. He knew I was coming and was glad."

The Jewish leaders: "You aren't even fifty years old - sure, you've seen Abraham!"

Jesus: "The absolute truth is that I was in existence before Abraham was ever born!"[9]

(Perhaps in this last verse Jesus refers to God's instructions to Moses, Exodus 3:14–15: "Just say 'I Am has sent me!' Yes, tell them, 'Jehovah [or 'the Living God': literally, 'I AM THAT I AM' the God of your ancestors Abraham, Isaac, and Jacob, has sent me to you.' This is my eternal name to be used throughout all generations." Interestingly, I AM THAT I AM is con-nected with both the crown of God and the creation of the universe).

At that moment the Jewish leaders picked up stones to kill him. But Jesus was hidden from them, and walked past them and left the Temple.[10]

However, it was not until after His crucifixion and resurrection that reality began to set in on the Jewish leadership. Despite their efforts, it seemed as though Jesus had dictated the terms of their actions. In this way, the Pharisees must have felt powerless; their arms had become useless. Perhaps they recalled the rest of the prediction in Zechariah 11: 15–17, "Woe to this worthless shepherd who doesn't care for the flock. God's sword will cut his arm and pierce through his right eye; his arm will become useless and his right eye blinded."[11]

And a justification for their fears must have come to them during the post-crucifixion appearances of Jesus to the masses. Yet, even more frighten-ing than the rumors of a risen Jesus was the unexpected change in those cow-ards He called disciples. Even today the agnostic historian finds this dramatic change in the followers of Jesus an unexplainable experience of human his-tory. Just previous to the crucifixion, these same followers had denied their discipleship to Jesus. But in an instant they became so bold and strong in their

YET, EVEN MORE FRIGHTENING THAN THE RUMORS OF A RISEN JESUS WAS THE UNEXPECTED CHANGE IN THOSE COWARDS HE CALLED DISCIPLES. EVEN TODAY THE AGNOSTIC HISTORIAN FINDS THIS DRAMATIC CHANGE IN THE FOLLOWERS OF JESUS AN UNEXPLAINABLE EXPERIENCE OF HUMAN HISTORY.

belief that the messianic truth must have been shockingly obvious even to, and I emphasize, particularly to these sages of the Scriptures - the Pharisees. Surely they realized the fullness Jesus' life brought to the mystical aspects of the Tanakh or Old Testament. After all, Jewish Theology dictates that: "The world was created only for the Messiah."[12]

Most readers are probably acquainted with many of the Old Testament messianic prophecies because they virtually reiterate those things known about Jesus. I will list a sampling of them:

The Messiah would be born of a virgin (Isaiah 7:14) in the town of Bethlehem (Micah 5:2). He would be the Son of God (Psalms 2:7) and known as Immanuel (Isaiah 7:14). Loosely translated Immanuel (Immanu-El) means 'God with us.' He is an eternal being (Micah 5:2) whose divinity is clear (Psalms 110:1). The Messiah will be a Holy King (Psalms 2:6) and a descendant of King David (Jeremiah 23:5). He will perform miracles (Isaiah 35:5–6) and teach in parables (Psalms 78:2). However, He will be betrayed (Psalms 41:9) for 30 pieces of silver (Zechariah 11:12) and abandoned by His followers (Zechariah 13:7). Then the Messiah will be crucified (Psalms 22:1–18) with thieves (Isaiah 53:12) for our sins (Isaiah 53:4–6). Darkness will cover the land (Amos 8:9). However, the Messiah will be resurrected (Psalms 16:10, Psalms 22:19–24, Psalms 30:3, Psalms 118:17–18 and Hosea 6:2). Though He would be rejected by the Jews (Psalms 118:22 and Isaiah 53:3), He will bring light to the Gentiles (Isaiah 49:6 and Isaiah 60:3).

The Biblical scholars identify more than three hundred such messianic prophecies. No other man, but Jesus, has come close to fulfilling just those few predictions listed above. However, Jesus fulfilled all three hundred plus prophecies. Though there are some messianic prophecies which He could have arranged, many, such as His lineage, were exclusively providential. Naturally, Jesus has dissenters. Yet, the historical evidence brings credibility to Jesus' divine nature. Nonetheless, one can learn these three hundred plus prophecies and still not comprehend the perimeters of this messianic dilemma.

Earlier in a discussion on pagan symbolism, we discovered the common world expectation (including the collective unconscious) for a Savior or Messiah who would be a great "hero" to mankind. Yet, the ancient Jewish prophets seem to have been on a different level of spiritual consciousness. And, their ability to communicate in this spiritual perspective is perhaps the first great indication they indeed received a favored position with God. These Jewish prophets not only received divine doctrine such as "Thou shall not murder," but also received accurate pictures or descriptions regarding the future. The Jews had one rigorous test to judge whether one's prophecies were from God. Prognostications had to be one hundred percent accurate. If the prophecies were not totally accurate then obviously, they were not from God. No other people seem to have received prophecies with the accuracy of the

Jews. There have been many societies who have found a degree of 'prophecy' in spiritual matters. For an example, some of the Native American tribes received 'prophecy' about the coming white man. Centuries later, some American 'spiritualists' claimed to have received messages about the coming death of President Kennedy. If the Kabbalahists' theories concerning the assent of the human spirit are even partially accurate, this ascension into the divine is a skill of thymos (that which delineates humanness) and is connected to the beginnings of human existence. In other words, by divine decree all humanity has the ability to rise into the spiritual world. That is part of humanness. Yet, there are no other spiritualists who have compared to the standards of accuracy achieved by the Jewish prophets.

Quite frankly, Jewish prophecy confounds the intellect of man. It cannot be explained away by agnostic rationalizations; Jewish prophecy is too accurate. Tanakh or 'Old Testament' prophets received many of their prophecies through dreams. However, these men were very sophisticated in their dream analysis. In fact, they seem to have been more sophisticated in their interpretation than dream therapist of today. Some theologians and scholars think these Jewish prophets were Kabbalists. (There are also many who do not think the prophets were Kabbalists. Kabbalah is controversial to orthodox Judaism). This mystical sect of Judaism attempted to mentally travel in other dimensions of time and space. And, if not approached in the correct manner, Kabbalah becomes a spiritual 'Tower of Babel' and thus is considered physically, psychologically and spiritually dangerous even by the Kabbalists. Interestingly, many noted western historical prognosticators, whether or not connected to Biblical prophecy, have studied Kabbalism. As an example, Nostradamus is often connected to Kabbalism. There are actually four levels of Rabbinic interpretation. Azilut is the fourth and highest level. According to researcher Vendyl Jones (known as the real 'Indiana Jones'):

(Azilut) deals extensively with the higher sphere concerned with the PARADISE of God, that sphere from which angels ascended and descended on Jacob's ladder (Gen. 28:10–12). This PARADISE of God is synonymous, in Jewish thought, with the Eternal Garden of Eden, called GaNehDeN. The Greek word PARADISE comes from the Hebrew word Pardes, which means 'an orchard.' Parades is symbolic of the four levels of interpretation known to Jewish hermeneutics. Hence, to go into PARADISE, or PARDES, means to go into the mystical level of interpretation, to enter the eternal Garden of Eden.

If a person in this temporal world ascends into that Paradise of God, the Garden of Eden, he will discover that all the things that this temporal world calls 'mystical' will become 'realities' and all the mate-

rial things of this temporal world will become only models, symbols, and facsimiles of the world to come.[13]

(Notice that these beliefs not only relate favorably with Plato's concepts, but to quantum reality).

Some of these prognosticators predicted that the Messiah would be the Savior of both Jew and Gentile and His identity would be a problem for the traditionalists of the day. This helps us to further understand the mystical meaning behind Jesus of Nazareth's claim that He was the fulfillment of Old testament Law and the Old Testament text and why this claim is in agreement with the ancient rabbinical comment, "All the prophets prophesied only of the days of the Messiah."[14]

JEWISH SOCIETY UNDER ROME

We will continue to look at messianic writings, but first, let us consider the sociological condition of the Romanized pre-Christ Jewish people. Most were very poor. However, they were also a proud and independent people. They attributed their very existence to the faithful word of their sovereign God. And they believed the land of Judah was theirs by divine right! However, for the time, the Jewish state was part of the vast holdings of a powerful and feared Roman Empire. As we have discussed, the Roman Legion was truly frightening to all who might consider rebellion. Because of this fact alone, the subservience of Judah to Rome was quite secure. I would compare the chances of a Jewish rebellion against the Roman military with the chances of a modern Rhode Island war against the United States. The first wave of F-15s and Rhode Island would plead for peace! Now consider this. If the F-15s flew in and leveled Rhode Island, would any other state consider rebelling? Perhaps subduing Rhode Island would take a nuclear weapon or two, but sooner or later all of the other states would realize the high cost of rebellion. Tragically, total destruction was the typical message of the Roman Legion. They would physically wipe out any opposition. The Roman Legion held the 'known world' in their fist and squeezed at their discretion! Although there was some leniency toward religious practices of conquered peoples, Caesar worship and the worship of the Roman Empire was the official religion throughout the Empire. You can see how a people dedicated to a spiritual God; (the God who was faithful, the God who brought them from the wilderness to the 'Promised Land') would object to being ruled by such a pagan empire. Furthermore, their God had made them specific promises. Genesis 49:8–12 reads, "Judah, your brothers will praise you. You shall destroy your enemies. Your father's sons shall bow before you. Judah is a young lion that has finished eating its prey. He has settled down as a lion - who will dare to rouse him? The scepter shall not depart from Judah until Shiloh comes, whom all people shall obey. He has chained his steed to the choicest vine, and washed his clothes in wine. His eyes are darker than wine and his teeth are whiter than milk." According to an interpreter's commentary, "The thought seems to be that Judah will exercise tribal authority (cf. Judges 1:1–2) until the monarchy is established with a Judihite on the throne, at which time peace and prosperity will become proverbial."[15] The scepter, of course, is the symbol of authority over the people. Although the Jewish people had been captives to other countries, they had never lost the scepter. The Jewish leadership knew YHWH was "good to His word." If He said it, He meant it. He had always been faithful to carry out all of His promises. This seems to be a historically correct statement. As we have mentioned, the fulfillment of God's prophecy is unexplainable by human thinking. Prophecy is one of the strongest proofs of the God of the Jews and of His Holy Word. But, for some reason, in this particular case, God forgot about His promise. For you see, the Romans took away the Jewish right to carry out death penalties. They released a decree which gave only the Roman government right to pronounce death. This power was considered to be part of the authority of that scepter and to the horror of the Jewish population, Shiloh (Messiah) had not shown up. YHWH had forsaken His people.

The Jewish leadership tried to cover up this dilemma. Josh McDowell relates this cover up by the following, "The Jews in order to save face, made up various reasons for eliminating the death penalty." He uses as an example the Talmud (Bab., Aboda Zarah, or Of Idolatry, fol. 8, recto.) which states, "The members of the Sanhedrin, having noticed that the number of murders had increased to such an extent in Israel that it became impossible to condemn them all to death, they concluded among themselves [and said], 'It will be advantageous for us to change our ordinary place of meeting for another, so we may avoid the passing of capital sentences.'"[16]

This is the only time God has not been true to his word. To this day, the Jewish fathers are still trying to cover up this fact with the same or similar excuses as their authoritative predecessors used. But, the undeniable fact is—all of the Jews knew God blew it!

This 'scepter tragedy' (Shiloh did not come) must have seemed dreadful. Historical documents describe grievous demonstrations. The Jews dressed in ashes and sackcloth and lamented or mourned in the streets. Rabbi Rachmon wrote the following about that time: "When the members of the Sanhedrin found themselves deprived of their right over life and death, a general consternation took possession of them; they covered their heads with ashes, and their bodies with sackcloth, exclaiming: 'woe unto us, for the scepter has departed from Judah, and the Messiah has not come!'"[17] Unfortunately for the Jews, the messiah prophecies have yet to be fulfilled. To this day the majority await the Messiah. And today, many of the Jewish religious leaders seem to feel it is time for the Messiah. I wish to point out the

Jewish authorities have predicted His coming many times before. (For them to be correct, there must have been a misunderstanding about the passing of the scepter.)

Another interesting prophecy dictates that the Temple will be rebuilt in Jerusalem before the Messiah comes to Israel. Because the Jewish leaders expect their Messiah to come soon, we can expect the construction of a new Temple; a third Temple. The Temple prophecy is found in various parts of the Bible. One such example is Malachi 3:1, "Listen, I will send my messenger before me to prepare the way. And then the one (literally 'the Lord') you are looking for will come suddenly to his Temple - the Messenger of God's promises, to bring you great joy. Yes, he is surely coming,' says the Lord of Hosts."[18]

But if the Messiah is the Lord who will suddenly come to His Temple, which Temple will the Messiah visit? Will He come to a new (third) Temple or was He to have visited an earlier Temple? The Scriptures written by Haggai and Zechariah hold the answer. Haggai seems to have been a member of the 'Great Synagogue,' or that group of scribes who interpreted the law; thus he was a Jewish scholar of great respect.[19] Therefore, Haggai's teachings are accepted as traditional Judaic thought. Haggai 2:3–9 comments:

Who among you can remember the Temple as it was before? How glorious it was! In comparison, it is nothing now, is it? But take courage, O Zerubbabel and Joshua and all the people; take courage and work, for 'I am with you,' says the Lord of Hosts. 'For I promised when you left Egypt that my Spirit would remain among you; so don't be afraid.'

For the Lord of Hosts says, "In just a little while I will begin to shake the heavens and earth - and the oceans, too, and the dry land - I will shake all nations, and the Desire of All Nations (literally, "The Treasures" or "that which is choice." But many commentators prefer this rendering: "The treasures of the nations will pour into this Temple, and I will fill it with splendor.") shall come to this Temple, and I will be greater than the splendor of the first one! For I have plenty of silver and gold to do it! And here I give you peace" says the Lord.[20]

From this writing, one could conclude the Temple of the Messiah referenced by Haggai would be the second Temple, a smaller Temple than the first. To justify this position we have only to look at secular records. Josephus, the Roman historian, reported that some Jews were worried about (Persian) King Darius' reaction to the construction of a temple which was to replace the destroyed first Temple. Josephus stated:

So they immediately wrote to him (Darius) about these affairs; but as the Jews were now under terror, and afraid lest the king should change his resolution as to the building of Jerusalem, and of the temple, there were two prophets at that time amongst them, Haggai and Zechariah, who encouraged them, and bade them be of good cheer, and to suspect no discouragement from the Persians, for that God foretold this to them. So, in dependence on those prophets, they applied themselves earnestly to building, and did not intermit one day.[21]

Interestingly, the prophets were correct, Darius supported the rebuilding of the Temple. In fact, Darius had the holy vessels, which were pillaged by Nebuchadnezzar, returned to the new Temple. Josephus further reported Darius prayed to God that, " . . . if any one attempted to hinder the building of the temple, God would strike him dead, and thereby restrain his wickedness."[22] The almost unanimous conclusion of all respected scholars is that both Haggai and Zechariah referred to the second Temple.

Zechariah's comments also indicate the Messiah will come to this second Temple, and furthermore, the Messiah will bring a new age, i.e., the Kingdom is now! In Zechariah 3:6–7 God declares to Joshua (the High Priest) that the priests should follow the paths that God has declared and keep the Temple holy. In Zechariah 3:8–9, God announces:

"Listen to me, O Joshua the High Priest, and all you other priests, you are illustrations of the good things to come. Don't you see? - Joshua represents my servant the Branch (i.e., the Messiah) whom I will send. He will be the Foundation Stone of the Temple that Joshua is standing beside, and I will engrave this inscription on it seven times. I will remove the sins of this land in a single day."[23] Zechariah 8:19–23 indicates a time of joy will come to Jerusalem and men from foreign nations (Gentiles) "will clutch at the coat sleeves of **one Jew** and say, 'Please be my friend, for I know that God is with you.'"[24] (Bold emphasis added)

The second Temple was built; it endured and later was destroyed. Yet, the Messiah did not appear. I am sure the reader is way ahead of me. These Scriptures predicted the historical timing of the awaited Messiah and are considered to be part of the three hundred plus prophecies that Jesus of Nazareth fulfilled. If Jesus was the Messiah, then the Sanhedrin did not have to dress in ashes and sackcloth and cry in the streets about God forsaking them; Jesus the Adonai, was alive and well! Of course, the second Temple was the one Jesus of Nazareth visited. As a last point about Scripture regarding God's plan for the Messiah, Jesus certainly did "shake all nations." He fills a great void, for a Messiah has always been and, to this day, is the "Desire of All Nations." As previously discussed, a definable pattern of ancient messianic god myths developed around the world. In fact, new messianic myths continue to surface.

Here is an interesting philosophical thought: Assuming Jesus realized His Holiness at an early age (as I believe He did), He must have thought that the contemporary Jewish leaders were foolish for putting on ashes and sack cloths, etc., and grieving. After all, His Father had given His Word - 'Ye of little faith.' As a young boy, when He visited the Temple and held theological debates (perhaps with some of these same lamenters), what do you suppose He most enjoyed discussing? My guess is that it was the sovereignty and reliability of God.

We also read that, at one point, Jesus appeared unannounced at the Temple and drove out the money changers and scolded, "The Scriptures say my Temple is a place of prayer . . . but you have turned it into a den of thieves."[25]

His actions could not have been expected nor guarded against. Therefore, His Temple appearance must have seemed to be 'sudden.' I also wonder if the Jewish people were familiar with Jeremiah 7:11 which states, "Is my Temple but a den of robbers in your eyes? For I see all the evil going on in there."

One can find other prophecies about the historical timing of the Messiah. Though Daniel 9:24–27 is usually discussed as one Messiah prophecy, it really is a two-part prophecy. The first prophecy, Daniel 9:24–25, speaks about the exact dates of certain events, including the appearance of the Messiah. Because this Scripture is quite complicated, I will use the Living Bible translation. However, I suggest the reader refer to an earlier translation for a more exact quotation. The Scripture reads:

The Lord has commanded 490 years of further punishment upon Jerusalem and your people. Then at last they will learn to stay away from sin, and their guilt will be cleansed; then the kingdom of everlasting righteousness will begin, and the Most Holy Place (in the Temple) will be rededicated, as the prophets have declared. Now listen! It will be forty-nine years plus 434 years (this totals 483 years not the 490 years mentioned earlier, leaving 7 years unaccounted for at the time of Messiah) from the time the command is given to rebuild Jerusalem, until the Anointed One comes! Jerusalem's streets and walls will be rebuilt despite the perilous times.[26]

Four hundred eighty-three years represents the prophesied length of time between the command given to build this second Temple and the arrival of the "Anointed One" or Messiah. Interestingly, this seems to correspond well with the birth of Jesus of Nazareth. Some Jewish and agnostic scholars argue the Scripture does not refer to the Messiah, but to another 'anointed one' such as Joshua. However, Joshua did not appear at the proposed time. Furthermore, Joshua (and other 'anointed ones') symbolize the literal Messiah.

We can also be certain about the accuracy of the time in question. Old Testament Scripture reveals that Nehemiah, who was of Jewish ancestry, served as an official to King Artaxerxes of Persia. Nehemiah asked and got permission to return to Jerusalem and help rebuild the city. The following date is given:

> *And it came to pass in the month Nisan, in the twentieth year of Ar-*
> *ta-xer'xes the king, that wine was before him: and I took up the wine,*
> *and gave it unto the king. Now I had not been before time sad in his*
> *presence. Wherefore the king said unto me, Why is thy countenance*
> *sad, seeing thou art not sick? This is nothing else but sorrow of heart.*
> *Then I was sore afraid, And said unto the king, Let the king live for*
> *ever: why should not my countenance be sad, when the city, the place*
> *of my fathers' sepulchres, lieth waste, and the gates thereof are con-*
> *sumed with fire? Then the king said unto me, For what dost thou make*
> *request? So I prayed to the God of heaven. And I said unto the king,*
> *If it please the king, and if thy servant have found favour in thy sight,*
> *that thou wouldest send me unto Judah unto the city of my fathers'*
> *sepulchres, that I may build it. And the king said unto me (the queen*
> *also sitting by him,) For how long shall thy journey be? and when wilt*
> *thou return? So it pleased the king to send me; and I set him a time.*[27]

I use the King James Version because the Living Version has interpreted the date ("in the month Nisan, in the twentieth year of Ar-ta-xer'xes the king") to be, "the twentieth year of the reign of King Ar-ta-xer'xes of Persia" (Nehemiah 1:1) and "One day in April."[28] If we use the Living Version's interpretation, then the 483 years would place the time of the Messiah to be those days of Jesus of Nazareth. This interpretation places the Messiah's appearance at about the time of the crucifixion and resurrection.

Interestingly, Sir Robert Anderson, using the early Jewish calendar which is composed of 360 days, and astronomic calculations from the British Royal Observatory, found the exact prophesied date (of the Messiah's appearance) to be April sixth 32 C.E. Mathematically, 360 days per calendar year multiplied by 483 years equals 173,880 days, or by calendar, April 6, 32 C.E. Anderson calculated this to be the exact date of Jesus of Nazareth's triumphant entrance into Jerusalem.[29] He rode in on a donkey while crowds lined the way shouting and singing, "God has given us a King! Let all heaven rejoice! Glory to God in the highest heavens!"[30]

St. Luke further validates these calculations through his unrelated account. Luke wrote: "In the fifteenth year of the reign on Emperor Tiberius Caesar, a message came from God to John (the son of Zacharias), as he was living out in the deserts."[31] As we read further we find St. Luke is referring to John the Baptist and the narration leads to John's baptism of Jesus. Caesar Tiberius is thought to have started his reign on August 19, 14 C.E. Most scholars speculate that Jesus' ministry began with His baptism in the fall of the fifteenth year of the reign of Tiberius Caesar. It is concluded that Jesus' ministry lasted only three and a half (3 1/2) years. Counting the Passovers which followed Jesus' baptism, the first would have come in the spring of 29 C.E. and the fourth and final would come in 32 C.E. In 32 C.E., the Passover fell on April 10th and, according to Robert Anderson and his calculations, the Sunday previous to the Passover of 32 C.E. was April 6th 32 C.E. In the book, *The Search For Messiah,* Mark Eastman and Chuck Smith explain: "That day, April 6, 32 C.E., was exactly 173,880 days after Artaxerxes gave the decree to restore and rebuild Jerusalem on March 14, 445 B.C.E! That day was the first day that Jesus of Nazareth allowed his disciples to proclaim him as Messiah!"[32]

Whether or not one accepts these astronomical calculations as accurate is only a secondary issue. The second Temple is obviously the referenced temple. Therefore, if these are messianic prophecies, Jesus was either the Messiah or there will be no Messiah, because there is no longer a second Temple. These prophecies can never again be fulfilled. Furthermore, if modern rabbis do not accept these words as a prophetic time table of the coming Messiah, Eastman and Smith believe previous generations did. They have stated, "However, it is well established that ancient Jews believed that this prophecy pinpointed the time of Messiah's coming. In fact, many in the Qumran community (the writers of the Dead Sea Scrolls) believed that they were living in the very generation to which this prophecy pointed!"[33]

The second part of Daniel's prophecy refers to destruction: "After this period of 434 years, the Anointed One will be cut off, his kingdom still unrealized . . . and a king will arise whose armies will destroy the city and the Temple." In the more accurate King James Bible this Scripture states "And after threescore and two weeks shall Messiah be cut off, but not for himself: and the people of the prince that shall come shall destroy the city and the sanctuary; and the end thereof shall be with a flood, and unto the end of the war desolations are determined."[34]

Anyone familiar with the life of Jesus realizes He fulfilled these verses. But, again the modern rabbis and sympathetic scholars do not accept

---

THEREFORE, IF THESE ARE MESSIANIC PROPHECIES, JESUS WAS EITHER THE MESSIAH OR THERE WILL BE NO MESSIAH, BECAUSE THERE IS NO LONGER A SECOND TEMPLE.

this as a reference to the Messiah, but suggest it refers to another 'anointed one' - perhaps Onias III (2 Macc. 3:1; 4:7–10, 33–35). However, as with the previous verses (Daniel 9: 24–25), these rationalizations fall short of neutralizing the obvious implications. Though there seems to have been some disagreement (about the characteristics and timing of the Messiah) between the ancient rabbis, Daniel 9: 26 is plainly messianic prophecy. Concerning the rabbinic confusion over the messianic implications, historian Paul Johnson wrote:

> *During the second and first centuries BC, this justice-dispensing rein-carnation of Davidic ruler fitted neatly into the notions, in the Book of Daniel, the Book of Enoch and other apocalyptic works, of an end of days and the Four Last Things - death, judgment, hell and heaven. It was at this comparatively late stage that the divinely chosen and charismatic figure was first called the Messiah or 'the anointed [king].' The word was originally Hebrew, then Aramaic, and simply transliterated into Greek as messias; but the Greek word for 'the anointed' is christos, and it is significant that it was the Greek, not the Hebraic, title which was attached to Jesus.*

> *The messianic doctrine, being of complex and even contradictory origins, created great confusion in the minds of the Jews.*[35]

Saint Stephen, a Jew and the first Christian martyr, spoke to the historical ineptness of the Jewish leadership and reminded them that the Jewish experience was to persecute the prophets of God. Stephen said, "You stiff-necked heathen! Must you forever resist the Holy Spirit? But your fathers did, and so do you! Name one prophet your ancestors didn't persecute! They even killed the ones who predicted the coming of the Righteous One - the Messiah whom you betrayed and murdered. Yes, and you deliberately destroyed God's Laws, though you received them from the hands of angels."[36] Thus, if we take a strict historical position, it seems that these Jewish scholars did not understand the perimeters of their Scripture, nor the breadth of God's promise.

Yet, in all fairness to the Pharisees, we can now look back and proclaim that Jesus fulfilled all three hundred plus messianic prophecies. However, Jesus' contemporaries did not have our perspective. The Scriptures about the Messiah were as confusing to them as the prophecies in the Revelation are to us today. Go to a Christian book store and buy any two books, written by any two authors, focused on the end time prophecies and I am confident that you will find major differences in their interpretations. Prophecies have often been written in a rather mystical matter. Many prophecies have been hard to comprehend before they were fulfilled, but distinguishable after the fact. This is a result of the always present deep spiritual symbolism. We recognize symbolism as the language of the spirit. Obviously, Jesus' interpretation of what the Messiah was to do differed drastically from the understandings of the Pharisees and the Sanhedrian. Evidence suggests that when Jesus died on the cross and rose again, some of the Jewish leadership (at least two members) believed He was the Messiah. Others probably did not believe He had fulfilled the messianic Scriptures and some may not have had strong feelings either way but tried to make excuses for what had happened. This is further indicated in Acts 5:34–40. Referring to these verses Johnson stated: "There is an important passage in the Acts of the Apostles describing how Gamaliel the Elder, grandson of Hillel, and at one time president of the Sanhedrin, dissuaded the Jewish authorities from punishing the early Christians, by arguing that the authenticity of their Messiah would be demonstrated by the success of their movement."[37] Gamaliel declared, "And so my advice is, leave these men alone. If what they teach and do is merely on their own, it will soon be overthrown. But if it is of God, you will not be able to stop them, lest you find yourselves fighting even against God."[38] If there were not some question as to Jesus' authenticity, there would not have been such a discussion. Assuming this view is accurate, it must have been a horrible time for Jewish leaders who witnessed Jesus' death and believed Jesus' claims (as Joseph of Aramathea apparently did). I do not think any of us can understand the depth of his grief.

But, there were other prophecies related to the Messiah which seemed not to have been fulfilled by Jesus of Nazareth. This would include the prophecies pertaining to the great wealth and peace and wonder which would come to Israel during the Reign of the Messiah. Jesus did not fulfill these prophecies, did He? There seems to be a two-part answer to this question.

First, much of the 'glamorous bounty' coming to Israel could be interpreted as spiritual blessings. For example, there is a peace in the soul of man that will only be filled through 'spiritual' communion with his Creator. This Divine gift, the permission to have a close spiritual relationship with the Creator, is indeed a special kind of richness. Many people who have lived their lives 'walking with God' have found joy beyond the realm of money and wealth. Jesus indicated such as He claimed heaven is now. When one accepts Jesus as Lord, that person is changed. They become a spiritually freed man or woman, and they are to live eternally!

The second point is much harder to understand. Jesus has not fulfilled all of the prophecies about the Messiah. It is not unusual for prophecy to unfold over a long period of time. In accordance with this understanding, Jesus will return and fulfill all remaining messianic prophecies.

Why did He leave before His work was over? The Jewish authors of the New Testament tell us, He was not ready to take over. The time of the Gentiles was not something just made up. Gentiles are being "saved."

EHYEH ASHER EHYEH - I AM THAT I AM is the Hebrew God, but He is also the only God. We are all part of His creation and therefore owned by Him. The Biblical explanation indicates that when He is through with the Gentile nations, He will allow our filthy world to collapse and He will return to establish a wonderful new existence.

Yet, there is the broader meaning to Scripture. We postmodernists are misguided if we confine our understanding to the literal meaning of prophecy. According to one of the most respected historical researchers on this subject, Alfred Edersheim, the validity of Jesus' Messiahship was not "confined" to the "fulfillment of certain prophecies."[39] Though the Jewish population did expect a man to satisfy the messianic predictions, there seemed to be another meaning which also needed to be discharged. That was an allegorical puzzle which had eluded human understanding previous to the life of Jesus. Edersheim presents a number of reasons to validate this view. The one most relevant to my subject is the satisfaction of Scriptural symbolism. According to Edersheim: "The Messiah and His history are not presented in the Old Testament as something separate from, or superadded to, Israel. The history, the institutions, and the predictions of Israel run up into Him."[40] How is that possible? Edersheim clarifies:

> *This organic unity of Israel and the Messiah explains how events, institutions, and predictions, which initially were purely Israelitish, could with truth be regarded as finding their full accomplishment in the Messiah. From this point of view the whole Old Testament becomes the perspective in which the figure of the Messiah stands out. Perhaps the most valuable element in Rabbinic comment about messianic times is that all of the miracles and times of deliverance in Israel's past would be reenacted, in an intractable manner, in the days of the Messiah. Thus, the whole past was symbolic, and typical of the future - the Old Testament was the glass through which the universal blessings of the messianic days were seen. It is in this sense that we would understand two sayings of the Talmud: "All the prophets prophesied only of the days of the Messiah." (The Talmudic Tractate Sanhedrin, on the Sanhedrin and Criminal Jurisprudence, 99a), and "The world was created only for the Messiah" (The Talmudic Tractate Sanhedrin, on the Sanhedrin and Criminal Jurisprudence, 98b).[41]*

The Jewish solution to the puzzle has been to separate the undesirable characteristics, such as the 'Suffering Servant' from the 'Victorious Messiah,' allowing the former to only express the historical state of Israel. However, this messianic division seems to have evolved well after the fall of the Roman Empire and thus, only after considerable reflection on the implications of Christianity. This may have resulted from the Jewish authorities trying to rationalize away their responsibility for killing what may have been the greatest leader the world has ever known. Eastman and Smith give a number of sample writings from ancient rabbinical sources which validate the Christian messianic concept as a traditional Jewish perception. In fact, they began with the following summary:

> *As we examine the various beliefs of the ancient rabbis we will find that not only are they in stark contrast with contemporary Jewish thought, but the ancient views are in almost perfect agreement with Christian beliefs regarding the character, lineage, birth, mission and destiny of the Messiah.*[42]

These early Jewish commentaries, of course, do not specifically regard the life of Jesus because they were written previous to His historical life. Therefore, they obviously are a bit like Christian commentaries on *The Revelation*. One would expect such writings to be somewhat mystical. Yet, they clearly illustrate that orthodox Judaic thought included messianic concepts indicative of the Christian understanding. Edersheim agrees:

> *There is, indeed in Rabbinic writings frequent reference to the sufferings, and even the death of the Messiah, and these are brought into connection with our sins - as how could it be otherwise in view of Isaiah 53 and other passages - and in one most remarkable comment (Yalkut on Isa. 9:1) the Messiah is represented as willingly taking upon Himself all these sufferings, on condition that all Israel - the living, the dead, and those yet unborn - should be saved, and that, in consequence of His work, God and Israel should be reconciled, and Satan cast into hell. But there is only the most indistinct reference to the removal of sin by the Messiah, in the sense of vicarious sufferings.*[43]

The 'Suffering Messiah' referenced above, as well as from other Tanakh or Old Testament Scripture, led to a somewhat popular belief that two Messiahs would come to Israel. From the Christian standpoint, this thinking is correct in a fragmentary manner. Yes, in a limited way, these rabbinical commentaries were right. However, the Suffering Messiah has already visited planet earth; the Victorious Messiah is coming soon. The difference is, to the Christian, the two are one in the same being! Jesus will come again. The fact

HOWEVER, THE SUFFERING MESSIAH HAS ALREADY VISITED PLANET EARTH; THE VICTORIOUS MESSIAH IS COMING SOON. THE DIFFERENCE IS, TO THE CHRISTIAN, THE TWO ARE ONE IN THE SAME BEING! JESUS WILL COME AGAIN.

that the messianic references in the Tanakh or Old Testament were written in the singular form lends credence to the Christian view. Furthermore, it is quite obvious that the inhabitants of Qumran contemplated that the one messiah would endure first suffering and, later, triumph and glory. Eastman and Smith state: " . . . the Qumran community apparently believed (based on biblical chronology) that the Messiah would come during their time, and that he would suffer initial defeat and be cut off (killed), only to return at a later time in glory!"[44] When relevant Qumran texts were circulated in 1991, Michael Wise, a professor of Aramaic at the University of Chicago stated:

We've known for a long time there are connections between ideas contained in the scrolls and Christianity. However, this particular idea - the idea of a dying Messiah - is new and explosive . . . it was always thought that Jews at the time of Jesus expected a Messiah who would restore Israel to dominance politically. Yet the newly released text shows that the Jewish scroll writers had the idea of a Messiah who would suffer and die . . . That shows this was not an idea unique to Christianity.[45]

Of course, Qumran also ties the Jewish prophecy of Psalm 22:16 (claimed by many modern Jewish scholars as indicating Jerusalem) to the death of Jesus by crucifixion.

Yet, other Dead Sea Scrolls seem to suggest Qumran accepted the most radical Christian variances from Judaism. Scroll 4Q246 is referred to as the Son of God Scroll. Though it has deteriorated to the point that it is only fragmented pieces, an extraction of it reads:

"He shall be called the son of God.

and they shall designate [call] him son of the Most High."[46]

On the strength of these above writings, some scholars theorize that the Qumran community accepted Jesus as the Messiah. If this is accurate, it would enforce my proposition that a large portion of the Jewish community knew Jesus was the Messiah, but were not willing to risk their lives for Jesus' revolutionary understanding of Judaism.

Interestingly, modern Jewish scholars did not release these writings to outside sources (they were 'leaked'). Could it be the scrolls were not released because they expose a messianic interpretation, antagonistic to modern Judaism, but authentic to ancestral Judaism?

Whether or not you accept Jesus of Nazareth as the Messiah, the Promised One, the Great One whom all mankind has been summoned by God to await, is your free choice, but make no mistake about the Pharisees - they must have faced a horrible thought . . . a nightmare of a thought. This man called Jesus did fulfill the prophecies. Perhaps He did not fulfill prophecy the way they had expected. Certainly, He did not fulfill them the way the Jewish leaders would have liked. But, nonetheless, the prophecies had been fulfilled. The Pharisees had tried time and time again to change the course of Jesus' life. They had tried to control His actions, His ministry, the way He lived, the way He died and the time of death, but they had failed. Eye witness accounts hint these men would have supported His efforts had He only done things their way. But Jesus was so brazen, too much of an authority figure to live in their times. He should have learned to be a good diplomat - that is, unless He was ready to lead a rebellion. He was given His chance to prove He was the awaited 'Victorious Messiah' and He did not take it. Yet, the outcome was scary.

CHAPTER 19

JESUS' MESSAGE

*"What he (Jesus) had to teach was for the most part conventional
Jewish ethics. But he went beyond this by placing exceptional
emphasis on the eligibility of sinners for the Kingdom."*[1]

There are indisputable differences between YHWH of the Old Testament and Abba of the New Testament. This contrast resulted from the teachings of Jesus Christ. It was the difference between the traditional Jewish understanding of divine words and the edification of Jesus; everyone who heard His teachings must have realized the uniqueness of His compassionate explanations. This alone made Him special. He took authority over the Scriptures like no one before or since.

Recently, a friend of mine began a discussion about the perceptions of God. In our exchange my friend stated, "The Bible seems to discuss two different Gods. The Tanakh's (Old Testament) YHWH is a God of vengeance who sometimes deals with people harshly and perhaps unfairly to our human understanding. However, the God of the New Testament is a God of love." Personally, if I were making this argument, I would stress that the New Testament God image is both a heavenly Father (Abba) and a God. This God image framed a revolutionary view of a loving kinship between humans and God. How can these two 'testaments' (Old and New) possibly be narratives on the same God? The answer to the question can seem complicated. However, I will simplify the task. The Old Testament is, among other things, a legal document. It is a legal description of the relationship between YHWH and Israel. The text also holds a formal description of God. Included is a depiction of His authoritative nature and His intolerance of sin. Thus, the Old Testament is, in part, the legal description of a factual relationship. However, if we can categorize the Old Testament as a legal document, the New Testament can be simplified and characterized as a 'Golden Parachute' by the following quote: "For God loved the world so much that he gave his only Son so that anyone who believes in him shall not perish but have eternal life. God did not send his Son into the world to condemn it, but to save it."[2]

One thing has become obvious regarding the human condition: Whatever issue God is making through our world and our human existence, human beings cannot live within the guidelines YHWH demands. Thus, God provides humanity with an escape from tragic destruction. The New

Testament proclaims: "There is no eternal doom awaiting those who trust him (Jesus) to save them. But those who don't trust him have already been tried and condemned for not believing in the only Son of God."[3]

Jesus is the fulfillment of the divine 'Golden Parachute' introduced to humanity through numerous ancient writings.

REALITY EXPOSED

And one of the elders saith unto me, Weep not: behold the Lion of the tribe of Juda, the Root of David . . . in the midst of the throne and of the four beasts, and in the midst of the elders, stood a Lamb as it had been slain, having seven horns and seven eyes, which are the seven Spirits of God sent forth into all the earth.[4]

The U. S. news media played it up big. Virtually all of our newspapers and television news broadcasts exposed the Jesus fable. Though they did not examine the nature of the study, the media eagerly reported that Jesus' disciples had embellished their stories regarding this simple carpenter. The resource for this news flash was an ongoing group of post-modern theologians commonly identified as the 'Jesus Seminar.' The smearing of Jesus' credibility was not based upon new archaeological finds or any other recent materials. How did these theologians determine that Jesus was not the special being Christians have portrayed Him to be? They voted! They cast their lots and voted that Jesus Christ had not said most of the things He was Biblically credited with saying. They further commented that much of what has been attributed to Jesus, came from 'Old Testament' documents. And finally, these 'theologians' decided, by vote, which Biblical statements were the actual words of Jesus and which were from other sources. The bases for their choices centered around the disciples. If the disciples had 'made up' sayings attributed to Jesus, they would have gotten their ideas from the Jewish and early Christian cultures. Thus, these theologians investigated what had been stated by early rabbis and Christian authors.

To begin with, it should be noted that the New Testament clearly confirms that Jesus quoted from the Old Testament. Moreover, if Jesus was the Messiah discussed in the 'Old Testament,' He would logically quote 'Old Testament' Scripture. Such diligence should not come as any great surprise. These ancient writings were *about* Him. In fact, Jesus claimed to be the fulfillment of the Law (Old Testament).

The true fallacy of the Jesus Seminar's premise comes from their assumption that Jesus said nothing original of great importance. The theologians assumed that the disciples were lying. As previously discussed, the disciples had no reason to lie for Jesus. To the contrary, even many of the liberal scholars cannot defend this view. For example, E. P. Sanders has written: "That Jesus' followers (and later Paul) had resurrection experiences is, in my judgement, a fact. What the reality was that gave rise to the experiences I do not know."[5]

Moreover, by the Jesus Seminar's rules, virtually anything said is automatically considered to be a falsehood. J. P. Morehead in discussing the 'Jesus Seminar' suggests:

> *If we applied this test to any historical figure, the only details allowed would be things that were utterly so out of touch with the rest of his culture, that one would wonder how the person could say it to begin with. Isn't it more likely to believe that when a person talked, they would say something related to what had been taught in their culture? Doesn't it make sense that when Jesus spoke on subjects, He talked about things that the rabbis would have also commented on - and maybe similarly? Doesn't it make sense that some of the apostles, after Jesus died, would end up teaching some of the same things Jesus taught?*[6]

This is a major flaw in the Jesus Seminar's reasoning. To begin with, these intellectuals must not have considered all of the texts. If we use the same Jesus Seminar guidelines on all related writings we find that Jesus' divine nature is, in fact, revealed in His teachings. The reason for this 'shocking' revelation is that a number of concepts accredited to Jesus do seem to originate from Him and are foreign to anything said by the rabbis or early Christians. For one, Jesus was the first person in the Jewish faith to claim to be the Son of Man. This is a very profound statement with far reaching implications regarding His divine nature. Secondly, though the Tanakh or Old Testament infers the 'mission of Israel' was 'the Kingdom of Jehovah.'[7] Jesus took control of the 'Kingdom' revelation. As an example, in St. Luke 11: 20, Jesus stated: "But if I am casting out demons because of power from God, it proves that the Kingdom of God has arrived." To this particular Scripture, Historian Michael Grant maintains, "This is a statement so alien to the thought of his time that once again it must be attributed to Jesus himself rather than to the Gospel writers or their sources."[8] Therefore, if these theologians were fair, Jesus' divinity passes the Jesus Seminar test. In fact, the radical differences which separate the Jewish and Christian religions must be attributed to Jesus' influence. Yet, the Jesus Seminar cannot recognize Jesus' nature as the source of this historical division of religions. Why? Because, Jesus' divinity does not fit within their biased starting assumption, i.e., Jesus was only a carpenter and not the initiator of theological growth and most certainly not the divine Son of God. This reasoning is both circular and baseless. Therefore, the Jesus Seminar's test is fallacious. Such rationalizations also explain why the Jesus Seminar (as a body) is considered atheistic by many. Is this a true picture of intellectualism today? Is our historical record based on the votes of a small group of idealists who give no quarter to cogent evidence? Naturally, because the group began with the proposition that Jesus was only a normal human, nothing about His divinity could be allowed. Nonetheless, beginning with this biased absolute is the only way the Jesus Seminar could hold their conclusion.

Another flaw in this Jesus Seminar's position is that these 'theologians' take the naturalist's proposition that there are no miracles. Of course, we have already discussed a number of such wonders. Morehead protests, "One of my fields is philosophy of science and I can tell you that science cannot even answer the question whether miracles can occur. It's not a scientific question."[9] At this time, the scientific world is virtually limited to natural events and therefore cannot confirm nor rule out supernatural events. Thus, I question the veracity of these 'Jesus Seminar' theologians. If they believe miracles are impossible, even though they have no such factual proof, then they must prejudicially believe that God is limited or perhaps non existent. Thus, one might conclude that the Jesus Seminar has lost the meaning of a Supreme Power. So, why are overtly biased men hired as Christian theologians?

It is unfortunate for academia when scholars look back in history and, with no good reason, dispute historical records. How can our academic institutions sit back and watch scholars examine what scores of witnesses proclaimed, i.e., that Jesus was the Son of God, and coolly state these witnesses not only made up the Jesus myth but went to their deaths to advance the cover up? Frankly, because of the above prejudices, the Jesus Seminar has lost much of its credibility with many other scholars.

Nonetheless, the news media often presents this radical group as a valid scholarly voice and tells the world the Jesus Seminar has found that Jesus was not the divine leader the Christian world claims Him to be. Because of their biased vote, many books and magazines and newspapers have been sold demeaning Jesus. Many names have become famous for such anti-Christ headlines.

A MOST IMPORTANT DISCOVERY

Before we go further into this particular discussion about Jesus Christ, I wish to take this opportunity to announce a most important discovery. Though this discovery is not about Jesus, it is of profound importance to American history; thus, I am sure, every reader will be more than happy to allow my findings at this time. What if I told you I had recently discovered a particularly sinister conspiracy. All records about Abraham Lincoln seem to

HOW CAN OUR ACADEMIC INSTITUTIONS SIT BACK AND WATCH SCHOLARS EXAMINE WHAT SCORES OF WITNESSES PROCLAIMED, I.E., THAT JESUS WAS THE SON OF GOD, AND COOLLY STATE THESE WITNESSES NOT ONLY MADE UP THE JESUS MYTH BUT WENT TO THEIR DEATHS TO ADVANCE THE COVER UP?

have been doctored to give Lincoln credibility beyond his limited capabilities. All of the eyewitnesses to the Gettysburg address misrepresented or lied about the event. Actually, Lincoln's famous speech was written and given by another man. Afterwards, historians decided to dignify this backward crass president. Mr. Lincoln could not have been the composer of those eloquent words which comprise what is often regarded to be our greatest American speech. Lincoln neither wrote nor gave that address. After all, Lincoln was a backwoodsman and a terrible speaker. The man who expressed interest in having all his generals drink the same whiskey as General Grant could not have spoken those insightful words which envisioned a nation of great character. Those two expressions are too divergent to have come from the same man. And, as a matter of fact, the persons responsible for this cover-up got all of their ideas for Lincoln's speech from the sayings of America's founding fathers. Most of what Lincoln was reported to have said was already alluded to by Washington, Jefferson and their friends.

Of course, I am using satire. Abe Lincoln did indeed write and recite the Gettysburg address. Furthermore, Lincoln is not alone in his diversity. I could have chosen a variety of statements from virtually anyone. General George S. Patton was profane in his speech. I could have included one of his many vulgar statements to suggest that he had little need for God. However, that would not be true. Patton was a spiritual man. He was quite candid about the fact that he studied the Bible. He so profoundly believed in the power of God that he had a chaplain compose a prayer for "good weather for battle." The 'theologian' who, centuries after the fact, states Jesus did not say something accredited to Him, only because the theologian does not think it sounds like something Jesus would say, has no business in academia.

Moreover, despite the headlines, the great majority of theologians have not said anybody made up anything about the Scriptures of Jesus. What creditable scholars have said is that many of the Scriptures attributed to Jesus can be found elsewhere. Furthermore, in a variety of cases, there seem to be discrepancies about specific events. Neither of these observations create theological hostilities toward Jesus' divinity.

As part of my explanation, I wish to turn to that great American pastime, baseball. I do not think many of us would find it surprising to hear a coach tell a batter, "Keep your eye on the ball." Keeping your eye on the ball is a fundamental concept of baseball. As a matter of fact, I have heard this same fundamental, 'keep your eye on the ball,' expressed in other ways. A coach might tell a batter, "You cannot hit what you do not see." Or he might tell a pitcher, "The batter hits what he sees." How many of us would be surprised to hear any of these phrases come out of the mouth of any particular baseball coach? Every baseball coach has probably said, "Keep your eye on the ball." This expression conveys a truth about baseball that all coaches should know.

In like manner, not everything Jesus said *originated* from Him. Unquestionably, some of the words and phrases Jesus used, appear not only in the Old Testament, but in other religions and philosophies. The difference between Jesus' statements and those of other ancient origins can be found in the dynamics of the messages. It is how the words and sentences are arranged into concepts. The meaning underlying Christianity is often the defining factor which separates it from all other religions. Certainly Jesus quoted Jewish Scriptures. He, most probably, enjoyed explaining the spiritual value (as opposed to the legalist value) of the sacred Jewish text. For some reason, some Jewish Scriptures are similar to ancient writings from other religions. This, of course, is further evidence that all humans intuitively know God's Laws. For example, most ancient religions had a concept similar to the 'Golden Rule' - "Do unto others as you would have them do unto you." Lao-tze the father of Taoism wrote, "To those who are good to me I am good . . . And to those who are not good to me I am also good. And thus all get to be good."[10] Confucius taught about Five Constant Virtues. The Virtue of Righteousness was expressed to be "Not to do unto others what you would not they should do unto you."[11] In Jesus' day, the Jewish perception of this 'rule' "called for men to avoid doing to others what they would not like to have done to themselves."[12] Jesus took a more extreme and humanly passionate position. Therefore, Jesus' version was radically different from any other known source. Jesus said:

> *If someone slaps you on one cheek, let him slap the other too! If some-*
> *one demands your coat, give him your shirt besides. Give what you*
> *have to anyone who asks you for it; and when things are taken away*
> *from you, don't worry about getting them back. (Now comes the*
> *Golden Rule.) Treat others as you want them to treat you.[13]*

The difference between Jesus' statement and everything else which might be considered a form of the Golden Rule is further separated through Jesus' following explanation:

> *Do you think you deserve credit for merely loving those who love you?*
> *Even the godless do that! And if you do good only to those who do you*
> *good - is that so wonderful? Even sinners do that much! And if you*
> *lend money only to those who can repay you, what good is that? Even*
> *the most wicked will lend to their own kind for full return!*
>
> *Love your enemies! Do good to them! And don't be concerned about*
> *the fact that they won't repay. Then your reward from heaven will be*

very great, and you will truly be acting as sons of God: for he (the Christian) is kind to the unthankful and to those who are very wicked.[14]

Jewish laws were difficult to keep, but Jesus' concepts were even more difficult. Marietta D. Moskin stated this point well: "Jesus went beyond the Jewish laws when he told his followers to turn the other cheek and to love their enemies." Moskin reasoned, "To forgive, to love and to share require a change in inner attitude and a strict honesty with oneself."[15]

Despite the negative aspersions of the American media, the nature of Jesus is deeply connected to the significance and revolutionary disposition of His message. It is quite obvious that Peter could not have been the creator of Jesus' message. Neither could Paul nor James nor Matthew, Mark, Luke nor John. His words were too bold for the day. As an example, the kingdom portrayed by Jesus is radically different from any religious thought conceived previous to His worldly experience. One cannot rationalize away the Truth of Jesus Christ's message. Furthermore, if we allow the extremism of these Jesus Seminar 'theologians' to prevail, then we throw out most of the wording and much of the message of the Christian movement. We would lose much of the New Testament depth and value, as well as all reason for a devout and faithful following. We lose the logic of the Messiah. We lose the passion of His love. We lose the reason for His sacrifice. Most important, we lose His divine nature; this loss comes not from truth, but from atheistic presumptions. I suggest such professors need to also ask, why did those Jews who followed Jesus radically change their concepts about reality? And why did Jews ask Gentiles to become their brothers and sisters? No other Judaic sect wanted to be associated with the 'unclean' Gentiles.

Additionally, philosophers, theologians, historians and anthropologists have searched for a connection between the theological message of Jesus and the religious sects of the day. There are similarities between Jesus' message and some of these sects. The Essenes are often referred to in this vein. However, Jesus' message is uniquely different from all Jewish sects and factions. No known group held His beliefs.[16] In this regard, Jesus stands alone in spiritual wisdom.

CHAPTER 20

JESUS OF NAZARETH AND THE HONESTY OF THE GOSPELS

"Jesus told him, 'I am the Way - yes, and the Truth and the Life. No one can get to the Father except by means of me. If you had known who I am, then you would have known who my Father is. ***From now on you know him - and have seen him!'"*** *(Bold emphases added)[1]*

The life of Jesus was, among other things, an exciting transcendental declaration to humanity. This 'message' was not foremost in Jesus' miraculous healings, or the virgin birth, or even His resurrection. Instead, these were unmistakable signs of His validation and acts of salvation. However, another important part of Jesus' life centered on the concepts He taught. It was His insights which revolutionize the Old Testament. His message was a radical departure from the traditional Jewish interpretation of God's wisdom. The Hebrew understanding is based on law. Jesus' message rests on love. This was a severe departure from the traditions of a proud people. Who could accept such a radical change? Who could follow such a revolutionary man? Yet, we have seen great evidence that the story of Jesus is true. We have discussed historical references which give credence to the Biblical accounts. We have questioned Peter, Thomas, Paul and others. We have wondered about their motives. We have attempted to understand their radical dedication even into death—their willing martyrdom even unto the vilest of tortures. Yet, this story seems too amazing for our human intellect to discern. Theology professors have rightfully asked tough questions: What is the real meaning of Jesus' words? What is Jesus' true message?

Let us consider some of the most commonly questioned Biblical references. One major point often discussed is: How accurate is our version of Mark, because part of his text may have been added as an after thought, perhaps by another writer? Who was the editing author and when was the text added? Without going into great detail, this point is not crucial because 1 Corinthians is older than any of the Gospels and states quite plainly "the old Christian formula," i.e., Jesus died, was buried, was raised and appeared. This is the same formula recovered in Mark and verified through the other Gospels. According to William Lane Craig, the formula probably reaches to "within the first five years after Jesus' crucifixion."[2] Furthermore, Paul clearly references the early nature of 1 Corinthians by writing: "After that (Jesus' resurrection and discovery by the apostles) he (Jesus) was seen by more than five hundred Christian brothers at one time, most of whom are still alive, though some have died by now."[3] Clearly, this statement alone pushes the Biblical message back to a time very close to the event. Certainly, in these early times, the story was collaborated by those referred to as "still alive." Had this not been the case, the religion would have died. Thus, we must give some level of credibility to the witnesses.

Another question involves the similarities among the four summaries of Jesus' life (Matthew, Mark, Luke and John) known as "The Gospels." Throughout these reports, we find uncanny agreement over the activities and messages of Jesus. We even find similarities in the wording. Many scholars now conclude that, if one considers all factors involved, no four writers could independently compose texts as consistent as Matthew, Mark, Luke and John. (Many exclude John from this criticism because there are more variances in his text and less chance for collaboration). Because Mark is considered to have been the first Gospel written, it is suggested that Matthew and Luke borrowed from Mark's text. However, because Matthew and Luke were thought to be written at approximately the same time in divergent lands, there does not seem to have been much chance for collaboration between these later Gospels. So, the thought process goes, Mark could have been used as a reference by Matthew, Luke and to a lessor extent John. Such a possibility erroneously leads atheists and agnostics to rationalize that there must have been blind acceptance of Mark's text and any additional information found in Matthew, Luke and John are riddled with embellishments.

However, all 'collaboration' accusations are purely speculative. No one knows for sure when these documents were written, although, with time, increased evidence continues to push all their dates of origin closer to the time of Jesus. Moreover, no one knows if there was any cooperation between these writers (except the conformation expressed by Luke in his opening explanation). We must assume that the events which did take place were observed by many and these 'many' saw the same things from different points of view. Thus, each writer found individuals testifying to identical things. Furthermore, all four Gospel writers may have visited with the same eye witnesses. Certainly all would want to visit with the major relations of Jesus. Included would be Mary - the mother of Jesus, Mary Magdalene - the close friend and follower of Jesus who witnessed some of the more dramatic events, James - the brother of Jesus, Peter - 'the rock,' etc. This would, to one extent or another, explain much of the duplication in the Gospel reports. Another important aspect is that none of the writers (with perhaps the exception of

---

WE MUST ASSUME THAT THE EVENTS WHICH DID TAKE PLACE WERE
OBSERVED BY MANY AND THESE 'MANY' SAW THE SAME THINGS
FROM DIFFERENT POINTS OF VIEW.

John) seem to be trying to spiritualize what was seen. The accounts seem primarily to be reports of facts. Facts do not vary. Most important, whether or not parts of Mark's work were used as a basis for Matthew, Luke or John is of little importance. Let us assume for the moment that both Matthew and Luke used Mark as their major source in their letters. What does that tell us about Mark? Such actions should be interpreted as approval. Both Matthew and Luke would be independently declaring that Mark's work was accurate. All one can credibly suggest, through this speculation, is that Matthew and Luke might have used Mark as a valid source. This is and has been a common practice for authors to authenticate and legitimize their works. When I use the ideas of Chuck Smith in a particular area of this writing, I am agreeing with Chuck Smith on that one particular point. When I use James Orr, I am in agreement with James Orr.

So comes another question: Did Matthew or Luke copy Mark? Why produce another version of the same story? If Mark's work was so good, why write any more letters about the life of Jesus? Perhaps the above speculation is wrong and Mark's version was not known to Matthew, Luke or John. Or, perhaps Mark's narrative was not long enough for Matthew, or descriptive enough for Luke, or spiritual enough for John. Luke states quite plainly his reason for writing another version of the Gospels:

DEAR FRIEND WHO loves God.

Several biographies of Christ have already been written using as their source material the reports circulating among us from the early disciples and other eyewitnesses. However, it occurred to me that it would be well to recheck all these accounts from first to last and after thorough investigation, to pass this summary on to you (literally, 'after these things'), to reassure you of the truth of all you were taught.[4]

It is likely that Mark's writing is one of the versions Luke is referring to. It is also interesting that Luke makes reference to "source material reports circulating among us from the early disciples." Perhaps there were other source documents known to all four of these writers, but lost to us. Nonetheless, it is important to remember that each Gospel report appealed to a different audience. In addition, these writers had different backgrounds and different writing skills. For example, Matthew was probably a common man while Luke was a physician with a high level of intelligence.

Now that we have stated realistic explanations for the Gospel similarities, let us consider the opposite problem. We find a few areas of these reports which do not seem to be completely consistent. It is not the intent of this book to resolve every problem of the variances in the Bible. However, these discrepancies are important in that they point to the independence of the reports. To find no problems would indeed be amazing considering the number of source witnesses and writers. To find total agreement would raise a huge red flag. Such consistency would suggest a 'cleansing' or collaboration beyond the point of honest reporting of objective truth.

One of the more serious variances, and one directly related to the resurrection, involved the discovery of Jesus' empty grave. It is obvious that each version is unique. Each version says something about the discovery that the others do not. To begin with, John's version has one woman going to the grave. Mark's has two women and Matthew's has at least three. Yet, Luke's letter states an unspecified number of women (all Galilean) went to the tomb. How could these discrepancies exist if the reports are true? The answer is evident. These story variances do not point to a contradiction of events or a foundational deficiency in Christian dogma; instead, they are related to a truism in the nature of reporting. Witness' reports of an event differ. First, let me remind you that this was perhaps the most surprising and exciting event of the entire Bible! For the people involved, it would have to be the highest of highs, the ultimate in exciting human experiences. Most definitely, there would also have been much fear and much confusion. As such, this event would be one of the hardest to accurately define. Sometimes we expect our benefactors to have had tape recorders and newscasters 'live on the spot' to get the story— the immediate and most accurate response. Unfortunately, there were no live cameras in those days and we had no 'on the spot reporters.' These writers were dealing with the greatest human discovery of all time. They were trying to relate an incredible event to a reader. One cannot expect each account to be word for word unless Mark was copied without exception.[5] Of course, the outcome of such universal acceptance would be only one historical account of the life of Jesus from the Christian standpoint. Second, each man may have gotten their information from different women. It is obvious John's major source was Mary Magdalene. Luke probably interviewed several women; thus, his report may have been a composite of experiences. It seems quite obvious Mary Magdalene was a major source for most, if not all, narrations. She most likely was close to Mary (Jesus' mother) and instrumental in planning and coordinating a procession of Galilean women to embalm Jesus. 'Mother Mary' most likely went as much to mourn her son's death as to embalm Him. I am sure her group of friends would want to console mother Mary during her time of need. In this regard, there could very well have been a small group of four or five compassionate women volunteering to help and comfort a grieving mother. Therefore, the writers would have interviewed a number of witnesses and had a variety of points of view. Each story may be

DESPITE A FEW EXCITED PEOPLE PERHAPS SEEING AND HEARING SLIGHTLY DIFFERENT THINGS, THE STORY DOES NOT CHANGE . . . JESUS IS RISEN!

true from a particular perspective. Because one story zeros in on a specific woman does not mean other women did not participate nor does it exclude a span of continued experiences of the Galilean women lasting an hour or more in time. Third, if the Scriptures were made up the authors would, most assuredly, have stated that men found the empty tomb. As we have seen in many middle eastern countries burdened with ancient traditions, women were treated harshly. Who would have allowed women to discover such a wondrous event? Thus, Biblical veracity must be unquestioned on this point. Despite the confusion, the focus of the message in all the Gospels are the same. And, its truth has been tested in the witnesses' blood. Despite a few excited people perhaps seeing and hearing slightly different things, the story does not change . . . Jesus is risen!

As for the actual wording of all the New Testament events, it is quite reasonable to understand why one might find some difference between Mark's quotations of Jesus and Luke's quotations. Yet, like the above rebuttal, the meaning behind the messages is the same. The message did not change because of wording. Everyone understood the ideas Jesus conveyed. This is quite obvious when you lay the Gospels out side by side to compare the intended meanings. Jesus is quite clear.

Finally, though the Gospels have given us an incredible account of miracles and other extraordinary events foreign to our human understanding, they must be extremely accurate. No one can validly criticize the accuracy of St. Luke's historical report, because he is accepted as an exceptional historian. As a scientist, Luke examined these events quite thoroughly. Clearly, his belief was not based on myths. Moreover, though we do not find the same detail in the other Gospel accounts, the honesty in all four reports is evident. It is hard to envision these men involved in a 'Jesus conspiracy.' Likewise, it is hard to believe that they blindly copied from a master text. To the contrary, the Gospels were sincere and candid reports which should not be taken lightly.

Jesus brought a message which revolutionized theological thinking. Judaism had become a legalistic society. Though some historians speculate that Jesus was a rabbinical Jew, His teachings ripped apart the Jewish 'legalism' traditions and revolutionized the human concept of God. Thus, His words were, of themselves, foundations for a new way of life for they introduced mankind to the 'Kingdom of God.'

CHAPTER 21

THE WILL OF GOD
IS PASSIONATE!

"Jesus, no doubt, had more than his share of kindly humane toler-
ance, but there was much more to his attitude than that. For, like
every other feature of his ministry and thinking, it was a logical
deduction from his inauguration of the Kingdom of God, to which
everyone possible must be prepared for admission by enabling them
to experience the necessary change of heart, whereupon their sins
would be forgiven them. It was therefore imperative to extend his
proclamation as far and wide as possible, and to take special steps
to bring in everybody without distinction."[1]

As we have briefly discussed, the authenticity of Jesus' deity was, in part, revealed through His teachings. Whether or not one accepts the New Testament narration as the precise words of Jesus is a moot point. Factually, the New Testament loses much of its exactness simply through translation. However, what is important is the value of Jesus' knowledge. His perceptions must be accepted or rejected on their merits of wisdom. In this respect, on these merits of wisdom, the authenticity of Jesus' message far exceeds the scope of any contradictory rebuttals. Enveloped in the Biblical text are repetitious patterns which many scholars feel genuinely describe Jesus' personality, His manner of teaching and the major themes and lessons of His message. These patterns point to the innate abilities and directness of Jesus. Regarding these distinguishing factors, Gunther Bornkamm wrote, "The important point is that in all of them the same feature recurs, by which the historical Jesus can be recognized."[2]

Jesus' cutting directness was a dominate feature of His personality. His demeanor was different from any of the other priests or 'holy men' because He expressed Himself as the ultimate 'authority' in matters of the spirit. Such deportment was unprecedented in the extremely formalized Judaic culture. Therefore, Jesus' authoritative nature must have been quite unsettling. Yet, from early on, Jesus acted in this distinctive manner. Perhaps His first definitive statement came in His hometown of Nazareth. Saint Luke wrote:

When he came to the village of Nazareth, his boyhood home, he went
as usual to the synagogue on Saturday, and stood up to read the

Scriptures. The book of Isaiah the prophet was handed to him, and he opened it to a place and read where it says:

"The Spirit of the Lord is upon me; he has appointed me to preach Good News to the poor; he has sent me to heal the brokenhearted and to announce that captives shall be released and the blind shall see, that the downtrodden shall be freed from their oppressors, and that God is ready to give blessings to all who come to him."

He closed the book and handed it back to the attendant and sat down, while everyone in the synagogue gazed at him intently. Then he added, "These Scriptures came true today!"[3]

It was apparent to all in attendance that Jesus was audaciously claiming to possess the attributes of the Messiah. Again and again throughout Jesus' ministry, He spoke as one who holds divine authority. It is only with this understanding, with this special relevance of His words to a broken society and through the messianic implications of His expressions, that we begin to perceive the emotional impact of His mien. St. Luke next discusses Jesus' authoritative manner in Capernaum:

Then he returned to Capernaum, a city in Galilee, and preached there in the synagogue every Saturday. Here, too, the people were amazed at the things he said. For he spoke as one who knew the truth, instead of merely quoting the opinions of others as his authority.[4]

St. Mark agrees with this account when he reports this same event:

Jesus and his companions now arrived at the town of Capernaum and on Saturday morning went into the Jewish place of worship - the synagogue - where he preached. The congregation was surprised at his sermon because he spoke as an authority, and didn't try to prove his points by quoting others - quite unlike what they were used to hearing![5]

Likewise St. Matthew wrote about Jesus' authority. An example is the following passage about the importance of His message:

"But those who hear my instructions and ignore them are foolish, like a man who builds his house on sand. For when the rains and floods come, and storm winds beat against his house, it will fall with a mighty crash." The crowds were amazed at Jesus' sermons, for he taught as one who had great authority, and not as their great Jewish

leaders. (Literally, "not as the scribes." These leaders only quoted others, and did not presume to present any fresh revelation).[6]

These are but glimpses into Jesus' authoritative manner. In actuality, the entire New Testament is abounding in the power of Jesus' authority! For a broader experience, read Matthew 5:1 through Matthew 7:29.

Bornkamm rightfully emphasized that Jesus' authority was "equally recognizable in his words and deeds."[7] This observation is very important in discovering the essence of Jesus. It was not just the abundance of 'signs' which pointed to Jesus as the anointed Son of God. Such signs were particularly important to the Jews. But, if one were to, in some way, excuse Jesus' miracles or discount Jesus' resurrection, if one were to assume these were faked, or question the validity of the virgin birth, or Jesus' fulfillment of prophecy, there would still be great reason to accept Jesus' Lordship, because much more evidence of the authority of Jesus lies outside the abundance of miraculous events. The spiritual upheaval of His message demonstrates His Messiahship. It was His miracles, but it also was His love. It was the authority He wheeled, and the comfort He brought. It was His knowledge of the spirit. It was the confidence of His words, and the wisdom of His teaching. It was His convictions, and His dedication. It was His innocence, and His suffering for the sins of Israel and the world. It was everything about Him! Jesus demonstrated His uniqueness. In essence, Jesus was the message of God. "To make the reality of God present: this is the essential mystery of Jesus. This making-present of the reality of God signifies the end of the world in which it takes place."[8]

Jesus ended conventional life on planet earth. Jesus shattered the concept of man reaching for God. His message was contradictory to all beliefs known to mankind. Even today, non-Christian traditions have a hard time understanding the passionate love and forgiveness of Jesus' message. They want to add human rationalizations to the equation. Even the cults which have grown out of traditional Christianity cannot fathom the power of God's message given through His Son, Jesus Christ. They, like virtually all world beliefs, stress man must work to 'earn salvation.' Bornkamm wrote, "This is why the scribes and Pharisees rebel, because they see Jesus' teaching as a revolutionary attack upon law and tradition. This is why the demons cry out, because they sense an inroad upon their sphere of power 'before the time' (Matt 8:29). This is why his own people think him mad.[9] But this is also why the people marvel and the saved praise God."[10]

JESUS SHATTERED THE CONCEPT OF MAN REACHING FOR GOD.

THE MESSAGE

Jesus' life marks both a warning to the ungodly and a unmitigated gift to the lovers of God. Jesus' message was, "Turn from sin, and turn to God, for the Kingdom of heaven is at hand" (or "has arrived.").[11] Outside the acceptance of His deity, this is the entirety of Jesus' message. One day the Pharisees asked Jesus, "When will the Kingdom of God begin?" Jesus replied, "The Kingdom of God isn't ushered in with visible signs. You won't be able to say, 'It has begun here in this place or there in that part of the country.' For the Kingdom of God is within you."[12]

> *When Pilate questioned Jesus before His crucifixion, he asked Jesus if He was indeed the awaited King of the Jews. The Scriptures state: Then Jesus answered, "I am not an earthly king. If I were, my followers would have fought when I was arrested by the Jewish leaders. But my Kingdom is not of the world."*
>
> *Pilate replied, "But you are a king then?"*
>
> *"Yes," Jesus said. "I was born for that purpose. And I came to bring truth to the world. All who love the truth are my followers."[13]*

Although the coming Messiah and the Kingdom of God were interrelated, the Jews expected a material kingdom "which (according to the New Testament) will find its fulfillment only at the end of time."[14] Thus, it is very plain why the Jewish leadership rejected Jesus as the Messiah. They anticipated an entirely different kind of messiah. If one examines the Kingdom prophecies, the Jewish position becomes understandable. Consider these examples: (King James Version)

Isaiah 59:20; God makes a very strong statement to the Hebrew: "And the Redeemer shall come to Zion, and unto them that turn from transgression in Jacob, saith the LORD."

This is obviously a reference to the coming Messiah. (The Messiah is the Redeemer).

Isaiah 59:21 continues: "As for me, this is my covenant with them, saith the LORD; My spirit that is upon thee, and my words which I have put in thy mouth, shall not depart out of thy mouth, nor out of the mouth of thy seed, nor out of the mouth of thy seed's seed, saith the LORD, from henceforth and forever." This is a reminder to the Jews of the significance of God's covenant to Jacob. God does not forget His word. The Jewish race is the chosen people of God. Through them (by way of a redeemer/Messiah) will come the redemption of sin and restoration of fellowship with God (lost by Adam).

Isaiah chapter 60, God tells of the great things which will happen to Israel when the Messiah comes.

Isaiah 60:1, "Arise, shine; for thy light is come, and the glory of the LORD is risen upon thee." The light is of the Messiah and the glory is what the Messiah brings to Israel.

Isaiah 60:2, "For, behold, the darkness shall cover the earth, and gross darkness the people: but the LORD shall arise upon thee, and His glory shall be seen upon thee."

Isaiah 60:3, "And the Gentiles shall come to thy light, and kings to the brightness of thy rising." This is a recognition of the position of power Israel will hold.

Isaiah 60:4, "Lift up thine eyes round about, and see: all they gather themselves together, they come to thee; thy sons shall come from far, and thy daughters shall be nursed at thy side." This prophecy is being fulfilled at this time, as the Jew returns to the homeland. More emphasis is placed upon the gathering of the Jewish people, including the accumulation of wealth. The Gentiles (all of the other races/nations) "shall build up thy walls."

Chapter 60:11, "Therefore thy gates shall be open continually: they shall not be shut day nor night; that men may bring unto thee the forces of the Gentiles, and that their kings may be brought."

Chapter 60:12, "For the nation and kingdom that will not serve thee shall perish; yea, those nations shall be utterly wasted." These verses are quite clear and speak of the power behind God's Word.

Great riches will come and the land will be made beautiful for God's sanctuary (temple).

Chapter 60:14, "The sons also of them that afflicted thee shall come bending unto thee; and all they that despised thee shall bow themselves down at the soles of thy feet; and they shall call thee, The city of the LORD, The Zion of the Holy One of Israel."

There will be no more violence in Judea, nor will there be violence on her borders. The LORD will provide the light for the land.

Chapter 60:21, "Thy people also shall be all righteous; they shall inherit the land forever, the branch of my planting, the work of my hands, that I may be glorified." The Jews will become a new and righteous people and they will multiply and receive the blessings of GOD.

Chapter 61 has a description of the perceived class system.

Chapter 61:5, "And strangers shall stand and feed your flocks, and the sons of the alien shall be your plowmen and your vinedressers."

Chapter 61:6, "But ye shall be named the Priests of the LORD; men shall call you the Ministers of our God: ye shall eat the riches of the Gentiles, and in their glory shall ye boast yourselves."

Now contrast those promises with Jesus' Kingdom promises: "And he lifted up his eyes on his disciples, and said, 'Blessed be ye poor: for yours is the kingdom of God.'"[15]

God's Kingdom is for the poor. What is meant by the blessed poor? This refers to the poor in spirit. These are the people who abandon their wills for the Will of God. Brennan Manning wrote, "The poor man and woman of the gospel have made peace with their flawed existence. They are aware of their lack of wholeness, their brokenness, the simple fact that they don't have it all together. While they do not excuse their sin, they are humbly aware that sin is precisely what has caused them to throw themselves at the mercy of the Father. They do not pretend to be anything but what they are: sinners saved by grace."[16]

Manning continues, "Getting honest with ourselves does not make us unacceptable to God, but draws us to him - as nothing else can - and opens us anew to the flow of grace. While Jesus calls each of us to a more perfect life, we cannot achieve it on our own. To be alive is to be broken; to be broken is to stand in need of grace. It is only through grace that any of us could dare to hope that we could become more like Christ."[17]

What kind of Kingdom is this? The Pharisees speak of a coming age when the Gentile will be the slaves of the Jews, where the money of the Gentiles will belong to the Jews and where the Jews will be the super race and be blessed by God. Yet, Jesus speaks of a Kingdom which is not of this world, but of the spirit, and not for the elite, but for the poor in spirit. Jesus speaks of a Kingdom where men and women no longer wish to live by their will, but seek the Will of God. Jesus asks us to love God with all our hearts. Jesus asks us to repent from our sins, to actually go and sin no more. Jesus asks us to love our enemies. Jesus prays we will become one (as a family is one) so the world will know He and God are one. We should live within a spiritual family no longer ruled by the color of our skin, or the color of our eyes or our I.Q. or "how cool" we are, or how rich we are, or any other measure so attuned to our materialistic society, but to live by the profession that Jesus Christ is the Son of God and Lord of our lives. The Christian's task is to become more like Jesus and obey the Will of Abba, the Father. Realizing what is expected of those who join Jesus' Kingdom, one might ask: "Where is the value to such a Kingdom?" Jesus grants eternal life. That would definitely be a reason to join. But, for the moment, let us eliminate eternal life. Assuming there is no eternal life aspect, what great value would come from a spiritual kingdom which begins now while one is alive and breathing on planet earth? The answer reaches past what is normally considered Theology and consumes all philosophical meaning to the human experience.

IMPLICATIONS OF THE KINGDOM

Jesus' revolution was not against the Roman legion, but against the ways of man. Because of Jesus' Kingdom concept and other teachings, He has become recognized by many modern scholars as one of the most important philosophers in human history. As such, His concepts reach beyond His religious teachings. If He were not recognized for His deity, if He had been only a common man, He would still be acclaimed for His liberating philosophy. Arguably, His philosophical concepts have had a greater effect on planet earth than any others. Even intellectually honest atheists must recognize that profound changes in the human vision sprang forth from the words of Jesus. These momentous changes vary from the virtual ablution of slavery in many countries, to the massive expansion of private institutions such as hospitals and universities. Virtually all of the oldest of these institutions in the United States were founded by Christian churches or Christian foundations. Additionally, Christian missionaries were sent world wide. The goal was, for the glory of God, to bring medical care and literacy to all of humanity. For those who question the validity of Jesus' Biblical statements, the conceptualization of the Kingdom of God on earth would be a good place to begin an investigation. This one idea exemplifies the sophistication of Jesus' logos because intellectually the concept is well beyond the logic of a simple carpenter from the wilds of an ancient world. In fact, it would be too profound for even the brightest scholar of that era.

Furthermore, Jesus' philosophy brought forth an amazing change in government. Jesus lived in a world composed of slaves and masters. Even 'free men' without an aristocratic post were essentially slaves. And, the Roman Emperor was considered a god. As backward as the Roman structure seems, it was far advanced over previous empires. After the 'fall of Roman,' the human race would experience feudal governments, monarchies and aristocracies, etc. Had Jesus been teaching during the Renaissance He would have found His message was yet premature in terms of the mind set of humanity. Jesus' concept of human freedom had not yet had much effect on civil and political government. However, the human understanding of freedom as practiced today in democratic and republic forms of government came from the teachings of Jesus.

We can examine the concepts of liberty and equality as presented by Hegel, Locke, Hobbes, Nietzche and others. Though each of their understandings held unique features, as each held his own values, it seems apparent that all would have agreed on one thing. These, and many other 'great' philosophers, would concur that the foundation of liberty, freedom and equality, and thus democracy, come from the philosophy of Jesus of Nazareth. Hegel called Christianity the 'absolute religion.' This declaration was the result of the "objective historical relationship" between Christian doctrine and the "emergence of liberal democratic societies in Western Europe." In fact, this causal

---

VIRTUALLY ALL OF THE OLDEST OF THESE INSTITUTIONS IN THE UNITED STATES WERE FOUNDED BY CHRISTIAN CHURCHES OR CHRISTIAN FOUNDATIONS.

relationship went undisputed through many later philosophers including Weber and Nietzsche. According to Hegel, freedom received its "penultimate form" as a result of Christian doctrine because Christianity initiated the axiom that all men are equal "in the sight of God" in relation to their moral choices in life. It was this concept of freedom that launched a great change in life in mankind. Fukuyama emphasizes this understanding with the following: " . . . free not in the formal Hobbesian sense of freedom from physical constraint, but morally free to choose between right or wrong."[18]

According to Fukuyama, "Christian equality" is predicated on the understanding that "all men are equally endowed" with the faculty to make moral choices. "All men can accept or reject God, do good or evil . . . The Christian God recognizes all human beings universally, recognizes their individual human worth and dignity. The Kingdom of Heaven, in other words, presents the prospect of a world in which the isothymia of every man - though not the megalothymia of the vainglorious - will be satisfied."[19]

To this point in Fukuyama's discussion I am in total agreement. However, like so many others, Fukuyama misconstrued the logos of Jesus' philosophy. This is apparent as Fukuyama continued: "The problem with Christianity, however, is that it remains just another slave ideology, that is, it is untrue in certain crucial respects. Christianity posits the realization of human freedom not here on earth but only in the Kingdom of Heaven. Christianity, in other words, had the right concept of freedom, but ended up reconciling real-world slaves to their lack of freedom by telling them not to expect liberation in this life. According to Hegel, the Christian did not realize that God did not create man, but rather that man had created God."[20] Fukuyama's perception is focused by way of the same atheistic argument that man created God because man needed a crutch. The problem with this thinking is that Jesus did not intend His philosophy to be a passive concept. It was not proposed to be put aside except when we feel sorry for our situation or our pain or suffering. He did not intend for us to say to ourselves, "Just wait until my suffering is over. I will be in heaven in God's Kingdom." No! Jesus essentially said, "Do not wait until you die; join my Kingdom now!"

Thus, when one accepts Jesus Christ as the Lord he or she immediately enters 'The Kingdom' of Heaven, and immediately becomes an 'ambassador' for God's Kingdom. The message of the Kingdom is that God has a plan for the salvation of all man including the rich, including the poor, including the free, including the bound. Without accepting His plan, man is lost in his sin. This, of course, does not mean a Christian's life struggle over right and wrong is finished just because he or she inters the Kingdom. "And there is not

---

THE CHRISTIAN GOD RECOGNIZES ALL HUMAN BEINGS UNIVERSALLY, RECOGNIZES THEIR INDIVIDUAL HUMAN WORTH AND DIGNITY.

a single man in all the earth who is always good and never sins."[21] Furthermore, the Kingdom is not passive, but a liberating philosophy, and includes a new contract with God. The Biblical explanation follows:

The day will come, says the Lord, when I will make a new contract with the people of Israel and Judah. It won't be like the one I made with their fathers when I took them by the hand to bring them out of the land of Egypt - a contract they broke, forcing me to reject them (a covenant they broke, even though I cared for them as a husband does his wife), says the Lord.[22]

Thus came a new age and a new day. Jesus of Nazareth, by His words and deeds, fulfilled the Scripture and changed the world. From this metamorphose in human logos grew the essence of human freedom. When the French Revolution (1789–1799) began the democracy movement, Jesus' philosophy became the basic tenant for Western civilization. The foundational principle of democracy being the equality of man - "All men are created equal."

From this preclusion we intuitively know it is wrong to live extravagantly when there are those in need. We intuitively know it is wrong to force slavery on another person. We intuitively know we should do unto others as we would have done unto ourselves. Therefore, Jesus' is an active and liberating philosophy. And seen from the Hegelian understanding of history (history is a line of experience where trends are determined and time is unimportant), Christianity liberated the masses. Emancipation of the human condition is commonly perceived to be a result of the spread of the Christian philosophy.

D. James Kennedy, referring to Biblical times, writes:

Half of the population of the Roman Empire was slaves. Three fourths of the population of Athens was slaves. The life of a slave could be taken at the whim of the master. Over the centuries, Christianity abolished slavery, first in the ancient world and then later in the nineteenth century, largely through the efforts of the strong evangelical William Wilberforce. It didn't happen over-night, and certainly there have been dedicated Christians who were slave owners. Nonetheless, the end of slavery, which has plagued mankind for thousands of years, has come primarily through the efforts of Christians.[23]

Thus, Fukuyama, the antagonist is wrong. Jesus, the Son of God who died for man's sins, became the 'great liberator.' Jesus liberated not only in theological terms, but in ways unimaginable to first century man. The United States of America, more than any other land, has put Christian philosophy into practice. Yet, consider the United States today. The world's wealth has come to this nation. The greatest opportunities for the common person to achieve recognition and wealth has been in the United States. More people have pulled themselves out of poverty here than anywhere else in the world. Even those people considered to be 'poor' in the United States seem wealthy when compared to others around the world. No other country provides the food that ours does. No other country has as generous a population as does the United Sates. Yet, no other country in the world worships Jesus Christ as we do. So, Fukuyama, perhaps you failed to notice the bi-products of the Christian philosophy. There is nothing passive about Jesus or the things He taught.

Thus, I conclude this short discussion on Jesus of Nazareth. Was Jesus Lord God on earth? Was His life the one humanity, throughout the ages, seemed to have been waiting for? Was He the Messiah not only for the Jews but for all mankind? Was His life predicted by priests and soothsayers, kings and wise men from the earliest days of man until this day? I say He was. One thing is certain, Jesus asked a question which each of us must answer. He said, "Who do you say I am?" When pondering the life of Jesus, consider more than the proclaimed miracles in the Bible and the 'hero' symbolism represented throughout the history of the world that He fulfilled. Remember also the things we can witness today. Recognize the many ways Jesus has changed human civilization. Then ask yourself, "Who was this great man called Jesus?"

SECTION FIVE:

MODERN TIMES

CHAPTER 22

A GLANCE AT THE REVELATION

"They were singing him a new song with these words: 'You are worthy to take the scroll and break its seals and open it; for you were slain, and your blood has bought people from every nation as gifts for God. And you have gathered them into a kingdom and made them priests of our God; they shall reign upon the earth.'"[1]

A brutal headline in a Dallas newspaper read: "Man gets 75 years for killing woman; He beat her with a bat, then burned her body."[2] Does a headline like this shock you? Probably not. We have been so numbed by violence that such articles are only matters of curiosity. I remembered this headline, not because of the brutal violence, but because of the interesting circumstances surrounding it. In addition to what the article revealed about our societal conditioning, it also supported the gun advocate position that violence is not a product of guns, but of man. Nationally, the violent deaths caused by poisoning, clubbing, stabbing and other miscellaneous methods outnumber shootings. Yes, such violence is a product of the post-modern human soul, not weapons. Furthermore, the desolation of the soul seems to be reflected throughout all aspects of modern civilization.

Interestingly, this gory story was placed on page thirty of the Dallas paper. The big story of the day on the front page was *(football player Emmitt) Smith, (and Dallas) Cowboys agree on $13.6 million deal.*[3] What a great point these two stories made. I suggest this juxtaposition of headlines, i.e., the interest in a glamorous sports story over the brutal killing of another human being, is a great example of American society's distortion of priorities. Thus, sports is yet another indicator of this same shift in human values. According to Sports columnist Roger B. Brown, " . . . religion is the one element where sports has seemed to reflect a growing intolerance in society." To this regard, Michael Jordan, retired superstar for the Chicago Bulls, commented: "Today's society is more infatuated with the anti-hero . . . It's really weird how some people can be so wrongfully tagged. And it's kind of funny how we as a society seem to run away from religion." David Robinson, of the San Antonio Spurs, concurred: "I think this country is in a post-Christian era . . . People who are setting the laws now don't really believe in the same things that the people who founded this country did. It's like nobody wants to say Jesus anymore . . . like it's a bad word or something . . . Nowadays, everything is kind of twisted, just like the Bible talks about." (I assume this to be a reference to the Biblical 'last days' prophecies such as those found in *The Revelation* and other NT books).[4] Kurt Warner, quarterback for the St. Louis Rams and MVP of Super Bowl XXXIV, claims that he was told by Ram coaches, "his Bible reading was hurting his on-field performance."[5] If this is the case, I must ask: Are these coaches prejudiced against Christianity? Warner says he was reading the same Bible when he lead the Rams to a Super Bowl victory. Furthermore, some of the greatest football players in the history of the game have been strong Christians. Ex-Dallas Cowboy, Roger Staubach, is considered one of the greatest of quarterbacks to have played the game. Perhaps his best attribute was his ability to make big plays in big games—to complete the winning drive and pull out a victory. It is well known that Roger has a deep faith in Jesus Christ. I am sure he read his Bible. For about 20 years (the late 1960's, 70s and early 80's) the Dallas Cowboys and the Pittsburgh Steelers were two dominate teams in pro football. As Staubach was a big reason for the Cowboys winning tradition, Rocky Bleier was a major factor in the Steeler success. Bleier was critically wounded in Vietnam and should not have recovered. Some call his return to health 'miraculous.' Applying lessons from his Catholic upbringing, dedication and hard work allowed him to, once again, play football. Obviously, Bleier's 'can do' attitude was a major inspiration in building the Steelers' legacy. Great running back Gayle Sayers' holds the personal philosophy that, "The Lord is first; my family and friends are second; I am third."[6] Mike Singletary, one of the hardest hitting linebackers in the history of football, is also a devoted Christian and often speaks of his love for his savior.

I mentioned these specific players because they are all inspired dedicated men of God and seemed to have advanced beyond their abilities. It is hard to believe that Warner's reading the Bible hurt his game. Some of the most honored coaches in football were also dedicated Christians. Tom Landry, Vince Lombardi and Knute Rockne were all men of faith. Lineman Mike Connelly of the Dallas Cowboys and the Pittsburgh Steelers was one of my inspirations. Mike played both center and guard but was very small for a professional lineman. Yet, he played nine years in the National Football League. Needles to say, he was (and is) an extremely tough man with an unrelenting dedication to all that he does. For several years, while I was in high school, Connelly and other professional players from various teams worked out at a Dallas YMCA weight room. Each gave me pointers about preparing for the game and inspiration to be a better player and person. It was Mike Connelly who introduced me to Fellowship of Christian Athletes. Certainly, a book could be written about many players and coaches with motivational stories founded on the strength they received through a relationship with God. However, the comments of Michael Jordan, David Robinson and Kurt Warner seem to be confirmed daily. Rayfield Wright is one of the greatest lineman in the history of football. However, he has been excluded from the NFL Hall of Fame. Rayfield was a member of Fellowship of Christian Athletes and I can attest to the fact that his relationship with Jesus Christ is the most important thing in his life. I have watched him show young athletes a Super Bowl ring as he witnessed about his love for Christ and his dedication to God's Will. One must wonder if his 'God centered life' has kept him out of the Hall of Fame. As a pro player, he had no weaknesses. He was the best in the game on one of the greatest teams to have ever been assembled. I doubt anyone in sports would say otherwise. Why would this magnificent player be excluded from his rightful place in football unless it is his religion?

To further demonstrate this change in attitude in our country, a federal court has ruled that the National Pledge of Allegiance must be banned from public schools. The ban is a result of the pledge's language—more *specifically,* the word "God." Such a judicial decision would have been outrageous just a few years ago. Yet, today our historic philosophical connection with the divine Creator is methodically being severed. In fact, if you were to start a conversation with a friend and bring up the point that we are "one nation under God" you might start an argument. I believe these examples point to a cause and effect relationship. As we have isolated God from an ever greater portion of our society, we have also realized an increase in violence, fraud and deceit. Thus, we have changed the environment which nourished our success. As explained in Chapter 21, we are the product of Jesus' Kingdom of God concept. Furthermore, if God's Will reigns over the universe, then we must consider the possibility that we have been shielded by God from many of the problems which have plagued other countries around the world. If such is the case, then I would assume that such divine protection might be related to our forefathers adoption of godly principles. From the historical eye, our forefathers acknowledged divine guidance, and prophesized that our country would challenge the morals of the world. For example, John Adams stated: "I always consider the settlement of America with reverence and wonder, as the opening of a grand scene and design in providence, for the illumination of the ignorant and the emancipation of the slavish part of mankind all over the earth."[7] These are very bold words from our second President. Moreover, this is absolute proof that people 'high up' in this experimental government, desired the abolition of slavery, not only in our country, but around the world. Other founding fathers voiced similar expressions. For Example, Thomas Jefferson stated, "I have sworn upon the altar of Almighty God eternal hostility against every form of tyranny over the mind of man."[8]

AS WE HAVE ISOLATED GOD FROM AN EVER GREATER PORTION OF OUR SOCIETY, WE HAVE ALSO REALIZED AN INCREASE IN VIOLENCE, FRAUD AND DECEIT.

Such intellectual valiance exalted our nation. The Biblical view is well expressed by the following: "Righteousness exalts a nation, but sin is a reproach to any people."[9] Biblically, the Church is considered to be preserving 'salt.' In a related matter, God states to His followers, "In everything you do, put God first, and he will direct you and crown your efforts with success."[10] Other powerful countries once held this symbolic 'salt' in high regard and later willfully eliminated its influence. Arguably, all such societies suffered great hardships and experienced major internal struggles. Those which have endured this decay lost personal freedoms as well as economic and military influence. Example countries are scattered throughout Europe. Again, we can read the words of Adams warning of such folly: "Remember, democracy never lasts long. It soon wastes, exhausts, and murders itself. There never was a democracy yet that did not commit suicide."[11] Adams further explained his position in another quote: "We have no government armed in power capable of contending with human passions unbridled by morality and religion. Our Constitution was made only for a religious and moral people. It is wholly inadequate for the government of any other."[12] Thus, I suggest, the success of the United States of America is a result of the spiritual direction of our country. More to apropos to Divine Authoritarianism as related to this above reasoning, the United States is circumstantial evidence that God is proactive in world affairs.

So, why would God allow suffering and human destruction? To this quagmire of a question, consider the earlier dichotomy: either God exists or God does not exist. Regarding the first possibility, we have reasoned that if there is no God then there is no explanation for existence. The best conclusion would seem that we are here by chance. Of course, suffering is a factor of existence. Therefore, if God does not exist, suffering has no real meaning because life itself has no meaning. From the scientific point of view, there are only various forms of matter and energy. Perhaps in its reduced state, matter is only a sophisticated form of energy. So, considering this true value reference, there are no differences between matter and energy, or even matter and a vacuum. Without an existence designed by God, these words are but meaningless divisions; nothing has an intrinsic rudimentary value. Can we sincerely propose that there is any objective difference in anything? Without God, nothing meaningful exists.

There is a more pragmatic view of this position which eliminates the cold dark phenomenal understanding. It is an existential interpretation of life. From our subjective position, we do exist and we have a conscience; therefore, we (humans) will judge reality. In a real sense, if God does not exist, our superior consciousness or 'thymos' (in the collective understanding - that spiritedness which distinguishes us from animals) makes us gods. Thus, we will make all the rules of life. Through thymos, we will continue to explore and conceive all that is and all that will be. Yet, if we are without a supernatural God, it is the superior man's responsibility to minimize pain, suffering and violence. Humanity must act according to this authoritative obligation.

Interestingly, the human thymos is not only responsible for human achievements of greatness, but is also accountable for much of the world's pain, suffering and violence. One of the most bizarre, yet, reflective probe into the 'evils,' resulted from man trying to become liberated from God. It came in Marquis de Sade's concept, "utopia of evil." De Sade demanded the freedom to experience the ultimate in decadence through the wildest of human perversions. What he found was a trenchant dark side of humanness. In this regard, what has been our experience with such unrestrained power? What has this human dark side done for existence? The Holocaust is an example of said fruits. We know of no examples of such aberrant rationalism in the non-human world. Thus, the Holocaust was beyond the scope of animal behavior and fits in the realm of perversion. The rulers of Nazi Germany, through 'empirical experiments,' claimed to had 'scientifically proven' the superiority of the Aryan race. Thus, they rationalized that killing or enslaving all other races was the right thing to do. Though we tend to consider this a unique inhumane action directed and choreographed by one perverted individual (Hitler), history presents many similar illustrations of human wickedness. Some obvious illustrations are the violence of the ancient Aztecs, the 'evil empire' of the USSR and recently, the warped logic of Osma bin Laden and the Taliban government of Afghanistan. This radical persuasion of an authoritarian religion finds it heroic to destroy innocent men and women, boys and girls. Obviously, God created all people for His purposes. Yet these self-chosen executioners of God's creatures rationalize that they kill for Allah or God. In so doing, they take the place of God. Would not this be the ultimate in blaspheme? Any thinking person must see the perversion in such actions. There are many other societies which provide further proofs. In fact, this evil factor is found within virtually every human society. The United States of America is no exception. Gang violence, for example, is derived from the same dark side of human (thymos) consciousness.

In the Hegelian proposition, 'humanness' is determined by one's capacity to risk his or her life for recognition. If this is true, one irrefutable mission of the humanism must be to discover a formula that will enable society to control the dark regions of thymos. Philosophers conclude we must find a way to bring recognition to human beings without risking violence.

But, if we do learn to control thymos in a peaceful manner, we will not have done much to solve the comprehensive problem because, when it

---

WHAT HAS THIS HUMAN DARK SIDE DONE FOR EXISTENCE?
THE HOLOCAUST IS AN EXAMPLE OF SAID FRUITS.

comes to violence, humans are only a part of the problem. Though animals do not contemplate genocide for the sake of purifying their species as the radical Muslims are doing, virtually all animals either kill for food or are hunted for food. Therefore, it is fair to say that we 'human gods' will never be able to solve the problem of pain, suffering and violence until we find a comprehensive solution which reaches all life forms. Moreover, if thymos is indeed founded on one's capacity to risk life for recognition, and thymos is that which separates us from the rest of the animal kingdom, then would the final solution to pain, suffering and violence be a human induced massive genocide of all life forms? If humans are gods because of a willingness to risk one's life for recognition or glory, then the calculated extermination of all life is the ultimate solution to pain, suffering and violence. Thus, extermination of all life is the magnanimous thing for us to do.

From yet another introspective position, total genocide would bring finality to the ever-occurring myth. It is the finishing of the 'divine mystery.' And, it shall make us whole—a man made resurrection from a world of decay. We will rise from the ashes of our physical frailties and shattered dreams and take our place on the plane of divine will. Now history will end by the hands of a new hero. This introspection and grandiosity of self-power may be the cause of many suicides and mass murders.

In truth, (if there is no God) recognition is a relative measurement discerned by humanness, for we (in arrogant deduction) are the only ones who 'know.' Therefore, the genocide of all life would bring us self recognition. We would know that we solved (perhaps permanently) our elemental problem. Only without life could there be a universe without pain, suffering or violence. Some would argue that we do not hold the moral capacity to make such a choice. The issue is greater than the human 'god' can allow, as we would also be the life form that brought about destruction of all life forms. If Hitler was unjust to command the extermination of a race (or a number of races), it would surely be unjust for a species to willfully eliminate all life. But, if there is no God, Hitler was right! Hitler was powerful enough to determine what was right in the world he conquered. And, if there is no God, Hitler was the closest human to achieving a 'god' status, because Hitler risked his life for much glory and came close to ruling the entire world. In this rational (philosophical) understanding, genocide of life is the ultimate solution. Total genocide overshadows one race or one religion over all others. Total genocide eliminates all problems. So, we now deliberate a higher level of moral conflict - one destined for the hands of some grand being.

On the other hand, if God does exist, perhaps God, too, has a plan for the extinction of pain, suffering and violence. Perhaps God's holiness is, in some way, based upon His ability to bring justice to His creation. If God destroyed His physical creation—that part of creation which quantum theory allows to be compared to Toonville—not only would there be meaning to the extinction of life, but there could be meaning to life after extinction. Perhaps this, in part, is what makes God God. Perhaps God will destroy pain, suffering and violence and all other obscenities, of which the human species might find some delight, at just the right time and in the right way, while allowing consciousness to continue in either a nonphysical or an altered physical realm. If this is Truth, then again, we find a deeper meaning to life's struggles; an omnipotent God is determining that which is Truth and reality. His creation, His validation of Truth and any salvation from the 'evils of the flesh,' would be based upon God's Will.

In regard to salvation, human beings hold at least one related intuition. Humanity seems to have a common understanding about the end times. We intuitively know, if there was a beginning there will be an end. Virtually all cultures, from ancient to modern man, have held end times myths or legends. If you will recall, this intellection is where I began my book. I discussed some of the fears I held as a college history major. I was and continue to be frustrated with the mindset of some of the militaristic countries holding horrific weaponry. Reading and trying to understand *The Revelation of The Bible* brought an unrestrained peace to my life and greater understanding of the wisdom of God. Through Biblical studies, I found confidence in God's plan for the end of life as we know it. I feel I also understand why we are in the state that we find ourselves in today and why it is necessary for God to 'conduct business' as He does. I am not a Revelationist who sets dates for both the destruction of the earth and the return of Jesus Christ. I do, however, expect *The Revelation* to come to pass–to be fulfilled, and I wait for Jesus' triumphant return.

IS THE UNITED STATES OF AMERICA PREPARED

I wish to convey my concern for my country, the United States of America. It is my personal belief that the United States of old stood for great rights and virtuous freedoms. I believe the USA was ordained by God and our fundamental concepts were spiritually inspired.

Furthermore, the true historic record of our country is yet another proof of God. When one examines the early history of the United States of America, it becomes obvious that we were a society based on a belief in God. The record demonstrates that God protected and nurtured our country. So important is this bond to our way of life that even an atheist who enjoys the liberties granted by our great nation should support its theistic foundation. The most used American tenet about religion and government is the misused tenet of 'Freedom of Religion.' The intent of this doctrine was not to afford government a way to do away with public prayer or worship or displays of thanksgiving, because such expressions have been common expressions of our society from the beginning of our national heritage. In fact, the First Amendment to the Constitution allows for "free exercise" of expression. Then, what was the intent of Freedom of Religion? 'Freedom of Religion' was a premeditated declaration forbidding government from supporting one religion over another. Our ancestors had suffered from the problems of state based religion in England. In like manner, today we recognize a number of limitations and excesses generated by state-based religions in the middle east.

Yet, on the other hand, our forefathers realized that the foundation of God was very much needed if the country was to survive. Thus, the backbone of the Declaration of Independence rests on the perception that human beings are "endowed by their Creator with certain unalienable Rights . . ." The architect, Thomas Jefferson, appealed to certain Biblical claims such as the equality of man.[13] Only through God will human rights become absolutes. Without the recognition of a Creator, all such rights become subjective to the whelms of government. As we have already confirmed through philosophy, a strong dictator could 'revolutionize' or do away with subjective rights. Thus, if there is a love for freedom, both the atheist and the God-fearing man should stand together in favor of divine absolute rights for man.

One reason we have no king is that Thomas Paine and others declared that God is our king. Paine wrote, "But where, say some, is the king of America? I'll tell you, friend, he reigns above, and doth not make havoc of mankind like the royal brute (king) of Great Britain." Paine continued by stating more practically that our divinely inspired law is king–divine law, absolute law.[14] Thus, through divine law and the Biblically referenced equality of man, the United States holds the position that all men are equal in the sight of the law and all men hold certain rights by the declaration of our Creator. No one is above the law as the law is absolute. No one can abolish the rights of man, because the rights of man are from God.

The USA has always experienced problems. However, our problems stem primarily from human politics and prejudices and not from the spirit of the law. Our founders were on the right track. Work within this godly system and stand for virtuous causes, right wrongs, strengthen weaknesses and build a future of goodness and greatness. Based in part on historical resolutions (including those discussed above), I thought of the United States as a great light to the world. My exact term was "God's Protectorate." As long as we sought the values of a godly nation, i.e., the right to search for truth, hold the freedoms of a moral society and maintain an underlying belief in God, God would bless us and allow us to continue to work within the human system–for the good of humanity. It is my sincere belief that, through God's blessings, we

---

ONE REASON WE HAVE NO KING IS THAT THOMAS PAINE AND
OTHERS DECLARED THAT GOD IS OUR KING.

hold the opportunity to pull the entire world out of decay. We were humanity's greatest chance and last chance to build a loving and God fearing world. One might counter that there is nothing occurring between God and the United States. In fact, the country is a secular nation, not a theocracy.

Interestingly, about 2000 years ago, Jesus prophesied that there would be a 'time of the Gentiles.' It would endure until 'the end times.' [15] Because the United States of America is secular, we would be defined as a Gentile nation based in Christian philosophy. It is interesting that our Gentile nation is the strongest country in the world. We are considered the world's lone superpower. As discussed earlier, this prestige was built on our Christian foundation. In fact, our population's most common prayer is most probably "God bless America."

In an attempt to understand how America's Christian heritage has interfaced with national secularism, let us consider several historical events. Arguably, the United States' most conspicuous moral problem involved its struggle with slavery. Yet, I remind the reader of the above John Adams quote regarding a moral conscience in our founding leadership, the belief in a divine quidance and the beginning of the end of slavery in America. Our nation has always gone to God in prayer. As with the slavery issue, the United States has historically endeavored to maintain moral values and forge a common national relationship with God. Internationally, we have generally treated our friends and enemies with compassion, generosity and judicial fairness. For example, recall the horrors of Nazi Germany. Consider the shock of our parents and grandparents when they realized the world was falling into the hands of another Nero. Freedom was quickly fading from the world and an ominous wake up alarm came in the form of massive deaths of unwanted peoples. The frightening reality is that a mad-man was extremely close to becoming the sole ruler on planet earth. He was perhaps one atom bomb away, and he was feverishly working on that bomb. Many people thought that Hitler was certainly the Antichrist referenced in 1 & 2 John, *The Revelation,* etc., in the Bible. Fortunately, a foundationally evil Nazi world was defeated by a foundationally good society. However, did Hitler hold a spiritual message for humanity?

I believe that the resurrection myths which circulated the world before and after Jesus of Nazareth were intuitive expressions of the collective unconscious–synchronistic signposts calling attention to one factual resurrection - The Resurrection of Jesus, the Christ. In like manner, Hitler, Stalin and others were divine warnings and synchronistic messages to humanity of a coming man who will gain power over a united world government. Hitler forewarned us of the perils of tomorrow. Like 'birth pains,' such tyrants have become more prevalent bringing higher apocalyptic threats of danger to our globe. Today's tyrants hold nuclear weapons, poisonous gasses and deadly viruses. Unlike the days of the super power's standoff of 'Mutual Destruction' when no one thought either side would take a chance and use these horrific weapons, most everyone today believes modern terrorists will not hesitate to ignite a super weapon. In addition, rogue nations like Iran and North Korea have developed or are developing such weapons. Unlike the defunct Soviet Union, the latest members around the Weapons of Mass Destruction (WMD) table seem to be less stable while more extreme. Furthermore, as the list of countries with such weapons grows, the threat of a nuclear war increases logarithmically.

THE UNITED STATES BECOMES A SUPER POWER

In World War II, the United States of America procured weapons of war at a much greater rate than the world could have hoped for. We surprised the Germans. We surprised the Britains. We even surprised ourselves. As liberated people lined the streets to watch the Allied forces roll through, they seemed amazed at the 'big guns' and the great numbers of our weaponry. (Remember, they had also seen the German's weaponry roll through). Had we not produced weapons at the unbelievable level which we did, World War II would have brought even greater devastation than it did and we may have lost our civilization to the mad man, Hitler.

I cannot imagine the fear of the day and the shocking reality of what a victorious Nazism would bring to planet earth. I recall discussions with my father about Hitler's visit to the 1937 Olympics, his snubbing of Jessie Owens and his obvious disgust with Jesse's day of triumph. People thought Hitler was arrogantly crass with Jessie. But, few really understood the seriousness of the message Hitler bore that portentous day. After the defeat of Nazi Germany, the severity of Hitler's Aryan message did come through loud and clear. The real horror hit home with pictures from Hitler's death camps. It was such a gruesome sight! Prisoners were deliberately starved and dehydrated . . . a Nietzscheian comment of the hideously obscene. The death camp victims found still alive were only alive because of their personal will to live! When I was a teenager, my father reluctantly allowed me to view historic pictures of the liberation of these grossly tortured human beings. I feel compelled to reiterate James Cantelon's thoughts on this atrocity:

> *I believe that the greatest sufferer in the awful carnage of the Holocaust was God himself. He loves Israel as a father. As a mother wails at the suffering of her children, so God sorrows at Jacob's troubles. And more so. For I think he suffers in proportion to his magnitude, as a mother suffers more than the sick or dying child she holds in her arms.*[16]

Words cannot relate nor depict the spiritual pain of those dreadful times . . . times seething with devastation, death, hatred, and gross injustices. Never before had such wickedness been brought to the world consciousness. However, when this war was over, under the auspicious leadership of United States, the allied nations did something unprecedented in the history of the world. We not only forgave our enemies, but we lifted them from their defeated and devastated state. There may have been political reasons or secret agendas or alternative motives behind our efforts but, the fact is, we were for-giving. In another period of history, the Germans, Italians and Japanese would have become slaves. They would have been taken from their homelands, put in chains and paraded through the streets of Washington D.C. Many would have been slaughtered. Those who remained would have lost all they owned and lived the rest of their lives as chattel. The USA, England and other allied nations would have occupied, divided up and owned Germany, Italy and Japan. Perhaps the Allies would have continued to press the war into the Soviet Union. Certainly, some of our military leaders were in favor of such an extended campaign. But, we are not a war-loving people. We are a peace-loving people and we forgave our enemies and went on with life. I believe God blessed us for our compassion. I think He smiled over the results of that conflict. In fact, He predetermined the results of that conflict.

From time to time, we have injected our foreign policy into areas which should have been off limits and, thus, we have made shameful agree-ments. But what major world power hasn't? Which dictator is better to work with, the one in power or the one who would replace the one in power? This is the type of question our leaders have had to ask. As a student during the Vietnam war, I experienced a personal confrontation: What should I do about the war? I agreed with our defense of South Vietnam. Though South Vietnam was governed by a corrupt government, it was not communistic and, during that time, communism was our greatest threat to freedom. Yet, like so many others, I had misgivings about the 'special' rules of combat. American troops put their lives in 'harms way' but could not properly defend against insurgent aggression. Nor could American forces properly aggress their adversary. Yet, contrary to the views of those who have been too blind to see the 'Big Picture,' there was a very strong moral reason to fight the conflict. We were fighting against 'human wickedness' and protecting the Judaic/Christian phi-losophy of moral freedoms for all mankind. Whatever the actual political rea-soning for the Vietnam conflict, constructive freedom was what the American troops defended. This included the freedom to seek and share a relationship with the Creator.

In years past, I placed a picture on my wall which was very disturb-ing to many of my friends. The picture was taken as the American military forces were pulling out of Vietnam. In the picture, two Vietnamese women held a crucifix up in the air. The women were crying and begging to be taken out of their country. The symbolism of this picture was quite obvious. If these ladies were Christian and were left behind, their fates were sealed. They died! All inhabitants, who were Christian or openly believed in God, were to be killed. If that sounds unbelievable, visitors to the region have claimed the victorious communists purged their countries of all 'western influences.' This included all freedoms and was one of many historic proofs that, without God, subjective freedom is tentative at best. Again, massive genocide was the preferred solution of a society turned evil. In similar fashion, the leaders of Cambodia killed every man, woman and child who had gone to school, if even for a day! 30,000 to 50,000 skulls were piled in one place as a sign to the people, denoting the seriousness of their oppression. They were to obey! They were dehumanized and conditioned to exist as property of the state. They were to ingest only ideals approved by their owner—the state. To these brutal masters, there was no such thing as human freedom primarily because there was no power greater than the state. God did not matter because they were atheists.

The 60's brought in a 'New Age.' We witnessed 'love-ins,' demonstrations, the birth of 'mind-expanding' drugs, the consciousness movement, the institutionalization of subjective thinking, and a 'new music' that seemed to search and expand the human psyche. In religion, we saw the dawning of the age of Humanism with an injection of Eastern mysticism. The message of the young was, "Look at the mess our parents are leaving us!" The word for the day was experimentation. Everything was open to change

Some of what grew out of this period was good. People began to love one another and accept one another, without regard to race, color or creed. However, had the Christian church worked within this avenue, perhaps they would have united the entire Christian family of God. In union, Christianity might have better addressed our most pressing social problems. Moreover, the Christian movement could have triggered the spiritual revolution that is so desperately needed by our world. However, the Christian body failed to recognize the opportunity facing them and lost the momentum of that day.

A relevant argument opposing this view might be 'only God can begin a spiritual revolution.' I will agree with this proposition. However, Jesus prayed that Christians would be one (as in a union) so the world would know that He and the Father were one. I think He was telling us (Christians, in particular) something very important about how we should live. But, Christians in the USA are neither hot nor cold.[17] As a result, we have 'lost many souls' and watched numerous people suffer needlessly. In fact, we continue to allow our morals to be compromised and our religious freedoms constricted. As the overwhelming majority, we have failed to stand for the values our fathers

IN FACT, WE CONTINUE TO ALLOW OUR MORALS TO BE COMPROMISED
AND OUR RELIGIOUS FREEDOMS CONSTRICTED.

placed at our feet. Thus, I fear, those 'days of the Gentile' are about over. Our moral society rots before us. Our media has failed us badly. The 'free press' is dead. Instead of thoughtfully reporting issues, we ingest a media's propagandized fantasy. Instead of adding value to our society, the media adds trash. Because of moral apathy, television mesmerizes us with human filth. Our computers bring new accesses to the exploitation of human frailties. Internet adult clubs and web pages promote every kind of sexual promiscuity. Additionally, illegal sexual activities are found on 'the net' such as child pornography and bestiality. Through the guise of human freedom, we find alluring addictions and temptations; perhaps the seduction of the dark side is too great a match for human decency. Thus, the unthinkable may be approaching. The end times ooze across our land and fill our cities with waste and decay. The time may soon come when the United States of America will fall from within. Darkness loots us of our prosperity and morality. As was the case in ancient Rome, "Our glory is fleeting." It is amazing how fast our beloved country is moving from a moral buttress in a world of depravity to a world model for moral bankruptcy. We join the world in darkness. The artists (Pretenders) sing:

> *Welcome to the human race,*
> *with its wars, disease and brutality . . .*
> *You, with your innocence and grace,*
> *with still some pride and dignity - to a world in decline.*[18]

American children fill the streets with cadaverous blood. Public schools preach existential humanism while many teachers expound upon the ideals of the godless. Scores of women have debased their souls by killing the unborn child nestled in their womb. Oligopolies and monopolies (the true expressions of American diversity) prey upon a 'new and improved' American society. Some Industrial chiefs pilfer their companies and leave penniless employees and stockholders in their wake, holding no regard for the sorrow that awaits these broken lives. Sexual promiscuity has become the practice of the day. Young children have been abducted, molested and, sometimes, killed for the joys of unfettered sex. While numerous 'celibate' male priests molest alter boys, major U.S. corporations protest the moral decision of the Boy Scouts to disallow homosexual scoutmasters. Moreover, this evolving politically correct culture is exterminating our freedom of expression, even in our worship. In the name of tolerance, the Holy Bible is becoming known as 'hate speech.' Canada has already declared that the scriptural arguments against a

---

IN THE NAME OF TOLERANCE, THE HOLY BIBLE IS BECOMING KNOWN AS 'HATE SPEECH.'

homosexual lifestyle are to be prosecuted as hate crimes. Thus, we might assume that, in some future date, such laws will be passed in the United States. Thus, if God gave awards for stupid people, we, the proponents of liberty, we, the abundantly blessed, might take first place.

Where is the spirit of loving one another? Where is the value of life? Where is the honor of the virgin who waits? What happened to the Boy Scout who does at least one good turn daily? Where is a virtuous hero? Are these now myths in a post-modern world? Does their passing signify the death of a moral society? Are the freedoms for which SHE once stood on their way to illegality - like a prayer or a pledge in a public school? Is this the liberty that our ancestors fought and struggled for? Or, is this a hellhound intent on doing us in?

A PARADOX ON PLATO'S ALLEGORY OF THE CAVE

Once upon a time, or perhaps it was today, the American people were ravished by the filth of a false reality and exploited by the Elite in a cave called Hollywood. In the old days, about 1965, the Elitists of a dark underground community, working together in complete harmony, began to seduce common men, women, boys and girls. Slowly but surely, say for 30 plus years, they led common folk down cave Hollywood to a specially arranged pit in the darkest and deepest cavern. In one corner was a large fire. In front of the fire sat rows of mesmerized common people, enslaved by the Elitists' seduction. The captives had their backs to the fire. They wore blinders and were bound in such a way that they could not see the fire behind them nor the other slaves to either side. All they could see was the cave wall directly in front of them. The light from the fire illuminated the wall and the slaves would sit for hours at a time watching the wall. Before too long, the laminated wall was the only thing that these people knew. Elitists' symbols of beautiful gods and goddesses were made and the shadows of these symbols would dance on the walls. Thus, the symbols become the people's reality. Meanwhile, the Elitists merrily took their drugs and changed partners in search of another high. Even the Elite continue to search for happiness because happiness does not come from owning everything.

New ideas for perverted pleasures were needed! By now the Elite had enslaved the common folk through mind control so they could play wicked games with the innocent young common children to see how perverted they become. One of the Elite sang "Girls just want to have fun" and let young boys covet her nakedness (in living color). Other Elite joined her wall of lust and produced a special performance; call it Sodomy and Glamora. The chil-

---

ONCE UPON A TIME, OR PERHAPS IT WAS TODAY, THE AMERICAN PEOPLE WERE RAVISHED BY THE FILTH OF A FALSE REALITY AND EXPLOITED BY THE ELITE IN A CAVE CALLED HOLLYWOOD.

dren began to emulate what they saw—in the name of 'intellectualism.' Some of the shyest girls were not ready for 'everything.' So, the excited boys raped them as a human sacrifice of innocence. And, girls searching for freedom learned to kill their unborn babies. (This perversion is especially gratifying to the power hungry Elite. Who would have thought girls would kill their own children? Perhaps anything is possible!) NOW, the Elites proclaim, girls and boys can have sex without consequences. After all, don't they have the right? And the children shout, "Oh hail Hollywood. We praise your glittering fires. Lead us to the pit, for we want to watch the wild dance. We want to feel like dogs in heat. Fill us with your Carnal Knowledge. Show us your symbol of the young stud Doogie Howser, for we are the young and the restless. Tell us, goddess Candice (Bergen), how we should live the new way, without the traditional family approval—for you know so much." Of course, the goddess Candice was born an Elitist, so she really didn't know anything about common life. She only knew the joys of the hedonistic Elite and the perversions of the cave called Hollywood. There was some question whether the common people were really brainwashed to the point where they would mind the Elite, 'no matter what.' So, the Elites allowed the common people to periodically pick a leader the Elites could control. But, of course, the Elites know who can best serve. So, one Elite (lets call her Barbara) sings God Bless America to show her sincerity, and arrogantly scolds, "If you slime balls don't pick the one I command, then I'm 'outta here' for England. Then, you cannot watch my symbol any more." Other Elite joined her commands by shouting, "We'll be outta here too! And, we're taking our kids." (Perhaps that is not arrogance, but is only an expression of the power of the cave).

This story should have ended with the common people relegated to slavery to the Elitists. Although they would know the perverse symbols, they were, in fact, real slaves, trained to be the gladiators of perversions. These slaves would have been toys for the Elite ever after, had it not been for a stubborn group of common people in the back of the cavern. They never did like the symbols or the walls. So they kept asking, "What is real and where is the Real Light? We must find our way back to Real Light. We want to feel the warmth of the Sun of God." So, they escaped and found their way back to the mouth of the cave. And at the mouth they stepped out of darkness into the Sun's Light. Everything was so beautiful. Words could not express their feelings. The Real Light was so much brighter and more beautiful then anything they had seen for as long as they could remember. And now they understood so much more than the people left below in the cave. They recalled that 'Freedom's not just another word for nothing left to do.' They could not allow the accesses of the Elitists to enslave those who seek the Light. The lesson: Our society must ardently demand access to Truth and limit our exposure to filth if we are going to be wise enough to know the true reality of our existence—the Ultimate Reality of the universe. Isolating God and His Will from our society is certainly not the way of the wise. It is the road to destruction. And, accepting the filth of the Elitists is not staying within the Will of the Father.

I suggest the United States' movie and television entertainment industry as well as the related news media sources make up the most pretentious elitist society in the history of our world. Corrupt Hollywood influences are not limited to the filth they produce. Their influence goes much deeper. It seems most elitists habitually defile their lives to the point that they are no longer capable of understanding human values. Perhaps, the individual elitists are ignorant about morality and do not understand that their values are skewed when they entice the public with their perversion.

French philosopher, Pierre Klossowski, in evaluating Marquis de Sade, stressed that, in order for de Sade's plan for an evil utopia to become viable, he would need thought controls. Klossowski wrote, "There is in the course of the Revolution a period of collective incubation during which the first transgressions the masses commit can make one think that the people have become open to all kinds of adventures. This period of psychic regression, which turns out to be quite temporary, plunges libertine minds into a sort of euphoria: there is some chance that the most daring elaborations of individual thought will be put into practice."[19]

It seems Marquis de Sade was correct. In fact, today, de Sade has his 'incubator' for violence and promiscuous sex. Television, movies, video games and other modern wonders have become thought control tools and validate de Sade's proposition. Not only have these proven to be superb forms of "collective incubation," but today, we have documented the progressive intensification of "daring elaborations" and a resulting "period of psychic regression." To this regard, there have been over 3,500 studies investigating the relationship between "media violence and violent behavior." All except 18 have indicated that there is a corresponding relationship.[20]

Among the organizations supporting these (violence and the media) conclusions are The National Commission of the Causes and Prevention of Violence, The Surgeon General's Scientific Advisory Committee on Television and Social Behavior, The National Institute of Mental Health, The American Psychological Association, The American Academy of Pediatrics, The American Academy of Child and Adolescent Psychiatry, The American Psychological Association, The American Medical Association, The American Academy of Family Physicians and The American Psychiatric Association.[21]

Viewing such activities in a controlled environment has numbed the masses to what, in earlier days, would have been considered out-of-control perversion. Thus, violence and sexual impropriety have become part of our way of life. Through the wonders of movies and television programming, we have witnessed the glorifying of such perverse activities as ultra-violence, illicit sex, drugs and virtually every obscenity of both word and deed known to man. Thus, our society seems to grow more violent and perverse on a daily bases. The National Association of Secondary Schools' position statement on "violence and destructive behavior in the media and entertainment industry," states: "The entertainment industry plays an important role in fostering destructive behavior by promoting instant gratification; glorifying casual sex, alcohol, tobacco and drug use; and encouraging the use of profanity, violence, killing, and racial and sexual stereotyping.[22] Robert Peters, of Morality in Media, writes that there is "a mountain of anecdotal evidence, often found in local newspaper accounts of crimes, which indicates that viewing antisocial behavior on film, TV or a video/computer game or listening to antisocial behavior being extolled in music or RAP lyrics negatively affect many young people." Peters concludes, "Finally, there is a mountain of social science research showing a link between viewing anti-social behavior on TV and real life anti-social behavior."[23]

The destruction of values through movie and television programming is obvious. To understand this truism, one only has to compare modern television 'family programming' with that of years gone by. Consider the differences in television portrayal of the family on television today, i.e., the Simpsons, etc., with the programs of the past such as Ozzie and Harriet, Leave It To Beaver or Father Knows Best.

In a recent study, the Henry J. Kaiser Family Foundation found sexual content on television has "significantly increased." Of the 1,114 programs considered between October 1999 to March 2000, two thirds of these programs "featured" sexual content, where "only about half" did in the same period in 1997–1998.[24] I am sure a study contrasting sexual content today and fifteen years ago would be even more skewed.

Though representatives of the media often categorically deny that they hold such powers, it is obvious they, in fact, do understand the awesome psychological forces at their command. Moreover, similar to de Sade's proposal, media elite intentionally use these forums to condition the masses. As an example, Daniel Lipman, the producer of Showtime's explicit program "Queer as Folk," reportedly stated: "The sexuality on our show is extremely important. Probably the most political statement that we make on the show [is] showing gay men and women having sex."[25]

In step with de Sade's decadent strategy, the Elitists encourage idolizing fans to destroy those things which make life significant. As one blatant example, recall television history: Candice Bergen declared that Vice-President Dan Quail was wrong when he proposed that two parent families were the most advantageous for children. As many watched in disbelief, Bergen marched unwed mothers across the television screen and led the viewers to believe children do not need their daddies and, in fact, were better off without men around the house. The media gaily celebrated her message on all channels. Apparently the vice president was wrong because an Elite personality said so. And, in slave-like manner, the American people bought it. The American people embraced Bergen's wisdom and ridiculed the Vice-President. Though a number of psychologists were aghast by the harmful nature of this position and spoke out against this Bergen, they were not heard. The media ignored the professionals and defended the Elite 'goddess.' In step with the Marquis de Sade's blueprint for a perverted world, the networks only aired the Elitist's twisted message. But, how many lives did this demonstration ruin? We see the aftermath of Bergen's position. It is common knowledge that the majority of men and women who are in prison for acts of violence come from broken homes. American streets are filled with gangs and the large majority of both the boys and girls involved come from single parent homes. A large percentage of the youth committing suicide are from broken or dysfunctional homes. Sexual discomfiture seems also to be related to either a broken home or a prolonged strained or unnatural relationship with a parent or trusted adult. A lacking or missing relationship with either mother or father seems to lead to problems of self-esteem, sexual confusion and defiance of authority. As a growing number of our citizenry come from broken relationships, we find a growing number of angry, defiant and confused youth who are inclined to experiment with everything from drugs to sexual perversion. Logic would suggest that, as broken and dysfunctional homes continue to be an American sociological phenomena, a correlating growth in youth crime, violence, suicide, sexual promiscuity, same sex and bisexual experimentation and miscellaneous degradations will persist. Moreover, as our society becomes more dysfunctional, these alternatives will become more 'main stream' and, thus, acceptable to a growing sector of the population.

I yearn for the innocence of the past. I yearn for a society that lets me grow and allows me the spiritual freedom to live in a union with all my spiritual brothers and sisters. I dream of the day when we will love one another and really mean it! But, Truth is a relic of days gone by. In an effort to modernize, to be relevant to the needs of a post-modern society, political correctness replaces historically tested qualities. And, the spiritual message is weakened and paganized.

A ONE WORLD GOVERNMENT?

As the United States continues to surrender pieces of its sovereignty to the United Nations, our world grows closer to forming a one world govern-

AND, THE SPIRITUAL MESSAGE IS WEAKENED AND PAGANIZED.

ment. From discussions with my co-workers, I believe people are beginning to accept such a government as an inevitable change. Consider our situation. Businesses in both Europe and the Far East own major corporations in the USA. In like manner, many businesses based in the USA own companies in other parts of the world. As these multi-national companies grow, they tend to make trade agreements among themselves. To encourage such trade, the North American Free Trade Agreement (NAFTA) has become law, making the entire continent of America a free trade zone. The General Agreement on Tariffs and Trade (GATT) has expanded trade globally. The World Trade Organization (WTO), organized in 1995 is a direct result of GATT and was organized to improve trade relationships between member nations. Even the remaining Communist countries are being courted by salivating world trade leaders. Most notably, China is expected to become a global economic giant. Thus, China has been treated in a very favorable manner. However, when it comes to money there seems to be 'no stone unturned.' Even smaller countries like Vietnam are included. In fact, many Americans were shocked when President Clinton traveled to Vietnam to hold the world trade door open for this notorious enemy of freedom. Yet, free trade is the great hope. Free trade will make living conditions better around the world. Free trade will make the uncivilized civilized. Some feel 'Utopia' awaits. However, a likely aftermath of the free trade organization is that the United States will become less important in directing world affairs. President Bill Clinton reflected this sentiment by stating that the United States will soon be replaced as the world's great power. He expects either China or the new European Union to become the "premier political and economic power."[26]

Interestingly, the attractiveness of a one world system has not been politically limited to either the Democratic or Republican parties, but has been bipartisan in scope. And, if we consider all of the changes being made in the financial world, a common monetary system would seem highly beneficial. In many ways, such a system already exists. Money 'floats' on an international monetary system; thus, virtually all international transactions are by computer. A VISA or Master Card easily makes an international purchase in most any country. If you own a Master Card, you can go shopping in France, Germany or China.

Dave Hunt holds an interesting perspective on this point. He wrote:

Revelation 13 declares that Antichrist will control all banking and commerce in the entire world. Once again that concept seemed unbelievable in the past. Then along came our generation and developed the computers and communications satellites with which to fulfill this prophecy. We are rapidly heading toward a cashless society for reasons of efficiency and crime control. Holdups, kidnapping, extortion, drug dealing, and money laundering as well as counterfeiting and cheating on income tax could all be eliminated by doing away with cash and requiring that all transactions be electronic. For these reasons such a system is inevitable.[27]

Other international changes necessitate a growing interdependence. For the first time in its history, the United States has relinquished its national sovereignty over certain environmental issues to the United Nations. Both Presidents George H. Bush and Bill Clinton made such ecological agreements. For another first, President Clinton put American troops under the direct command of the United Nations. In a related matter, a decorated United States soldier, Michael New, faced a court martial because he refused to wear the colors of the United Nations. He claimed that he had sworn to defend the United States of America, not the United Nations. In fact, he had religious convictions against defending the United Nations. Obviously, the United States government does not think serving the United Nations is voluntary. The implication is that a United States citizen also owes alliance to the United Nations.

President Clinton "authorized the United States to sign a treaty creating the world's first permanent international war crimes tribunal" or world court. Such a court would give new legal authority to the U.N.[28] At the time of this writing, the United States, under the presidency of George W. Bush, is trying to work out an agreement which would exempt or, at least, limit the U. S. from the authority of this court. Though such a court would hold authority over any American, it is our servicemen and women who would be most vulnerable, as our soldiers could be charged, tried and convicted of malicious and undefined "crimes against humanity" without the protection of the Constitution or the Bill of Rights.[29] With this one world trend, a world government could take greater control of both national and international affairs.

WHAT IS WRONG WITH A ONE WORLD GOVERNMENT?

What is so terrible about a one world government? For some societies a One World Government might be wonderful change. However, for a free and God fearing people—for the citizens of the United States of America, it could be horrendous. We would trustingly place our beliefs and values into hands of representatives of governments who have no foundational beliefs in innate God given rights like 'life, liberty and the pursuit of happiness.' In fact, a large percentage of countries enjoying clout with the United Nations seem to hold contrary convictions. Some of these countries might allow men restricted rights, but give no rights to women. Some countries treat women severely. Some kill or mutilate women for little or no reason. Do we want to place the well being of our women in these hands? Do we want our daughters stoned if they have premarital sexual relations? Many African and Middle Eastern and

Far Eastern societies still practice slavery. Regardless of the fact that we, the people of the United States, have resolved this slavery issue, a one world government, without God's absolutes, would likely continue to allow this sin. Do we want to take a chance that some of our children may have to live under this evil? Without the Constitution or the Bill of Rights to protect us, a court could easily make slavery a just sentence to personal bankruptcy or other situations. Furthermore, a percentage of nations show no desire to afford any of their citizens the least of human rights. The People's Republic of China will, most likely, have a growing influence on this body. Have we forgotten Tiananmen Square? However, to understand how fortunate we are with our freedoms, we only have to consider our neighbors. Do we not experience an appreciative number of Cuban and Haitian refugees each year? Are there not people from around the world begging the United States to give them asylum from injustices and atrocities occurring in their own countries? Allen Keyes, who served as United States Ambassador to the United Nations, has written about his concerns on Marxism - which is only one of many alternative systems in today's united world. Keyes said:

> *The Marxist view is intrinsically opposed to the doctrine of human rights, and to the doctrine of eternal justice that underlies it. Man is just an extension of the material world, in the Marxist view, and so all professions of respect for human distinctness are in bad faith in principle, because ultimately the only thing a consistent Marxist will respect is the power or matter unfolding itself in history.*[30]

Keyes continued by reflecting upon the Marxist influence on the United Nations:

> *And the decision to form an organization that included such a (Marxist) nation is the clearest possible sign that right belief on moral matters was never a defining characteristic of the community being formed . . . So, the U.N. has failed with respect to human rights because it is based on a false practical principle–it does not take seriously the requirement of moral principle in politics.*[31]

Perhaps one reason a world government does not seem distasteful to many of us today is because society has suppressed and re-defined our historical role with God—our Creator and our subsistence.

One day I was having a discussion with a friend about religion and world events. In the middle of my discussion I leaned over to my atheistic friend (now agnostic) and said: "Isn't it odd? We are moving into a political situation where a one world government seems like the most advantageous thing to do. Isn't it amazing that just a decade ago very few people would have thought a one world government would be the wiser choice for Americans than national sovereignty? Now, 'one worldism' seems like a very reasonable and logical direction. Isn't it strange that a number of our business and political leaders openly support the one world government vision. In the not so distant future, our country might volunteer to give up its sovereignty to a centralized worldwide government. Isn't that a little odd?"

My friend responded, indicating that he *did* think that a one world government seems logical and he did see the irony.

The irony rests in the before mentioned prophecy of Saint John. In his 'end of time' dream, *The Revelation,* he saw a time when ethnicity would rise up against ethnicity. The morals in the world would become worse and worse. The crime rate would rise rapidly across the earth. Additionally, the world would experience devastation from horrific diseases, starvation and natural disasters. To resolve many such problems, planet earth would be ruled by a world government that would have authority over all nations and all human beings. The world government would be controlled by a benevolent dictator. After a short period of rule, the dictator would turn into a madman who would cause the citizens or the world much pain and suffering. Finally, the end of the world would come in as the nations of the world position themselves for a final war against Israel. At that time, Jesus will return and end existence as we know it. If it were not for His return, all of humanity would be destroyed in this final war.

I often stop at places where I can browse through used books. Once, in Boston, I found an old book about 'legendary' Israel. This book was written in 1911. The author described religious writings of the Jews as poetic legends. While making his case, he reminded the reader that Jewish prophecy recognized that the Jews would govern on land owned (in 1911) by the Palestinians. The author pointed out that a Jewish nation no longer existed. Furthermore, Jews were scattered around the world. The Jews had been absorbed. They were citizens with roots in many nations. Obviously, Jewish prophecy was in error. However, in 1948, a relatively short time after this book was written, a nation of Israel was re-established in its traditional location. Later, in the war of 1967, the holy city of Jerusalem became Jewish property. A state of Israel does not seem strange to us, because we have grown up with an established Jewish nation. Yet, for Biblical scholars, this 'redistribution' seemed the conclusion of an incredible chain of events. Furthermore, this re-birth of a Jewish state has been touted, by many of these authorities to be the beginning of 'the end times.' An agnostic might argue that a people acquainted with Biblical prophecy may have influenced this placement.

MOREOVER, AS WE CONTINUE TO GATHER INFORMATION ABOUT OUR PLANET, WE FIND EVIDENCE THAT UNIQUE NATURAL FORCES ARE CONVERGING AND CREATING GREAT PRESSURES ON OUR DETERIORATING WORLD.

Whether or not this is the case is irrelevant. Today, the factual state of Israel exists in the ancient Biblical location. How strange! Since the establishment of Israel, a climate of war has threatened it's peace. In fact, the brewing conflict could easily lead to world wide destruction—just as John seemed to predict. Yet, perhaps this is not so strange because a Jewish prophet's commentary was expected to be 100% accurate. Otherwise, the prophet was considered a fake and was stoned to death. If John was a Judaic prophet of God, his vision should be as accurate as his predecessors. Anyone who is truly interested in seeing into the future should study Saint John's visions.

WORLD DISASTERS

The Revelation predicts that planet earth will experience widespread famine, disease, pestilence and an increase in natural disasters. When these catastrophes develop, some may appear to be linked together. Such apocalyptic events may have seemed unnatural in years gone by. Now, they are not quite so foreign to our understanding. In today's world, for example, we realize that a volcano will not only burn up much of the surrounding land area, but will also cause major air pollution. Moreover, as we continue to gather information about our planet, we find evidence that unique natural forces are converging and creating great pressures on our deteriorating world.

Actually, the Revelation recognizes these environmental 'cause and effect' relationships. As an example, the following prophecy seems to express the resulting effects of an asteroid's collision with the earth:

> *The third angel blew (his trumpet) and a great flaming star fell from heaven upon a third of the rivers and springs. The star was called "Bitterness" (Wormwood) because it poisoned a third of all the water on the earth and many people died.*[32]

Perhaps connected to this plight is a fourth angel (in the next verse) who causes the sun to be "blighted" and "daylight is dimmed."[33] We know each of these physical changes are likely if a large asteroid were to collide with the earth. Will such an event take place? Such asteroids have struck earth in the past and certainly will again. It is only a matter of time. In fact, near misses have become a topic of interest because some asteroids have passed dangerously close before we have realized that they are in our area.[34]

As for disease, we find new and more sophisticated strains of old diseases, such as tuberculosis and hepatitis, have become resistant to existing treatments. This makes them very deadly, especially to weaker systems. Virtually everyone is aware of the newer viruses. Legionnaire's disease and

---

AS FOR DISEASE, WE FIND NEW AND MORE SOPHISTICATED STRAINS OF OLD DISEASES, SUCH AS TUBERCULOSIS AND HEPATITIS, HAVE BECOME RESISTANT TO EXISTING TREATMENTS.

Lyme disease are two examples. The HIV virus, precursor to AIDS, is probably the best known. However, worldwide, this virus is much more deadly than
most Americans would believe. In the USA, the AIDS virus centers on people
who participate in homosexual activities and intravenous drug use. However,
it is less confined in other countries. According to Population Services
International, a world health organization focused in the South Asia, the
"largest conglomeration" of prostitutes in the world is in Bombay involving
approximately 70,000 females. "No population is more central to the spread
of AIDS in India than commercial sex workers and, in turn, their male clients
who often unwittingly transmit the disease throughout the rest of society."
over 100,000 of Bombay's "sex workers" were infected with AIDS.[35] Yet, on
November 2, 2000 The United Nations Programme on HIV/AIDS (UNAIDS)
made an even more alarming charge. It proclaimed 34.3 million people worldwide are either sero-positive or have AIDS. Furthermore, twenty million people had already died from AIDS. Of the deceased, fifteen million had lived in
sub-Saharan Africa. A representative of The Organization of African Unity
simply stated, "Africa is dying."[36] Three million people will die of AIDS this
year, and 2.4 million of those will be from Africa.[37] Yet, Africa is not alone.
Today, in China, there are an estimated 600,000 AIDS cases. By the year
2010, it is estimated 10 million Chinese will be infected with the disease.[38]
As startling as these statistics are, Russia may have claim to the fastest growing AIDS problem today.[39] Thus, the U.N. predicts that by the year 2020, 68
million people worldwide may have died from AIDS.[40] Some suggest one
third of the population of the world could die from this virus.

Other viruses are even more mysterious than AIDS. It is believed new
strains of Ebola, Marburg, Lassa and Crimean-Congo and others could result
in plagues of unthinkable proportions, even surpassing AIDS in casualties.
New diseases could also develop and spread worldwide before cures are
found. SARS generated such a scare. Moreover, terrorists are cultivating
deadly strains of diseases as biological weapons, including smallpox, bubonic
plague and Ebola. Interestingly, one theory about SARS is that is was "artificially created" in a Chinese laboratory and released accidently.[41] Anthrax has
already been used as a terrorist weapon via the U.S. Post Office. Ricin, a poisonous protein from the caster bean seed, was to be released in London's subway system. Fortunately, the instigators were detected and the attack was
neutralized. The United States and Britain were fortunate in these cases as
these bio-terror incidents could have been much worse.

Another great health concern involves diseases spread in the food we
eat. One example of many is Bovine Spongiform Encephalopathy, better
known as Mad Cow disease. It results from feeding cattle ruminant animal
parts. This illness made headlines over the last few years as it ran rampant in
western Europe. The possibilities of future outbreaks have kept the financial

sector on edge.[42] Often in such a crises, huge numbers of animals are slaughtered and their bodies destroyed. If this is not controlled properly a disease could wipe out a large portion of the food supply. In fact, in this day of change, a new lethal strain of bacteria could rapidly spread to herds around the world. This is a constant concern for ranchers and meat handlers. Additionally, terrorists synthetically strengthening strains of disease could possibly create a super-germ causing world wide starvation.

Chemical weapons are yet another concern. Such weapons have been used a number of times. Mustard gas, first introduced in World War I, seems to be the most common chemical weapon and has been used in several other conflicts. Chemical weapons would also include VX, tabun, sarin, chlorine, phosgene and cyanide gasses. Sarin was used by terrorists in the 1995 Tokyo subway attack. Unfortunately for the world, reports indicate that a growing number of countries have developed or are developing these and other chemical and biological weapons. Their use in both terror and battle bring new horrors not yet understood.

Another prophetic problem involves changes in weather patterns. The seasons do not appear to be as discernable as they once were. Two meteorological conditions have been blamed for most of these changes: Global warming and El Nino. Though there is some disagreement as to whether these conditions are intensified by human actions, we are aware that the warming and cooling trends on the earth are natural processes. That is way the earth has experienced natural Ice Ages. However, it is interesting that these two major forces are exerting pressure at the same time. Thus, the last ten years have seen some of the hottest days, worst flooding, longest droughts and devastating blizzards–virtually every imaginable category of weather recorded has brought unequaled disasters during this period. Though most of us do not think of the severity of weather until we are directly affected, such changes do create incredible problems for society. Perhaps the most devastating effect has been the loss of human and animal life, the destruction of crops and the resulting famine and disease.

To this regard, the Pentagon has done a study of current weather trends. According to their findings, there is a possibility that the current global warming cycle is leading to a change in the 'ocean-atmospheric condition.' The Pentagon paints a gloomy picture. They suggest that a change in the ocean currents is in the making. It (the Pentagon) theorizes that "the world's climate can lurch from one state to another in less than a decade." Simply put, such a change could flip the traditional flow of the warm Atlantic current which now streams from the Caribbean to Europe. This would cause an

UNFORTUNATELY FOR THE WORLD, REPORTS INDICATE THAT A GROWING NUMBER OF COUNTRIES HAVE DEVELOPED OR ARE DEVELOPING THESE AND OTHER CHEMICAL AND BIOLOGICAL WEAPONS.

"abrupt climate change" . . ."turning farmland into dust bowls and forests (into) ashes." If this occurs there would be a massive migration of people from United Kingdom and northern Europe to warmer climates. Of course, the middle east would find such migration into its borders. This would generally be comprised of Christians and Pagans 'invading' Muslim countries. There would probably be major food shortages, bad sanitation, great illness and incalculable climatic ramifications. Civil war would be the least of governmental worries. Anyone who doubts such changes are coming needs only to track the onslaught of weather changes happening around the world.

The front cover on a popular magazine read, "THE HOT ZONE - Blizzards, Floods & Hurricanes: Blame Global Warming." Inside the cover their report began, "As blizzards go, last week's snow was bad enough. But some scientists warn that the paralyzing storm may be a sign of catastrophic global warming. If they're right, weather will turn really extreme - more floods, worse hurricanes, longer droughts and, yes, heat waves."[43] Among the problems sighted over the previous twelve months is Siberia's five-degree increase in average temperature. Additionally, North East China and the Korean Peninsula both found that "summer rain and flooding led to famine."[44] North Korea, suffering severe food shortages since 1995, has experienced ruined crops from both floods and drought.[45] In November of 2000, North Korea appealed to other world governments for three times the food aid they required the year before.[46]

Of course, we can easily think of many other areas around the world that have been plagued by famine. Ethiopia, India and West and Northwest Africa are among the affected areas. Even the United States has experienced rising problems. Insurance companies around the nation claim growing losses are affecting their underwriting procedures. Besides the record-breaking droughts in the Southwestern United States during the summers of 1999 to 2003, calamitous forest fires sweep through our parks and wilderness areas. Although part of the blame was due to government mismanagement, we also have experienced hazardously dry conditions. Perhaps natural forest fires partly explain the following Biblical puzzle:

The first angel blew his trumpet, and hail and fire mixed with blood were thrown down upon the earth. One-third of the earth was set on fire so that one-third of the trees were burned, and all of the green grass.[47]

However, many Biblical scholars believe John is referring to a nuclear war. The Revelation implies the middle east will experience increased military movements. The antichrist will try to bring these forces together under a world government, but will finally fail.

Former President Bill Clinton made several bold moves hoping that the U. N. would bring peace to the middle east. However, after all of his council, all of his sending troops to diverse places, in all of his legalities and with all of his speeches, the middle east seems to be crumbling. Today's middle eastern headlines are about peace conferences which bring no lasting peace and the constructing of war machines - in every nation–in every sector–in every hamlet. Suicidal terrorists bombers aim at Jewish children. Dead women and children have become common daily expectations. It is as if everyone in this area of the world is expecting a major conflict. Past Israel Prime Minister Ehud Barak became unpopular with a large segment of his citizens because, on the advice of peace negotiators, he gave away Israeli land holdings to the Palestinians. This was his olive branch. He was hoping for peace. Yet, the Palestinians continued pressing for war.

President George W. Bush followed his predecessor with continued efforts for middle eastern peace. The prospects seemed workable up to September 11, 2001. Of course, on that day America felt the hand of terrorism on her shores like never before and, as of this writing, never since. In one moment, middle eastern peace may have been crushed. One of the exponents for peace, Prince Bandar bin Sultan of Saudi Arabia, exclaimed that on September 10th (a day before the American tragedy) he was "the happiest man on earth." But, on September 11th, he experienced a great crises. He said that he could not think of anything that would "do more damage or worse damage to Islam or to Saudi Arabia."[48]

For four thousand years, the middle east has been plagued by national, racial and religious conflicts. However, the conflicts of the past would pale when compared to a now possible nuclear, biological and chemical war. It is believed that a middle eastern terrorist network either hold or is trying to procure such weapons. Recently, the United States renewed the war with Iraq. The reasoning behind this conflict rests, in part, with the prospect that Iraq could spread these horrific weapons to these terrorists who will most certainly use them. Will defanging Iraq help avoid a great coming war? Or, is a super war inevitable? Isn't it interesting that a super war or final war in the middle east, the perpetual hot bed of conflict, is exactly what *The Revelation* predicts.

There are growing numbers of military organizations which could affect the complexion of a super war. These powers are generally thought to be regional entities. However, one can distinguish or categorize virtually all of them as examples from four diverse social-political philosophies. Like continental plates that push and grind against each other, these political forces

HOWEVER, THE CONFLICTS OF THE PAST WOULD PALE WHEN COMPARED TO A NOW POSSIBLE NUCLEAR, BIOLOGICAL AND CHEMICAL WAR.

probe, antagonize and violate each counterpart. Yet, by the nature of man, each must vie for world domination.

The traditional social-political categories have been Monarchism, Fascism, Communism and Democracy. However, I will sharpen these four distinctions allowing them to better fit the picture we see of an emerging world. Today we live in a world too economically driven for the 'old model' of Monarchism to compete. Moreover, most of the middle eastern Monarchies, which dominated this region, have been compromised by Islamic radicalism. Thus, Monarchism is a dying from of government. I will distinguish three of the four modern competing powers as Marxist, Islamic radicalism and Occultism.

As one would expect, there are vast differences in the core beliefs of these three movements. However, all three seem dictatorial in nature. Today, the Marxist model governs The People's Republic of China. Other Marxist states include Cuba and North Korea. The majority of these Marxist states seem to be have mounting internal problems and are becoming less stable.

Examples of Islamic radicalism are Iran and Sudan. The major powers behind this model are the radical Shiite, Islamo-fascists and Sunni Islamists. Forms of this model existed up through the middle ages, but were often replaced with despotic or monarchial rule. Though their historical resolution has always been, and now remains, to rule the world, the birth of modern Islamic radicalism came in 1979 with the fall of the Shah of Iran. Such extremism will certainly lead to massive destruction for masses of innocent people.

Today, the Occultism grouping seems limited to a hand full of backward countries such as Haiti. However, Nazi Germany is an example of a recent super power which fit within this category. Surprisingly, the emerging European Union is posed to recognize Paganism as never before. At this writing, the Preamble to the European Union's Constitution focuses on early Pagan traditions and ignores its Christian influences. Referring to the Preamble, Cardinal Roberto Tucci spoke the sentiments of many by stating, "The most unifying factor of Europe, which has been Christian culture, is missing."[49] Unfortunately, the incubator of Christian culture may be completely abandoning the religious foundation that once made it great.

The fourth modern force is entrenched in human rights and freedoms. Though 'pro-freedom' countries are often secular allowing a number of cultures and religions to coexist, this force was a by-product of the Christian philosophy. I will distinguish this form of government as a mix of Democracy and/or Republic or, for short, 'Democratic.' The United States of America is the preeminent example of this model. Britain is another sterling example of the Democratic state.

Clearly the above categorization is a generalization and not amenable to all situations. In fact, a number of countries are mixtures of several models. For example, Turkey could be distinguished as a mixture of moderate Islamic and Democratic models. France and Germany are becoming socialists countries which tends to be a mixture of the Democratic and Marxist models. However, regardless of the national mixtures and pressures, these four models seem representative of the major positions in modern civilizations.

To break these down further might soothe political or theological divisions, but it would also unnecessarily complicate this illustration. For example, one conspicuous exclusion is a Jewish model. However, the young Israeli state adopted a form of the Democratic plan and has rejected their ancestral model which could somewhat fit with the Islamic version. A vintage Jewish state would seem harsh and extreme by modern standards.

To realize the gravity and responsibility held by the above forces, one only has to recall Nazi Germany. If it were not for the strength of Democratic model, this Nazi Occultic version would have exterminated all of the competing forces. There would be no Marxist, Islamic radicalism or Democratic models. There would only be Nazism. Today, we find the Islamic radicalism and Democratic models colliding into each other. Islamic radicalism has a history of terrorizing other religious groups worldwide. However, when Islamic terrorists attacked the United States on September 11, 2001 the event was labeled a 'wakeup call' to the west. The United States seems to have decided that the best way to defend against such terrorism is to attack terrorist nations world wide. This further explains the above mentioned confrontation between the United States and Iraq. In addition, the United States intends to develop a middle eastern democratic society hoping to change the entire Islamic temperament toward individual rights and freedoms.

However, the Marxist movement makes world peace much more complicated. The Communist countries have murdered many believers of all faiths. This includes members of the Islamic, Christian and Jewish religions. The war between the Soviet Union and Afganistan is an example of these conflicts. Nonetheless, "cultural cleansing" has been a less publicized state activity common to all three of the dictatorial forces. It seems reasonable, if *The Revelation* is accurate, that the 'super war' or Armageddon will fester from the interactions of these four diverse forces. To illustrate this hypothesis, let us take a closer look at some of the forces at play on the world scene.

TERRORISM

Books are now being written about the al-Qaida movement, which has grown throughout the Islamic world, and its 'holy war' (Jihad) against

Western and Jewish influences. However, there are numerous other Islamic terrorist groups which are not as well publicized. Investigative writer, Alan Caruba, has stated: "Despite a long history of defeat and despotism, fundamentalist Islam now poses the greatest threat to freedom worldwide."[50] In support of this statement, the great majority of military conflicts and terrorist attacks, around today's world, result from Islamic radicalism. However, from the Islamic perspective, one can understand some of their hatred for our society. Their culture revolves around a reverence for Ali. Besides the decadence of the American way of life, many Muslims are greatly offended by abortion, homosexuality, premarital sex, eroticism (as in American advertisements), "adult" content in television, movies and so fourth. They do not want a pornographic and sinful society to corrupt theirs. Furthermore, our attempts to neutralize Islamic radicalism through forceful actions in Afghanistan and Iraq create an Islamic concern that the United States is 'empire building.' This perception is aggravated by the perception that the United States conquered Communism,[51]

The following groups are known terrorist organizations. Virtually all of these groups fit within the various geopolitical models above. However, notice how many are Islamic radical organizations. The terror organizations include the Abu Nidal Organization - split from the PLO in 1974; Abu Sayyaf Group–operating mainly in the Philippines; Armed Islamic Group–an Islamic terror militia from Algeria; Alex Boncayao Birgade–a Communist terrorist organization in the Philippines; Al-Gamma'a al-Islamiyya–Egyptian based Islamic militants but also found in other areas of middle east; Army for the Liberation of Rwanda–main goal is to overthrow the Rwandan government; Aum Supreme Truth–the organization that released nerve agent in the Tokyo subway system; Basque Fatherland and Liberty–a Marxist group from Northern Spain; Continuity Irish Republican Army–dissident group from the Irish Republican Army; First of October Antifascist Resistance Group–a Communist organization in Spain; HAMAS–a dominate Palestinian terrorist organization; Harakat ul-Mujahidin–Islamic group based in Pakistan; Hizballah–based in Lebonon and allied with Iran; Irish Republican Army–Irish organization to unite Ireland and expel the British; Islamic Movement of Uzbekistan–formed to overthrow the Uzbekistan government and replace it with an Islamic state; Jaish-e-Mohammed–Islamic pro-Taliban terrorists based in Pakistan; Japanese Red Army–Communist organization founded to overthrow the Japanese government and encourage world revolution; Al-Jihad–closely tied to al-Qaida and dedicated to overthrowing Egyptian government and replacing it with an Islamic state and world wide terror; Kach and Kahane Chai–a pro Israeli organization; Kurdish Workers Party–Originally and traditionally Communist; their goal is to establish a Kurdish state; Lashkar-e-Tayyiba–Islamic militants based in Pakistan known for their attacks against Hindu Indian interests; Liberation Tigers of Tamil Eelam–militants in Sri Lanka dedicated to the formation of a Tamil state; Loyalist Volunteer Force–Irish Loyalists terrorist movement; Mujahedin-e Khalq Organization–pro Iranian group; National Liberation Organization–Cuban inspired terrorist group in Latin America; New People's Army–Communist militants in the Philippines; The Palestinian Islamic Jihad–aim is to form a Palestinian state and the destruction of Israel; Palestinian Islamic Front–Pro PLO terrorists noted for their attack on the Achille Lauro; Popular Front for the Liberation of Palestine–Marxist group for a Palestinian state; Orange Volunteers–Irish Protestant militant organization; People Against Gangsterism and Drugs–Islamic terrorists in Cape Town, South Africa; Popular Front for the Liberation of Palestine-General Command - Islamic extremists in Palestine and aligned with Iran and Syria; Real IRA–Irish Republic militant group; Red Hand Defenders–Loyalist militants in Northern Ireland; Revolutionary Armed Forces of Colombia–Marxist group in Colombia, South America; Revolutionary Organization 17 November–Leftist's operating in Greece; Revolutionary People's Liberation Party–anti-American and anti-NATO group; Revolutionary People's Struggle–Greek Communist terrorists; Revolutionary United Front–militants working to overthrow the government of Sierra Leone; Sendero Luminoso (SL) - Tupac Amaru Revolutionary Movement–Marxists terrorists in Peru; United Self-Defense Forces of Colombia - paramilitary group protecting the drug trade around Colombia, South America.[52]

Moreover, many nations in the world are trying to play major roles in the struggles of these geopolitical forces. This, of course, further complicates the middle eastern region. Because of time and space, I will limit the majority of my discussion to one power–the People's Republic of China.

PEOPLES REPUBLIC OF CHINA

In the Revelation, there is a portion that reads as follows:

Release the four mighty demons held bound at the great River Euphrates." They had been kept in readiness for that year and month and day an hour, and now they were turned loose to kill a third of all mankind. They led an army of 200,000,000 warriors–I heard an announcement of how many there were.[53]

In the days of the apostle, John, this prophecy must have seemed impossible without a divine miracle to create 200,000,000 warriors. Fielding such an army has been impossible until recent times. However, China can fulfill the number of warriors in this prophecy any day she wishes. Interestingly The Revelation later reads:

The sixth angel poured out his flask upon the great River Euphrates and it dried up so that the kings from the east could march their armies westward without hindrance.[54]

What John seems to have stated is that, in the final days, a huge army of 200,000,000 will kill a third of the world's citizenry and armies from the east will be involved in a final battle. Never before has China's participation seemed more probable than today. Interestingly, China already has a large army in the middle east. They have 700,000 troops and forced servants in Sudan, one of the most volatile problem spots in the world.[55] Sudan's Islamic government has been involved in a violent civil war for over a decade. Because it has been particularly nasty, it is a major focus of human rights groups such as Human Rights Watch. Some of the reported atrocities include the bombing of schools and hospitals, the crucifixion of Christians and a scorched earth policy against Sudan's own populace.[56]

Dr. Charles Jacobs, member of an anti-slavery watch group, has claimed that the Muslim based Sudanese government has begun "a holy war" against Black Christians and others, leaving millions dead and others homeless. Government supported militias sweep African villages, killing males and enslaving women and children. Those captured are often sold or traded. A Sudanese soldier summed up the Islamic view of Christian people when he commented to a Christian slave, "We see you like animals."[57]

The Chinese forces are officially in Sudan to protect the oil fields. However, diplomatic correspondent, Christina Lamb, thinks they are to be used in a major "offensive" against the rebels. Lamb writes, "An internal document from the Sudanese military said that as many as 700,000 Chinese security personnel were available for action."[58]

Some readers might ask, "Why haven't we been better informed about this?" The first part of the answer is simple; the 'free press' is no longer 'free.' Our traditional press no longer reports much of the news; it seems to be more interested in propagandizing. In fact, many Americans now rely on alternative news sources to find quality coverage. Thus, the ratings for traditional networks continue to fall as internet news sites and radio 'talk shows' continue to grow. The second part of the answer is not so simple. Our government has taken a limited stand. However, there would be disastrous ramifications from an 'all out' war with China. The destruction of this rising giant, with its influences, would certainly hold negative results for the entire world.

Moreover, the United States helped China become a military giant. We gave them our advance missile, satellite and computer technology.

OUR TRADITIONAL PRESS NO LONGER REPORTS MUCH OF THE NEWS; IT SEEMS TO BE MORE INTERESTED IN PROPAGANDIZING.

Without help from the United States, China would not have obtained such precise nuclear delivery capabilities. For political reasons, our government allowed American business interests to sell China the needed technology. Furthermore, either as a reward for political campaign contributions, or through espionage, the Chinese procured all of our nuclear secrets.[59] Thus, today China can send advanced nuclear missiles onto American soil. Additionally, we have sent American military special forces to train Chinese regular soldiers in the art of advanced combat. These activities must have been related to our desire to show the Chinese that we are not their enemy; we are not a threat to them, but a partner for 'world peace.' According to General Peter Schoomaker, "You need to engage so you can develop rapport and understanding and have another method of dialogue."[60]

Will this gamble pay off? Will the Chinese become our working partners or will they surprise us with military conquest? Both Russia and China have threatened us with nuclear war. Ironically, both countries would use our (United States) nuclear technology in a nuclear war. Furthermore, China is arming Pakistan to neutralize India. It also has great influence on North Korea. Of course, North Korea is the latest country to develop a nuclear war program. Perhaps North Korea will have access to our nuclear secrets through the Chinese. Additionally, China now controls the Panama Canal and, through Sudan, could also control the Suez Canal. With socialist in control of South Africa, China could end our access to the materials we need to make fighter jets, space shuttles and "sheathe" reactor fuel and the like.[61]

Unfortunately, another problem looms over China. There seems to be an internal struggle for its national identity between China, the military bully of the far-east, and China, the industrial world partner. However, the Chinese may have serious financial troubles. If so, the country could become unstable. According to Gordon Chang, "High expectations for the Chinese economy are 'grossly exaggerated' . . . China's economic growth is declining and its banking system is in 'disarray posing a threat of destabilization to the international economy.'"[62] A financially unstable China could be a very scary thing. The military bully may gain control. Like a wounded animal, it might decide to strike out at its enemies, or try to take that which it does not own.

With the escalating changes around the globe, one can imagine a war pitting Israel and possibly the United States and the Unite Kingdom against the rest of the world. OPEC could hold the key. If the United States and the UK fail to stabilize the middle east, terrorists from Iran and Syria could overthrow Iraq, Kuwait and finally Saudi Arabia. Old allies have shown, through the United Nations' 'food for oil' program, that economic wealth takes precedent over the stability of the world. In fact, in the interest of money, France and Germany led the European Union in a compromise with Sudan on slavery issues.[63]

Of course, we might not be around to protect Israel. A number of Bible scholars theorize the United States is the 'great city' eulogized in the following prophecy:

Alas, that great city, so beautiful–like a woman clothed in finest purple and scarlet linens, decked out with gold and precious stones and pearls! In one moment all the wealth of the city is gone!

And all the shipowners and captains of the merchant ships and crews will stand a long way off, crying as they watch the smoke ascend, and saying, "Where in all the world is there another city such as this?"

And they will throw dust on their heads in sorrow and say, Alas, alas, for that great city! She made us all rich from her great wealth. And now in a single hour all is gone . . . [64]

Until September 11, 2001, most Americans believed the United States was invulnerable to nuclear attack. In the past, we similarly assumed Pearl Harbor was invulnerable. Then came December 7, 1941. On that day, the Japanese surprised our country. Using only 181 planes, they destroyed the American Pacific Fleet. Not only did they sink America's best war ships and 180 of our aircraft, they also killed 2,300 brave American service men and women.[65] This disaster left the United States' west coast ripe for invasion. Many Americans including President Roosevelt called on God for help. Perhaps those prayers prevented Japan's incursion on our mainland.

Of course, September 11, 2001 was another date which "will live in infamy." Again, the United States was caught by surprise; this time by terrorists. Because this event has been discussed so much I do not think it is necessary to relive the tragedy of the day. However, this attack left thousands of innocent citizens dead and many more in mourning. It was indeed a sad day for our nation.

Unfortunately, the United States may have a future date which "will live in infamy." It could be much more serious than the ones related to Pearl Harbor or '9/11.' Al-Qaeda and other Islamic terrorists organizations have made it clear they intend to bring terror to the USA. In fact, the possibility of nuclear strikes carried out by terrorists living in America with suitcase nuclear weapons is a real threat. The United States government has not dismissed any possible weapon, including nuclear or biochemical. These terrorists are not necessarily after military targets. They attack mothers, fathers and children. They attack grandparents. They attack young lovers. They attack the business

OF COURSE, SEPTEMBER 11, 2001 WAS ANOTHER DATE WHICH "WILL LIVE IN INFAMY."

people and laborers. They attack the weak, the young and the old. They attack the innocent.

There are a number of other potential adversaries who might be willing to attempt a future nuclear strike. Again, China comes to mind. This awakening giant is now working on advanced technology designed to incapacitate our electronic infrastructure. If they are successful, they could launch a first strike attack and catch us by surprise. Our nuclear strategy over the past forty or so years has been called Mutual Assured Destruction. This means that, if we are attacked by an arsenal of nuclear weapons we will retaliate and launch our nuclear might. This would be national suicide for both involved countries. However, said strategy is based on our ability to strike back. If China were to incapacitate our surveillance and launch capabilities they could destroy the bulk of our weapon systems and encounter minimal collateral damage.

Could we again go to God for protection? If we call on Him, why should He answer? We have taken down His laws from our courts and public buildings around the country. We have banned Him from our schools, our sporting events and even our workplaces. We destroyed His rules for family structures. We assault our religious institutions for their obtrusion into our lives. We attack organizations like the Boy Scouts for their required belief in God and high moral standards. Why would He protect us when we forsake Him?

Please do not misunderstand my point. I am not a prophet. I am not suggesting I know America's future or when the world will come to an end. I do not know how long it will be before we move into a worldwide government or when any other Biblical predictions will come to pass. We may very well solve all of the above problems and find new concerns. However, isn't it odd that the world seems to be making definite moves in the above directions, and all predicted by Saint John for the last days? As for the coming Antichrist, there are those who eagerly await his presence. Some of these people are ready to continue where Hitler left off. However, today's dictators and terrorists envision programs that will make Nazi eugenics look tame in comparison. Futuristic ideas include such things as mandatory abortion, mandatory euthanasia for the sick and elderly, as well as the reintroduction of eugenics to solve religious and racial differences.

When speaking of Jesus' return, St. Paul wrote:

If you hear of people having visions and special messages from God about this, or letters that are supposed to have come from me, don't

---

COULD WE AGAIN GO TO GOD FOR PROTECTION? IF WE CALL ON HIM, WHY SHOULD HE ANSWER?

believe them. Don't be carried away and deceived regardless of what they say.

For that day will not come until two things happen: first, there will be a time of great rebellion against God, and then the man of rebellion will come - the son of hell. He will defy every good there is, and tear down every other object of adoration and worship. He will go in and sit as God in the temple of God, claiming that he himself is God. Don't you remember that I told you this when I was with you? And you know what is keeping him from being here already; for he can come only when his time is ready.

As for the work this man of rebellion and hell will do when he comes, it is already going on (literally, "the mystery of lawlessness is already at work"), but he himself will not come until the one who is holding him back steps out of the way. Then this wicked one will appear, whom the Lord Jesus will burn up with the breath of his mouth and destroy by his presence when he returns. This man of sin will come as Satan's tool, full of satanic power, and will trick everyone with strange demonstrations, and will do great miracles. He will completely fool those who are on their way to hell because they have said 'no' to the Truth; they have refused to believe it and love it, and let it save them, so God will allow them to believe lies with all their hearts, and all of them will be justly judged for believing falsehood, refusing the Truth, and enjoying their sins.[66]

A FINAL VALIDATION OF *THE REVELATION*

A greatly simplified version of *The Revelation* was found in Qumran. This writing, Scroll 4Q246 - 'the Son of God Scroll,' was previously discussed for its messianic implications. It also describes the history of the world and the final conclusion. An extraction of Scroll 4Q246 reads:

Like the appearance of comets, so shall be their kingdom.
For brief years they shall reign over the earth and shall
trample on all;
one people shall trample on another and
one province on another until the people of God shall rise and
all shall rest from the sword.[67]

Interestingly, the prophet foresees providence or God's Will as the guiding force of human history. Also implied is a tyrannical reign of a world kingdom that shall rule for a brief time and, perhaps, a resurrection of the saints—all concepts found in *The Revelation*. What is so amazing is that, as far as scholars have determined, there was no connection between St. John and the person responsible for this scroll. A similar prophetic message must have been perceived by two independent sources at relatively the same time.

IN CONCLUSION

Again, we are faced with defining questions. Do we rationalize away *The Revelation* as we have done with so many other sources of information in numerous fields of human study? Do we credit the amazing historical events which continue to align with Biblical prophecy to blind luck? Do we continue to declare all enigmas in every field of study which do not seem to fit a 'by chance' existence to be meaningless and irrelevant? Does the philosophical need of a 'super' influence on the scientific laws which create the existence we experience, and all of the incredible synchronistic and symbolic oddities of the human psycho-dynamics, etc., prove we have no foundations? Do such puzzles prove our world is unpredictable, that science is a farce? No, rather these events point to a design and, thus, to a Designer. They point to a plan and, thus, a Planner. I believe science and math and history and medicine and many other fields of human understanding point to an order and to an awesome reality directed by a proactive God. At this juncture in time, those who study astronomy and see no need for God are unscientific. Those who believe in evolution and dismiss creation are inept. Those who study the human mind and neglect spiritual validity are unrealistic. Those who discredit the power of prayer must also reject 'the scientific method' of research. Those who do not believe in the supernatural must deny the existence of quantum reality. Objectivity and the related uniformity of nature are misconstrued by the limitations of humanness and are rejected by the humanist orthodoxy. However, those who reject God are short sighted. Those who hide their eyes will not see. It is written, "The fear of the LORD is the beginning of wisdom, and the knowledge of the Holy One is insight."[68]

Considering all that we know, there must be a loving Creator who is in touch with His creation. This Creator put laws like, "love one another," in the hearts of every human being. The Creator must also be our God as He communicates with us, asks that we communicate with Him and answers our prayers. He created food to nourish our lives, allows us freedoms not granted to any other creatures and provides for our salvation. What seems to be just as true is that our Creator is in control of everything involved with our existence. God seems to have known from the beginning of time that His laws would be broken. He has always known what wars would be fought, what forces would be victorious and what sorrow these wars would bring. God seems to have

---

CONSIDERING ALL THAT WE KNOW, THERE MUST BE A LOVING CREATOR WHO IS IN TOUCH WITH HIS CREATION.

known that the Gentiles would have a period of glory. Furthermore, He must have knowingly brought forth national founding fathers like George Washington, statesmen like Abraham Lincoln, world leaders like Winston Churchill and generals like George Patton.

Unfortunately, even with such overwhelming evidence proclaiming God's providence and majesty over our existence, most of us no longer rely on God's Will as a guide for our actions. As the Bible predicted for the end times, we now mock and defile all that is Holy within human comprehension. We block out Truth for relativism. We push God in a corner and demand that He stay out of places that He has no business. Thus, we live for nothing. And, for nothing, we will die.

WHAT IS REALITY?

Though much more could be written, this is my case for a divine God who is in control of all that is. The philosophers call this Divine Authoritarianism. We strive to understand the concepts of spiritual worlds like the forces of good and evil. A struggle between good and evil seems to test each person's fiber. Perhaps all spiritual beings, including our human spirits, participate in a spiritual 'showdown' in one form or another. Perhaps, the results will prove (to all) the wisdom of living harmoniously within the security of God's Will. It is argued God is a 'just and discerning God.' Therefore, He allows all creation to understand the reality of sin. In His wisdom, He knows that the shame of sin will defeat itself. When His creation witnesses the joy of living through His Will, as compared to the misery of living in sin, His point will be made. There will be no reason for the misery to continue. Furthermore, Jesus Christ is the major player in the fate of earth. In fact, in some way not understandable to human beings, the Son and the Father are one - Jesus is God. Thus, when Jesus does come again, it will not be to save the world. He will have already saved those who will be saved. On His return, He will attack sin with the vengeance of His God power. He will strike with an awesome force unknown from even in the beginning of time. When He raises His sword of judgment, the war will instantly be over and every creature will recognize and worship God Almighty. When we get to the point where humanity cannot escape from 'the cave,' then Jesus the Messiah, the Son of God will indeed come back. This time He will come to close the book on the conflict with sin. That is *The Revelation.*

POST-MODERN IMPRESSION

Sacred marriage is no more;
we play as harlots in days of yore,
but for 'N.O.W.'
fathers are meaningless.

Who cares if parents are real?
cause love is just something else to do
while we are the young and restless.
Life is learned on M T V
With help from Friends
like Jerry Springer.

We search through life for ecstasy -
or some other pill
that can drain
all of the pain
and make reality
UNreal

With Gang colors adorned
and other geopolitical porn,
Came a New (and improved)
One World of glitter and fluff
and other incredible stuff.

We watched tha people become slaves
to new provocative ways.
They wear it's leash of passion
in the classical chic
non-relevant
fashion.

Yes, one perceived and promoted
by a man with no name
and a company with no blame.
Yet, all are the same
In this ONE WORLD game.

The sacred rules are changed.
porn is no longer bad,
as long as it sells
And, kids are BUYING!
(that's the real REAL thing)

So give me a house; that's all I want
with a pool,
a Mercedes Benz,
and a cellular phone.
Add some booze . . .
and a broad
or two.

To hell with those who have no food,
no T.V. or cosmetics!
There's too much else to do
then to worry about some fool,
not worthy of me.
I have money!
Why doesn't he?

So I pop the question.
What sex is 'right' for you?
Civilization doesn't crumble
values do!
But life is cool, if you inhale
all that decadence can entail.

Yes, even death is cool
as long as its not you -
unless you're bored
and
really
really
want to!
So, what is life?
And how will we recognize it ?
We will soon know
We will SOON know.
We will SOON KNOW . . .

As filth covers us in dirty sin
rational lies become our outer skin.
In dead seriousness
all humanity cries
(the mourning scream)
"The preserving salt is GONE!"

As lightening breaks the darkened sky
and strikes with fear in those near by.
It is only in despair
that we look in the air
and impatiently await
the undeniable TRUTH.

If Providence is real
as is God's Will
then Fire will soon judge
EVERYTHING
Including me and you
and we will all inclusively
Know . . .
Jesus

EPILOGUE

Plato, Immanuel Kant, Albert Einstein and many other profound thinkers would agree that we are limited in our understanding of reality. We can only examine, with certainty, the physical crust of reality. We deduce from our inspections only what seems to be true at one moment in time. Such examinations are impersonal. In sympathy with philosopher Martin Buber's conclusions regarding relationships, the previous inquiry into the Ultimate Reality treated God like a thing. We picked up a model of reality, looked at it from various angles and drew conclusions, but from this inspection, we do not and cannot 'know' actual reality. We have determined that God's existence is probable.

So, what is lacking? You need to bring God into your life. Shed yourself of your 'glory,' your intellectualism and such. Shed yourself of your armor. You are no match for "I AM THAT I AM." Call on God to come into your life just as you are. The truth is, if we are honest with ourselves, we are all inadequate. We all have our wicked secrets and our dirt. We all have been hurt. We all have personal hates and fears. Sooner or later, we will all die and crumble into dust. However, God is the provider of strength. We know God answers prayers. Ask Him to hold you in His arms. Get to know Him personally. Accept His love and His forgiveness. You will be amazed how much He shares with you. You will be surprised how lovingly He confronts you. Accept the Messiah as your savior. Ask Jesus to "save you" from your sins. Ask Him to be with you, to be your shepherd and guide you through life's ups and downs. He knows you are not perfect. He knows that you are mixed up and unsure of yourself. He knows that all humans hold sin in their deeds and thoughts. Yet, He died an excruciating death for our salvation. Moreover, He died for you. If you were the only person in the world needing His salvation He would have died the same death for only you, because He loves you. Do not wait. Get real with God today.

If you do have such a relationship then develop it. Love God with all your heart, soul and might. Try to be a good Ambassador for God's Kingdom. Be God's servant and love your fellow man. As you serve others you serve God. Be one with your spiritual brothers and sisters so the world will know that Jesus and God are one.

When I played football in high school and college, my world revolved around the sport. I spent much of my time doing things like running sprints and lifting weights. In fact, I did just about everything I could do to be the best athlete I could be. I remember a time in my senior year in college when I played my last game. After the game, I sat down by my locker and cried. My football world was over. I wondered if I could have 'worked out' a little harder or a little smarter. Should I have ran more sprints, received more sleep or prepared for games in other ways? Was there anything that I could have done that would have made me a better player? This 'self interrogation' was not only about personal achievements. There was a higher value involved. My questions were also about the integrity of the game. Had I given to football all that I could give to make it more exciting and rewarding to my team mates, coaches, opponents and fans?

It is my belief that each of us, at the end of this life, will look back at our pasts. We will consider it from a spiritual point of view. We will be saddened by our shortcomings. We will consider those things that we should have done and did not do; and we will consider those things we did do that we wish we had not done. Many of our deeds will seem debased and disgusting. Most importantly, we will be sorrowful for our human neglect and arrogance toward God. We will wish we had another opportunity to be God's Ambassador and stand for God's interests. We will wish we had loved more and hated less. We will remember people we should have helped. We will be shamed by wasted assets and talents. We will not only be sorrowful from a personal bases, but for the integrity of the game 'life' and its Creator. Unfortunately, life will be over. Yet, I think this introspection will be a big part of the meaning of life. Perhaps that is why the Bible warns us in Ephesians 5:16 to not "be fools, be wise: make every opportunity you have for doing good."

Thus, the wise man or woman must work to change his or her shortcomings. Do not let human pride come between you and your relationship with God. Take the help God has given you. Jesus visited earth to be both our example and our savior. Dedicate your life to Him and accept His love and direction. May God bless you, warm your heart and make your life complete and meaningful.

WE WILL WISH WE HAD LOVED MORE AND HATED LESS.

ENDNOTES

INTRODUCTION

1. "Guess Who Doesn't Believe In God?," *Netscape What's New,* 5 March 2004, Netscape internet network, 5 March 2004 <http.chanels.netscape.com/new/html/live/scoop/ns/18.html?/query=believe+in+God>.

2. The Living Bible, Saint Luke 16:31. All Biblical references will be taken from The Living Bible unless otherwise noted.

3. See Chapter 17; What Happened to the Body?

4. James D. Bales, *The Biblical Doctrine of God* (Shreveport, LA: Lambert Book House, Inc., 1974) 3.

CHAPTER 1 - What is the Ultimate Reality?

1. Genesis 1:1.

2. Romans 7:15–17.

3. An example can be found in Thomas Anthony Harris' ground-breaking book of 1969 entitled *I'm Ok, You're Ok.* Harris' discussion of Transactional Analysis suggests that, in general, the healthy mind sees oneself and personal contacts, as being 'ok' as opposed to 'not ok.' Notice that Harris does not suggest 'I am perfect, you are perfect.'

4. Grant R. Jeffery, *The Signature of God* (Toronto, Ontario, Canada: Frontier Research Publications, Inc., 1996) 16.

5. Kitty Ferguson, *Stephen Hawking: Quest for a Theory of Everything* (New York, NY: BantamBooks, 1991) 14.

6. Ferguson, 14.

7. Neil deGrasse Tyson, "In the Beginning: Back in the Olden Days–The First Trillionth of a Second After the big Bang– Energy was matter, matter was Energy, and E=[mc.sup.2] ruled.(Universe))," *Natural History Magazine,* Sept. 2003: 19- 20.

8. If the reader perceives this Ultimate Reality to be related to the Eastern, early Persian and Greek religious tradition of everything being part of God, then you have misinterpreted the author's meaning. The inner relationship of all things is physical and philosophical, but it seems as though humanity is either the only spiritually oriented creature/thing in the universe, or at least the most spiritually oriented creature/thing that we are aware of.

9. Isaiah 59:9.

10. Matthew 6:22–23.

CHAPTER 2 - Philosophy of Life: The Two Views

1. Charles B. Thaxton, "In Pursuit of Intelligent Causes: Some Historical Back ground," (Originally presented June 23–26, 1988 at Sources of Information Content in DNA, Interdisciplinary Conference in Tacoma, WA, 1988, revised 1991), *Leadership University,* 13 September 2003 <http://www.leaderu.com/offices/thaxton/docs/inpursuit.html>.

2. Hugh Ross, *The Fingerprint of God* (Orange, CA: Promise Publishing, Co., 1989) 32.

3. This concept will be covered more thoroughly in Chapter 7, entitled Miracles - Something To Believe In.

4. I cover the fallacies of Kants' 'faith' position and its influence on other philosophers in Chapter 9: Philosophy - God's Will Be Done, Despite Human Resistance.

5. W. T. Jones, *Kant and The Nineteenth Century: A History of Western Philosophy* (San Diego, CA: Harcourt Brace Jovanovich, Publishers, 1952) 66.

6. Kenneth Boa and Larry Moody, *I'm Glad You Asked* (Wheaton, IL: Victor Books, 1982) 18–19.

7. Thomas B. Warren, *The Warren-Flew Debate on the Existence of God* (Jonesboro, AR: National Christian Press, 1976) 110–113.

8. Thomas B. Warren, 4.

CHAPTER 3 - God Almighty

1. Psalms 14:1.

2. *New Reasons To Believe,* dir. Hugh Ross and Alex Metherell, Reasons To Believe, 1992.

3. Jim Brooks, *Origins of Life* (Tring, Herts, England: Lion Publishing, 1985) 8.

4. Hugh Ross, *How Can You Believe In Creation with All the Facts That Support Evolution?*, Pasadena, CA: Reasons To Be- lieve, rec. 1990.

5. George Greenstein, *The Symbiotic Universe: Life And Mind In The Cosmos* (New York, NY: William Morrow and Com- pany, Inc., 1988) front cover.

6. Greenstein, 45.

7. Greenstein, 45.

8. Greenstein, 45–46.

9. Greenstein, 89.

10. Nancy R. Pearcey, "Our 'Tailor-made' Universe: New Scientific Study Begs the Philosophical Question, 'Who's the Tai- lor?,'" *Access Research Network,* 2 September 2000, September 13, 2003 <http://www.arn.org/docs/pearcey/p_tailormade090200.htm>.

11. These odds are figured more precisely by Guy Cramer at the

Trinity Report. Guy Cramer, "The Crutch of Atheism," *Trinity Report,* 14 September 1998, Trinity Consulting, 27 October 2003 <hhtp://www.direct.ca/trinity/crutches.html>.

12. Frank J. Tipler, *The Physics Of Immortality: Modern Cosmology, God and the Resurrection of the Dead* (New York NY: Anchor Books, 1994) 5.

13. Tipler, 3.

14. Tipler, ix.

15. Tipler, 17.

16. Grace Slick, Somebody To Love, *Jefferson Airplane,* RCA Victor, 1967.

17. R. C. Sproul, *Not A Chance: The Myth Of Chance In Modern Science And Cosmology* (Grand Rapids, MI: Baker Books, 1994) 12.

18. R. C. Sproul, *Reason To Believe: A Response To Common Objections To Christianity* (Grand Rapids, MI: Lamplighter Books, 1978) 112.

19. Sproul, *Reason To Believe,* 112.

20. Robert Shapiro, *Origins: A Skeptic's Guide To The Creation Of Life On Earth* (New York, NY: Summit Books, 1986) 71.

21. Shapiro, 18.

22. Shapiro, 18.

23. Sproul, *Not A Chance,* 152.

24. Boa and Moody, 22.

25. Boa and Moody, 22.

26. Sproul, *Not A Chance,* 158.

27. Bruce Bowen, "Behavior," *Science News* 158 (9 December 2000): 378.

28. Bruce Bowen, "Human Brains May Take Unique Turn," *Science News* 160 (1 September 2001): 132.

29. Sproul, *Not A Chance,* 158.

30. Sproul *Not A Chance,* 158.

31. Sproul, *Not A Chance,* 161.

32. Sproul, *Not A Chance,* 163.

33. Robert Gange, *Origins and Destiny* (Waco, TX: Word Books, 1986) 50.

34. Gange, 50.

35. Gange, 50.

36. Gange, 50.

37. Gange, 49.

38. Gange, 98.

39. Gange, 98.

40. John M. DeMarco, "Unlocking Darwin's Black Box," *New Man,* March-April 2003: 29.

41. William A. Dembski, *Intelligent Design* (Downers Grove, IL: InterVarsity Press, 1999) 159- 160.

42. Stephen Hawking, *A Brief History In Time* (New York, NY: Bantam Books, 1988) 152.

43. Hawking, 152.

44. Hawking, 115.

45. David H. Freeman, "The Mediocre Universe; Making Sense of Creation," *Discover Magazine,* February 1996: 71.

46. Freeman, 71.

47. Robert R. Caldwell and Marc Kamionkowski, "Echoes from the Big Bang," *Scientific American,* January 2001: 40.

48. Hugh Ross, "Quantum Mechanics, A Modern Goliath," *Reasons To Believe,* 14 September 2003 <http://www.reasons.org/resources/apologetics/quantummech.shtml?main>.

49. Nick Herbert, *Quantum Reality: Beyond The New Physics* (Garden City, NY: Anchor Press, 1985) 17.

50. Herbert, *Quantum Reality,* 164.

51. Menas Kafatos and Thalia Kafatou, *Looking In Seeing out: Consciousness and Cosmos* (Wheaton, IL: Quest Books, Theo- sophical Publishing, 1991) 64. Also, Lee E. Warren, "Has Science Found God in Non-Local Reality?," *The Power Latent In Man,* Sept/Oct 1996, 14 September 2003 <http://www.plim.org/nonlocal.htm>.

52. Herbert, *Quantum Reality* 214–215.

53. Herbert, *Quantum Reality* 214.

54. Lee E. Warren <http://www.plim.org/nonlocal.htm>.

55. Michio Kaku, *Hyperspace: A Scientific Odyssey Through Parallel Universes, Time Warps, And The 10th Dimension* (New York, NY: Oxford University Press, 1994) 172.

56. Michael J. Duff, "The Theory Formerly Known as Strings," *Scientific American,* February, 1998: 65.

57. Daniel C. Matt, *The Essential Kabbalah: the Heart of Jewish Mysticism* (Edison, NJ: Castle Books, 1997) 94.

58. Peter Weiss, "Constant Changes If A Constant of Nature Can Vary, Then S Might Laws of Physics," *Science News* 160 (6 October 2001): 222.

59. Weiss, 222.

60. Weiss, 222.

61. Hugh Ross, *Creation and Time: A Biblical and Scientific Perspective on the Creation-Date Controversy* (Colorado Springs, CO: Navpress, 1994), 130.

62. Quoted by john Noble in New York Times, *Readers Digest* 147 (December 1995): 215.

CHAPTER 4 - Science: Closing In On God

1. Philo, *Works Of Philo, On The Creation,* trans. C.D. Yonge (Peabody, MA: Hendrickson Pub., 1993) 7.

2. Robert Wright, "Science God and Man," *Time Magazine,* 28 December 1992: 40.

3. Ross, *How Can You Believe In Creation,* Audiocassette.

4. Hawking, 140–141.

5. Ross, *How Can You Believe In Creation,* Audiocassette.

6. Ross, *How Can You Believe In Creation,* Audiocassette.

7. Ross, *How Can You Believe In Creation,* Audiocassette.

8. Ross, *How Can You Believe In Creation,* Audiocassette.

9. Ross, *How Can You Believe In Creation,* Audiocassette.

10. Rae Corelli, Marci McDonald and Hilary MacKenzie, "Looking At God," *Maclean's Magazine,* 4 May 1992: 38–43.

11. Brooks, 40–41.

12. Wright, 42.

13. Wright, 42.

14. *The World Tomorrow,* Roderick C. Meredith and Richard Ames, syndicated television, 27 December 1993.

15. Job 38:1–41.

16. Job 40:6–14.

CHAPTER 5 - Evolution: A Big Horse With A Bunch of Guys Inside

1. Phillip E. Johnson, *Darwin On Trial* (Washington, D.C.: Regnery Gateway Inc., 1991) 110.

2. David Gold, *The David Gold Show,* KLIF Radio, Dallas, TX, 8 February 1993.

3. Phillip E. Johnson, *Debating Darwinism - II,* (Colorado Springs, CO: Focus on The Family, 1995), Audiocassette.

4. Phillip E. Johnson, "Pomo Science," *Access Research Network,* Social Text, 14.1–2, 1996, 14 September 2003
<www.arn.org/docs/johnson/sokal.htm>.

5. Gange, 118–119.

6. Gange, 117.

7. Don Lindsay, "Nebraska Man," *Don Lindsay Archive,* 14 September 2003
<http://www.donlindsay-archive.org/creation/nebraska.html>.

8. Gange, 117.

9. Erik Trinkaus, and Pat Shipman, *The Neandertals: Changing The Image Of Mankind.* (New York, NY: Alford A. Knopf, 1992) 378–392. Also

Hugh Ross, Facts and Faith vol. 9, number 3, 2. (We should not be very surprised if, for example, we find fossil humans appearing in the record before mammals are supposed to have evolved.)

10. Richard Dawkins, *The Blind Watchmaker* (New York, NY: W.W. Norton and Company, 1986) 225.

11. Carrol C. Calkins, ed., *Mysteries Of The Unexplained,* (Pleasantville, NY: Reader's Digest Association, Inc., 1882) 35.

12. Michael A Cremo and Richard L. Thompson, *Forbidden Archeology: The Hidden History Of The Human Race* (Los Angeles, CA: Bhaktivedanta Book Publishing, Inc., 1996) 455.

13. Cremo and Thompson, 455.

14. Cremo and Thompson, 455.

15. Calkins, 34, 37–38.

16. Cremo and Thompson, 811.

17. Calkins, 35.

18. Calkins, 35.

19. Calkins, 35.

20. Calkins, 35.

21. Calkins, 37.

22. Calkins, 38–39.

23. Calkins, 39.

24. Calkins, 41.

25. Calkins, 41.

26. Cremo and Thompson, 796.

27. Calkins, 36–37.

28. Dawkins, 225.

29. Dawkins, 230.

30. Institute For Creation Research, *Science, Scripture and Salvation,* syndicated radio program, 11 June 1995.

31. Job 40:15–24

32. *Great Dinosaur Mystery,* Dir. Paul S. Taylor, Films for Christ Production, video lecture, 1991.

33. Calkins, 39.

34. Shapiro, 257.

35. Shapiro, 257.

36. Dawkins, 225.

37. Shapiro, 257.

38. Francis Fukuyama, *The End of History and the Last Man* (New York, NY: Avon Books, 1992) 162.

39. Gordon Rattary Taylor, *The Great Evolution Mystery* (New York, NY: Harper and Row, 1983) 215.

40. Matt Crenson, "How the Earth Gave Birth: Origin of Life Remains Elusive," *The Dallas Morning News* 27 February 1995: 7D.

41. Taylor, *The Great Evolution Mystery,* 207.

42. Gange, 50.

43. Gange, 50.

44. Gange, 50.

45. Gange, 51.

46. Stephen C, Meyer, "DNA and Other Designs," *First Things Journal,* April 2000, No. 102, Institute on Religion and Pub- lic Life, 14 September 2003 <http://www.petersnet.net/browse/2971.htm>.

47. Charles B. Thaxton, Walter L. Bradley and Roger L. Olsen, *The Mystery of Life's Origin: Reassessing Current Theories* (New York, NY: Philosophical Library, Inc., 1984) 30.

48. Thaxton, Bradley and Olsen, *The Mystery of Life's Origin,* 33.

49. Michael Denton, *Evolution: A Theory In Crisis* (Bethesda, MY: Adler and Adler, 1985) 262.

50. Denton, 261.

51. Denton, 262.

52. Dan Ferber, "CELL BIOLOGY: Immortalized Cells Seem Cancer-Free So Far," *Science Magazine* 283 (8 January 1999): 155.

53. Hugh Ross, *The Genesis Question: Scientific Advances and the Accuracy of Genesis* (Colorado Springs, CO: NavPress, 1998) 41.

54. Crenson, "How the Earth Gave Birth," 6D-7D.

55. Crenson, "How the Earth Gave Birth," 6D-7D.

56. Johnson, *Debating Darwinism - II,* Audiocassette.

57. Fred Hoyle, *The Intelligent Universe* (New York, NY: Holt, Rinehart and Winston, 1983) 12.

58. Hoyle, 12.

59. Hoyle, 17.

60. Hoyle, 19.

61. Denton, 250.

62. Frank Zoretich, "Dan McShea and the Great Chain of Being: Does Evolution Lead to More Complexity?," *Santa Fe Insti- tute Bulletin,* fall 1996, Santa Fe Institute, 20 November 2003 <http://www.santafe.edu/sfi/publications/Bulletins/bulletin-fa1196/mcshea.html>.

63. Denton, 264.

64. Robert W. Faid, *A Scientific Approach To Christianity* (Green Forest, AR: New Leaf Press, 1982) 105–106.

65. Gange, 95.

66. Gange, appendix 6, 162.

67. Gange, 95.

68. Gange, 99.

69. Gange, 99.

70. Gange, appendix 6, 163.

71. Faid, 116–117.

72. James Gleick, *Chaos: Making a New Science* (New York, NY: Viking Penguin Inc., 1987) 239.

73. Gleick, 236.

74. Ian Stewart, *Does God Play Dice? The Mathematics of Chaos* (Oxford, UK, New York, NY, USA: B. Blackwell, 1989) 285.

75. Gleick, 261–262.

76. Dembski, 148.

77. Dembski, 148.

78. Dembski, 148–149.

79. Tom Siegfried, "Complexity May Be Starting Point in Unraveling the Mystery of Life," *The Dallas Morning News* February 27, 1995: 8D.

80. John W. Patterson, *Scientists Confront Creationism,* ed. Laurie R. Godfrey (New York, NY: W. W. Norton, 1983) 96.

81. Matt Censon, "How the Earth Gave Birth," 6D-7D.

82. Ross, *How Can You Believe In Creation,* Audiocassette.

83. Lynn Margulis and Dorion Sagan, *Microcosmos, Four Billion Years of Microbial Evolution From Our Microbial Ancestors* (Berkley, CA: University of California Press, 1997) 51–52.

84. Margulis and Sagan, 51–52.

85. "Scientists and other Intellectuals that Doubt Darwinism and other Naturalistic Theories of Origins," *Design and Evolution Awareness (IDEA) Club,* University of California at San Diego, 23 February 2004 <http://www-acs.ucsd.edu/~idea/scidoubtevol.htm>.

CHAPTER 6 - Science: The Biblical View

1. I Thessalonians 5:21.

2. Genesis 1:24.

3. Jeremy Black, *Gods and Demons and Symbols of Ancient Mesopotamia* (Austin, TX: University of Texas Press, 1992) 53.

4. Psalms 90:4.

5. Don England, "The Origin of Life," *A Critical Look At Evolution,* ed. Robert S. Camp (Atlanta, GA: Religion, Science and Communication Research and Development Corp., 1972) 101.

6. Johnson, *Debating Darwinism - II,* Audiocassette.

7. James D. Bales, *Evolution And The Scientific Method* (Searcy, AR: J. D. Bales, 1976) 53–54.

8. J. P. Moreland, *Christianity and the Nature of Science* (Grand Rapids MI: Baker Books, 1989) 198.

9. Francis Hitching, *The Neck of the Giraffe: Where Darwin Went Wrong* (New Haven, CN: Ticknor & Fields, 1982) 23.

10. Kenneth Jon Rose, *Classification of the Animal Kingdom: An Introduction to Evolution* (New York, NY: D. McKay Co., 1980) 9.

11. Denton, 172.

12. Robert T. Clark and James Bales, *Why Scientists Accept Evolution* (Grand Rapids, MI: Baker Books, 1966) 95.

13. Sid Perkins, "Fake Fossil Not One but Two New Species," *Science News* 159 (21 April 2001): 253.

14. Ann Gibbons, "Dinosaur Fossils, In Fine Feather, Show Link To Birds," *Science Magazine* 280 (26 June 1998): 2051.

15. Lian-hal Hou, Zhonghe Zhou, Larry d. Martin and Alan Feduccia, "A Beaked Bird From The Jurassic Of China," *Nature Magazine* 377 (October 1995): 616–618.

16. Gibbons, "Dinosaur Fossils, In Fine Feather, Show Link To Birds," 2051.

17. Hitching, 34.

18. Ann Gibbons, "Paleontology: Early Birds Rise From China Fossil Beds," *Science Magazine* 274 (15 November 1996): 1083–1090.

19. Ann C. Burke and Alan Feduccia, "Developmental Patterns And The Identification of Homologies In The Avian Hand," *Science Magazine* 278 (24 October 1997): 666–668.

20. Richard L. Deem, "Demise of The Birds Are Dinosaurs Theory," *The Y Files,* 8 November 97, Y92, Trinity Consulting, 20 October 03 <http://www.yfiles.com/dinobird.html>.

21. Ann Gibbins, "Plucking The Feathered Dinosaur," *Science Magazine* 278 (14 November 1997): 1229–1230.

22. Ann Gibbons, "Paleontology: New Feathered Fossil Brings Dinosaurs and Birds Closer," *Science Magazine* 274 (1 No- vember 1996): 720–721.

23. Hitching, 19.

24. Taylor, *The Great Evolution Mystery,* 230.

25. Denton, 162.

26. Denton, 165.

27. George Gaylord Simpson, *Evolution After Darwin, The Evolution of Life: The History of Life,* (Chicago IL: The University Of Chicago Press, Vol. 1, 1960) 149–159.

28. Taylor, *The Great Evolution Mystery,* 215.

29. Taylor, *The Great Evolution Mystery,* 186.

30. Taylor, *The Great Evolution Mystery,* 186.

31. Denton, 162.

32. Denton, 163.

33. Niles Eldredge, *The Miner's Canary* (New York, NY: Prentice Hall Press, 1991) 76.

34. Dawkins, 228.

35. Hitching, 20.

36. Denton, 164.

37. Taylor, *The Great Evolution Mystery,* 60.

38. Denton, 164.

39. Denton, 166.

40. Robert Augros and George Stanciu, *New Biology: Discovering the Wisdom in Nature* (Boston, MA: New Science Library Shambhala, 1987) 169–170; quote Stanley, New Evolutionary Timetable, xv.

41. Augros and Stanciu, 169.

42. Augros and Stanciu, 169.

43. Hugh Ross, *Species Development: Natural Process or Divine Action,* (Pasadena, CA: Reasons To Believe, 1990), Audiocassette 2.

44. Jan Klein, Naoyuki Takahata and Francisco J. Auala, "MHC Polymorphism and Human Origins," *Scientific American* December 1993: 82.

45. Gleick, 69–71.

46. J. P. Moreland, *Scaling the Secular City: A Defense of Christianity* (Grand Rapids, MI: Baker Books, 1987) 222.

47. Denton, 194.

48. Harold G. Coffin, "Creation: The Evidence from Science," *These Times* January 1970: 25.

49. Dawkins, 248–249.

50. Ernst Mayr, *Evolution and the Diversity of Life: Selected Essays* (Cambridge, MS: Belknap Press of Harvard University Press, 1976) 93.

51. Dawkins, 231.

52. Augros and Stanciu, 182.

53. John Rennie, "DNA's New Twists," *Scientific American* March 1993: 131.

54. Rennie, 131.

55. Jack Wood Sears, "The Problem of Mechanism," *A Critical Look At Evolution,"* ed. Robert S. Camp (Atlanta, GA: Religion, Science, and Communication Research and Development Corporation, 1972) 135.

56. See Chapter 5.

57. Allan C. Wilson and Rebecca L. Cann, "The Recent African Genesis of Humans," *Scientific American* April 1992: 71.

58. Hugh Ross, "Chromosome Study Stuns Evolutionists," *Facts and Faith,* 9.3 (1995): 3.

59. Ross, "Chromosome Study Stuns Evolutionists," 3.
60. Ross, "Chromosome Study Stuns Evolutionists," 3.
61. Ross, "Chromosome Study Stuns Evolutionists," 3.
62. Rennie, 131.
63. Augros and Stanciu, 191.
64. Augros and Stanciu, 191.
65. Augros and Stanciu, 191.
66. Augros and Stanciu, 15.
67. Thaxton, Bradley and Olsen, *The Mystery of Life's Origin: Reassessing Current Theories,* 201, (supernatural and science, quote from J. W. N. Sullivan, The Limitations of Science).
68. Genesis 2:7.

CHAPTER 7 - Miracles: Something to Believe In
1. Robert G. Jahn and Brenda J. Dunne, *Margins of Reality: The Role of Consciousness in the Physical World* (San Diego CA: Harcourt Brace Jovanovich, 1987) 83.
2. "Art Bell Interview with Michio Kaku," by Art Bell, *Coast to Coast AM,* syndicated radio program, 25 February 1998.
3. William L. Craig, "The Problem of Miracles: A Historical And Philosophical Perspective," *Gospel Perspectives VI,* 1986, 9–40, *Leadership University,* 20 October 2003 <http:www.leaderu.com/offices/billcraig/docs/miracles.html>.
4. Craig, "The Problem of Miracles."
5. Craig, "The Problem of Miracles."
6. Craig, "The Problem of Miracles."
7. Ross, *More Reasons To Believe.*
8. Hugh Ross, *Fifth Dimension and Beyond,* Pasadena, CA: Reasons To Believe, rec. 1990.
9. Hugh Ross, *Fifth Dimension and Beyond.*
10. Ross, *Fingerprint of God,* 50.
11. Ross, *Fifth Dimension and Beyond.*
12. C. G. Jung, *Synchronicity: An Acausal Connecting Principle,* trans. C. G. Hull, 3rd ed. (Princeton, N. J.: Bollingen Series, Princeton University Press, 1973) 65.
13. Paul L. Maier, *In the Fullness of Time: a Historian Looks at Christmas, Easter and the Early Church* (San Francisco, CA: HarperSan Francisco, 1991) 54.
14. Maier, *In the Fullness of Time,* 58.
15. Matthew 2:1–2.
16. Maier, *In the Fullness of Time,* 58.

17. James Thomas Flexner, *George Washington, The Valley Forge Experience 1732–1775* (Boston, MS: Little, Brown and Co., 1965) 128.

18. George Washington, "To John Augustine Washington," July 18, 1755, Letter, Library of Congress, Manuscript Division, Washington DC.

19. Tom Dooley, "America: The Lost Dream, an Incredible History Lesson," Hurst TX: *Master Media,* 1990, multimedia.

20. David Colbert, ed., *Eye Witness to America: 5,000 Years of America in the Words of Those Who Saw It Happen* (New York, NY :Pantheon Books, 1997) 45.

21. William Manchaster, *The Last Lion: Winston Spence Churchill, Visions of Glory 1874 - 1932* (Boston, MA: Little, Brown and Co., 1983) 300.

22. Manchaster, 319.

23. Manchaster, 322.

24. Brig. Gen. Brenton G. Wallace, *Patton and His third Army* (Harrisburg, PA: Military Service Publishing Co. 1946) 151.

25. Major General George S. Patton, Jr., *War As I Knew It* (Boston, MA: Houghton Mifflin Co., 1947) 387.

26. Wallace, 151.

27. Wallace, 232.

28. Wallace, 158–159.

29. Larry Dossey, *Healing Words: The Power of Prayer and the Practice of Medicine* (San Francisco, CA: Harper, 1993) 200- 201.

30. William James, *Selected Writings* (New York, NY: Book of the Month Club, 1997) 486.

31. Dossey, xviii.

32. Kenneth L. Woodward, "Medicine: Religious Aspects," *Readers Digest* July, 1997: 17.

33. Walter L. Larimore M.D., "Providing Basic Spiritual Care for Patients: Should It Be the Exclusive Domain of Pastoral Professionals," *American Family Physician,* 1 January 2001, American Academy of Family Physicians, 01 December 2003 <http://www.aafp.org/afp/20010101/medicine.html>.

34. Dossey, 205–206.

35. Will Oursler, *The Healing Power of Faith* (New York, NY: Hawthorn Books, Inc., 1957) 316.

36. James, *Selected Writings,* 485.

37. James, *Selected Writings,* 486.

38. Herbert, *Quantum Reality,* 24.

39. Nick Herbert, *Faster Than Light Superluminal Loopholes In Physics* (New York, NY: New American Library, 1988) 187.

40. James Redfield, *The Celestine Prophecy* (New York, NY: Warner books, 1993) 59.

41. Herbert, *Quantum Reality,* 19.

42. M. R. Franks, *The Universe and Multiple Reality: A Physical Explanation for Manifesting, Magick and Miracles* (New York: NY, iUniverse, 2003) 35 .

43. Franks, 39.

44. Bruce Bower, "Into the Mystic: Scientists Confront the Hazy Realm of Spiritual Enlightenment," *Science News* 159 (17 February 2001): 104.

45. R. C. Sproul, *Reason To Believe* (Grand Rapids, MI: Zondervan Publishing House, 1978) 21.

46. Sproul, *Reason To Believe,* 21.

47. Sproul, *Reason To Believe,* 21.

48. Sproul, *Reason To Believe,* 27.

49. 2 Peter 1:16. (This scripture is also referred to by Sproul in *Reasons to Believe,* 21).

50. Jung, *Synchronicity,* 41.

51. Rosemary Ellen Guiley, *Harper's Encyclopedia of Mystical And Paranormal Experience* (Edison, NJ: Castle Books, 1991) 409, 494–495.

52. Jeffery, 202.

53. Faid, 76–77.

54. Jeffery, 204.

55. Jeffery, 217.

56. Jeffery, 221.

57. Daniel 9: 25–27.

58. Art Bell interview with Dr. T. Charles Tart, *Coast to Coast AM,* syndicated radio program, June 3, 1998.

59. Jay Kesler, "The Paths of Righteousness," *Forest Home Christian Conference Center,* Family Camp 2, tape 932413.

60. Edward Geoffrey Parrinder, *Upanishads, Gita and Bible: A Comparative Study of Hindu and Christian Scriptures* (New York, NY: Association Press, 1962) 94–106.

61. Parrinder, 96–97.

CHAPTER 8 - For The Good Of Man God Must Exist

1. Blaise Pascal, "Pensees," 1660, trans. W. F. Trotter, *eserver.org,* 24 November 2003 <http://eserver.org/philosophy/pascal-pensees.txt>.

2. Erich Fromm, *An Anatomy of Human Destructiveness,* 2nd ed. (New York, NY: Holt, Rinehart and Winston, 1992) 6–7.

3. Fromm, 288.

4. Fromm, 281.

5. *Devil Worship: The Rise of Satanism,* dir. Pat and Caryl Matrisciana, Jeremiah Films, 1989.

6. *Devil Worship.*

7. Bill Scanlon, "Columbine Caused By Curriculum, Board Member Charges," *Denver Rocky Mountain News,* 6 April 2000, Scripps Howard News Service, 24 November 2003, <http://www.rense.com/general/columb.htm>.

8. John H. Marks, "The Book of Genesis," *The Interpreter's One-Volume Commentary on the Bible,* ed. Charles M. Laymon (Nashville, TN: Abingdon Press 1971) 6.

9. John A. Phillips, *Eve: The History of an Idea* (San Francisco, CA: Harper Row, 1984) 157.

CHAPTER 9: Philosophy–God's Will Be Done, Despite Human Resistance

1. The Doors (Musical Group), "You're Lost Little Girl," *Strange Days,* New York, NY: Elektra, rec. 1967.

2. James Boice, "Relativism," *The Bible Study Hour,* syndicated radio program, 13 October 1993.

3. Exodus 20:1–17, The Living Bible.

4. Joseph Gaer, *How The Great Religions Began* (New York, NY: Dodd, Mead, 1956) 361.

5. Gaer, 47.

6. Gaer, 72.

7. Parrinder, 121.

8. Parrinder, 121.

9. Marietta D, Moskin, *Search of God: The Story of Religion* (New York, NY: Atheneum, 1979) 58.

10. C. S. Lewis, *Mere Christianity* (New York, NY: Macmillan, 1952) 5.

11. Lewis, 60–63.

12. Francis A. Schaeffer, *The God Who Is There: Speaking Historic Christianity Into the Twentieth Century* (Downers Grove, IL: Inter-Varsity Press, 1968) 15.

13. Schaeffer, 17.

14. Schaeffer, 17.

15. William S. Sahakian, *History of Philosophy* (New York, NY: Barnes and Noble Books, 1968) 243.

16. Schaeffer, 18.

17. Hugh Ross, *Creation Vs Evolution,* Pasadena, CA: Reasons To Believe, rec. 1990.

18. Warren Young, *A Christian approach To Philosophy* (Grand Rapids, MI: Baker Books, 1954) 35.

19. Young, 35.

20. Jones, *Kant and The Nineteenth Century,* 233.

21. Walter Kaufmann, *Existentialism From Dostoevsky To Sartre* (New York, NY: New American   Library, 1989), 11.

22. Norbert O. Schedler, *Philosophy of Religion: Contemporary Perspectives* (New York, NY: Mac- millan, 1974), 122–123.

23. Young, 42.

24. Lewis, 108.

25. Jones, *Kant and The Nineteenth Century,* 209–210.

26. Jean Andre Wahl *A Short History of Existentialism* (New York, NY: Philosophical Library, 1949)2. Wahl reports dis- paraging remarks regarding existentialism by two well known existential philosophers. Jaspers has stated, 'existentialism' is the death of the philosophy of existence! Heidegger called it 'the domain of the inauthentic.'"

27. Immanuel Kant, *Religion Within the Limits of Reason Alone,* trans. Theodore M. Greene and Hoyt H. Hudson (New York, NY: Harper Row, 1960) lxxxii-lxxxiii.

28. Wahl, *A Short History of Existentialism,* 14.

29. Hazel Southam, "Church In England 'Will Be Dead in 40 Years Time,'" *The Independent, London,* 16 April 2000, NHNE, 24 November 2003 <http://groups.yahoo.com/group/nhnenews/message/200>.

CHAPTER 10 - Comparative Religion

1. Sproul, *Reason To Believe,* 39.

CHAPTER 11 - Theory #1: Noah Survived the Flood With True Revelations of God

1. Paul Johnson, *A History of the Jews* (New York, NY: Harper and Row, 1987) 6.

2. Tim F. LaHaye and John D. Morris, *The Ark On Ararat* (New York, NY: Thomas Nelson, Inc., 1976) 4.

3. David Fasold, *The Ark of Noah* (New York, NY: Wynwood Press, 1988) 23.

4. Charles Berlitz, *The Lost Ship Of Noah: In Search of the Ark at Ararat* (New York, NY: Putnam, 1997) 87.

5. Genesis 6:15.

6. John C. Whitcomb, *The World That Perished: An Introduction To Biblical Catastrophism* (Grand Rapids, MI: Baker Book House, 1988) 22. A discussion on projections of Frederick A. Filby, *The Flood Reconsidered,* 93.

7. Genesis 8:3–4.

8. Genesis 6:15.

9. Whitcomb, 25.

10. Alexander Heidel, *The Gilgamesh Epic and Old Testament Parallels* (Chicago, IL: The University of Chicago Press, 1946) 227.

11. Sarvepalli Radhakrishnan, *A Source Book In Indian Philosophy,* Sarvepalli Radhakrishnan and Charles A. Moore, ed. (Princeton, N. J.: Princeton University Press, 1957) 5–6.

12. Berlitz, *The Lost Ship Of Noah,* 118–119.

13. Bengt Sage, "Noah and Human Etymology," *Impact,* No. 83 (Santee CA: Institute for Creation Research, May 1980) 1.

14. LaHaye and Morris, 231.

15. LaHaye and Morris, 233–236.

16. Berlitz, *The Lost Ship Of Noah,* 110.

17. For a more involved discussion of these maps including a reproduction of the Buache map of Antarctica read Berlitz's chapter "Knowledge From Forgotten Sources" in his book *Atlantis: The Eighth Continent* (New York, NY: G. P. Put- nam's, 1984) 120–153.

18. John C. Whitcomb, in his book *The World that Perished,* wrote about the Beresovka study at the Leningrad Museum. He suggests that the best possibility for this catastrophe is the immediate freeze caused by the collapse of the vapor canopy. *The World that Perished,* 76–77.

19. Whitcomb, 76.

20. Genesis 7:19.

21. Whitcomb, 20.

22. Berlitz, *The Lost Ship Of Noah,* 115.

23. Seton Lloyd, *The Archaeology of Mesopotamia: from the Old Stone Age to the Persian Conquest* (London: Thames and Hudson, 1978) 92.

24. Lloyd, 105–106.

25. Genesis 6:4–6.

26. Bruce Bower, "Out On A Limb: The Science of Body Development May Make Kindling Out of Evolutionary Trees," *Sci- ence News* 158 (25 Nov 2000): 347.

27. Alexander Marshack, *The Roots of Civilization: The Cognitive Beginnings of Man's First Art,Symbol and Notation* (New York, NY: McGraw-Hill, 1972) 34.

28. Marshack, 70.

29. Lloyd, 24.

30. E. O. James, *Prehistoric Religion: A Study in Prehistoric Archaeology* (New York, NY: Frederick A. Praeger, 1957) 18.

31. James, *Prehistoric Religion,* 19.

32. James, *Prehistoric Religion,* 20–21.

33. Marshack, 21–32.

34. Berlitz, *Atlantis,* 29.

35. John Anthony West, *Serphant in the Sky: The High Wisdom of Ancient Egypt* (New York, N.Y.: Harper Roe, 1979) 199–215.

36. *The Mystery of the Sphinx,* host. Charlton Heston, dir. Bill Cote, Goldhil Home Media International, 1993.

37. *The Mystery of the Sphinx.*

38. *The Mystery of the Sphinx.*

39. Berlitz, *The Lost Ship Of Noah,* 130.

40. Berlitz, *The Lost Ship Of Noah,* 166–167.

41. Fasold, 230.

42. LaHaye and Morris, 239–240.

43. Fasold, 230–231.

44. Fasold, 231.

45. Keiji Nishitani, *Religion and Nothingness,* trans. Jan Van Brgt (Berkley CA: University of California Press, 1982) 24–25.

46. Nishitani, 25.

47. E. Raymond Capt, *The Great Pyramid Decoded* (Thousand Oaks, CA: Artisan Sales, 1971) 5.

48. Isaiah 9:19–20.

49. Capt, 11.

50. Capt, 13.

51. Capt, 78.

52. Charles H. Dyer and Angela Elwell Hunt, *The Rise of Babylon: Sign of the End Times* (Wheaton Il: Tyndale House Publishers, Inc., 1991) 49.

53. Dyer and Hunt, 53.

54. Genesis 11:9.

55. John Travis, "DNA Hints at origin of all language," *Science News* 180 (27 October 2001): 269.

56. Erich von Daniken, *Chariots of the Gods? Unsolved Mysteries of the Past,* trans. Michael Heron (New York, NY: Put- num, 1968) 32–34.

57. Julian Nott and Jim Woodman tested the hot air ballon theory. Hot air ballon experiment is recorded on web site. Julian Nott, "Nazca," *nott.com* <http://www.nott.com/nazca.htm>.

58. Erich von Daniken, *The Gold of the Gods* (New York, NY: G. P. Putnam's Sons, 1972), 121.

59. Melvin Morse, M.D. and Paul Perry, *Closer To the Light: Learning From the Near-Death Experiences of Children* (New York, NY: Ivy Books, 1990) 87.

60. Morse and Perry, 89.

61. Morse and Perry, 89–90.

62. Morse and Perry, 91–92.

63. Clifford Wilson, *Ebla Tablets: Secrets of a Forgotten City* (San Diego, CA: Master Books, 1977) 21.

64. Wilson, *Ebla Tablets,* 12.

CHAPTER 12 - The Human Intellectual Connection

1. James, *Selected Writings,* 532.

2. Genesis 25:5–6, The Living Bible.

3. Nishitani, 50.

4. Nishitani, 27–29.

5. E. O. James, *The Cult of the Mother-Goddess* (New York, NY: Barnes and Noble, 1994) 34–35.

6. James, *The Cult of the Mother-Goddess,* 35.

7. James, *The Cult of the Mother-Goddess,* 34–35.

8. As with the histories of many ancient peoples, there seems to be some disagreement as to the beliefs of the Indus people. Some investigators may suggest the Indus also envisioned a supreme being which led to the monotheistic theme. If that were the case, it would be an amazing discovery, for ancient Indus man is not considered to have been sophisticated enough to develop monotheism. If the Indus had such a belief, it would give great evidence of an ancient civilization preserving a form of 'Noahian' theology, not greatly influenced by the early outside perversions, i.e., little or no Babylonian influences).

9. Parrinder, 20.

10. Parrinder, 60.

11. Radhakrishnan, 17.

CHAPTER 13 - Theory #2: Every Human Being Intuitively Knows God

1. James, *Selected Writings,* 537- 538.

2. Sigmund Freud, *Totem and Taboo: resemblances between the psychic lives of savages and neurotics* (New York, NY: Moffat, Yard, 1919) 203.

3. It has been proposed that the most religious people have the largest God Nodules. The question then becomes, when an atheist converts to a belief in God, and, as has often happened, continues to grow more and more secure in his or her belief, (and in fact, often becomes 'fanatically religious') does the 'God Nodule' grow also?

4. Glyn Richards, *The Philosophy of Gandhi: A Study of His Basic Ideas* (London: Curzon Press; Totowa, N. J.: Barnes and Noble, 1982) 8–9.

5. Genesis 4:2–5.

6. Genesis 4:10–11.

7. Genesis 9:5–6.

8. Philo, *The Works of Philo,* 833.

9. Genesis 8:20.

10 . Exodus 12:1–13.

11. Sir James George Frazer, *The Golden Bough: a study in magic and religion* (New York, NY: The Macmillan Co., 1922) 355. Though this is a questionable source, the ritual is probably representative of actual ceremonies and was reminisced through numerous myths.

12. Noel Quinton King, *African Cosmos: An Introduction to Religion in Africa,* (Belmont, CA: Wadsworth Pub. Co., 1986) 65.

13. Brian Lane and Wilfred Gregg, *The Encyclopedia of Serial Killers* (New York, NY: Diamond Books, 1992), 296.

14. Lane and Gregg, 106–107.

15. Stephen Benko, *Pagan Rome and the Early Christians* (Bloomington, IN: Indiana University Press, 1984), 69–73.

16. Gaer, 268–269.

CHAPTER 14 - Myths, Dreams, Symbols and Religion

1. John Barela, "Spiritual Questioning," *The Front Page, Today, the Bible and You,* August 1993, 17.

2. Schaeffer, 182.

3. James A. Hall, *The Unconscious Christian: Images of God in Dreams,* ed. Daniel J. Meckel (New York, NY: Paulist Press, 1993) 17.

4. C. G. Jung, *Answer to Job,* 3rd ed. (Princeton, NJ: Princeton University Press, 1973), Gerhard Adler, Editorial Note, front of book (not numbered).

5. Jung, *Answer to Job,* x v.

6. Parrinder, 103.

7. Jung, *Synchronicity,* v.

8. Jung, *Synchronicity,* vi-vii.

9. Sproul, *Not A Chance,* 201–202, 213.

10. Lawrence Ferlinghetti, *Pictures of the Gone World* (San Francisco, CA: City Lights Pocket Bookshop 1955) 44.

11. Carl G. Jung and others (and others), *Man and His Symbols,* ed. Carl G. Jung (New York, NY: Dell Publishing, 1964) 3.

12. Joseph Campbell, *The Hero With A Thousand Faces* (Princeton, NJ: Princeton University Press, 1949) 19.

13. Jung, *Man and His Symbols,* ix.

14. Jung, *Man and His Symbols,* x.

15. John W. Drakeford, *Psychology in Search of a Soul* (Nashville, TN: Broadman Press, 1964) 130.

16. George Arthur Gaskell, *Dictionary of All Scriptures and Myths,* 2nd ed. (New York, NY: Avenel, 1981, c1960) 188.

17. An example closely tied to this discussion comes to us in Ezekiel 8:12–18.

18. Black, 54–55.

19. Black, 182.

20. Black, 184.

21. Black, 184.

22. Black, 184.

23. G. Rachel Levy, *Religious Conceptions of the Stone Age* (New York, NY: Harper Torchbooks, 1963) 180.

24. C. A. Burland and Werner Forman, *Feathered Serpent and Smoking Mirror: The Gods and Cultures of Ancient Mexico* (New York: G. P. Putnam's Sons, 1975) 95. Depiction of Panel of the Codex Fejervary-Mayer.

25. Han Biedermann, *Dictionary of Symbolism: Cultural Icons and the Meanings Behind Them,* trans. James Hulbert (New York, NY: Meridan, 1994) 80.

26. Biedermann, 84

27. *The Occult History of the Third Reich: T Enigma of the Swastika,* dir. Dave Flitton, Madacy Entertainment, 1991.

28. *The Occult History of the Third Reich: T Enigma of the Swastika.*

29. Jung, *Answer to Job,* 79.

30. von Daniken, *The Gold of the Gods,* 132.

31. von Daniken, *The Gold of the Gods,* 132–133.

32. Joseph Campbell, *The Power of Myth: Joseph Campbell with Bill Moyers,* ed. Betty Sue Flowers (New York NY: Doubleday, 1988) XVII.

33. Lewis, 3.

34. Schaeffer, 182–183.

35. Romans 1:18–19.

36. Romans 2:12–15.

37. Lewis, 5.

38. *The Occult History of the Third Reich: T Enigma of the Swastika.*

39. Gene S. Stuart, *The Mighty Aztecs* (Washington D.C.: National Geographic Society, 1981) 142.

40. Stuart, 33. (Assumed to be quote from Chichimecs - pre-Aztec writings regarding Huitzilopochtli's promises).

41. Stuart, 110.

42. Stuart, 110.

43. Burland and Forman, 80, 84–85.

44. Stuart, 50.

45. Alfonso Caso, *The Aztecs: People of the Sun* (Norman OK: University of Oklahoma, 1958), 75.

46. Nishitani, 40.

47. Nishitani, 40–41.

48. In one such occurrence Venus crossed in front of the sun. Montezuma must have thought it was a sign from Quetzalcoatl. Burland and Forman, 109–110.

49. Burland and Forman, 109.

50. Stuart, 148.

51. Burland and Forman, 112.

52. Stuart, 82.

53. Caso, 8.

54. Proverbs. 3:4–5.

CHAPTER 15 - Myths and Christianity

1. *Signs,* dir. M. Night Shyamalan, prod. Rob Mercer, M. Night Shyamalan, dist. Touchstone Pictures, perf. Mel Gibson, 2002.

2. Exodus 12:15.

3. Exodus 12:22.

4. Exodus 12:1–20.

5. John 19:31–33.

6. King James Version, Holy Bible, Psalms 34:20.

7. Exodus 12:5.

8. Jung, *Man and His Symbols,* 99–100.

9. Nishitani, 41.

10. Richard Cavendish, ed. *Mythology, an Illustrated Encyclopedia* (New York: Barns and Noble, Inc. 1993) 102.

11. Jung, *Man and His Symbols,* 135.

12. Luke 4:16–21.

13. Example used in Jung's book, *Man and His Symbols,* 99. However, there are many others.

14. Dembski, 40

15. Dembski, 34

16. Dembski, 44

17. Jung, *Answer To Job,* 79.

18. King James Version, Holy Bible, Genesis 3:15.

19. Henrietta C. Mears, *What The Bible Is All About* (Glendale, CA: G/L Publications, 1953) 21.

20. Josh McDowell, *Evidence That Demands A Verdict* (San Bernardino, CA: Here's Life Publishers, 1972) 116.

21. Matthew 1:22.

22. See Chapter 7.

23. 1 Timothy 1:3–5.

24. 1 Timothy 1:6–7.

25. 1 Timothy 1:8–11.

26. Jars of Clay, "Love song For A Savior," *Jars Of Clay,* New York, NY: Zomba Recording Corp., 1995.

CHAPTER 16 - Jesus of Nazareth

1. Craig, "The Problem Of Miracles: A Historical And Philosophical Perspective,"
<http://www.leaderu.com/offices/billcraig/docs/miracles.html>.

2. Craig, "The Problem Of Miracles,"

3. Paul L. Maier, "Jesus - Legend or Lord?," *Issues, etc.,* 1999, Lutheran Church-Missouri Synod, 14 September 2003
<http://www.issuesetc.org/resource/archives/maier4.htm>.

4. Fredric W. Farrar, *The Life of Christ* (New York: George H. Doran Co., 2nd ed. 1876) 675–676.

5. James C. G. Greig, "The New Testament and Christian Origins," *The Interpreter's One-Volume Commentary on the Bible,* 1187.

6. Maier, "Jesus - Legend or Lord?"

7. Maier, "Jesus - Legend or Lord?"

8. McDowell, 124.

9. McDowell, 124–125.

10 . Marvin Hunt, "The Mysterious Lack of Writings About Jesus Outside of the Bible," *The Daily Times Union,* 14 Septem- ber 2003
<http://www.biblehistory.com/133.htm>.

11. McDowell, 125.

12. McDowell, 81–82.

13. (c) 1993 by The Word For Today. Reprint from *The Search For Messiah* (page 248) by Mark Eastman and Chuck Smith, by permission of The Word For Today, P.O. Box 8000, Costa Mesa, CA 92628.

14. Eastman and Smith, 254.

15. Zechariah 9:9.

16. Zechariah 9:11.

17. John 11:47–50.

18. John 11:47–48.

19. John 11:49–50.

20. Peter Marshall, *The First Easter,* ed. Catherine Marshall (Carmel, NY: Guideposts Associates, 1959) 37–38.

21. John 8: 46–49.

22. T. F. Torrance, *Theology in Reconstruction* (London: SCM Press, 1965) 122.

23. Eastman and Smith, 253.

24. Farrar, 675–676.

25. Eastman and Smith, 253.

26. (c) 1981 by The Word For Today. Reprint from *The Credibility*

of the Resurrection and Resurrection (Sermon Tape No. T2094 and T3046) by Chuck Smith of by permission of The Word For Today, P.O. Box 8000, Costa Mesa, CA 92628.

27. Luke 24:50–51.

28. James Orr, *The Resurrection of Jesus* (London: Hodder and Stoughton, 1908) 33.

29. Orr, 34–35.

30. Acts 1:3.

31. William Lane Craig, "Contemporary Scholarship and the Historical Evidence for the Resurrection of Jesus Christ," *Truth 1,* 1985, 89–95, *Leadership University,* 20 October 03 <http://www.leaderu.com/truth/1truth22.html>.

32. Craig, "Contemporary Scholarship."

33. Paul Maier, "History, Archaeology and Jesus," *Issues, etc.,* 1999, Lutheran Church-Missouri Synod, 20 October 03 <http://www.issuesetc.org/resource/archives/maier3.htm>.

34. Craig, "Contemporary Scholarship."

35. Orr, 127.

36. Acts 2:41.

37. Acts 2:22–23.

38. Matthew 27:25.

CHAPTER 17 - What Happened To The Body?

1. Jars Of Clay, "Liquid," *Jars Of Clay,* Zomba Recording Corp., 1995

2. Paul L. Maier, *In The Fullness of Time,* 197.

3. Orr, 10.

4. Maier, *In The Fullness of Time,* 198.

5. Eastman and Smith, 190.

6. Eastman and Smith, 192.

7. Orr, 43.

8. Mark 10:28.

9. John 2:23–25.

10. Ernest C. Wilson, *The Week That Changed The World* (Lee's Summit, MO: Unity Books, 1968) 17.

11. Mark 14:71.

12. Marshall, *The First Easter,* 34.

13. John Shelly Spong, *The Easter Moment* (New York, NY: The Seabury Press, 1980) 47–48.

14. (c) 1981 by The Word For Today. Reprint from *The Credibility of the Resurrection* (Sermon Tape No. T2094) by Chuck Smith of by permission of The Word For Today, P.O. Box 8000, Costa Mesa, CA 92628.

15. Smith, *The Credibility of the Resurrection,* Sermon Tape No. T2094.

16. Faid, 65.

17. Flavius Josephus, *The Complete Works Of Josephus,* trans. William Whinton (Grand Rapids, Mi: Kregel Pub., 1960 c, 1981) 423.

18. (c) 1981 by The Word For Today. Reprint from *Resurrection* (Sermon Tape No. T3046) by Chuck Smith of by permission of The Word For Today, P.O. Box 8000, Costa Mesa, CA 92628.

19. Smith, *The Credibility of the Resurrection,* Sermon Tape No. T3046.

20. Ludwig Wittgenstein, *On Certainty,* ed. G. E. M. Anscombe and G. H. von Wright, trans. Denis Paul and G. E. M. An- combe (New York, NY: Harper Row, 1969) 2e-15e.

21. John 20:29.

22. Josephus, 379.

23. Maier, *In The Fullness Of Time,* 200.

24. Maier, *In The Fullness Of Time,* 200.

25. Luke 23:28–31.

26. McDowell, 191.

27. McDowell, 191.

28. McDowell, 192.

29. Acts 26:8.

30. (c) 1981 by The Word For Today. Reprint from *Resurrection* (Sermon Tape No. T3046) by Chuck Smith of by permission of The Word For Today, P.O. Box 8000, Costa Mesa, CA 92628.

31. Orr, 14.

32. Acts 2:24.

33. Romans 3:10–12; also reference Psalm 14:3.

34. (c) 1981 by The Word For Today. Reprint from *Call His Name Jesus* (Sermon Tape No. 3355) by Chuck Smith of by permission of The Word For Today, P.O. Box 8000, Costa Mesa, CA 92628.

CHAPTER 18 - Jesus, King of The Jews!

1. John 10:24.

2. Zechariah 11: 15–17.

3. John 9:39–41.

4. John 7:25–27.

5. Revelation 3:3.

6. John 7:46–52.

7. Refer to Mark 11:26–33.

8. Micah 5:2.

9. John 8:54–58.

10. John 8:59.

11. Zechariah 11:15–17.

12. The Talmudic Tractate Sanhedrin, on the Sanhedrin and Criminal Jurisprudence, 98b trans. Alfred Edersheim, *The Life & Times of Jesus the Messiah* (Peabody, MA: Hendrickson Pub., 1993) 115.

13. Vendyl Jones, *Will The Real Jesus Please Stand?* (Tyler, TX: Priority Publications, 1983) 1–3, 1–4.

14. Babylonian Talmud, Sanhedrin 99a, referenced by Eastman and Smith, 8.

15. Marks, "The Book of Genesis," *The Interpreter's One-Volume Commentary on the Bible,* 31.

16. McDowell, 169.

17. McDowell, 168–169.

18. Malachi 3:1.

19. Roger N. Carstensen, "The Book of Haggai," *The Interpreter's One-volume Commentary on the Bible,* 501.

20. Haggai 2:3–9.

21. Josephus, 233.

22. Josephus, 233.

23. Zechariah 3:8–9.

24. Zechariah 8:23.

25. Matthew 21:13.

26. Daniel 9:24–25.

27. Nehemiah 2:1–6, King James Version.

28. Nehemiah 2:1.

29. Recalculated by Eastman and Smith, 105–107, from Sir Robert Anderson, *The Coming Prince.*

30. Luke 19:38.

31. Luke 3:1.

32. Eastman and Smith, 107.

33. Eastman and Smith, 108.

34. Daniel 9: 26.

35. Johnson, *A History of the Jews,* 125.

36. Acts 7:51–53.

37. Johnson, *A History of T Jews,* 125.

38. Acts 5:38.

39. Edersheim, 113.

40. Edersheim, 114.

41. Edersheim, 114–115.

42. Eastman and Smith, 2.

43. Edersheim, 116.

44. Eastman and Smith, 125.

45. "Dead Sea Scrolls Mention death of Messianic Leader," *The Dallas Morning News* 8 November 1991: 18A.

46. Scroll 4Q246 as quoted from *The Signature of God,* 101.

CHAPTER 19 - Jesus' Message

1. Michael Grant, *Jesus: An Historian's Review of the Gospels* (New York, NY: Collier Books, 1992) 170.

2. John 3:16–17.

3. John 3:18.

4. Revelation 5:5–6.

5. E. P. Sanders, *The Historical Figure of Jesus* (New York, NY: Penguin Press, 1993) 280.

6. J. P. Morehead, "The Jesus Seminar," *Issues, Etc.,* syndicated radio program, 12/24/95.

7. Edersheim, 183–184.

8. Grant, 21.

9. Morehead, "The Jesus Seminar."

10. Gaer, 157.

11. Gaer, 139.

12. Howard Clark Kee, "The Gospel According To Matthew," *The Interpreter's One-Volume Commentary on the Bible,* 618.

13. Luke 6:29–31, The Living Bible.

14. Luke 6:32–35, The Living Bible.

15. Marietta D. Moskin, *In Search of God* (New York, NY: Atheneum, 1979) 60.

16. Suggested reading, *Jesus of Nazareth,* 27–52.

CHAPTER 20 - Jesus of Nazareth and the Honesty of the Gospels

1. John 14:6–7

2. William Lane Craig, "The Historicity of the Empty Tomb of Jesus," *New Testament Studies 31,* 1985, 39–67, *Leadership University,* 20 November 2003 <http://www.leaderu.com/offices/billcraig/docs/tomb2.html>.

3. 1 Corinthians 15.6.

4. Luke 1:1–4.

5. This might suggest an area where Matthew, Luke and John did find Mark inaccurate. Perhaps the event was remembered differently by the eyewitnesses. There could be a number of reasons for this problem, ex: perhaps some of the women did not walk with (mother) Mary but met her at the grave site.

CHAPTER 21 - The Will of God is Passionate

1. Grant, 52.

2. Gunther Bornkamm, *Jesus of Nazareth,* trans. Irene and Fraser McLuskey and James M. Robinson (New York, NY: Harper & Row, Publishers, 1960) 59.

3. Luke 4:16–21.

4. Luke 4:31–32.

5. Mark 1:21–22.

6. Matthew 7:26–29.

7. Bornkamm, 61.

8. Bornkamm, 62.

9. Matthew 3:21.

10. Bornkamm, 62.

11. Matthew 4:17.

12. Luke 17:20–21.

13. John 18:36–37.

14. Bornkamm, 65.

15. Luke 6:20, King James Version.

16. Brennan Manning, *Ragamuffin Gospel: Good News for the Bedraggled, Beat-Up, and Burnt Out* (Portland, OR: Multnomah Press, 1990) 80.

17. Manning, 85.

18. Fukuyama, 196.

19. Fukuyama, 196–197.

20. Fukuyama, 197.

21. Ecclesiastes 7:20.

22. Jeremiah 31:31–32.

23. D. James Kennedy, *What If Jesus Had Never Been Born? The Positive Impact of Christianity in History* (Nashville, TN: Thomas Nelson Publishers, 1994) 18.

CHAPTER 22 - A Glance at The Revelation

1. Revelation 5:9–10.

2. Steve Scott, "Man gets 75 years for killing woman," *Dallas Morning News* 17 September 1993: 30A.

3. Tom Cowlishaw, "Smith, Cowboys agree on 13.6 million deal," *Dallas Morning News* 17 September 1993: 1A.

4. Roger B. Brown, "Christian-bashing becomes all too frequent in sports," *Fort Worth Star Telegram,* 4 December 1996, section D: 2.

5. "Super Bowl MVP told Bible is harmful: Coaches said star quarterback's game suffered due to Christian belief," *WorldNetDaily,* 5 February 2004, 16 February 2004 <woeldnetdaily.com/news/article.asp?ARTICLE_ID=36944>.

6. "Gayle Sayers," *Christian Speakers and Artists,* 9 February 2004

<http://www.christianspeakers.com/speakers/showSpeaker.asp?mode=name&speakerID=126>.

7. Quotes by Author, *John Adams The Quotations Page,* 17 February 2004 <http://wwwquotationspage.com/quotes/John_Adams>.

8. Thomas Jefferson Famous Quotations, *Telemanage.ca,* 17 February 2004 <http://quotes.telemanage.ca/quotes.nsf/QuotesByCatPerson!ReadForm&RestrictToCategory=Thomas+Jefferson>.)

9. Proverbs 14:34.

10. Proverbs 3:6.

11. John Adams Famous Quotes, *Telemanage.ca,* 17 February 2004 <http://quotes.telemanage.ca/quotes.nsf/QuotesByCatPerson?ReadForm&RestrictToCategory=John+Adams>.)

12. John Adams Famous Quotes, *Telemanage.ca,* 17 February 2004 <http://quotes.telemanage.ca/quotes.nsf/QuotesByCatPerson?ReadForm&RestrictToCategory=John+Adams>.)

13. Steve Farrell, "Why One Nation Under God Matters," *NewsMax.com,* 27 June 27, 2002, Archives, 20 November 2003 <http:www.newsmax.com/commentarchive.shtml?a=2002/6/27/200936>.

14. Farrell, "Why One Nation Under God Matters."

15. Luke 21:24.

16. James Cantelon, *Theology for Non-Theologians* (New York, NY: Macmillan Publishing Co., 1988) 53.

17. A reference to Revelation 3:15.

18. Pretenders, "Show Me," *Learning to Crawl,* New York, NY: Sire Records, 1983.

19. Pierre Klossowski, *Sade My Neighbour,* trans. Alphonso Lingis (London: Quartet Books Limited 1992) 48.

20. Misia Landau, "How Media Violence Touches Children," *FOCUS* (Harvard Medical, Dental and Public Health Schools), 26 October 2001, 15 February 2004 <http://www.med.harvard.edu/publications/Focus/2001/Oct26_2001/child_health.html>.

21. "TV Violence," *Key Facts,* The Henry J. Kaiser Family Foundation, Spring 2003, 13 November 2003 <http://www.kfforg/content/2003/3335/TV_Violence.pdf>.

22. "Violence and Destructive Behavior in the Media and Entertainment Industry," *National Association of Secondary School Principals Position Statement,* 5 May 2001, 15 February 2004 <http://www.principals.org/advocacy/violence_destr.cfm>.

23. Robert Peters, "Violence in the Media–How it Affects our Young

People," *Morality in the Media,* 20 January 1999, 23 November 2003 <http://moralityinmedia.org/mediaIssues/njhearn.htm>.

24. "More TV Shows Include Sexual Content; Safer Sex Messages Most Common When Teen Characters or Sexual Inter- course Are Involved," *Henry J. Kaiser Family Foundation,* 6 February 2001, 27 December 2003 <http://www.kff.org/entmedia/3087-SexonTVPR.cfm>.

25. "The Rouges' Gallery of Television, 2001," [Source: Eric Erickson, "Still here, still queer," New York Blade News, 4 January 2002], Morality in the Media, 23 October 2003 <http://moralityinmedia.org/index.htm?mediaIssues.htm>.

26. "Clinton: China or Europe Will Replace U.S. as Top Power," *NewsMax.Com,* 2 May 2003. *NewsMax.com: Inside Cover Story,* 14 September 2003 <http://www.newsmax.com/showinside.shtml?a=2003/5/2/181207>.

27. Dave Hunt, *How Close Are We? Compelling Evidence for the Coon Return of Christ* (Eugene, OR: Harvest House Publishers, 1993) 260.

28. Lawrence L. Knutson, "Clinton Oks War Crimes Court Entry," *Associated Press,* 31 December 2000, *Yahoo! Groups icc-info (International Criminal Court-Information)* 01 December 2003 <http://groups.yahoo.com/group/icc-info/message/898>.

29. Wes Vernon, "Americans May Be Hauled Before International Court," *NewsMax.Com,* January, 6, 2001, *NewsMax.com Archives,* 14 September 2003 <http://www.newsmax.com/archives/arti-cles/2001/1/5/212756.shtml>.

30. Allen Keyes, "U.N.'s Shaky Foundation," *WorldNetDaily,* March 18, 2000, *WorldNetDaily Archive Exclusive Commentary,* 01 December 2003 <http://www.worldnetdaily.com/news/article.asp? ARTICLE_ID=18705>.

31. Keyes, "U.N.'s Shaky Foundation."

32. Revelation 8:10–11.

33. Revelation 8:12.

34. Dr. David Whitehouse, "Earth almost put on impact alert," BBC News/Nature 24 February 2004 <http://news.bbc.co.uk/2/hi/science/nature/351719.stm>.

35. "Commercial Sex Workers on Front Lines of Bombay AIDS Battle" *PSI* 4 August 2003, 28 December 2003 <http://www.psi.org/resources/pubs/bombay.html>.

36. "'Africa is Dying' Says OAU Representative As General Assembly Begins Review Of World wide Impact Of HIV/AIDS Pandemic," *United Nations* Press Release GA/9808, 2 November 2000, Fifty-fifth General Assembly, Third Committee, 1 December 2003 <www.un.org/News/Press/docs/2000/20001102.ga9808.doc.htm>.

37. "Mandela Issues World AIDS Day Plea," *CNN,* December 1,

2000, *CNN Europe,* 28 November 2003
<http://www.cnn.com/2000/WORLD/europe/12/01/aids.events/>.
    38. "Mandela Issues World AIDS Day Plea."
    39. "Russia Facing AIDS 'Catastrophe,'" *CNN,* 16 November 2000,
CNN Europe, 28 November 2003
<http://www.cnn.com/2000/WORLD/europe/11/16/russia.aids?>.
    40. Ed Susman, "40 Million Living With AIDS," *United Press
International,* 2 July 2002, *UPI Science News,* 28 November 2003
<http://www.aegis.com/news/upi/2002/UP020702.html>.
    41. Charles R. Smith, "China's Chernobyl: SARS Can Spread on
Imported Goods," *NewsMax,* May 5, 2003, NewsMax.com Archives, 28
November 2003 <http://www.newsmax.com/archives/arti-
cles/2003/5/5/154733.shtml>.
    42. Deborah Cohen, "Food, Agri-stocks on Mad Cow Watch-
analysis," *Reuters,* February 6, 2001, Prion Disease: Diagnostics Review, 1
December 2003 <http://www.mad-cow.org/00/feb01_last.html#hhh>.
    43. David A. Kaplan, "This is Global Warming?," *Newsweek,* 22
January 1996: 20.
    44. Kaplan, "This is Global Warming?" 20.
    45. "Lack of Funds Forces WFP To Cut Assistance to Hungry North
Koreans," *WFP news Release,* September 30, 2002, *World Food Program,* 1
December 2003 <http://www.nkfoodaid.org/situation/press_release.html>.
    46. "North Korea Faces Food Disaster, U.N. Says," *Reuters,* 30 Nov
2000, *CNN.com,* east asia, 1 December 2003
<http://www.cnn.com/2000/ASIANOW/east/11/29/nkorea.food.reut/>.
    47. Revelation 8:7.
    48. Bill Koenig, "Bush's Five Significant 'Same Day' Events in
2001," *Koenig's International News,* June 13,2002, *Koenig's Recent
Commentary* <http://www.watch.org/showart.php3?idx=29772&rtn=/index.
html&showsubj=1&mcat=4>.
    49. Mike Reilly, "Europe Returning to Pagan Roots,"
NewsMax.com, 30 May 2003, *NewsMax.com: Inside Cover Story,* 28
November 2003 <http://www.newsmax.com/showinside.shtml?a
=2003/5/30/152207>.
    50. Alan Caruba, *Arab Delusions and Arab Defeats,*
IntellectualConservative.com, 30 January 2004, 17 February 2004
<http://www.intellectualconservative.com/article3096.html>.
        51. Caruba, <http://www.intellectualconservative.com/
article3096.html>.
        52. "29 groups that currently are designated by the Secretary of
State as Foreign Terrorist Organizations (untitled)," *NewsMax.com,* 28

November 2003 <http://www.newsmax.com/archives/articles/2001/9/19/134417.shtml>.

53. Revelation 9:13–16.

54. Revelation 16:12.

55. Col. Stanislav Lunev, "Chinese in Sudan: Army of Workers or Army?," *NewsMax.com,* August 30, 2000, *NewsMax.com Articles,* 28 November 2003 <www.newsmax.com/archives/?a=2000/8/29/201616>.

56. Uwe Siemon-Netto, "World Ignores Atrocities in Sudan," *United Press International,* 5 April 2001, *NewsMax.com,* 28 November 2003 <http://www.newsmax.com/archives/articles/2001/4/4/202524.shtml>

57. Charles Smith, "China and Sudan: Trading Oil For Humans," *World Net Daily,* 19 July 2000, *WorldNetDaily Exclusive Commentary,* 28 November 2003 <http://www.wnd.com/news/article.asp?ARTICLE_ID=20575>.

58. Christina Lamb, "Chins puts '700,000 troops' on Sudan alert," *Telegraph.co.uk,* 27 August 2000, *News.Telegrahp.co.uk telegraph network,* 19 January 2004 <http://www.telegraph.co.uk/news/main.jhtml%3Fxml%3D%252Fnews% 252F2000%252Fwsud27.xml%26secureRefresh+true%26_requestid%3D26068>.

59. Richard Poe, "The Idiot's Guide to Chinagate," *NewsMax.com,* May 27, 2003, NewsMax.com archives, 14 September 2003 <http://www.newsmax.com/archives/articles/2003/5/26/214938.shtml>.

60. Anthony LoBaido, "U.S. to train 'Red Berets,'" *WorldNetDaily.com,* 15 December 1999, WorldNetDaily Exclusive , 16 January 2004 <www.worldnetdaily.com/news/article.asp?ARTICLE_ID=17292>.

61. Anthony C. LoBaido, "China's Strategic Deception," *WorldNetDaily.com,* Septemper 13, 2000, WorldNetDaily Exclusive Commentary, 20 January 2004 <http://www.worldnetdaily.com/news/article/asp?ARTICLE_ID=16421>.

62. Carl Limbacher, "Is China the Next Argentina?" *NewsMax.com,* July 3, 2002, NewsMax.com Archives, 14 September 2003 <http://www.newsmax.com/showinside.shtml?a=2002/7/2/202622>.

63. "Sudan - Human Rights Developments," *Human Rights Watch,* Human Rights Watch Wrord Report 2000, 29 January 2004 <http://www.hrw.org/wr2k/Africa-11.htm#TopOfPage>.

64. Revelation 18:16–19.

65. John A. Garraty, *1,001 Things Everyone Should Know About American History* (New York, NY: Doubleday 1989) 173.

66. 2 Thessalonians 2:2–13.

67. Scroll 4Q246 as quoted from *The Signature of God,* 101.

68. Proverbs 9:10.

Contact Jowell Peden
or order more copies of this book at

TATE PUBLISHING, LLC

127 East Trade Center Terrace
Mustang, Oklahoma 73064

(888) 361 - 9473

Tate Publishing, LLC

www.tatepublishing.com